Your Freedom and Mine

Abdullah Öcalan and the Kurdish Question in Erdoğan's Turkey

Edited by

**Thomas Jeffrey Miley
and Federico Venturini**

BLACK
ROSE
BOOKS

Montreal • Chicago • London

Black Rose Books No. SS391

Library and Archives Canada Cataloguing in Publication

Your freedom and mine: Abdullah Öcalan and the Kurdish question in Erdoğan's
Turkey / Thomas Jeffrey Miley, Federico Venturini, eds.

Includes bibliographical references.
Issued in print and electronic formats.
ISBN 978-1-55164-670-1 (hardcover)
ISBN 978-1-55164-668-8 (paperback)
ISBN 978-1-55164-672-5 (PDF)

1. Öcalan, Abdullah. 2. Kurds--Turkey--Politics and government--21st century. 3.
Turkey--Politics and government--21st century. I. Miley, Thomas Jeffrey, editor II.
Venturini, Federico, editor

DR435.K87Y68 2018   956.1'00491597   C2018-901211-0   C2018-901212-9

C.P. 35788 Succ. Léo-Pariseau
Montréal, QC H2X 0A4
CANADA
www.blackrosebooks.com

ORDERING INFORMATION:

USA/INTERNATIONAL

University of Chicago Press
Chicago Distribution Center
11030 South Langley Avenue
Chicago IL 60628

(800) 621-2736 (USA)
(773) 702-7000 (International)

orders@press.uchicago.edu

CANADA

University of Toronto Press
5201 Dufferin Street
Toronto, ON
M3H 5T8

1-800-565-9523

utpbooks@utpress.utoronto.ca

UK/EUROPE

Central Books
Freshwater Road
Dagenham
RM8 1RX

+44 (0) 20 852 8800

contactus@centralbooks.com

Black Rose Books is the publishing project of Cercle Noir et Rouge

DEDICATED TO THE MEMORY OF JUDGE ESSA MOOSA
(1936–2017)

Table of Contents

vii   Foreword. *Dilar Dirik*

x   Prefaces. *Thomas Jeffrey Miley and Federico Venturini*

xiv   Note from the Publisher. *Dimitri Roussopoulos*

xvi   Maps and Photographs

Part One: The Historical Context of the Conflict

3   The Turkish-Kurdish Conflict in Historical Context. *Thomas Jeffrey Miley with Cihad Hammy and Guney Yıldız*

122   Living Freedom: The Evolution of the Turkish-Kurdish Conflict and Efforts to Resolve It. *Adem Uzun*

Part Two: Campaigns of International Solidarity

167   Abdullah Öcalan: A Life of Four Decades of Resistance. *Havin Guneser*

176   My Encounter with the Kurdish Movement. *Kariane Westrheim*

182   The EU Turkey Civic Commission (EUTCC) and the Peace in Kurdistan UK Campaign. *Michael Gunter and Kariane Westrheim*

190   The Freedom for Öcalan Campaign and the British Trade Union Movement. *Interview with Simon Dubbins*

Part Three: The EUTCC İmralı International Peace Delegations

199   The Plight of the Kurds in Turkey and the Fate of the Middle East. *Thomas Jeffrey Miley after the First İmralı Delegation*

204   Joint Statement of the First International İmralı Peace Delegation *(Istanbul, Turkey; February 2016)*

213   Turkey and the Kurds: A Chance for Peace? *Jonathan Steele Reports from the Third İmralı Delegation*

221   State Terror, Human Rights Violations, and Authoritarianism in Turkey: Report of the Third İmralı International Peace Delegation *(Istanbul and Diyarbakır, Turkey; February 13–19, 2017)*

253   The Council of Europe and the Death of the Peace Process: Report from the İmralı Delegation to Strasbourg. *Thomas Jeffrey Miley*

Part Four: Reflections of the EUTCC İmralı Peace Delegates

265   Fighting the Lion Inside the Cage. *Janet Biehl*

270   My Tryst with the Kurdish Freedom Struggle. *Radha D'Souza*

274   A Basque Politician in Kurdistan. *Miren Gorrotxategi*

277   Still a Long Way to Peace: Changing Minds about the Kurdish Issue. *Andrej Hunko*

280   An Exercise in Understanding. *Ögmundur Jónasson*

285   "Please Tell My Story." *Joe Ryan*

288   Repressing Comedians, Journalists, and Politicians. *Ulla Sandbæk*

291   An Activist-Researcher as a Peace Delegate. *Federico Venturini*

296   The Experience of an Ignorant European Politician. *Julie Ward*

302   Ten Powerful Moments of an Outraging Experience. *Francis Wurtz*

Part Five: Analysing Democratic Confederalism

309   A Seeker of Truth. *Abdullah Öcalan*

317   Capitalism and the Kurdish Freedom Movement. *Reimar Heider*

324   Democratic Confederalism, Democratic Autonomy. *Havin Guneser*

331   Review of Abdullah Öcalan's *Manifesto for a Democratic Civilization*. *Donald H. Matthews and Thomas Jeffrey Miley*

347   Struggling Hand in Hand with the Kurdish Youth Movement: Dispatches from the Long March for the Freedom of Öcalan. *Mohammed Elnaiem*

360   The Perils and Promises of Self-Determination: From Kurdistan to Catalonia. *Thomas Jeffrey Miley*

Part Six: Geopolitics, Dilemmas, and the Scramble for the Middle East

371   Regional and Global Power Politics in the Syrian Conflict. *Jonathan Steele*

375   The War on Terror and Europe's Refugee Crisis. *Thomas Jeffrey Miley*

379   Dancing with the Devil. *Darnell Stephen Summers*

384   Delisting the PKK and the Resulting Benefits. *Michael Gunter*

387   Consolidating Peace, Democracy, and Human Rights after Raqqa: Prospects for the Region and the Kurds. *Panel Discussion*

394   Afterword. *Cihad Hammy*

403   Notes on the Contributors

408   Glossary of Acronyms

Foreword

Dilar Dirik

The following anecdote is often told among comrades in the Kurdish freedom movement. One day, young Abdullah Öcalan met an old Kurdish man and spoke to him about Kurdistan. Pointing at a lifeless, dry tree trunk, the old man asked resignedly: "The Kurdish people are like this dead tree. Can you make it become green again?" Öcalan knew what this was supposed to mean; the old man's words told a tale of the withering of a people faced with a history of denial, violence, and genocide. It was not only the Kurds who existed like a shrivelled tree trunk; the failures of existing socialism, social democracy, and certain national liberation movements had disappointed peoples' existential hopes in the promise of a free, democratic society that would lead us toward human emancipation. Over the next decades, this dead tree resurrected and grew into a garden of colourful diversity, luscious energy, and rooted resilience. This tale of hope and liberation is the legacy that Abdullah Öcalan's unshakeable convictions transmit to the generations to come.

In the tradition of the people's philosophers of the Middle East, he derived his insights from the pain and suffering of the oppressed who wandered the streets of poverty, misery, and despair. As a Kurd in Mesopotamia and as a worker in Turkey, as a socialist of the 20th century, as a freedom fighter in the mountains, and as a brother of enslaved women he found himself caught in the middle of a chaos of colonialism, patriarchy, and capitalism. It is in the midst of this chaos that he become a revolutionary in Kurdistan.

Inside the cold, worn down walls of a tiny brick house in the Fis village of Amed (Diyarbakır) were packed a few dozen young people, bright-eyed with ideals. They had come from nothingness and poverty, driven by their deep feelings for the wretched and forgotten. From the darkness of this dank room, the guerrilla flame of Kurdistan's revolutionary Newroz fire embraced, warmed, and enlightened the poor, the young, the wretched, the women, the workers, and the peasants; it was a flame that seemed to drive away all oppressors. Abdullah Öcalan and his comrades taught our parents the importance and meaning of struggling against colonialism, fascism, and state terrorism. Our parents were tortured in prisons, murdered in dark alleys, slaughtered in the village streets, burned alive in basements, and uprooted in exile. But they never surrendered. They taught us that resistance is life and that surrender is betrayal—betrayal to both our existence and our place in history. In order to exist, one first has to fight. But what is the meaning of such an existence?

Breathing life back into the veins of the marginalised required diving into the roots of history to understand the emergence of human enslavement: from the ancient ziggurats of the Sumerian city-state to the mansions of the ruling classes of today. Öcalan guides us through the universality of humanity's ancient struggle for freedom, from the stem cells of early society, born between the

Euphrates and Tigris rivers, to the techno-cultural ruptures in the history of civilisation, to the sociology of the quantum moments of freedom and the potentiality of every human being. But he does not leave it there. His vision is nothing less than a manifesto to build another world.

Perhaps this is nowhere clearer than in the most revolutionary task that he has set himself and his movement: the uncompromising liberation of women from all enslaving shackles of domination. The consequences of Öcalan's insistence on confronting patriarchy are nothing less than turning the course of history upside down. In a region where women can be traded off for a few goats or pieces of land, where a man's "honour" is considered more sacred than life itself, where the meaning of womanhood has been reduced to mere sexual enslavement and domestication, women, as the first rebels of history, are weaving life with their own hands, in their own colours. Abdullah Öcalan's paradigm—democratic nation and democratic confederalism based on democracy, women's liberation, and ecology—became the weapon of the women who, throughout history, had lost their power of self-defence as well as their means of politics, economy, creation, and culture. In the knowledge that Öcalan is their greatest comrade, women of Kurdistan faced towards the mountains, removing their shackles one step at a time, re-claiming their stolen thrones from history, and becoming the goddess-like pioneers of a culture of resistance, ethics, and beauty. The patience of Inanna and Tiamat is radiating from the labouring hands of women in Mesopotamia once again, from Sinjar to Kobane, Raqqa and Afrin (the latter of which is occupied since March 2018 by the Turkish army and its affiliated jihadists).

Today, the young generation of Kurds and their internationalist comrades are ready to stand on the front lines against international fascism. They are equipped with a philosophy of universal human beauty, a true internationalism based on the solidarity of peoples, ecological consciousness, and women's liberation, and they are armed with a will-power of uncompromising resistance. They are enacting a transformation from *hebûn*—mere existence—to *xwebûn*—independence; it is a tectonic shift from *merely being* to *being oneself*, creating autonomous means of self-determination by establishing one's own systems, life worlds, ecologies, economies, politics, and societies and to thus assert one's own terms of existence.

Today, under the banner of democratic confederalism, Kurdistan, once forgotten and denied, has become the centre of radical imaginaries. Inspired by the philosophy of Apo, there are Kurds, Turks, Arabs, Armenians, Turkmen, Assyrians, Syriacs, and Chechens jointly forming local administrations, cooperatives, assemblies, and academies in the spirit of peoples' solidarity. Led by Apo's thought, thousands of women—whose historic sacrificial resistance has led to the defeat of the so-called Islamic State in northern Syria—declared the victory of Raqqa's liberation as a gift to women around the world, in the same city squares that formerly served as the settings for 21st century sex slave markets for the patriarchal rapist male. The peoples of our beautiful region were once turning against eachother through the chauvinist, supremacist, racist, and authoritarian doctrine of nationalism; yet, now, they once again look each other in the eyes and, shoulder to shoulder, fight against fascism. Women and men, expelled from paradise, begin to re-build the foundations of a free life together, side by side as comrades and meaningful partners, beyond relationships of domination and subjugation, beyond marital concepts that serve to deceive, exploit, and enslave. The people, alienated from their own economy and natural world through neo-liberalism and industrialism, re-discover their connections to and love for their native lands by understanding themselves as part of an ecology of life.

Using his wisdom, knowledge, experience, and authority as a leader, Öcalan mobilised millions of people to develop their political consciousness on autonomous terms, guided by commitment to an ethical and political society. He provided a mass movement with the means of organising and leading itself. Today, with women having regained their wisdom and loving authority, society is returning to its ecological, ethical harmony, from the mountains of Kurdistan to the valleys and plains of the Middle East. A revolutionary culture based on *hevaltî*, on revolutionary, sacrificial comradeship, teaches us to deeply feel another being's suffering and to put oneself in the lines of hellfire for them. This is the legacy of the Kurdish freedom movement for us, especially as young Kurdish women; and this is the magical attraction that draws millions of Kurdish people and internationalists to this struggle today, making it the heart of the international war against fascism.

Through Öcalan's thought and practice, starting with the shrivelled tree in the streets of Kurdistan and reaching into the roots of history, a legacy of resistance sprouted. With the unity of many peoples, it grew into a tree with many branches; and it has flourished, crowned by a women-led struggle and an ecology of universal liberation. Alive and magnificent, this tree is ready to bring fresh political life to the entire world.

May this book explode the walls of the military-carceral complex of İmralı Island with the metaphysical power of the human imagination. As long as we awaken our love for freedom and bring it to life through action, this imprisoned philosopher will remain the freest among us.

Freedom for Abdullah Öcalan!

Preface

Thomas Jeffrey Miley

The idea of this book originally came from Dimitri Roussopoulos, the long-time Canadian political activist and publisher with Black Rose Books. I remember first discussing the possibility of such a book with him, along with Federico Venturini, in February of 2017 on a mini-bus from Istanbul. As the EUTCC international peace delegation, we were on a three hour bus ride to Edirne Prison, near the Greek border, in what would be an unsuccessful attempt to visit the HDP's co-chair Selahattin Demirtaş, the inspirational Turkish parliamentarian of Kurdish and Zaza descent and co-chair of the progressive and pro-Kurdish Peoples' Democratic Party (HDP). He was then, and still remains, unlawfully imprisoned. His trumped-up terrorism charges consist of a combined sentence of 183 years in prison.

Demirtaş lives in conditions that are similar to, though not as extreme as, those of Abdullah Öcalan, the leader of the Kurdish freedom movement who has been imprisoned on İmralı Island for nineteen years. The official objective of our delegation was to attempt to meet with Öcalan, to advocate for his release, and to encourage a restarting of the peace negotiations between the Turkish government and the PKK, though we harboured no illusions about our chances for success. Later that evening of this trip to Edirne, at our hotel back in Istanbul, we shared our nascent plan about a book project with the rest of the delegation who received it with enthusiasm. And so began a labour of love.

This book is very much a collective effort and an extension of an international solidarity campaign—but a solidarity campaign of a different sort. The problem with solidarity, at least as it is usually conceived and practiced, is that it is often nearly indistinguishable from charity. We have all seen the posters: the camera tilted down, focusing our sovereign gaze upon a victim, an object. Tears flowing, hands outstretched. "Save the children." "We are the world." Donate some cash, sign a petition, attend a march, sing a song, feel good about yourself—and little else.

However, the campaign of international solidarity with the Kurdish freedom movement operates in accordance with different parameters—the values of democratic confederalism: mutual solidarity and the ambition to build a free society beyond hierarchy and oppression. At least this has been my experience. I first encountered the movement through the efforts of Dilar Dirik, who is nominally my student but who in reality has been one of my greatest teachers. Since then, I have been consistently impressed with the movement's communal ethos and collective will to struggle. Indeed, I have found the movement's radical democratic, revolutionary praxis to be nothing short of contagious.

Today, I count among my closest friends and intellectual collaborators people who I have come to know through my engagement with the Kurdish freedom movement and its struggle. The joy and seemingly endless insights from near-daily conversations with people like Estella Schmid and Cihad Hammy; the opportunity to collaborate with a core of committed young scholars like Mohammed Elnaiem, Luqman Guldive, Jerome Roos, Rebwar Salih, and Güney Yıldız; the privilege to come into contact with and learn from the examples of experienced scholars and activists like Janet Biehl, Radha D'Souza, Simon Dubbins, Nick Hildyard, or Les Levidow; and the satisfaction of bringing role models and elders like Donald Matthews or Darnell Stephen Summers into dialogue with the movement. All these experiences, which have broadened my ethical and existential horizons substantially, I owe to my involvement with the Kurdish cause.

It is my hope that this book will help raise international consciousness about the plight, the bold inspirational example, and the political project of Abdullah Öcalan and the Kurdish freedom movement. We in "the West" have so much to learn from this movement. First and foremost, we can learn from them how to resist, how to struggle—even against all odds. For struggle we must if humanity, and perhaps even life on the planet, is to survive the ongoing onslaught, the tyranny of the plutocrats, and the war-mongers. Democratic confederalism or catastrophe, such are the stakes.

It is an honour to have had the chance to work with the team at Black Rose Books on this volume. It is a publishing house which, as many readers will know, has done so much to promote the work of Murray Bookchin, to help make his important ideas about communalism and social ecology known to a broad audience. Among Bookchin's readers, perhaps the most influential is Mr. Öcalan, whose own articulation of these ideas, in the form of democratic confederalism, inspires the valiant struggle of the Kurdish freedom movement.

Special thanks are in order to Nathan McDonnell at Black Rose Books for his belief in and dedication to this project; to David Cann for his meticulous proofreading and editing; and perhaps, above all, to my partner, Johanna Riha, and to our sweet baby James, both of whom, in desperate times, have filled my life with so much love.

— *Moshi, Tanzania*
  April 2018

Preface

Federico Venturini

Your Freedom and Mine began with the idea of shining a brighter light on the work of the EUTCC International İmralı Peace Delegations. Given the complexity of the situation, we soon realized that much more needed to be said, with the result that the book expanded rapidly beyond its original scope. Although it wasn't possible to include all of the original material in the final version of the book, we believe that we have managed to outline the Kurdish question, deepen the debate, and provide some answers on the battles still to be fought.

The book has several different goals. The first is to present an informed historical account and political analysis of the Kurdish question, drawing on original material and first-hand accounts. To embrace the diversity of experience, we have given space to authors with different styles and different backgrounds, including activists, lawyers, politicians, journalists, and academics. Only a plurality of voices will serve to depict the complicated jigsaw of the Middle East. This collection seeks to highlight both the intricacy of the current situation and its international ramifications.

It is also intended to breach the wall of silence on recent events in the Middle East, highlighting the tragedy and hopes of the Kurdish people. In the aftermath of the Kurdish combatants' heroic resistance in Kobane and their struggle against ISIS, a renewed blanket of silence has dropped once again over their aspirations for freedom as well as those of other minorities in the Middle East. This book reveals the very real nature of human rights violations and calls for the peace process in Turkey to be restarted as soon as possible, in which Abdullah Öcalan must play a prominent role.

As my co-editor Thomas Jeffrey Miley has pointed out several times, *Your Freedom and Mine* is a labour of love. All the people that contributed did so because of their connections and commitment to social change. As a famous Aboriginal saying of the 1970s puts it: "If you have come here to help me, you are wasting your time. But if you have come because your liberation is bound up with mine, then let us work together." This is fundamental to our work: we look at this book project not only because we want to help the Kurdish movement, but because we believe our own struggles are intimately linked with theirs and those of many others in the world.

The final and most important goal of this book is to inform in order to inspire change. We hope that readers are inspired by the Kurdish example to fight for a different world. The Kurdish people know their situation intimately because they live it, in their skin, every day; this book shares their experience with the rest of the world. It has been said that the Kurds have embarked on the most advanced and successful movement for social transformation in recent decades. *Your Freedom and Mine* urges us to support, learn from, be inspired, and transformed by their experience. We cannot abandon them and, in these dark days, we must take inspiration from them to build change in our own cities, neighbourhoods, and streets.

One person who embodied this ethos to the end was the late Judge Essa Moosa, former Supreme Court judge of South Africa and lawyer for Nelson Mandela. Essa devoted his life to fighting apartheid and never stopped. He was on the front line of promoting and protecting human rights around the world. While he was the leader of the İmralı Peace delegation, we worked together, and he taught us to be patient, precise, focused, committed, and open-hearted. From him, we learned that struggles need a holistic vision in which everyone has a specific part to play.

I want to thank Thomas Jeffrey Miley for offering me the chance to be part of this project; Nathan McDonnell at Black Rose Books for his crucial assistance; Josie Hooker for translations, proofreading, and editing; and the Asrın Law Office and Ms. Didar Erdem for their tireless work for justice and truth.

This book is just a drop in the ocean, but what is the ocean made of if not of drops? Ours is just one effort among millions of others who, like ants working patiently piece by piece, open cracks in history. The reader will judge if we have fulfilled our aims. We tried our best to do our part, now let's go out and transform our society, in a collective, bottom-up pursuit of an ecological and democratic future.

— *Udine, Italy*
  April 2018

Note from the Publisher
Dimitrios Roussopoulos, Co-Founder of Black Rose Books
June 2018

I am often asked why I am so passionate about the Kurdish question when there are many other peoples in the world who are also denied their human rights through repression and domination. My reply is that it is not because I pity the Kurds in their suffering, but that I am inspired by their resistance and vision.

As the world's largest stateless population, the Kurds have been an obvious victim of humiliation by the imperalist and Nation-State system. So they, of all peoples, have good reason to call such a system into question. Today, the Kurdish freedom movement is audaciously building a new society beyond State and nationalism, a new economy beyond capitalism, a new gender relations beyond patriarchy, and a new ecological symbiosis beyond industrialism. This utopian political imagination is progressing in leaps and bounds in the north of Syria, a region of four million people known as "Rojava". As witnessed by several visiting delegations, these populations, including Kurds but also many other diverse ethnic groups, have instituted a directly democratic decision-making process based on local community organising, neighbourhood and street assemblies, and a remarkable program of citizen education. This experiment in a new society has attracted scores of people from around the world to study it and support it. In a word, a social revolution has unfolded in this territory, notwithstanding ongoing military incursions by imperialist and fundamentalist forces intent on crushing this new-born society. Meanwhile, the Western mass media have generally ignored the situation, and it was only when the fanatics of ISIS began their vicious butchery and were effectively defeated by heroic Kurdish militias, including many women, that the mainstream media sat up and took notice.

The major inspiration for the Kurds' pioneering ideas comes from the work of the jailed leader of the Kurdish freedom movement, Abdullah Öcalan. During his two decades of isolated imprisonment, he studied the writings of many radical intellectuals to rethink the politics of the very movement he founded and led, searching for new answers to old questions and new questions to old answers. Among the books he read were *The Ecology of Freedom* and *Urbanization Without Cities* by the genius social theorist Murray Bookchin, two books that we at Black Rose Books are proud to have published. Öcalan was deeply impacted by Bookchin's epic analysis of the millenia-old struggle between freedom and domination from pre-history to modern cities and the need for a utopian liberatory politics, centred on local democratic community organising, to save humanity from the social and ecological crises. Such ideas would greatly help the Kurdish movement navigate its way out of the morass of statism, militarism, and Marxist-Leninism. Upon Bookchin's death, the PKK issued a statement which read in part, "He introduced us to the thought of social ecology, and for that he will be remembered with gratitude by humanity... We undertake to make Bookchin live in our struggle. We will put this promise into practice as the first society which establishes a tangible democratic confederalism."

In early 2016, I was invited by the EU Turkey Civic Commission to participate in an international peace delegation to Istanbul; we would investigate human rights abuses committed against the Kurdish population of Turkey and explore the prospects for a return to the peace process between the government and the PKK. A second delegation followed in 2017, but this time it also visited Diyarbakır in the south-eastern part of Turkey. Throughout both visits we met scores of individuals and organisations who recounted difficult and often painful experiences. Our task was to bring to the attention of the world that this NATO "ally" was in fact dominated by a regime which repressed the most basic human rights. What we witnessed was a society in the cruel crucible of authoritarianism.

The Kurdish struggle is important for all of us as their destiny is intimately bound up with our own, and the threats they face are being felt across the modern world. The terrifying rise of patriarchal autoritarianism with a venomous cult of violence and often a penchant for religious fundementalism is a product of the crisis of capitalist modernity; this is true for the hypernationalist neoliberal Turkish state as much as for the ativistic brutality of ISIS, the thanatocratic Assad government, and the strong-man rule of Trump and Putin. Caught in the crossfire of such Apocalyptic political forces are the humble Kurds aspiring to change the world and overturn 5,000 years of patriarchy and domination, though they face the threat of genocidal extinction. As with much of the political turmoil in the Middle East, there is the temptation to recoil in confused horror at what seems like senseless tragedy. But it is actually a glimpse into the extreme crisis that the world is sliding into, reminding us of the old leftist slogan "socialism or barbarism". With the international storm of fascism, fundamentalism, nationalism, obscene inequality, and ecological crisis, it is imperative that we act in solidarity for a democratic, feminist, and ecological outcome to the Kurdish question and closely learn from this audacious movement—for their sake as much as for our own.

During the 2017 delegation's three hour van trip from Istanbul to Edirne Prison, I suggested to Thomas Jeffrey Miley that we work on a book project emerging from the work of our delegation. He, and later the whole delegation, enthusiastically agreed to the idea. Initially, the objective was to collect the variety of documentation emerging from the EUTCC fact finding missions. In the end, the project would go so much further than this. The result is that this important book is perhaps the most authoritative overview of the contemporary politics of the Kurdish freedom movement and their proposals for a political solution to the Turkish-Kurdish conflict, as well as a rare documentation of the inspiring realm of international solidarity initiatives linked to this cause.

We dedicate this book to the memory of Judge Essa Moosa and to my dear friend Osman Kavala, an Istanbul intellectual and philanthropist devoted to freedom, democracy, and culture who has sat in jail since October 2017. This book would have been impossible without the devoted intellectual work of Miley, who is largely responsible for its contents, nor would it have seen the light of day without the determined drive of my assistant and colleague at Black Rose Books, Nathan McDonnell.

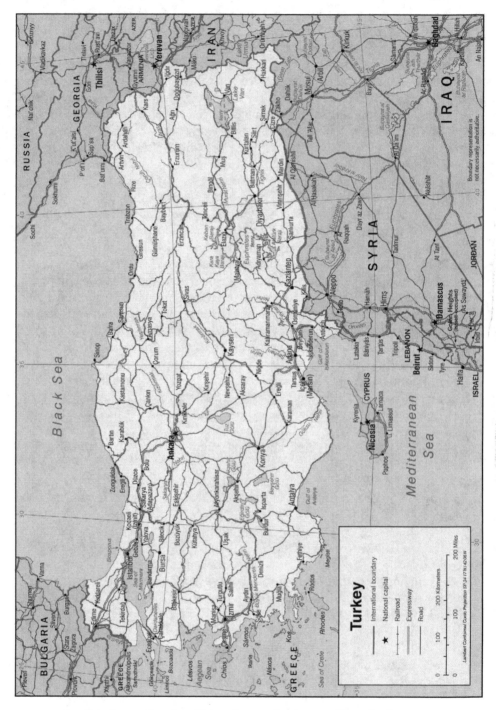

A political map of modern Tukey. Source: the CIA World Factbook; 2006.

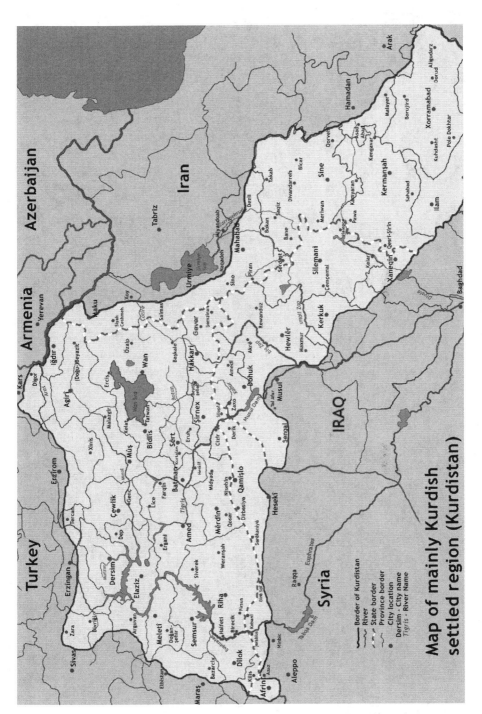

A map of Kurdistan with Kurdish place names. Source: TATORT Kurdistan.
Available at: http://tatortkurdistan.blogsport.de/.

Thomas Jeffrey Miley and Judge Essa Moosa; February 2016. Judge Moosa, formerly Nelson Mandela's lawyer, was the original proponent and leader of the İmralı Peace Delegation. In the absence of Moosa, Miley was the delegation's spokeperson.

Group photo of the first İmralı Peace Delegation with several local organisers, Istanbul; February 2016. Composed of a diverse group of intellectuals, politicians, journalists, and academics, the delegation composition slightly changed between the different missions. From left to right: Father Joe Ryan, Federico Venturini, Francisco Velasco, Thomas Jeffrey Miley, Judge Essa Moosa, Andrej Hunko, Eirik Eiglad, Dimitri Roussopoulos, Ibrahim Bilmez, Ceylan Akca, Elly Van Reusel, Janet Biehl, Nathan McDonnell, and Didar Erdem.

Delegation members with DTK co-president Leyla Güven and board member Moussa Fayasullani; Diyarbakır/Amed; February 2017. The DTK is a radical democratic platform of Kurdish associations and movements working toward democratic confederalism. It is based in the south-east of Turkey. From left to right: Father Joe Ryan, Francis Wurtz, Jonathan Steele, Thomas Jeffrey Miley, Federico Venturini, Leyla Güven, Dimitri Roussopoulos, Miren Gorrotxategi, Ulla Sandbaek, Moussa Fayasullani, Ögmundur Jónasson, and Nathan McDonnell.

Delegation members holding a press conference outside Edirne prison with HDP MP Huda Kaya and activist Ayşe Berktay, after having been refused entry to visit the imprisoned HDP co-president Selahattin Demirtaş; February 2017. He was unlawfully jailed on trumped-up terrorism charges with a combined sentence of 183 years in prison. During the 2018 presidential elections, he would run as a presidential candidate from within his prison cell.

Delegation members with lawyers Ibrahim Bilmez, Rezan Sarica, and Mr. Serbay Köklü from the Asrin Law Office in Istanbul; February 2017. As the attorneys of Öcalan, they work tirelessly advocating for the improvement of his conditions. Öcalan has been unable to meet with his lawyers since July 27, 2011. They have since applied to see him over six hundred times; each request has been denied on the grounds that "the boat is broken" or "the weather is bad".

Ferhat Encü, one of the thirteen HDP politicians imprisoned since late 2015, with Ögmundur Jónasson, Iceland's former Minister of Justice. We met with Encü on the evening after he had been released from prison; Jónasson was particularly enthused as he had been an advocate for Encü's cause for several months. In this photo, he shows Encü an opinion piece he wrote in an Icelandic newspaper raising awareness about the issue. Our initial elation turned to disappointment, however, when Encü was again imprisoned a few hours later.

Father Joe Ryan, Federico Venturini, Bert Showenburg, Jonathan Steele, and MEP Julie Ward at the public forum "Peace Delegation Calls for the Return to the Peace Process in Turkey," organised by the Centre for Kurdish Progress and Peace in Kurdistan in the Houses of Parliament, Westminster, London; February 2017.

In collaboration with the European United Left/Nordic Green Left European Parliamentary Group (GUE/NGL), the EUTCC organises the annual conference "The European Union, Turkey, the Middle East and the Kurds" at the European Parliament in Brussels.

PART ONE
The Historical Context of the Conflict

The Turkish-Kurdish Conflict in Historical Context

Thomas Jeffrey Miley with Cihad Hammy and Güney Yıldız

Editors' Note: This is a synthesized overview of the history of state denialism, state terror, and human rights atrocities committed by the Republic of Turkey against its Kurdish citizens over the last century. It must be noted that the chapter relies nearly exclusively on accounts of historians and social scientists that are available in the English language. The evidence presented here of deeply-entrenched, systemic oppression against the Kurdish people is overwhelming, all the more so when we keep in mind that the record upon which we rely remains doubly biased against the perspective of those whom Eric Wolf once called "the people without history."

Genocide Haunts the Turkish National Imaginary

Understanding the long and bloody conflict between the Kurdish freedom movement and the Turkish State requires some awareness of the historical context. For, among other reasons, the insurgency of the Kurdistan Workers' Party (PKK) against the Turkish State is one of the longest-lasting insurgencies in the Middle East, spanning over three decades to date.

It would be too easy to ascribe the ongoing conflict to nationalist mentalities and/or a penchant for violence—such mentalities are never born in a vacuum. They may be causes, yes, but they are also symptoms and consequences inextricably linked to a deeper historical process—propelled by war and trauma—and by the brutal dynamics of dependent capitalist development, which has resulted in a social psychosis of sorts.

The Turkish Republic was born like a phoenix. It emerged out of the ashes of its predecessor—the Ottoman Empire—in the wake of the unprecedented and appalling death and destruction—not to mention the defeat and humiliation of the First World War. Some of the bloodiest battles of that terrible war were fought on the Ottoman-Russian front (Halliday 2005, p. 81). In addition, the Ottoman authorities unleashed a genocidal assault upon the Armenian population, the culmination of a decades-long pattern of pogroms and cleansing, which, in the 1890s, had been perpetrated by special Kurdish regiments created explicitly for the task of ethnic repression (Anderson 2008, p. 407). Nor were the Armenians the only victims of ethnic cleansing and mass deportation—many of the perpetrators and their supporters suffered a similar fate among their ranks. Refugees and exiles hailing from the Northern Caucasus and the Balkans, ethnic Turks yet also Circassians, in the hundreds of thousands had been expelled to Anatolia in successive waves over the last half of the nineteenth century. Many remained full of "bitter memories of their treatment by Christians" (Anderson 2008, p. 407)—yet another instance of victims who became killers, or supporters of killers (Mamdani 2002).

Even so, what happened to the Armenians in 1915 was unique in its brutality. As Anderson summed up, "ostensible deportation, brutal enough in itself, was to be the cover for extermination—systematic, state-organized murder of an entire community" (Anderson 2008, p. 407). This was the first state-sponsored genocide of the twentieth century. This was a genocidal assault unleashed in the midst of punishing defeats along the Ottoman-Russian front that was motivated by a mixture of hatred and fear—fear that the Armenians had rallied to support imperial Russia's troops.

The Turkish national imaginary remains haunted by the ghosts of the Armenian genocide—the unmentionable—that which must still be vehemently repressed and denied. As Frantz Fanon famously documented in Algeria, those traumatized by wars can include the perpetrators of violence, the oppressors, as well as the oppressed (Fanon 2001). The enormity and sheer scale of the crimes that were committed against neighbors in the course of the war are crimes that can be denied, but never fully erased or forgotten. Thus, the social imaginary remains plagued by what Stephen Casmier has, in the context of the United States (US), referred to as "perpetrator trauma" (Casmier 2015). The trauma in this case was caused by a trail of egregious collective and individual crimes in which many Kurds were complicit, with their authors unrepentant and unpunished.

A Long and Bloody Record of Militarism and Authoritarianism

The ongoing conflict between the PKK and the Turkish State can only be understood when embedded within such a deeper historical context—a context characterized by a long record of militarist authoritarianism, and considered in connection with a "longstanding and pervasive pattern of political violence" that has frequently plagued, even brutalized, the Republic, and is inflected and reinforced within dominant social imaginaries (Orlow 1982, p. 53).

As the leader of the Kurdish freedom movement, Abdullah Öcalan has contended that, from the very early years of the Republic, the exclusion of a Kurdish collective voice—especially one that called for democratic autonomy—has always ranked highly on the agenda of anti-democratic forces within the Republic of Turkey; for this reason, he claims that "[t]he PKK's fight is not with the Republic but with the anti-democratism aimed at the Republic" (Öcalan 2012, pp. 48–51).

The Ottoman Empire was dismantled at the end of the First World War, and the remaining territories over which it long ruled were reorganized into the system of the "modern nation-state," a system more or less in place in the region ever since. By the end of the "Great War," the Empire had "succumbed to military pressure, of Russia in the east, and Britain and its Arab allies in the south." In the Arab regions from which the Ottomans were forced to retreat, "the British and French defined a set of new territorial entities which later became states: Lebanon, Syria, Iraq, Transjordan, and Palestine" (Halliday 2005, p. 81).

At the same time, out of the Anatolian hinterland of the Empire, "a new Turkish state was created." This new Turkish State was "initially subjected to severe external controls, formalised in the Treaty of Sèvres of 1920." The Treaty of Sèvres, enforced by the Great Powers, not only "ceded areas in the West to Greece and placed the straits under international control," it also, crucially, recognized the "possibility of a separate Kurdish State" in the East. However, the Sèvres settlement did not hold. Instead, "a nationalist movement, led by Mustafa Kemal Pasha, rejected this settlement and, in a series of successful campaigns, reasserted Turkish independence," ultimately forcing a new agreement in 1923—the Treaty of Lausanne. In the new Treaty, the "boundaries and independence of the new Turkish State" were established, and with it the promise of Kurdish autonomy, or a Kurdish State rescinded (Halliday 2005, p. 81; see also Yadırgı 2017, pp. 5–6).

The machinations of the Great Powers have not been forgotten to this day. Their attempt to divide and distribute the spoils of victory at the end of the First World War, in the Treaty of Sèvres and, in particular, their promise in Sèvres to recognize autonomy or even statehood for the Kurds, continues to generate fears and paranoia among Turkish nationalists when it comes to the "Kurdish question," and still helps account for the "tendency to assess the demands of the Kurds in Turkey along conspiratorial lines" (Yadırgı 2017, p. 6). Indeed, as Fred Halliday once remarked, in reference to his own experiences interviewing Turkish government officials in the late 1990s—after decades of membership in the NATO alliance—when asked about the rights of Kurds they "would lean across their desks in Ankara and lecture Western visitors … about the "Sèvres syndrome," the tendency, as understood in Turkey, of western governments to divide, weaken or interfere in the affairs of Turkey and its neighbours" (Halliday 2005, p. 92).

Kemal, too, had originally promised the Kurds political autonomy and respect for their language and cultural identity, at least in the thick of the War for Independence, while the outcome of the campaign was "still in the balance." But as soon as "victory was assured, Kurdish areas were stocked with public officials, Kurdish place-names were changed and the Kurdish language banned from courts and schools" (Anderson 2008, p. 418; Natali 2005, p. 73).

Still, bonds of religion had served to unite Turks and Kurds, even potentially into one "nation." However, by 1924, with Kemal's decision to abolish the Caliphate, all common symbolism came crashing down. It was the abolition of the Caliphate that thus triggered the first major Kurdish revolt, that of *Shaykh Said*, which broke out in 1925 (McDowall 1996; Romano 2006). The full weight of the Turkish military came crashing down on the Kurds, not just the rebels— a bloody fit of collective reprisal: "Whole villages were burnt or razed to the ground, and men, women, and children were killed" (McDowall 1996, p. 196).

The brutal repression of the Kurds marked the onset of—and set the tone— for what has been called "implacable Kemalism." Indeed, it initiated the young Kemalist Republic's authoritarian, militarist, one-party state turn. Control of the Kurdish region became the military's prime function—its *raison d'être*. The press was censored, journalists were intimidated and arrested; trade unions and civil society associations were suppressed, their freedom of expression limited, and opposition political parties were banned (McDowall 1996, p. 198). In sum, it "was the signal for the imposition of a dictatorship" across the Republic (Anderson 2008, p. 419).

Meanwhile, in the Kurdish region, "repression was followed by deportations, executions and systematic Turkification." After 1925, the Kurds officially ceased to exist and Kemal himself never publicly uttered the word "Kurd" again. Thus was consummated and institutionalized the Republic of Turkey's greatest ethno-nationalist fiction, the fiction that "the nation was composed of one homogenous people," a Turkish nationalist fiction and utopia which continues to be enforced and imposed by the State to this day (Anderson 2008, pp. 418–419).

From the time of Kemal through to the present, Republican ideals in Turkey have been consistently distorted by an aggressive and militant Turkish ethno-national consciousness, a dominant social imaginary unwilling and unprepared "to acknowledge the ethnic and cultural distinctiveness of the Kurdish minority" (Cleveland 2004, p. 182). This is an important part of the legacy of Kemal—a towering figure in Turkish national consciousness, the hero of the War of Independence, the founder of the Republic, the father of the Turkish nation—the worship of whom remains the order of the day, as a visit to any school in the country makes abundantly clear.

The Emergence of Turkish National Consciousness and the Nationalist Turkish State

"Atatürk" literally means "father of the Turks," a title that was officially bestowed upon Kemal by the Grand National Assembly in 1934, just four years before his death. Although may be considered by many to be the father of the nation, it was not he who suddenly and solely conjured the Turkish national consciousness from thin air.

Turkish national consciousness had already developed gradually over the course of the nineteenth and early twentieth centuries. It percolated originally among the Turkish-speaking elite, evolving out of earlier Ottomanist commitments associated with "reformist" and "modernizing" tendencies, before transforming into a fully-fledged Turkish ethno-nationalism by the last decades of the Ottoman Empire. The secular bureaucrats, the Westernizers, the would-be "modernizers" of an imperial order in decline, had proven themselves the unwitting midwives of a Turkish nation. And the military was its vanguard, the defenders of the nation's honor, most emblematically embodied by the so-called "Young Turks," whose core group was organized in the Committee for Union and Progress (CUP).

In the summer of 1908, in Monastir and Salonika, amid fears and rumors that the British and the Russians had reached an agreement to divide up the remaining Rumelian territories, a military revolt broke out and quickly spread (Anderson 2008, p. 400). The insurgent officers, known as the Young Turks, were motivated by patriotic conviction, and were especially upset about Sultan Abdul Hamid II's dangerous neglect of investment in the military. They were moved to act by an urgent sense of need to defend the territorial integrity of the Empire—even over obedience to the sultan.

At the outset, the source of popularity of the Young Turks had been their call for a restoration of constitutional government. But once in power, the Young Turks turned out, perhaps unsurprizingly, to be pure opportunists when it came to respecting the constitution.

The Young Turks were emulators of the West, who demanded recognition and respect, a seat at the table, in the image and likeness of the Great Powers. But for that to happen, they knew "a transformation of the Ottoman State was required, to give it a modern mass base of the kind that had become such a strength of its rivals" (Anderson 2008, p. 401). To mobilize the masses in support of the State, the Young Turks believed that explicit appeal to the category of the nation was required. And so the social imaginary came evermore to be defined in relation to a Turkish nation, terms ever more propagated and diffused by the Empire, especially in the school system (Hammy 2016).

The Young Turks in the CUP may have been opportunists when it came to constitutionalism, but they were true believers when it came to the subject of the nation, and theirs was a virulent, aggressive, exclusionary brand of Turkish na tionalism (Yadırgı 2017, p. 5; Hanioğlu 2011, p. 64).

Turkish ethno-national imaginaries flourished in response to the limits and contradictions, and the successive failures of the Ottoman project. Such ethno-national imaginaries emerged even more forcefully in dialectical relation with the trends and traumas of imperial fragmentation and separatist agitation. This helps explain why—from the outset—Turkish nationalism has always been inflected with a considerable dose of understandable paranoia about the vulture-like angling of the Great Powers. In turn, and predictably, the "gradual conversion of Ottomanism into Turkish nationalism further accelerated the secessionist tendencies among the non-Turkish populations" (Rustow 1965, p. 177). But it was only in the wake of the Great War, with the death of the Empire, that the Ottomanist notions were vanquished once and for all—and that void soon came to be filled by a newly-hegemonic Turkish ethno-nationalism, incarnated in the figure of the war hero Kemal, and institutionalized in his Republic.

Indeed, the ethno-nationalist "mythology" propagated by the Kemalist regime ranked among the most "extravagant" in the interwar period, a period abundant in extreme nationalist frenzies. As Anderson has succinctly described (2008, p. 420):

> By the mid-thirties, the state was propagating an ideology in which the Turks, of whom Hittites and Phoenicians in the Mediterranean were a branch, had spread civilization from Central Asia to the world, from China to Brazil; and as the drivers of universal history, spoke a language that was the origin of all other tongues, which were derived from the Sun-Language of the first Turks.

Yet, as Anderson also concludes, the extravagant myths of Kemalism, the reflexes of "ethnic megalomania" were also always reflective of "the underlying insecurity and artificiality of the official enterprise." This in accordance with the great Turkish sociologist Çaglar Keyder's by now classic interpretation of "the retroactive peopling of Anatolia with Ur-Turks in the shape of Hittites and Trojans as a compensation mechanism for its emptying by ethnic cleansing at the origin of the regime" (Anderson 2008, p. 420).

What's more, Keyder's interpretation helps explain why the reflex to repress the Kurdish rebellion in 1925 was so ruthless. Indeed, Keyder considers this a defining moment as well as a crucial turning point in the trajectory of the young Republic, serving to accentuate its militaristic, authoritarian, and ethno-nationalist bent. According to Keyder, the Kurdish rebellion was "a potent reminder that, despite the Armenian deportation and the Greek exchange, the new country still had not attained the degree of national homogeneity desired by the bureaucracy." Consequently, the "rebellion put the government back on the war footing, with independence courts enjoying extraordinary powers to repress Kurdish demands in the east, and using them with impunity." Amidst the wave of severe repression in the East, "a new Law for the Maintenance of Order" was promulgated and put into effect across the country, thereby "provid[ing] the government with an institutional framework for authoritarian rule," and thus "eliminating potential channels of opposition." Such channels were, "with the exception of a brief period in 1930," destined "to remain closed during two decades of single-party rule" (Keyder 1987, pp. 83–84). And from the 1930s, Italian fascism provided the model for emergent State/party relations, under the catch cry of "unifying the forces" (Houston 2008, p. 127; Keyder 1987, p. 100).

Over that period, the regime took advantage of the effective silencing of opposition to construct and consolidate a highly "centralized, secular, Turkish nationalist state." A nationalist state whose reflex response to revolts in the Kurdish regions was aggressive and repressive, even sadistic, including "resettlement schemes and other laws designed to dissolve Kurdish ethnic identity" (Angrist 2004, p. 390)—a nationalizing state, dominated by an "integral" brand of nationalism, assimilationist in principle, exclusionary more often than not in practice (Brubaker 1996).

Its nationalist mentality was captured well by the famous words of the then-prime minister, Ismet Inönü, whose father was a "Turkified Kurd," and who was destined to succeed Kemal as president after Kemal's death in 1938. He insisted, in 1925, in the midst of the wave of brutal repression, "In the face of a Turkish majority other elements have no kind of influence. We must Turkify the inhabitants of our land at any price, and we will annihilate those who oppose the Turks or 'le Turquisme'." A supremacist and ultimately exclusionary mentality captured even more bluntly by Kemal's Minister of Justice, who boasted in 1930, "We live in a country called Turkey, the freest in the world. As your deputy, I feel I can express my real convictions without reserve. I believe that the Turk must be the only lord, the only master of his country. Those who are not of pure Turkish stock can only have one right in this country, the right to be servants and slaves" (Özcan 2006, p. 70).

This nationalizing state was willing to physically annihilate those it designated as internal enemies, and engage in state terror to suppress any and all signs of renewed Kurdish resistance, perhaps most brutally in Dersim in 1938, where whole villages were razed, and "aerial bombing, gas and artillery barrages" were used. The British pro-consul reported at the time, "It is understood from various sources that in clearing the area occupied by the Kurds, the military authorities have used methods similar to those used against the Armenians during the Great War: thousands of Kurds including women and children were slain; others, mostly children, were thrown into the Euphrates; while thousands of others in less hostile areas, who had first been deprived of their cattle and other belongings, were deported to Vilayets in Central Anatolia" (quoted in McDowall 1996, p. 209).

Turkish nationalism became institutionalized and propagated primarily, perhaps, in the education system where all students were forced to repeat on a daily basis, "I am a Turk, I am honest, I am hard working. My law is to protect the children, to respect the elderly and to love my country and my nation more than my own being. My ideal is to elevate myself and to advance. May my existence be sacrificed to the Turkish existence" (Natali 2005, p. 86). Though the nationalizing effect of such indoctrination was destined to be limited in the Kurdish region, especially given the fact that, as late as the 1960 census, "an average of 85 per cent of the populations in fifteen Kurdish provinces" remained illiterate (Natali 2005, p. 97).

From the Death of Kemal to the Alliance with NATO

In terms of foreign policy, the Kemalist regime long maintained a position of independence and neutrality. There had been a brief glimmer of hope among socialists, in the years just after the First World War, when "it appeared that the Bolshevik revolution would spread" across the Middle East, when the Congress of the Peoples of the East "called for *jihad* against imperialism," when Moscow gave its "backing to radical forces inside Turkey;" but by 1921, the pro-Soviet forces "had been defeated, and the USSR ... sought to make peace" with the Kemalist regime. And from 1923 forward, the Kemalist regime in turn maintained a studious "neutrality in the growing conflicts of Europe," which lasted until "the initial phases of World War II" (Halliday 2005, pp. 84–85).

Kemal's death in 1938 signaled a significant realignment in international relations, "away from neutrality and towards an alliance with the [W]est," especially as the War's outcome became easier to predict. Though, tellingly, "no Turkish shot was fired in the fight against fascism" (Anderson 2008, p. 429).

In anticipation that Russia would emerge from the war "in a more powerful and threatening mood," and expecting Stalin to "demand from Turkey... strategic and other concessions," such as those he did, in fact, impose throughout Eastern Europe, Kemal's successor, Ismet Inönü, effectively embraced the West to secure his country's territory and "independence." Inönü's fears were not unfounded. At the end of the war, a triumphant Stalin proposed "revisions of the territorial agreement concerning the eastern frontier," and a revision of the 1936 treaty governing access to "the straits linking the Black Sea to the Mediterranean." It was even rumored that Stalin "was demanding a base on the straits." Inönü was quick to request help from the US, as would be reflected and enshrined in the 1947 Truman Doctrine—the effective declaration of the new Cold War. Loyal allies to "the west," the Republic of Turkey sent troops to the first hot war within the Cold War—the war in Korea. Thus in 1952, Turkey secured membership in NATO, "remote as it was from the North Atlantic" (Halliday 2005, pp. 106–107).

Incorporation into the NATO alliance signified a historic casting of the dice. It proved a fateful and long-lasting realignment, signifying a dramatic alteration of the terms of "independence" from the parameters and project of the Republic's founder, in exchange for inclusion in the Marshall Plan, and for military assistance. This meant subordination to the west, and an end to any anti-imperialist image, unconscionable, even unforgivable, to important segments of the citizenry, both on the Islamist right and on the secular left (Halliday 2005, p. 107).

For the NATO alliance, the geostrategic advantages of incorporating the Republic of Turkey into its fold were obvious. The Republic "represented the most eastern land post of NATO during the Cold War. Nobody else… was closer to Moscow." And so, the Turkish State was effectively commissioned a role on the front lines of the Cold War, guarding the boundaries of the "Free World." Indeed, "a third of NATO's total borders with Warsaw Pact countries" were guarded by the Turkish State. Consequently, military assistance flowed in abundance. The Republic was "equipped with high tech gear" and "used as a listening post," and "billions of US aid" was handed over to the Turkish elite, who soon "became an excellent defense contractor for the United States military." The result: the second largest armed forces in NATO, and the "largest in Europe" (Ganser 2004, p. 225; Yadırgı 2017, p. 186). In Turkey, as in the US, the chickens of so much military spending eventually came home to roost, as militarist motifs within dominant social imaginaries were inevitably reinforced.

Not coincidentally, the shift towards alliance with the "Free World" coincided with the end of single-party rule. A rigged election in 1946, followed by a real one in 1950, in which Kemal's Republican People's Party (RPP) lost—Inönü was thus voted out of office. A peaceful transition of power to the Democratic Party ensued, with Celal Bayar elected president, and Adnan Menderes his premier.

The Transition from a Single-Party State to Competitive Party Politics

The pressure coming from the NATO countries to adopt competitive elections—to maintain at least the façade of freedom in exchange for the billions in aid ostensibly dedicated to protecting "the Free World"—played an important role in persuading Inönü to undertake this transition. Nevertheless, the transition to a competitive representative system was a transition within Kemalism. Only a limited pluralism was allowed; the leaders of the Democratic Party (DP) all hailed from the ranks of the Kemalist establishment. Thus the transition of power was from one faction of Kemalism to another.

Definite limits to opposition endured—Socialism remained beyond the limits of legal toleration, and the Kurdish question remained unmentionable. Official policy was still anchored in repression and denial. The new government made "no changes" when it came to "the official ideology of Turkish citizenship" (Natali 2005, pp. 92–93). Under Democratic Party rule, "the Kurds still could not legally use the term "Kurd" in public or speak their language without the risk of repression" (Natali 2005, p. 96; Yadırgı 2017, p. 192).

Indeed, the Democratic Party shared and continued to propagate the very same exclusionary and virulent Turkish ethno-nationalism as that of the RPP. It even championed its resurgence when, at the request of Britain, the government "took up the cause of the Turkish minority in Cyprus, reclaiming rights of intervention in the island relinquished at Lausanne," and even "unleashed a savage pogrom against the Greek community in Istanbul" (which had been officially exempted from the 1923 "exchange"). The penchant for nationalist violence and aggression came naturally to the new president, Bayar, who, back in the day, "had been an operative of the CUP's Special Organization responsible for ethnic cleansing of Greeks from the Smyrna region, before the First World War had even begun" (Anderson 2008, pp. 434–435).

Even so, the transition to a partially-competitive electoral regime brought with it a certain relaxation of the Republic's militant secularism, in an overture to religious sensibilities among the new governing party's overwhelmingly peasant base. As has been rightly emphasized by Saribay, since the majority of the country remained peasants, and the majority of them remained devout Muslims, "the acquiescence of the government towards religion, permitting wider grounds for religious practice and education, was both a natural result of democracy and a necessary adjustment to it" (Saribay 1990, p. 123). The same "democratic" logic did not, however, apply to the Kurds, since they were a minority. Though, crucially, the Kurdish countryside again emerged as "the stronghold of Islam" (with the exception of Dersim, where "Alevis feared Sunni revivalism") (McDowall 1996, p. 397). Still, in class terms, as Kurdish leader Abdullah Öcalan framed it, "the DP brought a section of the Islamist gentry into the system," but this in turn triggered fears among the Kemalist establishment about "the decline of secularism" (Öcalan 2012, p. 50).

Somewhat paradoxically, given its peasant-based populism (although perhaps not, given the new geopolitical alignments), the Democratic Party also led the transition from a statist economy towards a somewhat more liberalized economy. Such economic liberalization also came naturally to the Democratic Party's leaders, who were less dependent on the State for their status among the elite. Bayar may have been a rabid Turkish nationalist, but he was also a banker; while Menderes was a large land-owner, and "a wealthy cotton planter." At the same time, the government managed to placate the discontent among its popular base by using abundant "American assistance to supply cheap credit and assure high prices to farmers, building roads to expand cultivation, importing machinery to modernize cash-crop production, and relaxing controls on industry." As a result, "per capita incomes jumped in the countryside" (Anderson 2008, p. 434).

Military Interference in Civilian Politics, Round One: The 1960 Coup

The Democratic Party remained in power for a decade, before being violently removed from office in 1960, through the first of the Republic's coups. What were the motives behind the coup?

By the middle of the decade, aid-induced prosperity began to give way to "spiralling inflation, shortage of goods and black marketeering" (Saribay 1990, p. 126). Menderes managed to score a third electoral victory in 1957 nonetheless, though with continued inflation and mounting public debt, "he turned to increasingly repressive measures, targeting the press and parliamentary opposition to maintain his position" (Anderson 2008, p. 435). In terms of its democratic credentials, the "Bayar-Menderes regime" was now beginning to appear "at least as arbitrary as the regime it had ousted" (Sugar 1964, p. 172).

Against this backdrop of economic crisis and repressive measures against opposition, the Democratic Party became increasingly "associated with the resurgence of Islam" in the countryside; the "more the DP became associated with the Islamists, the more it was regarded as part of the peripheral religious movement opposed to the centralizing and secularizing bureaucracy" (Saribay 1990, p. 124). The government was thus increasingly perceived as flouting the limits of Kemalist core ideas and doctrine, especially in urban and elite circles, among the state bureaucracy and, crucially, the military. "The officers came to see the problems of Turkey in the way they were articulated by the Republican opposition and the press" (Ahmad 2014, p. 117).

Repression can often lead to violence; in this case it certainly did. Increased restrictions on channels for legal opposition, free expression, and peaceful criticism engendered an increase in violent protest, which "occurred with increasing frequency in Turkey's cities during [the] spring [of] 1960." To quell the violence, Menderes called upon the army, and as if that weren't onerous enough, he even assigned the armed forces "the task of disrupting Republican Party campaign rallies" (Cleveland 2004, p. 280). In so doing, he overstepped his bounds.

The military had been at the vanguard of westernizing, modernizing reforms well before the establishment of the Republic. But after his victory in the War for Independence, in annunciating the principles of his Republic, Kemal always "insisted on a clear separation of military and civilian affairs." Other military leaders-cum-politicians from the Republic's first generations, including Kemal's successor Inönü, had followed Kemal's example by stepping down from their military posts upon assuming positions in government. But Kemal had a definite utopian vision for the Republic—one whose basic foundations had never been challenged to this extent before. As a result, the military's attitude about intervention in the realm of civilian political life began to shift. In an essay published in the mid-1960s, the eminent German-American political scientist, Dankwart Rustow, who had lived in Istanbul as a refugee after his family fled Berlin in 1933, captured well the ethos and mentality of the military, its ambivalence and sense of dilemma, around the time of the coup:

Kemal Atatürk's doctrine and practice required abstention of the army from politics and obedience to civilian authorities. But what if the civilian superiors abandon and betray the Kemalist heritage of reform—as the Menderes government did at an accelerating pace in the 1950s? The events of 1959–1960 forced the army's hand in the dilemma. The civilian superiors, after gradually undermining the secularist ethos of the Atatürk reforms, were now systematically violating the constitution which the soldiers were duty-bound to uphold and were attempting to use the army as a tool in these designs. General Gürsel's parting advice in resigning his army post in April 1960 echoed Atatürk's precept of soldierly abstention from politics. But in fact, the army by then had no choice about abstaining: if it obeyed the orders issuing from Menderes, it would be deeply in politics on his behalf; if it refused to obey, it would be even more deeply in politics against him. In the revolution of May 27, 1960, the army chose the second alternative. Although a civilian constitution was restored in the fall of 1961, the sentiment persists among younger military officers that Turkey is not politically mature enough for competitive parliamentary politics, and that only an authoritarian regime under military aegis can accomplish the necessary tasks of social, cultural, and economic reform. (Rustow 1965, pp. 186–187)

In sum, in the spring of 1960, the military revealed in no uncertain terms that it "would not allow itself to be turned into a tool of political repression against the legacy of Atatürk. Nor, as it turned out, would the army allow the government to stray too far from that legacy" (Cleveland 2004, p. 280).

Though the coup was led by a General, Cemal Gürsel, "It was not the work of the high command, but of conspirators of lesser rank" (Anderson 2008, p. 435). Different factions and different ranks jostled among the 38-officer junta, which called itself the National Unity Committee (NUC). The members of the NUC were united in their determination to enforce fidelity to the principles of Kemalism from which the government of Menderes had, in the opinion of the military, strayed (Cleveland 2004, p. 280). Beyond that, there was little agreement—only few "had any preconceived notions of Turkey's political future" (Ahmad, p. 119). Colonel Alpaslan Türkes (1917–97) constituted a prominent exception, a man with an ultra-nationalist agenda, who later went on to found the country's neo-fascist party, the Nationalist Movement Party (*Milliyetçi Hareket Partis*) (MHP). The majority, however, had no such ambitious plans. "Most of the officers wanted to return to their barracks after holding 'just and free elections' and restoring power to the politicians" (Ahmad 2014, p. 120).

The Kurdish Question in the 1960 Coup

The secular and Kurdish questions were still very much intertwined, certainly in the eyes of the military. Salient among the grievances expressed against the Democratic Party and its leaders was the perception that they had "allowed the Kurds to get out of hand" (McDowell 1996, p. 404). And in the immediate aftermath of the coup, "[t]he state elite deployed commando units in Kurdish villages, terrorizing local populations and institutionalizing the military's role in the Turkish political apparatus" (Natali 2005, p. 97).

The junta wasted no time before adopting "a much more doctrinaire policy of denial towards the Kurds." It immediately passed a law to systematically "change Kurdish place names into Turkish ones, 'names which hurt public opinion and are not suitable for our national culture, moral values, traditions and customs,'" and, shortly thereafter, "another law providing for the establishment of regional boarding schools with the specific intention of assimilating Kurds" (McDowall 1996, p. 404). The concurrent uprisings of the Kurds under Mullah Mostafa in Iraq raised tensions further, prompting General Cemal Gürsel to warn the Kurds in Turkey that if they were to emulate such uprisings, "the Turkish army would not 'hesitate to bomb their towns and villages into the ground'" (Entessar 1992, p. 88).

Indeed, Cemal Gürsel, the general who led the coup, and who later served as "president, head of State, prime minister, and commander in chief" (Ahmad 2014, p. 121) in the interim before the re-establishment of civilian rule in the fall of 1961 (and remaining president through to 1966), was emblematically emphatic in his denialism vis-à-vis the Kurds. In the spring of 1961, he wrote the "foreword to the second edition of M. Sherif Firat's *Dogu Illeri Varto Tarih*," a book written by a Turkish-identifying Kurd, in which it was argued that "the Kurds were in fact of Turkish origin and that there was no such thing as the Kurdish nation." Gürsel now went on the record to declare "that no nation exists with a personality of its own, calling itself Kurdish," and to insist "that the Kurds were not only compatriots, but also racial brothers of the Turks" (McDowall 1996, p. 404).

The president's declaration prompted "major protest demonstrations" in cities across the Kurdish region, from Mardin, to Diyarbakır, to Severik, to Bitlis, and to Van. A new generation of Kurds appeared on the streets, bravely foisting banners that defiantly proclaimed, "We are not Turks, we are Kurds ... The Turkish government must recognize our national rights." But the demonstrations ended in a bloodbath: "[a]ccording to Kurdish sources, 315 demonstrators were shot dead, and another 754 wounded" (McDowall 1996, pp. 404–405).

The Birth of the Second Republic

But the junta was divided "between hardliners and moderates" and "[d]espite his attitude to the Kurds, Gursel supported a return to civilian rule." Indeed, he even "handed the task of drafting a new constitution to a group of intellectuals, a remarkable act for any general" (McDowall 1996, p. 405). The new Constitution, written by law professors and ratified by referendum in July 1961, was "designed to prevent the abuses of power that had marked Menderes' rule." It established a new Constitutional Court as well as a new Upper Chamber; it also "introduced proportional representation, strengthened the judiciary, guaranteed civil liberties, and academic and press freedom." Yet at the same time, it "created a National Security Council dominated by the military," and granted this new Council "wide-ranging powers" (Anderson 2008, p. 436).

The NSC's purpose was spelled out in Article III of the new Constitution. Its function was to assist the cabinet "in the making of decisions related to national security and co-ordination" (Ahmad 2014, p. 123)—an embedded military prerogative sufficient to significantly qualify the new Constitution's democratic credentials, at least in accordance with criteria of the most influential literature in comparative political science (e.g. Linz and Stepan 1996). The problem for representative democracy was compounded by the fact that "[t]he term 'national security' was so broad and all-embracing that the generals were able to interfere in virtually every question before the cabinet." To make matters worse, military prerogatives were further enshrined, via Article 110, by increasing the powers of the NSC and rendering the Chief of the General Staff directly accountable to the Prime Minister, thus bypassing any subordination to the Minister of War (Ahmad 2014, p. 121).

Thus was born the Second Republic. Despite the military guardianship enshrined in the new Constitution and the continuing denial of the rights (and even existence of the Kurds), in many other ways it made significant advances in a liberalizing direction (Romano 2006, p. 41). The new Constitution guaranteed wider limits of toleration for "freedom of thought, expression, association and publication, promised social and economic rights, and even granted trade unions limited rights to strike." It also allowed, "for the first time in the [R]epublic's history, for the establishment of a socialist party, the Turkish Workers' Party" (McDowall 1996, pp. 405–406).

Among the first things General Gürsel ordered, after seizing control of Istanbul and Ankara, was the arrest of leading government officials, including Premier Menderes and President Bayar. In total, over 600 officials associated with the Democratic Party were rounded up, and subsequently tried on a variety of counts, including "political and financial corruption and subversion of the [C]onstitution" (Cleveland 2004, p. 283). The trials "resulted in the conviction and imprisonment of some 450 individuals ranging from one year to life." Before the new election was held, the junta presided over the controversial execution of the "still-popular" former Premier Menderes, along with two members of his cabinet, "sentenced to death and hanged," thereby serving notice prior to the reintroduction of competitive party politics about the fate awaiting any politician who dared to breach fundamental Kemalist principles (Cleveland 2004, p. 283). Former President Bayar, too, was sentenced to death, but his sentence was commuted to life in prison, before being ultimately freed by an amnesty law in the mid-1960s (Zürcher 2017, p. 251).

Democratization and Social Polarization in the Second Republic

The democratizing tendencies of the Second Republic were accompanied by ever-increasing social polarization. The entrance of the Turkish Workers' Party into the public realm may not have made a huge impact on the hearts and minds of the Turkish toiling masses, but on university campuses a critical mass of revolutionary students emerged (Zürcher 2017, p. 249).

Turkey has a long tradition of student activism dating back to "late Ottoman times," and "Atatürk, in a form of Turkish cultural revolution, consistently encouraged the youth of the nation to spearhead the Kemalist modernization efforts." Indeed, it had been student riots that effectively precipitated the coup—their motivation was to prevent what "the students saw as an attempt by Menderes and the Democrat Party to dismantle the Kemalist reforms" (Orlow 1982, p. 57).

But the process and nature of student radicalization that percolated throughout the late 1960s was different; as the decade proceeded, it became increasingly inflected with influences from the "First, Second, and Third Worlds." The Turkish Republic intersected with all three—"Europe to the west, the USSR to the North, the Mashreq to the south and the east"—and "Turkish students were galvanized by ideas and influences from all three: campus rebellions, communist traditions, guerrilla imaginations, each with what appeared to be their own relevance to the injustices and cruelties of society around them, in which the majority of the population was still rural and nearly half were illiterate" (Anderson 2008, p. 437).

Despite never receiving more than a minimal percentage of electoral support, the Turkish Workers' Party nevertheless helped transform the terrain of Turkish politics in several ways. It "forced the other parties to define themselves more clearly in ideological terms." It also attracted support from young intellectuals, "served as a legal home for quite a few important cadre members of the outlawed Turkish Communist Party," and more generally, "served as a kind of laboratory for the Turkish left," out of which "innumerable factions" emerged (Zürcher 2017, p. 250).

Meanwhile, on the other end of the ideological spectrum, by the late 1960s, two significant developments had occurred. First, the emergence of an ultra-nationalist, neo-fascist flank, spearheaded by Colonel Alpaslan Türkes, who had been one of the main protagonists of the coup before being purged by the moderate faction within the junta in the fall of 1960. Türkes' National Action Party openly adopted fascist methods, including the creation of a youth organization and a paramilitary force named the Grey Wolves, in reference to "a figure in pre-Islamic Turkish mythology." Its "mission was to conquer the streets (and the campuses) from the left." The Grey Wolves' "ideology and strategy" was spelled out in its official magazine: "What is the creed of the Grey Wolf? We believe that the Turkish race and the Turkish nation are superior. What is the source of this superiority? The Turkish blood" (Ganser 2004, p. 228).

With the goal of conquering the campuses and the streets, in December 1968, the Grey Wolves initiated "a campaign to intimidate leftist students, teachers, publicists, booksellers and, finally, politicians" (Zürcher 2017, p. 260; Anderson 2008, p. 438). Thus commenced a wave of violence and counter-violence between the far right and the left, which continued to "accelerate" through the 1970s, contributing considerably to the "destabilization of the constitutional form of government" (Orlow 1982, p. 63; Romano 2006, pp. 43–44).

The second significant development on the right of the political spectrum took the form of a new, more intransigent brand of political Islam, championed by Professor Necmattin Erbakan, a member of a mystical Sufi order with a large network among Istanbul business circles, and whose National Order Party would not refrain from denouncing the Turkish government for its supine posture vis-à-vis the Americans (Zürcher 2017, p. 260; Anderson 2008, p. 438).

The centre of the political spectrum from the mid-1960s was dominated by Süleyman Demirel and his Justice Party—often accused in more orthodox Kemalist circles of "being a continuation of the Democrat Party"—a "winning asset among the electorate" (Levi 1990, p. 138). Indeed, the overlap in electoral base was clear. Even so, there were important differences between Demirel's JP and Menderes' DP. For one thing, Demirel paid heed to the warning of Menderes' execution, and was kept in line by the new constitutional checks and balances as well. Furthermore, Demirel was a self-made man from the countryside. Unlike Menderes, he did not hail from the Kemalist elite. This gave him a certain populist credibility, regardless of his program, since many people in the countryside "could identify with his background and see his career as the embodiment of their hopes" (Zürcher 2017, p. 253).

The electoral fortunes of Demirel and the centre were facilitated by the recovery of the Turkish economy—throughout most of the 1960s, growth rates were "high, and real incomes went up almost continually, by an average of 20 per cent in the years between 1963 and 1969" (Zürcher 2017, p. 254). The recovery was fuelled by the implementation of policies of Import Substitute Industrialization, combined with the continuing inflow of US economic and military aid, as well as increasing remittances from the burgeoning number of Turkish workers who had migrated to Europe (Anderson 2008, p. 438; Keyder 1987, p. 180).

Kemal's own Republican Peoples' Party, still under the leadership of former President Inönü (but increasingly influenced by the up-and-coming Bülent Ecevit), attempted—rather unsuccessfully—to reorient towards the centre-left. This provoked anti-communist smears from Demirel—"left of centre is the road to Moscow," so the slogan went—and ultimately triggered a split in party ranks (Zürcher 2017, p. 256).

Developments in the Second Republic and the Dynamics of Global Capitalism

The split in the RPP was symptomatic of the broader tendency towards political fragmentation that plagued the Second Republic (Ahmad 2014, p. 132). Such fragmentation was, in turn, a "super-structural" manifestation of an underlying rapid and "complex process of social, economic, and demographic change"—a process that had begun in the 1950s and continued at an accelerated pace throughout the

1960s and into the 1970s. Indeed, between 1950 and 1975, the country's population nearly doubled in size, from 21 million to over 40 million. The period saw rapid urbanization as well, with the proportion of the population residing in cities of over 100,000 inhabitants up from a mere 8.4 per cent in 1950 to close to 25 per cent by 1975, with Istanbul swelling from 1 million to 5 million, Ankara grew from 290,000 to 2.2 million, "with shantytowns inhabited by unemployed or underemployed migrants [becoming] a prominent feature of Turkey's urban landscape." Together, these transformations "placed severe strains on Turkey's political structure" (Cleveland 2004, pp. 282–283).

One of the points upon which the great Turkish sociologist Çaglar Keyder famously insisted was the importance of the world-systemic dimension, i.e. where and how the Turkish Republic came to be incorporated into the global capitalist system. More specifically, Keyder argued that "turning points of the world economy" act as critical junctures, in which the contours of domestic political and economic dynamics are successively shaped and reshaped, and the dice are thus loaded in struggles for domestic advantage. According to Keyder:

> At the end of World War II, Turkey, along with other countries of the "free world", was under considerable pressure to adopt parliamentary reforms. This conjuncture and the booming world economy permitted the bourgeoisie to constitute its own political rule, and to reconstruct the administrative apparatus accordingly. Development of capitalism gradually made way for an industrialization strategy similar to the post-1945 experiences of other middle-income peripheral countries under the hegemony of the manufacturing bourgeoisie. (Keyder 1987, p. 3)

External pressures alone do not seem sufficient to explain the transition towards competitive if limited pluralism in the Turkish Republic. After all, the Salazar regime in Portugal and the Franco regime in Spain lasted well into the 1970s, as Anderson has noted. Anderson himself hones in on the comparison with Spain, and goes on to suggest that Turkey's earlier—if incomplete—step towards democratization, understood as the competitive circulation of elites—was only possible because "there was no comparably explosive class conflict to be contained, nor radical politics to be crushed." Framed thusly in comparative perspective with the trajectory of Spain, domestic dynamics come to appear more decisive, at least to Anderson, who attributes the lack of comparatively "explosive class conflict" to a variety of domestic factors, such as: (1) that "most peasants owned land;" (2) "workers were few;" (3) "intellectuals marginal;" (4) "a left hardly figured;" and, crucially, (5) "the lines of fissure in society, at that stage still concreted over, were ethnic more than class in nature" (Anderson 2008, p. 433).

This last claim of Anderson's, that the lines of fissure in society were "ethnic more than class in nature" betrays his own orthodox Marxist bias and sympathies for the militant secularism of Kemalism, the dominant state ideology, and therefore downplays the salience of the secular-religious divide, not to mention its intersection—indeed intimate intertwining—with both class and ethnic divisions. Anderson seems here to surreptitiously underestimate the problem of Turkish nationalism, even to downplay its virulence, what he elsewhere labels "integral nationalism." Not only because he frames it as reflecting an "ethnic rather than class" division, as if the two dimensions were not inextricably sutured, as if the class dimension were not crucial for understanding the plight of the Kurds.

In doing so, Anderson thus seems to overestimate the extent to which "democratization" can be said to have taken place. He also arguably betrays a certain lingering Leninist admiration for the anti-colonial dimension of Turkish nationalism, even if he is emphatic, with Keyder, about how the ghosts of the Armenian genocide still haunt the contemporary Turkish national imaginary. He not only crucially, if momentarily, downplays the virulence of Turkish nationalism; he also tends to treat it as if its continuing virulence were the result of endogenous Turkish dynamics alone.

In thus subtly disputing the first prong of Keyder's world-systemic interpretation, in favor of a more domestic-oriented, Brennerian-style, class-analytic approach, Anderson also conveniently ignores the second prong of Keyder's account—namely, Keyder's argument about how "the establishment of US hegemony following World War II provided an important dimension to the global context" (Keyder 1987, p. 4). In his concrete account, Keyder reveals himself to be well aware of the comparison with Spain, and for that matter Greece, Portugal, and Italy as well, but he emphasizes a very different dimension of comparison. Keyder points out that between the mid-1950s and the early 1970s in Spain, "revenue from tourism increased from one-third of export earnings to 100 per cent in 1965, and then declined relatively to stabilize around two-thirds at the end of the decade." By contrast, the Republic of Turkey brought in virtually no revenue via the tourist industry. Instead, "US economic and military aid provided the single most important credit item (after exports) each year until 1969," and covered "about one-half of the trade deficit until 1974." Importantly, albeit parenthetically, he added, "such a dependence on American funds significantly coloured the country's political environment" (Keyder 1987, p. 180).

Militarism and Para-Militarism in the Second Republic

From its inception, the Republic of Turkey had never tolerated Communist opposition. Indeed, the Communist Party had been banned, and its leaders murdered, by Kemal during the War for Independence, in 1921. But the anti-communist motif in Turkish nationalism was accentuated from the outset of the Cold War, thanks in no small part to the Republic's incorporation into NATO and its dependence on American military aid.

More concretely, in 1959, the Americans helped to organize, pay, arm, and train a "counter-guerrilla" force, deploying cadres from the Grey Wolves and the Turkish military secret service (MİT). According to Zürcher, the counter-guerrilla force was set up "to organize resistance in the event of a communist takeover" (Zürcher 2017, p. 263). However, the organization had a penchant for acting pro-actively. According to Ganser, it "received its first training in torture techniques" while "'interrogating' people from the Socialist countries, especially Yugoslavia and Bulgaria." The counter-guerrilla force soon came to operate "notorious torture chambers," which played a significant role in the extra-legal suppression of the left (Ganser 2004, pp. 229–230).

Nor was the impact of militarism limited to the extra-legal activities of the paramilitary far right. On the contrary, the Second Republic witnessed the birth and expansion of military involvement in mainstream Turkish "political and socio-economic life." Not only were the "pay and living standards" of the officer class "increased substantially," so as to safeguard the military brass from the deleterious effects of inflation; so too were "retired generals sent as ambassadors or appointed directors of corporations and banks." Perhaps most consequentially, "the military entered the world of business and industry" with the creation of the Army Mutual Assistance Association (or OYAK), which aimed gradually, but continuously, to "expand and diversify," to the point where it could be found "in virtually every area of the economy from automobile production to insurance and banking," and even came to be described as the "third sector of the economy," alongside the "state and private sectors" (Ahmad 2014, p. 123). Thus was born the American-subsidized, Turkish version of the military-industrial complex.

The crucial link between militarism and nationalism, rightly stressed long ago by the great revolutionary thinker Rosa Luxemburg, is certainly evident in the case of Turkey, as is the incorporation, even subordination, of the Turkish coercive state apparatus into the broader anti-Communist obsessions and machinations of the NATO alliance in the context of the Cold War. Indeed, the southern frontier separated the "free world" from the Soviet sphere. The Americans not only helped bankroll and equip the Turkish military and foster Turkish militarism in general; they also trained and armed far-right paramilitary groups willing and eager to conduct a dirty war even beyond the bounds of the Republic's repressive laws.

The importance of these connections between the coercive apparatus of the Turkish Republic, the Americans, and the State-sponsored paramilitary terror squads have been rightly emphasized by Abdullah Öcalan, who, in a line of argument not far from the perspective of Keyder (though bringing him up to date), insisted:

> The history of the Republic can be divided into three phases. The first phase, from 1926 to 1950, was characterized by a one-party authoritarian bureaucratic oligarchy. The second phase, from 1950 to 1980, was characterized by a fierce rivalry between the bureaucratic oligarchy and the landowners, the trade bourgeoisie and the import-substitution industrialists, in order to reallocate state profits. The third phase, from 1980 to 2010, saw the explicit inclusion of global finance capital in state profits as a result of its own direct intervention. The common feature of all three phases is the system established by the state and private capital monopolies, which subjected both society and people. Harsh oligarchic methods struggled with state-centered political parties and unions. The hegemonic power that kept the struggle under control was mainly the British Empire from 1925 to 1945 and the United States from 1945 to 2010. After 1950 Europe, the IMF, and the World Bank were partially included as well. But NATO's Gladio is the real ruler. (Öcalan 2012, pp. 54–55).

The Turkish Left and the Kurdish Question in the 1960s

The Turkish Workers' Party, the socialist party allowed for the first time under the 1961 Constitution, proved "highly attractive to many Kurds as the political atmosphere acquired a more strongly rightist flavour… It was only with the left that the Kurds felt they were treated more or less as equals." Moreover, Kurdish intellectuals had tested the new freedoms guaranteed in the more liberal constitution, publishing a variety of bilingual journals on pro-Kurdish themes, but had soon been disabused about the definite limits to pluralism tolerated by the new constitutional order when these journals were promptly shut down, their "editors and leading contributors arrested, and denounced as 'communists and separatists.'" The sense of mutual persecution further strengthened the affinities between the Kurdish activists and the Turkish left. "The closure of one Kurdish or leftist journal after another was a symptom which thoughtful Kurds could hardly ignore" (McDowall 1996, pp. 405–407).

Over the course of the 1960s, these affinities increased and came to take the form of organic links, through the Turkish Workers' Party and its affiliated unions, to which many Kurds were understandably attracted, since these "offered a means of organizational power for ordinary people." Indeed, these organizations claimed to represent the toiling masses, the oppressed, and the marginalized, categories in which most Kurds could undeniably recognize themselves. McDowall has eloquently described the fierce hostility, condescension, and racism which the Kurds were—and continue to be—up against:

> While the State denied that Kurds were anything but Turks, many Turks denied even this fiction by repudiating them. To be Kurdish was, as being Turkish had been a century earlier, to be a primitive rustic or, worse, a Caliban. "Where is your tail?" Kutahya school children had teased Mehmet Altunakar at secondary school in the 1930s. Such taunts were commonplace for every exiled Kurd. By the 1960s racism was still overt and undiminished, those living east of Malatya "being regarded in all but official circles as foreigners". One journal, *Otuken*, stated "Kurds do not have the faces of human beings" and advocated their migration to Africa to join the half-human half-animals who lived there. It went on to warn "They can learn by asking their racial fellows, the Armenians, that the Turks are very patient, but when angry, no one can stand in their way." Others made their hints at genocide more forthright, "We need a solution [to the Kurdish question] as sharp as a sword. Bring the Cossacks or Kirghiz immigrants with their weapons. This will solve the problem once and for all" (McDowall 1996, p. 407).

Only on the Left could Kurds hope to find any modicum of respite from such a climate of hate in Turkey. There were, nevertheless, some signs of increased toleration and even sensitivity toward the plight of the Kurds in some liberal Turkish circles of the time. Perhaps the biggest splash in the mainstream was made by Ahmet Hamdi Bashar, in his new journal *Barish Dunyasi* (World of Peace). In its second issue (May 1962), the new journal included "an article which argued that no real development could take place in 'the East', while certain subjects are forbidden, or in a context of prohibition and violence" (McDowall 1996, p. 405).

The article generated much debate, even began to break through the defences of rampant denial. But the terms of mainstream Turkish debate about the problems in "the East" remained a far cry from full-fledged recognition and support for cultural and political rights for the Kurdish community. Indeed, the Turkish chauvinist mentality was still so deeply ingrained that even the Turkish left would all too often disappoint.

Even so, the zeitgeist effect of the New Left and its burgeoning sympathies for minority nationalities, soon made an impact, spreading from the West. By the late 1960s, both within the Turkish Workers' Party, and especially among radical student circles, mainstream concerns about the "economic backwardness of the East" were transformed and interpreted through the lens of internal colonialism; and thus, "the first calls to recognize the Kurdish nationality problem were made" (Zürcher 2017, p. xiv).

The Political Economy of Kurdish Insurgency

The social and economic transformations that underlay the radicalization and polarization of the 1960s were felt with particular intensity in the Kurdish region. These transformations unleashed class conflict in the region, which in turn undermined and destabilized the patterns of elite co-optation that had emerged in response to electoral incentives introduced with partial democratization. As Yadırgı has recently emphasized in his important contribution to our understanding of the political-economic foundations of the Kurdish freedom struggle, compared to the 1950s, under Democrat Party hegemony, and with memories of 1938 (the brutal suppression in Dersim) still haunting Kurdish collective consciousness, the traditional Kurdish elite proved susceptible to the carrot of co-optation. In Yadırgı's words, "the agriculture-led development strategy during the Democrat decade marked the beginning of two inter-related processes: the economic incorporation of the Kurdish region into the Turkish economy, and the co-opting of the old Kurdish elite into Turkish political life" (Yadırgı 2017, p. 193).

But with this incorporation of the elite, inequalities among Kurds were greatly exacerbated. The "DP government used Marshall Plan aid to subsidize the importation of agricultural machinery" and to ostensibly distribute land, though mostly from state-owned lands that "were already in use for grazing." None of this led to an improvement in living conditions for Kurdish peasants. On the contrary, with the introduction of market imperatives, the established elites—especially large landowners—accumulated more and more land, triggering a rise in the number of landless peasants and forcing many to migrate to urban centres for work. The pattern was evident in most rural areas of the still solidly-rural Republic, but the highest proportion of landless peasants was in the Kurdish region. Indeed, as Yadırgı reports, throughout all of "Turkey," the proportion of peasant families without land rose from a mere 5.9% to fully 30.7% between 1950 and 1960; but in the province of Diyarbakır, the numbers went from an already high 37.1% to 47% in the same period (Yadırgı 2017, p. 194).

Thus, class divisions in the Kurdish countryside were exacerbated. The objective conditions ripened for an outburst of revolutionary insurgency among landless peasants, though such pressures were perhaps softened, if not siphoned off, by outmigration in large numbers to shanty towns and the ranks of the burgeoning (though still relatively small) urban proletariat and under-employed.

Then, "a section of the well-educated children of this traditional rural class" began to defect alongside some other, more upwardly-mobile Kurdish students, in Ankara and Istanbul. They effectively took up the banner of the Kurdish cause, ever more stridently by the end of the 1960s, positioning themselves against the capitulations and co-optations of their parents' generation (Güneş 2012, pp. 50–64), and migrant Kurdish workers were soon successfully recruited for activism as well (Yadırgı 2017, pp. 197-198). The organic links between Kurdish intellectuals and the downtrodden majority of Kurdish peasants and workers proved much easier to suture, much more difficult to sever, than those linking students to the toiling masses in the rest of the Republic, not to mention Paris or New York. Their message struck a chord.

Organic links were thus forged between radicalized students and workers, and perhaps especially under-employed youth. The "under-employed," also known as the *lumpen-proletariat*. Throughout all of the Republic, the population was growing rapidly, outpacing growth in the job market and the education system (Ahmad 2014, p. 132). But the rates of population growth and of under-employment were even higher among the Kurds (Yadırgı 2017, p. 207). As a result, there emerged, among the shanty towns surrounding the urban centres, a growing segment of Kurdish youth with nothing to lose but their chains.

The *lumpen*, had been long distrusted, even ridiculed, by the ideologues of proletarian consciousness, though famously championed by Fanon in the context of the anti-colonial struggle. The *lumpen*, those who "circle tirelessly around the different towns, hoping that one day or another they will be allowed inside." Fanon predicted, "[i]t is within this mass of humanity, this people of the shanty towns, at the core of the *lumpen-proletariat*, that the rebellion will find its urban spearhead." In the *lumpen*, "that horde of starving men, uprooted from their tribe and from their clan," Fanon believed he had found a revolutionary subject—indeed, "the most spontaneous and the most radically revolutionary forces of a colonized people" (Fanon 2001, pp. 102–103).

Öcalan, too, reflecting on the radicalization of the 1960s and into the 1970s, from prison, has highlighted the importance of the under-employed in the shanty towns. "Unemployment intensified in the second half of the twentieth century," he insists, "providing the material bases for the modern freedom movements." In addition to this spontaneous element, based in local material conditions, Öcalan has also stressed the importance of the "external stimulus" provided by witnessing "national liberation movements and class struggles elsewhere in the world gain strength." The zeitgeist effect, amplified and accelerated by "the progress of modern information technology" (Öcalan 2001, p. 50). This was a self-fulfilling prophecy of sorts, the conviction that the flame of revolutionary consciousness was being ignited not only among Kurdish and Turkish youth, but around the globe—part of a broader trend, part of a worldwide revolutionary awakening bound to gain momentum.

This zeitgeist effect proved especially strong among the youth, inspired by images of "student movements in Germany, the United States, and especially France (where students had come close to launching a revolution and toppling General de Gaulle in May 1968)" (Zürcher 2017, p. 258). Such images from around the globe helped ignite the flame of revolutionary imagination.

The Emergence of the Internal Colonial Thesis

Among the Kurds, the conditions for igniting the fire were particularly ripe, and so they were especially receptive to such mediated suggestions. Not only were class divisions in the Kurdish countryside stark and getting worse, with shanty towns and urban centres brimming over with displaced and under-employed Kurdish youth, but also inequalities in living conditions between the Kurdish region and the rest of the country were increasing all the time.

Indeed, as Yadırgı has documented, "throughout the long period of planned import substitution, the national income share of the seventeen eastern and south-eastern provinces continually decreased: in 1965, it was 10.39%, in 1975, it reduced to 9.56% and by 1979, it further dropped to 8.17%," despite the fact that the population of the Kurdish provinces was growing faster than the rest of the Republic. In sum, as Turkey progressed in its pursuit of the path of "ISI development," it appeared to be leaving the Kurdish region behind, or even worse— it appeared to be pushing it down. A case of "massive underdevelopment born of state negligence and paranoia" (Yadırgı 2017, p. 206, 213).

The appeal of the internal colonial thesis was more than partly a product of the zeitgeist, but it certainly rang true to many Kurds, and for good reason. By the late 1960s, the thesis was being explicated with aplomb by the Kurdish intellectual and activist, Dr. Sait Kirmizitoprak, a man who had been imprisoned with dozens of other Kurdish intellectuals by the Menderes government back in 1959, in the so-called "49-ers incident," an act of Turkish nationalist repression that was not forgotten. He emerged as "one of the leading figures of the pro-Kurdish movement in the 1960s." A man who helped paved the way for Abdullah Öcalan, encouraging him "to look to the anticolonial liberation struggles in Asia and Africa" for inspiration. In 1978, Öcalan included a sketch of the thesis in the foundational Manifesto of the PKK (Yadırgı 2017, p. 36).

However, the Kurdish national-liberationists were not alone in their denunciation of the intrigues and machinations of imperialism—the Turkish nationalists were quick to blame the surge in pro-Kurdish consciousness on the intrigues of foreign powers as well. The recurrent crises in international relations for the Kemalist State caused by the situation in Cyprus, together with calls to protect the autonomy of the Turkish minority on the island amidst fears that *enosis* would come to pass with fellow NATO-member Greece, proved very effective in fanning the flames of Turkish chauvinism, even allowing it to resuscitate long-forgotten anti-imperialist motifs, despite Operation Gladio and NATO.

While the Turkish far-right were thus galvanized by the ability to combine its ruthless anti-communism with a newfound anti-American veneer, on the left divisions were beginning to abound, especially among Marxists. As elsewhere, "the Soviet invasion of Czechoslovakia caused a crisis of consciousness among the Turkish Left." It even caused the Turkish Workers' Party to split.

The internal colonial thesis with respect to Kurdistan was part of a broader debate on the Turkish left. The debate about revolutionary tactics was intimately linked to the debate about the proper diagnosis of the disease plaguing the body politic. At one end, there were those who argued that the Republic of Turkey was a "feudal society" that was "ripe for a socialist revolution," and that, furthermore, this revolution "could be brought about by democratic means." At the other, there were those who insisted instead that "Turkey was an Asiatic society with feudal characteristics, that the proletariat was too weak" to impose its will through democratic means.

These latter groups in turn were divided over whether the Turkish Republic was one in which the social formation was primarily "Asiatic" or "feudal." Whereas the defenders of the feudal thesis "saw the state (for state, read *army*) as a potential ally in a progressive coalition to fight feudal and 'comprador' interests;" the defenders of the "Asiatic mode of production" thesis, by contrast, conceived of "the struggle as being between an oppressive state (including the armed forces) and the population" (Zürcher 2017, pp. 258–259).

From 1970 onward, the defenders of the "Asiatic mode of production" thesis responded to the increasing levels of violence and provocations of the Turkish far-right by deciding "that agitation was not enough and that only 'armed propaganda' (in other words terrorist attacks) and an armed guerrilla struggle could bring about a revolution." And so began a campaign of "urban guerrilla warfare, aimed at destabilizing the country" (Zürcher 2017, p. 259).

In these same pro-paramilitary revolutionary circles, sympathy for the plight of the Kurds, and "demands that attention be paid to it," blossomed. But still there were limits to the sensitivity towards the Kurdish question on the Turkish left, and a near-ubiquitous insistence that "ethnic identities should be submerged in classed solidarity," an insistence that Kurdish intellectuals and activists increasingly interpreted as evidence of institutionalized and hegemonic Turkish national chauvinism. Thus the seeds for further divisions were sown.

As for the "feudal thesis" folks, as well as those on the Turkish left who had staked their faith in a national-popular front, both groups set out to reclaim the mantle of older Kemalist anti-imperialist ideals that had been thoroughly perverted, especially since the Republic's ruling elite had "accepted the Truman Doctrine and the Marshall plan" (Ahmad 2014, p. 130). The plausibility of both groups' tactical positions, their belief in a democratic route or in the potential for support within the ranks of the military, was seriously tarnished in June 1970, "when large-scale demonstrations of workers in Istanbul were dealt with heavy-handedly by the troops" (Zürcher 2017, p. 259). And where there had been successful contacts with radical officers, these officers were quickly identified and purged.

Against such seemingly empirical verification of the limits of the "national-popular" front and "neo-Kemalist" tactics, support for the alternative tactic of "guerrilla warfare" was bolstered in radical circles, both among Turks and among Kurds. This local dialectic was once again conditioned by a powerful zeitgeist effect. For the trend towards guerrilla warfare was, indeed, global in scope, especially across the so-called "Third World," to which the Republic of Turkey also pertained, even if its location in the world-system could be more precisely described as "semi-peripheral" rather than "peripheral." As Hobsbawm once put it, "in the third quarter of the century all eyes were on the guerrilla," whose "tactics … were strongly propagated by ideologues on the radical Left," especially among radical critics of Soviet policy" (Hobsbawm 1994, p. 439). The name Chairman Mao should ring a bell, as should Fidel Castro, or for that matter, Ho Chi Minh.

Indeed, this point about the zeitgeist must be stressed. To understand the trajectory of the Turkish and the Kurdish left at the time, it is crucial to situate it within this global historical context. This was the moment of Régis Debray, *cause célèbre*, jailed by the same thugs in Bolivia who had martyred his friend, Che Guevara. It was the moment when he famously argued that, in Cuba with Che, he had glimpsed the future, that the guerrilla tactic provided the answer to the question: "How to overthrow the power of the capitalist state?" Indeed, the guerrilla could become "the nucleus of a people's army" and harbinger of "a future socialist state" (Debray 1967, p. 24). Thus, he could confidently dismiss not only "those who are addicted to the electoral opium, for whom socialism will come on the day when half plus one of the electorate vote for it," but also even those committed revolutionaries who remained believers in the "old obsession," those who believed that "revolutionary awareness and organization must and can precede revolutionary action" (Debray 1967, p. 83). This was a moment when it was increasingly fashionable to conclude, with Debray, that "[r]evolutionary politics, if they are not to be blocked, must be diverted from politics as such," that "[p]olitical resources must be thrown into an organization which is simultaneously political and military" (Debray 1967, p. 123).

This was the moment when Frantz Fanon's last book and testament, *The Wretched of the Earth*, was all the rage as well. A book in which Fanon had eloquently defended the recourse to armed struggle on psychological grounds, as a "cleansing force" and practice capable of "mobilizing the people," indeed, a practice that "binds them together as a whole, since each individual forms a violent link in the great chain, a part of the great organism of violence which has surged upwards in reaction to the settler's violence in the beginning." What's more, Fanon insisted, the practice of violence, "when it arises out of a war of liberation, introduces into each man's consciousness the ideas of a common cause, of a national destiny and of a collective history;" that "it frees the native from his inferiority complex and from his despair and inaction"; that "it makes him fearless and restores his self-respect" (Fanon 2001, p. 74).

"Restoring Law and Order" and Crushing the Left

The violence on the far-right, especially, picked up pace from the end of 1968 onward. The scene was set—a spiral of violence and counter-violence between far-right and left was already underway (Camara 1971). By early 1971, the Demirel government was overwhelmed, "paralysed," and "powerless to act to curb the violence on the campuses and in the streets" (Zürcher 2017, p. 261).

On March 12, the military intervened, in what came to be called a "coup by memorandum." The Chief of General Staff presented the Prime Minister with a memorandum denouncing the situation of "anarchy" in the country, and threatened that the military would be forced to "take over power itself," in accordance with its "constitutional duty," in order to "carry out reforms 'in a Kemalist spirit'" should order not be quickly restored. Some on the left initially welcomed the news of military intervention, hoping it could trigger movement in a progressive direction; they were soon disabused of this naïve notion. For, unlike the coup in 1960, this time around the orders came directly from the high command—not to mention a high command that "was mesmerized by the spectre of a communist threat" (Zürcher 2017, pp. 261–262).

Consequently, the military mandate of "restoration of law and order" was little more than code for "crushing the left." The Turkish Workers' Party became banned, "its leaders accused" not only of "carrying out communist propaganda," but also, crucially, "supporting Kurdish separatism." In this regard, the event that triggered the party's proscription is significant: a resolution in its party congress "expressing support for the 'democratic aspirations of the Kurdish people'" (Ahmad 2014, p. 135). The message came across loud and clear: any recognition of the rights of Kurds to exercise their collective voice remained well beyond the bounds of what the Kemalist establishment was willing to tolerate.

Political Islam, as well, was at least partially suppressed. Necmettin Erbakan's National Order Party was ordered to disband, but he was not prosecuted. So he effectively proceeded to rename it the National Salvation Party, and had no further problems with "the forces of law and order," who instead concentrated their wrath upon the Turkish left and the Kurds.

As for the lawlessness of the far-right, the military command expressed no objection—far from it. Not only was the far-right MHP not proscribed, but the "counter-guerrilla, who were paid and armed by the army," played a prominent role in "the suppression of the left" (Zürcher, pp. 262–263). The main aim of their brutal attacks was to "intimidate the workers and curb union militancy" (Ahmad 2014, p. 135).

The legal and extra-legal repression of the left, however, did little to restore "law and order." Instead, an escalation of the spiral of violence ensued. Indeed, from 1969, when the violent skirmishes with the far-right began, young Turkish and Kurdish left-wing militants began going to Lebanon, where they received paramilitary training by the Palestinian National Liberation Movement at Fatah camps. Around the same time, "a network of cultural clubs were established" across the Kurdish region, but also in Ankara and Istanbul, called the Revolutionary Eastern Cultural Hearths (McDowall 1996, pp. 408–409; see also Güneş 2012, pp. 66–69).

The Deterioration of the Human Rights Situation in Bakur

One of the main manifestations of real lawlessness (if not "anarchy") in the months and years before the high command's coup-by-memorandum was the rapidly deteriorating human rights situation in the Kurdish East. The cultural clubs in the East "implicitly stood for the Kurdish national movement," and so were targeted by the far right in "connivance with the State." By the beginning of 1970, the government in Ankara had "despatched commandos to the [Kurdish] region to begin searching villages for separatists or signs of separatist activity"—security operations characterized by their penchant for "arbitrary brutality and torture." The peace accord between the Kurdish nationalist leader Barzani and the governing Ba'ath party in Iraq, consummated in March 1970, served to "heighten Ankara's apprehensions concerning its own Kurds." By early fall, many involved in the network of Kurdish cultural clubs had been arrested, and "major trials took place," both in Istanbul and Diyarbakır, leading to heavy sentences—some in "excess of ten years" (McDowall 1996, p. 409).

Then, in the beginning of 1971, the newly formed Turkish Popular Liberation Army (TPLA) and the Turkish Popular Liberation Front (TPLF) together upped the ante by carrying out a series of bank raids and abductions of US military officers—it was action-reaction, as if in a vicious spiral. When the Interior Minister spoke in March 1971 to explain the military intervention, he alleged that, in the ongoing raids in the East, "a large number of weapons had been found," and accused Iraqi Kurdish leader Barzani of "assisting the separatists" in Turkey (McDowall 1996, p. 410).

Needless to say, the suppression of legally-permitted avenues for political expression only strengthened the hands of those on the left and in the emergent Kurdish movement who believed the guerrilla option was the superior option. Thus, the campaign of kidnappings was ratcheted up; martial law was soon declared, and the liberalizing provisions of the 1961 constitution were suppressed. The right to strike was suspended, while suspected "terrorists" were rounded up to be brutally and systematically tortured. More acts of "terrorism" ensued, which in turn unleashed "a veritable witch-hunt against anyone with leftist or even progressive liberal sympathies," and so forth. (Zürcher 2017; p. 262; Ahmad 2014, pp. 135–137).

And yet, the military found itself in a dilemma. It was reticent to take over power directly, and the difficulties and disrepute of the military junta in neighboring Greece only reinforced such reticence. But at the same time, "memoranda and ultimatums" could not be produced on a "daily basis to keep the politicians in line," at least not without losing face. So slowly but surely, the civilian politicians, and especially Demirel, eventually regained the upper hand in the struggle for control over the executive cabinet, and in October 1973, elections were held (Zürcher 2017, p. 264).

For the rest of the 1970s, the Republican People's Party (firmly controlled by Ecevit) see-sawed with Demirel and his Justice Party in forming a series of weak and unstable "coalition governments," which at times depended on the support of both the fascist MHP and Erbakan's Islamist National Salvation Party (Anderson 2008, p. 438; Zurcher 2017, p. 266). The successful invasion of Cyprus in 1974 further fanned the flames of Turkish nationalist chauvinism. Meanwhile, the process of underlying social polarization continued apace, with the torture and violence on the far-right outweighing by far any human rights violations by the left.

The Turkish Workers' Party was banned throughout the period, and under clandestine conditions, ultimately disintegrated. A myriad of guerrilla factions competed for hegemony on the left—among them, the Albanian-inspired Popular Liberation Army, the *Guevarista* Popular Liberation Front, and the Maoist Communist Party of Turkey/Marxist-Leninist (Özcan 2006, pp. 76-77).

All the while, violence by the far-right "steadily increased," especially in the Kurdish region. "State security forces also renewed their operations" in the region, "ostensibly to curb the violence but in practice turning a blind eye to rightist activities," and concentrated on persecuting the left. "By the end of 1978, 20 to 30 were being killed daily in the East" (McDowall 1996, p. 413).

Economic Crisis and Neoliberal "Stabilization"

To make matters worse, as the decade wore on, economic conditions in the country had begun to deteriorate considerably as well. This was the result of a combination of factors, among them the "worldwide economic downturn," intimately intertwined with "the oil-price shock of 1974," not to mention, crucially, the "US embargo and European sanctions" that followed on the heels of the Turkish invasion of Cyprus," as well as "the cost of occupation" itself (Ahmad 2014, p. 146). In economic terms, the intra-NATO conflict with Greece turned out to be quite costly (Durmaz 2014). At the same time, the economic downturn in Germany made a serious dent in remittances from Turkish expat workers (Zürcher 2017).

Revolutionary developments in Iran and the Soviet invasion of Afghanistan caused the Americans and Europeans to reaffirm solidarity with Turkey, and so the embargo and sanctions were lifted by the end of the decade. In the meantime, much damage had already been done. Indeed, according to Durmaz's well-documented and meticulous study, "the embargo had a serious impact on the Turkish economy and defense capability because the Cyprus campaign required continuous logistical support, and Turkey was dependent on the United States for many of its military supplies" (Durmaz 2014).

By the end of the decade, Prime Minister Ecevit found himself forced to request a bail-out from the IMF, which demanded painful structural adjustment programs in return. The age of neoliberalism had come, and the Republic of Turkey was among the first to be forced to abandon the dream of Import Substitution Industrialization, and to suffer the social consequences of imposed economic austerity in order to avoid default on a debt that had ballooned "almost fivefold" in less than a decade (Yadırgı 2017, pp. 214–215).

The stabilization program agreed upon in January 1980 proved a critical turning point for the country, both economically and politically (Ahmad 2014, p. 147). The imposed austerity was incredibly unpopular. The opposition of the unions and of left-wing activists made it very difficult for the government to implement "the neoliberal economic package." By September, the military had intervened for a third time, again under the high command. The military junta "endorsed the neoliberal economic policies and made a point of keeping [the American-trained undersecretary of economic affairs Türgut] Özal in the government," and gave him the title of "deputy prime minister in charge of economic affairs." Özal was "a man who had worked in the World Bank and was known to financial circles in the West" and trusted by the business community in Turkey. Özal "thereafter became a towering figure in Turkish politics," future prime minister and president of the Republic. Özal's program, a kind of "Chilean solution," was endorsed and enforced by the military. The onset of neoliberalism in the Republic thus worked hand in hand with authoritarian reaction. Indeed, the latter made possible the former (Yadırgı 2017, pp. 217–218; White 2000, pp. 104–106).

The Birth of the PKK

In 1978, against this background of economic crisis combined with extreme repression and violence in the Kurdish region, a group of Kurdish (and Turkish) university students in Ankara founded the Kurdish Workers' Party—the PKK. Among them stood Abdullah Öcalan.

Öcalan had been radicalized by events that occurred in the aftermath of the 1971 coup-by-memorandum, especially the so-called "Kizildere" incident in March 1972, when the Turkish military bombed a village house where leftist guerrillas were holed up with three hostages (English NATO technicians). The guerrillas were demanding, as ransom, that the founder of the Turkish People's Liberation Army, Denis Gezmis, referred to by many as the Turkish Che Guevara, not be executed. All but one in the house were killed (Ertugrul Kurkçu).[1] Needless to say, Gezmis was eventually executed for his role in the kidnapping of US soldiers before the coup.

Öcalan took part in a protest organized by radical students at the University in Ankara against the Kizildere massacre, at which he was arrested and then imprisoned for seven months. This was his first direct experience with state repression. Öcalan was a first-year student, involved in the Federation of Revolutionary Youth, and was a personal friend of Mahir Cayan, the leader of the Turkish Popular Liberation Front and one of the militants killed in the Kizildere massacre. Those seven months in prison served as an "incubator" of sorts for Öcalan. He became further radicalized by the experience and used the time to reflect (Özcan 2006, p. 78). Upon his release from prison, Öcalan began to organize actively, determined to form his own group. As Öcalan recalled:

> Towards the end of the year [1972] we were released. I still remember; the first thing I had to do was to pass my exams in fifteen days and have the right to

attend the second year of the faculty. As soon as I achieved that, I had one-to-one meetings in the utmost secrecy with each individual probable person for the nucleus of the group. The idea of colonialism was emerging at that time. 'The Kurdish question is a colonial matter', I said. Nobody had thought of such a diagnosis [about Kurdistan] if you remember. But the terms 'Kurdistan', 'colony' came to my mind…do you believe that when I was going to tell someone I used to go to the deepest room, if there were two doors I shut them both, and I was simply whispering into the ears (Quoted in Özcan 2006, p. 80).

After an amnesty by Prime Minister Ecevit in 1974, Öcalan brought together "six political colleagues to initiate a specifically Kurdish national liberation movement based on Marxism-Leninism." The following year, the group left Ankara, to proselytize and gain recruits across the Kurdish region, with a special focus on the different areas from which each of the six founding members came: Urfa, Elazig, Tunceli, Gaziantep, and Maraş (McDowall 1996, p. 418).

At the time of this initial phase of organization and recruitment, the group was known simply as "the followers of Apo," a still widely-used term of affection for Öcalan (White 2000, p. 135). Their gospel consisted of a simple but powerful message that many people were ready to hear, and so spread rapidly across the Kurdish countryside. The message was this: the Kurdish people have "the right to self-determination." They understood this at the time to mean "the establishment of an independent and united Kurdistan, and a socialist transformation of society." However, to realize this utopia, they preached, would require much sacrifice, blood and fire. Indeed, the "followers of Apo" were emphatic: nothing less than "a prolonged people's war against colonization by Turkey, Iran, Iraq, and Syria could bring about the desired societal change" (Jongerden and Akkaya 2016, pp. 3–4).

The "Prolonged People's War" and the Struggle for Kurdish "Self-Determination"

The idea of a "prolonged people's war" can be traced back to the political thought and praxis of Mao Zedong, who invoked it as a military-political tactic in the course of the long Chinese civil war that preceded his successful rise to power. It was subsequently imitated by guerrilla groups operating in a variety of different contexts—Fidel Castro in Cuba, the Freedom Fighters in Bangladesh, the Naxalites in India, the New People's Army in the Philippines and, more recently, the People's Liberation Army in Nepal and the Shining Path in Peru.[2]

But it was the example of Ho Chi Minh and the Viet Cong in the Vietnam War that probably weighed on Öcalan's mind most during his "incubation" in prison and thereafter. Keep in mind that the Americans were forced to pull out of Vietnam in August 1973—a crippling blow by the Viet Cong that was certainly impressive, dominating headlines around the globe. Just maybe a similar blow could be struck by the "colonized" Kurds against their colonizers. The thought could not have failed to fuel Öcalan's imagination regarding the revolutionary possibilities.

The basic idea behind a prolonged peoples' war, as a military tactic, was to exploit the few advantages that a small guerrilla group can presume to have in a fight "against a state with a large and well-equipped army." Among these potential advantages was, crucially, "broad-based popular support." In this respect, a "prolonged people's war strategy" can be distinguished from Régis Debray's related "foco" theory—so fashionable at the time in the West—which Debray developed as a result of his experiences with Che, and suggested that popular support need not precede, but could be progressively built, in the course of the guerrilla struggle.[3] (An "innovation," by the way, intimately linked to Che's unfortunate demise.)

The "prolonged people's war" strategy makes a point of "avoiding decisive battles," and is conceived in principle as a three-stage process. In the first stage, the guerrilla should establish its initial base for operations in "remote areas or otherwise difficult terrain in which its enemy is weak." In a second stage, "as it grows in power," the guerrilla "establishes other revolutionary base areas and spreads its influence across the countryside." And finally, in the third stage, "the movement has enough strength to encircle and capture small cities, then larger ones, until finally it seizes power."[4]

From the outset, the "followers of Apo" were distinguished "from all previous Kurdish groups in Turkey (or elsewhere)" in two very important respects: first, "they were drawn almost exclusively from Turkey's growing proletariat;" and second, "they were filled with anger at the exploitation of both the rural and the urban proletariat at the hands of the *aghas* [wealthy landlords], merchants and the ruling establishment" (McDowall 1996, p. 418; Romano 2006, p. 89). As such, their conception of national liberation was already inflected with, and bled into, the praxis of class war.

Indeed, the working-class origins and working-class mentality of this initial group of revolutionary evangelists was among their most effective recruitment tools, and certainly more convincing to Kurdish peasants than any vague and abstract Marxist---Leninist notions (White 2000, pp. 155–156; Van Bruinessen 1988, p. 42). As Öcalan himself remarked decades later, reflecting (again) from prison, "The early organization was a group of people with no great organizational talents and who were also not particularly aware of social issues. All came from a poor background and were honest people. The community appreciated these qualities, which became the social bases of the organization. The political struggle was dominated by oral propaganda" (Öcalan 2011, p. 113).

Their strategy was not very elaborate in the beginning; nor was a sharp distinction drawn between Kurdish and Turkish fronts for liberation and struggle. On the contrary, as Jongerdon has explained, the "followers of Apo" "considered themselves Marxists engaged in making a revolution, with Kurdistan as their focal area and with the intention of uniting the revolutionary left in Turkey" (Jongerdon 2017, p. 247). The geography of Kurdistan, "marked by two important mountain ranges, the northwestern Zagros and the eastern Taurus," combined with the history of brutal repression by the Kemalist establishment, made it seem an ideal location for a revolutionary base camp, appropriate for launching "stage one" (Jongerdon and Akkaya 2016, p. 1; O'Ballance 1996, p. 146).

The May 1977 murder of Haki Karer, a "follower of Apo" of Turkish origins, shot dead by a member of an ostensibly rival left-wing group, but with links to the Turkish intelligence service, triggered the decision in 1978 to officially establish a party, the Kurdish Workers Party or PKK (Öcalan 2011, p. 113; Özcan 2006, p. 84; Güneş 2012, p. 79).

The PKK soon became "the first political-military organization transcending regional and tribal ties capable of appealing to a wide range of Kurds residing in different parts of the country," and consistently displayed "an enormous capacity to mobilize Kurds both within and without Turkey." Over the course of the following decades, according to some estimates, it enrolled some "10,000 well-armed insurgents and could command the loyalty of 50,000 militia and, according to government estimates, 375,000 sympathizers" (Ozkahraman 2017, p. 5). According to other estimates, "membership grew from a few hundred fighters in the early 1980s to between 15,000 to 20,000 in 1994" (Yıldız and Breau 2010, p. 18).

Originally, the PKK was organized along classic democratic-centralist, Marxist-Leninist lines. In the party's founding manifesto, *The Road of Revolution in Kurdistan*, the new party denounced those factions on the Turkish left who still refused to recognize the status of Kurdistan as an "inter-state colony" or the centrality of the Kurdish question for revolutionary struggle. And it went on to sketch "two main objectives: (1) the transformation of Kurdish society through the elimination of relations of exploitation; and (2) the unification of Kurdistan and the establishment of an independent state" (Jongerdon 2017, p. 249; Özcan 2006, pp. 87, 98–101). To achieve these goals, the PKK called for a determined struggle against three groups, considered existential enemies of the Kurdish people: (1) the paramilitary fascist Right (the Grey Wolves, etc.); (2) agents of the State and their supporters; and (3) "the exploitative Kurdish landlord class." However, in practice, at least at first, they concentrated efforts on the class struggle within Kurdistan (McDowall 1996, p. 419).

The PKK and the Praxis of Class War

The region was certainly ripe for class struggle. As Jongerdon succinctly described, "[r]elations of exploitation were mainly defined by division of labor and hierarchy based on the distinctions between agricultural laborer, tenant farmer, and landowner. The large landowners, sometimes also both tribal and religious leaders, maintained close relations with the State and regarded peasants and villagers as their subjects" (Jongerdon 2017, p. 250). The PKK's first targets in this class war were these large landowners in Öcalan's home province, Urfa. In August 1979, the party committed its first act of revolutionary violence, when it "tried to assassinate Mehmet Celal Bucak," a man who personally "controlled 20 villages" as well as the town of Siverek, for which he served as Justice Party representative. The PKK's violent determination to stand up to this "hated local mag-nate" did much to ensure the sympathies of the poor peasants and the workers in the feud that ensued (McDowall 1996, pp. 419–420; Saeed 2017, p. 40; Romano 2006, p. 75).

But the PKK's revolutionary violence was not always limited to class enemies. Amidst the turmoil of violence and counter-violence between left and far-right throughout the Republic, clashes between rival leftist groups were not altogether uncommon, and the PKK was no exception in this regard. Indeed, the "followers of Apo" were rumored to have run all potential rivals out of Öcalan's home turf of Urfa province (McDowall 1996, p. 419; White 2000, p. 148). The fact that the PKK distinguished itself from other leftist groups by both the aggressiveness of its revolutionary attitude and the class composition of its cadres, with their work-ing class and even *lumpen* origins, led it to discredit and dismiss other leftist groups, both Turkish and Kurdish, as "revisionist and reformist"—even if this was not always the case (White 2015, p. 17). Indeed, in its initial years, the PKK was often accused of having "physically attacked" members from rival organiza-tions. The organization expressed repentance for such acts very early on, includ-ing "self-criticism" on the subject in its first party congress. Even so, "occasional armed confrontations" with rival groups on the left continued to "take place for some years" (White 2015 p. 17; Marcus 2007, p. 41).

The PKK was not only a revolutionary agent of violence, it must be recalled that it also found itself prominently targeted as an object of violence. The turmoil of violence and counter-violence, the vast majority of which was committed by the far-right in cahoots with the "deep state," led to a daily death toll of 20–30 by the end of 1978. In one instance, the Maraş massacre, the Grey Wolves militia murdered over 100 Alevi Kurds in one day. As a result, the PKK employed armed members for protection, which meant that any skirmish could quickly turn bloody (McDowall 1996, p. 413).

Sometimes violence was committed at the explicit behest of Kurdish landowners, such as the murder of Halil Çavgun, killed by police forces in May 1978, while putting up posters and graffiti commemorating the one-year anniver-sary of Haki Karer's assassination (Orhan 2015, p. 111).[5] Çavgun was certainly not the only such victim. Indeed, "it is estimated that at least 20 cadres and senior militants of the party were killed in 1977 and 1978" (Orhan 2015, p. 110). Thus, even before the PKK was officially named, it was already producing revolutionary "martyrs." Hundreds more were killed between 1978 and 1980 (Orhan 2015, p. 111).

The 1980 Coup and the State of Emergency

Then came the September 1980 coup and the declaration of the state of emer-gency. In its aftermath, fully 1,790 people suspected of being PKK members were rounded up and arrested, including several members of the central committee, and charged with promoting separatism. A mass trial of those rounded up was held (Zürcher 2017, p. 285), but the key leaders, including Öcalan, managed to "slip over the border," and "continued preparations for insurgency from neighboring Syria and Lebanon" (McDowall 1996, p. 420; Romano 2006, p. 50). The coup and the crackdown only strengthened the PKK's resolve, and consolidated its commitment to revolutionary war (Entessar 1992, p. 96; Güneş 2012, p. 98).

The round-up of suspected PKK members was part of a much broader crackdown on the left in the days and weeks following the coup. Indeed, a massive wave of repression swept the country: "In the first six weeks after the coup 11,500 were arrested; by the end of 1980 the number had grown to 30,000 and after one year 122,600 arrests had been made. By September 1982, two years after the coup, 80,000 were still in prison, 30,000 of them awaiting trial" (Zürcher 2017, p. 284; Romano 2006, p. 80). Alongside the mass arrests, systematic abuse, and torture occurred.

Meanwhile, the generals immediately set about to purge the political system, and to "reconstruct the entire political system on new foundations" (Ahmad 2014, p. 149). All party leaders were arrested, "the parliamentarians sent home and the parties abolished," and "all mayors and municipal councils (over 1700 in all) were dismissed" (Zürcher 2017, p. 283). The generals established a National Security Council; they suspended the Constitution; they suspended "professional associations, such as those of lawyers and doctors," as well as the trade unions; "strikes were declared illegal and striking workers were ordered back to work" (Ahmad 2014, p. 150).

But this was not the full extent of the wave of repression. The universities were "put under tight centralized control," and university professors with progressive views were targeted—more than 300 were purged in late 1982, "followed by a second wave of dismissals early in 1983" (Zürcher 2017, p. 285).

Needless to say, "the regime also adopted a pro-Western foreign and military policy." Meanwhile, domestically, the generals gave priority to "crushing all aspects of 'the Left'"—not only radicals, but "social democrats, unionists, and even members of the Peace Association who included the very elite of Turkish society." To this end, the regime also attempted a re-equilibration of official Kemalist ideology, and began to promote a "Turkish-Islamic synthesis" (Ahmad 2014, pp. 150–151). "Laicism does not mean atheism," the junta now insisted (Anderson 2008, p. 441). Emblematic of the regime's ideological re-equilibration was that religious courses were "made compulsory for school children for the first time in the history of the republic." The "Turkish-Islamic synthesis" introduced in the wake of the 1980 coup has continued to gain strength ever since, in no small part because, "by inflicting a serious defeat on the left, the military inadvertently made it possible for the Islamist movement to rally [nearly] all discontent among the poorer strata of society," at least outside of Kurdistan (Savran 2015, p. 60).

The 1982 Constitution

In October 1981, just over a year after seizing power, the National Security Council "appointed a consultative committee to write a new constitution," though it forbade "former politicians from engaging in public political debate" about it.

The draft constitution proposed to get rid of the Assembly's upper chamber, and to "centralize power in the office of the president." To this latter end, it granted the president powers to dissolve parliament, as well as to "rule by decree, and virtually appoint the constitutional court." Alongside these presidentialist innovations, the military sought to further enshrine perpetual constitutional prerogatives for itself, in the guise of a new "presidential council." Other provisions created constitutional limits with respect to "freedom of the press and the unions." This was "democracy without freedoms," in Ahmad's (un)felicitous turn of phrase or, more precisely, an even more limited version of competitive pluralism (Ahmad 2014, p. 151).

The scope of competitive pluralism became further restricted by "a new electoral law [that] denied parliamentary representation to any party that did not receive 10 per cent of the total vote" (Cleveland 2004, p. 285)—an extremely large threshold in comparative perspective.

Despite these glaring flaws from the perspective of rights and democracy, the new constitution was overwhelmingly approved via referendum by a citizenry eager to regain a modicum of liberties; but tellingly, no debate was allowed. With the passage of the new constitution, General Kenan Evren, who led the coup, "automatically became president for the next seven years" (Ahmad 2014, p. 152).

"Only in the Kurdish southeast were relatively high percentages of 'no' votes recorded" (Zürcher 2017, p. 227). Needless to say, the new constitution also doubled-down on the Republic's hostility towards any manifestation of the Kurdish language or culture, in three separate Articles (26, 28, and 89), which banned the use of any "prohibited language" from use in print documents, the media, or other publications, and prohibited any political party from defending or promoting any "non-Turkish language" (Entessar, p. 96). Alongside these came Article 66, which adamantly declared, "[E]veryone bound to the Turkish State through the bond of citizenship is a Turk" (Gunter 1997, pp. 51–52; Natali 2005, p. 107). Further, Article 14 "prohibited political struggles based on language, race, class and sect" (Yadırgı 2017, p. 219).

In addition to the "new constitutional prohibitions against the use of the Kurdish language" and expression of Kurdish identity, the junta also revised the penal code to criminalize any such expression before formally returning power to civilian control (Entessar 1992, p. 96). This came on top of the "ban on the use of the terms 'Kurd' or 'Kurdish'"; and alongside frequent recourse to the use of "draconian measures," such as Articles 141 and 142, which "prohibited organizing 'communist' and/or 'separatist' organizations," and Articles 158 and 159, which "prohibited 'insulting' the president of the Republic, the Parliament, and government and military authorities." "Even lawyers who defended Kurds accused of promoting separatism were prosecuted" (Entessar 1992, p. 96).

In the climate of repression and reaction, crude Turkish nationalist myths about the Kurds resurfaced, even flourished, such as the unfounded claim that "Kurds were simply another Central Asian Turkic tribe and were, therefore, of Turkish origin" (Entessar 1992, p. 97). Such bogus myths were even officially propagated by the State, as "official state publications [systematically] denied the authenticity of Kurdish ethnic identity," and "Turkish nationalist writings" even claimed that "the Kurdish *Newroz* celebration was really a Turkish holiday" (Natali 2005, p. 109).

An ex-minister of public works, a man of Kurdish origin, Şerafettin Elçi, who had caused a scandal in April 1979 by publicly stating "There are Kurds in Turkey, I too am a Kurd," was put on trial by the junta, and "sentenced to prison for 'making Kurdish and secessionist propaganda'" (McDowall 1996, p. 413; Entessar 1992, p. 97).

After Elçi's conviction came the show trial of 30 Kurdish activists accused of belonging to the PKK. The public were prepared for these trials by the broadcasting of a 90-minute television program that featured "numerous testimonies" of "peasants denouncing the goals, programs, and activities of the PKK." Indeed, they were portrayed as terrorists "bent on aggrandizing their own fortunes at the expense of the Kurdish population." One peasant featured in the program even went so far as to claim "that the PKK was worse than the European invaders," that it had "forced his son to murder his mother and sister" (Entessar 1992, p. 97). In sum, the PKK was not just criminalized and brutally repressed, but also demonized to the point of being public enemy number one. Soon enough, rumors abounded that the PKK leader, Abdullah Öcalan, "was really an Armenian and that the PKK's goal was to annihilate Sunni Muslims" (Natali 2005, p. 109). In sum, the junta fantasized that, via repression and reactionary propaganda, it could nip in the bud all expression of Kurdish ethnicity and national consciousness. They may have succeeded for a short while—but soon things would devolve into a spiral.

Neo-Liberal Re-Equilibration in the Balance of Class Power

Meanwhile, the military regime set about to dismantle the Import Substitution Industrialization model, and "give free rein to market forces" (Anderson, p. 441). With the crushing of the left, a "radical makeover of the economy could be embarked upon with minimum resistance" (Keyder 2004, p. 67). Predictably, the unleashing of market forces led to increasing levels of inequality; wages and salaries as a share of national income dropped from around 30 per cent in the 1970s to around 20 per cent in the 1980s. So too, a wave of privatization, deregulation, and "flexibilization" decimated public-sector manufacturing jobs, which had "constituted the core of the labor movement of the 60s and 70s," and "informal and diversified conditions of work" began to spread (Keyder 2004, p. 67).

The resultant re-equilibration in the balance of power between labor and capital worked well for the latter—alongside declining wages, "exports trebled in value, new enterprises sprang up, profits rose" (Anderson 2008, p. 441). And crucially, new geographies of development began to emerge. Smaller Anatolian cities soon became "regional industrial centers," the so-called "Anatolian tigers," which benefitted from the turn towards "labor-intensive manufacturers," especially given their "craft traditions and non-unionized workforces," and budding entrepreneurs "contacted directly with retail chains and volume buyers in Europe." This new class of entrepreneurs tended to view "dealings with the economic bureaucracy of the State" as "a burden rather than a benefit;" and "did not share the westernized style and militant secularism of their more entrenched counterparts in Istanbul" (Keyder 2004, p. 68). The seeds for a future Islamist rival to Kemalist hegemony were certainly being sown (Savran 2015, p. 61).

In sum, the period of military rule witnessed a rather thoroughgoing "authoritarian neoliberal restructuring" across the Republic. Among the inequalities that were exacerbated by this turn of events were those between the Kurdish southeast and the rest of the Republic. Not only did the military regime double down on the repression and denialism of the Kurdish collective voice; it also neglected "the sector on which the predominately rural Kurdish regions were heavily dependent: agriculture." The "eradication of subsidies and price support programmes after 1980, combined with the trends in the international market to create a severe deterioration in the sectoral terms of trade." As a result, peasant farmers faced "increased and even extreme indebtedness to cover costs" (Yadırgı 2017, p. 218). Capitalist development in the Anatolian heartland thus went hand in hand with economic neglect of the Kurdish periphery.

Having laid new authoritarian and neoliberal foundations, the military was ready to step back and allow once again competitive-electoral politics, albeit of an even more limited variety. After the adoption of the new constitution at the end of 1982, a new law on political parties was introduced. New parties could be formed, providing they were approved by the National Security Council. To make matters worse, "[s]tudents, teachers, and civil servants were barred from party membership." Nor were new parties "allowed to form roots in society because they were not allowed to found women's or youth branches, to develop links with trade unions or to open branches in villages." (Zürcher 2017, pp. 286).

12 out of 15 applications for party status were either unsuccessful or revoked within the first few days. Those proscribed included the successor to Demirel's Justice Party as well as a social democratic party founded by the son of Inönü (Ahmad 2014, pp. 152-153). Just three parties were allowed to compete in the November 1983 election: (1) the Party of Nationalist Democracy (closely associated with the generals); (2) the Populist Party (largely Kemalist and formed out of the old Republican Peoples' Party); and (3) the Motherland Party (the party of Turgut Özal, "the man behind the economic reform program") (Zürcher 2017, p. 287). Özal, the victor, was a man who, despite his World Bank background and his ruthless neoliberal agenda, was, like Demirel before him, "the kind of politician with whom the average Turk could identify"—a "self-made man" from a provincial town "whose own career" incarnated so many bootstrap hopes and dreams. Significantly, he was also "known to have connections with the *Naksibendi*" religious order, and proved determined to "use state control of religion to promote it as never before" (Zürcher 2017, p. 288; Anderson 2008, p. 442).

The PKK Goes on the Offensive

Throughout "the period of military rule," for the most part, "the PKK lay low," safe beyond the Turkish border, though it did make "occasional raids" to kill Turkish soldiers manning that border. In addition to its safe havens in Syria and the Beqaa Valley in Lebanon, the PKK also managed to come to an agreement with Barzani's KDP in Iraq, thus facilitating access to a third safe haven, in the Qandil mountains in Iraq, where it remains to this day (McDowall 1996, p. 420; Güneş 2012, p. 99).

Meanwhile, it "prepared for its return to Turkey." In its Second Congress, in 1982, the PKK further formulated and specified its tactic of a prolonged people's war, emphasizing that, at least in the first phase, guerrilla actions were to focus on "demonstrating the limits of state control" (McDowall 1996, p. 420; Güneş 2012, pp. 99–100). The offensive began in August 1984, beginning with a series of "spectacular ambushes against the security forces." In October, "three members of a unit responsible for guarding President Evren" were murdered while he was touring Yüksekova, before "ambushing and killing eight soldiers" in the province of Hakkari (McDowall 1996, p. 421).

The military coup and the commencement of the PKK's armed campaign opened a "new chapter of violence in the region." According to most estimates, since 1984 more than 40,000 have been killed, around 4 million displaced, and over 3,000 villages evacuated and destroyed—a Hobbesian nightmare of grave proportions. In 2001, a UN Special Rapporteur on extrajudicial, summary or arbitrary executions was appointed to visit Turkey. Official figures that describe the violence since the declaration of the state of emergency in 1987 were provided by Turkish Authorities: "over 23,000 suspected PKK militants killed, more than 4,400 unarmed civilians killed and 5,400 wounded, more than 5,000 police officers and gendarmes killed and 11,000 injured" (Yıldız and Breau 2010, pp. 16, 277 footnote 99).

The State responded with wounded pride and determination—launching the so-called "Operation Sun," which soon "developed into a cross-border excursion into Iraq" (O'Ballance 1996, p. 155). Throughout "most of 1985 the Turkish army operated an intensive manhunt in the south-eastern provinces for active subversives" (O'Ballance 1996, p. 156). The PKK dominated national headlines again in spring of 1985 after "a major battle in Siverek" cost the lives of over 60 guerrillas, troops, and civilians (McDowall 1996, p. 421). By summer, the State boasted that it had killed 97 subversives and captured 309, and in a three-week period in the fall, rounded up over 1,000 more (O'Ballance 1996, p. 156). Other estimates put the number of deaths at nearly 200, and the number of armed incidents at 70 (McDowall 1996, p. 421). Still other estimates put the number of PKK-linked "operations against Turkish forces and their Kurdish collaborators" at around fifty, between June and November (Entessar 1992, p. 99).

All the while, "mass trials of subversives continued" apace, "attracting overseas media attention and that of Amnesty International." The demonization by the State, combined with the organization's "competent propaganda section," helped the PKK consolidate its reputation in international circles, as well as on the ground in Kurdistan, "as the predominant Kurdish resistance group in Turkey" (O'Ballance 1996, p. 157).

Prominent among the PKK's targets were powerful landlords. Through deeds of the pistol, revolutionary violence, it sought to show Kurdish peasants that there were alternatives to subservience in "dealing with the enemy class," at the same time that it "demonstrated the inability of the State to protect its own" (McDowall 1996, p. 421). Yet, according to McDowall, the PKK's violence, and the wave of repression and intimidation that it provoked, "created great ambivalence among ordinary Kurds"—"most feared it;" a few "loathed it," either because "it threatened their secure position within the system," or because it threatened "their traditional worldview." And yet, "others secretly (or not so secretly) admired its daring" (McDowall 1996, p. 421).

An important component of the Turkish State's arsenal of repression, in response to the attacks on its local supporters, was its decision "to arm villagers so that they could protect themselves" (McDowall 1996, p. 421). The so-called "village guard system" sought to exploit clan-based loyalties and divisions, and quickly incorporated "those identified with the Right and far Right political parties" already in conflict with the PKK (McDowall 1996, p. 422). In April of 1985, General Evren made a point to "amend the Village Law to allow for the maintenance and arming of village guards at the government's expense" (Yıldız and Breau 2010, p. 16). The State recruited *en masse*: according to McDowall, "by 1990, there were approximately 20,000 village guards, by 1993, 35,000." Its main method of recruitment included economic incentives—guards were paid "several-fold above the average per capita income in the area" (McDowall 1996, p. 422; Romano 2006, p. 83). Other estimates put the figures even higher. According to Yıldız and Breau, "by 1987, Turkey had recruited 70,000 village guards." The human rights situation deteriorated rapidly, as "the village guard system exacerbated lawless violence in the region, particularly against civilians" and, in turn, the "village guards became targets of the PKK" (Yıldız and Breau 2010, p. 16). In sum, the State's response created the conditions for the outbreak of a full-fledged civil war in the southeast, one inflected with both strong class and clan-based divisions.

In 1985, the Turkish authorities "constructed a wire mesh fence alongside its border with Syria," rendering it more difficult for the PKK to organize cross-border raids. However, the border with Iraq that ran through precipitous mountain terrain was impossible to fence, such that the State was forced to rely more on village guards "as a means of blocking PKK access and supply routes" (McDowall 1996, p. 423). The PKK responded with a "ferocious assault" on the village guard system, beginning in 1987. "During the next two years it deliberately wiped out village guard and agha families, men, women, and children, without compunction, in Mardin, Siirt, and Hakkari provinces." This in turn led to "counter-reprisals on PKK 'supply villages', in which the village guards demonstrated they were no less ruthless than the PKK" (McDowall 1996, p. 423). Action–reaction, as if in a spiral—but on the whole, village guards "proved no match for the PKK" (Zürcher 2017, p. 307).

So they were supplemented by the army, which become a central target as well. In March 1986, a PKK representative accused the government "of greatly understating the losses sustained by the army," claiming that "at least 1500 Turkish soldiers had been killed" since August 1984. Government figures, by comparison, put the number of dead at a mere 84 soldiers, alongside 125 guerrillas and 66 civilians (O'Ballance 1996, p. 159). The number of army casualties swelled in the wake of the effective 1987 PKK offensive against the village guard system. By November 1986, the Minister of Information was forced to admit the numbers were somewhat higher than previously estimated; and also confirmed that "there had been over 20 Turkish air strikes on insurgent camps in Iraqi territory, as well as two land excursions" (O'Ballance 1996, p. 159).

In particular, there was an airstrike on August 12, 1986, in which "ten aircraft attacked alleged Kurdish insurgent camps near the border," on the heels of "the publication of a decree amending martial law and emergency regulations to authorize 'hot pursuit' into neighboring countries." Prime Minister Özal even went so far as to brag, "These bandits will be pursued until their hiding places are destroyed. If need be we will do so again" (O'Ballance 1996, p. 159). The cross-border strikes ratcheted international tensions, especially with Iran, who declared them a violation of Turkish neutrality in the ongoing Iran–Iraq war. Especially after October, when the Turkish media began to report that "Turkey planned to occupy the oil-rich Kirkuk region" should Iraq be defeated, a claim vehemently denied by the Turkish foreign minister (O'Ballance 1996, p. 160).

In addition to its guerrilla operations, the PKK also formed the Kurdistan Popular Liberation Front (ERNK), "intended to be the nucleus inside Kurdistan, to provide civil networks for supply routes, bases, urban warfare and intelligence, and finally the kernel to mobilize the masses," and its ranks "rapidly expanded." Perhaps even more effectively than the PKK's capacity for lethal violence, the "burgeoning mass support" for the political project of self-determination is what rendered "the PKK so dangerous to the State" (McDowall 1996, p. 424; Güneş 2012, pp. 109–111).

The Turkish Reaction to the PKK Offensive: An Escalation of State Terror

The spiral of repression and violence continued apace—repression through the legal apparatus, as well as by the security forces. Already in 1982, the Minister of Education had mandated that folk songs could only be sung in Turkish. The following year, a law prohibiting the use of Kurdish managed to avoid even mentioning the taboo word. Even those who gave their children Kurdish names were expressly prohibited from legally registering them, on the grounds that such names "contradict the national culture, morality and traditions and insult the public ... By 1986, 2,842 out of 3,524 villages" in the provinces of "Adiyaman, Gaziantep, Urfa, Mardin, Siirt and Diyarbakır had been renamed" (McDowall 1996, p. 425).

All the while, the presence of the coercive military apparatus on Kurdish soil continued to increase. By the early 1990s, the number of government soldiers in Kurdish regions reached 200,000 (McDowall 1996, p. 425). However, among the rank and file stationed in the region, "demoralization" was a big problem—so much so, that "the army had to threaten with sharp counter-measures in order to forestall mass desertions" (Zürcher 2017, p. 307). Article 72 of the 1982 constitution had mandated a compulsory military service system for all males of

Turkish nationality, complemented by the Law on Military Service (No. 1111) (Yıldız and Breau 2010, pp. 12–13). The standard duration of such compulsory service was 18 months. This translated, in addition to high levels of "demoralization" among those stationed in the Kurdish region, into widespread fear and hatred of the "terrorist menace" among their families.

One way the Turkish government responded to low morale among soldiers was by recruiting far-right extremists to help out. After the military coup in 1980, the junta had repressed the far-right paramilitary forces, too. The Turkish intelligence agency (the MİT) now "came to visit their former brothers in arms and made them an attractive offer: the release from prison plus assured income if they agreed to fight the Kurdish minority" (Ganser 2004, p. 240). Among the operations of the counter-guerrilla were "false flag operations in which the counter-guerrilla dressed up as PKK fighters, attacked villages, raped and executed people randomly" (Ganser 2004, p. 241).

The Turkish authorities long tried to maintain "the fiction that the PKK operated [exclusively] from over the border." Eventually, however, they were forced "to recognize that the PKK could draw on local support and that the 'kidnappings' that were constantly reported in the press were really instances of people joining the guerrilla." The Turkish army was thus presented "with the classic guerrilla situation." As Zürcher puts it, "It was clear that most of the local population supported the PKK and that the guerrillas simply merged into the village population." This led to hostilities and atrocities committed against the local population (Zürcher 2017, p. 308).

A governor-general was "appointed over the eight Kurdish provinces" in July of 1987, and a state of emergency was declared there. The governor-general's "powers were extensive, including the evacuation of villages and pasturage where this was deemed necessary" (McDowall 1996, p. 425). Torture was commonplace. When "Turkish soldiers were unable to distinguish between rural civilian populations and armed insurgents, it was reported that they drove the villagers off their land, burned down their homes, and destroyed their crops, orchards and livestock"—accusations later "corroborated by judgments of the European Court of Human Rights, which found Turkish security forces responsible for torturing civilians, extra-judicial killings of non-combatants, abductions and disappearances and the destruction of Kurdish villages, property and crops" (Yıldız and Breau 2010, p. 17). Few villages "escaped the trauma or frequency of security operations" (McDowall 1996, p. 425). As McDowall vividly recounts:

> In some cases "capture and kill" orders were issued. In the words of one asylum-seeker, 'The children became so fearful that whenever a policeman came to the house they would immediately put their hands on their heads as a gesture of surrender.' Those detained were kept in inhumane conditions and frequently received bastinado, electric shocks or sexual abuse. In the words of one peasant, 'I was ready to confess that I had killed one hundred men, because they brought my wife and sister, stripped and threatened to rape them right there' (McDowall 1996, p. 425).

Likewise, as Yıldız and Breau report:

> An atmosphere of intimidation and violence prevailed. State security forces targeted the PKK, although Kurdish rural communities were often caught in the crossfire. Security operations in Kurdish villages were accompanied by arbitrary arrests, looting of movable property, beatings, torture and "disappearances" ... In detention, Kurds were frequently subjected to extra-judicial execution, ill-treatment and torture, including *falaka* (beating the soles of the feet), electric shock treatment and rape. This was facilitated by the relative ease with which public authorities could subject Kurds to prolonged, incommunicado detention and a climate of impunity among the police and gendarmerie in which convictions for such acts were rare and sentences, when imposed, were light. The ensuing terror caused thousands to flee their homes. Mass internal displacement was compounded by a deliberate policy of village evacuation by the government. Between 3 and 4 million villagers were forced from their homes [by the end of the 1990s] ... Reports of mass graves where the bodies of the disappeared had been dumped by security forces started to appear as early as the late 1980s. (Yıldız and Breau 2010, p. 17)

Partial Steps towards "Democratization"

But even as the conflict in the southeast continued to escalate, rife with state-sponsored terror and human rights atrocities, in other respects the Republic appeared to be proceeding slowly towards "further democratization." There was pressure from the old political class to be allowed to participate openly in politics again, though they had been banned from doing so by the new constitution. Özal gave into this pressure, and allowed a referendum on the issue, campaigning against the reform, but lost by a very narrow margin in early September 1987. The old political leaders were allowed back into the electoral arena. Demirel and Ecevit thus resumed their careers in public life (Zürcher 2017, p. 289).

In the months before the referendum, Özal applied for membership to the European Community (EC), which was accepted in April 1987. The EC nevertheless registered concerns "about journalists having been sentenced to imprisonment for mentioning 'Kurdish separatism.'" In addition, the Council of Europe "passed a resolution in which it "called on the Turkish government to recognise its 'Kurdish problem,'" though no explicit mention was made of the extent of state terror and human rights atrocities in the region. In January 1988, Turkey signed the Council of Europe's agreement on the Prevention of Torture, though this made little difference on the ground (O'Ballance 1996, pp. 165–166).

On the domestic front, the referendum result forced new elections, in which Özal emerged again the victor. But the political spectrum had broadened. Özal even hinted that the ban on communist politics built into the penal code might soon be lifted, which led to increased tensions between the prime minister and the military (Zürcher 2017, p. 290). In 1989, Özal managed to get himself elected by his majority in Parliament to become the Republic's eighth president, despite flagging support for him and his Motherland party.

The opposition parties were highly critical of the repression of wages that had occurred in the wake of neoliberal restructuring. This caused Özal to espouse a "populist" turn of sorts, which included increases in public-sector wages, and large investments in the countryside. This was no panacea. To the contrary, it caused spiking deficits and rising inflation (Yadırgı 2017, p. 221). By the end of the decade, rates of inflation were back to pre-1980 levels—around 80 per cent (Zürcher 2017, p. 291)—exacerbating his already diminishing popularity.

Between 1989 and 1991, the Turkish government gradually embarked on further "liberalization of the political system." In April 1989, several liberalizing reforms were passed, including "a reduction (from 15 days to 24 hours) of the period people could remain in police custody—which was when most torture took place." However, the measures were not enacted. More substantially, two years later, in April 1991, at the government's request, the assembly "decided to allow the use of the Kurdish language in private" (Zürcher 2017, p. 296). Two months later, the ban on the DISK trade union confederation was finally lifted, after 11 years.

Significantly, around the same time Özal breached one of the biggest taboos for the Turkish national imaginary, when, after meeting members of the Armenian community, he posed a question to diplomats and journalists: "What happens if we compromise with Armenians and end this issue? What if we officially recognize the 1915 Armenian genocide and own up to our past? Let's take the initiative and find the truth. Let's pay the political and economic price, if necessary."[6]

And yet, on the issue of the "war on terror," the regime did not budge. "[T]he new anti-terrorism law … defined the concept of 'terrorism' very broadly," including even "verbal or written statements." On such draconian grounds, "countless trade unionists, lawyers, human rights activists, journalists, and prosecutors" were prosecuted on trumped-up charges of "terror" (Zürcher 2017, p. 296).

Meanwhile, in the 1991 assembly elections, Demirel and his Party of the True Path emerged victorious. Özal's own Motherland party came in second, surprisingly. The Social Democratic Party, "which included the votes for the Kurdish People's Labour Party whose candidates had contested the election on the Social Democratic Party slate because the PLP could not participate, not having candidates in every province," finished a disappointing third, just ahead of Erbakan's Welfare Party, which contested the election in tactical alliance with the ultra-nationalist far right (Zürcher 2017, pp. 296–297).

The Escalation of State Terror Atrocities in Bakur

While the competitive-electoral arena was thus moving in a liberalizing direction, ever more competitive, the unofficial war in the southeast continued to escalate "at frightening speed" (Zürcher 2017, p. 297). In this regard, 1990 was a watershed year. "Bourgeoning civil resistance" against the security forces came to complement the guerrilla campaign. "For the first time families of PKK martyrs dared collect the corpses for burial from authorities and arranged public funerals which rapidly became opportunities for mass protest" (McDowall 1996, p. 427; White 2000, p. 164). In spring, in Cizre, over 10,000 Kurds came out for a public demonstration. In response, security forces imposed curfews "on 11 towns in Mardin and Siirt provinces" (McDowall 1996, p. 427). With the surge in civilian resistance came a corresponding surge in civilian deaths at the hands of security forces. Over 100 were killed in March alone, compared with only 16 in the first three months of 1989 (McDowall 1996, p. 427).

The subject of the insurgency became, for the first, time a salient issue in public debate. The old taboos were broken as it became harder to doubt that "the Kurdish question was the most serious domestic challenge the republic faced" (McDowall 1996, p. 429). The hegemonic view remained that "the only language the Kurds understood was that delivered by the security forces, and that even tougher action was required." Yet, among an increasing number of politicians there was "growing recognition that the military had no answer to the progressive loss of 'hearts and minds' in the south-east" (McDowall 1996, p. 427).

The military did not take kindly to such humane conjectures. After an emergency cabinet meeting in April 1990, the government recurred to a policy of censorship to "ensure people remained ignorant of developments," a move which not only "outraged the press" but also implied that the Turkish security forces had serious atrocities to hide (McDowall 1996, p. 427). At the same time, in an even more draconian manoeuvre, the government granted the governor-general "wider powers to forcibly resettle 'those persons whom it is deemed necessary … in places which the Ministry of Interior shall determine" (McDowall 1996, p. 427). Özal publically embraced the measures as his own, but it was rumored that the military had drafted it.

Just like that, the governor-general put these tyrannical powers to use. As McDowall documented, "the number of villages razed and people deported soared: nineteen villages in Dersim were razed in April, 27 villages and 81 hamlets in Şırnak were evacuated and razed in August–September, rendering over 30,000 homeless; in Buhtan alone 300 villages and hamlets were evacuated in the period up to November, with the displacement of 50,000. Many victims had simply refused to join the village guards" (McDowall 1996, p. 428).

The State's tactic was brutally clear: in order to deny the PKK support from the villagers, they decided to physically remove the village population from areas not easily kept under surveillance. (Van Bruinessen 1999). Such a principled commitment to human rights' atrocities wherever necessary indicated the State's resolve to cleanse the territory of the enemy of the nation at any cost. And still, the worst was yet to come.

In July 1990, the Social Democratic Party, which now included a significant Kurdish contingent, published a controversial report on the situation in the southeast, where it had made an unprecedented and "startling recommendation: free expression of identity and linguistic freedom of expression, abolition of the village guards, the governorate-general and state of emergency, and a major programme of regional development." In McDowall's estimation, a "Kurdish viewpoint was beginning to find a voice." And not just on the left (McDowall 1996, p. 428). In early 1991, Mesut Yılmaz, the man who replaced Özal as prime minister after Özal became president, was reported to have "opined that Kurdish should become Turkey's second official language." Around the same time, Özal himself "announced his acceptance of the idea of an autonomous Kurdish region in northern Iraq" (McDowall 1996, p. 428). In some ways even more boldly, after Demirel became prime minister again, he announced that it was his "wish to recognise Kurdish cultural rights and provide extra investment for the under-developed south-eastern provinces," and even claimed "that allegations of human rights abuses would be investigated" (O'Ballance 1996, p. 209). But by spring 1992, the Prime Minister was forced to admit that he could not make good on such promises.

The situation in Iraq complicated matters further. To add to the tensions and social turbulence of the undeclared war in the southeast, two major waves of Kurdish refugees entered Turkey from Iraq: the first in 1988, after the genocidal use of chemical weapons on the Kurdish population by the Hussein regime to-wards the end of the Iran–Iraq war, and again in Spring 1991, after Hussein again attacked the Kurds in the aftermath of the uprising against him—an uprising that the US had encouraged, before effectively leaving the Kurds to their own fate (Entessar 1992). In this second wave, nearly 500,000 Kurds pressed against Turkey's southeast frontier. The refugee camps inside Turkey were horrible and "unfit for human habitation. ... living quarters resembled prison units ... [and] movement of refugees was strictly controlled" (Entessar 1992, p. 109). However, Ankara also established formal relations with the two main Kurdish parties there, Barzani's KDP and Talabani's PUK (McDowall 1996, p. 430), raising alarm bells in military and far-right circles.

Özal's "Reversal"

By 1992, the half-Kurdish President Özal, had come out in the open in favor of a dramatic reversal—"an amnesty for the guerrillas and recognition of the PKK as a participant in Turkey's political system" (McDowall 1996, p. 431; White 2000, p. 162; Romano 2006, p. 55)—a position that likely cost the President his life.

Such unprecedented signals of willingness to compromise led the PKK to return the overtures in kind. As early as 1988, clear messages from Öcalan indi-cated that he was willing to negotiate. In an interview in the Bekaa Valley for the Istanbul newspaper *Milliyet*, he "offered a cease-fire to the Turkish government if it would recognize the PKK." Many speculated at the time that the offer was made under duress from his hosts, who feared that "a major Turkish military in-vasion into the Bekaa Valley was in preparation" (O'Ballance 1996, p. 168). Nev-ertheless, the interview caused quite a splash, at least for its humanizing effect regarding perceptions of the much-demonized PKK leader. As Zürcher recounts, "The man who had been for years as Turkey's public enemy number one (which in a sense he was) and as a true demon, turned out to be a man of flesh and blood who was a fan of the Galatasaray football club" (Zürcher 2017, pp. 307–308).

In 1990, coinciding with the systematic evacuation of villages, Öcalan warned of even greater bloodshed. Nevertheless, he was careful to emphasize, for the first time, "There is no question of separating from Turkey. My people need Turkey. We can't split for at least 40 years" (McDowall 1996, pp. 428–429).

The following year, similar hints from the PKK about their willingness to negotiate were dropped. In March 1991, "at the height of the Iraqi Kurdish uprising, a spokesman indicated that the PKK might welcome a federalist solution within Turkey." And then again, in November, "the journalist İsmet Imset asked Öcalan whether he might accept a federal solution to which the latter replied, 'Unquestionably this is what we see'" (McDowall 1996, p. 430; Imset 1992, p. 342). President Özal responded to this gesture in a manner that "shocked Ankara," by remarking that "he would be willing to talk about a federal system if only to oppose it." The willingness to talk was what shocked. Öcalan jumped at the opportunity. Within a month he "offered Ankara a ceasefire and negotiations if the latter released all PKK prisoners, ceased its 'secret war' in Kurdistan, permitted free political activity in Turkey and announced its own adherence to a ceasefire" (McDowall 1996, p. 430; Romano 2006, p. 56).

All the while, despite such verbal overtures, the spiral of violence and repression continued to escalate. The spring of 1992 marked another ominous watershed—when security forces massacred around 100 civilians during the *Newroz* festival—"the annual focus for Kurdish national expression" (McDowall 1996, p. 435; White 2000, p. 166). Then, in August, security forces assaulted the town of Şırnak, following (unsubstantiated) reports of PKK activity. The result was brutal: the entire population of around 20,000, fled *en masse*, and many buildings were destroyed. Two other Kurdish towns, Dargecit and Çukurca suffered similar fates (McDowall 1996, p. 435; White 2000, p. 167). The PKK responded with a dose of brutality of its own. In September, over two successive days, "it wiped out 40 members of a village guard clan near Van" (including many women and children), then "ambushed and killed 29 troops." The escalating violence reached unprecedented levels. Official figures put the numbers at 3,000 dead between 1984 and 1990. In 1991 alone, the official number of deaths stood at 1,000, followed by close to 2,000 in 1992. As the violence increased, "any illusion of government authority" was shattered (McDowall 1996, p. 435). As Yıldız and Breau summarize the course of 1992:

> Government reports of PKK attacks were used as justification for the security forces' retaliation against the civilian population. The PKK attacked security forces deployed in towns in the Kurdish region, and the state security forces retaliated with such ferocity that the town's inhabitants were killed, wounded or forced to flee in terror. State security forces opened fire and shot randomly at houses, shops and vehicles, and fired on civilian residential areas with panzers and other tanks and heavy artillery. During security operations the offices of human rights defenders, journalists and lawyers were raided and destroyed, and forces waged house-to-house campaigns to root out members of the PKK. … 1992 also saw a substantial increase in targeted assassinations by unknown assailants, including of high profile doctors, lawyers, teachers, political leaders, journalists, human rights activists, and business people. The then minister of the interior reported 881 casualties that year in the 13 provinces under emergency rule in southeast Turkey where the victims' attacker was unknown (Yıldız and Breau 2010, pp. 17–18).

Meanwhile, civilian resistance continued apace. Throughout 1991 and 1992, a series of large uprisings known as the *serhildan* took place. In most towns across the region, in Diyarbakır, Batman, Şırnak, and Siirt, shop closures and boycotts were organized. The State responded with more "forced evacuations of Kurdish rural settlements," ostensibly "to cut off logistical support to the PKK." The answer to collective voice and collective punishment became the norm (Güneş and Zeydanlioğlu 2014, p. 4).

The PKK's First Ceasefire and its Breakdown

The emergent relations between the Turkish State and the new Kurdish Regional government (KRG) in Iraq led to a devastating blow against the PKK when, in late 1992, the KRG coordinated and collaborated with invading Turkish troops "in a massive offensive against the estimated 5,000 or so PKK guerrillas hidden in the ravines of Bahdinan," in which hundreds of guerrillas perished. In the aftermath of the combined Turkish–KRG assault, "there was considerable speculation that the backbone of the PKK had now been broken" (McDowall 1996, p. 436).

Such rumors multiplied in March 1993. In an interview with Iraqi Kurdish leader Jalal Talabani, he confirmed that he had met with Öcalan and the PKK "was now ready to abandon the armed struggle," and was even willing to condemn any further terror tactics, in return for a negotiated solution. And just a few days after the interview was published, Öcalan made another unprecedented gesture, announcing "a unilateral ceasefire" intended to last from Newroz until 15 April, "during which time his forces would only defend themselves if attacked." Öcalan also added that, if Turkish authorities responded positively, "There is no reason we should not extend our ceasefire … I personally would like to be able to return unarmed to the southeast in order to engage in political activity." Indeed, on April 16, Öcalan extended the ceasefire indefinitely, together with a remarkably moderate plea: "We should be given our cultural freedoms and the right to broadcast in Kurdish. The village guard system should be abolished and the state of emergency legislation lifted. The Turkish authorities should take the necessary measures to prevent unsolved murders and should recognize the political rights of Kurdish organizations" (McDowall 1996, p. 436; Güneş 2012, p. 133).

The indefinite ceasefire and the surprisingly moderate overtures of Öcalan were received by the Turkish military as but a sign of weakness. Their reflex was to finish off the lion while he was wounded (White 2000, p. 168). President Özal, however, agreed to negotiate. Then, suddenly, the president died in suspicious circumstances, officially suffering a heart attack. Close to 20 years later, his body was exhumed and examined, and it was finally proven what had long been suspected—President Özal had, in fact, been poisoned, just as his wife had always claimed.[7] It was a covert coup to eliminate any possibility for peace.

After Özal's death, Demirel became President, and Ms. Tansu Çiller, a former professor of economics and minister in Demirel's previous government, became the new prime minister. Çiller made it clear from the start that she had no intention of interfering in the military's plans for eradicating the PKK from the southeast. And so, the onslaught escalated and the human rights situation deteriorated as Turkish security forces sought to make it lethally and viciously clear that they were in no mood to negotiate with what they perceived to be a weakened foe. They zeroed in for the kill.

For its part, towards the end of May, "a group of PKK stopped a bus near Bingöl and killed the 35 off-duty troops aboard." It was widely speculated that the operation "was the work of a rogue PKK commander intent upon sabotaging the ceasefire." Either way, "Öcalan now had little alternative but to declare the ceasefire formally over" (McDowall 1996, p. 437; White 2000, p. 169). And so, hostilities recommenced, on both sides. A second unilateral ceasefire was called by Öcalan in 1995, and was again perceived as a sign of weakness; the response was a cross-border assault in the mountains of Northern Iraq (Çelik et al. 2015, p. 8).

Just after Çiller became prime minister, the military renewed its offensive, including terrible and "destructive assaults on the towns of Kulp and Lice" (McDowall 1996, p. 438). The death toll again soared. Massacres against civilians by security forces continued with total impunity. In one example, "a military operation carried out by gendarme soldiers of the Bolu Commando Brigade in October 1993" "led to the disappearance of 11 Kurdish men following their detention during the operation." In another case, three men from the village of Çaglayan in Diyarbakır were "disappeared" following the forced evacuation of the village. Both instances were later condemned by the European Court of Human Rights, in which "Turkey was found to have violated the right to life" (Yıldız and Breau 2010, p. 18).

Alongside the stepped-up military assaults, the Turkish government banned the Kurdish political party HEP, which had emerged after splitting from the Social Democratic Party (Güneş 2012, pp. 156-164). Moreover, the Constitutional Court decided to strip "one of the most moderate Kurds in the Assembly" of his parliamentary immunity. Further removals of parliamentary immunity soon followed. Moreover, these legal measures were complemented by extra-legal ones: assassinations of Kurdish politicians, bomb attacks on their headquarters and branch offices, and arrests of party members (McDowall 1996, p. 439). The window of opportunity for a negotiated, political solution to the ongoing human rights' tragedy in the Kurdish region was thus slammed shut.

The PKK responded for the first time by carrying its struggle into Turkish areas and launching a series of attacks against tourist sites along Turkey's south coast. It even began to attack Turkish targets beyond the borders of Turkey, in Western Europe. The first was an attack on the Turkish embassy in Bern.

To put this tactical escalation on the PKK's part in context, the extent of the ongoing atrocities in the Kurdish countryside to which it was responding cannot be forgotten. By the end of the 1990s, fully 3,500 villages and hamlets had been forcibly evacuated, and many more were "voluntarily" evacuated because inhabitants could not survive the conditions of onslaught (Van Bruinessen 1999). The countryside was devastated, the demography decimated. Already by the end of 1993, the figure of 10,000 total deaths was widely cited; by the end of 1994, this figure had climbed to 20,000, as well as 2,000 villages destroyed. By that time, "an estimated one million refugees from the countryside had sought shelter" in Diyarbakır, "a pattern repeated in town after town across Kurdistan." Meanwhile, up to another 20,000 more "fled across the border" into the Kurdish region of Iraq (McDowall 1996, p. 438).

1993 as a Turning-Point in the War

1993 was a turning point for the PKK. Its attacks on Turkish targets in Western Europe "led to the banning of the PKK and affiliates in Germany, and the detention of a number of PKK supporters in France, steps which threatened the PKK's financial resources" from the ever-growing Kurdish diaspora (McDowall 1996, p. 438).

In the following year, the State managed to mobilize no less than 300,000 troops in the southeast, in an attempt to eradicate the PKK "once and for all." In their wrath, with ruthless determination to root out all remnants of the organization, "torture and shootings of ordinary villagers became so widespread" that many "abandoned their homes in fear for their lives" (McDowall 1996, p. 438). Yıldız and Breau documented the atrocious human rights situation at the time in grim detail, as subsequently corroborated by the European Court of Human Rights:

> Records of Turkish military operations, submitted by the Turkish government to the European Court in *Orhan v. Turkey*, indicate that 30 operations took place in the province of Diyarbakır from 2 to 31 May 1994. Although there were no records of troop numbers, the Court noted evidence that large numbers of military units took part in military operations in Diyarbakır. Reports detailed helicopters and jets bombing Kurdish villages in 1994, resulting in 26 civilians being killed, including at least 17 children. Witnesses reported that in the days leading up to the attack, gendarmes had subjected the villagers to death threats for having refused to join the village guard corps.

> European Court judgments also established a pattern of abductions and extrajudicial killings by state agents or people acting on behalf of state authorities at this time. The European Court of Human Rights, in its judgment, found a large number of cases where Turkey had violated the right to life and liberty. A report of the Turkish Parliamentary Commission on Unsolved Political Killings, leaked to the press in 1995, confirmed that the village guards were involved in extrajudicial killings along with a wide range of other illegal activities, such as extortion.

> In addition to extrajudicial killings, cases before the European Court of Human Rights also highlighted the systematic nature of the destruction of villages in the southeast, including the burning of houses, destruction of crops, and the killing of livestock. Following its fact-finding investigation, the European Commission on Human Rights in *Mentes and others* described the officially sanctioned lawlessness in southeast Turkey in the 1990s: "The Commission considered that the burning of the first three applicants' homes constituted an act of violence and deliberate destruction in utter disregard of

the safety and welfare of the applicants and their children who were left without shelter and assistance and in circumstances which caused them anguish and suffering. It noted in particular the traumatic circumstances in which the applicants were prevented from saving their personal belongings and the dire personal situation in which they subsequently found themselves, being deprived of their own homes in their village and the livelihood which they had been able to derive from their gardens and fields" (Yıldız and Breau 2010, pp. 18–19).

There would be no let-up throughout the rest of the decade. Indeed, the years between 1992 and 1999 were the bloodiest years of the conflict by far. Official Turkish figures show that, of the 31,000 security forces, civilians and PKK guerrillas who lost their lives in the period before Öcalan's capture (i.e. 1984–1999), fully "27,410 died between 1992 and 1999" (Yadırgı 2017, p. 223). The human rights atrocities committed by the Turkish security forces—the recourse to collective punishment—can hardly be overestimated. The security forces appeared intent on much more than just eradicating the PKK; instead, it hoped to alter the demography of the region once and for all. Ethnic cleansing and collective dispersal was the goal, along with a permanent silencing of Kurdish collective voice. As Yadırgı persuasively makes the point:

> Mass village evacuations were multifaceted processes and involved more than the professed aim of combatting the PKK. They formed part of the Turkish State's enduring desire to break up the Kurdish communities in the predominantly Kurdish provinces and to consolidate control in Kurdish heartlands. In addition, disseminating the Kurdish population would not only advance the long-standing goals of assimilating Kurds into the dominant Turkish culture and attenuating the Kurdish identity, but it would exasperate calls for autonomy (Yadırgı 2017, p. 225).

The brutality of the Turkish State in the southeast had repercussions, especially in Europe, where the increasingly numerous and vocal Kurdish diaspora, despite legal bans, successfully raised European consciousness about the depths of the ongoing human rights catastrophe being perpetrated against the Kurds. The new diplomatic strength of the Kurds in the European diaspora was on display, for example, in June 1998, when "a Kurdish rally in Dortmund was addressed by a former Danish prime minister, a former Greek minister, as well as the Green Party" (Ahmad 2014, p. 165). The Turkish authorities began to be cast as particularly odious villains in international human rights circles. Even the Clinton administration began to chastise the Turkish government on the extent of its human rights abuses.

But the repercussions in terms of reputation and moral opprobrium were not limited to Europe or to international human rights circles alone. The ongoing atrocities in the southeast also led to the eventual exposure by the Turkish press of the close "alliance between elements of the State and the criminal element, or 'mafia' … [a.k.a.] the 'deep state'" (Ahmad 2014, p. 166). A fatal car crash in November 1996, known as the Susurluk incident, vindicated the journalists who had gone out on a limb to insist upon such dirty connections. In the same car were killed an infamous neo-fascist militant and a deputy chief of police involved in state security matters, and a Kurdish tribal chief with links to the village guards was injured. The incident caused something of an uproar. The general Turkish public was at last alerted of "the complicity between the State and criminals" (Ahmad 2014, p. 166). Nevertheless, such public uproar did little to change the dynamics of criminality on the ground; collective punishment of the Kurds continued unabated at the hands of the security forces and the "deep state."

Meanwhile, against a backdrop of economic liberalization and the abolition of barriers to capital flows since the late 1980s forward, the Turkish State was rendered susceptible to crises of capital flight—in 1991, 1994, 1998, and, again, in 2000–2001 (Yadırgı 2017, pp. 225–226). Alongside bouts of soaring inflation and burgeoning public-sector deficits, these multiple strains on the economic fabric were a source of mounting concern, especially in Turkish business circles. Soon the costliness of the ongoing war against the PKK-cum-Kurdish people— estimated at a full two billion per year between 1984 and 1999—became a matter of discontent. "Calls for alternative," less costly, and more humane "means of addressing the Kurdish question" became more common (Yadırgı 2017, p. 226).

The Rise of Erbakan's Brand of Political Islam

Such proliferating sensibilities among the Turkish general public and, perhaps especially, the business community notwithstanding, the Kemalist political establishment remained remarkably belligerent vis-à-vis the Kurdish question. But that establishment, in turn, found itself increasingly besieged, particularly from the Islamist flank. Necmettin Erbakan's Welfare Party made tremendous advances in the 1994 municipal elections, most shockingly in urban areas, where it took control of "six of the 15 largest Turkish cities, including Istanbul and Ankara" (Zürcher 2017, p. 319). Future prime minister and president, Reçep Tayyip Erdoğan, made his debut on the national scene as the flamboyant and outspoken mayor of Istanbul. The winds of change were beginning to blow and it then seemd that the rising Islamist Welfare Party was "inclined to take a more conciliatory line" with respect to the Kurds, with Erbakan himself repeatedly hinting at the need for negotiation and compromise (Zürcher 2017, p. 310).

The December 1995 general election confirmed the rising popularity of Erbakan's brand of Islamist politics, when his Welfare Party claimed the largest share of votes. In the aftermath of the election, it became clear "that no stable government could be founded without the participation of the Islamists." Even Western-oriented business circles prioritized stable government over the secularist alternatives. And so, the secular Republic came to be ruled by an openly Islamist prime minister (Zürcher 2017, pp. 322–323).

However, relations between Erbakan's Welfare Party and the military deteriorated rapidly. At the end of February 1997, the military "presented the cabinet with a long list of demands (officially 'advice') aimed at curbing the influence of the Islamists in the economy, in education and inside the state apparatus" (Zürcher 2017, p. 324). By mid-1997 Prime Minister Erbakan had been forced to step down and, at the beginning of 1998, the Constitutional Court banned him and his party from participation in public life. Mesut Yılmaz and the Motherland Party stepped in to fill the void, in another weak coalition that included Ecevit's Democratic Left Party. The military thus "succeeded in executing what was called in Turkey at the time the 'first postmodern coup'" (Zürcher, p. 325). But they could only hold back the rising Islamist tide for so long.

The Kemalist establishment also went after Recep Tayyip Erdoğan, accusing the mayor of Istanbul of "inciting religious hatred" for having read an old poem by Ziya Gökalp comparing minarets with bayonets during an election rally, for which he was "sentenced to ten months in prison" (Zürcher 2017, p. 325). But, in Erdoğan's case, persecution strengthened his popularity and resolve. By 2002, he struck back with a vengeance. With the Welfare Party banned, the Islamist forces were forced to reorganize, which they did—first as the Virtue Party, which was also banned in 2001, and then as the Justice and Development Party (AKP), under the leadership of Erdoğan and Abdullah Gül.

The Abduction of Abdullah Öcalan

In 1998, under increasing pressure and even military threats from the Turkish government, PKK leader Abdullah Öcalan was forced to leave Syria, where he had been exiled for close to two decades (Romano 2006, p. 58). Thus began a tortured odyssey, which led him first to Russia, then Italy and Greece. While on the run, in August 1998, Öcalan declared a third unilateral ceasefire, which subsequently ended when he was captured in Kenya, en route to South Africa, on February 15, 1999 (White 2000, pp. 185-186; Güneş 2012, pp. 134-135).

Öcalan's capture caused an outpouring of emotions, unleashing "a wave of terror" that included "the assassination of a regional governor and a firebomb that killed 13 people" (Yıldız and Breau 2010, p. 19; White 2000, p. 188). The emotion was, perhaps, especially visible among Kurds in the diaspora (Romano 2006, p. 163). Protests were organized around the world at Greek and Israeli embassies and consulates (both implicated in the arrest, along with the CIA). In Berlin, three Kurds were killed and sixteen injured in an attack on the Israeli consulate, after which the German government threatened deportations should the protests continue.[8]

Öcalan was taken back to Turkey, and held in solitary confinement at a prison on İmralı Island, in the Sea of Marmara, where he remains to this day. Over 1,000 Turkish military personnel were stationed on the island to guard public enemy number one.[9] A military court charged him with treason and separatism, and by June he was convicted and sentenced to death.[10] Öcalan immediately appealed the decision.

During the trial, Öcalan struck a surprisingly conciliatory chord. He called for an amnesty for himself and for his organization, but in exchange, declared that he was ready and willing to serve the "Democratic Republic" (Gunter 2011, p. 73). Along these lines, he submitted to the court as part of his defense a text titled, "Declaration on the Solution of the Kurdish question," in which he first announced his commitment to a project "aimed at reforming the political constitution of Turkey," and attempted to "dissociate the idea of a republic from the idea of nationalism." In his words: "In the constitution of the Republic of Turkey, citizenship has been equated with Turkishness, historically making Kurds invisible. A new constitution, it follows, has to define citizenship in civil terms" (in Akkaya and Jongerden 2014, pp. 189–190).

Alongside this gesture at the level of ideology, Öcalan also made important conciliatory moves at the level of tactics—including the declaration of another unilateral ceasefire, accompanied by an explicit call for the PKK to move outside the borders of Turkey. The PKK agreed to this call, and on August 2, 1999, effectively began to retreat. But its show of goodwill was met with brutal force on the part of Turkish security forces who ambushed the retreating guerrillas, resulting in hundreds of deaths (Çelik et al. 2015, p. 9).

Emotions surrounding the capture and trial of Öcalan were not limited to the Kurds. A sense of nationalist euphoria spread among many Turks, as reflected in the outcome of the April 1999 election in which the far right MHP received unprecedented levels of electoral support. The new government was led by the increasingly nationalistic Ecevit, who had abandoned any hints of leftism, while the Islamist forces were temporarily pushed back and the "centre" collapsed. In the southeast, by contrast, the pro-Kurdish People's Democracy Party (HADEP) did extremely well, winning control of Kurdish cities such as Diyarbakır, Batman, Bingöl, Hakkari, Siirt, and Snark (Ahmad 2014, p. 173; Güneş 2012, p. 166).

Turkey as a Candidate for EU Membership

In December 1999, after years of delay, at a summit in Helsinki, the European Council finally declared "Turkey a candidate for membership in the EU." A customs union had been in effect since 1995, but now the Council made clear that the results of the Turkish candidacy for full membership would ultimately depend on "Turkey making satisfactory progress with meeting the EU's Copenhagen political criteria, which explicitly included: 'the stability of institutions guaranteeing democracy, the rule of law, human rights and respect for and protection of minorities'" (Yadırgı 2017, p. 227). In effect this meant that the Republic would have to recognize and respect the human rights of the Kurds, including the right to exercise their collective voice. Or, as former Prime Minister Mesut Yılmaz put it at the time, "The road to the EU passes through Diyarbakır" (Gunter 2011, p. 94). Significantly, the Copenhagen criteria also included a ban on the death penalty.

Towards the end of November 1999, the Turkish Supreme Court of Appeals rejected Öcalan's appeal of his death sentence, at which point the European Court of Human Rights intervened. The ECHR requested Turkey to suspend the execution until it could rule on his appeal. It was increasingly clear that membership in the EU depended on not just "a satisfactory solution of its Kurdish problem" in general, but also, "specifically its suspension of Öcalan's death sentence." As the German ambassador to Turkey put it bluntly, "If you execute Öcalan, you can forget Helsinki" (Gunter 2011, p. 82).

In August 2002, "as part of its drive to win a date for EU accession talks to begin," Turkey abolished the death penalty, and at the same time, commuted Öcalan's death sentence to a sentence of life imprisonment (Gunter 2011, p. 89). Even so, in December 2002, it was concluded that the Copenhagen criteria had not yet been met, and so Turkey was not included among the ten new countries offered membership by 2004 (Zürcher 2017, p. 336).

As part of its efforts to meet the Copenhagen criteria, in October 2001, the Ecevit government adopted some 34 amendments to the 1982 constitution, removing prohibitions on the use of languages other than Turkish. These constitutional amendments facilitated the adoption of a subsequent sequence of harmonization laws aimed at aligning Turkish law with certain EU standards, including abolishing "numerous restrictions on freedom of expression and association" (Yadırgı 2017, p. 228).

Yet, excessive use of force and extrajudicial killings by Turkish security forces continued, as documented by human rights organizations. Further, Kurdish detainees were led to protest following violent events in December 2000. Yıldız and Breau report:

> A security forces' operation to transfer prisoners in 20 prisons to new "F-type prisons," holding one to three occupants, resulted in the death of 30 inmates and two gendarmes. This was followed by a hunger-strike by more than 1,000 inmates across Turkey lasting for 61 days to protest the planned transfer of prisoners. The inmates maintained that the new institutions would lead to increased isolation of prisoners and expose them to abuse and torture. The prison system with F-type cells was to end the collective ward life of political organisations, which had reportedly become uncontrollable (Yıldız and Breau 2010, p. 20).

Meanwhile, in September 2000, just over a year after the vicious ambush by Turkish security forces while retreating, the PKK called for an end to armed conflict with Turkey. This gesture was followed, in April 2002, with an official change of name, from the Kurdistan Workers' Party (PKK) to the Kurdistan Freedom and Democracy Congress (KADEK), as a tangible sign of the organization's ideological and tactical re-orientation, in accordance with Öcalan's expressed desire (Yıldız and Breau 2010, p. 20; Güneş 2012, pp. 140-141). Turkey then lifted the state of emergency in the southeast and, following the European Court of Human Rights' judgments against Turkey, from this point to June 2004 the conflict remained at a lower level. Indeed, violence had been waning ever since Öcalan's unilateral ceasefire in 1999. As Yıldız and Breau have meticulously documented:

> While 194 police and gendarmes were reported killed in 1999, the corresponding figure for the year 2000 was 27. The same figures for suspected PKK militants were 1,202 and 365, respectively. The number of deaths of unarmed civilians was 64 in 1999 and 43 in 2000. Over the next few years, killings continued to decline. It was reported that between January 2000 and July 2003, 161 PKK members and 39 Turkish soldiers were killed in operations in the southeast. The number of incidents of extrajudicial killings also fell sharply, but the phenomenon by no means disappeared. Village evacuations slowed in pace, and what is often referred to by international bodies as a process of "normalisation" began (Yıldız and Breau 2010, p. 20).

Yet conflict did not cease. Turkey's own Human Rights Association reported the number of deaths during this period at around 100 per year (Yıldız and Breau 2010, p. 20).

The Rise of Erdoğan and the AKP

In the meantime, against the backdrop of the ongoing economic crisis, in November 2002 an electoral "earthquake" took place—including a near complete collapse of the parties that had been in power. Erdoğan's new Justice and Development Party (AKP) was a soaring success, garnering over 34 per cent of the vote. The electoral landscape revealed a clearly divided country: the Kurdish southeast (where the new pro-Kurdish party, HADEP, dominated); the south and west coasts, as well as European Turkey, were secularist Kemalist strongholds of Denis Baykal's CHP; and the rest, including Ankara and Istanbul, supported the AKP (Zürcher 2017, pp. 338-339). Erdoğan was unable to become a member of parliament because of his prison sentence. Therefore, Abdullah Gül was appointed prime minister, but largely regarded as a caretaker until the constitution was amended to allow Erdoğan to take his place in March 2003 (Ahmad 2014, p. 182).

Less than two weeks later, there was a momentous and, in some ways, "traumatic" defeat of the government's motion to permit the deployment of 62,000 US troops in Anatolia—intended to open a northern front in the war against Iraq (Ahmad 2014, p. 183). Over 100 AKP MPs defected on the issue and a major breach in relations with the US was thus consummated, continuing to this day. That decision resulted in dramatic implications for the evolution of the Kurdish issue in Iraq as well, since the US ended up using the Kurdish region there as an alternative base of operations (Gunter 2011, p. 90).

The Erdoğan government may have been in control of the legislature, but it was up against a hostile state: the bureaucracy, "judiciary, police and army" remained beyond its control (Zürcher 2017, p. 339). The struggle for hegemony within the state apparatus commenced. "Chipping away at the autonomy of the state and establishing political control over its organs," would be Erdoğan's top priority. His first move was to adopt the role of liberalizer, under the watch of his ally, the European Union. His mantra: the Copenhagen criteria must be met. Between October 2003 and July 2004, parliament passed 261 new laws, many of which concerned the military's role in the political system, legal procedures, and human rights. The next year, a further 166 such laws were passed. In the torrent of liberalization, the role of the National Security Council was reined in; official military prerogatives were progressively undermined. But its de facto power remained strong. Still, in combination with other liberalizing measures expanding the realm of press freedoms and civil liberties, the Republic of Turkey began to meet European standards, "at least on paper" (Zürcher 2017, p. 340–341; Eccarius-Kelly 2011, p. 130). The addendum "at least on paper" is significant, as the implementation of these laws has since been broadly questioned (Ozkahraman 2017, p. 6).

Among the liberalizing measures were some gestures towards the Kurds. In 2002, new legislation permitted limited broadcasting in Kurdish. As a result, "the state-run television channel … began broadcasting in Kurdish for thirty minutes per week" (Yadırgı 2017, p. 228). Perhaps more significantly, the state of emergency in the southeast was finally lifted. These moves, alongside the commuted sentence for Öcalan, "raised hopes that the protracted and brutal conflict with the PKK might at last be entering a more peaceful and productive phase" (Yadırgı 2017, p. 228).

Such hopes were premature. By 2004, the commander of the Turkish Land Forces, General Ilker Basbug, broke the military's silence to respond directly to European Commission President Jose Manuel Barroso's call "to ensure both cultural and political rights for the Kurdish people of Turkey." Basbug retorted indignantly, "Nobody can demand or expect Turkey to make collective arrangements for a certain ethnic group in the political arena, that would endanger the nation-state structure as well as the unitary State" (Yadırgı, pp. 228–229). The precedent of the foundation of the KRG in Iraq weighed heavily on the general's mind. Basbug expressed his clear concern that the KRG had "brought a political, legal, military, and psychological power to the Kurds of the region," and, indeed, that "this situation may create a new model of belonging for a segment of our citizenry" (Yadırgı 2017, p. 230).

On the heels of this response, in June 2005, another General, Hilmi Özkök, complained in the popular periodical *Cumhuriyet* "that the army's powers had been limited in the fight against terrorism," prompting the government's justice minister to assure him that "the government and the army were on the same side as far as terrorism goes," and to add, for good measure: "We don't want any pressure from the EU, we want cooperation" (Ahmad 2014, p. 191). Then, in August, during a speech in Diyarbakır, Erdoğan made the unprecedented recognition that "[t]hough Turkey has a Kurdish problem we have the confidence to face it with democratic courage." This provoked a sharp reply from the military brass, this time from the Commander of the First Army, Hursit Tolon, who warned the prime minister that when he "spoke of democracy and made concessions to the EU and the PKK he was abandoning the position of the Kemalists who had founded the Republic in 1923" (Ahmad 2014, pp. 191–192). The military's grumblings were enough to convince Erdoğan to back down and to steer clear from pursuing more liberalizing reforms with respect to the Kurds.

Even so, Erdoğan and the AKP were riding high. The economic crisis of 2000–2001 had helped bring the AKP to power; it also led Turkey to seek, for the eighteenth time, the assistance of the IMF. In exchange, the IMF mandated "a programme centred on fiscal discipline and large budget surpluses." This time, forced austerity seemed to unlock the key to neoliberal boom. Public sector debt decreased, though a closer look at the numbers reveals that current account deficits continued to grow throughout the period. And yet, the economy was flush. "After falling by 9.5 per cent in 2001, Turkey's GDP increased by about 35 per cent during the next four years." Inflation was, for the first time in a while, brought into check. "By the end of 2005, annual inflation fell to less than 8 per cent, a level not seen since the 1960s" (Yadırgı 2017, pp. 233–234; 237).

In the spring of 2007, the AKP's Abdullah Gül was the party's candidate for president. This triggered a reaction among secularist forces, including the sitting president, Necdet Sezer, who actively mobilized opposition to the alleged threat to the secular republic. The military again chimed in, with the general staff warning that "nobody should forget that the army was a participant in the secular nature of the State and that it would clarify its position when needed" (Zürcher 2017, p. 342). The general staff's public intervention was reminiscent of its "postmodern coup" against prime minister Erbakan in the previous decade. But Islamist forces were much stronger now, and the military's prerogatives much weakened. Consequently, the AKP's response was very different, reacting "with a sharply worded statement in which it said that the general staff was subordinate to the prime minister and that in a democracy it was unacceptable for a general staff to criticize its own government" (Zürcher 2017, p. 342).

In May 2007, the constitutional court, acting on advice from the army and the sitting president, declared the April parliamentary election and the presidency of Abdullah Gül as null and void. Prime Minister Erdoğan responded with fury—calling for snap elections and proposing a number of constitutional amendments, including the possibility that in the future the president would be directly elected by the people. Both the snap election and the subsequent constitutional referendum constituted "resounding victories for the AKP" (Zürcher 2017, pp. 342–343). In the general election, it now polled fully 46.5 per cent of the vote; and its constitutional referendum passed with 69 per cent support. These represented serious setbacks for the secularists. The AKP's power consolidated even further the following spring, after the leading public prosecutor attempted to have the party banned "on the grounds that it had become a centre of anti-secular activities," but the claim failed by one vote in the constitutional court (Zürcher 2017, p. 343).

Öcalan's Articulation of the Democratic Confederal Model

The grumblings of the military over the AKP government's alleged softness with respect to the Kurdish question had come against the backdrop of the May 2005 European Court of Human Rights' decision that Abdullah Öcalan needed to be retried, his case re-opened, "in order to satisfy the principle of fair trial" (ECHR 2005, paragraph 210). As part of his defense case before the ECHR, Öcalan submitted a long and elaborate text, which he described as "problematizing capitalist modernity" (Özcan 2006, pp. 123–132; Saeed 2017, pp. 96–102). The text was later published in four volumes, appearing in Turkish for the first time in 2009–2010. In this text, Öcalan went beyond the call for a "democratic republic," arguing for what he termed "democratic confederalism," in a nod to Murray Bookchin, with whose work Öcalan had become intimately familiar while confined to solitary life in prison in İmralı (Güneş 2012, p. 136).

According to Öcalan, the project of democratic confederalism "builds on the self-government of local communities and is organized in the form of open councils, town councils, local parliaments, and larger congresses." Crucially, he adds, "the citizens themselves are agents of this kind of self-government, not state-based authorities" (Akkaya and Jongerdon 2014, p. 190). A radical redefinition of self-determination was on display, one which has reinvigorated ideological commitments within the ranks of the Kurdish freedom movement, giving "political orientation to the contemporary struggle" of Kurds in Turkey, and crystallized most powerfully in the revolutionary developments in Rojava since 2012.

The democratic confederal model, as articulated by Öcalan in theory and as constructed by the Kurdish freedom movement in praxis, is especially innovative in two respects: first, in the vanguard role and self-governing guarantees it grants to women; and second, in the self-governing guarantees it grants to cultural and religious minorities. With respect to the first of these innovations, it should be noted that "women have traditionally played a significant role in the PKK, and comprised approximately a third of PKK armed forces in the early 1990s" (Yıldız and Breau 2010, p. 15).

From 2005, "the PKK and all affiliated organizations" becomes restructured on the basis of the democratic confederal model, under "the Union of Kurdistan Communities (*Koma Civaken Kurdistan*, KCK)," and organized alongside the Democratic Society Congress (*Demokratik Toplum Kongresi*, DTK), conceived as "part of the attempt to forge a new political paradigm, defined by the direct and continual exercise of the people's power through village, town, and city councils" (Akkaya and Jongerdon 2012, p. 193; Saeed 2017, pp. 90–91).

The re-organization of the PKK and of the Kurdish freedom movement was accompanied by a good dose of self-criticism as well. Indeed, Öcalan denounced in the second volume of his *Prison Writings* the existence of "warlordism within the PKK." In quasi-confessional terms, he advanced the strong critique, "Within the organisation there was a tendency to misuse the armed struggle for personal political goals and ambitions contrary to the party line and regardless of any moral concerns…we were no longer very different from our opponents and this mentality became characteristic of our struggle" (Öcalan 2011, p. 118).

All the while, however, Turkish raids against the PKK continued, its bases and militants suffering a further 700 attacks since the ambush.[11] Öcalan remained formal leader of the PKK but, in his absence, Cemil Bayık allegedly called the shots in day-to-day military operations (White 2000, p. 191). By May 2004, Bayık and the PKK were warning that the "unilateral ceasefire would end soon, due to what it alleged were 'annihilation operations' against its forces" (White 2015, p. 44). And by the following month, the ceasefire was formally called off. It was reported at the time, however, "that there were splits within the organisation over the use of armed violence" (Yıldız and Breau 2010, p. 15).

To assess claims about such splits, it is useful to keep in mind both the original organizational structure and the subsequent transformations of the PKK. Öcalan's denunciation of "warlordism in the ranks of the PKK" came as part of a broader critique of the Marxist-Leninist organizational form of "democratic centralism" around which the guerrilla/party was originally built.

From the start, the PKK had attracted working class, youth, and "lumpen" elements with nothing to lose but their chains, and very eager to take up the armed struggle. Almost by definition, they could be difficult to control, as a former general-secretary appointed for the Malayta-Elazig confessed to anthropologist Aliza Marcus. Recalling the early days, "As general secretary of a committee you might even say no to a planned attack, and it would still happen… the youth were like that. For example, people on their own would decide to go and stage a robbery to get money, or steal guns or something sensationalist like attacking someone who was an agent of the state" (Marcus 2007, p. 47).

Like so many other left-wing militants at the time, Öcalan originally conceived of the democratic centralist structure as an effective means of imposing discipline and control over the organization. As such, from the start, in classic Marxist-Leninist fashion, the PKK was organized with a central committee responsible for making decisions, alongside "regional preparations committees across the regions of Turkey to oversee local actions." In addition, from the time Öcalan was forced to flee to Syria, there was established a Presidential Council whose task was "to coordinate the implementation of Öcalan's decisions." The Presidential Council initially included seven members: Riza Altun, Cemil Bayak, Duran Kalkan, Mustafa Karasu, Murat Karayılan, Osman Öcalan, and Nizamettin Tas. As for the guerrilla units, they operated under the orders "of a hierarchy of commanders," and were "subject to a strict system of internal discipline, including "imprisonment in camps" and even executions for transgressors (Yıldız and Breau 2010, p. 15; Marcus 2007, p. 332, footnote 1).

The precise relation between the Presidential Council and Öcalan after the latter's exile has long been the subject of considerable contention. In fact, in his *Prison Writings*, Öcalan insisted that, at one point, he considered withdrawing from the organization out of a sense of frustration, especially over his dependence on unreliable information about what was taking place on the battlefield, so to speak: "This situation gnawed away at me, but I was in no position in the organization to impose my will. At one stage I even contemplated withdrawal, as I told an Italian journalist" (Öcalan 2011, p. 55).

Even so, Öcalan stands accused of having committed considerable abuses of power within the PKK during the period before he was forced into exile. According to Aliza Marcus' conclusions, largely drawn from interviews with disenchanted militants around the time of Öcalan's capture, Öcalan had been quick to "fight against real and potential critics inside the organization," and had fostered an organizational culture highly critical of manifestations of dissent (Marcus 2007, p. 96). A grave enough accusation in its own right, but to which, Marcus added, even more gravely:

> This unforgiving view toward dissent helped the PKK avoid the ideological splits that fatally weakened other Kurdish organizations. But it also strengthened the already dictatorial powers of Öcalan and quickly became a tool he and senior PKK militants freely used to dispose of those who displeased them, who seemed untrustworthy, or who simply were a burden on the battlefield. (A. Marcus 2007, p. 96; see also the allegations about murder of internal critics in White 2000, pp. 144–146)

Be that as it may, beginning in 2000, from his lonely cell in İmralı, Öcalan made repeated calls "for reformation and internal change," "deliberate and willed," complete with a thorough "analysis and criticism of the past." Indeed, in his second volume of *Prison Writings*, Öcalan insisted in no uncertain terms: (1) that "the armed struggle can only be the last resort;" (2) that "[t]he guerrilla war and the armed rebellions that we fought in the past went both politically and militarily beyond our legitimate right to self-defence;" (3) that "we will only live up to our responsibility for the past when we build up a comprehensive register of all the crimes perpetrated in this war by us and our opponents;" and even (4) "that we will have to account for all the crimes committed by us or in our name, and all individuals and institutions involved in such crimes must be held accountable" (Öcalan 2011, pp. 122–123).

This self-critical posture on the part of Öcalan led him to detect the roots of the PKK's transgressions in its "state-like hierarchical structure"—a structure which he now believed "causes a dialectic contradiction to the principles of democracy, freedom and equality." According to this self-diagnosis, despite the PKK's "freedom-oriented views we had not been able to free ourselves from thinking in hierarchical structures" (Öcalan 2009, p. 28).

In addition, and intimately related to the cult of hierarchy, the PKK had been guilty of participating in the cult of war. As Öcalan forcefully put the point:

> Another main contradiction was the value of war in the ideological and political considerations of the PKK. War was understood as the continuation of politics by different means and romanticized as a strategic instrument. This was a blatant contradiction to our self-perception as a movement struggling for the liberation of society. According to this, the use of armed force can only be justified for the purpose of necessary self-defense ... The PKK believed that the armed struggle would be sufficient for winning the rights that the Kurds had been denied. Such a deterministic idea of war is neither socialist nor democratic, although the PKK saw itself as a democratic party ... The supposed defeat of the PKK that the Turkish authorities believed they had accomplished by my abduction to Turkey was eventually reason enough to critically and openly look into the reasons that had prevented us from making better progress with our liberation movement. The ideological and political severance undergone by the PKK made the seeming defeat a gateway to new horizons. (Öcalan 2009, pp. 29–30)

Nevertheless, such a self-critical verdict and urgent call for reform was undoubtedly a bitter pill to swallow for many PKK militants who had sacrificed and suffered so much over the years. In a short time, the organization's tactics and strategy had been fundamentally re-oriented. Even the idea of an independent nation-state for Greater Kurdistan had been explicitly denounced in principle. A period of internal soul-searching and party conflict understandably ensued. Needless to say, not everyone in the organization understood Öcalan's conclusion that "a gateway to new horizons" had been opened; for many of Apo's erstwhile followers it was exceedingly difficult to admit as much.

In November 2003, at another party congress, the PKK renamed itself again—this time changing from the Kurdistan Freedom and Democracy Congress (KADEK) to the People's Congress of Kurdistan or *Kongra-Gel* (KCK). Reorientation implied a significant degree of disorientation. Indeed, according to some accounts, as many as 1,500 militants left the organization during the period.[12] Other accounts speak of a divide between "reformist" and "traditionalist" wings inside the organization, even inside the Presidential Council—a divide that allegedly split "traditionalist" leaders Cemil Bayık, Murat Karavilan, and Fehman Huseyin from "reformist" leaders Kani Yılmaz, Nizamettin Tas and Öcalan's younger brother Osman, ultimately leading the latter group to leave the organization.[13]

The ban of the HADEP, pronounced by the Turkish Supreme Court in March 2003, and the imprisonment of its leader, Murat Bolzak, helped tip the balance in favour of the more "traditionalist" view that continuing guerrilla insurgency remained a prerequisite for the organization's survival and success.

According to Paul White, more than any other high-ranking member of the Central Committee or the Presidential Council, it was Cemil Bayık who managed to "assert his authority in Öcalan's absence." White also contends that Bayık "in some ways represents the 'old' PKK," but adds that, "ironically, it is Bayık's legacy as a PKK 'hawk'" that rendered him valuable in Öcalan's strategy for negotiating peace with the Turkish State. This was because, as White sees it, "Öcalan seems genuinely to want a lasting peace, but he also perceives the need to keep pressuring Ankara to keep its word." White nevertheless also concedes that Bayık's authority and, therefore, autonomy is ultimately limited, since it was derived "substantially from his historical closeness to Öcalan" (White 2015, pp. 24–25).

At the 2003 party congress, the "traditionalist" wing gained the upper hand, and by June 2004 the ceasefire had been called off. The reason adduced: "ongoing state military operations against the organisation's fighters." Between June and August 2004, over 50 clashes between PKK fighters and Turkish security forces were reported. By the end of August, however, the PKK communicated that "it would be prepared to halt attacks if Turkey's government agreed to a truce." But then, in September, "a major outbreak of violence" in Siirt province occurred, "with government forces announcing they were expanding their operations" to target the PKK. Clashes continued sporadically, amounting to 166 battle deaths by year's end (Yıldız and Breau 2010, p. 21).[14]

Escalation of Clashes

In 2005, as clashes continued, the PKK officially reverted to its original name. Turkish fears about developments in the North of Iraq, triggered by the emergence of the KRG, combined with the nomination of Kurdish leader Jalal Talabani as Iraqi president, "led the military to escalate the number of clashes and operations carried out in the southeast near the Iraqi border". In May, Turkish security forces undertook a major operation in the Dersim region involving some 10,000 troops pursuing 350 PKK members. The following month, 2,000 to 3,000 troops were involved in another series of security sweeps in Dersim (Yıldız and Breau 2010, p. 21).

Then, on July 2nd, "six people were killed and fifteen injured by a bomb planted by 'Kurdish guerrillas' on a train" in Bingöl province; throughout the month, "attacks attributed to Kurdish nationalists multiplied" (White 2015, p. 44). The PKK denied involvement in many of these incidents, some of which were undoubtedly the work of a new group called the Kurdistan Freedom Fighters (TAK), with which the PKK has consistently insisted it has no links.

The TAK's origins and nature remain shrouded in mystery. It has been alleged to be "a splinter group of former PKK members disgruntled with the organization's perspective of seeking a peaceful settlement," and with the PKK's renunciation of the goal of an independent nation-state for Greater Kurdistan (White 2015, p. 45; see also Eccarius-Kelly 2011, pp. 35–37). Even so, and despite Öcalan's repeated calls for peace and negotiation, the TAK repeatedly pledged its allegiance to "Chairman Apo our historical leader." However, the group's signature targeting of civilians—including bombings at "a supermarket; a tourist resort near Antalya; the coastal resort town of Çesme; a bus station in Istanbul; a district office of the Justice and Development party in Istanbul; and in Kislay," as well as burning forests—has led others to suspect false flag operations coordinated by elements within the "deep state" intent on discrediting Öcalan and the PKK and undermining any potential peace settlement. If this was the TAK's intention, it was certainly effective, since its terror tactics served to "heighten anti-PKK feelings among ordinary Turks," and also triggered violent Turkish ultra-nationalist retaliations in kind (White 2015, pp. 46–47; Güneş 2012, p. 149).

Whatever relations between the PKK and the TAK may have been, the wave of terror that broke out in the summer of 2005 was used to justify yet another major Turkish military operation in October, with around 10,000 troops deployed in the southeast, which in turn provoked multiple clashes in the provinces of Mardin and Van, and led to another serious deterioration of conditions in the cities of Diyarbakır and Van (Yıldız and Breau 2010). The situation was further exacerbated by protests and violence at the end of the year, associated with commemorations of the sixth anniversary of Öcalan's capture. This was followed by events in March 2006, when four days of rioting, including seven casualties, followed protests at the funeral of four PKK members killed in a military operation in Mus (Yıldız and Breau 2010, p. 21).

In August 2006, the TAK initiated another major bombing campaign, including a bank in Adana, a school in Istanbul, and tourist resorts—this time provoking explicit condemnation by the PKK, which officially declared another ceasefire on October 1st, following calls by Öcalan to that effect.[15] The Turkish Chief of Staff, however, rejected the ceasefire, and demanded that the PKK "lay down its arms unconditionally." And so, violence continued apace, "including a bomb attack in Diyarbakır, which killed ten people, mostly children, and a grenade attack on a café in the southwest city of Izmir". Then, in December, "at least four soldiers were killed in mine explosions, and one soldier was killed when a helicopter was bombed in Bingöl." The assassination of Armenian community leader, Hrant Dink, an "outspoken proponent of human and minority rights in Turkey," in January 2007, triggered yet "further unrest" (Yıldız and Breau

2010, p. 21). In May 2007, a bombing in Ankara that killed six people and injured 121 was attributed by the Turkish government to the PKK, invoking anger and fear among ordinary Turks. The following month, a PKK suicide bomb at a military base in Tunceli killed seven soldiers and wounded six.[16]

Meanwhile, tensions at the border of the KRG in Iraq remained high, as Turkey escalated troop levels along the border, deploying as many as 140,000 by July 2007. Alongside this, a partial state of emergency was re-imposed in so-called temporary security zones between the provinces of Şırnak, Siirt, and Hakkari. The heightened presence of Turkish troops led, predictably, to sporadic clashes with the PKK (Yıldız and Breau 2010, p. 22).

By this point, there was a long history of Turkish forces pursuing military operations against the PKK on Iraqi soil. In fact, ever since the PKK established de facto control over the Qandil mountains back in the early 1990s, major raids had been commonplace, along with indiscriminate shelling and bombings, which had led to the death and displacement of many civilians. In 1992, 1993, and 1995, such raids had taken place, with the ostensible aim of "ousting PKK bases in the area," and had even been granted a legal veneer "by the presence of a 'hot pursuit' agreement with Iraq." The 1992 raid had been coordinated with Iraqi Kurdish leader and future Iraqi President Jalal Talabani's Patriotic Union of Kurdistan (PUK), under pressure from the United States (Yıldız and Breau 2010, p. 23). In 1995, the Turkish State's incursion took place against the backdrop of a power struggle between the PUK and Barzani's Kurdistan Democratic Party (KDP), which Ankara claimed had led to a breakdown in the policing of the PKK in Iraq. By the late nineties, it was widely reported that "Turkish forces provided assistance to both the PUK and KDP" in the fight against the PKK, even as Turkish jet bombings continued to kill Kurdish civilians in Iraq (Yıldız and Breau 2010, p. 24).

After the defeat of the Ba'ath regime and the consolidation of the KRG under the hegemony of Barzani's KDP, however, coordination and collaboration were tempered by fears of the precedent and potential contagion that Kurdish autonomy and even potential independence in Iraq might have on the Kurdish population in Turkey. As early as March 2003, "more than 60,000 Turkish troops and heavy artillery" had been deployed at the border; by April 2006, continued skirmishes in the southeast had led to significant reinforcement of the presence of Turkish troops; and by August 2006, cross-border operations had "resumed," with "Turkish planes targeting PKK positions" on the Iraqi side of the border (Yıldız and Breau 2010, p. 25).

These incursions into Iraqi Kurdistan were expanded in 2007, after continuing clashes in the southeast led Prime Minister Erdoğan to "call for concrete measures" against PKK forces in the Qandil mountains, and to forcefully assert "Turkey's right to combat terrorism." By May, Erdoğan had "signalled that Parliament was ready to support any decision by the military to launch cross-border attacks on the PKK;" by June, the "temporary security zones" had been established, and from these zones the build-up for a potential invasion took place (Yıldız and Breau 2010, p. 25). After four Turkish soldiers were killed by landmines while pursuing the PKK on Iraqi soil, the Turkish army responded with indiscriminate shelling "which damaged nine Iraqi Kurdish villages and forced residents to flee."[17]

The victory of Erdoğan and his AKP in the July 2007 general election strengthened the prime minister's hand, but he still opted for the path of military aggression. In August, just three days after the new parliament had been sworn in, Iraqi Prime Minister Maliki came to Ankara, and the two countries "signed a memorandum of understanding in regard to ending PKK access" to its Qandil mountain base. But on the 7th of October, some "40–50 PKK fighters ambushed a Turkish commando unit in the Gabar mountains" near the Iraqi border, "killing fifteen and injuring three," in "the largest concentration of PKK force since the resumption of the armed campaign in June of 2004" (Jenkins 2007). In response, Erdoğan threatened another major Turkish incursion unless KRG and Iraqi national authorities, as well as the Americans, took decisive measures to root out the guerrillas. Erdoğan even took the case to the Turkish Parliament, where he received a 507–19 vote in favour of his official request "to order strategic strikes and large-scale invasions of Iraq for a one-year period" (Yıldız and Breau 2010, p. 26). The drums of war were beating loudly by now. Calls for a buffer zone inside the Iraqi border by politicians across the mainstream began to gain momentum.

Then, on October 21, "an estimated 150–200 [PKK] militants attacked a 50-strong infantry battalion in a military outpost close to the village of Daglica," in the Hakkari province, again right next to the border with Iraq. This time "12 soldiers were killed and 17 wounded," while another 8 were taken hostage, taken over the border into camps in Northern Iraq. The seizure of hostages, for the first time since the mid-nineties, was interpreted at the time as an attempt to force the Turkish authorities into negotiations (Jenkins 2007). But if that was the intent, it seems to have backfired. "Mass protests against 'Kurdish separatism' were held across the country," as well as among "the Turkish nationalist movements in the diaspora" in Europe. Meanwhile, the Turkish military took advantage to present its ongoing operations as if they were "defensive" in nature (Yıldız and Breau 2010, p. 26). It responded "by bombing PKK bases" on the 24th, and stepped up preparations for another "major cross-border military operation."[18]

Assurances made by US military and civilian leaders with respect to "intelligence sharing" along with promises to put pressures on KRG authorities calmed the tense situation somewhat; though in November, "shelling by the Turkish armed forces of areas located between Duhok and the border with Turkey" led to more Iraqi Kurdish civilian displacements. The following month, "over fifty Turkish fighter jets hit PKK positions in Zap, Hakurk, and Avasin." "Local Iraqi officials" claimed that amid the attacks, 10 villages had been targeted and at least "one woman killed" (Yıldız and Breau 2010, p. 26). Eight more Iraqi Kurdish villages were reported to have been attacked, and two more civilians killed, later in the same month.

Aerial attacks continued in January 2008, while the "army and government reiterated threats of major military operations" across the border, "while NATO and the European Union called for restraint," though failed to comment on the fact that the on-going cross-border operations constituted "a violation of Turkey's obligations under international law" (Yıldız and Breau 2010, p. 27). Towards the end of February 2008, the long-threatened "major cross-border offensive" called Operation Sun commenced, involving somewhere between 3,000 and 10,000 Turkish troops.[19] But by the end of the month, these ground troops were already pulling out. The PKK was quick to claim that their fierce resistance had effectively forced the Turkish troops to withdraw. Some outside analysts have concurred, such as Paul White who refers to Operation Sun as "a total failure," adding the claim that it "served only to reinforce Erdoğan and weaken the army" (White 2015, p. 49).

The Ergenekon Conspiracy

White's additional claim about the conflict between Erdoğan and the army makes sense against the broader backdrop of what has been described as "a struggle for power with no holds barred between the old Kemalist establishment and the AKP" that had broken out in 2007 (Zürcher 2017, p. 343). Developments with respect to the Kurdish conflict inevitably were calculated and played into the machinations of both sides in the struggle for hegemony in Turkey.

Among the measures that the Erdoğan government had passed in its bid to meet the Copenhagen Criteria had been the abolition of generals' immunity. Starting in 2007, the AKP government instigated "a string of criminal investigations that identified highly placed officers in what became known as the so-called Ergenekon conspiracy" (White 2015, p. 107). "Ergenekon" is originally an "ultranationalist, pan-Turkist name for the Turks' mythical homeland in Central Asia;" in the late-nineties, especially after the 1996 Susurluk incident had definitively exposed its existence, it came to be a name used to refer to the illegal underground network connecting Turkish security forces with far-right militias, the *kontregerilla*, a synonym for the "deep state" (Zürcher 2017, p. 344). The same "deep state" that was responsible for so many human rights atrocities in the Kurdish region. The prosecution now charged several highly placed officers with participation in this illegal network, which it insisted had been "involved in one or more conspiracies aimed at a *coup d'état* against the AKP government" (Zürcher 2017, pp. 344–345).

On the July 10, 2008, 86 "individuals, including generals, heads of police departments, businessmen and persons from the secular press, were indicted on charges of conspiracy," accused of belonging to the infamous Ergenekon (Yıldız and Breau 2010, p. 274 footnote 20). In the course of the hearings, many sordid details of the dirty war against the PKK and the collective punishment of the Kurds emerged: among them, the existence of mass graves, some of which were excavated during the trial, revealing for the first time to the general public the vast extent of extrajudicial executions that had taken place (Yıldız and Breau 2010, p. 17).

More high-profile arrests followed, as the criminal investigation against the Ergenekon network expanded. Some of the left-wing media took advantage of the revelations from the trial to publicize explosive claims about impending coup plots by the old Kemalist establishment (Zürcher 2017, p. 345).

The investigations surrounding the Ergenekon cases continued for six years, and dominated Turkish headlines throughout the period. In 2010, the investigations escalated further, when the periodical *Taraf* received a suitcase containing some 8,000 documents related to alleged plans within the Turkish army to pull off a coup, the so-called "Operation Sledgehammer." Many of the documents were of questionable authenticity, and some were later proven to be falsifications, but nevertheless, "the public prosecutors brought two cases against top military officers" on the bases of the documents (Zürcher 2017, p. 345). Indeed, "[b]y September of 2011, over 15% of all generals were in prison" (White 2015, p. 107). The Sledgehammer case would conclude in 2012; the Ergenekon cases the following year. The "deep state" had been thoroughly exposed; though the irregularities in the court proceedings surrounding the Sledgehammer case in particular led many to suspect that the outcome had been a foregone conclusion; that Erdoğan and the AKP were determined to break the back of any and all "countervailing forces" to its grip on power and designs (Zürcher 2017, p. 346).

And indeed, in the wake of the Ergenekon and Sledgehammer trials, the military seemed to have been effectively put in its place, subordinated at last to the civilian authorities. The proof was in the pudding: in July 2013, "it kept silent" when article 35 of its Internal Service Law, an article that had long constituted the legal basis for military interventions in politics, was amended. The article had declared that "the task of the Turkish armed forces is to guard and defend the Turkish fatherland and the Turkish republic, as described in the constitution." Now the article was changed to circumscribe the military's tasks. No longer was any "duty to defend the republican order" included among them. Instead, its task was now limited "to the defence of 'the borders of the nation'" (Zürcher 2017, p. 346).

The Oslo Process

The Ergenekon investigations did not initially affect the dynamics of the ongoing military conflict in the southeast. Violence continued throughout 2008. Indeed, the conflict took on increasingly international dimensions when, in early July, the PKK kidnapped "three German tourists while they were climbing Mount Ararat," and claimed that "the three climbers would be held until Germany abandoned its 'hostile policies towards the PKK.'" The German authorities were quick to insist that they would not negotiate with "terrorists;" even so, "there were reports that the German government had communicated with the hostages." The PKK asked the Red Cross to mediate; and after two weeks, the hostages would be released (Yıldız and Breau 2010, p. 22). The very next week, a double-bombing took place in Istanbul, one which killed 17 and injured 154. The government pointed the finger at the PKK, but for its part, the PKK denied any involvement.[20]

Then, in October 2008, news "that Abdullah Öcalan had been ill-treated in prison" circulated, leading to the outbreak of demonstrations across the southeast, "in which one protestor was killed and many injured" (Yıldız and Breau 2010, p. 22). In addition, violent clashes in the Hakkari province again broke out, with the PKK launching an attack on "the Aktutun border post in Şemdinli on the night of the 4th, killing 15 Turkish soldiers and injuring another 20, with reports of 23 PKK fighters dead in the process as well.[21]

But, behind the scenes in Oslo, meetings "between high-level representatives from the National Intelligence Agency (MİT)" and representatives for the PKK, including such prominent figures as "Zübeyir Aydar, Sabri Ok, Remzi Kartal and Adem Uzun," alongside the "presence of an international mediator," had begun in September 2008—a process that would last through the middle of 2011. The Turkish side even "asked the PKK for a list of demands," and no less than "three protocols would be prepared" (International Crisis Group 2014, p. 2). According to Güney Yıldız, the Oslo talks, which would last on and off through the middle of 2011, would include PKK leadership from Qandil, PKK officials in Europe, Prime Minister Erdoğan's representative Hakan Fidan (later appointed head of the MİT), alongside representatives from the MİT, and would be mediated by British intelligence officers (Yıldız 2017, pp. 33–34).

Yıldız also traces the origins of the secret "Oslo process" to "a decision taken at a National Security Council meeting in 2007, which brought together the Turkish Armed Forces and the government. On the Turkish side, the process was thus relatively inclusive, insofar as it brought together both the AKP governing party and anti-AKP "secular-nationalist factions," especially within the Turkish Intelligence Service (MİT) (Yıldız 2017, p. 34).

From the start of 2009, with the Oslo Process now well underway, Erdoğan and the AKP began to make more liberalizing gestures towards the Kurds, with leading government officials, including the prime minister himself, repeatedly referring openly to "the Kurdish issue."

A "democratic opening," even the birth of a "Kurdish initiative," was hailed. "The government set up a Kurdish-language state TV channel in early 2009 and permitted private institutions to open and teach Kurdish in December" (International Crisis Group 2014, p. 2). In addition, Erdoğan proposed renaming Kurdish villages which had been given Turkish names; and even announced plans to "expand the scope of freedom of expression, restore Turkish citizenship to Kurdish refugees, and extend a partial amnesty for PKK fighters."[22]

Even so, the government's sincerity would soon be called into question, after thousands of Kurds were arrested in April 2009, "accused of links with the movement's umbrella organization, the Kurdistan Communities Union (KCK) ... including elected serving mayors, political activists, lawyers and students" (International Crisis Group 2014, p. 2). Such legal persecution was followed up in December by a constitutional court ban on the pro-Kurdish party DTP, which led to over 1,400 DTP activists being rounded up, and its leaders being put on trial for "terrorism."[23] The Crisis Group puts the number of activists rounded up higher still, in the thousands (International Crisis Group 2014, p. 2).

The PKK, for its part, had declared its sixth unilateral ceasefire in April 2009, after Öcalan called on the organization to put down its weapons and prepare for peace. And in October, it had even sent a "peace group," totaling some 34 people, 8 of whom were PKK guerrillas, from Qandil and the Maxmur refugee camp in northern Iraq, across the border into the town of Silopi. "The group members were welcomed by several ... thousand enthusiastic Kurds making victory signs in a welcoming ceremony organized" by the still-legal DTP, and attended by several DTP mayors and parliamentarians (Casier, Jongerdon and Walker quoted in White 2015, p. 52).

The ceremony was perceived by the Turkish public as a "victory parade," and it sparked the ire of Turkish nationalists. "Protests against a perceived sell-out to Kurdish nationalists occurred in several Turkish cities," and CHP opposition leader Deniz Baykal even complained, "Terrorists have become heroes" (White 2015, p. 52). The Kemalists went on the offensive against the AKP government for its concessions to the Kurds, causing the government to backtrack and postpone further conciliatory gestures.

Then, in early December 2009, the PKK effectively broke its ceasefire, by ambushing Turkish soldiers in Resadiye, in Central Anatolia, killing seven and wounding three. There were mixed reports about whether the ambush had been the work of a rogue unit, or if the action had been approved by Qandil. Nonetheless, four days later came the ban on the pro-Kurdish DTP, which triggered "major riots by Kurds all over Turkey and resulted in violent clashes between pro-Kurdish and security forces as well as pro-Turkish demonstrators," causing several deaths and injuries.[24] By the end of the month, arrest warrants had been issued for 80 leaders and representatives of the newly formed BDP, set up to replace the now-banned DTP. The wave of repression against Kurdish political representatives would continue into the new year—"a total of 151 Kurdish politicians and activists were eventually charged with 'aiding the PKK'" (White 2015, pp. 53–54).

The PKK would kill two and wound five more Turkish soldiers in clashes in the Hakkari, Batman, and Siirt provinces on the same day in mid-March 2010, in which two PKK militants would be killed as well. The very same week, two Turkish police officers would be killed by PKK fighters "in the northern Turkish province of Samsun" (White 2015, pp. 54–55). But even after all this violence, still, the "Oslo process" sputtered on.

On the 1st of May 2010, the PKK officially declared an end to its ceasefire and carried out "an attack in Tunceli that killed four and injured seven" Turkish soldiers.[25] At the end of the month, "Abdullah Öcalan added a dramatic flourish to this announcement from his prison cell, declaring that he was formally abandoning all attempts at rapprochement with the Turkish authorities, and handing that task to his military commanders." Given his previous repeated calls for restraint on the part of the PKK command, this was interpreted at the time as "a calculated move against his Turkish jailers, designed to shake them with a spectre of the return to total war on both sides" (White 2015, p. 55). The result: an upsurge in violence—including a missile attack by the PKK "on a naval base in Iskenderun," and more clashes between the PKK and Turkish soldiers in Hakkari and Elazig provinces.

As the summer of 2010 progressed, however, the Kurdish guerrillas again expressed a desire to negotiate, this time from the mouth of PKK commander Murat Karayılan, who in an interview with the BBC emphasized that the PKK was willing "to disarm in return for political and cultural rights"; however, he also warned, "If the Turkish state does not accept this solution, then we will declare democratic confederalism independently" (White 2015, p. 55). Perhaps not independence, but a unilateral exercise of self-determination nonetheless as the strategy, should dialogue fail. On the eve of Ramadan, the PKK proceeded to declare another formal ceasefire, which it later extended until the June general election of 2011, though military operations and sporadic retaliations would not cease.[26]

In the months leading up to the general election, Erdoğan veered towards an increasingly belligerent attitude to the Kurds, "refusing any concessions to PKK demands and stepping up military operations" in the southeast. Shortly before the election, the "Oslo process" collapsed altogether.

Enter Demirtaş

But the collapse of the secret peace negotiations in the run-up to the June 2011 election did not mean an end to politics, or that only guns and bombs could speak for the Kurdish freedom movement once peace negotiations had collapsed. To the contrary, the more exclusively "political" wing of the movement seemed to be gaining an autonomous momentum of its own, a momentum encouraged by Öcalan in his efforts to restructure the Kurdish movement along democratic-confederal lines—a restructuring that did not seek to supplant the role of the PKK, but that did push for a proliferation of autonomous, bottom-up, participatory initiatives from within Kurdish society. At the same time, the struggle for electoral support in the sphere of the representative arena, despite so much persecution, had begun to generate prominent new figures—figures who, though they did not wish to, nor could they, compete with the appeal of Öcalan and the PKK, did nevertheless generate a good deal of enthusiasm in their own right. Perhaps most prominent among these, a man sometimes called by Western commentators "the Kurdish Obama," Mr. Selahattin Demirtaş.

Mr. Demirtaş had begun his political career in 2007, when he first stood as one of the "Thousand Hope Candidates," on a list bringing together the Kurdish Democratic Society Party (DTP) alongside other candidates from a broad variety of left-wing organizations across Turkey. This is how he first became a parliamentarian, and at the age of 34, the Parliamentary Chief Officer for the party. After the party was banned by the constitutional court in 2009, Demirtaş helped found the new Peace and Democracy Party (BDP), and along with Gültan Kışanak, would be elected co-chair. In 2011, Demirtaş formed part of the "Labour, Democracy, and Freedom" list, a list which had been endorsed by his BDP, in coordination and coalition with fully 18 other left-wing organizations across Turkey, an electoral coalition which would soon crystallize into the Peoples' Democratic Party (HDP). This time around, Demirtaş would be elected as representative for the province of Hakkari.[27]

The campaign took place against a backdrop of intensifying hostilities between the Turkish military and the PKK. Just less than two months before the election, led by Kurdish deputies and mayors, Demirtaş prominent among them, several thousand Kurds took to the streets of Diyarbakır, to "demand their rights and to call for an end to the conflict with the PKK" (White 2015, p. 57). Demirtaş addressed the crowd, and emphasized four demands: (1) "the right to education in Kurdish;" (2) "the release of imprisoned activists;" (3) "the end of operations against the PKK;" and (4) "the removal of the electoral threshold of 10 per cent of votes required to enter parliament" (White 2015, p. 57).

In April 2011, the Turkish High Election Board intervened to ban twelve BDP candidates, among them the icon Leyla Zana, the first Kurdish woman parliamentarian, who had already served ten years in prison after being stripped of her parliamentary immunity back in 1994 and convicted of treason after having spoken in Kurdish in the Grand National Assembly. This new wave of arrests triggered "angry protest by thousands of Kurdish demonstrators," again in Diyarbakır, as well as Van, and even a protest in Taksim square in Istanbul. Civil disturbances ensued, after the police resorted to heavy-handed methods to disperse crowds. This in turn worried President Abdullah Gül so much that he personally summoned Demirtaş. Mr. Demirtaş, however, would decline the invitation, citing the death of a protestor, and accusing "police of opening fire on demonstrators," an accusation later confirmed to be true. At a campaign rally the same day, Prime Minister Erdoğan, for his part, would "denounce what he termed 'vandalism'" and would "accuse the BDP of encouraging young Kurds to protest violently and throw molotov cocktails" (White 2015, pp. 57–59). A few days later, some 35 Kurdish activists, "including local leaders of the BDP," would be arrested, "accused of belonging to the so-called urban network of the PKK, the KCK" (White 2015, p. 60). An escalation of both civil demonstrations and armed clashes would ensue. Meanwhile, the BDP had begun to threaten it would boycott the election should the climate of intimidation and repression continue.

On the very same day that the activists and politicians were rounded up, in Northern Turkey, the police escort of Prime Minister Erdoğan was ambushed, resulting in one police officer killed, another wounded. In a stroke of fortune for Erdoğan, perhaps, he was not in the convoy at the time of the attack. Even so, Erdoğan and his supporters were incensed in the aftermath of the attack. Security sources immediately pointed the finger at the PKK, which "did not initially claim the attack" (White 2015, p. 60). Nearly ten days passed before the PKK finally announced "that the assault 'was made by our members in retaliation for the terror exercised by the police on the Kurdish people'," but was nevertheless careful to note that "the attack 'targeted police ... not civilians or the prime minister'" (White 2015, p. 60).

Still, now it was more personal for Erdoğan; and in the aftermath of the attack, he lashed out with vehemence against the pro-Kurdish BDP, repeating the charge that "the BDP are terrorists," while stepping up military operations against the PKK, too (White 2015, p. 61). Some commentators at the time began to speculate that Erdoğan had decided to compete for the far-right Turkish nationalist base of support. But then, less than two weeks before the election, at the very beginning of June, and despite the recent total collapse of the secret Oslo negotiations, Erdoğan appeared to veer back again towards a predilection for negotiations and compromise on the Kurdish question, announcing at an election rally in the heart of Kurdistan, in Diyarbakır, that "we have prepared the ground for a resolution process" (White 2015, p. 63).

The election results were an overwhelming success for Prime Minister Erdoğan, "his best result ever, almost 50 per cent of the vote." The main opposition party, the Kemalist CHP, only managed about half that, at 26%, despite having undergone a long-awaited generational renewal in its leadership, which had led to (what turned out to be unfounded) high hopes. Meanwhile, the far-right MHP had faired relatively poorly, down to 13%; while the pro-Kurdish BDP registered a fairly impressive 6.5% of the vote across the whole country, obtaining an unprecedented 35 parliamentary seats (Zürcher 2017, p. 348). A moral victory of sorts for the Kurdish freedom movement, after which the figure of Mr. Demirtaş in particular became ever more prominent on the Turkish political scene. Indeed, in the Kurdish southeast, the BDP had outperformed the ruling AKP.

Continuing Repression against the Kurdish Freedom Movement

Six of the BDP representatives elected remained in jail. Only one of these, Hatip Dicle, would be released "due to his election to parliament in the constituency of Diyarbakır (East)," but the constitutional court was quick to intervene to strip him of elected office, and the High Council of Elections had him "subsequently returned to jail" (White 2015, p. 64). Dicle was a historic figure in the movement, a man with a long history of political persecution. He had had his parliamentary immunity lifted and had been imprisoned alongside the icon Leyla Zana back in 1994, on the charge of "belonging to the PKK," released a decade later, under pressure from the EU, only to be imprisoned again in 2007, this time for "terrorism," for a statement in which he advocated a peaceful resolution to the ongoing conflict with the PKK, and again in April 2010, as part of a state crackdown on the movement's Kurdistan Communities Union (KCK), charged with being "the urban wing of the PKK."[28]

The belligerent action towards Dicle on the part of the Turkish authorities provoked in turn a response from the Kurdish freedom movement. Ahmet Türk, who had been banned from joining the BDP or any other party after the dissolution of the DTP in 2009, and now a leading figure in the movement's Democratic Society Congress (DTK), intervened on behalf of the DTK, "warn[ing] that the decision to strip Dicle of his office was 'a decision to take Turkey into chaos ... to push our people to an environment of conflict." He continued, accusing "the State government and judiciary of trying to block our efforts to create a democratic political base," in a word, of trying to keep the movement excluded from the arena of representative democratic politics by any means necessary. In light of this action, Mr. Türk even claimed that the elected representatives of the BDP should "again consider boycotting parliament" (White 2015, p. 64).[29]

The boycott soon came, while "clashes between the security forces and the PKK further intensified" in the wake of the election. In July the PKK managed to kill 20 Turkish soldiers in just two weeks, losing 10 of its own fighters in these violent altercations. In August, the Turkish Armed Forces upped the ante once more, "launching multiple raids against Kurdish rebels, striking 132 targets," including "six days of air raids" in the Kurdish Region of Iraq. The General Staff boasted of having killed 100 guerrillas, and wounding 80 more. Simultaneously, the Iranian government, with the consent and even collaboration of Iraqi Kurdish leader Barzani, conducted strikes in Northern Iraq as well, targeting the Kurdistan Free Life Party (the PJAK), "widely described as an offshoot of the PKK." A branch of the Kurdish freedom movement extending into "East Kurdistan" in Iran, the PJAK had been founded in 2004 as part of the movement's attempt to reorganize itself along "democratic confederal" lines. By the end of September, the PJAK had been dealt a decisive blow at the hands of the Iranian armed forces, "conceded defeat and agreed to retreat one kilometre away from the Iranian border and to refrain from military activities on Iran's soil."[30] This meant, in effect, that the PKK ranks were from thereon reinforced with PJAK cadres for the fight against the Turkish State. The Turkish military and intelligence services, at least, claimed as much, reporting "a sharp increase in Iranian citizens among insurgents killed" in the ensuing months.[31])

In the meantime, in July, the Democratic Society Congress (DTK) had held an "Extraordinary Congress" in Diyarbakır, with the participation of over 850 delegates, including many BDP parliamentarians and mayors, in which it openly declared its support for the project of "democratic autonomy." DTK chairwoman and parliamentary deputy Aysel Tuğluk attempted to stress in declarations to the media made just after the Congress that though "the Kurdish people had declared autonomy," they nevertheless "yet remained loyal to Turkish national unity and respected the country's territorial integrity," careful to emphasize this crucial point on which Öcalan had insisted (White 2015, p. 67). Her words, exactly: "As the Kurdish people we declare our democratic autonomy in the light of the rights provided by international human rights agreements in a common country based on territorial integrity and within the perspective of a democratic nation with the peoples of Turkey" (Çelikkan et al. 2015, p. 10). Even so, the reports in the media emphasized not the point about respecting territorial integrity, but rather, the unilateral nature of the declaration, and therefore contributed to yet another bout of Turkish nationalist backlash.

By the end of July, Öcalan again intervened, this time at least feigning despair with both sides (the Turkish government and the PKK), blaming both sides for "intransigence," even going so far as to declare, "Both parties use me for their interests. I am ending this intermediary role … There can be no peace talks under the current conditions" (White 2015, p. 69).

Turkish military assaults and PKK counter-violence continued to escalate into September. Human Rights Watch issued a statement at the beginning of the month about the late-August air raids into Iraqi Kurdistan, directly contradicting the government's claims, insisting that many of the areas targeted "were not used by armed groups, but were inhabited by civilians" (White 2015, p. 70).

Peace seemed ever further away. And then, in the middle of September, 2011, a taped recording was uploaded to the internet, capturing the voices of the Turkish deputy undersecretary of the prime minister, Mr. Hakan Fidan (a man who would later be appointed head of the MİT), alongside the MİT's deputy undersecretary, meeting with three European representatives for the PKK.[32] The government was thus forced to admit "that it had engaged in secret direct negotiations with the PKK," about which the far-right Turkish nationalist press was predictably apoplectic, going so far as to accuse Mr. Fidan of treason (White 2015, p. 73).

The hysteria thus generated on the Turkish nationalist far-right was of course infectious, working to intoxicate the climate of public opinion, and thus to condition the prime minister's calculations of the costs and benefits of repression and coercion versus accommodation and compromise, tilting the scale even further towards the former. The predictable result: action, reaction, again the spiral. And so, PKK violence also spiked. Weeks after the vicious air raids in Iraqi Kurdistan, the PKK responded with an attack in Çukurca and Yüksekova, in Hakkari province, killing 26 Turkish soldiers and wounding 18 more.[33]

October 2011 witnessed as well yet another wave of legal persecution against the Kurdish freedom movement, targeting leaders of its umbrella organization, the Kurdistan Communities Union (KCK), again rounded up for "belonging to the PKK." 150 activists and representatives were arrested on the 4th of October, raising the number of Kurdish political prisoners at the time to over 2,500 (White 2015, p. 79).

At the beginning of October, there was nevertheless some hope that the peace process could recommence, engendered in large part by the Turkish President, Erdoğan's ally and AKP partner, Abdullah Gül. On the first day of the month, President Gül had instructed the Turkish Grand National Assembly "that one of its 'main tasks' was to draft a new Constitution," one that would be "ultimately approved by referendum" (White 2015, p. 78). Because the President was also keen to stress "that the current Constitution 'does not meet the aspirations of the Turkish people,'" many were optimistic that he was pushing for liberalizing reforms, which might even include compromise and recognition of political rights for the Kurds. The more astute and honest among such optimists, however, would soon be disabused of such hopes, as violence continued to escalate, and especially after President Gül responded to PKK attacks in the middle of the month with an outburst of rage, "promising 'very great revenge.'" In the President's unequivocal words the echoes of Kemalist belligerence towards the Kurds were clear for all with ears to hear. The President threatened, "No one should forget this: those that inflict this pain on us will endure far greater pain; those that think they will weaken our State with these attacks or think they will bring our State into line, they will see that the revenge for these attacks will be very great and they will endure it many times over" (White 2015, pp. 78–80). A violent rhetorical outburst, to say the least. And a signal for things to come.

Meanwhile, not only the far-right, but the main opposition party CHP, continued to attack the President and the prime minister for being too soft on the Kurds, with some even continuing to suggest that the Oslo peace talks had been nothing short of treasonous. Even so, for most of the opposition, the more press-ing concern with respect to the proposed Constitutional reform had to do with matters of secularism, and with the AKP's ever firmer grip on power. Against the backdrop of the AKP's consolidated hegemony within the parliamentary arena and its decisive advances in the state apparatus, the proposed Constitu-tional reforms triggered "increased fears among secularist sections of Turkish society that the [ruling] party would push through the Islamization of the coun-try" (Zürcher 2017, p. 349). Such fears were further reinforced by the additional fact that EU-accession talks had come to seem definitively stalled. It cannot be forgotten, the Kurdish question was always ultimately a pawn in a bigger game, considerations of justice and human rights always subordinated to the logic of the struggle for power, to the machinations and Machiavellian calculations among the main contenders in conflict, the different fractions of the Turkish rul-ing class, and the "deep state."

The Turkish State again escalated on the front of legal persecution against the Kurdish freedom movement in November, arresting another 70 activists, accusing them of belonging to the PKK, this time including not only many BDP members but Öcalan's lawyers as well (White 2015, p. 83). However, even amidst this spiral-ing escalation of repression, Prime Minister Erdoğan was still capable of throwing the Kurds at least a symbolic bone—towards the end of November, "when he pre-sented a historic apology to members of his ruling AKP on behalf of the Turkish State for the murderous repression of the 1937–1938 rebellion in Dersim," a re-pression that had "forced the exodus of tens of thousands Alevis." "If there is need for an apology on behalf of the State, I would apologize, I am apologizing," he de-clared, though he mentioned nothing about more recent, indeed ongoing, mas-sacres (White 2015, p. 83).

December 2011 marked another low point. On the 15th, in the province of Bïngol, "Turkish soldiers stormed a house, killing eight alleged PKK fighters." This was followed by nearly a week of open war between the Turkish armed forces and the PKK in the province of Diyarbakır, in which "Turkish ground troops, supplemented by helicopter gunships," murdered an estimated 50–70 PKK fighters (White 2015, p. 84).

Then came the infamous Roboski airstrike. In the middle of the month, American drones had captured images of alleged PKK militants moving towards the Turkish border from Iraqi territory. On the 28th, near the same spot as the drone footage, some 40 villagers were targeted and bombed by Turkish F16s. They were mostly local teenagers who were smuggling cigarettes, diesel fuel, and other such "black market" products across the border. Only four survived the brutal massacre, which triggered a wave of protests across the Kurdish region, and even spread to Ankara and Istanbul. PKK commander Bahoz Erdal spoke out to "urge the people of Kurdistan to react after this massacre and seek a set-tling of accounts through a series of uprisings." On behalf of his party, the Peace and Democratic Party co-chair Selahattin Demirtaş quoted verbatim President Erdoğan's claim about Syrian President Bashar Al-Assad, that, "A leader who kills his own people has lost his legitimacy," though he was also careful to insist that

Kurds should "respond through democratic means." Even the Kemalist opposition, the Republican People's Party (CHP), expressed disapproval of the massacre.[34]

As White summarizes the sense of hopelessness at the time, "The year 2011 thus ended as it had begun—with bloody violence on both sides. As the year drew to a close, it seemed that nothing could prevent Turkish Kurdistan descending into a deepening bloody cycle of violence" (White 2015, p. 85).

The Erdoğan government promised to pay reparations to the victims of the Roboski airstrike, but the evidence surrounding the case was immediately declared an "official state secret." The Turkish Grand Assembly would establish an Investigatory Committee into the massacre, but it would be granted only limited access to the minister of interior's report. Nor would it be allowed to interview high ranking government and state officials implicated in the chain of command. To this day, no legal judgment has been made against any state officials implicated in the massacre (Çellikan et al. 2015, p. 10).

The pattern of armed confrontations would continue throughout 2012. In early February the armed forces would kill 13 alleged guerrillas, and in the middle of the month Turkish warplanes would again strike alleged PKK targets in Iraqi Kurdistan. For its part, the PKK would kill policemen in Central Anatolia and in Istanbul, in May and June, respectively. The summer months would witness a further increase in tensions triggered in no small part by events in the north of Syria, also known as "Western Kurdistan" (or Rojava); on the 19th of July, in the midst of the Syrian Civil War, the Assad regime retreated, effectively ceding control to revolutionary forces inspired by Abdullah Öcalan and organically linked to the Kurdish freedom movement.

Meanwhile, inside Turkish Kurdistan (or Bakur), conflict would be especially heavy, concentrated in the Hakkari province. In early August, the PKK opted for an uncommon, arguably reckless, tactic of "frontal battle," blockading roads leading from Iran and Iraq into the town of Semzinan, and the Turkish armed forces responded with more assaults from the air, resulting in reports of over 115 guerrillas killed, compared with 6 mortalities among Turkish armed, and two village guards. This would be followed, in mid-August, with a mine explosion which killed another 15 guerrillas and two Turkish soldiers, again in Hakkari province, and then, a car-bomb close to the police station in Gaziantep, which wounded fifty-six, and killed nine civilians, including four children (White 2015, p. 86).

The Turkish State responded with special vehemence to the civilian deaths, unleashing "six days of intense bombing of PKK bases in the Qandil mountains," with reports of assistance by US intelligence. There were also reports of civilian casualties and an official condemnation by KRG President Barzani, which were brushed off by Erdoğan, who "declared that his government had 'run out of patience' and vowed to continue the attacks" (White 2015, p. 87).

All told, the summer months were especially deadly. Between June and the beginning of September, nearly 800 people died, including "some 500 PKK fighters, more than 200 security personnel, and 85 civilians." In mid-September, forty-four Kurdish journalists, imprisoned since the previous December, faced terrorism charges in an Istanbul court. By early December, Erdoğan was threatening that the same fate could well await the Parliamentary deputies of the BDP, that their parliamentary immunity could be cancelled, again accusing them of being but the political wing of the PKK (White 2015, p. 87).

In the meantime, in October, several hundred Kurdish political prisoners went on hunger strike to demand an improvement in Abdullah Öcalan's treatment, including the right for him to meet with his lawyers who had been barred from visiting him since early 2011. The hunger strikes would last for six months until March 2013. The Turkish minister of justice would intervene behind the scenes, holding confidential interviews with the hunger-strikers, while taking precautions to keep this measure out of the public eye. The Turkish authorities did not give in to the demand for Öcalan to be able to meet with his lawyers (indeed, they have still not been able to meet with him, to this day). However, they would concede a visit between Öcalan and his brother, Mehmet, in which Öcalan would request that the hunger strikes end (Çellikan et al. 2015, p. 11).

The "Solution Process" Commences

At the very end of 2012, Erdoğan changed course once more, delivering a bombshell to the Turkish public, when, in a television interview, he announced that the Turkish intelligence service (MİT) was in the midst of conducting negotiations with Öcalan in İmralı prison. Thus commenced the so-called "solution process," sometimes referred to as the "İmralı process." It was the much-publicized successor to the failed "Oslo process," though would ultimately come up against similar structural obstacles and, in the spring of 2015, meet the same fate as its secret predecessor.

Erdoğan's public announcement and sudden embrace of the "solution process" was met with considerable optimism verging on enthusiasm in Western foreign policy circles, with the International Crisis Group claiming that the talks "enjoy wide political support," and expressing the hope that they could "offer a genuine opportunity to end Turkey's longstanding Kurdish conflict" (quoted in White 2015, p. 101). And indeed, the chairman of the main opposition party, the Kemalist CHP, Kemal Kılıçdaroğlu, "declared his support for the government in its negotiations with Öcalan," in the form of a terse commandment to "solve the problem" (Çelik et al. 2015, p. 64). Indicative of the window of opportunity that had thus opened, an opinion piece was published in January 2013 in the Gülen-funded English-language periodical, *Today's Zaman*, by İhsan Dağı, who emphasized, "Öcalan is an aging man and in the era of post-Öcalan Kurdish politics it will be impossible to find or create a leader like him to make peace with" (quoted in White 2015, p. 103).

In the first week of January, 2013, BDP parliamentarians Ahmet Türk and Ayla Akat Ata were allowed an initial visit with Öcalan on İmralı. Throughout the "solution process," BDP-cum-HDP parliamentarians would be assigned the task of go-betweens, serving as interlocutors and relaying messages between Öcalan and Qandil. The second such visit came on February 23, this time made by BDP parliamentarians Pervin Buldan, Sırrı Süreyya Önder, and Altan Tan. The third such visit, in April 2013, would include BDP and HDP co-chair Selahattin Demirtaş (Çellikan et al. 2015, p. 11).

Even so, Erdoğan's embrace of the "solution process" did not bring a cessation of hostilities on the part of the Turkish authorities. To the contrary, the day after the first BDP visit with Öcalan at İmralı, Turkish interior minister, Idris Nahim Sahin, "announced that military operations against the PKK would continue;" and two days after that, Erdoğan would reiterate the interior minister's point, insisting, "It is out of the question for us to cease our struggle against the separatist terrorist organization without disarmament." As if to drive the point home with more than mere rhetoric, on the very same day, the Turkish armed forces "carried out an air operation on the Pülümür Valley in Dersim" (Çelik et al. 2015, p. 64).

Nor would the violence of the Turkish state against the PKK be limited even to Turkey. To the contrary, on the 9th of January, the Turkish National Intelligence Organization (MİT) murdered, execution style, three women Kurdish activists, including the only female co-founder of the PKK, Sakine Cansız, alongside a representative for the HDP in Europe, Fidan Doğan, and Leyla Söylemez.[35] The brutal triple-murder took place at the *Centre d'Information sur la Kurdistan*, in the heart of Paris. It would be interpreted by many as "a provocation apparently aimed at derailing the PKK/Ankara peace process" (White 2015, p. 112). This was met with an impressive wave of mass protests by the Kurdish diaspora in France and in Germany, who chanted slogans such as "We are the PKK," and carried signs such as "Women are murdered, Europe is silent" (White 2015, p. 114).

Tensions between Erdoğan and the Gülen Movement

The timing of the provocation suggested that elements of the Turkish deep state were determined to see the "solution process" fail. Matters related to the deep state are by definition opaque; however, it is certainly noteworthy that the triple-murder in Paris coincided quite closely with a serious escalation in tensions between the Erdoğan government and its long-time ally, the Gülen movement, which had long been rumored to have collaborated closely with elements in the deep state. Indeed, these connections were no doubt useful to the AKP government throughout the first decade of its rule, the "years of symbiosis" between the Gülen movement and the AKP (Zürcher 2017, p. 347).

From the 1980's, the Gülen movement, through its "network of preparatory schools, high schools, colleges and even universities," had managed to "buil[d] a large cadre of well-educated—and pious—economists, managers, lawyers, and administrators," who came in handy to the AKP in its attempt to curb the hegemony of the Kemalist establishment "in the judiciary, public prosecution service, police and public administration;" accordingly, "[m]any 'Fethullacis' rose quickly within the party and, especially after 2007, acquired key positions in the judiciary, police and administration." The "symbiosis" came quite naturally, since, at the ideological level, there was a high level of convergence between the two—"[t]hey both favored a combination of Islamic values with a capitalist free market economy" (Zürcher 2017, pp. 346–347).

Even so, on the question of Turkish nationalism, the Gülen movement—despite its Islamism—was well-connected within the deep state, and correspondingly rigid and strident in its Turkish nationalist convictions. Indicative in this regard, an incendiary speech was delivered in the fall of 2011, titled "Terror and Agony," in which Gülen prayed, in deliberate reference to the PKK and its supporters, "O God, unify us, and as for those among us who deserve nothing but punishment, knock their homes upside down, destroy their unity, burn their houses to ash, may their houses be filled with weeping and supplications, burn and cut off their roots and bring their affairs to an end" (Quoted in White 2015, pp. 115–116).

In February 2012, Special Prosecutor Sadrettin Sarakaya—closely linked to Gülen—had taken advantage of a judicial inquiry into the Kurdish KCK, to order the man who Erdoğan had recently appointed the head of the National Intelligence Organization (MİT), Hekan Fidan, to "give a statement on meetings he had had—as the government's special envoy—with PKK leaders" during the Oslo process (Özcan 2016). The Gülen movement had not been privy to the Oslo talks, and had reacted with furor to the revelation of such negotiations, since to many Gülen members, especially those with the strongest "links with ultranationalist circles," such negotiations were "tantamount to high treason." Erdoğan responded to a warrant for Fidan's arrest by getting the legislature "to pass a law that exempted the MİT from prosecution," and promptly dismissing "the public prosecutors involved in the case" (Zürcher 2017, p. 357).

Erdoğan would later claim that "this moment 'was the day we saw the real face of the parallel structure', using the term used by government supporters to describe and define the Gülen movement" (Özcan 2016). In the months that followed, Erdoğan would respond forcefully to what he took to be a direct attack on him by the Gülenists, perhaps most notably, by "demoting suspected Gülenist police chiefs," as well as by eliminating "special-authority courts, supposedly controlled by Gülenists," prompting Gülen, in turn, to call Erdoğan "Pharaoh" (White 2015, p. 117). With the commencement of a new round of negotiations, tensions between the Erdoğan government and the Gülen movement flared even further, with "rumours appear[ing] in the press about imminent government actions against the Gülen movement" (Zürcher 2017, p. 357).

The "Solution Process" Gains Momentum

In the first meeting at İmralı in early January 2013, Öcalan had been quick to warn that "[t]he putschist clique will try to sabotage this process" (quoted in Yıldız 2017, p. 37). Less than a week would pass between the first meeting and the triple-murder in Paris. In the wake of the triple-murder, Öcalan initially refused to continue with the talks, but changed his mind after "concluding that the Paris attack was carried out by a faction within the State" in an attempt to "prevent talks between the PKK and the Turkish state" (Yıldız 2017, p. 37). As for the view from Qandil, the PKK's Cemil Bayık would later tell an interviewer that the head of the MİT, Fidan, "accepted the responsibility of his organization in being behind the assassination, but put the blame on clandestine factions" operating independently. Even more specifically, HDP MP Pervin Buldan would relay to

Öcalan in a subsequent visit to İmralı that Mr. Fidan had told the HDP delegation that he suspected either the Gülenist or a secular-nationalist faction within the organization to have been behind the murderous provocation in Paris. More recent interviews with PKK officials by Yıldız, however, show that the PKK suspects that Mr. Fidan was well-aware of the preparations for the triple-murders in Paris all along (Yıldız 2017, p. 37).

Despite the provocation, the "solution process" seemed to be gaining momentum. On the 24th of January, 2013, in a sign of goodwill to the Kurdish freedom movement, the Erdoğan government passed a law allowing for people to defend themselves in court in their "mother tongue." Two weeks later, Erdoğan announced to the Turkish public that the head of the MİT, Mr. Fidan, had met with Öcalan at İmralı. On the 19th of February, in another show of goodwill to the Kurdish freedom movement, ten members of the Kurdistan Communities' Union (KCK), including co-mayor elect of Diyarbakır, Fırat Anlı, would be released from prison. On the 23rd, the second BDP delegation would visit Öcalan at İmralı. By the 13th of March, the PKK would reciprocate the government's signs of goodwill when it released eight public officials it had been holding captive. Two days later, PKK commander Murat Karayılan confirmed that the organization was indeed willing "to strongly participate in Öcalan's solution perspective" (Çelik et al. 2015, p. 65).

As the "solution process" gained momentum, attempts to sabotage continued as well. Five days after the BDP delegation visit to İmralı, the minutes of the meeting would be leaked in the *Daily Millet* in another counter-move by deep-state elements. Even more disturbingly, on the 20th of March, the justice ministry and Erdoğan's office at the AKP headquarters in Ankara would both be bombed.[36]

But the drums of war could not drown out the calls for peace. The very next day, Erdoğan would announce that he was working on forming a committee of 63 "Wise Persons" to oversee the negotiations. In addition to this, a final verdict of non-prosecution was declared, regarding MİT head Mr. Fidan and four other MİT staff for their role in the Oslo process (Çelik et al. 2015, p. 65).

Öcalan's Newroz 2013 Letter

Even more promising, from the Kurdish side, was a historic letter by Abdullah Öcalan, read out at the Newroz celebration in Diyarbakır, in which Öcalan called on the PKK to declare another ceasefire and to withdraw across the border.

The letter is indicative of Öcalan's vision of democratic confederalism as a democratic alternative to the tyranny of the Nation-State, a vision intended to appeal not only to Kurds, but to all the peoples of the Middle East and beyond. Öcalan begins his letter by saluting "all the people of the Middle East and Central Asia" who celebrate Newroz festivities, to which he refers as a day of "awakening, revival and resurgence," a day uniting the peoples of the region. On this historic occasion, Öcalan predicted, this day would be remembered as "the dawn and turning point of a new era," one of "democratic tolerance." Öcalan next salutes "all people on the grand path towards democratic rights, freedom, and equality," before turning to address the Kurds in particular, as "an ancient people, dwellers in the sacred lands of Mesopotamia and Anatolia, mother to all agriculture, village and urban civilization."[37]

He recognizes a discourse of a people with ancient origins, located in the very birthplace of "civilization," a civilization "several thousand years old," but far from homogenous; indeed, he notes that they are composed of "diverse races, religions, creeds," in which Kurds "have taken part in friendship and accord," a civilization "which we have built together." Öcalan goes on to emphasize that such "coexisting communities" have "more recently"—by which he means "for the past two hundred years"—"been pitted against one another," via "military conquests, western imperialist interventions, and policies of repression and denial," ultimately intent on "submerging the Arabian, Turkic, Persian, and Kurdish communities" to the logic of the "nation-state," and its "imaginary borders and artificial problems."[38]

Öcalan thus begins by succinctly communicating a vision of a region long cohabitated by multiple, co-constitutive, ancient communities, with a deep history mostly characterized by harmonious inter-ethnic relations, but lately divided and conquered by the machinations of imperialism, combined with the tyranny of the Nation-State.

Öcalan continues by heralding a great "awakening" among the peoples of the Middle East and Central Asia that promises to bring the demise of "exploitative regimes" and the end of their "repression and denial." This awakening heralds a "return to the roots" as the peoples of the region begin "to cry for peace and amity" and "to demand a solution, a halt to the blinding and seditious wars and conflicts against one another."[39]

The theme of struggle comes next—more specifically, the struggle of the Kurds. Öcalan begins by speaking of his own individual struggle: his "rebellion against the despair, ignorance and slavery into which [he] was born," but quickly blurs the reference into the collective struggle of the Kurds, the "effort to create a new consciousness, a new understanding and a new spirit." The collective struggle of the Kurds, a struggle which Öcalan is quick to emphasize, "has not been and cannot be against any specific race, religion, sect, or group;" to the contrary, the struggle is directed "against repression, ignorance and injustice, against enforced underdevelopment as well as against all forms of oppression."[40]

Öcalan makes special reference to both the youth and the "eminent women;" he calls out to them, and to "anyone who can hear my voice," before announcing, most optimistically, "The period of armed struggle is ending, and the door is opening to democratic politics."[41]

To his followers, to Kurdish militants, he offers the reassurance, "None of our sacrifices, none of our struggles, have been in vain." Thanks to such struggles, "the Kurdish people have recovered their identity and their roots." Nevertheless, he insists, "We have now reached the point to silence the weapons and to let ideas and politics speak;" indeed, the time has come to "withdraw our armed forces" beyond the borders of Turkey. The end of armed conflict, he emphasizes, "is not an end, but a new beginning." A new struggle begins, "to create an equal, free and democratic country of all peoples and cultures." A project distinct from "the creation of geographies based on ethnicity and a single nation, a fabrication of modernity that denies our roots and our origins." A project that can and should be embraced by all the peoples of the region, by "Armenians, Turkmen, Assyrians, Arabs, and all other peoples," as well as by Kurds.[42] A project of democratic freedom and equality.

Öcalan then turns to explicitly address the broader Turkish public. What is called Turkey today, he begins by pointing out, is the "ancient Anatolia," in which Turkish people have long lived in common with Kurds, and especially "under the flag of Islam," have long done so in a spirit of "amity and solidarity." The logics of "conquest, denial, rejection, forced assimilation, or annihilation" have been superimposed much more recently, only in the last century, introduced along with imperialism and the Nation-State, at the onset of "capitalist modernity," and reflecting the "effort of the ruling elite" to divide and conquer the populations over whom they rule, in order to consolidate their "grip of tyranny" over majorities and minorities alike.[43]

Öcalan also appeals to key events which resonate and are ritually reproduced in the Turkish national imaginary, to events from the period of the immediate prehistory and foundation of the Republic, to the Battle of Gallipoli and the War of Independence, in which, he recalls, Turks and Kurds "fell as martyrs together," and to the 1920 opening of the assembly, which he insists, Turks and Kurds opened together. The common past, a reality; a common future, a necessity. The very same spirit that "established the Turkish Grand Assembly," he proclaims, "leads the way to a new era."[44] The new era as a restoration not only of the ancient, then, but also as a restoration of the Republic, more specifically, of the democratic impulse at the foundation of the Republic, which was all too soon distorted into ethno-nationalist and tyrannical form.

Having thus addressed both his own constituency in the Kurdish freedom movement and the broader Turkish (re)public, Öcalan finally turns to address "all oppressed peoples," including women, to whom he refers as "the most longstanding colonized and subjugated class;" to "all marginalized and excluded creeds, and cultures;" and to "the working class and all subordinated classes." An intersectional appeal, as the sociologists would say, and an internationalist one as well. He calls out to all of those who have been excluded and dominated by the hierarchies entrenched and perpetuated by the logic of capitalist modernity, invoking in the process an alternative logic, and vision, that of "democratic modernity."[45]

Öcalan then again hones in on Anatolia and Mesopotamia as providing an appropriate "geography" and "culture" for building this alternative model: one which the peoples of the region desperately need, as much as they need "bread and water." Indeed, he proclaims, the region finds itself in the midst of "a more complicated and more profound version of the War of Independence," one which requires unity and solidarity among the constituent peoples of the region, among "Kurds, Turkomans, Assyrians, and Arabs." It is high time, he insists, that the peoples of the region reclaim the term "We" from the "narrow and ruling" reduction of "We" to mean "One." He pronounces, in a prophetic tone, "We shall unite against those who want to make us divide and fight one another." As if to emphasize further and more explicitly the prophetic nature of this prediction and urgent call, he continues, "The Newroz is a beacon to us all. The truths in the messages of Moses, Jesus, and Mohammed are being implemented in our lives today with new tidings," as the peoples of the region struggle "to regain what they have lost."[46]

To conclude, Öcalan hails the beginning of a "great democratic leap forward," one which brings with it the promise of Enlightenment values such as freedom, equality, justice, and peace, synthesized with "our own existential values and lifeways."[47] A powerful and radically democratic message, one that simultaneously bears witness to and articulates a revolutionary democratic impulse and an impulse towards a democratic peace.

Tentative Steps in the Direction of a Peaceful Solution

Öcalan's message was read out at the Newroz celebrations on the 22nd of March; the PKK declared a ceasefire the next day. Notably, Öcalan's letter had proposed a ceasefire and withdrawal of the PKK from Turkish territory; but he did not call for disarmament. The imperative of self-defense remained.

Given the scale of violence and atrocities that the Turkish state had exercised against the Kurdish freedom movement, calls for disarmament on the part of the Turkish authorities were understandably interpreted in pro-Kurdish circles as calls for unconditional surrender, which would only render the movement utterly defenseless against Turkish tyranny. But disarmament is precisely what the Turkish authorities demanded. Thus, negotiations came up again and again against this intractable contradiction. Indeed, according to the International Crisis Group, the roadmap presented by the Turkish authorities was as follows: first, the PKK should declare a ceasefire and withdraw from Turkish territory, "leaving its weapons behind;" and only after this had happened would the government take steps towards democratization, which in turn, would have to be followed by "total disarmament and demobilisation of the PKK." By contrast, the International Crisis Group continues, "the PKK expected the government to make legal and constitutional reforms, and take steps such as allowing evicted Kurds to return to their native villages, at the same time as the PKK declared a ceasefire, released hostages, and withdrew armed insurgents" (International Crisis Group 2014, p. 5).

By the end of March, Erdoğan found himself insisting that "the process was developing as planned," while the Kemalist opposition in the Grand Assembly wasted no time criticizing him for his weakness in defending the nation's interest. The prime minister was forced to clarify that, though Öcalan's prison condition had been improved, any further concessions, such as house confinement, were out of the question, and that all rumors about a "transition to autonomous administration in the Southeast did not reflect the truth." He would further clarify, on the last day of the month, that the PKK "had to first disarm and then withdraw," which, in turn, provoked a response by Qandil that "disarmed withdrawal was not part of their agenda," with PKK commander and KCK Executive Council Member Cemil Bayık adding for good measure: "the guerrilla force cannot take a single step back without receiving legal assurance" (Çelik et al. 2015, p. 66).

A curious constellation of forces was beginning to emerge: Öcalan was increasingly thrust into a role of mediator between the PKK in Qandil, which registered consistent and thoroughgoing distrust and caution, on the one side, and the Turkish authorities, on the other, whose intransigence was no doubt conditioned by hardline elements within the deep state attempting to disrupt the negotiations by any means necessary, and by a parliamentary opposition ready to seize on any and all concessions by the Erdoğan government as weak and misguided at best, treasonous at worst.

More must be said about this constellation of forces represented in the "solution process", which included a somewhat narrower spectrum of representation than the Oslo precedent. Representation for the Kurdish freedom movement included Öcalan, several MP's from the left-wing, pro-Kurdish BDP-cum-HDP, and, albeit *in abstentia*, the PKK high command in Qandil. This amounted to an important difference from the Oslo negotiations, which took place outside the country on "neutral ground," which thus allowed PKK representatives from Qandil to meet and negotiate directly with state authorities. By contrast, this time around, negotiations took place in İmralı, in the presence of Öcalan but, obviously, not the PKK high command. BDP-cum-HDP representatives were given the task of delivering communications back and forth: to and from the Turkish authorities as well as to and from Öcalan with the PKK high command. Moreover, all communications between BDP-cum-HDP representatives and Öcalan took place in the presence of Turkish authorities, which further constrained effective deliberation and frank communication among the different actors representing the Kurdish freedom movement.

Meanwhile, on the side of the Turkish state, representation was also more limited than it had been in Oslo in important respects. The far-right, ultra-nationalist MHP was not the only party excluded this time around; so too was the country's second largest party, the Kemalist CHP, absent at the negotiating table. As such, Yıldız explains, the actors implicated included only "Turkish intelligence officers, Justice Ministry Officials" an AKP minister and several AKP MPs. Moreover, as Yıldız perceptively notes, the Gülen faction in the state apparatus was excluded, too (Yıldız 2017, p. 34).

Öcalan argued from the outset that it would be best to broaden representation in the negotiations to include other actors from civil society, such as human rights organizations, trade union officials, business community representatives, and the like. But, aside from the creation of the wise persons' committee, such advice would go unheeded (Yıldız 2017, p. 36).

At the beginning of April, after the fourth BDP delegation to İmralı—this time consisting of co-chair Selahattin Demirtaş, alongside Pervin Buldan and Sırrı Süreyya Önder—the delegation would leave with a letter by Öcalan for the PKK high command in Qandil, "asking it to comply with the instruction to withdraw to positions beyond Turkey's borders" (Çelik et al. 2015, p. 66).

For its part, the Turkish government would move ahead with its plan to form a wise persons' committee, including "artists and writers such as Orhan Gencebay, Kadir İnanır, Yılmaz Erdoğan, and Baskın Oran among its members." In a sign of goodwill, on the occasion of his first meeting with the committee, Erdoğan would declare, "Now is not the time to settle accounts, but the time for both sides to give each other their blessings. Now is the time to realize the law of fraternity. Now is the time to emphasize not differences but shared values" (Çelik et al. 2015, p. 67). Later that day, in a parliamentary vote notably boycotted by the Kemalist opposition CHP and the far-right ultra-nationalist MHP, a "Solution Process Commission" would be formed with votes in favor from the governing party AKP and the representatives of the Kurdish freedom movement.

Such a symbolic gesture on Erdoğan's part would be followed in the second week of April, with a baby-step in the direction of ameliorating the legal repression against the movement, by expanding the limits of free expression. The Grand Assembly passed a "liberalizing" reform, according to which "in sentencing those who carried out propaganda for a terror organization, or printed and broadcast their announcements and declaration, 'legitimizing and praising methods involving force, violence or intimidation, or the encouragement of the employment of such methods' was set as a condition" (Çelik et al. 2015, p. 67). Likewise, the Ministry of Justice announced that it had released some 200 suspects under arrest in relation to the so-called "KCK operations" of November 2011, in which over 8,000 people were arrested. Another baby step.

Disturbingly, however, around the same time, "news appeared on media that the construction of *kalekols*—fortress-like high security military stations" had accelerated in the wake of the ceasefire. Thereby reinforcing those with more skeptical temperaments in the pro-Kurdish camp about the true nature of the Turkish authorities' endgame. Two baby steps forward, one big step back?

Even so, the Kurdish freedom movement would continue to register its commitment to the process. After a fifth meeting with BDP-cum-HDP representatives at İmralı, a letter from Öcalan would be delivered to PKK headquarters in Qandil, prompting a press conference there on the 25th, attended by a large group of Turkish and international press, at which PKK commander and KCK Executive Council Member Murat Karayılan would announce a gradual withdrawal beginning from the May 8, though at the same time insisting that "the organization would take the decision to disarm only as a part of a process in which, (1) constitutional changes were made," (2) "Abdullah Öcalan was freed completely," (3) "Special Forces and similar organizations operating within the body of security forces of Turkey" were disestablished, and (4) the village guard system was abolished.

As announced, the PKK did begin its gradual withdrawal on the May 8. Though KRG Prime Minister Barzani had registered his support for the "solution process," the "Iraqi Foreign Ministry now announced its opposition to the entry into Iraqi territory of PKK members withdrawing from Turkey" (Çelik et al. 2015, p. 68). US President Barack Obama, however, chimed in to push the process forward, simultaneously sending a message to the Iraqi government, albeit one predictably couched in an extremely misleading and biased, "war on terror" frame, by "commend[ing] the Turkish people for your courage in seeking an historic and peaceful resolution of the PKK violence that has plagued Turkey for so long" (Çelik et al. 2015, p. 69).

On the 25th and 26th of May, an historic conference was held in Ankara, one that had been proposed by Öcalan, dedicated to the theme of "Democracy and Peace." The event provided some grounds for optimism about the "solution process," no doubt.

Enter Gezi Park

Then came the Gezi Park protests, the wave of demonstrations that spread across the country, affecting nearly all 81 provinces, including hundreds of thousands of protestors. This wave was triggered by citizen indignation at police forces' thuggish tactics and violent eviction of a peaceful sit-in of environmental activists who had been protesting an "urban development" plan that effectively entailed the elimination of the very last green spaces in central Istanbul.[48] According to a report by Amnesty International, "[t]he nationwide protests were fanned by the authorities' aggressive dismissal of the integrity of those originally protesting in Gezi Park and the crude attempts to deny them the right to peaceful protest altogether. The widespread police use of tear gas, water cannon, plastic bullets and beatings of protestors during what were overwhelmingly peaceful protests added to the anger" (Amnesty International 2013, p. 6).

A pattern of spiraling protest and "fresh violence and increasingly hardline government rhetoric" ensued, continuing throughout June and July. The Amnesty report documents how at the height of the protest wave, Turkish "authorities repeatedly showed total intolerance for any form of protest, however passive. Even solitary figures, standing alone and silent in Taksim Square were detained for participating in what became known as the 'standing man' protests." Indeed, Erdoğan would go so far as to "suggest that banging pots and pans in solidarity with the demonstrators would also be considered a crime, and at least one criminal case was opened on such grounds. The repression would extend beyond the protestors, too, to include "journalists reporting from the protests," as well as "doctors treating the injured and lawyers defending their rights, [who] were also arrested and subjected to arbitrary and abusive use of force." The authorities even threatened to crack down on "business owners who opened their doors to protestors fleeing police violence" (Amnesty International 2013, p. 6).

The state violence unleashed against the protestors was certainly not of the intensity of the human rights atrocities that had long characterized its treatment of the Kurds; even so, the violence was very real and very disturbing nonetheless. By the middle of July, according to the Turkish Medical Association, "there had been more than 8,000 injuries at the scene of demonstrations;" and by "the end of August, five people had died during the course of the protests," with "strong evidence linking three of these deaths to the abusive use of force by police." The number killed would later be revised upwards to nine (Zürcher 2017, p. 356).

Perhaps even more disturbingly, the authorities were quick to make use of anti-terror legislation to target non-governmental organizations, "political groups and professional bodies" who had come out in support of the protests, a factor which seriously inhibited the ability of Turkish groups to investigate the abundant "allegations of abusive police violence" (Amnesty International 2013, pp. 6–7).

The Amnesty report emphasized that "[t]he authorities' response to the Gezi Park protests ... in many ways represents a continuation of long standing patterns of human rights abuses in Turkey; the denial of the right to peaceful assembly, excessive use of force by police officers and the prosecution of legitimate dissenting opinions while allowing police abuses go unchecked." It also highlighted the relative novelty of the events, noting that the wave of protests was "unparalleled in terms of the numbers of people taking part, their duration for over two months and the fact that they spanned virtually every province in the country." The Gezi Wave was distinguished by class differences that dramatically contrasted with previous patterns of protests and repression. Indeed, according to Amnesty, not only were "[m]any of those taking part ... in their 20s and had not previously been involved in any form of political protest;" but also, crucially, "[m]any came from the more affluent sections of society." The demographic profile of those repressed, in Amnesty's judgment, helped shed light on the State's endemic repressive reflexes, bringing "a more visceral awareness of the human rights abuses previously experienced by people demonstrating on politically sensitive issues such as Kurdish rights and politics to a broader audience within Turkey" (Amnesty International 2013, p. 7).

The distinctiveness of the protestors' demographic profile was simultaneously a strength and a weakness. The wave of Gezi protests of course brought together "many different groups and grievances," including "environmentalists, secularists, trade unions, Kurds, Alevis, women's rights activists, [the LGBT movement], socialists, communists, and liberals;" even so, the wave of protests was clearly dominated by middle-class youth (Zürcher 2017, p. 355).

Erdoğan responded to the outbreak of the protests with fury, "insist[ing] they be brought to an immediate end." Some of the members of the AKP had initially "called for reconciliation and dialogue;" but Erdoğan insisted instead on a policy of "confrontation." He referred to the demonstrators as "'vandals' and unbelievers who had no respect for the 'national will' as expressed in the AKP's election victories;" he treated "the demonstrations as the work of conspirators;" as for the protestors, he considered them "puppets in the hands of mysterious international financial interests aiming to undermine Turkey's economy" (Zürcher 2017, p. 356).

The prominent role of the urban middle-class youth, along with their skillful use of the social media in coordinating the wave of mobilization, led many commentators to draw the comparison with the Tahrir square movement of 2011 in Egypt that had proven capable of bringing down President Hosni Mubarak; however, as Zürcher has rightly noted, the balance of popular forces was different in the Republic of Turkey. In Egypt, the opposition to Mubarak had included "a broad coalition from left to right in which the Muslim Brotherhood played a decisive role," along with the labor movement. By contrast, in Turkey, "[t]he great mass of Sunni conservatives and the urban proletariat remained mostly loyal to Erdoğan," rendering the movement much weaker demographically, composed "essentially [of] a coalition of urban, middle-class groups and minorities like Alevis and Kurds" (Zürcher 2017, p. 356). Thus, the popular base of support for Erdoğan were much greater, and so the wave of protest ultimately much weaker.

However, the protests were widely recognized at the time as "the most significant nationwide disquiet in decades," and among "the most challenging events" faced by the Erdoğan government in power.[49] Öcalan, too, recognized their significance early on, responding in early June to the outbreak of protest by "saluting the Gezi resistance," though simultaneously cautioning that "no one should allow themselves to be used by nationalist circles, or circles favoring a military coup" (Çelik et al. 2015, p. 69).

Öcalan's warning was indeed perspicacious. One of the more interesting details of the responses to the wave of protest was the discrepancy between Erdoğan's fury and the conciliatory position adopted and urged by Fethullah Gülen who, "from his headquarters in Pennsylvania, reject[ed] violence and call[ed] for a fraternal dialogue"—in "yet another sign that the relationship" between the two leaders and two movements "was deteriorating fast" (Zürcher 2017, p. 356).

Not only did the strains between the Erdoğan government and the Gülen movement come to the surface around Gezi; the prospects for peace with the Kurdish freedom movement were diminished as well. This was because, as Yıldız has observed, "The protests made the Erdoğan administration less confident and more authoritarian than before." It was a point of inflection, no doubt, perhaps even a point of no return. Several AKP party officials who Yıldız interviewed openly blamed the Gülen movement for the wave of protests, insisting "that factions that wanted to target the government and spoil the peace process came to support the Gezi Protests financially, politically and through the media organisations they control[led]." Notably, the PKK remained committed to the peace process and never openly broke from negotiations with Erdoğan throughout the wave of protests. Even so, the more authoritarian bent of the government would inevitably have negative repercussions for all forces struggling for democratization, especially those aligned with the HDP and therefore the Kurdish freedom movement (Yıldız 2017, p. 39).

The fate of Sırrı Süreyya Önder, the iconic Turkish film director and actor-cum-BDP MP, who became a symbolic figure of the Gezi resistance after he was hit by a tear gas canister and hospitalized, is illustrative in this regard.[50] For Önder had been among the BDP representatives who visited Öcalan at İmralı in February and April 2013; but after gaining notoriety for his involvement in Gezi, the government would refuse to let him participate as a member of further delegations (though the government would later recant) (Çelik et al. 2015, p. 69).

The wave of Gezi resistance coincided with foot-dragging on the part of the PKK when it came to withdrawal. By September, the organization would announce that it was ceasing its withdrawal, citing government inaction on promises to propose laws to begin decriminalizing members of the guerrilla. However, government officials interviewed by Yıldız advanced a different interpretation, one reflective of a certain paranoid and Manichean mindset that increasingly pervaded the ruling party in the wake of Gezi. These sources insisted that the PKK had decided to halt withdrawal "due to the start" of the anti-government protests—adopting a wait-and-see tactic in case the protests proved capable of toppling the government, as the more hopeful among observers were predicting at the time.

The "Solution Process" Stalls

The Gezi protests, interpreted through the lens of the escalating feud with the Gülenist movement, worked to exacerbate the repressive reflexes of the government. That feud, in turn, forced the government to search for alternative alliances, which would ultimately lead to a significant rapprochement with the secular-nationalist forces on the far Right—forces who had been previously targeted by Erdoğan during the Ergenekon trials (Yıldız 2017, p. 40). From one ally hostile to the Kurdish freedom movement, to another, even more hostile.

As the Erdoğan government began to veer ever more to the authoritarian right, its legitimacy was further diminished in the eyes of the more liberal elements in Turkish society. This too posed an obstacle for the "solution process", as reflected in the demise of the Wise Persons' committee, which suffered a series of resignations by members who were critical of the government's posture vis-à-vis Gezi, including those of the writer Murat Belge, the journalist Kürşat Bumin, and the political scientist Baskın Oran (Çelik et al. 2015, p. 70).

In late June, on the day of the last meeting of the committee, in which the Wise Persons presented their reports on prospects for the "solution process" based on research in seven regions, Erdoğan complained that "only 15% of PKK members had withdrawn from Turkey." That same week, at a demonstration in Lice against the construction of a fortress-style military station (kalekol), soldiers murdered one of the protestors; while in Diyarbakır, a crowd at a rally "organized by the BDP with the slogan, 'It's the government's time to take a step' was attacked by the police with water cannons and pepper gas," to which protestors would respond "by setting off fireworks and throwing stones" (Çelik et al. 2015, p. 70).

Throughout July, the "solution process" stalled, and by the end of the month, in a meeting with his sister at İmralı island, Abdullah Öcalan even threatened to withdraw from negotiations should the government fail to take any steps by the beginning of October. By August, Murat Karayılan, PKK commander and head of the recently constituted "People's Defence Force" (HPG), sounded an early alarm about mounting tensions over the saber-rattling of the Turkish state in response to developments in Rojava, not to mention the brutal embargo it had imposed, one notably adhered to by the KRG in Iraq as well. Tensions would escalate much further the following year, during ISIS' long siege on Kobane.

Even so, in the summer of 2013, co-chair Salih Muslim of the Democratic Union Party (PYD), an organization organically linked with the Kurdish freedom movement in Turkey, would be invited to Ankara twice by the Turkish Foreign Ministry. There was even talk at the time that the PYD might be allowed to open a representative office in Ankara. Soon enough, all such talk would cease. But even as such talk persisted, both Karayılan as well as Cemil Bayık, from Qandil, were already denouncing the "attacks [which] continue on the Rojava Revolution from multiple fronts" (Çelik et al. 2015, p. 72).

At the end of September, Erdoğan finally announced a much-awaited "Democratization Package," which would be received with much disappointment in Kurdish circles and dismissed by BDP representatives as an empty gesture devoid of any tangible democratizing content. The "solution process" remained stalled throughout the fall, into the winter. In this regard, come early December, the Solution Commission of Turkey's Grand National Assembly would present a report to the Parliament, during which Commission Chairman Naci Bostancı lamented, "[I]t has been determined that the solution process has established a negative peace, and that something needs to be done to orient it towards a positive peace" (Çelik et al. 2015, pp. 77–78).

Easier said than done—especially in an increasingly polarized climate, in which the Erdoğan government felt itself squeezed on many sides, its legitimacy and its ability to survive in doubt. The paranoia, the sense of siege, in government circles would be further heightened after a judicial investigation into charges of corruption would be launched in December 2013—an investigation which "initially targeted four cabinet members and their sons but then widened to include Erdoğan's family, including his son and his son-in-law." The forces pushing forward the investigation were widely rumored to be aligned with the Gülenist movement, occupying "senior positions in the security apparatus, the civilian bureaucracy, and the judiciary" (Yıldız 2017, p. 39).

At the time, Öcalan, too, in discussions with BDP/HDP MPs at İmralı, also warned that the corruption cases under way could well amount to an attempted coup, and asked his movement to take a clear stance against any such attempt. In Öcalan's words, "Those who want to turn the country into bedlam by igniting the fire of a coup should know that we will not pour gasoline onto such a fire. We will stand in the way of every attempt at carrying out a coup, as we have done until now" (Çelik et al. 2015, p. 79).

But such efforts on Öcalan's part were not sufficient to counter the force of attraction pulling Erdoğan into the orbit of the far-right, given he was in "survival mode." Now that he was at war with the very elements in the State who had previously protected him, he was increasingly convinced that if he wanted to survive, he had little choice but to make amends with the secular-nationalist forces he had previously targeted during the Ergenekon trials. A much-publicized visit to the hospital bed of a retired general "who had been sentenced to 18 years for plotting against [him] by Gülenist judges" was emblematic of the prime minister's new survival tactic (Yıldız 2017, p. 39).

The government had already announced a take-over of the Gülenist network of schools in November; now, with the onset of the corruption trials, the government would mount another counter-offensive in "the form of massive transfers and demotions of police personnel with known Gülen ties." So too would Erdoğan begin waxing eloquent about the need to "eradicate the 'parallel structure', the State within the State," while accusations proliferated linking the machinations of the Gülen movement to the intelligence agencies of the United States (where he lives), as well as with Israel. In turn, "public prosecutors with Gülen sympathies reacted by ordering gendarmes to open trucks destined for Syria and to have them searched," thereby revealing the Erdoğan government's complicity in the supply of arms to the "Islamic resistance" to the Assad regime, forcing the government into a very uncomfortable position with its NATO partners, to say the least (Zürcher 2017, pp. 358–359).

A New Election Cycle

Against this backdrop of no-holds-barred conflict between the Erdoğan government and the Gülen movement, the local and presidential elections would be celebrated in the spring and summer of 2014, respectively. Over the course of the electoral campaigns, Selahattin Demirtaş and the rest of the leadership of the pro-Kurdish HDP did their very best to put to rest any lingering rumors among the Turkish secular left that the Kurdish freedom movement would be willing to support Erdoğan's hyper-presidentialist ambitions in exchange for the recognition of greater Kurdish rights (Yıldız 2017, pp. 40–41).

In the run-up to the election, the "Democratization Package" would be passed in the Grand National Assembly. The package did include some advances in terms of cultural rights, including allowing "private schools to provide education in Kurdish, and election propaganda in Kurdish at elections," but little else in terms of "democratization" more broadly understood (Çelik et al. 2015, p. 81). In messages delivered through members of the delegations who continued to meet with him at İmralı, Öcalan consistently urged an acceleration of the peace process. However, less than two weeks before the local elections, a less patient message would be delivered by Qandil, declaring that "the government was no longer an interlocutor for the democratization movement." This would bring differences of sensibility within the Kurdish freedom movement to the surface as leading BDP-cum-HDP co-chair Selahattin Demirtaş retorted, "It was Mr. Öcalan who initiated the process, and any statement that can end it can also only come from him" (Çelik et al. 2015, p. 82).

The same week, the European Court of Human Rights would render a verdict in a case that had been filed by Abdullah Öcalan's lawyers about the conditions of their client's detention on İmralı. The Court ruled that "Turkey had 'partly violated' the European Convention of Human Rights," at least in the period up to 2009, when the leader of the Kurdish freedom movement had been held in total isolation; and perhaps more importantly, with respect to his life sentence without possibility for parole. Both ruled violations of Article 3, the famous prohibition on torture, which states that "No one shall be subjected to torture or inhuman or degrading treatment or punishment" (Çelik et al. 2015, p. 82). This verdict was received as but a provocation by the Turkish nationalist far-Right, and one to which the Turkish state has yet to respond, despite its obligation to comply.

The elections would be held on the 30th of March. There had been much speculation that the internecine feud between Erdoğan and the Gülenist movement would hurt the former's prospects in the new electoral cycle. From the start of the campaign season, Erdoğan would strike a consistently aggressive tone, "denounc[ing] both the liberal opposition and the Gülenists as conspirators and agents of foreign interests," and enemies of the people (Zürcher 2017, p. 358). The polarization served to mobilize Erdoğan's core constituency, and so the AKP performed better than expected, holding onto control of both Ankara and Istanbul, managing to reproduce an electoral map with the "now familiar pattern— a fringe of CHP red along the west coast and in Thrace, green in the southeast, which was dominated by the Kurdish party [now HDP], and all the rest AKP yellow" (Zürcher 2017, p. 358)

Erdoğan would interpret the electoral success in the local election as vindication for his assault on the Gülenists, which he would ratchet up further in the run-up to the presidential contest. In this period, he would remain non-stop on the campaign trail, delivering incendiary speech after incendiary speech against the "Gülenist conspiracy," while simultaneously unleashing "large-scale purges of the police and public prosecution," extirpating elements identified as agents of Gülen (Zürcher 2017, p. 358).

The Kemalist CHP opted for a joint candidate in electoral coalition with the far-right MHP, strangely, a relatively unknown candidate by the name of Ekmeleddin İhsanoğlu, a man with considerable conservative Islamic credentials, dubbed by some of his more secularist detractors as "Erdoğan lite" (Zürcher 2017, p. 359). Meanwhile, the Kurdish freedom movement put forward Selahattin Demirtaş as presidential candidate, at the head of the new Peoples' Democratic Party (HDP), a platform uniting the pro-Kurdish Peace and Democracy Party (BDP), now renamed the Democratic Regions' Party (DBP), in coalition with a broad array of figures and organizations on the Turkish Left. Throughout the campaign, Demirtaş struck a consistently principled tone of strident opposition to Erdoğan's hyper-presidentialist ambitions, emphasizing his praise for the Gezi park protestors, even displaying photos of himself participating in the events.[51]

By May, the PKK was again warning, in the words of Executive Council member Duran Kalkan, that "if no steps are taken, if there is no response to Leader Apo's projects, and if the oppression of the people continues, then both the guerrillas and the people will intervene in the process." Nor was this the only sign of an impending resumption of hostilities. The day after the statement from the PKK, reports surfaced in the media that "the Turkish state had built 341 new military stations and 900 kilometers of military roads, and that two thousand new village guards had been trained." Throughout the month, clashes between police forces and Kurdish youth protesting *kalekol* constructions in Diyarbakır,

Şırnak, and Mardin would take place, while, for his part, Erdoğan responded with the threat, "You will go and bring back the young people who have taken to the mountains, if you do not do that, we will launch our B and C plans" (Çelik et al., pp. 83–85).

Even more ominously, the spill-over effects of the ongoing war in Syria were becoming increasingly evident (Ozkahraman 2017, p. 13). Not only did the number of refugees from Syria in Turkey surpass 1.5 million in the month of May, so too did clashes in Rojava between Kurdish revolutionary forces and Islamist rebels impact upon the public consciousness; this was especially the case after the Kurdish People's Protection Units (YPG) publicized the confession of an arrested ISIS-member about Al-Qaeda having "a military recruitment bureau in the Reyhanlı district in Hatay" on the Mediterranean coast of Turkey, where Islamist militants were being hosted before being shuttled across the border to fight in Rojava. By the end of the month, the government had introduced a broadcast ban on reports of trucks owned by the Turkish intelligence services intercepted at the Rojava border carrying weapons to Islamist militants in Syria (Çelik et al. 2015, pp. 84, 86).

Notably, in the same month, the Öcalan-inspired Democratic Islam Congress, organized by the Kurdish freedom movement, would be held in Diyarbakır, to which Öcalan would address a letter in which he insisted that a pluralist, egalitarian, and democratic Islam is necessary, that the interpretation of Islam "on the side of the government and the State contradicts the very essence" of the principles of the Muslim faith (Çelik et al. 2015, p. 84).

In the run-up to the presidential election, the construction of military fortresses across the Kurdish region continued apace. There were reports that Öcalan was increasingly frustrated with the government's failure to take any serious steps in the direction of peace. Time was running out, he seemed to foresee, and the window of opportunity for peace would soon be slammed shut.

On the 10th of August, Erdoğan would receive 52% of the vote, thereby winning the majority in the first round. The result was another demonstration of the continuing popular appeal of the prime minister-cum-president, even amidst the feud with the Gülenists, and it was another step towards the consolidation of his grip on power and the realization of his hyper-presidentialist ambitions. But at the same time, it also demonstrated the definite limits to his appeal, and confirmed the deep divisions in the country (Zürcher 2017, p. 358).

In the week after the election, tensions would escalate further on the Kurdish front. In the district of Lice, in the province of Diyarbakır, a statue of Mahsum Korkmaz, the PKK commander who had led the first attack on Turkish soil in 1984, was erected in his honor on the 30th anniversary of the event. Korkmaz had been killed by Turkish forces in 1986, and his memory has been much honored in the Kurdish freedom movement ever since. A court ordered the statue, located in a cemetery, be removed; the gendarmerie intervened; youth protesters tried to stop the demolition from taking place and altercations ensued, in which a 24-year old protestor Mehdi Taşkın would be shot in the head, killed.[52] After which, both the government and the Kurdish freedom movement would cry provocation, with Deputy Prime Minister Beşir Atalay alleging, "What [happened] today was necessary. We can't tolerate such incidents. As one in charge of the peace process, I can say that we see this as a direct provocation;" while for its part, the Kurdistan Communities Union (KCK) issued a warning: "It is clear that the AKP government is playing with fire. They know too well Korkmaz's importance for the Kurds… Their decision to attack our cemetery and displace the statue is [only intended to] dynamite the peace process."[53]

At the end of August, the newly appointed prime minister, Ahmet Davutoğlu, would present his new cabinet. Notably, the comparatively dovish Deputy Prime Minister Mr. Atalay would not be reappointed; however, the new cabinet would include the known hardliner, a war on terror crusader, Yalçın Akdoğan. (Çelik et al. 2015, p. 87). The new deputy prime minister was rumored to be a vocal proponent of the so-called "Sri Lankan model" for dealing with the Kurds, in reference to the Sri Lankan army's aggressive strategy of counterinsurgency and measures of repression verging on genocidal war crimes, including "repeatedly shelling civilians, targeting hospitals, and trying to prevent the world from finding out about it," according to Human Rights Watch.[54]

As if the prospects for peace were not complicated enough, the day after the announcement of the new hawkish deputy prime minister, the Turkish military would chime in, through the Chief of General Staff, Necdet Özal, who publicly complained, "The government did not ask our opinion regarding the road map [for peace], we are finding out about it from the press. We wish that our view had been sought. The government said the problem would be solved without arms, but we do not want mothers to cry. If the red lines of the solution process are transgressed, we will give the necessary answer" (Çelik et al. 2015, p. 87).

The Siege of Kobane

The prospects for peace would be diminished much further from mid-September of 2014, with the onset of the long siege by ISIS on Kobane, a siege that would last for over six months. By the 20th of September, at least 60,000 displaced Kurds had crossed the border separating Syria from Turkey, into the district of Suruç, province of Şanlıurfa, despite clashes with security forces on the Turkish side of the border (Çelik et al. 2015, p. 89).[55] By the first days of October, after ISIS had "succeeded in capturing over 350 Kurdish villages and towns in the vicinity of Kobane," the number of displaced who had made their way into Şanlıurfa stood at 300,000; and by January 2015, the number would reach fully 400,000.[56]

On that same 20th of September, advancing ISIS "forces came within 15 kilometers of the city of Kobane;" while on the side of the defense, more than 300 Kurdish fighters reached the besieged city, crossing over the border from Turkey, to serve as reinforcements for the beleaguered Syrian-Kurdish Peoples' Protection Units (YPG). For his part, senior PKK commander Karayılan made an open appeal to Kurdish youth in Turkey to emulate this precedent and join Kurdish forces in Syria to defend the Rojava revolution from the onslaught of ISIS thugs.[57]

The ensuing clashes at the border between Kurds attempting to go to the aid of Kobane and Turkish security forces, combined with the nonchalance of the Turkish authorities in response to the siege on Kobane, indeed, the lack of response, infuriated especially the more militant among the Kurdish population in Turkey; so too did it lead to considerable dismay in Western political and diplomatic circles (International Crisis Group 2015, p. 4). An article in *The Guardian* quoted Joost Lagendijk, former Dutch MEP and expert on Turkey, as saying, "The pictures of the Turkish army as a spectator and bystander, doing nothing while Kurds are being killed in front of their eyes, has created a world-wide perception of Turkey as a cynical and calculating player." In a similar vein, an Obama administration official affirmed, "There's growing angst about Turkey dragging its feet to prevent a massacre less than a mile from its border … This isn't how a NATO ally acts while hell is unfolding a stone's throw from their border."[58]

War can produce strange bedfellows. A good example is the case of the alliance between the revolutionary Kurdish forces in Rojava and the U.S.-led aerial coalition, which had begun bombing ISIS targets in Iraq in the wake of the latter's impressive and threatening surge in the summer, after ISIS captured Mosul in June and made it within 40 kilometers of Erbil in early August. The US had taken note of the bravery, discipline, and efficiency of PKK and YPG forces, who combined to break ISIS' genocidal siege of the Yazidis on Sinjar Mountain in early August, a siege which also triggered the new round of American airstrikes in Iraq.[59] On the 23rd of September, the US extended its aerial campaign against ISIS targets to Syria, near Raqqa; and on the 27th, it launched its first air strikes on ISIS near Kobane.[60] [61]

Even so, by the 6th of October, the situation in Kobane looked particularly bleak for the YPG, with the Western media paying close attention. *The Independent* ran a story quoting the director of the Syrian Observatory of Human Rights reporting, "They are fighting inside the city. Hundreds of civilians have left. The Islamic State controls three neighborhoods on the eastern side of Kobani. They are trying to enter the town from the south west as well."[62] The headline of the same article, however, cast attention just across the border, on President Erdoğan, who, while addressing a group of refugees in Gaziantep, had waxed prophetic, predicting that Kobane was about to fall.

In Kurdish circles, the president's prediction was widely interpreted as basically an endorsement. Indeed, in Yıldız's estimation, "[t]he tone Erdoğan used in his speech was perceived to be celebratory by many Kurdish actors inside and outside of Turkey." The fact that Erdoğan had also insisted that "for us, the PKK and IS are the same" further incensed Kurdish sentiment (Yıldız 2017, p. 42).

Öcalan would issue a statement of his own on Kobane on the same day, in which he assured that "[o]ur people in Kobane are going to resist until the end, [that] resistance will be manifest everywhere," and added, for good measure, in apparent allusion to Turkey, "[w]hichever country is supporting ISIS will itself suffer damage."[63] Two days later, he would further elaborate that he "considered the Kobane reality and the peace process in Turkey as an "indivisible whole... in a democratic journey and struggle for humanity that has cost everyone a lot." More explicitly, he would also warn, "Should this massacre attempt succeed (in Kobane), it would both bring an end to the ongoing resolution process and lay the foundation for a new coup that will last long."[64]

In the days following the statements from Erdoğan and Öcalan, and in response to calls from both the KCK and the HDP for "permanent action," Kurds took to the streets *en masse*, in the tens of thousands, in Bakur and beyond, throughout Turkey, across Europe, to protest government inaction in the face of the ongoing massacre in Kobane, along with its obstruction of Kurds trying to cross the border to help defend Kobane. Clashes with Turkish security forces, as well as with members of the so-called Kurdish *Hizbollah*, ensued. After "incidents that led to the deaths of 49 people in around 40 cities," curfews would be imposed in many urban areas, including Diyarbakır, where Turkish "tanks and infantry forces roamed the streets" (Çelik et al. 2015, p. 89).[65] As Yıldız has insightfully observed, "Compared with the Gezi protests, which lasted for months and resulted in the death of 9 civilians, the extent of casualties is striking" (Yıldız 2017, p. 42).

Only after Öcalan would send another message, in effect calling off the protests for the sake of renewed efforts at peace, would the demonstrations subside.[66] But not before the Bingöl deputy police chief and superintendent were shot and killed, which in turn triggered the extrajudicial execution of four suspected "terrorists," and had brought tensions to the boiling point before Öcalan intervened to defuse the situation.

The wave of protests may have ended after Öcalan called them off, but the Turkish authorities remained disturbed by the events even after they had subsided. One Turkish official interviewed by Yıldız in the spring of 2017 would claim, in retrospect, that the demonstration of the Kurdish freedom movement's "ability to mobilize masses so quickly across more than a dozen cities … shook the government and possibly other nationalist factions within the State, making them think that the PKK [had not] lost any of its ability to persuade Kurdish masses to confront violently the Turkish security forces, despite the ongoing peace talks" (Yıldız 2017, p. 42).

In Öcalan's message calling off the wave of protests, he warned of "provocateurs."[67] Provocateurs there undoubtedly were, and there would continue to be, for one, among the Turkish security forces, who, on the 23rd of October, would kill "three PKK members in a moving vehicle in the Kagizman district of Kars," in the northeast of Turkey. The following day, in apparent retaliation, "[i]n the Yüksekova district of Hakkari, three soldiers were killed by masked persons in the market place." However, the PKK was quick to issue a statement insisting that it had not ordered the attack, after which "a broadcast ban was imposed on the incident" (Çelik et al. 2015, p. 90). Hard-line elements within the deep state were likely now seizing the initiative to attempt to derail definitively the peace talks.

The Turkish authorities did eventually allow for reinforcements to reach Kobane from Turkish soil, on the 29th of October, but rather than allow volunteers associated with the Kurdish freedom movement to do so, it opted instead to let Peshmerga fighters associated with KRG President Masoud Barzani (International Crisis Group 2015, p. 4). Any further collaboration in any way with the Kurdish freedom movement on either side of the border had been ruled out.

As both the International Crisis Group and Yıldız have emphasized, on the 30th of October, the Turkish National Security Council would meet, under President Erdoğan's chairmanship, and decide that, "The Turkish State will struggle to fight against illegal structures which operate under a legal appearance ... and determination will be shown to prevent provocative actions geared towards harming the positive atmosphere created by the peace process, and all measures to ensure public safety and security will be taken" (International Crisis Group 2015, p. 5; Yıldız 2017, p. 43). This signalled an impending re-criminalization of the Kurdish freedom movement *tout court*, justified by a return to the security paradigm above all else.

In conveying Öcalan's message, HDP representatives had added that they "hoped the leaders of the Kurdistan Communities' Union (KCK) ... would also repeat their call to demonstrators to refrain from violence," an addition which suggested, highly plausibly, that there existed considerable differences within the movement in terms of sensibilities about recourse to counter-violence. Yet no such possible differences would be admitted, much less exploited, by Turkish authorities after the onset of the siege of Kobane. Instead, the government veered again towards an attitude of utter intransigence, and again began to employ very broad definition of "terror," while nevertheless systematically denying the ongoing reality of state terror, indeed, a return to the "war on terror," "public-security paradigm" (International Crisis Group 2015, p. 4). Remarks made by Prime Minister Davutoğlu less than a week after the October 30th National Security Council decision, would be illustrative in this regard. Addressing the HDP, Davutoğlu would strike an accusatory tone: "Our negotiations will continue if the HDP continues to act within the framework of the laws. We will address them only if they remain outside incidents involving violence, terror, unpermitted actions, and actions that lead to the loss of life and property, and take a stance against such actions." HDP MP Sırrı Süreyya Önder replied, in no uncertain terms: "We have done everything in our share for the peace process, and we declare to the whole world that we are prepared to continue doing so" (Çelik et al. 2015, p. 91).

In sum, as the International Crisis Group concluded, "Ankara's delayed reaction to Syrian Kurds' need for military help... was a turning-point for the Turkey-PKK conflict." The combination of Turkish government inaction with definite obstruction of Turkish Kurds' attempts to cross the border to defend the Rojava revolution from onslaught by ISIS "ignited outrage" among the base of the Kurdish freedom movement (International Crisis Group 2015, p. 4). In turn, the movement's capacity to mobilize mass demonstrations across the south-east and in Kurdish ghettos in urban areas throughout Turkey reinforced fears in the Turkish security apparatus that the Rojava model could spread to Turkey. The determination of hard-line elements within the deep state to apply the "Sri Lanka model" correspondingly stiffened and their influence spread, as reflected in the "war-on-terror-mongering" of the National Security Council decision of October 30th and the belligerent language of government ministers thereafter.

Of course, such talk of applying the "Sri Lanka model" was hyperbolic at best, delusional at worst. For the Kurdish freedom movement was much strengthened by its power in Rojava. The siege of Kobane served to demonstrate the bravery and tenacity, the revolutionary discipline, of Syrian Kurdish forces. Revolutionary fighters possessed the courage of their convictions and a will to sacrifice, even a cult of martyrdom, definitely something ISIS had never been up against before; this is not to mention the experience of a guerrilla force that had been at war with NATO's second biggest army (Turkey) for close to four decades. All of this was duly noted by the US (with the largest army in NATO), and Putin too, as the Syrian Kurds displayed remarkable resilience over the course of the siege. During and after this siege, the Americans and later the Russians would come to collaborate ever more closely with Syrian Kurdish forces, which they recognized as the most reliable boots on the ground for accompanying their aerial campaigns against the *jihadis*. Strange bedfellows, indeed.

Towards the Dolmabahçe Palace Accord

In early November, the Syrian Kurdish forces began regaining ground; by mid-January, they had recaptured the city of Kobane in its entirety; and by mid-March, the combined efforts of the forces on the ground and the Americans from the air had managed to break the siege. This was the first major defeat of ISIS; the signal of things to come.

As the momentum was turning against ISIS, for a time it appeared that a breakthrough in the "solution process" might take place as well. Öcalan himself had announced, from the middle of October, just after he had called off the wave of demonstrations, that a new phase of the peace process had commenced. By mid-November, HDP honorary president and MP Ertuğrul Kürkçü would insist that even though "a return to a security policy on the pretext of the Kobani protests had increased oppression, 'We are nevertheless making an effort to revive the process';" and towards the end of the month, HDP Deputy Chairperson Pervin Buldan announced the formation of an "expanded negotiation delegation and secretariat," while co-chair Demirtaş was arguing that the main Kemalist opposition party, the CHP, should be included in the negotiations as well, thereby implying that the peace talks were again gaining momentum (Çelik et al. 2015, pp. 90, 92, 93).

However, around the same time, from Qandil, PKK Commander Murat Karayılan would strike a more confrontational chord. In response to a claim by government spokesperson Bulent Arinç's statement that "We are not obliged to carry out a solution process," Karayılan quipped, "As if we are desperate for it. That is not the case. The hand of Kurdish politics is stronger than it ever has been. Bülent Arinç and all state officials should know that the PKK has many options. Especially in this period when the Kurdish question is now on the agenda in all aspects and has gained public support, all barriers of the past have been demolished. The PKK needs no one in this period." Though he would be sure to add, "However, there can be no doubt that the Kurdish people and the people of Turkey feel the need for peace, fraternity, friendship and coexistence." Before concluding for good measure, "Yet everyone should know that no one needs the AKP" (Çelik et al. 2015, p. 93).

Even so, by the beginning of December, Prime Minister Davutoğlu was claiming that "a new environment had emerged in the solution process," adding that the government was hoping "to reach an outcome by the general election in June 2015." On the first day of the month, Öcalan had submitted a "Draft for Peace and Democratic Negotiation Process," and on the 9th, a HDP delegation including "Idris Baluken, Pervin Buldan, Sırrı Sürreyya Önder and Hatip Dicle (who had been released from prison in July) held a meeting with Deputy Prime Minister Yalçin Akdogan," in which they discussed Öcalan's draft. By the 19th, Akdogan was insisting that "significant developments could take place," and even that "we are now in the home stretch" (Çelik et al. 2015, pp. 94, 96).

And yet, even while negotiations seemed to be intensifying, the AKP government was simultaneously proposing draconian amendments to the Law on Police Duties and Powers as well as a number of other repressive laws and legislative decrees in line with the war-on-terror, public-security paradigm. This prompted HDP co-chair Demirtaş to warn, "This is a law that they are trying to bring into force on the pretext of the Kobani incidents. It carries the potential to gravely undermine the negotiations process. If the draft becomes law, then the prime minister will order 'shoot', the police will shoot a person in the head, and then say, 'his face was covered, he was carrying a Molotov cocktail, or had a stone in his hand', and our children will be murdered in the streets. We will oppose it both in Parliament, and will raise Cain to try to prevent it in protests and marches in the streets." Prime Minister Davutoğlu responded with a threat: "Demirtaş will be responsible for the blood that flows." In turn, HDP MP Sırrı Sürreyya Önder would second Demirtaş' criticism the internal security draft law, on the floor of the Grand National Assembly, insisting, "You cannot achieve peace by preparing for war. This is worse even than martial law, it is a law fit for a coup" (Çelik et al. 2015, p. 95).

With negotiations intensifying and levels of animosity and distrust simultaneously peaking, the matter of disarmament emerged as a major bone of contention. government officials insisted that "the road map of the solution process would sooner or later inevitably involve disarmament." By contrast, from Qandil, PKK commander Cemil Bayık replied in no uncertain terms: "We will on no account lay down arms before we discuss the negotiations draft, finalize it according to dates we have determined, and reach an agreement on this subject. No conditions for us to lay down our arms have been met. Which problem has been solved for us to consider laying down our arms? Neither arms can be laid down, nor can the guerrilla abandon its positions before the democratic political solution of the Kurdish question is realized" (Çelik et al. 2015, pp. 94, 98).

At the end of December 2014, violence again spilled over from the war in Syria to the Kurdish region of Turkey. This time the trigger was the funeral of four Turkish Kurds-cum-YPG soldiers, killed in Kobane and Sinjar, now "repatriated" from Habur to Cizre. At the funeral, a fight would break out between members of the Patriotic Democratic Youth Movement (YDG) who were "keeping guard at the condolence tent set up in the Nur neighbourhood" and persons affiliated with HÜDA PAR, the so-called Kurdish *Hizbollah*. The fight quickly escalated into an armed confrontation, which would last into the early morning hours, including several acts of arson, and resulting in three deaths—a 65-year-old affiliated with HÜDA PAR, on the one side, and a 19 and 15-year-old affiliated with the YDG, on the other.

Denunciations of provocateurs ensued once more, this time with government officials leading the way. Prime Minister Davutoğlu used the occasion to make a public pitch for the draconian amendments to the Law on Police Duties and Powers, arguing, "Whenever the solution process has progressed on track, elements that try to use it have appeared. These provocations will have no impact on the Solution Process. This is why the internal security reform package is important. We will not allow persons wearing masks to set the place on fire." Even more aggressively, Deputy Prime Minister Akdogan added, "Just when we were saying everything is on track, Qandil made a statement saying, 'If anyone covers their faces during an action and throws Molotov cocktails, they are not on our side, they are agents'. A day later incidents took place in Cizre. Some persons covered their faces and went and threw Molotov cocktails, they tried to burn down people's homes. They were clearly cocking their snoot at Qandil, saying 'I don't recognise you'. So what I mean is, whenever we get close to an outcome, provocateurs enter the frame and immediately want to disrupt the process."

In turn, the male and female wings of the Patriotic Revolutionary Youth Movement would together issue a statement in which they insisted that the Turkish State itself had provoked the confrontation. According to the joint YDG statement, "It was the State itself that we faced in Cizre. An operation jointly launched by *Hizbul-Kontr* (the so-called Kurdish *Hizbollah*) DAESH (ISIS) and JITEM (the gendarmerie intelligence organization) faced the resistance of the youth movement. This operation ... was entirely coordinated by the hand of the State" (Çelik et al. 2015, pp. 98–99).

The Patriotic Revolutionary Youth Movement had grown rapidly over the course of the "solution process," during which the Kurdish freedom movement had made a concerted effort to mobilise the urban youth. The Youth Movement would emerge as a major protagonist in the clashes surrounding the demise of the peace talks. So long as negotiations continued, the Turkish authorities would accuse Qandil of not being able to control the urban youth; once the negotiations had ended, the urban youth would quickly come to be depicted as but an appendage of the PKK, the guerrilla's urban youth network, plain and simple, a new generation of "terrorists" living in urban settings, but obeying direct orders from Qandil.[68]

From the wave of protests during the siege of Kobane had emerged the tactic of digging trenches to declare certain neighborhoods "autonomous zones," cutting off access to Turkish security forces. The "democratic autonomy" route, a unilateral declaration and prefiguration of "democratic confederalism," born of insurrection, in accordance with Öcalan's emphasis on the right to self-defense. After the new wave of violence in Cizre, more trenches were dug. But what is born of insurrection is all too often extinguished via brutal state repression. On the 6th of January, 2015, Turkish police killed a 14-year old in Cizre. According to a report in VICE news at the time, "The YDG-H has been acting as a paramilitary force in Cizre for the past few months and has closed off several Kurdish neighborhoods with armed checkpoints and patrols. The group's members, mostly in their teens and early 20s, told VICE news they've been doing this to protect their streets after gun battles broke out in December between them, the police, and the Turkish Hizbullah group, HUDA PAR (no relation to Lebanon's Hezbullah). After several days of intense fighting, the YDG-H agreed to put down their weapons on Janauary 6 and allow the roads into their neighborhoods to be unblocked. The day the YDG-H stood down, however, authorities moved in. Police water cannon trucks and military APCs pushed into the Cudi area of Cizre, as the special forces allegedly opened fire. Three people were wounded and [one] killed."[69]

The boy they killed was named Ummit Kurt. He was gunned down "walk[ing] home from his job as a painter and decorator," while he was "passing through an area previously controlled by the Patriotic Revolutionary Youth Movement (YDG-H)." As VICE aptly put it in its headline, "anger simmered" in the wake of this police murder. On the 7th, "an armored police vehicle parked in front of the Dicle Police Station at the Silopi exit of Cizre district" would be the object of a rocket-launch attack, allegedly by the PKK, injuring two officers. A gun battle ensued (Çelik et al., p. 101).[70]

Clashes between the YDG and the police continued over the next several days and weeks. On the 9th, an HDP delegation would visit İmralı, after which they would communicate a direct plea from Öcalan for the youth in Cizre to stand down. The youth "responded immediately, stopping all armed activity in the streets."[71] But on the 14th, another young boy—this time, a 12-year-old—Nizan Kazanhan, would be shot in the head and killed by the police, again in Cizre. The confrontations predictably recommenced.

The surging violence was by now capturing ever more attention in the Western media. At the end of the month, *Foreign Policy* would publish an article warning that the clashes in Cizre were "threaten[ing] to undermine peace talks," more specifically, that "the violence threatened to harden public opinion on both sides of the conflict during the run-up to Turkey's crucial June Parliamentary elections."[72]

And yet, negotiations seemed still to progress, even amidst the surging violence. On the 9th of February, Deputy Prime Minister Yalçin Akdogan announced that "a favourable point had been reached" in the Solution Process, adding, "My impression is that we are close to an outcome." Two days later, he would meet with HDP İmralı Delegation members Pervin Buldan and Sırrı Sürreya Önder in the prime minister's office, though after the meeting HDP co-chair Figen Yüksedag would warn that the government's proposed draconian "internal security package" was disrupting the solution process (Çelik et al. 2015, p. 104).

The following week, a debate about the "internal security package" on the floor of the Grand National Assembly would descend twice into physical brawls between the government and the main Kemalist opposition party, the CHP, many of whose members feared that Erdoğan would use the new bill to create a police state.[73] In relation to the bill, HDP representatives would again warn that "the AKP is casting the peace process into a very dangerous course" (Çelik et al. 2015, p. 105).

Amidst all the escalating conflicts and confusion, reasons for optimism about the fate of the Solution Process remained. Perhaps foremost amongst these was the unprecedented collaboration between the Turkish military and the Kurdish freedom movement in the north of Syria that took place between the 21st and 22nd of February, in the so-called "Operation Shah Euphrates," an operation to relocate the tomb of Suleyman Shah, the grandfather of Osman I, the founder of the Ottoman Empire.[74] The tomb had been surrounded by ISIS forces, and the YPG formed a 5-kilometer security corridor to help the Turkish armed forces transfer the remains to a new mausoleum, located in the Kurdish-controlled village of Eshme (Çelik et al. 2015, p. 105). Öcalan himself would hail this feat as a "symbol of the new history of our peoples." Such collaboration, however, would be very short-lived; indeed, by March, the Turkish army would even deny that it had ever happened (Yıldız 2017, p. 45).

Then, on the last day of February, in what seemed at the time an historic breakthrough, after another meeting between HDP representatives and Deputy Prime Minister Yalçin Akdogan, HDP deputy Sırrı Sürreya Önder would read out a message by Öcalan sketching an outline for a definitive peace (later dubbed the Dolmabahçe Agreement). According to Öcalan's words that day, "In taking this 30-year process of clashes to permanent peace, our main target is reaching a democratic solution. On principles that form the least common denominator, I invite the PKK to summon an extraordinary congress in spring in order to make the strategic and historic decision on the basis of ending the armed struggle. This invitation is a historical declaration of intent aimed at replacing armed struggle with democratic politics" (Çelik et al. 2015, p. 106).

Önder then went on to list the headings of 10 clauses included in the framework of the Agreement: (1) democratic politics, its definition and content; (2) recognition of the national and local dimensions of the democratic solution; (3) legal and democratic reassurances for free citizenship; (4) the relationship between the State and society and democratic politics and heading aimed towards its institutionalization; (5) socioeconomic dimensions of the solution process; (6) treatment of the democracy-security relationship in a manner that protects public order and freedoms throughout the process; (7) legal solutions and reassurances for women's, cultural, and ecological problems; (8) development of a pluralist democratic approach regarding the recognition of the concept, definition and recognition of identity; (9) definition of the democratic republic, common homeland and nation on the basis of democratic criteria, and the introduction of legal and constitutional reassurances within the pluralist democratic system; and (10) a new constitution with a vision to internalize all these democratic moves and transformations (Çelik et al. 2015, p. 106).

Deputy Prime Minister Akdogan, present at the reading of the message, in turn remarked, "We find important this statement on the acceleration of work towards disarmament, the realization of a complete state of non-action and prioritization of democratic politics as a method" (Çelik et al. 2015, p. 107). For his part, Turkey's prime minister, Ahmet Davotoğlu, referred to Öcalan's statement as marking the beginning of a new phase in the peace negotiations.[75] President Erdoğan, too, appeared to hail the accord, declaring, "It was a very, very important call for us" (Quoted in Yıldız 2017, p. 47).

However, by the end of the first week of March, the government was already distancing itself from the Accord, and by the 15th of March, President Erdoğan was rapidly backtracking, denying altogether the existence of a Kurdish question in Turkey (Çelik et al. 2015, p. 109). The last time HDP representatives were allowed to meet with Öcalan was on 5 April.

Öcalan's 2015 Newroz Message

At the Newroz celebration in Diyarbakır, held on 21 March 2015, one of the last messages from Öcalan before his return to near-total isolation was read to the public, again by Sırrı Sürreya Önder. The message communicated effectively and in equal measure both a sense of urgency and of hope. Öcalan began by greeting "all our people and friends who are on the side of peace, equality, freedom and democracy," before turning to diagnose a "crisis caused by neoliberal policies imposed upon the whole world by imperialist capitalism and its despotic local collaborators," a crisis in which "ethnic and religious variations among our people and within our cultures are being erased by meaningless and brutal identity wars." He argued that "history and our people demand peace and a democratic solution," and that "we are faced with a mission to start a new process on the basis of ten articles which are officially declared in the historic Dolmabahçe Accord." This agreement, Öcalan insisted, has rendered it "historically necessary to hold a congress to bring a stop [to] the nearly 40-year old armed struggle carried out by the PKK against the Turkish Republic." To help achieve this end and thereby usher in a new era, one based on "free and equal constitutional citizenship in a democratic society," Öcalan called for a truth and reconciliation commission.

Next, he turned to strike a regional and even internationalist chord, emphasizing that "what is right for our people and our country should at the same time be valid for our whole region"—a region that for too long, especially during the last hundred years, was subjected to the divide and conquer machinations of imperialist capitalism that, "on the basis of nation-state nationalism, set ethnic and religious identities against one another." He then addressed directly the issue of ISIS, an organization whose image reflects "the old brutality of the Imperialist powers, who did not give up their ambitions in the Middle East," and which "exemplifies the meaning of brutality, slaughtering Kurdish, Turcoman, Arabian,

Yezidi, and Assyrian people." Öcalan emphasized, "The day has come to terminate this brutal assault." In order to be successful in this urgent task, Öcalan called on nation-states "to engage in new type of democratic process," and "build a new democratic collective abode in the Middle East."

Öcalan concluded with an appeal to "the women and the youth who beat the wings for freedom" by "saluting the resistance and victory of Kobane," which, he insisted, "Has great significance for the region and the whole world." Finally, he greeted "the spirit of Eshme" (in reference to the collaboration between Turkish and Kurdish forces in the relocation of the tomb of Suleyman Shah), which he hailed as "a symbol of a new era." His very last, hopeful words were, "Long live Newroz! Long live the fraternity of all peoples!"[76]

However, the "spirit of Eshme" was neither repeated nor reciprocated by the Turkish authorities. On the contrary, the day after Öcalan's message, President Erdoğan declared that he was against the Dolmabahçe Accord, provoking HDP co-chair Demirtaş to quip, "This Newroz has proven who wants democracy and who embraces dictatorship." The day after that, the Turkish army issued a harsh statement on their official webpage, in which they expressly denounced any mention of such a "spirit," denied any collaboration with the Kurdish freedom movement in the relocation of Suleyman Shah's tomb, and implicitly disavowed any respect for the Solution Process itself *en passant*. According to the army:

> Broadcasts and news reports that have been published in certain press and broadcast outlets regarding the changing of place within the territory of Syria of the Suleyman Shah Post of Reverence in reference to an expression by the head terrorist—a person that we have never addressed and will never address—about the "Spirit of Eshme," claiming that "the Turkish armed forces and PYD/PKK collaborated" which is entirely unsubstantiated. In the presence of the Great Turkish nation we strongly condemn these people and media organs who made such an imputation about the honorable, dignified and noble National Army, the Turkish Armed Forces, that has seen thousands of martyrs fall, and thousands of soldiers injured in carrying out an armed struggle against a terrorist organization that for 31 years has aimed to change the Constitutional order of the State of the Republic of Turkey. (In Çelik et al. 2015, p. 110)

The June 2015 General Election and the End of the "Solution Process"

In retrospect, the Dolmabahçe Accord appears something of a last-ditch effort on the part of the factions within the Erdoğan government in favor of a negotiated peace; Erdoğan himself soon threw his lot in with demands for a return to the security paradigm *tout court*—in effect, a return to war. Likely, this was not out of any illusions that the PKK, much less the Kurdish freedom movement, could be defeated by means of repression alone but, rather, out of some combination of geostrategic maneuvering and electoral calculation. After all, the dice were loaded by still-deeply entrenched Turkish ethno-nationalist imaginaries, hegemonic both in the state apparatus as well as among broad swathes of the general public, who were for so long exposed to the propaganda of the war-on-terror (Çiçek and Coşkun 2016; Ozkahraman 2017; Yıldız 2017).

The consolidation of the collaboration between the Kurdish freedom movement in Syria and the US (and later Russia, too) in the war against ISIS (during and after the siege of Kobane) certainly set off alarm bells within the Turkish national security apparatus, which no doubt reverberated up to President Erdoğan, influencing his calculation of the costs and benefits of pursuing peace. The dialectical clashes between the governing party and the HDP in the run-up to the June general election were probably what sealed Erdoğan's animosity towards charismatic HDP co-chair Selahattin Demirtaş. By extension, this is what convinced him to abandon any lingering commitment to the Solution Process and to embrace instead the so-called Sri Lankan model.

Polls taken in the months before the election revealed two interrelated and disturbing facts for Erdoğan: (1) that the principle electoral beneficiary of the ongoing peace process appeared to be the HDP, with surveys predicting a historic crossing of the extremely high 10 per cent threshold for securing a proper parliamentary group; and (2) that the other main electoral beneficiary appeared to be the far-right, ultra-nationalist MHP. By contrast, compared with the previous general election of 2011, the ruling AKP was on course for a disappointing result, with its appeal among the electorate down nearly 10 per cent.[77] Erdoğan's party nevertheless remained the Republic's most popular political force, but to secure a governing majority—in order to reform the Constitution—it would need some sort of coalition.

Long-time rumors within Kemalist circles suggested that Erdoğan was willing to grant the Kurds autonomy in exchange for Kurdish support for his hyper-presidentialist ambitions. However, over the course of the electoral campaign, which coincided with the final months of the peace process, HDP co-chair Selahattin Demirtaş repeatedly insisted that no such "dirty deal" was on the table for the Kurdish freedom movement. Indeed, in a speech to his parliamentary group on 17 March, Demirtaş responded in no uncertain terms:

> I want to remind here our promise to the people not to abandon the principles of democracy, peace, and freedom. We are not a movement of bargaining, a party of bargaining. There has never been a dirty deal between us and the AKP and there will never be. I will keep today's parliamentary group very short. I will, in fact, express my message in just one sentence: Mr. Recep Tayyip Erdoğan, you will never be able to be the head of the nation while the HDP exists and as long as the HDP people are on this soil. We will not make you president. We will not make you president. We will not make you president.[78]

Prime Minister Davutoğlu promptly replied to this provocation: "It is the Turkish people who will decide whether our president becomes the head of the nation."[79] Nor did President Erdoğan remain silent. To the contrary, he hurled a barrage of insults, accusations and threats against Demirtaş and the HDP. For example, he dismissed the HDP as "a party of gay people and atheists, pandering to the prejudices of the AKP's largely poor, devoutly Muslim working-class base," and repeatedly insisted that the HDP "supported terrorism and was in league with the PKK," as reported in *The Guardian* at the time.[80]

Indeed, over the course of the campaign, the prospects that the HDP would block Erdoğan's ambition for a new hyper-presidentialist constitution led the president to escalate animosity towards the Kurdish freedom movement. In the middle of March, Erdoğan denied the existence of a Kurdish question. By the end of March, in response to criticism of this denial, he defended his record as committed to peace and to "the solution of my Kurdish brothers' problems," despite the "numerous coup attempts, numerous attacks, the Gezi events, the 17–25 December coup attempt," all of which had been "staged to prevent" such a solution, according to the president. The president depicted himself as a lone advocate for peace, a man stuck between a rock and a hard place—between coupmakers on the one side, and intransigent, untrustworthy, terror-prone Kurdish militants on the other. As for the stalled peace talks, the president insisted that the blame lay squarely with the PKK, for refusing to put down its weapons. In his words, "You can make no contribution whatsoever if you do not put away these weapons. In an environment where promises made were broken time and again, we cannot progress any further without seeing concrete steps" (Çelik et al. 2015, p. 110).

By the end of April, however, the president was no longer depicting himself as a frustrated broker of peace but, rather, as the enforcer of the ideals and the will of the sovereign Turkish nation-state. Three sides had been reduced to two. The HDP were basically equated to the PKK, with its imminent criminalization threatened, if not openly pronounced. A definitive end to further negotiation was certainly hinted at. The president now reframed the issue:

> Saying "There is a Kurdish question" constitutes, from this point on, separatism. The Kurdish question is caused precisely by those who say that there is a Kurdish question. There is no longer a Kurdish question in our country. There is the State in this country. The existence of a table at which we sit facing each other means that the State has collapsed. The State does not lay down its arms, and if a terrorist bears arms, the State does what is necessary. The HDP resorted to illegal methods to make our work difficult (Çelik et al. 2015, p. 117).

Needless to say, these were not mere empty threats on the part of the president. Early in the campaign, Demirtaş warned that such verbal violence was likely to be translated into physical violence; he urged his comrades in the Kurdish freedom movement not to retaliate in kind, no matter the provocation. As Demirtaş put the point, poetically, "Look, if anything happens to us during the election campaign period, which is a possibility, it is my special request for all our friends; this ship must be sailed to the harbor" (Çelik et al. 2015, p. 112).

Certainly, over the course of the campaign, the Kurdish movement became a target of legal and extra-legal acts of persecution. On the legal front, the draconian "internal security package" was passed at the beginning of April, the same week that the very last HDP Delegation to İmralı Island was allowed. The security package, combined with the deliberate silencing of Abdullah Öcalan, returned to near-total isolation, signaled that the government had pivoted back towards a clear preference for war—a preference registered by ultra-nationalist street thugs and *jihadis*, both of whom unleashed their fury on the HDP in the polarizing run-up to and aftermath of the June election. In fact, according to the Human Rights Association, during the campaign HDP election offices and activists were the targets of harassment, intimidation and violence on over 170 occasions. Fully 185 HDP members were detained, 33 of whom declared they had been tortured while detained (Çelik et al. 2015).

The climate towards freedom of expression was unpropitious, to say the least. Concerns about the possibility of electoral fraud began to abound. Despite the intimidation and violence, HDP members repeatedly expressed their commitment to both a peaceful resolution to the Kurdish question and a deepening and strengthening of democracy throughout Turkey, even in the face of murderous provocations.

Once more, Turkish security forces went on the offensive. At the end of March, a military operation commenced in the Mazidagi rural area of Mardin. The day after the operation was announced, the Armed Forces alleged that the PKK had been "carrying out mortar shelling, and that the army had responded." The PKK, through the People's Defense Forces' (HPG) Central Headquarters, replied that the Armed Forces had been "intentionally and deliberately increasing military mobility, and that fire had been opened from certain military bases and stations along the border in violation of ceasefire regulations." For its part, the PKK Command insisted that the HPG were "acting in accordance with the 'democratic solution strategy'" and that it was ensuring that "the requirements of ceasefire regulations" were met. The HPG's Central Headquarters accused the Armed Forces and AKP of "implementing an election policy with the purpose of receiving votes from nationalist circles" (Çelik et al. 2015, p. 111).

Around the same time, the HPG issued a statement detailing the number of provocations and attacks by Turkish security forces over the past three months: "197 reconnaissance flights, 2 Kobra attacks, and 134 tank and artillery attacks." Furthermore, "14 enforced clashes took place during operations," resulting in the deaths of two soldiers, alongside two soldiers injured, and five military vehicles damaged. By the first week of April, the PKK was alleging that the "Turkish army [was] increasingly carrying out ambushes," in a deliberate attempt "to draw guerrillas into clashes" (Çelik et al. 2015, pp. 112–113).

In the second week of April, tensions escalated further after a confrontation between the PKK and military units close to the Yukaritütek village of Agri, where a tree-planting event was to be jointly held by the HDP and the DBP. The clash resulted in the deaths of an HDP member and a guerrilla, with four soldiers injured. Immediately after the clash, President Erdoğan accused the PKK of trying to "dynamite the peace environment and sabotage the solution process." For its part, the HPG denied allegations by the Agri Governate that the PKK opened fire first, insisting that "the clashes began when Turkish forces opened fire on PKK forces in the area" (Çelik et al. 2015, p. 114).

The government responded by trying to force Demirtaş to side with the forces of "law and order," and thereby drive a wedge between him and the Kurdish freedom movement. To this end, Prime Minister Davutoğlu posed a loaded question: "Is [Demirtaş] the Chairperson of a legitimate political party, or a defender of terror who defends and seeks to legitimize this type of terrorist activity carried out by armed elements of separatist terror organizations through pressure and in order to manipulate the people? ... Today is the day for everyone to clearly declare their positions" (Çelik et al. 2015, p. 115).

In the second week of May, the pressure on Demirtaş increased further when police in Diyarbakır raided his home. This was completed under the pretext of searching for a person wanted for involvement in various crimes and supposedly registered as residing at his address—a pretext later discarded as a mistake. Demirtaş responded, "It is not normal for police to come knocking at my door at a time so close to the election and in the middle of such a critical process" (Çelik et al. 2015, p. 119). The same week, Demirtaş lamented that "the solution process was now frozen, that the party delegation had not been able to visit İmralı Island for over a month, and that at the moment isolation was imposed on Öcalan."

For its part, the PKK suggested that the process was not just "frozen" but, in fact, over. In Executive Council member Duran Kalkan's ominous words, "We are under attack as a movement and as a people following President Erdoğan's anti-solution stance, especially since Newroz. We declare this is the beginning of a new process." PKK Commander Murat Karayılan was, nevertheless, quick to add, "We are carefully observing the process, and are trying to prevent provocations. Our actions are based on unilateral ceasefire. The isolation in İmralı constitutes for us a cause for war. We are waiting for leader Apo's orders, and are continuing to observe the unilateral ceasefire within this framework. However, everyone should know that there is a limit to everything" (Çelik et al. 2015, p. 120).

The following week, with three weeks to go before the election, the HDP's İmralı Delegation met with the PKK high command in Qandil, and subsequently held a press conference in Diyarbakır, in which they relayed that preparations for the extraordinary Congress "that would have focused on the solution process" had been frozen, "due to the conduct displayed by President Erdoğan and the AKP government." KCK Executive Council Co-Chair Bese Hozat quipped, "The dialogue process has been stopped at this stage. And in its current state, it has been abolished." To which PKK Commander Cemil Bayık added, "Erdoğan's intervention in the process, his rejection of negotiations, his rejection of coming to the table, his rejection of one of the parties, and his statement that 'There is no Kurdish question, it is separatism, whoever speaks of negotiations and parties, this means bringing down the State of Turkey', abolished in essence the conditions to realize the Congress" (Çelik et al. 2015, p. 121).

In the final weeks of the campaign, the harassment and violence targeting the HDP escalated further, culminating in a bomb attack at the HDP's final election rally in Diyarbakır, allegedly carried out by an ISIS member, killing five people and injuring over 400.

Nevertheless, the HDP scored a great victory in the June election, surpassing the 10 per cent threshold by a wide margin, winning close to 13 per cent of the vote and 80 delegates in the 550-seat Turkish Parliament. In Diyarbakır, close to 80 per cent of votes were for the HDP. The impressive performance of the HDP in the election temporarily checked Erdoğan's hyper-presidentialist ambitions— a fact that does much to explain the escalation of conflict and brutal crackdown on the Kurdish movement ever since.

Just two days after the election, three HDP supporters were gunned down at a coffee house used as an election bureau during the campaign. Thus the election result was far from delivering a miraculous end to the climate of intimidation and violence. Erdoğan had been stymied in his ambition to increase his grasp on power, but the AKP remained the number one party in Turkey, with over 40 per cent of the vote. Perhaps even more disturbingly, the country's third party was the ultra-nationalist MHP, which captured close to 17 per cent of the vote.

The result was a hung parliament. After the AKP failed to negotiate a coalition government with any of the main opposition parties, Erdoğan called a new snap election for 7 November. In the run-up to this second election, the AKP veered to the far-right—pursuing brutal policies of collective punishment and committing crimes against humanity—and took advantage of renewed hostilities with the PKK in July in a blatant appeal to Turkish nationalists who voted for the MHP.

The End of the Peace Process and the Return of the Spiral of Violence

The detonator for the descent into virtual civil war arrived on 20 July, when a local Kurd with links to the Islamic State blew himself up with a cluster bomb in the Suruç district of the Şanlıurfa Province, killing 33 and injuring over 100. This was the first such attack on Turkish soil for which ISIS officially claimed responsibility. Most of the victims were members of left-wing Turkish political organizations who had gathered for a press conference announcing plans to help reconstruct Kobane, just 10 km away, across the border.

Demirtaş blamed the government for the massacre, accusing the AKP of complicity with ISIS. The PKK concurred. Two days later, two police officers were found dead in Şanlıurfa. A local PKK unit claimed responsibility, calling it an act of revenge for the bombing in Suruç. The government responded with an escalation of repression. Thus commenced anew the spiral of violence and repression. Since then, the Kurdish region has witnessed a rapid descent into virtual civil war. It has been plunged into an intense violent conflict, surpassing even the atrocities of the 1990s.

On 24 July, just four days after the Suruç bombing, the government announced it had reached a new "military and security cooperation pact" with the Obama administration, for the first time allowing the US and Britain to launch airstrikes against ISIS from the İncirlik airbase in Adana, as well as drone strikes from Turkish soil.[81] In exchange for this, and for promises of collaboration in the fight against ISIS, it soon became increasingly clear that the Turkish authorities were given a green light to wage a simultaneous war against the PKK, not only inside Turkey, but beyond its borders as well.

On the same day of the security pact announcement, the Turkish State carried out its first airstrikes against ISIS positions inside Syria near the Turkish border. Simultaneously, a much more intense campaign of airstrikes was launched against PKK camps in the Qandil Mountains, located in the Kurdish region in the north of Iraq, and targeted YPG fighters just west of Kobane in Syria. This occurred despite the close collaboration between Kurdish and coalition forces that had been forged since the defense of Kobane in the course of the ongoing struggle against ISIS.[82]

Alongside the bombing campaigns, the Turkish authorities proceeded to conduct a major police operation within its borders, rounding up hundreds of people suspected of links to "terrorist organizations"—again with a clear, near exclusive focus on the PKK.

The conflict soon escalated, with the PKK targeting members of the Turkish security apparatus across the country in retaliation, as well as killing civilians. The Turkish military responded by ratcheting up the repression, including aerial bombardments against PKK convoys in the Hakkari Province in the east.[83]

Things intensified further in August. Local youth in Şırnak dug trenches to stop police and soldiers from entering. In the town of Silopi, on the morning of the seventh, police deployed snipers on local buildings, who opened fire; bullets rained on homes and six houses were set on fire in the Zap neighborhood, killing two residents. Police arrested the many injured who sought assistance at hospital.[84]

Three days later, local assemblies organized by the Kurdish movement in Silopi and in the town of Cizre, another stronghold, declared self-rule. In the weeks that followed, 13 other towns and neighborhoods followed suit, including Batman's Baglar neighborhood, Diyarbakır's Sur district, Van's Hacı Bekir neighborhood, as well as the districts and towns of Lice, Silvan, Varto, Bulanık, Yüksekova, Şemdinli, Edremit, Doğubayazıt and, remarkably, Istanbul's Gazi neighborhood. Locals formed self-defense units, but were soon crushed by security forces, with reports of police "roam[ing] streets in armored vehicles and firing indiscriminately" in many locales.

The spiraling of action and reaction, repression and counter-violence, gained unstoppable momentum. By early September, nearly a hundred military or police personnel had been killed, and authorities ratcheted up the repression further still. On 4 September, Turkish security forces sealed off the city of Cizre and placed it under curfew for eight days. This was the first of some 58 sieges on urban neighborhoods and cities across the Kurdish region in Turkey to date that security operations had justified as attempts to "flush out" insurgents.[85]

The violence was not limited to the Kurdish region. In the week following a PKK attack that killed 16 Turkish soldiers on 6 September, far-right groups of ultra-nationalists retaliated by ransacking 128 HDP offices across the country, setting several ablaze, in coordinated attacks that co-chair Figen Yüksekdağ insisted had been "carried out under police supervision."[86]

On 10 October, two bombs at a peace rally in the center of Ankara killed 109 people and injured over 400. The rally was organized by supporters of the pro-Kurdish HDP, and many HDP flags and logos could be seen at the rally. President Erdoğan immediately condemned the bombing: "I strongly condemn this heinous attack on our unity and our country's peace. No matter what its origin, aim, or name, we are against any form of terrorist act or terrorist organization. We are obliged to be against it together."

Pro-Kurdish sympathizers objected to the equivalence drawn between the PKK and ISIS in the comment. Meanwhile, the HDP not only complained about lack of security at the rally, but openly accused the State of complicity in the attack. Demirtaş declared, "This attack is not targeting our State and national unity, it is perpetrated by the State against the people. We are witnessing a massacre here. A cruel and barbarian attack was carried out. The death toll is high." He added that he did not expect that "those responsible for the bombings would be brought to justice."[87]

As the snap-election neared, the curfews in Kurdish areas and counter-terror operations continued apace. In a move befitting his hyper-presidentialist ambitions, Erdoğan stepped up the persecution of Kurdish activists and other political foes. Several opposition journalists were jailed, and in the week before the November election, police stormed the offices of an opposition media group.[88]

On election day, the AKP was rewarded for the government's right turn tactic of polarization and repression of the Kurdish movement. This time they regained a parliamentary majority, with close to 50 per cent of the vote, in no small part by winning over a significant chunk of the former constituency of the far-right MHP, apparently now sufficiently convinced of Erdoğan's nationalist credentials. The MHP's share of the vote fell from 17 per cent to 12 per cent.[89]

As for the HDP, it lost nearly 3 percentage points, but still just over the 10 per cent threshold. Co-Chair Figen Yüksekdağ attributed the setback to Erdoğan's deliberate strategy of polarization, but emphasized that the HDP's threshold-passing performance in such a climate was still a significant achievement, and a success.[90] In one sense it certainly was, since the ruling party remained 13 seats shy of the super-majority needed for unilateral constitutional reform. Even so, Demirtaş insisted that, given the climate of violence and intimidation, the election could not be considered "fair or equal."[91] Results were greeted with much anger across the Kurdish region, with riots breaking out on the streets in Diyarbakır.

The spiral of violence and repression did not end with the election results. To the contrary, feeling vindicated by the surge in electoral support but still frustrated in his hyper-presidentialist ambitions, Erdoğan stepped up attacks on the Kurdish movement, vowing in his first post-election speech that "Turkey would continue its fight against Kurdish insurgents until every last militant was 'liquidated.'"[92]

Less than three weeks later, on 22 November, Demirtaş survived an assassination attempt in Diyarbakır, when a bullet hit the bulletproof rear window of the official vehicle in which he was travelling.[93] Six days later, an assassin's bullet silenced the head of the Diyarbakır lawyers' association, Tahir Elçi, who was a prominent Kurdish advocate for peace.[94]

Against the backdrop of spiraling violence and ever-increasing repression, the government repeatedly criticized the HDP, alleging that it had failed to distance itself sufficiently from the PKK. This was despite the fact that HDP leaders had remained consistently on-point and adamant in their commitment to restarting the peace process, calling again and again on both sides to return to the negotiating table. Illustrative of the HDP's official position is the following exchange from an interview given by Demirtaş to *Der Spiegel*, near the beginning of the descent into virtual civil war, on the last day of July:

> **Der Spiegel:** And what about the deadly attacks against Turkish security forces by the Kurdistan Workers' Party? Don't these attacks simply confirm even more that the PKK is a terrorist organization?
>
> **Demirtaş:** I don't know why the PKK did that, but they shouldn't have. That's not the proper way to act. We urgently call on the PKK and the Turkish government to put down their weapons. There should be a mutual ceasefire.
>
> **Der Spiegel:** The PKK executed two policemen—and that was before the Turkish bombardment began.
>
> **Demirtaş:** That act was indeed a dark, dirty chapter. It was revenge for the attack in Suruç, committed by a local PKK unit. The broader organization did not claim responsibility. It seems to me that individual elements were looking to provoke the Turkish State.
>
> **Der Spiegel:** Your detractors claim that HDP and PKK are affiliated with one another. Are you closely connected somehow?
>
> **Demirtaş:** Of course there have been meetings. We sat at the same table during the peace negotiations in the last few years. We also spoke to the PKK leader, Abdullah Öcalan, in his prison cell on the island of İmralı in the Sea of Marmara. His words carry great weight in his movement. For us, it's about mediating within the framework of the law. Other than that, there is no structural connection between us. We are definitely not the political arm of the PKK that our detractors accuse us of being.[95]

With respect to the unilateral Declarations of Autonomy in the 15 neighborhoods and districts, actions which triggered curfews and effectively escalated the levels of violence, both the HDP on the whole, and Demirtaş in particular, were much more equivocal. In mid-December 2015, Demirtaş came out in support of those who dug trenches, framing the unilateral declarations of self-rule as acts of legitimate resistance against Erdoğan's "coup" and "dictatorship." According to Demirtaş:

> The region has embraced autonomy. The people are standing behind autonomy, they should see this well. In these [military] operations, especially the HDP's Kurdish grassroots are forced to obey. They made a coup after June 7…
>
> Turkey's west especially needs to understand this. The thing that you despise by saying "ditch" and "barricade" is actually a resistance against the coup. Should people act like lambs to the slaughter in the face of all pressures? What

did people do against the blockade during the Sarajevo resistance, which you mention with praise and enthusiasm? They dug ditches and they dug tunnels … The autonomy is against dictatorship. If Cizre people had declared "dictatorship and presidential system," instead of autonomy, they would send a celebration delegation there. If they had declared "dictatorship," it would be welcomed in Ankara with a flourish of trumpets.[96]

Along similar lines, in late December, the Democratic Peoples' Congress (DTK)—composed of non-governmental organizations associated with the pro-Kurdish movement and with which the HDP maintains close ties—called for self-rule at the local level throughout all of Bakur (North Kurdistan), and simultaneously called for the formation of an autonomous Kurdish region. The final resolution of the DTK's two-day meeting in Diyarbakır stated, "The rightful resistance mounted by our people against the policies that degrade the Kurdish problem, is essentially a demand and struggle for local self-governance and local democracy."[97]

President Erdoğan responded furiously, in characteristic fashion, combining the classic Kemalist motifs of territorial integrity and national unity with a simultaneous invocation of the Lord on High: "Now they are talking about separating our land in this country. With God's permission, we will never allow a surgery on the unity of our country."[98]

The furor of the Turkish government and of other state officials towards the actions and statements of the HDP was not limited to rhetorical flurries. By January 2016, 18 HDP co-mayors, and overall 29 HDP local elected officials, were jailed in relation to the unilateral Declarations of Self-Rule, accused of treason and collaboration with a "terrorist organization," namely the PKK.[99] In April, the government proposed a bill in Parliament intended to remove immunity from prosecution of members of Parliament, a move widely interpreted as targeting parliamentarians from the HDP.[100]

Among those targeted for prosecution, co-chair Demirtaş was charged in September 2015 by the Chief Prosecutor's Office in Diyarbakır, with offences ranging from "openly insulting the Turkish nation, the State of the Turkish Republic, the State's institutions and organs" and "openly instigating to commit crime," to "defaming the president," not to mention "producing propaganda of a terrorist organization." These charges stemmed from a press conference at which Demirtaş had reacted indignantly to the ransacking and burning of HDP offices across the country by organized ultra-right nationalist lynch mobs, alleging that "the gangs employed on the streets" had acted under the "coordination" of the ruling AKP and the Turkish Intelligence Service, and accusing the government of using any means necessary to convey the message: "If you do not give us 400 deputies [in the election], you will pay the price."[101]

Several months into the rolling curfews, and with the threat of prosecution looking more and more imminent, by April 2016, Demirtaş was striking a more self-critical and conciliatory tone on the subject of the unilateral declarations of self-rule. At a meeting in Berlin on 11 April, Demirtaş criticized the "ditch wars" for having "threatened public security and escalated violence," emphasizing nevertheless that such confrontations "should be resolved through dialogue, not by tanks, cannons, and weapons." He went on to distance himself and his party from such unilateral declarations, stating that they "could not achieve any results." Furthermore, when a question was posed to him about the PKK's "change of strategy" and its "resorting to violence after the June 7 parliamentary elections," he again stressed his party's principled commitment to peace: "Why did the PKK change strategy? This needs to be asked to the PKK. We are a democratic party and we reject all kinds of violence." This before adding, in no uncertain terms, "By itself, violence narrows politics' range of motion. We demand an end to violent incidents. No matter where it takes place, whether in the east or in the west, violence cannot be accepted. We will make our struggle through democratic means."[102]

The Kurdish Question and the Struggle for Democracy in Turkey

The close connection between the Kurdish question and the struggle for democracy throughout Turkey became all the more apparent on 14 January 2016, when police "detained 27 academics over alleged 'terror propaganda.'" Their crime: having signed a petition (one that included international left-wing intellectual celebrities such as Noam Chomsky and Slavoj Žižek), in which they called for an end to the "deliberate massacre and deportation of Kurdish people," in objection to the collective punishment and repressive crackdown on the Kurdish movement still underway. President Erdoğan came out furiously against the signatories of the petition and appealed explicitly to the judiciary to act against such "treason."[103]

In the aftermath of the incident, many of the signatories were targeted, subjected to threats, and intimidation by extreme Turkish nationalist groups. Moreover, by mid-March, at least thirty of the academics who had signed the petition had been dismissed with another 27 suspended from teaching activities.[104] This frontal assault by Erdoğan on the freedom of expression of Turkish academics additionally elicited the condemnation of the usually-silent American embassy, with Ambassador John Bass issuing the following terse statement: "While we may not agree with the opinions expressed by those academics, we are nevertheless concerned about this pressure having a chilling effect on legitimate political discourse across Turkish society regarding the sources of and solutions to the ongoing violence."[105]

One of the more incisive contributions to an edited volume published in 2010 by the Royal Institute of International Affairs at Chatham House was titled, "The Missing Moderate" (Watts 2010). This is a fundamental problem for the Turkish nationalist mentality—its missing moderates. There is an absence, a silence, which renders difficult any attempt to accommodate the Kurdish question within a peaceful and democratic Turkey, within a republic capable of respecting minority rights and tolerating ethnic and religious diversity. A problematic silence such as this becomes all the more difficult to correct or resolve in a context where dissident views are conflated with "terrorist propaganda," and intellectuals and academics, as well as journalists, are persecuted and suppressed for daring speak out against their government's criminal "war on terror."

The few that speak out in Turkish "civil society" have thus been silenced. When those who advocate for peace are harassed and detained as terrorist accomplices, when advocates of peace—like Co-Chair Demirtaş—are targeted for assassination, and when Diyarbakır's most prominent pro-Kurdish lawyer and peace advocate is gunned down in the streets with impunity, the spiral of repression and counter-violence succeeds in imposing its murderous and polarizing dynamic on Turkish society *tout court*. Such repression and violence intimidates, marginalizes, and eliminates those on all sides who urge peace and advocate democracy and respect for human rights, including the most fundamental right of all rights: the right to life.

Bibliography

Ahmad, F. 2014. *The Making of Modern Turkey* (London: Oneworld Publications).

Akkaya, A. and J. Jongerden. 2012. "Reassembling the Political: The PKK and the Project of Radical Democracy," *European Journal of Turkish Studies*, No.14: pp. 1–17.

Akkaya, A. and J. Jongerden. 2014. "Confederalism and Autonomy in Turkey: The Kurdistan Workers' Party and the Reinvention of Democracy," in C. Güneş and W. Zeydanliogu, eds., *The Kurdish Question in Turkey. New Perspectives on Violence, Representation, and Reconciliation* (London: Routledge), pp. 186–204.

Amnesty International. 2013. "Gezi Park Protests. Brutal Denial of the Right to Peaceful Assembly in Turkey" (https://bit.ly/2sqRgcy).

Anderson, P. 2008. *The New Old World* (London: Verso).

Angrist, M. 2004. "Turkey. Roots of the Turkish-Kurdish Conflict and Prospects for Constructive Reform," in U. Amoretti and N. Bermeo, eds., *Federalism and Territorial Cleavages* (Baltimore: The Johns Hopkins University Press), pp. 387–416.

Brubaker, R. 1996. *Nationalism Reframed. Nationhood and the National Question in the New Europe* (Cambridge: Cambridge University Press).

Camara, H. 1971. *The Spiral of Violence* (London: Sheed and Ward Stagbooks).

Casmier, S. 2015. "Ferguson, Meaning, and Walter Ong." Unpublished paper delivered at *Race and Expression. A Saint Louis University Symposium*. Saint Louis, MO. 8th April.

Çelik, A. et al. 2015. *Towards a Resolution: An Assessment of Possibilities, Opportunities and Problems* (Turkey Peace Assembly and Heinrich Böll Stiftung, www.turkiyebarismeclisi.com)

Çellikan, M. et al. 2015. "The Trajectory of the Peace Process," in A. Çelik et al., *Towards a Resolution: An Assessment of Possibilities, Opportunities and Problems* (Turkey Peace Assembly and Heinrich Böll Stiftung, www.turkiyebarismeclisi.com).

Çiçek, C. and V. Coskun. 2016. *The Peace Process from Dolmabahçe to the Present-Day: Understanding Failure and Finding New Paths*. Istanbul: Baris Vakfi (Peace Foundation).

Cleveland, W. 2004. *A History of the Modern Middle East* (Westview Press, Third Edition).

Debray, R. 1967. *Revolution in the Revolution?* (New York, NY: Monthly Press Review).

Durmaz, M. 2014. "The US Arms Embargo of 1975–1978 and its Effects on the Development of the Turkish Defense Industry," Monterey Naval College Masters' Thesis (https://bit.ly/2KNBUbd).

Eccarius-Kelly, V. 2011. *The Militant Kurds. A Dual Strategy for Freedom* (Santa Barbara, CA: Praeger).

Entessar, N. 1992. *Kurdish Ethnonationalism* (London: Lynne Reinner Publishers).

European Court of Human Rights (ECHR). 2005. *Case of Öcalan vs. Turkey.* Judgment, 12 May. (Strasbourg) (http://bit.ly/2tEBoTh).

Fanon, F. 2001. *The Wretched of the Earth* (London: Penguin Modern Classics).

Ganser, D. 2004. *NATO's Secret Armies. Operation Gladio and Terrorism in Western Europe* (London: Routledge).

Güneş, C. 2012. *The Kurdish National Movement in Turkey. From Protest to Resistance* (London: Routledge).

Güneş, C. and W. Zeydanlioğlu, eds. 2014. "Introduction: Turkey and the Kurds," in C. Güneş and W. Zeydanlioğlu, eds., *The Kurdish Question in Turkey: New Perspectives on Violence, Representation, Reconciliation* (London: Routledge), pp. 1–20.

Gunter, M. 1997. *The Kurds and the Future of Turkey* (London: Palgrave).

Gunter, M. 2011. *The Kurds Ascending. The Evolving Solution to the Kurdish Problem in Iraq and Turkey* (New York, NY: Palgrave MacMillan, Second Edition).

Halliday, F. 2005. *The Middle East in International Relations. Power, Politics and Ideology* (Cambridge: Cambridge University Press).

Hammy, C. 2016. "AKP: A Marriage between Turkish Nationalism and Authoritarian Islam," *Kurdish Question* (https://bit.ly/2v4OGbD).

Hanioğlu, M. 2011. *Atatürk. An Intellectual Biography* (Princeton: Princeton University Press).

Hobsbawm, E. 1994. *The Age of Extremes. The Short Twentieth Century. 1914–1991* (London: Abacus).

Houston, C. 2008. *Kurdistan. Crafting of National Selves* (London: Bloomsbury Publishing).

Imset, Ismet G. 1992. *The PKK. A Report on Separatist Violence in Turkey (1973–1992).* Ankara: Turkish Daily News Publications.

International Crisis Group. 2014 "Turkey and the PKK: Saving the Peace Process," Europe Report No. 234, November (Brussels).

International Crisis Group. 2015. "A Sisyphean Task? Resuming Turkey-PKK Peace Talks," Europe Report No. 77, December (Istanbul/Brussels).

Jenkins, G. 2007. "PKK Changes Battlefield Tactics to Force Turkey into Negotiations," *Terrorism Focus*, Vol. 4, Issue 34 (https://bit.ly/2IRF7BD/).

Jongerdon, J. 2017. "The Kurdistan Workers' Party (PKK). Radical Democracy and the right to Self-Determination beyond the Nation-State," in G. Stanfield and M. Shareef, eds., *The Kurdish Issue Revisited* (London: Hurst), pp. 245–257.

Jongerden, J. and A. Akkaya. 2011. "Born from the Left. The Making of the PKK," in J. Jongerdon and M. Casier, eds., *Nationalism and Politics in Turkey. Political Islam and the Kurdish Issue* (London: Routledge), pp. 123–142.

Jongerden, J. and A. Akkaya. 2016. "Kurds and the PKK," in J. Stone et al., *The Wiley Blackwell Encyclopedia of Race, Ethnicity, and Nationalism* (London: Routledge), pp. 1–5, (https://bit.ly/2KGP3mx).

Keyder, Ç. 1987. *State and Class in Turkey* (London: Verso).

Keyder, Ç. 2004. "The Turkish Bell Jar," *New Left Review*, July-August, pp. 65–84.

Levi, A. 1990. "The Justice Party, 1961-1980," in M. Heper and J. Landau, eds., *Political Parties and Democracy in Turkey* (New York, NY: I.B. Tauris), pp. 134–151.

Linz, J. and A. Stepan. 1996. *Problems of Democratic Transition and Consolidation* (Baltimore, MD: The Johns Hopkins University Press).

Mamdani, M. 2002. *When Victims Become Killers* (Princeton, NJ: Princeton University Press).

Marcus, A. 2007. *Blood and Belief. The PKK and the Kurdish Fight for Independence* (New York, NY: NYU Press).

McDowall, D. 1996. *A Modern History of the Kurds* (London: I.B. Tauris).

Natali, D. 2005. *The Kurds and the State. Evolving National Identity in Iraq, Turkey, and Iran* (Syracuse, NY: Syracuse University Press).

O'Ballance, E. 1996. *The Kurdish Struggle, 1920-1994* (London: Palgrave MacMillan).

Öcalan, A. 2009. *War and Peace in Kurdistan. Perspectives for a Political Solution to the Kurdish Question* (Cologne: International Initiative).

Öcalan, A. 2011. *Prison Writings. The PKK and the Kurdish Question in the 21st Century* (Cologne: International Initiative).

Öcalan, A. 2012. *Prison Writings III. The Road Map to Negotiations* (Cologne: International Initiative).

Orhan, M. 2015. *Political Violence and Kurds in Turkey. Fragmentations, Mobilizations, Participations, and Repertoires* (London: Routledge).

Orlow, D. 1982. "Political Violence in Pre-Coup Turkey," *Studies in Conflict & Terrorism*, Vol. 6, Issue 1-2, pp. 53-71.

Özcan, A. 2006. *Turkey's Kurds. A Theoretical Analysis of the PKK and Abdullah Öcalan* (London: Routledge).

Ozcan, G. 2016. "The Bully's Rise to Power: Erdoğan's Conquest of Turkey," *Roar Magazine*, 18th May (https://bit.ly/2mIYYue/).

Ozkahraman, C. 2017. "Failure of Peace Talks between Turkey and the PKK: Victim of Traditional Policy or of Geopolitical Shifts in the Middle East?," *Contemporary Review of the Middle East*, 4(1), pp. 1–17.

Romano, D. 2006. *The Kurdish Nationalist Movement. Opportunity, Mobilization, Identity* (Cambridge: Cambridge University Press).

Rustow, D. 1965. "Turkey: The Modernity of Tradition," in L. Pye and S. Verba, eds., *Political Culture and Political Development* (Princeton, NJ: Princeton University Press), pp. 171–198.

Saeed, S. 2017. *Kurdish Politics in Turkey. From the PKK to the KCK* (London: Routledge).

Saribay, A. 1990. "The Democratic Party, 1946-1960," in M. Heper and J. Landau, eds., *Political Parties and Democracy in Turkey* (New York, NY: I.B. Tauris).

Savran, S. 2015. "Class, State, and Religion in Turkey," in N. Balkan, et al., eds., *The Neoliberal Landscape and the Rise of Islamist Capital in Turkey* (New York, NY: Beghann Books).

Sugar, P. 1964. "Economic and Political Modernization in Turkey," in R. Ward and D. Rustow, eds., *Political Modernization in Japan and Turkey* (Princeton, NJ: Princeton University Press), pp. 146-175.

Van Bruinessen, M. 1988. "Between Guerrilla War and Political Murder: the Workers' Party of Kurdistan," *Middle East Report*, No. 153, July–Aug., pp. 40–46, 50.

Van Bruinessen, M. 1999. "The Kurds in Movement: Migrations, Mobilisations, Communications, and the Globalisation of the Kurdish Question," (https://bit.ly/2KA94fd).

Watts, N. 2010. "The Missing Moderate: Legitimacy Resources and pro-Kurdish Party Politics in Turkey," in R. Lowe and G. Stansfield, eds., *The Kurdish Policy Imperative* (London: The Royal Institute of International Affairs, Chatham House).

White, P. 2000. *Primitive Rebels or Revolutionary Modernizers? The Kurdish National Movement in Turkey* (London: Zed Books).

White, P. 2015. *The PKK. Coming Down from the Mountains* (London: Zed Books).

Yadirgi, V. 2017. *The Political Economy of the Kurds of Turkey: From the Ottoman Empire to the Turkish Republic* (Cambridge: Cambridge University Press).

Yıldız, G. 2017. "How Did Turkey's Peace Process with the PKK Rebels Fail? How Can It Be Resurrected?" MPhil Thesis, Department of Sociology, University of Cambridge.

Yıldız, K. and S. Breau. 2010. *The Kurdish Conflict: International Humanitarian Law and Post-Conflict Mechanisms* (London: Routledge).

Zürcher, E. 2017. *Turkey. A Modern History* (London: I.B. Tauris. Fourth Edition).

Notes to Internet References

1. Wikipedia. 2018. "Ertuğrul Kürkçü" (https://bit.ly/2IEElI0).
2. Wikipedia. 2018. "People's War" (https://bit.ly/2MvgWuM).
3. Wikipedia. 2018. "Foco" (https://bit.ly/2IIbLW6).
4. Wikipedia. 2018. "People's War" (https://bit.ly/2MvgWuM).
5. Wikipedia. 2018. "Kurdish-Turkish conflict (1978–present)" (https://bit.ly/2njnyk7).
6. Wikipedia. 2018. "Turgut Özal" (https://bit.ly/2dozfmL).
7. Ibid.
8. Wikipedia. 2018. "Abdullah Öcalan" (https://bit.ly/1FatBZU).
9. Ibid.
10. BBC News. 1999. "Text of the Öcalan verdict" (https://bbc.in/2Nc81zN).
11. Wikipedia. 2018. "Kurdish-Turkish conflict (1978–present)" (https://bit.ly/2tW80Y2).
12. Ibid.
13. Wikipedia. 2018. "Kurdistan Workers' Party/Cease Fire 1999–2004" (https://bit.ly/2KwFfYF)
14. Wikipedia. 2018. "Kurdish-Turkish conflict (1978–present)" (https://bit.ly/2njnyk7)).
15. Ibid.
16. Ibid.
17. Ibid.
18. Ibid.
19. Ibid.
20. Ibid.
21. Ibid.
22. Ibid.
23. Ibid.
24. Ibid.
25. Ibid.

26. Ibid.
27. Wikipedia. 2018. "Selahattin Demirtaş" (https://bit.ly/2lJfwBC)
28. Wikipedia. 2018. "Kurdistan Communities Union /Detentions and court cases of alleged members"
29. Wikipedia. 2018. "Ahmet Türk" (https://bit.ly/2tQppRG).
30. Wikipedia. 2018. "Kurdistan Free Life Party" (https://bit.ly/2tG4GAD).
31. Wikipedia. 2018. "Kurdish-Turkish conflict (1978–present)" (https://bit.ly/2tG4GAD).
32. Hürriyet Daily News. 2012. "Chronology of Oslo Dialogues with PKK" (https://bit.ly/2tCRyfR).
33. Wikipedia. 2018. "Kurdish-Turkish conflict (1978–present)" (https://bit.ly/2tG4GAD)
34. Wikipedia 2018. "Roboski airstrike" (https://bit.ly/1NXc1mh).
35. Wikipedia 2018. "Triple murder of Kurds activists in Paris" (https://bit.ly/2KysXzc).
36. Wikipedia. 2018. "Kurdish-Turkish conflict (1978–present)" (https://bit.ly/2njnyk7).
37. The Kurdistan Tribune. 2013. "Öcalan's historical Newroz 2013 Statement" (http://bit.ly/2KoIoNp).
38. Ibid.
39. Ibid.
40. Ibid.
41. Ibid.
42. Ibid.
43. Ibid.
44. Ibid.
45. Ibid.
46. Ibid.
47. Ibid.
48. Wikipedia. 2018. "Gezi Park Protests" (http://bit.ly/2K9QgmN).
49. Ibid.
50. Wikipedia. 2018. "Sırrı Süreyya Önder" (http://bit.ly/2Kcbxwh).
51. Wikipedia. 2018. "Turkish presidential election, 2014/Demirtaş campaign" (http://bit.ly/2Kp7UCg).
52. Hürriyet Daily News. 2014. "Soldier and protester killed in clashes during operation to remove statue of PKK founder" (http://bit.ly/2K9m7nH).
53. http://bit.ly/2tIp2Zt
54. http://bit.ly/2KcFqws
55. https://bbc.in/2KcbyjP
56. Wikipedia. 2018. "Siege of Kobanî" (http://bit.ly/2lAtm9n)
57. Ibid.
58. Constanze Letsch in Suruç and Istanbul, Ian Traynor in Brussels, "Kobani: anger grows as Turkey stops Kurds from aiding militias in Syria", The Guardian, Oct 8, 2014, (http://bit.ly/2tIoDGr)
59. Wikipedia. 2018. "Genocide of Yazidis by ISIL" (http://bit.ly/2KdQcCD)
60. Craig Whitlock, "U.S. begins airstrikes against Islamic State in Syria", The Washington Post, September 23, 2014, (https://wapo.st/2tEtwAh
61. "Battle for Kobane: Key events", BBC News, 2015, (https://bbc.in/2KcbyjP)

62. Heather Saul, "Erdoğan warns Kobani is 'about to fall to ISIS' as militants advance on Syria-Turkey border town", *Independent,* October 7, 2014 (https://ind.pn/2KmovXj)

63. "As Kobane Makes Last Stand, Öcalan Gives Turkey Deadline for Peace Process", *Rudaw,* 2014, (http://bit.ly/2KlDwIX)

64. "Öcalan Warns Kobane Fall Would Kill Kurdish Peace Process in Turkey", *Rudaw,* 2014, (http://bit.ly/2KccSDj)

65. Özlem İlyas Tolunay , "Behind the Kobane Tragedy: The Kurdish Political Movement and Turkey", *New Politics,* October 14, 2014 (http://bit.ly/2KmoB17)

66. Ibid.

67. Ibid.

68. Humeyra Pamuk, "A new generation of Kurdish militants takes fight to Turkey's cities", *Reuters,* September 27, 2015, (https://reut.rs/2KccUuV)

69. Jake Hanrahan, "Kurdish Anger Simmers as Turkey Accused of Killing Unarmed Teenagers", *Vice News,* January 21, 2015 (http://bit.ly/2KcGpfR)

70. "Suspected Kurdish militants attack Turkish police in southeast", Reuters, January 8, 2015 (https://reut.rs/2KlDz7B)

71. Vice News, "PKK Youth Fight for Autonomy in Turkey", YouTube, February 13, 2015 (http://bit.ly/2KccVyZ)

72. Noah Blaser, "Trench Warfare in Turkey", *Foreign Policy,* January 29, 2015 (http://bit.ly/2KlDxwv)

73. Daily News, "Opposition deputy falls from stairs at Turkish parliament amid fight over security bill", February 20, 2015, (http://bit.ly/2lE3o4Y)

74. Wikipedia 2018, "Tomb of Suleyman Shah", (http://bit.ly/2lB1t0Y)

75. http://www.ft.com/cms/s/0/5d305c18-bf67–11e4–99f8–00144feab7de.html#axzz47X3Uqh9r

76. Öcalan, Abdullah. "Newroz Message Abdullah Öcalan." The Kurdish Institute of Brussels. March 25, 2015. Accessed June 27, 2018. http://bit.ly/2lB1thu.

77. "Opinion Polling for the Turkish General Election, June 2015." Wikipedia. June 19, 2018. Accessed June 27, 2018. (http://bit.ly/2KbCRuq)

78. "We Will Not Make You the President, HDP Co-chair Tells Erdoğan." *Hürriyet Daily News.* March 17, 2015. Accessed June 27, 2018. http://bit.ly/2KonfmM.

79. Ibid.

80. Tisdall, Simon. "Turkish Election Outcome Is Blow to Erdoğan and Breakthrough for Kurds." *The Guardian.* June 07, 2015. Accessed June 27, 2018. http://bit.ly/2lEWEno.

81. Tisdall, Simon. "US Deal with Turkey over Isis May Go beyond Simple Use of an Airbase." *The Guardian.* July 24, 2015. Accessed June 27, 2018. http://bit.ly/2tHCIUF.

82. "2015 Suruç Bombing." Wikipedia. June 21, 2018. Accessed June 27, 2018. http://bit.ly/2KfKy2H.

83. "Kurdish–Turkish Conflict (2015–present)." Wikipedia. June 26, 2018. Accessed June 27, 2018. http://bit.ly/2KccV1X.

84. "Turkish Kurdistan: Town after Town Declares Self-government in Face of War." *Green Left Weekly.* August 21, 2017. Accessed June 27, 2018. http://bit.ly/2KbCRdU.

85. Winter, Chase. "Turkey Prepares Controversial Military Siege of Two Kurdish Cities | DW | 13.03.2016." DW Akademie. March 13, 2016. Accessed June 27, 2018. http://bit.ly/2lB1u52.

86. MacDonald, Alex. "Far-right Activists Attack HDP Offices across Turkey after Anti-PKK Demos." *Middle East Eye.* September 9, 2015. Accessed June 27, 2018. http://bit.ly/2Kp4teJ.

87. Letsch, Constanze, and Nadia Khomami. "Turkey Terror Attack: Mourning after Scores Killed in Ankara Blasts." *The Guardian*. October 11, 2015. Accessed June 27, 2018. http://bit.ly/2lB1mCv.

88. Reuters in Istanbul. "Turkish Police Storm Opposition Media Offices as Election Looms." *The Guardian*. October 28, 2015. Accessed June 27, 2018. http://bit.ly/2KdQgST.

89. Weaver, Matthew. "Turkey Election: Erdoğan's AKP Wins Outright Majority—As It Happened." *The Guardian*. November 01, 2015. Accessed June 27, 2018. http://bit.ly/2KbBZpG.

90. Ibid.

91. "Turkey Election: Ruling AKP Regains Majority." BBC News. November 02, 2015. Accessed June 27, 2018. https://bbc.in/2Kp7YSw.

92. Agencies in Ankara. "Turkey's President Erdoğan Says New Constitution Should Be Priority." *The Guardian*. November 04, 2015. Accessed June 27, 2018. http://bit.ly/2lBODiT.

93. Mezzofiore, Gianluca. "Selahattin Demirtaş: Pro-Kurdish Leader Says He Escaped Assassination Attempt." *International Business Times UK*. November 23, 2015. Accessed June 27, 2018. http://bit.ly/2Kcd5GB.

94. Malsin, Jared. "What the Murder of Tahir Elçi Means for Turkey and the Kurds." *Time*. November 30, 2015. Accessed June 27, 2018. https://ti.me/2KccVit.

95. Kazim, Hasnain. "Turkey's Demirtaş: 'Erdoğan Is Capable of Setting Country on Fire'SPIEGEL ONLINE—International." SPIEGEL ONLINE. July 31, 2015. Accessed June 27, 2018. http://bit.ly/2KaKocR.

96. "HDP Co-leader Justifies Declarations of 'Autonomy' as Fight against the 'Dictatorship.'" *Hürriyet Daily News*. December 22, 2015. Accessed June 27, 2018. http://bit.ly/2KfNQmz.

97. "Turkey's Kurds Call for Self-Rule amid Violence in Southeast." Reuters. December 27, 2015. Accessed June 27, 2018. https://reut.rs/2KqLIHO.

98. Ibid.

99. "HDP: Arrest of Co-Mayors Is Expel of Elected Ones." Bianet—Bagimsiz Iletisim Agi. January 6, 2015. Accessed June 27, 2018. http://bit.ly/2lB1ty0.

100. Solaker, Gulsen. "Turkish opposition backs immunity bill that Kurdish MPs say targets them." Reuters. April 14, 2016. Accessed June 27, 2018. https://reut.rs/2KlDxfZ.

101. "Investigation Launched into HDP Co-chair Demirtaş for 'Insulting the Nation.'" *Hürriyet Daily News*. September 10, 2015. Accessed June 27, 2018. http://bit.ly/2lB1stW.

102. "HDP's Demirtaş engages in self-criticism on autonomy barricades," *The Journal of Turkish Weekly*. April 13, 2016. Website now defunct. http://bit.ly/2KccVPv

103. Weaver, Matthew. "Turkey Rounds up Academics Who Signed Petition Denouncing Attacks on Kurds." *The Guardian*. January 15, 2016. Accessed June 27, 2018. http://bit.ly/2lACnPH.

104. "Turkey: Academics Jailed For Signing Petition." Human Rights Watch. March 16, 2016. Accessed June 27, 2018. http://bit.ly/2KomsSS.

105. Weaver, Matthew. "Turkey Rounds up Academics Who Signed Petition Denouncing Attacks on Kurds." *The Guardian*. January 15, 2016. Accessed June 27, 2018. http://bit.ly/2lACnPH.

Living Freedom: The Evolution of the Turkish-Kurdish Conflict and Efforts to Resolve It

Adem Uzun

Kurdish Diplomat and Executive Committee Member of Kurdistan
National Congress (KNK), Brussels

Editors' Note: This section includes relevant excerpts from a report prepared in 2014 by Mr. Uzun for the Conflict Transformation Research Programme at the Berghoff Foundation in Berlin. The full report was originally published in the Berghoff Transitions Series (No. 11). These excerpts provide a good overview of the transformations inside the PKK from the perspective of the most prominent representative of the movement in Europe.

The Rise of the PKK and its Armed Struggle

The PKK began with a group of young activists in Ankara led by theoretician Abdullah Öcalan who were first known as the 'Apoists' (from 'Apo', or 'uncle', Öcalan's nickname). In March 1973, the group's structure began to be formalised, and by 1975–1976, its influence had spread across Turkish Kurdistan. Its tremendous success in such a short time indicated how much Kurdish society thirsted for freedom: the notion of freedom resonated with people of the region, especially the youth. The PKK was officially founded on 27 November 1978, largely because its cadres believed that all legal ways of organising a national movement had been exhausted, leaving only armed resistance to combat the colonialist powers. They felt that only an all-encompassing revolution could enable the threatened Kurdish identity to flourish. The PKK declared that legal struggle was impossible in a country that thoroughly denied Kurdish identity: only armed struggle could successfully resist its annihilation. The PKK aimed to create a new Kurdish society through a popular uprising.

The Turkish State's Approach to the PKK

The Turkish state responded to the international leftist youth movements of 1968 and the PKK-led Kurdistan independence movement by staging a military coup on 12 September 1980. Shortly before the coup, PKK General Secretary Öcalan had fled through Syria to a Palestinian refugee camp in Lebanon, but most PKK cadres in Turkey were captured and sent to the military prison in Diyarbakır. News of the cadres' torture and persecution and their subsequent struggles, as well as preparations for guerrilla warfare under Öcalan, ensured mass support for the PKK (Öcalan 2004). The demands of the imprisoned cadres in Diyarbakır led to the PKK's first military operation: on 15 August 1984 guerrilla units infiltrated all the Kurdish provinces in Turkey. Popular support for the PKK grew gradually in northern Kurdistan because of Turkey's denial and annihilation policies against the Kurds. Many people joined the PKK guerrilla, which they considered a legitimate defence force against Turkish repression. At first, the Turkish state did not take these attacks seriously, announcing that the perpetrators would be dealt with quickly. Finally recognising in 1987 that it was confronted with a struggle that was broadly supported by the Kurds, Turkey declared a state of emergency. All powers were vested in a "super" regional governor, which meant that the struggle was delegated from the State to the Turkish Armed Forces. With full authority, the governors waged a vicious war, introducing special tactics such as extra-judicial killings and the deployment of paramilitary "village guards".[1] Turkey also sought foreign allies for its dirty war, using counterinsurgency methods learnt abroad to fight the Kurds.

The Kurds' Legal Political Struggle and Turkish Military Operations

The Turkish state policies of denial and annihilation were unable to defeat the PKK; on the contrary, mass support grew for the PKK, with the struggle waged not just by the guerrillas but also by people in the street. The most extraordinary examples of this were the (forbidden) mass celebrations of the Kurdish New Year, or "*Newroz*".[2] In the 1990s all public celebrations were banned, and the Turkish army attacked people who gathered without permission, killing hundreds. Yet the Kurds overcame their fear of the Turkish state and continued to celebrate Newroz each year.

The Kurdish struggle also reached the political realm. In 1989, in a defining moment, Kurdish Members of Parliament (MPs) Ahmet Türk, Adnan Ekmen, Mahmut Alınak and Salih Sümer were expelled from the Social Democratic People's Party (*Sosyaldemokrat Halkeı Parti*, SHP) for attending a Kurdish conference in Paris. The next year, the same MPs formed a new political party called the People's Labour Party (*Halkın Emek Partisi*, HEP) and in 1991, for the first time, 18 members of the pro-Kurdish HEP were elected to the Turkish Parliament. Among them was Leyla Zana, who later received the Sakharov Prize from the European Parliament. The HEP was outlawed by the Constitutional Court in 1993 (Fendoğlu 2011)[3]; its MPs' diplomatic immunity was revoked the year after. While Leyla Zana, Hatip Dicle, Selim Sadak and Orhan Doğan were sent to prison the other HEP MPs fled to Europe, where they were granted political asylum and formed the Kurdistan Parliament in Exile (PKDW). With Kurds in Europe organising mass rallies, demonstrations and international conferences, support for the Kurdish people reached new heights.

The combined efforts of the people's uprisings in Northern Kurdistan (Turkey), the diplomatic initiatives of Kurds in Europe and the influx of guerrilla fighters and their new offensives all threatened the Turkish state, which reacted by staging major military operations in the guerrilla strongholds of Botan, Dersim, Amed (Diyarbakır) and Serhat (the largest Kurdish cities in Northern Kurdistan). Since 1991, the Turkish state has also flaunted international law by carrying out cross-border military operations at the border of Turkey, Iran and Iraq. Such operations have generally been carried out two or three times a year—using tens of thousands of soldiers, village guards and counter-insurgents. Each operation costs Turkish citizens millions of dollars.

All kinds of weapons have been used against the guerrillas, including chemical weapons, which allegedly are still being used (Steinvorth and Musharbash 2010). Marks and scars indicative of chemical weapons have been found on guerrillas' corpses.[4] Similar violence has been and continues to be used against the civilian population. It is estimated that since the beginning of the armed struggle in the 1980s, more than 40,000 people have lost their lives, with 17,000 people 'disappeared' in custody or assassinated by state agencies in extra-judicial killings. These crimes remain unresolved. In November 2011, 120 mass graves containing the remains of civilians and guerrilla combatants were discovered (Kurdish Human Rights Project 2011).

The Turkish state has attempted to isolate the guerrillas by forcing the Kurds to emigrate. Between 2,000 and 4,000 villages have been forcefully evacuated by security forces since the beginning of the armed struggle; some 3 to 3.5 million people are internally displaced. Villagers who are forced to move to urban centres face severe economic and social challenges and limited political will to assist them (Kurdish Human Rights Project 2011).

The Pursuit of Dialogue and the International Conspiracy against Öcalan

After thousands had died, the two sides realised that they could not win by using violent means and began to search for political approaches. Confident of his massive political backing, PKK General Secretary Öcalan began to reorient his movement both structurally and strategically (as will be further described in the next section). Meanwhile, certain Turkish government circles began to seek a negotiated solution.

The Beginning of the PKK's Transition and the 1993 Ceasefire

Changes within the PKK began with Öcalan's political messages in 1993, and became official with the report he presented at the PKK's Fifth Congress from 8 to 27 January 1995. At the same time, circles within the Turkish state began to seek paths for dialogue. President Turgut Özal sent a message to Öcalan, and in response, the PKK declared its first unilateral ceasefire at a press conference in the Lebanese town of Bar Elias on 20 March 1993 (CNNTURK 2010). For one month, both sides stopped all hostilities: not a single shot was fired. The Turkish and Kurdish people greeted this lull with relief. Then Öcalan held another press conference to extend the ceasefire, explaining why the PKK had taken up arms in the first place, the mountain guerrillas' ambition and how the struggle should be conducted in the future. Given the significance of his speech, it is worth citing at length:

First of all, this process of ceasing fire has led to historical consequences; the ceasefire has started a new era. What is asked of us is to deepen this process. There is no doubt that our responsibilities are great. The Kurdish people are going through their roughest period in history. The Kurdish people have been subjected to persecution that has resulted in genocide and more. We never just took up arms for the sake of it. All we did was to open a road for our nation to freely develop. But we had no other means of struggle to adopt: that is why we had to take up arms and have brought the struggle to this stage. The Kurdish situation is, at heart, a Turkish-Kurdish situation. Our struggle has come to the point of the Turkish public accepting the Kurdish identity; it has seen it necessary to recognise Kurdish existence and solve the problem. [...]

We all support the development of this process. We hereby announce that with certain conditions the limited ceasefire could be made indefinite. These conditions are as follows: primarily, the ceasefire cannot be one-sided. All military operations should be ceased. The intense persecution of the people, arrests and extra-judicial killings must stop. If military operations persist, whether in three days or three months, we will have no choice but to effectively defend ourselves. This is the first point I would like to make. The government has some requests regarding the guerrillas coming down from the mountains. Our forces in the mountains have taken all possible risks to attain our political ambitions. They are there in support of our national existence and an honourable solution. If these ambitions are fulfilled, if our basic requirements are honestly fulfilled and the proper circumstances are arranged, then the problem of the armed guerrillas will be dealt with very easily. In this sense there is no problem with the guerrillas. Secondly, we have some immediate requests regarding the ceasefire process. I spoke of the cessation of all military operations. This goes not only for the guerrillas, but for the people in general. The third is a general amnesty. We do not see ourselves as guilty people, and expect all political prisoners to be freed. Of course we also expect certain cultural rights to be put in to practice. These are rights to a free press and media, Kurdish radio, television, newspaper and books, etc.

In short, the Kurdish language should be freed. We demand that the people who have been forced out of their villages be able to return and be compensated. We expect the state of emergency in the region to be lifted and the village guards to be disbanded. To pave the way to a solution, we declare a general amnesty for the village guards. This means that if they abandon their arms we will not touch them. All Kurdish organisations should be legalised. We demand the right to political association and organisation. In short, these are our expectations that will ensure a calmer, more peaceful atmosphere.

A further step that needs to be taken is the constitutional recognition of the Kurdish identity. All the above-mentioned points pave the way for a democratic federation. We would like these sorts of debates to be carried out with mutual respect.[5]

While these demands were still being enthusiastically discussed in public, Turkish President Turgut Özal suddenly died. Everyone, including his family, believes that he was poisoned (Seibert 2012).[6] At a meeting of the Turkish-American Businessmen Council, Stephen Kinzer of the *New York Times* stated that he had suspicions regarding Özal's death (Kinzer 2001). Forces in Turkey that were hostile to peace killed President Özal to reignite the war. After his death, the

Turkish Armed Forces restarted their military operations against the guerrillas, then the PKK killed 33 soldiers—and the negotiations were ended.[7] Military operations escalated: the war was rekindled. With Öcalan continuing to insist on changing policy, the PKK declared eight unilateral ceasefires in 1993, 1995, 1998, 1999, 2005, 2006, 2009 and 2010. Unfortunately, none of these ceasefires led to a durable peace. Instead, the Turkish state viewed them as signs of weakness and responded to them with conspiracies and provocations.

The PKK's Unilateral Ceasefires of 1995 and 1998

Following the end of the 1993 ceasefire, Turkey developed a new concept of war against the PKK by seeking diplomatic backing from the USA and Britain through the 'Dublin Process' (Serxwebun 1995), and military backing from Kurdish organisations in Iraq, namely, the Kurdistan Democratic Party (KDP) and the Patriotic Union of Kurdistan (PUK). But before the new concept was announced, in August 1995 the KDP and the PKK began hostilities that were to last three months.

This war was ended by a mutual ceasefire on 11 December 1995. Öcalan did not want to limit this ceasefire to the two Kurdish parties, and attempting to open a path for a political solution to the Kurdish question, declared that their ceasefire was intended to also stop Turkish state operations. Regrettably, his attempt was in vain and attacks against the Kurdish people continued at full pace. In spring 1996 the Turkish state launched an extensive military operation throughout Kurdistan—demonstrating its total disregard for the PKK ceasefire. On 6 May 1996, a commando ordered by then-Turkish Prime Minister Tansu Çiller tried to assassinate Öcalan in a house in Syria—but he was not at home. After such a provocation, the PKK resumed hostilities.

On 1 September 1998, the PKK declared its third unilateral ceasefire. Later it was understood that many circles in Turkey had been in dialogue with the PKK—indirectly. The Turkish Prime Minister Necmettin Erbakan and the commander of the Turkish Armed Forces had requested that the PKK declare a ceasefire, and the Turkish government had indirectly informed the PKK about a mechanism for administering the peace process and said that the people should be prepared for peace. However, this positive atmosphere was short-lived: it was immediately followed by an international conspiracy to capture Öcalan.

The Conspiracy against Öcalan and his Subsequent Arrest and Resistance

Although the PKK continued to insist on talks, the Turkish state never truly believed in bilateral political dialogue, and used every opportunity to attempt to eliminate PKK members. Extra-judicial killings carried out by the Turkish state between 1990 and 1999[8] aimed to incite the PKK to spread the war to Turkish cities. The Kurdish people generally supported Öcalan's policies, but from time to time they criticised the PKK leadership for not further escalating the war. Despite the pressure, Öcalan continued to pursue a political solution and declared four more unilateral ceasefires before 1999. The Turkish state viewed these ceasefires as signs of weakness and defeat, and escalated its military operations against the PKK. With political and military support from EU states and the USA, Turkey pressured Syria to force Öcalan to leave the country. In 1998, First Army Commander General Atilla Ateş made a fiery speech at the Syrian border. With American and Israeli warships offshore, it appeared that Turkey was preparing to go to war against Syria (Bila 2010).

Believing that these manoeuvres were in protest at Öcalan's residence in Syria, the Syrian government asked him to leave the country. As he later explained, Öcalan decided to leave Syria to spare the country being victimised because of him and to search elsewhere for a political solution to the Kurdish question. On 9 October 1998, Öcalan began a four-month odyssey through Russia, Italy, Greece and Kenya, where he was finally kidnapped and handed over to Turkey: the "fate of the Kurds of the past few centuries was [...] relived" (Rojbas 2011).

Many observers expected that if Öcalan was captured, the Kurdish movement would suffer a major blow and its struggle would wither away. Then-US Secretary of State Madeline Albright addressed the US Senate, calling on the countries that had welcomed Öcalan to put him on trial (US Senate 1999). After Öcalan's capture, she had to admit her surprise at the Kurdish people's hefty reaction to her words: apparently those who had sought Albright's support had not briefed her on Öcalan's significance. The Kurdish struggle did not let up and nobody surrendered; on the contrary, the Kurdish people demonstrated unprecedented defiance. The slogan "You Cannot Eclipse Our Sun" served to strengthen the resistance and support their leader, Öcalan. For some weeks, demonstrations were held daily, along with hunger strikes. Many Kurds set themselves committed acts of self-immolation, including mothers and a 10-year-old girl in eastern Kurdistan, despite calls from Öcalan and the PKK to stop.

A few Greek MPs had met Öcalan in Syria and invited him to Greece. However, on 9 October 1998, Öcalan was refused entry there. He then went to Moscow where he stayed for a month. During this time, Turkey offered Russian Prime Minister Primakov a deal: Turkey would not meddle in any Russian affairs if Russia stopped meddling in Turkey's Kurdish question and stopped helping Öcalan. Primakov agreed, and ignoring the Russian Parliament's invitation to Öcalan when he was still in Syria, began to assist Turkey. Öcalan realised that he had to leave Moscow, and went to Rome.

European states did not want Öcalan to stay in Europe because of Turkey's geopolitical status and their military, political and economic relations. Öcalan's application for political asylum was accepted by the Italian authorities, but never made official. Tens of thousands of Kurdish people camped in Rome in freezing weather to demand permission for Öcalan to stay and for a peaceful solution to the Kurdish question. In Rome, Öcalan made various statements declaring that he was ready for a peaceful solution to the Kurdish question and that European states should play an active part in promoting and supervising a peace process. However, the Europeans had decided that they wanted Öcalan to leave and started to pressure Italy to this end. When Öcalan saw that he was not being accorded the protection usually accorded political refugees, he decided to leave Italy. On 16 January 1999, on the basis of certain assurances, Öcalan returned to Moscow. But once again, he was not allowed to stay in Russia: on 29 January he left for Athens.

The Greek government had just one wish: for Öcalan to leave the country. They convinced him that it was not safe for him to remain there, and announced that they were making preparations for him in South Africa. A small jet was readied in Corfu and the flight to Africa took off. Onboard, Öcalan was informed that he was being flown to Kenya. On 1 February 1999, he was brought to a house in Nairobi belonging to the Greek Embassy. At Greece's request, a delegation consisting of the Kenyan president's son, members of the secret service and officials from the Ministry of Foreign Affairs were in constant contact with Öcalan. On 15 February, the Greek Embassy told Öcalan that everything was ready for him to go to the Netherlands and made assurances that he would be safe there. While Öcalan reluctantly accepted, believing the Greek government's promise, their spokesperson issued a statement that "Öcalan had left the house of the Greek Embassy on his own accord". Öcalan was escorted to one car and the rest of his party to the car behind it. However, Kenyan officials and secret services separated Öcalan's car and drove him straight to the airport, where they handed him over to Turkish secret service agents and officials of the Turkish Armed Forces who were waiting aboard a plane.

The world had united to conspire against Öcalan. For days he had roamed the skies, was refused asylum, and in defiance of the norms of international humanitarian law, he was handed to Turkish state officials, who imprisoned and isolated him in a jail of his own on İmralı Island.[9]

Meetings with Öcalan in Prison

At the time of Öcalan's arrest, the PKK was holding its Sixth Congress. It decided not to choose a new leader, declaring that "rather than disregard our imprisoned leader, we will embrace him even more than before". Kurdish people's anger at the international conspiracy inspired them to hold daily mass protests (demonstrations, marches, sit-ins, meetings, hunger strikes, etc.) in Turkish and European cities to demonstrate their support for and allegiance to Öcalan. There was even talk of a Turkish–Kurdish war. To diffuse the situation, the Turkish state retreated slightly: officials met with Öcalan in prison and stated that if he would calm the protests, they would take some positive steps. Öcalan later told the European Court of Human Rights (ECHR) that he had accepted the State's offer in order to avoid a Turkish-Kurdish conflict and create the proper foundation for the transition and reconstruction he envisioned. He called for protests to end. The atmosphere calmed and a new era began.

On 2 August 1999, the PKK declared that it would withdraw its forces from Turkey; it did so on 1 September 1999. The following month, in a separate show of goodwill, again following a suggestion from Öcalan, the PKK sent two 'peace groups' to Turkey, one from the mountains in Southern Kurdistan (Northern

Iraq) and one from Europe. Unfortunately, these goodwill gestures went unheeded. The entire guerrilla group that went to Turkey was immediately arrested and each member sentenced to a minimum of 10 years. One of them died in prison. The members of the group from Europe were all given prison sentences of 15 years. Some of them are still imprisoned.

Despite these developments, Öcalan continued to seek a paradigm shift and to reconstruct the PKK. He stated that, "[W]ithout expecting the state to change, the PKK must take the first steps to change—not as a simple step, but rather, as a strategic development. The current paradigm has realised its ambitions. What is needed now is a new paradigm to fulfil the demands for a solution." The PKK showed its determination to solve the Kurdish question peacefully, by launching a Peace Project in its Seventh Extraordinary Congress on 20 January 2000. Other initiatives calling for peace and dialogue followed, including: the Urgent Action Plan for Peace and Democratisation (4 November 2000); the statement of urgent demands to prevent war and develop the process of solution (19 June 2001); the Charter for Urgent Solution (22 November 2002); and numerous letters enunciating PKK views on how to solve the Kurdish question and addressed to the president, prime minister, general commander of the army and all political parties—in both 2000 and 2002.

Despite these active efforts towards peace and dialogue, the Turkish state continued its efforts to annihilate the PKK. The coalition in power, namely the Nationalist Movement Party (*Milliyetçi Hareket Partisi*, MHP), the Democratic Left Party (*Demokratik Sol Partisi*, DSP) and the Motherland Party (*Anavatan Partisi*, ANAP), wanted to exploit the international conjuncture dominated by the post-11-September 2001 'war-on-terror' rhetoric. Believing that it provided the opportunity to secure enough international support to eradicate the PKK, they froze the dialogue process. PKK overtures were interpreted as signs of weakness or evidence that the problem was 'finished'. The usual official Turkish policy was, "If guns are not firing, then the problem does not exist". So, besides a few regulations regarding democratisation, the Turkish state did not address the root causes of the Kurdish question and the constitution drawn up after the military coup of 12 September 1980 remains in effect.

International Obstacles to Resolving the Kurdish Question

In May 2002, just as a channel for dialogue was being opened between Öcalan and the Turkish authorities and intelligence services, the EU put the PKK on their list of 'terrorist organisations', overlooking the fact that an armed conflict has been raging between the Turkish Armed Forces and the PKK since 1984. The PKK fulfils the characteristics of a military structure as specified by the 1949 Geneva Protocols and has signed an agreement compelling its obedience to the laws of armed conflict (Breau 2002).

Including the PKK in the EU list of terrorist organisations is a case of the EU disregarding its own rules because it did not clarify why the PKK was included (Breau 2002). The EU decision dealt a massive blow to peace efforts.

Not only did it strengthen the hand of the Turkish state in applying its usual repressive tactics (allowing the government to stamp any Kurdish organisations and activists as 'terrorists' or 'terrorist supporters'), but the timing was most unfortunate. The PKK had just started its period of transition: clearly they were no longer using arms and had abandoned separatist aspirations in favour of searching for a solution within Turkey. Three years previously, the PKK had declared a unilateral ceasefire and withdrawn its armed forces outside Turkey's borders. Moreover, the PKK was gradually giving up its aspirations for a Kurdish nation-state, aspiring instead to a decentralised political system based on equality, enhanced cultural and linguistic rights, popular and social freedom, and the active participation of citizens in shaping their society. In fact, in January 2002 the PKK had officially dissolved itself during a press conference in Brussels attended by many international journalists. The EU decision, which seemed to ignore all the positive steps taken by the Kurdish movement, caused many Kurds to lose faith in the EU and question why the EU was working against them. The European states' historical role in dividing up Kurdistan, the broken promises of the 1923 Treaty of Lausanne, the EU's treatment of Öcalan and finally labelling the PKK a 'terrorist organisation' confirmed Kurds' belief that the EU supported the Turkish state's war against them. The saying, "Kurdish people have no friends but the mountains", was shown to be true once again.

The AKP government, who had just come to power in Turkey, interpreted the EU decision to list the PKK as a terrorist organisation as international support for taking a violent approach to the Kurdish issue. It repeated the same mistake when the United States invaded Iraq in 2003, calculating that after the US had removed Saddam's threat to the region, they would cooperate with Turkey against the PKK as part of the 'war on terror'. Turkey discarded its policy of dialogue and stepped up its violent persecution of the Kurdish freedom movement. On 1 June 2004, the PKK decided to shift from 'passive self-defence' to 'active self-defence'. It also changed its method of struggle from continuous to periodic conflict, whereby PKK guerrilla forces staged attacks to dissuade the Turkish Armed Forces from attacking and oppressing the people—and to protect themselves. PKK activity was accompanied by mass demonstrations showing the Kurdish people's support for its new policy.

The PKK's Transformation and the New Paradigm

The capture of their leader by means of an international conspiracy dealt a massive blow to the PKK and the Kurdish people, causing them to be embroiled in internal arguments from 2000 to 2004. Some cadres (with support from external forces such as the US government), sought to destroy the very essence of the PKK and failing to do so, left the movement and started a propaganda campaign against it. In response to the internal disputes, Öcalan developed a new strategy that was embraced by the mainstream PKK (the founding cadres) and created a new sense of direction that revived the movement.

Since the early 1990s, Öcalan had been aware of the changing balance in world politics, especially the disintegration of the bipolar (East/West) world system. He believed that the PKK had to adopt certain strategic changes in order to survive as an independent movement. Formed in the late 1970s, the PKK was strongly influenced by the Real-Socialist system that had moulded global revolutionary movements and national liberation struggles. It had adopted the jargon of that age and the Marxist-Leninist approach to a nation's right to self-determination through state formation. Within this framework, the PKK adopted the slogan of 'independent, united and democratic Kurdistan'—meaning it aspired to form a nation-state. Its political and military wings were organised accordingly.

The subsequent end of the Real-Socialist system, along with new global developments and practical experiences in Kurdistan, forced the PKK to search for a new strategy. After introducing the Kurds of Turkey, Syria, Iran and Iraq to the international arena, the movement had to analyse global and regional developments anew and revise its quest for change into a comprehensive strategy: to that end, it redefined itself within Kurdistan, the region and the world.

Establishment and Features of the KCK System

Educational activities and discussions based on Öcalan's defence to the ECHR led to changes in the PKK. The movement developed the thesis of 'democratic modernity', based on a democratic, ecological and gender-emancipatory system, and switched from being a party to a congressional system.

During its congress in April 2002, the PKK dissolved itself and a new Kurdistan Freedom and Democracy Congress (KADEK) took its place. Öcalan continued to reflect and analyse the situation, and as part of the ongoing quest for change, KADEK dissolved itself in 2003 and was replaced by the Kurdistan People's Congress (*Kongra-Gel*, KGK). This was an important stage in the search for a new paradigm. Öcalan, who was writing his book, In Defence of the People (2004), deemed *Kongra-Gel* an appropriate structure, but insufficient on its own.

In 2004, the PKK was reconstructed with a new identity: it became the ideological centre of the new system. The Union of Communities of Kurdistan (*Koma Komalên Kurdistan*, KKK) was established as the umbrella organisation of the new system at Newroz in Diyarbakır in 2005. One year later, the Kurdish name was changed to *Koma Civakên Kurdistan* (the Kurdish Communities Union, KCK), reflecting a slight change in emphasis. *Kongra-Gel* became the legislative assembly of the system, which continues to develop as an ideological, political and organisational tripartite.

The PKK's transformation into the KCK was based on historical analysis, and also represented an ideological and political revolution embodying the effort to create an organisational model suited to the new paradigm and ideological outlook that Öcalan described in his writings. The movement developed specific solutions for each part of Kurdistan; the thesis of 'democratic autonomy' was developed for Turkish Kurdistan: a voluntary joint existence that did not require changing the borders of the current nation-state or demanding a separate state was desirable. Chairman of the KCK Administrative Council, Murat Karayılan, outlined the reasons for such a transition:

> The KCK system represents a new understanding, a new mentality, a new organisational method, a new school and a new democratic understanding. Civilisation that developed out of the eco-system from the agricultural revolution in the Zagros region attained the Industrial Revolution in the 19th century. Along with the Industrial Revolution came the nation-states as a reality of human life. In our day, the nation-states that derived from the Industrial Revolution are hindering development in the face of a globalising world. Although financial capital that has developed under the system of nation-states is trying to shape the globalising world towards its own interests, it is unable to surpass the chaos the system is undergoing. Solutions proposed in capitalist systems are unable to solve the problem. This is because the State and especially the Nation-State are now retrogressive factors in Syria. Therefore, to find a fundamental solution—namely, an escape from the chaotic reality of the system—we need to approach the problem with a new mentality and method of organisation. Just like in the past, when Mesopotamia was the site of the first revolution in human history, today it will be the locale for the intervention to the current crisis of the system. Our leader (Abdullah Öcalan), through his practical struggle and his theorisations, has developed 'democratic confederalism' as the formula for the solution to the current crisis faced by humanity. We see the KCK as a model for its solution.[10]

It was not easy for an organisation that for so long had aspired to and struggled for an 'independent, united and democratic' Kurdistan to change its aspirations. At first, PKK cadres and movement sympathisers found the change difficult to comprehend. Along with misconceptions and misunderstandings, certain cadres were dismissive. The Turkish media—under unofficial state control—misconstrued Öcalan's appeals for a peaceful solution and presented them as if he had "surrendered to the state and was sorry" (Milliyet 1999). Efforts were made to destroy Öcalan's character and values. Meanwhile, various Kurdish cliques wanted to take advantage of this momentous period of transition and, using various derogatory terms for the PKK and Öcalan, tried to depict themselves as alternatives. However, the backbone of the PKK—made up of the leading cadres, guerrillas and enthusiastic masses—embraced the transition and declared that despite all the efforts to smear Öcalan, they were determined to effect change. They announced the formation of organisational mechanisms in conformance with the transition, as well as reconstruction committees to support it. The KCK declaration presented at Newroz 2005, explained the new system and the means needed to construct it. Here are a few excerpts from this document:

> [...] 2. The principle of a nation's right to self-determination as developed in the beginning of the 20th century, has been interpreted to mean the right to form a state. The nation-states formed on this basis are now a hindrance to development. The United Nations model is no longer an effective institution. The Gulf War and the situation in Iraq are proof of this.

3. The way out of this situation is not globalisation on the model of the Na-tion-State, but rather the democratic confederative system that is supported by the people. The state is not eternal, nor is the nation-state immortal. Today, the nation-state is being superseded by globalisation. However, because the imperialist powers have been unable to develop a significantly new model, the crisis of the current system has deepened into chaos.

[...] 6. The self-determination of Kurdistan is about the aspiration to form a democracy that is not concerned with political borders—rather than the for-mation of a state on nationalist principles. Kurdish people in Iran, Turkey, Syria and Iraq will form their own federations and unite in a confederal su-perstructure.

Democratic confederalism aspires to turn the State into an institution sensitive to democracy by removing all barriers to its democratisation. Three systems of law now rule Kurdistan: EU law, unitary state law and democratic confed-eral law. As long as the unitary states of Iran, Turkey, Iraq and Syria recognise the Kurdish people's confederal law, the Kurdish people will reciprocate by recognising their laws so that a consensus can be reached.

Democratic confederalism aims to solve all problems through peaceful means and relies on peaceful politics. Any hostile actions against the land, the people or their liberties will result in legitimate acts of self-defence. (Foreword of the KCK agreement)

As for the international level, it is important to mention the establishment of the Kurdistan National Congress (*Kongra Netewiya Kurdistan*, KNK) in Amsterdam in May 1999, which aims to: incarnate the moral unity of the Kurdish nation, without ignoring how Kurdistan has been divided between Turkey, Iran, Iraq and Syria; resolve disunity or conflict between Kurdish political parties; elaborate norms of solidarity and develop a concerted strategy for democratic solution to the Kurdish question. Membership is also open to the Assyrian Syriac-Chaldean, Armenian, Jewish, Arab, Turkmen, Azeri, Turkish and Persian minorities in Kurdistan.[11]

The PKK and the Women's Struggle

The participation of women in the PKK's founding congress anchored the attitude that women's struggle for liberation is the basis of the social struggle. Starting in 1987, Kurdish leader Öcalan concentrated on writing about women, family, society, patriarchy and the social, philosophical, cultural, economic and psychological effects of women's colonisation. He determined that women's en-slavement is the fundamental contradiction preventing societal freedom and championed women's liberation as the only way to bring about social enlighten-ment, democratic change and an emancipatory mentality. Women guerrillas are not just provided with military education, they are also encouraged to become the new individuals of a democratic free society. The Kurdish women's movement has developed into a philosophical and social movement and female PKK militants have become its leading social force. The women's movement takes its own decisions, democratically choosing its goals and administration in its congresses and conferences. Among the numerous parties and organisations pursuing this ideology of women's liberation under the umbrella organisation, the High Women's Council (*Koma Jinên Bilind*, KJB), are: the intellectual and strategising Kurdistan Women's Liberation Party (*Partîya Azadîya Jin a Kurdistan*, PAJK); the grassrootslevel Unions of Free Women (*Yekitîyên Jinên Azad*, YJA); the Free Women's Units 'Star' (*Yeknîyên Jinên Azad Star*, YJA Star) which employs strategies of legitimate self-defence; and the Committee of Young Women who engage in organising their peers. Women's struggle for liberation is not viewed as a mere fight for equality—since constitutional equality is meaningless if the cultural structure and mentality of the society remain unchanged. The struggle must address every aspect of the revolution. Women must decide for themselves, meaning that the women's struggle must organise throughout Kurdistan using a more horizontal organisation and overcoming marginal party politics. The Kurdish women's movement helps guarantee the social transformation required for a free society.[12]

The PKK and its Policy of Armed Resistance

The PKK considers that its most significant transition was in its approach to war and violence. At first the PKK was a movement that aimed at power and statehood using armed struggle to achieve this end. Later, the principle of national liberation was understood as self-defence, since global examples of the past 70 years showed that using arms had not helped people liberate themselves.

On 15 August 1984, six years after its establishment, the PKK formed the Kurdistan Liberation Forces (*Hêzên Rizgarîya Kurdistan*, HRK), acting as the army of the liberation movement. In 1986, the HRK was replaced by the People's Liberation Army of Kurdistan (*Artêşa Rizgarîya Gelê Kurdistan*, ARGK), which idealised the 'guerrilla' army. Following Abdullah Öcalan's entrapment, the ARGK pulled out of Turkey on 2 August 1999, and relocated to South Kurdistan (Northern Iraq), where it underwent a period of transition and was replaced by the People's Defence Force (*Hêzên Parastina Gel*, HPG) in 2000.

The HPG announced that rather than fighting a war of liberation it would organise around the principle of self-defence described by the United Nations, stating: "[W]herever there is a degradation of humanity, where justice does not prevail and violence diminishes human values, the people being victimised have the right to defend themselves in every way possible". Organisational, war and defence tactics were reorganised. The movement endorsed and signed the Geneva Convention and the additional protocols of June 1977 on the protection of victims of armed conflicts. On 18 July 2006, *Kongra-Gel* and the Swiss NGO, Geneva Call, signed a 'deed of commitment' banning anti-personnel mines which is supported by the UN, in the Alabama Room at the Geneva Town Hall, where many historical agreements have been signed:

International humanitarian law and human rights include all sides to armed conflicts… Acknowledging the norm of a total ban on anti-personnel mines established by the 1977 Ottawa Treaty […we] solemnly commit ourselves to the following terms (Ongan and Aktas 2006).

Unilateral Ceasefires, Indirect Dialogue, and Political Repression

Although the Justice and Development Party (*Adalet ve Kalkınma Partisi*, AKP), which came to power in 2002, hesitated at first, eventually it began to dialogue with the PKK. As a result, the PKK declared unilateral ceasefires in 2006, 2008, 2009 and 2010. Unfortunately, none of these steps brought about a lasting peace, mostly because of the AKP approach: the government took steps just before general and local elections, attempting to create conflict-free periods. But it was obvious that the AKP was aiming to strengthen its grip on power by developing tactical short-term relations and temporary steps—not a strategy to bring about a lasting solution. This section describes the period 2005–2010, marked by a series of attempts at conflict resolution, along with periods of renewed confrontation characterised by state repression of Kurdish political activities.

From the KCK's Declaration of Military Inaction to the October 2006 Ceasefire

Following the PKK's return to 'active self-defence' in 2004, some Turkish and Kurdish intellectuals concluded that the conflict was heating up because of the AKP government's faulty analyses. In August of 2005, they visited the Turkish prime minister and demanded a democratic solution to the Kurdish question. A few days later, Erdoğan visited the city of Diyarbakır, where he stated that the "Kurdish problem is my problem and … will be solved with the deepening of democracy".

His statement raised hopes in the Kurdish community, and there were calls for the PKK to declare a ceasefire. In response, on 19 August 2005 the KCK Administrative Council declared a month-long period of military inaction that was later extended for another month. However, at the same time, the Turkish army declared that "military operations will continue until there is not one single person in the mountains" and stepped up attacks. Heavy clashes ended the PKK's declared period of military inactivity. Intense clashes followed in spring and summer of 2006, accompanied by ongoing talks. Iraqi President Jalal Talabani and the president of the Kurdistan Regional government, Masud Barzani, were in dialogue with both sides and called for a ceasefire. The US Secretary of State made similar calls. Most importantly, the Turkish state was talking with the Kurdish Democratic Society Party (DTP)—the first time that the Turkish state accepted Kurdish names. Meetings with Öcalan also took place. The concrete steps needed to resolve the issue were discussed at these meetings, which included two PKK peace groups (one from Europe and one made up of PKK militants deployed in South Kurdistan); in return, the Turkish state was supposed to begin amending certain laws. In light of the positive news the PKK declared a ceasefire on 1 October 2006.

These positive developments occurred just before a general election in Turkey, causing some of the Kurdish electorate to interpret them as the Kurdish freedom movement's approval of the AKP. As a result, the AKP gained in Kurdish areas in the 2007 elections. But once again, the AKP misread the situation by pointing at the support it received from Kurds and claiming to be the number one party in the region and the representative of the Kurdish people.

After using opportunities offered by the PKK to win the elections, the AKP began to change its stance on the Kurdish question. The quest for a peaceful solution was replaced by policies of armed annihilation and views that "There is no Kurdish question if you do not think about it" and "Our security forces will do whatever is necessary regardless of whether it involves women or children".[13] On 17 October 2007, a bill was passed giving the military permission to conduct cross-border offensives attacking the PKK. On 5 November 2007, seeking international support, Prime Minister Erdoğan visited US President George W. Bush in Washington, DC, who declared that the PKK was their common enemy and that the US government would support Turkey's war against the PKK by all possible means, including supplying intelligence. Predator drones began to monitor the mountains of Kurdistan and Turkish bombings caused numerous civilian casualties. The Turkish state also shared intelligence received from the United States with Iran, who bombed civilian settlements in Iraqi Kurdistan, trying to hit guerrillas of the Free Life Party of Kurdistan (*Partiya Jiyana Azad a Kurdistanê*, PJAK), an Iranian Kurdish movement. The 'enemies'—Iran and the USA—became allies against the Kurdish people. The Turkish military then conducted operations on both sides of its borders and met with even bigger offensives from the guerrillas. After a year or so, a new quest for peace began to emerge, leading to renewed calls for a ceasefire. Both the Turkish and Kurdish people were feeling the painful consequences of war and started to call for a peaceful solution.

The Unofficial Ceasefire of December 2008 and the Declared Ceasefire of April 2009

In order for the people to be heard and to allow the 2009 general elections to be securely conducted, the PKK ceased fire unofficially in December 2008. The Turkish state learned of this decision through intermediaries and, with the Turkish Armed Forces also generally inactive, the elections were held in a peaceful atmosphere. En route to Iran, on 10 March 2009, the president of Turkey made a very positive speech about the Kurdish question to journalists, stating, "Good things are about to happen". This raised expectations and created a positive atmosphere.

In March 2009, the DTP won 99 local councils, doubling its share of votes. The AKP, who had not expected the Kurdish party to be so successful, displayed its discomfort in a speech by the Deputy Prime Minister Cemil Çiçek, who said,

"[The DTP has] pushed to the border of Armenia". Indeed, the Kurdish party had won the city council of Iğdir, a Kurdish city on the Armenian border. Throughout history, Armenians and Kurds have been described as "enemies wishing to divide Turkey".[14] In the PKK's early years, the Turkish state and army claimed that although Kurds were Muslim, the PKK was actually an Armenian (non-Muslim) organisation bent on dividing Turkey. The Çiçek statement shows that this mentality persists. People threatened by the Kurdish party's success claimed that Kurds and Armenians were going to join forces to avenge history and divide Turkey, a view that is still heard in Turkey.

Despite these negative developments and encouraged by the DTP's electoral success, the PKK made its ceasefire official on 13 April 2009. However, the State sabotaged its decision: just as everyone was expecting a positive response from the AKP government, 52 key members of the DTP, including deputy leaders, were arrested. Since then 1,700 Kurdish politicians have been arrested, including Hatip Dicle, the co-chair of the civil-society movement, Democratic Society Congress (Demokratik Toplum Kongresi, DTK).

While arrests were ongoing, the government announced the 'process of democratic opening' and conducted a 'Kurdish workshop' at the Ankara Police Academy on 1 August 2009. Although in some quarters this was seen as a positive development, these attempts occurred when persecution was intensifying, causing others to understand that the government had no serious project for a solution, but was hoping to stall the process. The government was seen as trying to ensure a period of military calm for a referendum on changes to the constitution—just as it had before the local elections in March 2009.

Discussions about military inactivity, a democratic opening and a solution were being held at the same time as the 'KCK Operations'.[15] On 11 December 2009, the Constitutional Court banned the DTP and expelled 37 Kurdish MPs including party co-chairs Ahmet Turk and Aysel Tuğluk. In response, the remaining Kurdish MPs that had been elected as independent candidates boycotted Parliament and returned to Diyarbakır, effectively cutting all relations between Kurds and the Turkish state, and sending a strong message that Parliament did not represent Kurds in Turkey. The AKP government was so shocked by this move that it immediately sent representatives to visit Öcalan in prison. They argued that they were aiming to make changes but that the judiciary were preventing them, and that they were unhappy with its ruling and planned to discuss the matter in Parliament. Öcalan responded that Parliament was the address for a solution. Kurdish politicians called off their boycott—but the AKP government soon forgot its promises and continued its repressive policies, leading Öcalan to state, "[I]f no positive steps are taken as soon as possible, on 31 May I will pull out of everything". The AKP took no note of him, and the KCK released a statement on 1 June 2010, declaring that all the steps they and their leader had taken for a peaceful and democratic solution had been rebuffed, and were even being used against the PKK. For this reason, the decision to halt military activity had to be reviewed: their forces returned to the position of active self-defence.

The Unilateral Ceasefire of August 2010

In summer 2010, major clashes occurred all over Turkey and Kurdistan. The Turkish media was filled with reports of disturbances and the heavy loss of life. On 12 September 2010, a major referendum was scheduled on constitutional amendments, and the government wanted to conduct it in a calm atmosphere. For that, they had to talk with Öcalan and urge him to declare a ceasefire. Many civil society organisations, intellectuals, the DTK and also the Peace and Democracy Party (BDP) that had replaced the banned DTP, called for a mutual ceasefire. Taking note of these requests, Öcalan stated that he was still "hopeful of peace, and if a serious and sincere approach to peace develops then I will be more than happy to play my role". Believing that dialogue was a sign of progress, he called upon both sides to engage in sincere dialogue. His call was made at a time when clashes were leading to all-out war.

Öcalan's message led the KCK to declare that for the referendum on 12 September to be conducted in a peaceful atmosphere during the sacred month of Ramadan, in response to calls from various quarters, including the DTK and the BDP, they had taken a meaningful decision. The KCK listed a number of conditions that had to be met before it would declare a unilateral ceasefire, some of which had to be urgently implemented, while others were about principle. The KCK stated that from 13 August to 20 September their forces would not conduct any military offensives but would defend themselves against any hostilities to themselves or the people. It further stated that in order for this temporary process to be permanent, the Turkish state should cease all military and political operations. Another demand was the release of all 1,700 imprisoned Kurdish politicians and members of peace groups. It further stated that the time had come for Öcalan to be a party to the negotiations.

The Muslims of Turkey enjoyed a peaceful Ramadan. The ceasefire also strengthened the AKP government's effort to push through certain constitutional amendments: 58 per cent of the voters approved amendments on judicial reforms, abolishing protection for leaders of the 12 September 1980 coup and for military personnel, as well as economic and social rights and individual freedoms. However, the BDP and over half the population of southeast Turkey boycotted the referendum (Wikipedia 2010), because it included nothing to satisfy the Kurdish people. In particular, it did not address their demands for democratic autonomy, or their fundamental rights and freedoms. Yet the AKP read voter approval as encouragement to increase its repressive policies rather than take steps towards a peaceful solution.

The Oslo Meetings: Official Dialogue between the Turkish State, PKK and Öcalan

Although state repression intensified during 2009 and 2010, the referendum had indicated that the public favoured the two sides reaching a peaceful solution. Many intellectuals were publishing articles that called for an open dialogue instead of closed-door meetings. It was becoming clear that both the Kurdish and Turkish people wanted to move from violence to peace. Finally, secret communication with Öcalan was replaced by a series of official meetings. Although he had had many direct and indirect contacts with the State since 1993, these meetings were far more significant and substantial—especially because they had the approval of the Turkish public. Öcalan was also allowed to meet regularly with his lawyers (who were flown to İmralı Island by helicopter), whereas in the past their meetings had always been blocked by trivial excuses.

Parallel to these meetings, high-level talks were being conducted between the Turkish state and the PKK in Oslo, Norway—although they were only disclosed to the public later. The PKK had already conducted meetings with Turkish officials, but the State had always sought to gain time for new offensives. Its approach to the Oslo meetings was similar. According to Prime Minister Erdoğan, "[I]ntelligence agents met the Kurdish representative to gain information, and to act accordingly" (Korucu 2014). For its part, however, the Kurdish freedom movement approached the meetings seriously, seeking to prepare society and the State for a solution, and repeatedly declaring ceasefires.

The PKK Roadmap

In 2010, after initial talks with the government delegation, Öcalan announced the need for a roadmap to solidify the dialogue and quest for a peaceful solution. He called upon all parts of society to consider the project and inform him of their thoughts and opinions. The Kurdish people began a period of discussion and presented their views to Öcalan. Similar excitement inspired democratic quarters and columnists in Turkey and hopes and expectations grew. For the first time Turks and Kurds believed that a solution was close. On 15 August 2009[16] Öcalan declared that he had finished the roadmap and given it to the prison administration to be sent to the ECHR. But the Turkish state held on to the document for fourteen months. Many well-known authors and columnists commented that the PKK had presented its project for a peaceful solution but the Turkish state did not appreciate its roadmap and had no counter-proposal. Öcalan declared that despite the State's apparent lack of a project or game plan, he would take further steps in order to break the impasse.

The Peace Groups

With the aim of opening dialogue between the government and the PKK, under Öcalan's leadership, a peace group composed of 34 people from the United Nations (UN) Mahmur refugee camp and eight guerrillas from Kandil (both in South Kurdistan) entered Turkey on 19 October 2009. After being questioned at the border, they left for Diyarbakır, escorted by hundreds of thousands of jubilant people. Interpreting joyous cries as provocative triumphalism on the part of the PKK, Turkish nationalists and government members ensured that the joy was short-lived. Once the peace groups had arrived, the main opposition—the

Nationalist Movement Party (*Milliyetçi Hareket Partisi*, MHP) and the Republican People's Party (*Cumhuriyet Halk Partisi*, CHP)—began to advocate repressive measures. Some members of the peace group were arrested while others declared that they could not safely remain in the country and returned to South Kurdistan. Because the government lacked any serious project for a solution, they characterised the displays of joy as a crisis of the 'democratic opening',[17] claiming that the "PKK's and the Kurdish people's joy thwarted us". That joy should have been interpreted as an ecstatic response to the approach of peace. The Turkish state's reaction and declaration that any other peace group would face similar consequences caused another peace group planning to come from Europe to cancel its journey.

Operations and Pressure Against Legal Kurdish Politics

In the operations against Kurdish politicians that had begun in April 2009, hundreds of people were arrested—including former MPs, local mayors, representatives of civil institutions and party activists. The DTP was banned, and its MPs forbidden to be politically active.

The Kurdish movement had anticipated the DTP's banning and quickly formed the BDP. But it, too, was unable to escape the State's repressive measures. In order to overcome the 10 per cent threshold in the general elections of 12 June 2011, the BDP entered independent candidates in a coalition with a few other political parties, and succeeded in getting 36 of its candidates elected to Parliament.[18] Six of the candidates were in prison and were not released.[19]

The Turkish state wants the BDP to sever its ties with the PKK and declare the PKK a terrorist organisation. Officials in the EU and USA second this demand. The BDP maintains that it has no organic ties with the PKK but that the overwhelming majority its supporters also support the PKK. The BDP views the PKK as armed opposition to the State, and claims that its relationship with the PKK helps it pressure the latter into renouncing arms, although the BDP does not regard that as its role. The BDP argues that if the State really wants to solve the Kurdish question, it must negotiate directly with the PKK. The BDP supports the Turkish state meeting with Öcalan in İmralı Prison and with PKK officials in Oslo. However, the State overlooks the party's positive stance, and constantly pressures the BDP, claiming that it is "supporting terrorism".

Cessation of Dialogue

Within the framework of the peace talks, the government committee had accepted Öcalan's proposal for a three-step process to resolve the conflict (ceasefire, constitutional reform and normalisation, with the PKK becoming a political actor in Turkey); a positive approach was expected after the general election in June 2011. However, using the death of soldiers who were on a military operation in the Silvan region of Amed (Diyarbakır) and the DTK's declaration of 'democratic autonomy' (see below) as excuses, the AKP government declared, "[N]othing will be the same as before, they will pay a heavy price: nobody should expect good will from us"—and implemented its long-planned policy of asymmetric war. From 27 June 2011, the government stopped meeting with Öcalan and also prevented him meeting with his lawyers and family.

The government then used the state-controlled media to promote the idea that the "PKK had cut off the meetings". On 5 October 2011 Murat Karayılan, president of the KCK Administrative Council, wrote a letter to the editor of Taraf, a newspaper that vigorously upheld the State's claims. His letter explained the reasons for ending the meetings and exposed the manipulation and disinformation surrounding the Kurdish question. It also shed light on what had transpired in the Oslo talks and what is needed to create an atmosphere conducive to forging a lasting peace.

The Search for Alternative Democratic Methods

When its efforts at dialogue were rebuffed, the Kurdish movement declared that if the State refused a democratic constitutional solution, it would seek to force one upon the AKP through alternative democratic methods—and if this did not succeed, the Kurdish people would have to create their own democratic political solution. Expecting nothing more from the State, the DTK declared the Kurdish people's 'democratic autonomy' on 14 July 2011. This model for autonomy for Kurds in Turkey is not about power: the PKK has distanced itself from ruling. But it believes this is the way for Kurdish society to develop its political will and achieve basic democratic rights.

Apparently these developments threatened the AKP because it had no proposals of its own for a democratic solution. Why else would it be so afraid of Kurds attempting to develop democracy by structuring their own democratic autonomy? The government attempted to annihilate the will of the Kurdish people who were demanding a democratic solution by using the judicial system against the BDP. It sought to make it impossible for Kurds to demand a democratic solution.

Then the 'KCK operations' begun in 2009 were revived, leading to thousands of arrests (Yüksekova Haber 2013). Most of Öcalan's lawyers were arrested, along with many Kurdish journalists. Since April 2009, 8,000 people, including MPs, mayors, journalists, solicitors, human rights activists, intellectuals, writers and academics, have been arrested; hundreds of Kurdish children languish in Turkish prisons for throwing stones at the police during demonstrations.

The Power Struggle Within the State Structure

On 13 September 2011, a recording of the secret meetings in Oslo between PKK officers and Turkish officials was leaked on the Dicle News Agency's website without the knowledge of the site's administrators. Later, the Bianet website reported that in a meeting with Turkish journalists in early 2013, Murat Karayılan, president of the KCK Administrative Council, had stated that the 'Oslo Meetings' had actually started in 2005. The manner in which the tape was leaked on the Dicle website and subsequent announcements made clear that a third party was involved. Yet Prime Minister Erdoğan blamed the KCK for leaking the tape and announced that the meetings had ended (Milliyet 2012). Soon after, the AKP government further isolated Öcalan by postponing meetings with his lawyers.

On 7 February 2012, state prosecutors called on Hakan Fidan, the director of the National Intelligence Service (*Milli İstihbarat Teşkilatı*, MİT), MİT assistant director, Afet Güneş, and former MİT director, Emre Taner, to issue statements about their meetings in Oslo regarding the "case of the KCK" (Aynaheber 2012). The prosecutors clearly intended to send state officials who had attended the meetings to prison.

Concerned that he himself was being targeted, Erdoğan insisted that neither Fidan nor any other MİT officials would provide statements. The friction between the executive and the judiciary made it clear that the Oslo meetings were ended because of a conflict within the State structure. However, believing it was being cornered, the AKP once again changed its approach and opened a new battlefront with the KCK. Two days later the government passed a law requiring the prime minister's permission to try MİT officials.

The Status Quo: Fear of Peace

Instead of opting for peaceful and democratic means to resolve the conflict, the Turkish state has repeatedly shown its contempt for democracy by arresting, detaining and repressing legal political representatives of the Kurds (e.g. denying them the right to express themselves in their mother tongue). But Kurdish leaders have taken the initiative once again by launching a bold programme of democratic negotiations aimed at introducing long-due legal and judicial reforms.

The 2013 İmralı Peace Process: A New Hope?

In the second half of 2012, imprisoned PKK members began an indefinite hunger strike in response to the AKP government's aggressive approach (Bestanuce 2013). On 17 November 2012, as the hunger strikers were nearing death, Öcalan called on them to stop. He also warned of serious developments in Rojava or Western Kurdistan (Syria).[20] Öcalan's call was heeded; the imprisoned PKK militants ended their strike. Shortly thereafter, Erdoğan announced that a new dialogue process between state officials and Öcalan had started on İmralı Island.

On 23 February 2013, Öcalan told the BDP delegation visiting him on İmralı Island that the state prosecutor's efforts to bring the MİT officials to trial five months earlier were an attempted coup. He said that he had subsequently written to the government, an effort that led to a new dialogue process.

Öcalan stated that he was going to submit written documents to the KCK administrators and the BDP and make a public announcement at the 2013 Newroz celebrations in Diyarbakır.[21]

That is indeed what happened. Öcalan's historic manifesto was read to more than a million people gathered in Diyarbakır for the Newroz celebrations on 21 March 2013. Öcalan declared the start of a new era (Sendika 2013). He called upon the KCK to declare a ceasefire and withdraw its armed units from North Kurdistan. He also made detailed suggestions to the government, noting the necessary legislative amendments and steps required to advance the process.

In response to Öcalan's call, the KCK declared a ceasefire on 23 March 2013. In May 2013 its announcement of preparations for a retreat—the beginning of the guerrillas' withdrawal from North Kurdistan—was observed by the international press.

Unfulfilled Obligations in the New Peace Process

The peace process that the KCK negotiated with the government was supposed to consist of three stages. The first stage consisted of a bilateral ceasefire, trust-building steps and the implementation of practical mechanisms. The second stage was concerned with the legal and constitutional amendments that are at the heart and root of the Kurdish question. The third and final stage, described as 'normalisation', foresaw the prisons being emptied, the return of Kurds in the mountains and in exile, and everyone being permitted to take part in politics.[22] Unfortunately, the government did not stick to its agreement, deeming the calendar 'ineffective'.

While the Kurdish side has taken gradual and strategic steps forward, the AKP government has not moved at all. By now, a truth and reconciliation committee should have been formed, Parliament should have passed legal amendments in support of the process, terminally ill prisoners should have been released and an advisory group formed. All these steps have been prevented by the government, which passed a law to protect its own civil servants but did not take any similar measures to protect the peace process. As it stands, anyone taking part could be accused of breaking the law and be jailed at any moment.

The AKP's active insistence on hindering the main actors of the peace process shows that it has an ulterior motive. In particular, the fact that Öcalan, the architect of the process, continues to be prevented from having any contact with the outside world casts doubts on the government's sincerity. BDP Cochair, Selahattin Demirtaş, announced, "[T]he government promised to assist the retreat of the guerrillas and enable Öcalan to have contact with the public; but these promises were not kept" (Haber 2013). The government has not refuted his statement. Instead of making legal amendments to enable a smooth process, it actually has enforced arbitrary measures to raise its stature within the dialogue; for instance, it banned publication of photographs taken on İmralı Island of Öcalan and the BDP delegation.

The AKP, or more precisely, Prime Minister Erdoğan, formed a group of experts that also amounted to nothing. The group included 62 'wise people' (including 12 women)—artists, politicians, academics, journalists, business people and civil society delegates, from Turkey's seven regions. The group prepared a report that was presented to the prime minister with the expectation that the recommendations would be addressed by Erdoğan's 'democratisation' packet. That did not happen. Professor Baskın Oran, a member of the group, announced that he quit because the government did not take the legislative steps promised after the guerrillas had begun their retreat. The group is presently inactive (Milliyet 2013).

Instead of the promised legislative amendments, the AKP government is pressing ahead—building more fortress-like military barracks in Kurdistan and stepping up military activity. It appears that the government intends to maintain the military option. The Turkish military practically ended the ceasefire by killing a civilian during a protest against one of the barracks in Şırnak. In response to the governments' tactics aimed at dragging out the peace process, on 9 September 2011 the KCK announced that the ceasefire was being held but the guerrillas' retreat would be halted. At the same time that a ceasefire was implemented in Turkey, the government was supporting the war against the Kurds in Syria by supporting Al-Qaeda-affiliated jihadist organisations such as the Al-Nusra Front.

In a meeting with his family on 18 November 2013, Öcalan described the government's stance:

> We told them to make the legal amendments and the guerrillas would leave the country. They could have left sooner, in just two months. But the state and the government did nothing. Because they did nothing, this is the most that could have happened. No legal framework was prepared. Had the state done this, the guerrillas could have even left in buses, retreating comfortably. But the framework was not prepared. This is why the process is continuing like this today.[23]

Conclusion

When it was founded, the PKK believed that there was no possibility of mounting a political campaign on behalf of the Kurdish people when even small-scale activism was severely punished. Inspired by other national liberation movements and agreeing with their tactics, the PKK adopted their ideological and military approaches. It opted for waging a long-term people's war to defeat Turkish colonialism and force the Turkish government to acknowledge the Kurds.

Over the years, the PKK's view of war evolved and it adopted a new strategy to replace the classic "defence, balance, attack" mentality of a revolutionary people's war. After 1990, the Kurdish people's struggle was characterised by guerrilla war and mass uprisings. Since the turn of the millennium, the democratic political struggle has grown in importance, and along with mass uprisings has become as important as guerrilla warfare, which was reoriented towards acts of legitimate self-defence. The PKK struggle has become more complex, with a broader array of strategies. Especially since 1993, PKK leader Öcalan has emphasised the importance of a democratic political solution by declaring various unilateral ceasefires. The global situation, the Kurdish people's organisational maturity and consciousness, as well as the broader general awareness of the Kurdish question—including on the part of the Turkish public—all make a democratic political solution possible. A need no longer exists to defeat the Turkish state and its army through the methods of war alone.

Despite all these efforts, however, the Turkish state has shown no interest in a democratic political solution and has attempted to exclude the PKK from a possible solution. The AKP has repeatedly claimed that it would solve the Kurdish question, yet it refuses to accept the Kurdish people as a national community with a democratic will that can determine its own fate. Kurdish demands for education in their mother tongue, the use of Kurdish in the public domain and cultural freedom have never been taken seriously. The Turkish state apparently believes that it could make a few minor reforms and allow some individual rights and the problem would disappear. It has never touched on the roots of the problem or sought to understand its history. As a result, the proposed solutions have continued the usual state policies of suppression, elimination and annihilation.

Although Turkey is considered to be one of the most modern states in the region, its rulers are unable to resolve a problem democratically. They regard the Kurdish struggle for democracy as a threat that will eventually rock their authority. The same problem confronts Iranian and Arab states, where one nation and one religion are prioritised and other ethnic and religious groups are alienated and prohibited from forming their own democratic civil organisations. Any activity that is not part of the official ideology, the official nation, the official language, the official culture and the official politics is viewed as a crime, and labelled 'treacherous'.

When one compares the tools available to the Turkish state with those available to the PKK, it is obvious that the State is far better equipped to take larger and more significant steps. However, the State has almost always wanted to come out on top by expecting the Kurds to 'surrender' or be satisfied with minimal compromises, supposedly because of a need to satisfy the opposition. But 90 per cent of the people and the opposition support the government taking positive steps towards a peaceful solution. Occasionally the government claims that its own laws obstruct progress, which is nonsense given the fact that the ruling party received 50 per cent of the general vote in an election when it promised to draft a new constitution. All opinion polls show that the people of Turkey support solving the Kurdish question through a new constitution.

In an article in *Taraf* from 5 May 2012, Turkish journalist Roni Margulies explained why the Kurdish question has not yet been resolved:

The problem is neither the Kurds, the PKK, nor arms. The problem is the attempts, since 1926, by the state to resolve this issue using violence. We must not forget this. The solution remains stopping the injustice. As long as the state attempts to resolve the issue using a military approach, those seeking justice with arms will not stop, cannot be stopped and will continue. There is no example in history where people have been oppressed forever with guns and military methods. For this war to end it is the responsibility of everyone who is Turkish, righteous and mindful to demand rights for everyone who is demanding their rights—and to explain that the only way for this war to end is for the people who are demanding their rights to be given them. To appeal for one side in the war to lay down their arms while the war is going on is pointless. Arms can only be put down after certain conditions are met and guarantees given. The responsibility of intelligent Turks is not to call for one side to lay down their arms, but to call on the other side to recognise that side's rights.

The Turkish people are ready for a solution, but there is no courageous political will to solve the problem.

The history of the Turkish and Kurdish people could be transformed into a tremendous forward march towards democracy that is as important, if not more, for the people as water and petrol. A future based on democratic norms is crucial for the Turkish, Iranian and Arab peoples. Kurds do not seek to threaten; they want to live in peace with others. Rather than being used as a tool to 'divide and rule' they want to be a unifying force on a strong and free basis. They do not want to be the tools of oppressive forces but rather deserve to be viewed as a democratic force in the region's march towards democracy. This project could serve as a role model for the whole Middle East.

Institutionalising democracy requires sensitivity. Sovereign religions and sovereign nations represent similar mentalities that are ill suited to democracy. Transitioning to democratic institutionalisation is particularly difficult because democratic institutions define themselves in terms of the State. The new democratic version of the Turkish nation-state presupposes freedom of language and culture.

At this stage, the EU and the US are as important as the Turkish government in solving the Kurdish question. Unfortunately, their support encourages the Turkish state to leave the problem unsolved. Were this support to become conditional, the road to peace would be smoother. The most significant step which might be taken in support of a peaceful solution would be to remove the PKK from the so-called EU terrorist list.

When we regard the Kurdish struggle and its current phase, we can see that a solution to the Kurdish question is forcing itself onto the global agenda. However, it cannot be solved using a narrow national approach: the Kurdish people want to forge a common future with other people of the region. The roots of the problem are universal in nature and the solution to the problem must be universal. Only a broad perspective can ensure a permanent solution to the Kurdish question. The dialogue process between the Turkish state and the PKK and Öcalan must be restarted. No solution that excludes Öcalan and the PKK is possible.

Notes:

1. Some 90,000 Kurdish villagers were first paid and provided with arms to defend their villages, then were used by the Turkish army to carry out domestic and cross-border military operations. Some of these 'village guards' are now being tried for their crimes. Village guards were used by the State for approximately 17,000 extra-judicial killings.

2. According to the legend in the Middle East, Newroz ('new day') symbolises the resistance and liberation of the blacksmith Kawa against the brutality of the tyrant Dehag—representing the liberation of subjugated people (Ayman 2013).

3. This policy continues today: 27 parties have been banned because of the Kurdish question. But each banned Kurdish party is replaced by a new one

4. For instance, the Turkish army is alleged to have used chemical weapons in the Kazan Valley (Geliyê Tiyarê) where 36 combatants were killed in clashes in the Çukurca district of Hakkari on October 22-24, 2011. Online at www.kurdishinfo.com/ turkish-army-claims-they-didnt-use-chemical-weapon-in-kazan-valley.

5. Online at www.serxwebun.org/arsiv/136/

6. "Rumours that Özal was murdered, possibly from members of the state security forces who resisted his efforts to find a peaceful solution to the Kurdish problem, have lingered for years. Media reports have said that shortly before his death, Mr Özal opposed the adoption of a counter-guerrilla strategy by the State, including the deployment of right-wing hit men, to hunt down leaders and alleged sympathisers of Kurdish rebels" (Seibert 2012).

7. The killing of these soldiers has always been a contentious matter: Öcalan himself, as well as certain advocates of peace in Turkey, have requested an independent inquiry into the incident. Many believe that Turkish soldiers reported their comrades' route to the PKK because they wanted the conflict to continue.

8. Attacks carried out by state-sponsored counter-guerrilla forces (under various names) claimed the lives of 17,000 civilian Kurds including women, children, businessmen, intellectuals, journalists, academics and non-PKK-militia members.

9. For Öcalan's own recollection and interpretation of this conspiracy, see Öcalan (2010).

10. Online at https://bit.ly/2O9nxgj.

11. The KNK could be perhaps best compared with the African National Congress (ANC) in apartheid South Africa, or with the Palestine Liberation Organisation (PLO) prior to the Oslo Accords—although it is not a military organisation.

12. A more detailed description of various women's organisations established throughout the Kurdish struggle is found in Appendix II (Chronology).

13. Prime Minister Recep Tayyip Erdoğan, at the Turkish Grand Assembly in March 2008.

14. At the time of the dissolution of the Ottoman Empire, in the name of creating a homogenous nation, the Turks massacred Armenians and forced hundreds of thousands of them to flee. Since 1923, Turkey's official history and schoolbooks have taught that the Armenians were trying to divide the country and brought about 'conflict'. The Turkish nation has always been poisoned with nationalism and hatred towards the Armenian people.

15. This refers to massive repression of any kind of Kurdish activism in Turkey—that began in 2009 and continues today.

16. This represents a symbolic date in the Kurdish struggle: on this date in 1984 the PKK launched its guerrilla war.

17. The government first announced a process of 'Kurdish opening' but in reaction to nationalists' rejection later called it the 'democratic opening'. The name had to be changed once

more to 'the process of national unity and fraternity'. But 'national unity' defines all people living in Turkey as 'Turkish'.

18. The 10% threshold is an anti-democratic measure introduced to keep Kurdish politicians out of Parliament and forces Kurdish parties to present independent candidates. Without that threshold, the same proportion of votes would have yielded the BDP closer to 60 MPs. In the previous election, the Kurdish party had also entered independent candidates and obtained 22 seats in Parliament.

19. Four of the six elected MPs started open-ended hunger strikes in prison on 15 February 2012, the anniversary of Öcalan's capture, demanding that negotiations be restarted with Öcalan and a peaceful solution be found to the Kurdish question. The court was forced to release all the MPs in January 2014.

20. For a description of the ongoing revolution in Syria and Western Kurdistan, see Appendix I.

21. For the full text of the declaration in english, see https://bit.ly/2uH6lGZ.

22. Online at http://firatajans.com/news/guncel.

23. Ibid.

Bibliography

Ayman, M. Nuri (2013). *Newroz'un anlamı ve ateşin kutsallığı* (The meaning and sanctity of Newroz fire). Ozgur Gundem, 13 March.

Ayheber (2012). *Türkiye ve dünyadaki bugünkü gündem* (The agenda in Turkey and the world). 15 February. Online at: www.ayhaber.net/yazar.asp?yaziID=8014 (link broken).

Bestanuce (2013). *Van F Tipi'nde 32 tutsak süresiz dönüşümsüz açlık grevinde* (32 prisoners on unlimited hunger strike in Van). 29 October. Online at www.bestanuce.org/haberayrinti.php?id=66749 (link broken).

Bila, Fikret (2010). *Öcalan'ın yakalanma süreci nasıl başladı?* (How did the process of catching Öcalan begin?) Nethaberci, 7 July. Online at: http://nethaberci.com/sondakika-dunya-haberleri/Öcalaninyakalanma-sureci-nasil-basladi-4351.html (link broken).

Breau, Susan C. (2002). The situation in south-east Turkey: Is this an armed conflict for the purpose of international humanitarian law? Online at: http://campacc.org.uk/uploads/seminar_breau2.pdf

CNNTURK (2010). *Geçmişten bugüne PKK ateşkesleri* (Past to present PKK ceasefires). 28 June. Online at: https://bit.ly/2mz1sLk

Fendoğlu, Hasan Tahsin (2011). *Parti Kapatma, HADEP ve AİHM* (Closing Party, HADEP and the ECHR). Institute of Strategic Thinking (SDE). 3 January. Online at: www.sde.org.tr/tr/haberler/1344/partikapatma-hadep-ve-aihm.aspx (link broken).

Haber (2013). Selahattin Demirtaş. Online at: www.internethaber.com/selahattin-demirtas/

Kinzer, Stephen (2001). *Turgut Özal'ın Ölümü Şüpheli* (Suspicious death of Turgut Özal). Iktibas, 23 October. Online at: http://iktibas.net/metin.php?seri=482 (link broken).

Korucu, Bülen (2014). *Yeni başlayanlar için 7 Şubat rehberi* (Guide for beginners on February 7). Zaman, 12 January. Online at www.zaman.com.tr/pazar_7-subatta-ne-oldu-biliyor-musunuz_2192873.html (link broken).

Kurdish Human Rights Project (2011). 'Displacement in the Kurdish regions'. Presentation, Kurdish Human Rights Project. Online at: www.khrp.org/khrp-news/human-rights-documents/briefing-papers.html (link broken).

Milliyet (2012). *Başbakan Erdoğan'dan 'Oslo görüşmeleri' açıklaması* (Declaration by Turkish Prime Minister Erdoğan concerning the Oslo meetings). 26 September. Online at: https://bit.ly/2JIcsiR.

Milliyet (2013). *İşte Akil İnsanlar Heyeti* (Wise people delegation). 4 April. Online at: https://bit.ly/2JLAadW.

Ongan, Ali and Murat Aktas (2006). Agreement with Kongra-Gel to ban landmines. 19 July. Online at: www.savaskarsitlari.org/arsiv.asp?ArsivTipID=5&ArsivAnaID=34067 (link broken).

Öcalan, Abdullah (2004). *Bir Halkı Savunmak* (Defending a People). Online at: www.abdullah-ocalan.com/savunmalar/4/birhalkisavunmak.html (link broken).

Öcalan, Abdullah (2010). 'A conspiracy against peace'. Il Manifesto, 13 February. Online at https://bit.ly/2uWL1fX (link broken).

Rojbas (2011). *Komplonun Ayrıntıları* (Conspiracy details). 11 August. Online at: http://rojbas1.wordpress.com/2011/08/11/komplonun-ayrintilari/ (link broken).

Seibert, Thomas (2012). Turkey hunts for what, or who, killed premier Özal. The National, September 28. Online at https://bit.ly/2NDabrC.

Sendika (2013). *Abdullah Öcalan'ın Newroz mesajının tam metni: "Bu son değil, yeni bir başlangıçtır"* (The full version of Öcalan's declaration: "This is not the end just a new start"). 21 March. Online at: https://bit.ly/2JMATeZ.

Serxwebun (1995). Dublin'den Kürdistan ve Ortadoğu'ya (From Dublin of Kurdistan and the Middle East). Online at: www.serxwebun.org/arsiv/164/files/assets/pages/page0004.swf (link broken).

Steinvorth, Daniel and Yassin Musharbash (2010). Shocking Images of Dead Kurdish Fighters: Turkey Accused of Using Chemical Weapons against PKK. Spiegel Online, 12 August. Online at: https://bit.ly/1LaNdoa.

Wikipedia (2010). Turkish constitutional referendum, 2010. Online at: http://en.wikipedia.org/wiki/Turkish_constitutional_referendum,_2010

Yüksekova Haber (2013). KCK operasyonlarının başladığı gün! (The day of the KCK declaration). 14 April. Online at: www.yuksekovahaber.com/haber/kck-operasyonlarinin-basladigi-gun-98888.htm (link broken).

Appendix I: The Revolution in Syria and Western Kurdistan (Rojava)

The peace process in Turkey cannot be separated from developments in other parts of Kurdistan and the Middle East. Any development, whether positive or negative, directly impacts the peace process. The Turkish state continues to oppose any positive developments in the rest of Kurdistan on the grounds that they will inspire its Kurdish population. This can easily be seen in Syria where the Turkish state secretively supports Al-Qaeda-affiliated groups, both logistically and militarily. In return for its support of rebels, Turkey demands that the Syrian National Coalition not recognise the Kurds. The British magazine, The Economist, wrote in October 2013 that the subject with the greatest potential to derail the peace process between the Turkish government and Abdullah Öcalan is government support for the Al-Qaeda-affiliated groups fighting the Kurdish Democratic Union Party (Partiya Yekitîya Demokrat, PYD) in in northern Syria, also called Western Kurdistan or Rojava.[1]

It has been three years since the uprising started in Syria, and it seems that its fate will determine the destiny of the Middle East. Although it appears to be a war between the Baath regime and an armed opposition, the US, Russia, Iran, Saudi Arabia, Qatar, Jordan, Turkey and many European states have become involved. Some of these states are supporting the regime, while others are backing the opposition—causing the war to drag on, and leading to tens of thousands of people dying, millions fleeing and Syria being destroyed. Hatred among various peoples and inter-faith violence grows by the day. Since the beginning, however, the Kurds have insisted that they prefer peaceful methods for solving the current problems, and refuse to side with either the regime or the opposition, because neither recognises the Kurdish people's natural and democratic rights. All contacts between the Kurdish people and the opposition have come to nought because of the latter's chauvinist demeanour.

In an interview with the Turkish daily newspaper *Taraf*, Veysel Ayhan stated:

> When the initial movements began against Bashar Assad in Syria, Turkey was saying that it was prepared to support the rightful demands of the people of Syria. Today there are regions that are being governed by the Syrian National Council (SNC). Funnily enough, we are not demanding the abolishment of these administrations, yet we are calling for the disbandment of the administrations in the Kurdish regions. We are opposing the autonomous administrations established in the Kurdish regions, yet we are not demanding anything similar for the administrations in the Sunni Arab regions. We do not say that Arabs "should not form autonomous regions". Syria is home to Christians, Alawites and Druse. Maybe an autonomous Alawite region will be formed. If the Alawites and the Druse say, "[W]e will form an autonomous region" will Turkey also oppose them?[2]

The Kurds have distanced themselves from both violent sides, preferring their own 'Third Way', which proposes fair representation of all peoples and identities within a unitary Syria; it welcomes a diplomatic solution, regards no one as an enemy and seeks only to defend itself against external hostilities. It works for the application of the democratic autonomy project founded on the principle of the peoples' shared destiny. The Kurds have chosen an alternative that foresees a joint future, not only for ethnic groups such as Kurds, Arabs, Armenians, Assyrians, Chechens and Turcomans, but also for religious identities such as Christian, Muslim, Yezidi, Sunni and Alawite. The Kurds did not take part in the war and only organised themselves both socially and militarily to defend their regions. On 19 July 2012, the Kurdish People's Protection Unit (Yekîneyên Parastina Gel, YPG) stormed government buildings in the Kurdish city Kobanê[3] and forced government forces to leave the city. The city administration fled without a fight, and the town was handed over to the People's Assembly of Western Kurdistan (MGRK). The same later happened in two other Kurdish border towns, Efrîn and Cizrê: both towns were ceded to the people. What has now gone down in Kurdish history as the 'Revolution of Western (Rojava) Kurdistan' has consolidated Kurdish aspirations: The Kurds have reinforced their autonomy and organised themselves in a bottom-up fashion—from civil organisations for doctors, engineers, teachers and youth, as well as trade unions and women's assemblies, to general assemblies. They have also formed economic committees. Now the Kurds want to be granted political status, or at the very least, want the areas they defend and control to be recognised.

It would be useful to take a look at the history of the situation to better understand the current circumstances and the feasibility of the Kurdish project. Syria was formed as a result of the 1921 London Agreement between France and the Kemalist administration. As a consequence of this agreement, a border was drawn between the Kurds of the North and the Kurds of the southwest: the former group was ruled by Turkey, the latter by the French mandate power in (Arab) Syria. The nearly three million Kurds living in Syria were never granted citizenship by the Baath regime. The Kurds mostly live in the Cezîre, Kobanê and Efrîn regions, sandwiched between North Kurdistan (Turkey) and South Kurdistan (Iraq), with a 700-km-long border with Turkey. Familial relations exist between the Kurds in Syria and the Kurds in Turkey, despite the border that runs right through the centre of some cities. Artificial borders have not prevented the Kurds from maintaining cross-border relationships.

When the Baath Party seized power in Syria in 1963, the situation of the Kurds took a turn for the worse. The Baathists singled out the Kurds from the Cezîre region, seeing them as a potential threat, and adopted a policy of displacing them and repopulating the region with Arabs; this was the beginning of the 'Arab Belt'.[4] The Baath Party even went as far as forcefully seizing land from the Kurds and handing it over to the new Arab settlers, forcing tens of thousands of Kurds to flee to Aleppo and Damascus. Furthermore, the regime made it illegal for Kurds to use Kurdish in school and refused to grant them citizenship or passports; the Kurds became an oppressed, stateless minority. They could neither buy land nor attend university.[5]

Despite oppressing the Kurdish people, the Baath regime always turned a blind eye to Kurdish leaders residing in Syria, a stance that had to do with Syria's problems with Iraq and Turkey: it saw Kurdish organisations as useful bargaining chips against neighbouring states. This is why many Kurdish organisations that were unable to get established in neighbouring countries settled in Syria and why the Kurds of Rojava Kurdistan have always been close to the centre of Kurdish politics and been able to remain active throughout the years. The PKK leader, Abdullah Öcalan, lived in Syria between 1979 and 1998, when the PKK was founded, and led the PKK armed struggle and mass mobilisations from Syria. According to PKK records, thousands of Kurds from Rojava Kurdistan have joined the PKK. The PYD, which adopted Öcalan's ideology and projects, is the most widely supported party in Rojava. The People's Assembly of Western Kurdistan (Meclîsa Gelê Rojavaya Kurdistan, MGRK) and the National Assembly of Syrian Kurdistan (Encumena Niştimaniya Kurdên Sûriyeyê, ENKS) signed the Erbil Agreement forming the Kurdish Supreme Council (KSC) on 24 July 2012, in Qamishlo, the largest Rojavan city. The KSC carries out military, civilian and political work. On 21 January 2014, the KSC declared the Kurdish cantons—inspired by the Swiss model—to be autonomous, in a step towards democratic autonomy. The Turkish daily newspaper Milliyet announced this news on 18 February 2014:

> The Autonomous Rojava Legislative Assembly declared that it had divided the region into three cantons which are Cezîre, Kobanê and Efrîn. Each canton will form its own autonomous administration. The Legislative Assembly accepted the Social Contract. According to this, the four pillars of the new system are the Canton system, the Legislative Assembly, Administration, Justice and the Supreme Election Council. The Legislative Assembly, as the representative of the Kurds, Arabs, Assyrians, Chechens and Armenians, see Rojava Kurdistan as an integral part of a future decentralised Syria.[6]

Kurds from Rojava Kurdistan, who regard themselves as part of a democratic Syria, must fight against regime forces and Al-Qaeda-affiliated Salafist groups such as Jabhat Al-Nusra (formed in July 2011 as the initially-unofficial Syrian wing of Al-Qaeda in Iraq) and ISIS. Kurdish military forces of the YPG and the Women's Protection Unit (Yekîneyên Parastina Jin, YPJ) have successfully repelled these Salafist organisations, although it has reportedly cost the lives of some 600 Kurdish fighters. The Salafists aim to establish an Islamic state in the Kurdish regions. According to the news portal ntvmsnbc.com: "[A] general of the Free Syrian Army … stated that Al-Qaeda is beginning to implement an Islamic state in the north of the country". Considering the aspirations of these organisations and the Syrian regime, it is clear that the Kurdish people have their work cut out for them. The KSC was not invited to the second Geneva Conference held on 22 January 2014. But the Kurds insist that they are not hostile to anyone and just want to live freely among all the peoples of a democratic Syria. For the peace process to succeed in Turkey (North Kurdistan), the Turkish state must change its attitude towards Rojava Kurdistan. Öcalan has always stated that the Turkish state should adopt a more friendly approach to the Kurds of Rojava Kurdistan. To assure stability in the Middle East, the status of the Kurds of Rojava must be recognised.

Notes for Appendix I:

1. Online at https://bit.ly/2uEARRO.

2. Online at www.taraf.com.tr/nese-duzel/makale-veysel-ayhan-kurtler-ucuncu
   -yolu-tercih-etti.htm (link broken).

3. Kobanê is a city in West Kurdistan on the Turkish border with only Kurdish inhabitants.

4. The 'Arab Belt' is the name of the policy of arabising the Kurdish regions. Since 1963,
   the Baath Party, under the slogan 'Protecting the Arabness of Cezîre', began to move Syrian
   Arabs to the Cezîre region. See http://guernica.tv/rojavada-savas-vedevrim/ (link broken).
   For example, the town of Til Ebyad, located between Cezîre and Kobanê, now populated by
   both Kurds and Arabs, is part of the Arab Belt. It has been controlled by the terrorist organisation Islamic State of Iraq and al-Sham (ISIS) since March 2013.

5. See www.zaman.com.tr/yorum_suriyede-kurtlerin-kalbini-kazanma-mucadelesi
   _1247081.html (link broken).

6. Online at https://bit.ly/2uD7peT.

Appendix II:

CHRONOLOGY: From the PKK to the KCK

1973   Abdullah Öcalan, a sympathiser of the leftist movement in Turkey, meets with a few of his friends to discuss the need to organise independently.

1977   After Hakki Karer, a leading member of the group, is murdered, the PKK is formed.

1978   In the Kurdish city of Maraş, fascists encouraged by the Turkish state massacre one thousand Alevis. Prior to the attack the homes of Alevi citizens were marked. Öcalan's group gains mass support. State-backed feudal landowners begin to attack the group and both sides suffer heavy casualties—especially in the region of Hilvan–Siverek. 26–28 November: The PKK (Kurdistan Worker's Party) is officially founded.

1980   12 September: A military coup is staged; the prime minister, leader of the opposition, government ministers, and tens of thousands of people are imprisoned. Many prisoners are sentenced to death and most of the sentences are carried out. The Army Chief who led the coup then drafts a new fascist constitution and declares himself president. 1980–1984 Abdullah Öcalan and a few other PKK cadres go to the Bekaa Valley in Lebanon (under Palestinian control) for political and military education.

1981   22–27 September: The First Congress of the PKK is held.

1982   21 March: One of the founders of the PKK, Mazlum Doğan, commits suicide to protest the treatment suffered by prisoners in Diyarbakır Prison. On the Kurdish holiday of Newroz, traditionally celebrated with bonfires, he lights three matchsticks, calling on the Kurdish people to revolt, then hangs himself.
17 May: Four PKK prisoners (Ferhat Kurtay, Eşref Anyık, Mahmut Zengin and Necmi Öner) hold hands and burn themselves alive to protest their inhumane treatment in Diyarbakır Prison.
14 July: PKK prisoners in Diyarbakır announce that they are going to fast to death. This is a turning point in Kurdish politics; a death fast is being conducted for the first time on Kurdish lands. The leading cadres of the PKK, Hayri Durmuş, Kemal Pir, Ali Çiçek, and Akif Yılmaz, die in September. Witnesses relate, "There was a battle of wills. That battle was won by those people who put their lives on the line for their people".
20–25 August: The PKK's Second Congress is held near the Turkish–Jordanian border. Major decisions are taken on such issues as returning

to Kurdistan, cooperating with leftist movements, undertaking diplomatic activities, establishing military and political organisations, and Abdullah Öcalan's continued leadership.

25 August: The Kurdistan Liberation Forces (HRK) are formed. Öcalan states that the only response to the struggle in Diyarbakır Prison is to step up the struggle. Kurdish artists in Europe form HUNERKOM, a cultural organisation (now known as "TEVCAND").

1983   In the first elections since the military coup, Turgut Özal is elected prime minister of Turkey. (He later becomes president and in 1993 initiates a dialogue with the PKK.)

1984   16 August: Under Mahsum Korkmaz's command, the PKK launches its guerrilla war by attacking Turkish army bases. The State first claims that this was carried out by a few bandits; later it is obvious that this was not so.

1985   The Turkish state begins to understand that it needs to deal with the PKK and forms a militia called the 'village guards'.
21 March: The National Liberation Front of Kurdistan (ERNK) is formed in Kurdistan and later opens diplomatic bureaus in many European countries.

1986   28 February: When the Swedish prime minister is assassinated, the Turkish state and Swedish intelligence service seek to blame the PKK in order to criminalise the organisation in Europe. Swedish intelligence later admits that the PKK was not involved.
28 March: Commander Mahsum Korkmaz ("Agit") is shot in the back and is killed. This represents a major setback for the organisation. The People's Liberation Army of Kurdistan (ARGK) is formed in his remembrance.
25–30 October: The PKK holds its 3rd Congress, which is remembered as bringing ideological clarity to the PKK, in Lebanon's Bekaa Valley.

1987   A state of emergency that gives the regional governor all authority is declared in Kurdish towns. Women take interest in the struggle and their numbers increase. A meeting with 2,000 female delegates is organised in Cologne, Germany; the Kurdistan Patriotic Women's Association (YJKW) is formed. The name is later changed to the Kurdistan Women's Freedom Movement (TAJK). The Union of Kurdish Youth (YCK) is formed (now called TECAK).

1988   The German government begins police operations against the PKK in February. Leading cadres are arrested and tried in what is later called the Düsseldorf Case. (Duran Kalkan and Ali Haydar Kaytan are released from prison in 1993.)

1989   21 March: The first mass Newroz celebrations take place. Despite being forbidden, thousands of people attend and are attacked—many are killed—by Turkish security forces.

1990   26–31 December: The PKK holds its 4th Congress in the mountains of Kurdistan. At this congress, it is decided that guerrillas should aim to control land.

1991–1992 State-backed counter-insurgency forces start to carry out extra-judicial killings. Eventually, more than 17,000 people are eliminated, including human-rights activist, Vedat Aydın, 74-year-old Kurdish intellectual Musa Anter, MP Mehmet Sincer, and Kurdish businessmen, Behçet Canturk and Savaş Buldan.

1992   21 March: Newroz celebrations are again attacked by state forces. More than 100 people die in the towns of Cizre, Şırnak, and Nusaybin.
May: The first Kurdish daily newspaper *Ozgur Gundem* is founded; bombs kill 13 employees in its offices.
Elections are held for the Kurdistan National Assembly (in Iraq), with a turnout of 90,000 voters. Delegates are elected from Kurdistan and Europe. The Turkish state—with US backing and 300,000 soldiers—conduct a cross-border military operation against 10,000 guerrillas in Iraqi Kurdistan. NATO forces fight the PKK for the first time. Kurds living in Germany organise a Kurdish Cultural Festival that is attended by 60,000 people.

1993   20 March: The PKK declares a unilateral ceasefire in response to a call from Turkish President Turgut Özal. The German state bans the PKK and its activities and closes down 34 Kurdish centres.

1995   8–27 January: In Kurdistan the PKK conducts its 5th Congress, during which the PKK's programme and flag are changed.
8 March: Female guerrillas congregate in the Medya Defence Region's Metina area and in a meeting with 200 delegates (and no men) announce the formation of their autonomous "Free Women's Union of Kurdistan" (YAJK). In 1999 some 300 women meet and change the YAJK's name to the "Kurdistan Women Worker's Party" (PJKK).
The PKK signs the Geneva Convention, promising to abide by international rules of war. The PKK announces a second unilateral ceasefire.
The Kurdish Parliament in Exile (PKDW) is formed and the first Kurdish TV station (MedTV) goes on air.

1996   Failed attempt to assassinate Abdullah Öcalan in the city of Sam. The PKK resumes hostilities against the Turkish state.

1998   8 March: PKK leader Öcalan presents his perspectives on women's struggle as the "Woman's Liberation Ideology".
1 September: The PKK declares a third unilateral ceasefire.

1999   15 February: The international conspiracy that had forced Öcalan out of Syria on 9 October 1998 eventually delivers him to Turkish officials in Nairobi, Kenya.
The PKK holds its 6th Congress in Kurdistan. Öcalan's capture is announced during the Congress, and the congress participants declare an all-out struggle.
24–26 May: The Kurdistan National Congress (*Kongra Netewiya Kurdistan*, KNK) is formed in Amsterdam.

1999–2000 Öcalan's trial begins on İmralı Island. He is sentenced to death but the ECHR intervenes to prevent the sentence being carried out. Öcalan announces strategic changes and advises the PKK to pull its armed forces out of Turkey. It does.

2000   23 January: The People's Defence Force (HPG) is established as part of the PKK's strategic transition with a military strategy based on self-defence.

2002   May: The EU lists the PKK as a "terrorist organisation", strengthening the hand of the Turkish state just when the PKK had declared that it would quit active war. The decision of the EU strikes a blow to peace.
4–10 April: The PKK dissolves itself and forms the Kurdistan Freedom and Democracy Congress (KADEK).

2003   27 October–6 November: KADEK is replaced by the People's Congress (*Kongra-Gel*), open to all, not just cadres, and presided by a civilian.

2004   The PKK declares that it is going to concentrate on ideological activities and not deal with administrative matters. The Party of Free Women (PJA) changes its name to the Kurdistan Women's Liberation Party (PAJK). The leading ideological party in the Kurdish women's revolution, its programme focuses on free life, free women, free men and society, and militant leadership.

2005   17 May: The Kurdistan Communities Union (KCK) is established as a result of Öcalan's theories. Representing Kurds from all parts of Kurdistan, it is run by an administrative council.

2006   7–18 April: The establishment of the High Women's Council (KJB) strengthens the Kurdish women's movement.
October: The KCK declares a ceasefire at the request of government circles. However, the Turkish Armed Forces immediately launch military operations.

2007   Indirect dialogue between the Turkish state and the PKK is initiated by intermediaries in Oslo.

2009–2011 Öcalan meets regularly with the same Turkish delegation that meets with PKK officials in Oslo and agrees to write a roadmap for peace. However, the State confiscates the roadmap and only releases it 14 months later.

2011   Öcalan prepares a protocol requested by the Turkish government delegation. He presents it to the PKK, which accepts it; he then presents it to the government, which leaves it unanswered and continues with its usual persecution and suppression.
September: A Turkish news agency releases audio recordings of failed peace talks secretly held in Oslo between the MİT and senior PKK officials.
October: Kurdish rebels kill 24 Turkish soldiers in one of the deadliest attacks in years.
December: Thirty-four civilians are killed in a botched Turkish airstrike in Roboski near the Iraqi border.

2012   September: Hundreds of imprisoned Kurds launch a hunger strike, demanding language rights and better prison conditions for Öcalan.
December: Ankara acknowledges nascent peace talks between the MİT and Öcalan with the goal of disarming the PKK.

2013   January: Two Kurdish lawmakers pay a landmark visit to Öcalan in prison.
Three Kurdish activists, including PKK co-founder Sakine Cansız, are shot dead in Paris.
23 February: A second delegation of Kurdish lawmakers visits Öcalan in prison as part of the new peace efforts.
13 March: Kurdish rebels free eight Turkish prisoners in response to the peace push.
21 March: Öcalan calls for a ceasefire in a letter issued to mark the Kurdish New Year, telling militants to lay down their arms and leave Turkey.

A History of Banned and Reformed Legal Kurdish Parties

1990   7 October: The People's Labour Party (HEP) is founded by 15 Kurdish MPs from the Social Democratic People's Party (SHP) of Turkey who were kicked out for attending a Kurdish conference in Paris.
1991 The HEP wins 18 seats in general elections.

1992   The Constitutional Court bans the HEP. The Freedom and Democracy Party (OZDEP) is formed to replace it. Soon after, the court also bans OZDEP.

1993   7 May: With the HEP case ongoing, the Democracy Party (DEP) is formed.
1993 July: The Constitutional Court outlaws the HEP; all its MPs join the DEP.

1994   2 March: Kurdish MPs Leyla Zana, Hatip Dicle, Orhan Doğan, Ahmet Turk, Sırrı Sakık, and Mahmut Alınak lose their diplomatic immunity and are tried in the State Security Courts. They are sentenced to a total of 895 years.
16 June: The DEP is banned. Most Kurds boycott the local elections.
May: The People's Democracy Party (HADEP) is founded under the leadership of Murat Bozlak.

1995   24 December: HADEP takes part in the general elections in a coalition with a few leftist parties, but falling short of the 10% election threshold, is not represented in Parliament.
October: The Democratic People's Party (DEHAP) is formed under the leadership of Tuncer Bakırhan.

1999   18 April: DEHAP wins no seats in Parliament due to the 10% threshold, but wins 37 local councils in the local elections.

2003   13 March: HADEP is banned by the State and 46 of its activists are banned from politics. HADEP was the longest lasting legal Kurdish party. Threatened by banning efforts, DEHAP dissolves itself.

2005   The Democratic Society Party (DTP) is founded and wins 69 local councils. It introduces the co-chair system to Turkish politics: Ahmet Turk and Aysel Tuğluk are appointed.

2007   22 July: The DTP decides to participate in general elections by running independent candidates in an effort to pass the threshold: it wins 22 seats in Parliament.

2008   May: The Peace and Democracy Party (BDP) is founded.

2009   November: A case is opened against the DTP. The party wins 99 local councils.
11 December: The Constitutional Court bans the DTP and expels Ahmet Turk and Aysel Tuğluk from Parliament.

2010   The DTP MPs join the BDP. Kurds boycott a referendum on amending the constitution because no amendments aim to solve the Kurdish question.

2011   12 June: The BDP takes part in the general elections by supporting independent candidates through the "Labour, Democracy and Freedom" bloc. The party wins 36 seats in Parliament (including six imprisoned candidates who are not released).

Appendix III: Kurdistan National Congress (KNK)
Excerpts from KNK Statement, January 1, 2014

The KNK's founding congress was held in Amsterdam on 24th May 1999 as a result of four years of discussions and planning within the Kurdish movement. The event marks a major breakthrough in the political organization of the Kurds, bringing together representatives from all parts of the divided Kurdistan with the common aim to solve the disunity between Kurdish political parties.

The Kurdistan National Congress was created to embody the moral unity of the Kurdish nation and to elaborate a concerted strategy for a democratic solution to the Kurdish question within the existing states. The KNK Charter, adopted on 26 May 1999, outlines its aims and objectives:

> For the sake of strengthening cooperation and the common struggle among the parts of Kurdistan, the Congress works on the basis of national unity and the main interests of the people of Kurdistan.
>
> The Congress tries to solve the problems among the people of Kurdistan and the neighboring countries peacefully and in a friendly manner.
>
> The Congress rejects all forms of violence, but supports defensive measures.
>
> The Congress recognizes the social reality of Kurds and Kurdistan, and supports and implements the principle of positive discrimination towards women's participation in all its activities, projects and organizations.
>
> The Congress supports the national liberation struggle of Kurdistan in all parts (Turkey, Iran, Iraq and Syria) and regards the provision of any kind of necessary support for the sake of achieving political organization as its duty.

The Congress, as a representative establishment of the people of Kurdistan, works on an international level for the sake of obtaining and maintaining its interests and cooperates with the political organizations of Kurdistan.

The Congress supports the preservation of freedom and liberation for all the religions, sects, and beliefs in Kurdistan.

The Congress works for the revival and progress of the Kurdish language and culture.

The Congress tries to achieve peace in the Middle East and the world, as well as working against all forms of discrimination and extremism.

KNK Activities

The Congress resides temporarily in Brussels until their return to Kurdistan. It is expanding its activities worldwide and now has offices in many major cities. Its work consists of:

- The political lobbying of governments, the EU, the European Parliament, Council of Europe, the UN and other international institutions;
- Disseminating regular information about the changing situation in Kurdistan to the media and public;
- Organizing meetings, seminars, conferences and events promoting Kurdish history and culture;
- Publishing materials, including an official KNK bulletin;
- Working alongside politicians, NGOs, human rights group, women's groups, trade unions and others to raise awareness about political issues and human rights violations in all parts of Kurdistan.

Main points decided at the 13th General Meeting of KNK, held in Brussels on 25–26 May 2013

Kurdistan as a nation has the right to live and create their own destiny as a Kurdish nation in their own land. Democratisation of Middle East can be achieved through the recognition of Kurdish identity and Kurdistan as a nation. Therefore, those countries that are either directly or indirectly involved have to recognize this problem, change their position on this important and sensitive issue, and listen to the Kurdish people's wishes. On these grounds Kirkuk and other parts of the Kurdish region that were taken have to be included again in the map of Kurdistan, and these countries have to show their respect for the map of Kurdistan and its territory.

In this very important gathering the Kurds have paid particular attention to the developments in western Kurdistan (within Syrian state territory). We fully support our Kurdish brothers and sisters who are right now fighting for their freedom.

In the northern part of Kurdistan, there is a peace process initiated by Kurdish leader Mr. Öcalan. We are calling on the Turkish government and other countries that may have interest in this process to listen very carefully to the wishes for a democratic solution for the Kurdish nation. Therefore, the peace solution or road map, proposed by the Kurdish leader, has to be taken into account in order to achieve a permanent peace in the country. Therefore, we are calling on Turkey to release Mr. Öcalan and all other Kurdish political prisoners.

The national struggle of the eastern part of Kurdistan has to develop further, and we are ready for a new process to achieve our goals through peaceful means. We have to be ready for these changes and the national unity of our people.

Our meeting clearly declares that there are other ethnic groups living among our national geography, and these nations and ethnic minorities are to be protected, respected on their religion, creed, and beliefs etc., and we are to establish a secular democratic system, which will respect every other people in the region

Abdullah Öcalan and the Peace Process

Following the interruption of talks in 2011, the Turkish National Intelligence Service (MİT), acting on behalf of Prime Minister Erdoğan, the AKP government, and by extension the full authority of the Turkish State, restarted dialogue at the end of 2012 with imprisoned PKK leader Abdullah Öcalan, who remains the representative of the Kurdish people. These talks were acknowledged in public at the time of the Newroz celebrations in March 2013. The main Kurdish demands remain a political solution to the Kurdish question and the democratisation of the region. The proposed solution put forward by Abdullah Öcalan and adopted by the Kurdish movement is for self-administration by the local people of their affairs through a system of 'Democratic Autonomy'.

In order to turn the process of dialogue into serious negotiations, three steps would be necessary: the implementation of a legal framework for negotiations, the formation of supervisory bodies, and the establishment of a permanent commission to oversee the negotiations. Abdullah Öcalan has to be released from the "Turkish Guantanamo" in İmralı in order to be free to negotiate on an equal basis with the Turkish side. This is an essential prerequisite before any successful outcome can be reached by the participants. To date, no serious proposals from the Turkish state have been presented for consideration on the way forward. In addition, there have been many serious provocations aimed at derailing the peace process such as the arrest of leading KNK politician Adem Uzun, the Paris assassinations, the violent response to the Gezi Park protests, the Lice and Yüksekova massacres, the Roboski incident, as well as ongoing political operations and heightened tensions against Kurds. Turkish military operations on the border have seen frequent clashes with Kurdish guerrillas despite ceasefires in which they have sought to avoid confrontation and taken up defensive positions. Infighting amongst Turkish rivals for power, the AKP, and the Gülen Movement have also led the peace process to an impasse.

Despite these setbacks, Abdullah Öcalan and the Kurdish side have remained consistent in their aims for peace based on guaranteed rights for the Kurds in a new constitution. They are determined that a democratic solution can be achieved by peaceful means and have resisted provocations to be drawn into conflict, remaining steadfast in self-defence. [...]

Appendix IV: Rojava and Kurdish Unity
Excerpts from KNK Statement (January 1, 2014)

The Kurdish people of Rojava issued a declaration of Democratic Autonomy in November 2013 when three multilingual and multicultural cantons were established by the Kurdish Supreme Council in the liberated region of Syria.

The Kurds appointed a governing council for the canton of Jazeera on 21 January 2014. This is one of the three cantons in the country's northeast which is called "Rojava" and which came under the control of Kurds as the civil war raged elsewhere in Syria. "Soon similar councils will be named for Afrin and Kobani, the two other cantons of the Kurdish regions in Rojava," Saleh Muslim, head of the Democratic Union Party (PYD), was quoted as saying.

Saleh Muslim said the 22-member council for Jazeera was a necessary step "to ensure there is no political vacuum." The PYD has been leading the struggle against jihadi opposition groups such as the Islamic State of Iraq and the Levant (ISIS) which have sought to drag the Kurds into the wider conflict.

The 22-member Jazeera council includes representatives with defence, security, planning, and finance portfolios. "We cannot wait until there is a political solution for the Syrian crisis to start running our affairs on the ground. People have to have their basic needs covered," said Saleh Muslim, who stressed that the council was made up of representatives from the different communities that live in the region and was not exclusively Kurdish. "Muslim and Christian Arabs are also taking part. The idea is not for self-rule to be exclusive at all."

With the support and recognition of Rojava, the time has come for the realization of the unity of all Kurdish groups. This can be achieved through a Kurdish National Conference which a preparatory committee is working to organize in an attempt to bring together representatives of Kurds from all the different parts of Kurdistan. Developments in Rojava have inspired Kurds everywhere and the fate of the region will have a dramatic impact on Kurds living in Iran and Turkey. It is anticipated that it should help guarantee the official status for all the Kurds. [...]

PART TWO:
Campaigns of
International Solidarity

Abdullah Öcalan: A Life of Four Decades of Resistance

Havin Guneser, journalist and spokesperson for the International Initiative
"Freedom for Öcalan—Peace in Kurdistan"
February 2015

Editors' Note: *In this article, Havin Guneser of the International Initiative, "Freedom for Öcalan—Peace in Kurdistan", explains the history relevant to the International Initiative's solidarity campaigns. Originally published in August of 2014 in German in* The Kurdistan Report, *this article was modified and published in English in* The Kurdish Question *in February 2015, and updated for this book in 2018.*

What makes people go on resisting and struggling despite the hardships, oppression, and threats to their lives? It must be what makes us human: our ability to imagine—to imagine that another world is possible. This is exactly what Abdullah Öcalan and his early group of friends including Haki Karer, Sakine Cansız, Kemal Pir, Mazlum Doğan, and others began doing in the late 1960s and early 1970s. Imagining. Who could escape the revolutionary power and the after-effects of 1968? The global rebellions of 1968 entirely transformed how people viewed the world and exposed the pretences of liberalism. Öcalan and his fellow activists were lifted up by this wave, as was the Left in Turkey (especially Mahir Cayan, Deniz Gezmis and Ibrahim Kaypakkaya), and felt themselves connected to other radical liberation movements, such as the Vietnamese National Liberation Front.

The early group that formed around Öcalan's inspired thinking consisted not only of Kurds, but revolutionaries from several ethnic groups. Women were included from the beginning in this grouping that would become the Kurdish Workers Party, known as the PKK. They imagined that there could be a life without oppression, exploitation of women, colonisation, and nationalist chauvinism. They rejected the false imaginings of the Kemalist state that the Kurdish people did not exist and did not have the right to continue their existence. They substituted their own imagining that they had a right to exist and that their liberation was tied to liberation of all people in Turkey. While imagining the right of a people to exist may sound simple today, back then, the genocidal policies (in both physical and cultural forms), the extent of auto-assimilation, as well as the internal political structures established by the colonisers—through political parties and collaborators—made it very difficult to imagine anything at all.

These simple, but daring, imaginings cost them dearly. It cost the wider Kurdish society dearly too. If freedom were so easy to attain, human society would not have been fighting for it for the past five thousand years. This is why capitalism, more powerfully than all other patriarchal political systems, tries to blunt our imagination. Its masters insist that liberation is not possible, that this freedom-less life is the only life. To prove this, they point to the collapse of the Soviet Union, the standstill of feminism, and the inability of alternative movements to construct an alternative life.

Many different social movements around the world simply refused to stop imagining that another world is possible. Öcalan and the Kurdish freedom movement belong to this category. Despite all attempts by Turkey, and then by the world powers, to suffocate this newborn movement, Öcalan and his fellow comrades, have managed to survive and continue their struggle. The Kurdish freedom movement may be unique in sustaining itself through persistent assault, as well as the ups and downs, not only of capitalism, but also the collapse of state socialism and the subsequent helplessness that discouraged many revolutionaries. Other national liberation movements succeeded in gaining control of the countries whose rulers they once resisted. The PKK saw the result of this; these revolutionaries turned into rulers themselves. Other critical lessons were learned. The PKK itself, Öcalan says, experienced "real socialism"—complete with bureaucracy and centralization—while still a movement and this was highly instructive. The women's movement, at its height in the 1980s and 1990s, also influenced the PKK at a time when the former was still engaged in radical women's liberation. These experiences and conditions shaped and sustained the PKK as it adapted following its open and critical analysis of its own shortcomings and those of other liberation movements.

Today, while we enjoy great achievements against enslavement, colonisation, and fascism, we are also witnessing the revival of these evils. This calls for a major re-analysis of these oppressive structures, and also of the alternative movements themselves. What revolutionary ideas and practices were, or are, wrong? Most alternative movements have not struggled to understand this situation, but instead have either plunged into dogmatism, been co-opted by liberalism, or have vanished. But Öcalan and his comrades asked: how could we act differently? Again, the key element is imagination. They refused to accept the world as it was—that there was nothing more to imagine. Increasingly, and more so after 1994, Öcalan spent most of his time searching for answers. Already in the 1980s, he had become quite critical of the Soviet Union and socialist states. He was also highly critical of the Turkish Left in the aftermath of the military coup of 1980. Perhaps the complexities of the Kurdish question, and the fact that the PKK had the ability to act independently of "the Left," made it easier to seek the truth. The circumstances gave no room for false answers or deception, because a wrong step would mean elimination by one power or another.

Öcalan is anything but dogmatic; he is a true dialectician. He understands that all systems have lifetimes and, thus, are temporary. They come into existence, but not because they are pre-determined, necessary or natural. They continue on the basis of certain rules before they reach an equilibrium. Later, they shift from that equilibrium until it is no longer possible for the status quo to remain stable. This is exactly what we are going through at the moment. Capitalism is in a structural crisis and our world is in a chaotic situation. Öcalan has been writing about this extensively since the 1990s, but even more so in his prison writings authored from his cell on İmralı Island since 1999. This chaotic situation, he warns, may evolve in unexpectedly progressive ways. Not only is there an opportunity to change the 500-year-old hegemonic rule of capitalism, but there is also the chance to change the patriarchal system altogether. He, along with other intellectuals such as Immanuel Wallerstein, predicts that the struggle will be fierce and will determine our lives for least another century, if not longer. And looking at what is going on around the world and in the Middle East currently, there is apparently truth to this vision. Thus, from his one-person cell in an island prison, he is trying to ensure that all oppressed peoples, including the Kurds, are able to implement an alternative political system, and that they are protected from the bloodbath that is prepared for them at each step of the way.

They say that beginnings determine the end. The PKK began as a multi-ethnic organisation. Under the guidance of the PKK, the Kurdish people achieved their right to exist as a people; yet also, under its guidance, they have struggled both externally and internally against sexism and patriarchy, both of which are hierarchical and state-based ideologies. The Kurdish freedom movement simply refuses to be assimilated into the capitalist system—a resistance built from the lessons learned from what befell other national liberation movements. Because of this refusal, they have been the victims of immense antagonistic propaganda that has perpetuated an erasure of their existence.

Let us give the example of Rojava (the Kurdish-majority part of Syria). At first there was much reaction against the Kurds by the superpowers of the world because the Kurds refused to fall into the trap that so many other uprisings did in Egypt, Libya, and elsewhere around the world. The Kurds refused to participate in wars that only brought bloodshed. Instead they opted for Öcalan's third way: to unite with all the peoples that lived in the region in order to form self-governance based on radical democracy, women's freedom, an alternative economy, and an ecological life. They were ignored and excluded from any discussion that was held to resolve the conflicts in Syria. But the newly formed cantons are persisting and are trying to establish a sphere of peoples' governance that assures that all identities can flourish. This is a sphere of freedom.

Against this sphere of freedom is the sphere of fascism represented by ISIS. ISIS is fundamentally opposed to the plurality of diverse identities in the region. This is why it so fiercely attacks the Kurds (including Sunni Kurds), Assyrians, Turkmen, Yezidis, Shias, and Christians and attempts to ethnically and culturally cleanse the region. It is a strategy for the total militarisation of the society. ISIS promotes complete and total male supremacy, pushing women back to sub-servient roles in society and uses sexual violence as its strategy of war. Indeed, ISIS is a perfect embodiment of Öcalan's concept of the system of the dominant male. No matter how ISIS disguises itself, it is nothing but pure fascism at work. Öcalan's paradigm of freedom is just the right antidote whether we look at it from the point of view of religious, ethnic, or women's freedom. He has been trying to break the vicious cycle of divide and conquer through demonization of adversaries and acts of vengeance. This is the goal of his profound analysis of state, power, and hierarchy and how they form the basis of the freedom-less life.

İmralı Island Prison and Öcalan

Öcalan is now 69 years old and has been kept at İmralı Island Prison in the Turkish Marmara Sea, guarded by 1000 soldiers, for 19 years. For almost 11 years, from 1999 to 2009, he was the sole prisoner on the island. Since July 2011, he has not seen his lawyers. Two of his lawyers were arrested in the early batch of raids targeting Kurdistan Communities Congress (KCK) representatives, while 34 lawyers were arrested after 27 July 2011. All the lawyers were released in 2014 but since July 2011, none of Öcalan's lawyers have been able to see their client. Since October 2014 his family has been barred from the island except for a very short meeting that was permitted with his brother in September 2016. Following heightened warfare and a massive hunger strike by political prisoners, a rare political opening in early 2013 allowed for talks between Öcalan and political delegations from the Turkish government and the HDP (Peoples' Democratic Party). In April 2015 Turkish President Erdoğan halted talks and the political delegation of HDP parliamentarians could no longer confer with him.

The same restrictions also apply to the other few inmates of İmralı Island Prison. As a result, we have no way of knowing how Öcalan and his three other comrades are. The European Committee for the Prevention of Torture and Inhuman or Degrading Treatment or Punishment (CPT) described the situation to be "indisputable isolation." Literally anything can happen or has happened there. Despite obvious international human rights violations evidenced by this treatment, the rules of the game are still arbitrarily determined by the Turkish state, and human rights organizations remain largely silent on his case. Political processes to resolve "the Kurdish question" cannot and should not stand in the way of Öcalan's legal and human rights. He is, essentially, under these conditions, a prisoner of war. Thus, we have always maintained that political talks cannot continue as they have been: they must turn into negotiations. And for that, Öcalan must be free. Mandela has a befitting quote for this situation: "Only free men can negotiate. A prisoner cannot enter into contracts."

The Turkish state's treatment of Öcalan is a precise indicator of the Turkish state's attitude towards the Kurds. The demand for more self-determination of the Kurdish regions, a topic of negotiations, has been answered by pure state violence and terror. The current total isolation of the whole İmralı Island Prison— which is now spilling over to other prisons—is not only unprecedented in the history of Turkey, and a grave violation of the European Convention on Human Rights (ECHR). It is also very likely foreshadowing a massive escalation of the conflict. Present isolation, together with the removal of two inmates from İmralı, raises even more concerns and alarm in the aftermath of collapse of negotiations in early 2015. 2016 saw unprecedented state violence and terror in Kurdish cities in Turkey and in neighboring Syria. Kurdish towns and cities are besieged by the Turkish army and dozens of civilians have been killed. Under winter conditions, water and electricity supplies were cut off and food became scarce due to round-the-clock curfews—all with an intention of forcing the population out and changing the demographics of Kurdish towns. Historical sites and ecological resources are also being targeted and destroyed. The Turkish army invaded and occupied the Afrin canton in Northern Syria in March 2018 with the help of jihadist gangs, and is setting up military bases in Kurdish areas of Northern Iraq. With new powers gained through the constitutional referendum and the recent snap election, the AKP is reconstructing the Turkish state together with MHP towards even more undemocratic and fascist rule with a direct aim of attacking Kurdish aspirations everywhere.

Despite this, and with an understanding of what is at stake in such a chaotic political situation, Öcalan has continued to focus on resolving the Kurdish question and the democratisation of Turkey and the Middle East. To this end, he has continued to build bridges between peoples. Despite his aggravated isolation, the Kurdish people endorse his leadership in recognition of his foresight and ability to make decisions that strengthen the position of the Kurds and promote the amity between peoples. His strict incarceration has not reduced his stature, nor the respect in which he is held. The reason is very simple and must be seen in the context of his leadership over the years and in light of the rapidly changing political conditions. The fact that Öcalan and the freedom movement were able to lead the Kurdish people from a condition of "nonexistence" to a potent resistance and quest for another form of living, despite many life-threatening obstacles is what has made the trust in him unshakeable. The prison bars have never stopped him overcoming colonisation and raising demands for freedom. He has inspired, and continues to inspire, the Kurdish peoples' demand for freedom. He is the symbol of their struggle against denial and colonialism, and, as a result, most Kurds view him as a guardian of peace and democracy.

A World-Wide Campaign: Freedom for Öcalan

From the first day it was formed in March 1999 (not even a month after Öcalan's abduction), the International Initiative has never lost its belief in the possibility of his freedom, and the possibility of peace in Kurdistan. The International Initiative—thanks to the support it has received from ordinary people, intellectuals, and personalities around the world—has worked non-stop to achieve a just peace by helping to repair ties between the Kurdish and Turkish peoples, as well as all other peoples of the region. The work has taken many shapes and many different tools have been used.

When the International Initiative decided to start a worldwide signature campaign in September 2012, Öcalan had already been kept under eight months of total isolation in what has become the Guantanamo prison at the heart of

Europe. There was no indication as to when this total isolation would end. Human rights organisations either had no mandate to act, were lost in bureaucracy, or simply viewed this as a precedent for our diminishing rights. After all, who would argue in favour of a person deemed a 'terrorist' by state powers? This continues to be the case today. Although the death penalty was no longer legally available, this was a time when it was the most used rhetorically.

Given the gravity of the situation, preparations began six months in advance of launching the world-wide signature campaign. In Brussels on 6 September 2012, International World Peace Day, the official start of the campaign was initiated by one thousand preliminary signatories including Gerry Adams, Prof. Antonio Negri, Prof. Immanuel Wallerstein, Prof. Achin Vanaik, and other intellectuals, politicians, MPs, and NGOs from South America, Europe, Asia, Russia, and the Middle East.

The goal was ambitious: to shatter the silence of the international public and to break the total isolation, which had never been so intense and long since Öcalan was abducted in 1999. This was the reason behind the demand for the release of him and all other political prisoners. We had arrived at a point where we were no longer just talking about a political leader or an individual—he was at the centre of the destiny of the Kurdish people and even the Middle East.

Before the International Initiative began, the Kurdish Human Rights Group in South Africa (KHRG) was also consulted and their support was attained, which numbered in the tens of thousands. At the same time, NGOs, trade unions, and political parties from the Basque country, Cyprus, Peru, Philippines, Germany, England, and France supported the signature campaign. It is important to recognize the work by Fidan Doğan, who was murdered in Paris in 2013 by Turkish agents. Her efforts resulted in strong support from the French Communist Party as well as many well-known NGOs and individuals.

The Real Influence of Such Campaigns

To date, many signature campaigns, protests, and marches demanding Öcalan's freedom have been realised. Since 25 June 2012, a continuous vigil for his freedom has been held in Strasbourg in front of the Council of Europe buildings. In February 2015 a demonstration for freedom for Öcalan marched for 12 days in extreme winter cold from three different starting points: Luxemburg, Frankfurt, and Bern. All these have helped to improve his situation and that of the Kurdish people in general. When we look at the world of the 1970s, Kurdish people were invisible and denied their rights, not only in Iran, Iraq, Syria, and Turkey, but also in Europe and around the world. By contrast, now Kurds are recognized as not only the most dynamic and revolutionary movement of Turkey, but perhaps also that of the Middle East and the world. The reason is simple: the Kurds are not just rebelling, they are organised, and like their sister resisters, the Zapatistas of Mexico, have a clear picture of their alternative. In that light, since 2012 Challenging Capitalist Modernity conferences have been held bi-annually bringing together intellectuals, activists, movements, journalists, students and other who convene to discuss in depth the parameters of what a free life may be and to organize international solidarity.

For the last several years, there have been many campaigns by many different organisations and each and every campaign has brought its own focus. For example, the Free Citizen Movement in Turkey started a signature campaign that declared "Öcalan represents my political will," and in 2005–2006 it gathered 3.5 million signatures despite the arrests, imprisonments, oppression, and confiscation of signatures in both Turkey and Europe. Given that the Kurdish people have no recognised collective right as a people to elections or referendum, such campaigns have huge significance in declaring their demands and will.

Indeed, the campaign that ran from 2005 to 2006 was a response to the colonialist insistence by Turkey and European states that the Kurds: "Find yourselves another leader." The result of that campaign enabled the Kurds to invalidate such demands. While on the one hand, a racist-colonial regime may attempt to invent statistics and narratives to legitimise its own goals, the Kurds and others, including intellectuals, responsible politicians, and progressive NGOs, have mobilised to shatter these projections. The Kurds have thus added to the declaration that Öcalan is their 'political representative' the additional demand for his freedom.

The signature campaign has continued around the world, with a renewed aim to undo prejudices towards him and the Kurdish people's struggle for existence and freedom. We have tried to correct misinformation and to educate society about the truth of the struggle and its events from its beginning to the present. As a result of official colonial policies, Öcalan and the Kurdish people have been cast in a poor light, and even criminalised in much of the world. It has thus been important to find creative methods and exert effort to counteract this negative propaganda. It is time for the European states to enact policies that recognize the political, social, and cultural rights and standing of the Kurdish people.

In addition, despite the oppressive conditions in Rojava and other parts of Kurdistan, we are happy to say that many ordinary Kurds have recently joined the campaign. In Turkey in particular, people have yet again been arrested for collecting or giving signatures. Yet many inspiring and brave people have come forward to support the campaign. It was possible to see people from many nationalities in trams, in front of universities, or in city squares and shopping centres collecting signatures. Some found methods to make their signature collection more creative. In Sweden, for example, those who gave their signatures were given a lemon with the word "terrorist" written on it. Why? Because, in Turkey, whoever was caught with a lemon was immediately arrested as lemon juice was effective in counteracting the burning effects of pepper spray used by the Turkish security forces against protesters.

Although initiated and led by the International Initiative, we are proud to say that the campaign has become everyone's. Many Kurdish organisations as well as the French Communist Party, KHRAG–South Africa, other world-wide organisations, institutions, and personalities from the Philippines, the Basque country, Germany, and Britain among others have given the campaign top priority. There has been participation from all continents around the world. This is what makes it a world-wide campaign.

We often have people ask us whether our signature campaigns and protest actions have any effect at all. These actions, and the solidarity displayed by all Kurds around the world (simultaneously) when Öcalan was abducted, not only prevented the imposition of the death penalty, but also paved the way for future dialogue. We would like to once again acknowledge the efforts and work of individuals around Europe and the allies of the Kurdish people around the world for their effort, creativity, and persistence in this petition campaign which officially ended in 2015. The campaign reached 10,328,623 signatures and may be the biggest signature campaign for the freedom of a political prisoner that the world has ever seen. Connecting with so many people, explaining the Kurds' situation to them, and obtaining so many signatures was in itself a significant accomplishment. To this end, many different materials in many different languages were prepared by the International Initiative. These can be found at our websites www.freeocalan.org or ocalan-books.com. The materials created from such campaigns will be used for many years to come.

The Art for Öcalan Campaign

In parallel we have also initiated an "Art for Öcalan" campaign to stimulate creative expression of the relationship between Öcalan, the Kurdish people, free life, and women's freedom. It also aims to educate the wider public on the history of the movement, the demands of the Kurdish people, and Öcalan's philosophical contribution. We already have an extensive body of work that has come in from Brazil, South Africa, the USA, South America, Italy, and Germany, as well as from Kurds from different parts of Kurdistan. The artwork has included print postcards which we used to send Öcalan twenty thousand birthday cards for his 64th birthday in April 2013. We also printed selected works on T-shirts and on canvas and made them available for a solidarity sale. We plan to organise exhibitions that will display the work that has been done and we are in search of music to be the official song of the campaign. And there is still more that we can do. The details on this campaign can be found at http://art-for-ocalan.org/.

The Time Has Come—Freedom for the Kurdish People

One man stands in the centre of this: Abdullah Öcalan. He is accepted by friends and foe as the leader and political representative of the Kurdish people. He is the most high-profile Kurdish politician. More than 3.5 million Kurds have signed a declaration recognising him as their political representative in 2006 despite severe repression. TIME magazine chose him to be among the 100 most influential persons in 2013. The campaign for his freedom collected more than 10 million signatures. Everyone agrees that a political solution to the Kurdish issue must be negotiated with him.

Since the peace talks in early 2013 and Öcalan's Newroz message of that same year, the Kurdish question had officially taken a new turn. The official policies of Turkey, other countries, and international bodies that deny the political rights of the Kurds have been shattered to pieces. In their place, they have begun the fiercest struggle to determine their destiny and that of other peoples of the region. The new negative developments in Syria and Turkey as well as the new power equations in the region between that of the USA, Russia and Iran are further destabilising the entire region. Although the imminent danger that threatens to eliminate the Kurds lingers on, the hopeful shift to implementing an alternative system involves a change of mentality of each and every individual. An alternative society is not an abstract concept. Just as there is a chance that the Middle East will become a graveyard of cultures and beliefs, there is an even greater chance that it will witness the widening of the sphere of freedom. How the struggle evolves will determine the end result. Thus, on the one hand, imagination is necessary in order to design our dreams. On the other hand, we must articulate these dreams and have the courage to implement them.

Indeed, the Freedom for Öcalan campaign is not just about demanding freedom for an individual, but also it strives to guarantee the irreversible freedom of the Kurdish people and amity between all peoples generally. As has been the case for worldwide struggles against racism and colonialism—Öcalan's freedom shall necessarily mean the freedom for Kurdish people, democracy in Turkey and peace in the Middle East.

My Encounter with the Kurdish Movement

Professor Kariane Westrheim, Department of Education, University of Bergen, Chairperson of the EU Turkey Civic Commission (EUTCC)

Editors' Note: *This is Professor Westrheim's personal reflections on her involvement with the Kurdish freedom movement, as well as her perspective, as the chairperson of the EUTCC, on the organisation's genesis and trajectory, including the inception and goals of its İmralı Delegations.*

The aim of our İmralı Delegations is to monitor the political and human rights situation in Turkey and to place high-level attention on Mr. Abdullah Öcalan's situation in İmralı prison by requesting permission to visit him. The intense psychological and physical torture, suffered by Öcalan for the last 18 years under conditions of solitary confinement, have accelerated with further restrictions imposed on his internment. At present, there are serious concerns for his life.

The İmralı Delegations' ultimate goal is therefore to contribute to the resumption of the peace talks. Since July 24, 2015, Turkey and Kurdistan are experiencing a serious war of attrition; everything and everyone connected to the Kurds or Kurdishness is a target. Since 2015, municipalities in the south-east have been seized and the deputy mayors and Members of Parliament, including the co-leadership of the HDP Selahattin Demirtaş, Figen Yüksekdağ, and 12 HDP deputies, have been placed under arrest together with hundreds of thousands of Kurdish and Turkish civilians.

After years of fighting in the 1980s and 1990s, the Kurdish freedom movement sought to find a political solution to the conflict. Since March 17, 1993, when the General Secretary of the PKK declared its first ceasefire, numerous initiatives have been declared ranging from ceasefires, calls for peace, or setting up a road map for a political solution. There have been times of openings and great hope, but in general all peace initiatives have broken down as a result of Turkey's lack of will to stretch out a hand to its number one state enemy. Being committed to and convinced of the necessity of a peaceful solution of the Kurdish question, the leader of the PKK, Mr. Öcalan, has repeatedly called for peace talks since 1993. Between 2013 and 2015, Mr. Öcalan was the main actor in this process. The talks led to a period of ceasefire until April 2015, the creation of a political atmosphere for the discussion of a solution, and a pluralist and tolerant socio-political platform. However, the peace process that continued in İmralı Island has been replaced by a bloody war that has taken over since July 2015. After the election loss of the AKP government on June 7, 2015 and President Erdoğan's coup in 2016, Kurdish towns such as Cizre, Sur, Nusaybin, Şırnak, Varto, and Silopi were destroyed using tanks, heavy artillery, and helicopters, and curfews were imposed in cities and towns. Approximately 1.5 million people have been affected by this violence. Nearly three thousand people have been killed. The İmralı Delegation has reported from these areas.

My first encounter with the Kurdish freedom movement was nearly fifteen years ago, in the summer of 2002, when I went on a study mission to Turkey accompanied by a former US Ambassador and a leading expert on Kurdish issues, international law, and negotiation. The Rafto Foundation in Norway, better known for its advocacy of human rights, undertook to explore whether such a mission might make a contribution to the process of post-war reconciliation and to advancing dialogue between Turkey and its Kurdish citizens. Rafto became involved in the Kurdish question in 1994 when it awarded Leyla Zana its annual prize at a time when Kurdish political leaders and parliamentarians (of the PKK and others) languished in prison or remained exiled in Europe unable to return home lawfully.

I was excited to take on this mission to Diyarbakır, Ankara, and Istanbul to accompany an experienced diplomat in meeting with more than 40 Turkish and Kurdish interlocutors. In 2002, Turkey tried to align with EU standards and the New Civil Code brought some changes in the areas of gender equality, protection of children and vulnerable persons, and freedom of association. Moreover, the death penalty was abolished. These reforms were welcomed by the Kurdish and Turkish interlocutors. However, the Turkish government had failed to address the root causes of the Kurdish rebellion: the institutional denial of a Kurdish national identity, legal prohibitions on the use of the Kurdish language in the broadcast media and schools, the denial of Kurdish cultural rights, the suppression of normal political activity by Kurdish political leaders, and the grinding poverty in Kurdish majority southeast Turkey. These Kurdish-specific problems were compounded by the legacy of military rule (and the continuing military interference in the political process), in which citizens, and particularly Kurds, had been harassed, imprisoned, and killed for exercising human rights or claiming political rights that are considered standard in western countries.

Kurdish leaders at the time stressed the importance of resolving issues growing out of the 15 year armed conflict in the southeast. These included conditions for the reintegration of PKK combatants, reconstruction of destroyed villages, and the permission for exiled Kurdish leaders (including those from the PKK) to undertake lawful political activity. While some of the Turkish interlocutors we met were sympathetic to all these points, they felt that the first was not essential and the last unrealistic. But they all endorsed the idea of a sponsored dialogue, and indicated an eagerness to take part. The opinion of the Turkish interlocutors were that such a dialogue should supplement the already substantial interchange on human rights between Kurds and other Turkish citizens, and would need to draw in individuals close to the actual power in Turkey, notably the military, the foreign ministry, and the more nationalist political parties. At a minimum, participants would benefit from exposure to negotiating theory and techniques. The interlocutors urged that the first meeting should be followed up as soon as possible after the Turkish elections in 2003,[1] with particular urgency if the more progressive parties prevailed. However, this was not to happen, as Recep Tayyip Erdoğan came into power with his Justice and Development party (AKP). From a rather hopeful political beginning in 2002, Erdoğan turned out to become a totalitarian president in 2014 and with the much questioned referendum in 2017, he won the increased presidential powers that we know have resulted in political and human disaster. This civil attempt for a peace dialogue between Kurdish and Turkish interlocutors stalled due to lack of further funding. The Kurdish movement was ready for dialogue—as it has been up until this day—but possible funders, such as the Ministry of Foreign affairs in Norway, found that the initiative was not important enough for further support.

However, this failed attempt to initiate a peace dialogue definitely motivated me to a new and important initiative in 2004. Some organisations working on Kurdish issues decided to set up a platform or an annual international conference where civil society organizations, academics, European, Turkish, and Kurdish politicians, policy-makers, and activists could come together in order to analyse and discuss crucial issues linked to the Kurdish question in Turkey. The initial sponsoring organisations were the Human Rights Project (UK), the Bar Human Rights Committee of England and Wales, Medico International (Germany), and the Rafto Foundation (Norway). The founding organisations and Kurdish representatives came together for the first time in Brussels to constitute themselves and plan for the first conference in the European Parliament on issues that would hopefully bring Turkey closer to a peaceful democratic solution. The first conference on the EU, Turkey, and the Kurds, entitled "Human Rights Violations and Democratisation in Turkey," took place in 2004, at the very beginning of the accession talks on Turkey's membership to the European Union (EU). The first speakers were well-known names such as Pervin Buldan, now a central figure in the peace talks between Turkey; the Kurdish leader Abdullah Öcalan; Hatip Dicle, one of the MPs that was imprisoned with Leyla Zana in 1994; and Akin Birdal, co-founder of the Human Rights Association of Turkey. Birdal barely survived an assassination attempt in 1998, when 13 shots were fired at him in his office. Birdal was a member of the Grand National Assembly of Turkey for the Democratic Society Party (DTP) from 2007 until 2009 and the Peace and Democracy Party (BDP) from 2009 to 2011. Also present were Francis Wurtz, then Member of the European Parliament, and Denzil Potgieter, an advocate of the High Court of South Africa and member of the Truth and Reconciliation Commission. Archbishop Emeritus Desmond Tutu accepted the invitation to become the first Patron, and opened the conference with a video message in which he gave his name to the Kurdish struggle for peace.

For 14 years now, the EU Turkey Civic Commission (EUTCC) has organised these international conferences in the European Parliament, supported by different political groups. The conference has received international attention and media interest as it has managed to stay close to political developments in Turkey. Having been involved in the organizing of the conferences since their beginning, it is particularly interesting to see that while speakers in 2004 did not even dare to speak about the PKK, or Abdullah Öcalan, this topic now numbers among the most crucial in 2016, with discussions about the resumption of the peace process and about developments in Rojava, North Syria.

One of the people who put the peace process issue on the conference agenda was Judge Essa Moosa, who first joined the conference in 2010 and became a member of the EUTCC in 2011. Judge Moosa was one of Nelson Mandela's first lawyers, a central figure in the African National Congress, and a judge in the Supreme Court in South Africa. Judge Moosa himself experienced, in body and in mind, the dehumanizing Apartheid regime. He and other ANC colleagues regarded the Kurdish movement as having major similarities with the ANC. His huge effort for the promotion of peace and democracy in Turkey and for the re-sumption of the peace process is widely known. Judge Moosa supported the Kurdish struggle with all his heart and used his experiences from the ANC struggle in his sincere efforts for the promotion of peace and the resumption of the peace talks between the Turkish government and Mr. Öcalan. He had a gen-uine belief in people and their ability to stand up against injustice, and he used to say that, even if the road to peace is paved with stumbling stones and hardship, one must never give up hope, as hope is what keeps the struggle on track. Another lesson from Judge Moosa was his firm belief in the power of friendship. A letter[2] from Nelson Mandela to Judge Moosa said: "Dear Essa, Many friends have rallied around us these last 26 years and left us with a lot of courage and hope. (…). Sincerely, Madiba."[3] The tone of the letter shows how close Mandela was to Judge Moosa and how much he trusted him.

Judge Moosa believed in dialogue and referred to his friend Archbishop Emeritus Desmond Tutu who said: "Dialogue between the parties is the only way to secure a peaceful resolution to the conflict, and peace is a precondition for establishing a democratic Turkey. Successful dialogue will make all other methods unnecessary."[4] Encouraged by Judge Moosa, in 2012 Archbishop Tutu issued an international call for the resumption of the peace talks and for the peaceful resolution of the Kurdish question in Turkey. Archbishop Tutu's call was endorsed and supported by leading international political leaders and Nobel Peace Prize Laureates. Amongst them are His Holiness the Dalai Lama, the former presidents Jimmy Carter and Jose Ramos Horta, Sinn Fein leader Gerry Adams, and former prime minister of Norway, Kjell Magne Bondevik. In the wake of the call, Judge Moosa, in cooperation with the EUTCC, established the International Initiative for Peace and Reconciliation (IPRI) at a press conference in the Residence Palace of the European Union in Brusselson December 3, 2012.

In February 2014, the EUTCC and IPRI jointly established the İmralı Delegation, led by Judge Moosa. So far, four delegations have been sent on fact-finding missions to Turkey, Kurdistan, and Strasbourg. Ahead of the 1st Delegation Judge Essa Moosa applied to the Turkish Minister of Justice, requesting a meeting with Mr. Abdullah Öcalan on İmralı Island. He also headed the 2nd İmralı Delegation in April 2016 to the Council of Europe, which I had the chance to also join. In a meeting between the Delegation and staff from the European Committee for the Prevention of Torture and Inhuman or Degrading Treatment or Punishment (CPT), Judge Moosa urged them to pay a visit to İmralı, which the CPT actually did, but they never reported to him as promised.

Judge Essa Moosa had warmth and a way of approaching people that came from his sincere belief in hope, friendship, love, and solidarity; no one who worked with him was left untouched. To watch this humble man so full of affec-tion, passion, and political conviction for the Kurdish cause was for me an un-forgettable learning experience.

Judge Moosa was supposed to lead the Third Delegation to Kurdistan and Turkey February 14–19, 2017, but due to his illness he could not participate. Essa Moosa's former letter was resent to the Minister of Justice who, unfortunately for Turkey did not respond positively to this legitimate request. Tragically,

Turkish authorities chose another direction and violence, killings, repression, military assaults, curfews, countless arrests, infringements of civil rights, and human rights atrocities followed in its wake. Turkey missed its opportunity to welcome Judge Moosa, a unique and experienced mediator for peace. He died in his home in late February 2017. In his spirit we, his friends and colleagues, will continue to put pressure on Turkey to resume peace talks with Mr. Abdullah Öcalan—and we will never give up.

Judge Essa Moosa's love for people in the midst of the struggle surrounded him with an aura you will find only among people who have themselves faced hard struggles. When people trust each other, have faith in each other, and stand firm together, they make eachother strong in order to persevere and hopefully one day succeed. This way of relating to others is also clearly expressed within the Kurdish freedom movement, whether you are in North Kurdistan (Bakur), the refugee camp Maxmur[5], Rojava, or the diaspora. You experience this in political meetings, the co-organization of conferences, campaigns, and events, or, in my case, when conducting my research fieldwork. I am always affected by the positivity, energy, and friendship of those in the movement. Despite all the political tumult, the hardship, and the challenges ahead, the Kurds continue to work, continuing to hope for a peaceful solution ahead—or at least a light in the tunnel. Every time I leave from an encounter with the movement I am filled with new energy and a desire to work further.

As a professor of educational science, knowledge and learning are key issues for me. My experience working with the Kurdish freedom movement over the last 15 years has convinced me that the movement must be regarded as an arena for learning, with prospects for personal growth. For tens of thousands of adults and youth the movement is a school that has provided alternative paths to education; whether the educational activity takes place in the mountains, the streets, in the Kurdish communities, in organisations, or in the Kurdish media. As a researcher, over the years I have visited some of the PKK camps in the mountains. It has been an interesting but also emotional experience to watch how much the guerrillas value education, knowledge, and learning. One of the women fighters that I met had spent more than 25 years in the mountains. She was eager to tell me that she, and many of her comrades, always carried a book in their pocket. She read every day and if she, for different reasons, could not, she felt that she had not worked that day.

Later, when I went to Maxmur, a refugee camp outside Erbil in the Kurdistan Region of Iraq, I encountered the same approach. Young people, whether they were in lower or upper secondary school or vocational school, were proud to tell me how much they valued education. Many of them had participated in the building of their own school. Two young students living in Maxmur told me that they wanted to study; they regarded it as an obligation to get an education in order to help their parents and the community who had done so much in order that the children could to go to school. Their parents never even had the chance to learn to read and write when they lived in Turkey, and their sons and daughters felt that they, by educating themselves, compensated for the injustice committed to their parents. The young students described the cohesion in Maxmur. They would not dream of leaving it in order to fulfill their individual dreams—"either we leave this camp all together, or none of us leaves! At least not until our leader Abdullah Öcalan is released." Without the active involvement of the Kurdish freedom movement, Maxmur would not have survived given all the surrounding political pressure from Turkey and other parties; from a small territory provided to the Kurdish refugees from Turkey, Maxmur has developed into a green and democratically governed oasis.

During a third piece of fieldwork among YPJ fighters in Rojava in 2015, I was met with much of the same attitude to education and learning as I was in the mountains and in Maxmur, all based on trust, friendship, and strong cohesion between the women fighters. They strongly emphasized that in order for women in the Middle East to liberate themselves, education is necessary, and friendship and solidarity is the glue that binds it all together.

That education is a threat for the AKP and President Erdoğan, a fact which became very clear after the so-called coup in Turkey in 2016, the aftermath of which saw thousands of teachers and students expelled from schools and universities, mainly in the Kurdish regions. In areas of political unrest and in politicised fields, schools often become sites for political struggle.[6] In Turkey, many Kurds find educational institutions oppressive and irrelevant. It should be possible to imagine that an educational system that is not seen (and experienced) as relevant will alienate its students. Over the years, many young Kurds have looked beyond formal institutional education towards educational sites that offer alternative education, values, and belief systems, whether these are political, religious, or both. The Kurdish freedom movement has provided knowledge and education to millions of Kurds—and they will continue to do so.

Notes:

1. Recep Tayyip Erdoğan was embraced by the West when he came to power in 2003. He was prime minister until 2014 when he succeeded in becoming president. Initially, he was regarded as a dazzling and charismatic reformer, seeming to embody the promise that Islam and democracy could coexist.

2. Judge Essa Moosa shared with us a personal letter from Nelson Mandela dated August 21, 1989, Victor Verster Prison, South Africa. See the "Joint Statement of the First International İmralı Peace Delegation" in this book for a facsimile of the letter.

3. "Madiba" is the name of a Thembu chief who ruled in the Transkei in the 18th century in a clan of which Mr. Mandela was a member. A clan name is much more important than a surname as it refers to the ancestor from which a person is descended. "Madiba" would be used as a name in "an intimate context." See: www.nelsonmandela.org/content/page/names

4. The EUTCC's message in remembrance of Judge Essa Moosa (February 25, 2017).

5. Maxmur is a refugee camp with approximately 12,000 refugees who fled from Turkey after the military had destroyed and burnt 3–4,000 villages. Maxmur today is a big village or small town founded on Abdullah Öcalan's ideas of democratic autonomy.

6. Grande, S. (2000). "American Indian Identity and Intellectualism: The Quest for a New Red Pedagogy." *International Journal of Qualitative Studies in Education*, 13(4), 343–359.

The EU Turkey Civic Commission and the Peace in Kurdistan UK Campaign

Michael Gunter (Secretary General, EUTCC) and
Kariane Westrheim (Chairperson, EUTCC)

Editors' Notes: This is a joint statement by Professors Gunter and Westrheim in which they provide a brief sketch of the history and purpose of the EU Turkey-Civic Commission. Below is a summary of the Peace in Kurdistan UK campaign and the Campaign Against Criminalising Communities.

The EUTCC was established in November 2004 following what became its first of now 14 international conferences titled "The European Union, Turkey, the Middle East and the Kurds", held at the European Parliament in Brussels, Belgium. The Rafto Foundation (Norway), Kurdish Human Rights Project (UK), Medico International (Germany), and Bar Human Rights Committee of England and Wales (UK) were the organizations that founded the EUTCC, but are no longer involved.

During these years the European United Left/Nordic Green Left (GUE/NGL) Group in the EU Parliament was the first political group to support the new international initiative and continues its crucial support. Stefano Squarcina, a staff member of the GUE-NGL, has provided invaluable logistical support since 2004. Other political groups joined later, such as the Progressive Alliance of Socialists and Democrats (S&D) and Group of the Greens/European Free Alliance.

What we experienced was that prominent individuals were eager to support the initiative: among them Nobel Prize Peace Laureates Archbishop Emeritus Desmond Tutu (South Africa) and Shirin Ebadi (Iran), as well as Noam Chomsky (United States) and Leyla Zana (Turkey), who have served as patrons since the very beginning. Recently, just to show the breadth of support, Baroness Helena Kennedy QC House of Lords, UK, Simon Dubbins, UNITE International Director, and Doug Nicholls, who is the General Secretary of the General Federation of Trade Unions in the UK, have also supported the EUTCC as patrons.

The EUTCC works closely with international human rights organizations, the Kurdish Institute in Brussels, significant NGOs and foundations, international campaigns such as the UK-based Peace in Kurdistan Campaign, and the Campaign Against Criminalising Communities (CAMPACC), co-founded by Estella Schmid; she is also a founding member of the EUTCC and a member of its board of directors (see Appendices I, II, and III).

The initial goal of the EUTCC is to promote Turkish accession to the EU as a means to help solve the Kurdish problem in that country through guaranteed respect for human rights and minority rights and a peaceful, democratic and long-term solution to the Kurdish problem. Thus, the EUTCC monitors and conducts regular audits of Turkey's compliance with the EU accession requirements as listed in the Copenhagen Criteria, although the work of the EUTCC extends beyond Turkey. The last couple of years it has had a particular focus on the situation in Syria, specifically on the Democratic Federation of Northern Syria (Rojava). The EUTCC also makes recommendations, acts as a point of contact, and exchanges information with the institutions of the EU and other governmental and non-governmental organizations inside and outside of Europe.

Over the years, a host of government practitioners, scholars, journalists, lawyers, NGOs and community activists, among many others, from Europe, the Middle East, South Africa, India, and the United States, to name a few, have presented a wide variety of speeches dealing with Kurdish issues in all parts of Kurdistan. Each annual conference has a specific thematic title reflecting the current phase of developments regarding the issues. The EUTCC provides an international platform where Kurdish politicians and spokespersons can discuss crucial issues with European politicians as well as representatives from international politics and organizations. Turkish political parties and organizations are always invited to the EUTCC conferences, but so far, Turkish political representatives, for example from the AKP, have never accepted the invitation.

Conference presenters have included the top levels of Kurdish politics: Selahattin Demirtaş, lawyer and co-chair of the pro-Kurdish Peoples' Democratic Party (HDP) in the Turkish parliament, who was arrested on groundless accusations together with co-chair Figen Yüksekdağ in November 2017; Osman Baydemir, the well-known former Kurdish mayor of Diyarbakır; and Salih Muslim and Asya Abdullah, the former co-chairs of the Democratic Union Party (PYD) in Syria. Others who have contributed include David Phillips, the Director of the Peace-Building and Human Rights Program at Columbia University; Michael Rubin, a resident scholar at the American Enterprise Institute think-tank in Washington, DC; Lincoln Davis, a former US Congressman and co-chair of the Kurdish Caucus in the US Congress; Cengiz Çandar and Hasan Cemal, both renowned Turkish journalists; Josef Weidenholzer, a MEP and vice-president of the Progressive Alliance of Socialists and Democrats in the EU Parliament; Gabi Zimmer, a MEP and Chairwoman of the European United Left-Nordic Green Left Group in the EU Parliament; Hamit Bozarslan and Abbas Vali, two renowned Kurdish academic scholars; and Jonathan Steele, a veteran British foreign correspondent. These, among many others, have all participated.

What, then, is the significance of these annual EUTCC conferences internationally and for the Kurds themselves? Have the annual conferences contributed to any significant changes? Although the situation in Turkey is worse than ever and the Kurds are targeted in all parts of Kurdistan, these insightful talks have served as consciousness-raising vehicles and have been well covered by the international press, especially given their venue in the European Parliament. They have offered the Kurds an international platform to have their case presented by distinguished, well-known persons. Indeed, people around the world have been introduced to the Kurdish question and been made sympathetic to its macro-importance for international politics, as well as nuances of significance for individuals on the micro level. Many have asserted that they first became aware of the Kurdish dilemma and its significance for world politics because of these annual conferences with their wide scope and great variety of speakers, all devoted to the one larger cause, namely, that of justice for the Kurds within existing international legal norms.

At the conclusion of its most recent 14th annual conference at the EU Parliament on December 6–7, 2017, the EUTCC released recommendations, endorsed the vision of the democratic confederal model for a just future for the Kurdish people, and called upon their friends and supporters to endorse the new vision.

Professor Kariane Westrheim (Norway) has been the chairperson of the EUTCC since its inception in 2004, while Professor Michael Gunter (United States) has been the secretary general since 2009. Professor Joost Jongerden (Netherlands), Dr. Dersim Dagdeviren (Germany), Estella Schmid (United Kingdom), and Professor Thomas J. Miley (United Kingdom) join them as members of the organization's board of directors. In addition, Adem Uzun (Belgium), a member of the Executive Council of the Kurdistan National Council (KNK) works closely with the board. The late Judge Essa Moosa (South Africa/died 2017) formerly served on the board to which he brought the invaluable experience of South Africa's national liberation struggle. Jon Rud (Norway and Spain) was the first secretary general, but is no longer active in the organization.

Appendix I: History of the Peace in Kurdistan UK Campaign

Since it was launched in October 1994, the UK-based Peace in Kurdistan Campaign (PIK) has established itself as a vital and tireless campaigning organisation dedicated to advancing the rights of the Kurdish people and campaigning for a political solution to the Kurdish question. It has won the support of politicians, academics, lawyers, journalists, and writers including distinguished figures with international reputations such as Noam Chomsky, John Berger, Lady Antonia Fraser, Michael Holroyd, Margaret Drabble, Edward Bond, Edward Albee, Gareth Peirce, Michael Mansfield QC, and the late Arthur Miller and Harold Pinter.

PIK performs its work on a completely voluntary basis. It has never been in receipt of any subsidy or grant from any local or national government authorities or other funding agencies. PIK was the first ever Kurdish solidarity group formed in Britain.

Over the years we have mobilised support for innumerable campaigns in defence of the Kurdish community in Britain and Europe and publicised countless cases of Kurdish political prisoners—journalists, artists, lawyers, politicians, and trade unionists.

Peace in Kurdistan has played a crucial role in the success of the Ilisu Dam Campaign (1998–2002). It was through our initiative in cooperation with the Kurdish community in UK that awareness of the alarmingly destructive potential of the dam was first raised. In 2002 the Ilisu Dam Campaign started another campaign: the Baku-Ceyhan Campaign.

One other important initiative was the Refugee Project (2003–2009), a campaign of a broad coalition of groups and individuals who came together to highlight the roles that UK foreign policies and investments overseas play in creating refugee and asylum seekers. The project provided a platform from which refugees can voice their concerns, as is clearly shown in its book, *Listen To The Refugee's Story* (co-published by Ilisu Dam Campaign Refugees Project, The Corner House, and Peace in Kurdistan Campaign).

The campaign aimed to show that the vast majority of migrants are fleeing from conflict zones or from social and economic oppression. In many cases, the British government, UK companies and taxpayers are directly or indirectly responsible for their plight. Investments take not just the more obvious forms of waging war and exporting arms, but also include work on infrastructure projects: hydro-electric and irrigation dams, oil and gas pipelines and mines, and government support for policies that put free trade before food security, health, and human rights.

We work with communities in the UK that are suffering most from current foreign, economic, and immigration policies to highlight the social, political, economic, and ecological root causes of migration; how aid and development strategies act to create conditions that generate forced migration; the discriminatory practices and human rights violations inherent in current asylum and immigration policies.

Other important aspects of our work has been the assistance we have provided with the co-ordinating and organisation of many delegations to the Kurdish regions in Turkey and Iraq and delegations of Kurdish politicians, lawyers, and journalists visiting the UK. These direct contacts and eyewitness observations have proved invaluable for British and other European friends to understand and chronicle the effects of particularly Turkey's war against the Kurds and the continuing human rights violations against Kurds from all social groups, be they political representatives, activists, women, journalists, lawyers, and others, many of whom have been 'disappeared', killed, tortured, or are incarcerated in Turkish jails.

Our many other activities in support of the Kurdish people include:

- Lobbying for the rights of the Kurds to be recognised by the political parties in Britain. We work constantly lobbying, briefing, and informing Members of Parliament about developments in Kurdistan. We hold regular public meetings in Westminster and since the founding of the Welsh Assembly and Scottish Parliament we have increased our activities by forging links with representatives of those two bodies and have organised meetings in these institutions.
- Publishing reports, briefing papers, translations, a weekly Kurdish news bulletin, press releases, and letter writing campaigns. We compile and publish reports on various human rights violations and legal issues relating to the

Kurds and distribute this information via mail-outs and the electronic media. We assist with the compilations of regular human rights submissions on violations inside Turkey to ongoing UN sessions.

- Joint work with other organisations active on the Kurdish issue, for example, the Kurdistan National Congress, human rights groups, NGOs, and trade unions.
- Work in association with the Kurdish diaspora community and their organisations in the UK. We assist and offer advice to members of the community in their activities.
- Close monitoring of press reports on the Kurdish question and responding promptly to errors, inaccuracies, and occasionally downright distortions.

As you can see our interventions cover a wide spectrum of issues and the burden of responsibility and demands on our very small staff of volunteers has been considerable. We hope you find our work important and worthy of support.

Campaign Demands:

1. International recognition for the fundamental right of the Kurdish people to self-determination and achieving their ability to exercise that right without fear of retribution and repression in Kurdistan in Turkey, Iran, Syria, and Iraq.
2. Another fundamental right is to live in peace and without fear of persecution. The Kurds more than any other nation deserve to be allowed the peace that for so long has eluded them. To this end we call for a negotiated political solution to the Kurdish question, with the participation of the legitimate representatives of the Kurdish people.
3. The winning of civil, political, social, cultural, and economic rights of the Kurdish people. These rights should be fully respected and enshrined in law in the countries where they reside.
4. Unrestricted freedom for the Kurdish press and broadcast media.
5. Preservation of the Kurdish language and ethnic identity through developing their right to freedom of expression.
6. Kurdish children and students to have the right to education in their mother tongue.
7. Equal rights for Kurdish women to allow them to fully participate at all levels in their society and calling for an end to the atrocity of honour killing.
8. The release of all Kurdish political prisoners, foremost among them Abdullah Öcalan.
9. To support Kurdish efforts to challenge Turkish state terror, as well as demands to remove the PKK from the banned "terrorist" list in the UK and Europe.

10. The refusal of Turkey's entry into the European Union until full and equal rights are granted to its Kurdish citizens.
11. Turkey to grant compensation to the millions of Kurds forcibly evacuated from their villages and to enable them to rebuild their homes.
12. For UN Special Rapporteurs and other international bodies to investigate allegations of genocidal state and military actions against the Kurdish people, including Turkey's dirty war against PKK guerrillas and the notorious Iraqi Anfal campaign.
13. To investigate and report into human rights violations in all parts of Kurdistan, including incidents of torture, arbitrary detention, extra-judicial executions, and for the perpetrators to be brought to justice.

Founding Statement:

The time has come for a political solution to the eleven year war between the Turkish state and the Kurdish people.

Since 1984, an increasingly destructive war has been raging between the Turkish state and the armed Kurdish opposition in the southeast, where the majority of the inhabitants are Kurds. As many as 3 million people have been displaced

Peace in Kurdistan regularly organises panels in the Houses of Parliament, Westminster, London. On this panel, Federico Venturini, MP George Howarth, Janet Biehl, and Rahila Gupta discuss "Democratic Confederalism and the Kurdish Case in Turkey"; April 2016.

from their homes, some to become refugees in Europe, and others to live in poverty or destitution in the cities of western Turkey, or the shanty towns of Diyarbakır.

This war has been accompanied by the endemic torture, extra-judicial killings, disappearances, and arbitrary imprisonment of tens of thousands of people suspected of 'separatism', including MPs, writers, journalists, trade unionists, lawyers, and human rights activists.

Justice Michael Kirby, a distinguished international jurist, has said that "the notion that a people can be ruled indefinitely against their will by governments comprising a majority of other peoples is as offensive as colonialism was". The armed opposition in Kurdistan have said that they want to exercise their right of self-determination, not by creating a separate Kurdish state, but through home rule within the Kurdish region. No threat exists to the integrity of Turkey, when a negotiated peace could lead to an amended Turkish constitution.

We believe that, as Turkey edges closer to Europe, she must comply with the European Human Rights Convention and the Organisation for Security and Cooperation in Europe's Copenhagen Declaration of June 1990, which requires states to "protect the ethnic, linguistic and cultural identity of national minorities on their territory, and create conditions for the promotion of that identity".

We appeal to the governments of Europe, to urge the authorities in Ankara to solve the problems of the southeast by negotiation with representatives of the people. We ask the OSCE and the government of Turkey to discuss the help the OSCE could give in restoring and maintaining peace in the region. We invite the people of Britain to join us in reaching out to all the people of Turkey— Turk, Kurd, Lazi, Abkhaz, and many others—so that together we can stop the war.

— Lord Avebury, Harold Pinter, John Austin MP, Estella Schmid, October 1994

Original signatories: *Tony Benn, Jeremy Corbyn MP, Lord Avebury, Baroness Sarah Ludford MEP, Lord Dholakia, Lord Hylton, Lord Rea, Lord Kilbraken, Lord McNair, Neil Ascherson, journalist; Noam Chomsky, writer; Julie Christie, actress; Lady Antonia Fraser; Arthur Miller, writer; Margaret Drabble, writer; Michael Holroyd, writer; Prof Ernst Gombrich OM, art historian; Tom Stoppard, playwright, Edward Bond, playwright; Edward Albee, playwright; Naguib Mahfouz, writer; Moris Farhi, writer; Dr Robert Olson, Professor of Middle East and Islamic History, University of Kentucky, US; Esmail Khoi, Iranian writer; James Kelman, writer; Reza Baraheni, Iranian writer; Dafyyd Iwan, Welsh singer and composer; Tim Gospill, editor 'Journalist'; Bruce Kent, International Peace Bureau; Desmond Fernandes, writer and genocide scholar; Gareth Peirce, solicitor; Mike Mansfield QC, barrister; Mark Muller QC, barrister; Timothy Otty QC, barrister; Frances Webber, barrister; Ian A. McDonald QC, barrister; Louise Christian, solicitor; Verena Graf, Secretary General of International League for the Rights and Liberation of Peoples, Geneva; Bill MacKeith, president Oxford Trade Union Council; etc (plus 500 supporters)*

Appendix II: Campaign Against Criminalising Communities (CAMPACC)

A growing resistance network has opposed the entire anti-terror legislative framework, its political agenda, and its exceptional powers. Since 2001 (CAMPACC) has brought together migrant groups, civil liberties campaigners, lawyers and journalists. The campaign has built solidarity with people targeted by anti-terror powers through protest actions, public meetings, petitions, seminars, and submissions to consultations (e.g. by Parliamentary committees and the Home Office), meanwhile collectively developing critical analysis of the securitisation agenda. CAMPACC raised the slogan, "We are all terror suspects", also printed on T-shirts. All these activities reinforce and build solidarity networks, which have been central to effective opposition.

For building solidarity, a crucial strength has been a long-term working relationship with numerous organisations which can bring greater resources. These include: the Haldane Society, solicitors' group practices (especially Garden Court Chambers and Birnberg Peirce), Statewatch, Cageprisoners, Cordoba Foundation, London Guantanamo Campaign, Peace in Kurdistan Campaign, Kurdish community centres, British Tamil Forum, Tamil Youth Organisation UK, London Somali Youth Forum, Hands Off Somalia, Peace and Justice in East London (PJEL), the College of Law (Birkbeck College), State Crime Project (University of Westminster), and the National Union of Journalists. Those co-operative efforts provide the basis for our analysis of securitisation strategies and collective resistance. See our website for more information: www.campacc.org.uk.

Appendix III: The Biography of Estella Schmid

Estella Schmid is a political activist. She is a co-founder and a spokesperson of the Peace in Kurdistan Campaign and the Campaign Against Criminalising Communities (CAMPACC). Her interests include global and social justice, women, civil rights, social and environmental movements, in particular liberation and anti-imperialist movements and people's struggles for self-determination.

Since the 1970s she has been active in international campaigns in solidarity with struggles of the Irish, South African, East Timorese, Palestinian, Eritrean, Kashmiri, Tamil, Baloch, Basque and, in particular, the Kurdish people. She was a co-founder of the first Kurdish solidarity group in the UK in 1990, the Kurdistan Solidarity Committee, the Kurdistan Information Centre in 1991, and the Peace in Kurdistan Campaign in 1994. Her other main projects have included the Ilisu Dam Campaign founded in 1997, CAMPACC in 2001, and the Refugee Project in 2002. She is a vice-president of the Haldane Society of Socialist Lawyers.

Estella was born in Vienna where she studied philosophy, theatre, film, and arts at the University in Vienna. She has been a director, producer, literary consultant, playwright, translator, and actor in the theatre and worked with companies in Vienna, Munich, Berlin, Cologne, Dusseldorf, New York, and London. She has lived in London since 1974.

The Freedom for Öcalan Campaign and the British Trade Union Movement

Interview with Simon Dubbins, Director of International—UNITE

Editors' Note: On the 27th of January, 2018, both Simon Dubbins and Thomas Jeff Miley were in London, participating in the emergency "Hands Off Afrin" Demonstration. After the demonstration, the two discussed at the Kings Cross/St. Pancras station about the implication of the British trade union movement in the Freedom for Öcalan campaign, in which Simon has been a crucial figure. Dubbins' speech at the 14th EUTCC Conference at the European Parliament in Brussels in December 2017 can be accessed at: https://bit.ly/2A85iVI.

Thomas Jeff Miley: What were your first impressions of the Kurdish movement, and how did you come to get involved in solidarity campaigns with the Kurds?

Simon Dubbins: I first came in to contact with the Kurdish political movement around 1992. Although I had heard about them before, the first time I actually saw them in person was when I saw the Kurdish groups on the 1st of May and other demonstrations in Germany. They used to march in a disciplined manner with red flags and pictures of their leaders. I also worked with a couple of Kurds while working on the production line of the *Frankfurter Rundschau* newspaper in Frankfurt Germany. As a person of the left, I naturally sympathized with the Kurdish cause. I knew they were of a clear Marxist-Leninist political perspective but the time was one in which the Soviet Union had just collapsed, and so the context was, 'what does that mean for you in the Kurdish struggle?' So yes, I guess my first real awareness was through the Kurdish diaspora in Germany.

I also remember very clearly when Öcalan was arrested. At that time I was living in Brussels but visited Germany regularly and kept contact with a Turkish friend who I had worked with at the Rundschau. I remember very clearly visiting him at home at the time Öcalan had been arrested and being struck by his mother watching the news of his capture, and saying: "There he is, they will have to execute him." I remember being shocked by this attitude and how demonised he was among the general Turkish public.

For whatever reason, though, despite being aware of the issue, the Kurdish question at that time was never really a central focus. In the following years I started to become more and more interested in Turkey. Despite all we now know about Erdoğan, at that time, when he first came to power, there was this perception of an opening and modernisation in the country. Turkey was an accession country to the European Union, so the unions started reaching out to sister unions and making an effort to hold conferences there. I went to Istanbul as part of congress delegations and immediately found it a very interesting place.

Then you start to become more aware of some of the very real underlying tensions, and although the situation was calmer than it had been in the past, and later a peace process existed, with hindsight it was naïve of many of us to think that Turkey was on the road towards a democratic settlement.

Later on of course Syria erupted. At that time, the real focus of the union's direct solidarity work was basically Palestine and Colombia, and other worthy causes too, such as supporting the progressive changes in Latin America. I was always sympathetic to politics of the Kurdish political movement, but I don't think I really understood the situation in Syria even when the Syrian government forces withdrew from the Kurdish areas in the North East of the country. What suddenly brought everything into sharp focus was when the murderous thugs of ISIS were attacking Kobane, and Erdoğan was refusing to let Kurdish fighters cross Turkish territory to support those resisting in the city. As soon as that happened you just knew something was badly wrong, so at work I immediately said that we need to draft a statement from the union calling on the Turkish government to allow the Kurdish fighters to cross to help the Kurds in Kobane.

Then I started to follow events much more closely and started to meet and talk to more people involved in the Kurdish movement. Soon I came to understand that women had been at the forefront of the struggle to defeat ISIS in Kobane and I found that inspirational, and I started to see and understand better the link between this struggle and the wider international left, you could see the centrality of the Kurdish struggle in this context.

I started to hear more about the radical ideology that was behind the Kurdish political movement and how it had developed and evolved over time. We started to include a section on Turkey, the Kurds and Middle East in the International Report to the UNITE Executive Committee, started to show a couple of maps on the screens and to explain why solidarity with the Kurds was important. We started the process of raising understanding and awareness of why this was vital to us as trade unionists in terms of women's rights, inclusiveness, multicultural and tolerant societies, explaining that these are the people we need to support.

At that time, the peace process in Turkey was starting to unravel, but the HDP still did magnificently in the general election of June 2015. I happened to be in Turkey again the day after that election at an international union congress and the atmosphere amongst the progressive Turkish unions was jubilant and full of optimism. Back in the UK I started to read more about the Kurdish movement and learnt a huge amount through conversations with Ibrahim Dogus, Adem Uzun, Estella Schmid, and many other activists, and I started to understand better the importance of Öcalan's long stay in Syria and the roots that had been planted there. I just hadn't realised that so many of the Syrian Kurds had been so widely influenced by Öcalan's ideology.

Then Erdoğan started to go ballistic after the great result of the HDP in June 2015. It pretty quickly became clear he wasn't going to accept it and then he effectively abandoned the peace process entirely and started arresting and attacking Turkish civil society and the Kurds. The bomb attacks happened against the union demonstrations and the activists in Suruc and Ankara during July and October 2015 killing more than 130 people. The young Kurds fearing they were going to be attacked dug the trenches in various Kurdish cities and declared autonomous zones and Erdoğan went completely crazy and just declared war on part of his own population. With Bert Schouwenburg, the International Officer at the GMB, we were talking and discussing: "What can we do? How can we get more involved? These are the people we need to be supporting."

Through those discussions there emerged the view that we needed to focus on freedom for Öcalan, as the figurehead, which was not a straightforward decision. We decided in February of 2016 that we would go on a delegation. We went to Ankara, met the unions, the HDP, I was particularly impressed with KESK, who have, as you know, many Kurdish members; DISK was in a similar boat.

Then we flew to Diyarbakır. I don't know what I was thinking at the time. Having been to Palestine and Colombia, you think you know what it is like to be in a conflict zone. This was February of 2016, right in the middle of the siege, so much shooting going on. I remember speaking to my wife on the phone, she was asking, "what's that banging?" All night, explosions, in the city you could hear the sniper fires down the street and see the front line of the conflict, it was definitely one of the hairiest delegations I have ever been involved in. Not even regular army units, but paramilitaries, were engaged in the assault. There were reports that a lot of Arabic was being spoken and a strong suspicion that Erdoğan had let ISIS fighters loose on the Kurds in a number of areas.

All I came away with was the idea that the Syrian Civil War was in actually in Turkey. Ibrahim was so calm and good in that situation. I was very impressed. But the fact is, the experience, it shook us, it really shook us.

I was immensely impressed as well, as I learned for the first time when we met the mayors of Diyarbakır, both of whom are now in jail, to understand the co-chair system, and thinking, they are more advanced than us. And the women's centre, we came across some very emancipated and motivated women. I thought, I love this movement, these are our values, this is what we stand for, we need to be helping these people in any way we can.

We came back from the delegation, and started to work on the Freedom for Öcalan campaign, which we launched with Dilek Öcalan, Öcalan's niece, and with Kamuran Yuksek, the leader of the DBP, the local-level party under the HDP umbrella. The Turkish embassy tried to stop our meeting in Parliament, but it was packed and we launched it, the two biggest unions in the country. And two weeks later, Kamuran was arrested, with the Turkish authorities using what he said in Parliament against him.

So they asked me, would I come to the trial, and I did, with Kate Osamor, the MP from Edmonton, London. It was a lot calmer in Diyarbakır by then, the military operation was over, though the Sur district remained off limits. In the court house, we were over the moon, but also surprised that he unexpectedly got freed. I think the presence of a foreign delegation certainly had an influence,

Unionist Bert Showenburg, Jonathan Steele, MEP Julie Ward, and unionist Simon Dubbins during a public forum in the Houses of Parliament, London, February 2017. The UK union movement is now at the forefront of Kurdish solidarity campaigns.

but a couple of months later, in typical Turkish fashion they knocked through a court order and sentenced him to 28-years jail while he was in Brussels, effectively forcing him into exile.

In July 2016 at our union's Policy Conference, we held the first fringe meeting on the situation in Turkey and solidarity with the Kurds. The HDP MP Ertugrul Kurkcu addressed the packed fringe meeting, and then in the international debate that afternoon the union passed a motion calling for solidarity with all progressive forces in Turkey, with the Kurdish people, and freedom for Öcalan. A young female Iraqi Kurdish member of ours moved the motion and spoke brilliantly and got a standing ovation. We were over the moon, this was the first time that we were really starting to build awareness and get the issue out there to the activists, bringing a complex far away thing to our conference and making it relevant.

The GMB also took the initiative at their Congress in Dublin where they held what was probably the first ever 'Freedom for Öcalan' fringe meeting at a trade union conference. The meeting was chaired by Bert Schowenburg their International Officer and was fully supported and addressed by their General Secretary, Paul Kenny, as well as by Ibrahim Dogus.

Later that same year, in 2016, a motion was tabled at the TUC conference concerning the situation in Turkey and we got it amended to include support for freedom for Abdullah Öcalan and civil rights, union rights and democracy, and with that freedom for Öcalan became the official policy of the British trade union movement. Following that we organised a fringe meeting at the Labour Party Conference and we invited Feleknas Uca, a Kurdish HDP MP from

Diyarbakır, who again spoke to a packed fringe meeting, a couple of hundred people, on the subject of the Middle East, the struggle for democracy, and the Kurds, as well as of course Freedom for Öcalan.

Since then we've continued to build the campaign amongst the British trade unions. The following year, in 2017, UNITE tabled the motion to the TUC conference. This time we specifically committed the TUC to encourage affiliates to support and join the Freedom for Öcalan campaign and obliged the TUC to organise a delegation to Turkey including a visit to Diyarbakır. We were delighted that the motion was unanimously supported, and to be fair, they are already implementing it.[1] The campaign now already has formal affiliations from the GMB, UNITE, NEU, ASLEF, RMT, FBU, CWU, EIS, and GFTU, and many other unions are in the process of affiliation. Although we have a long way to go still, the structure is really starting to take shape now.

As all of this is happening, I am starting to read Öcalan, and as I started to read him, I was stunned, that a man in solitary confinement was capable of producing such profound reflections on 5000 years of history. He had me watching you-tube videos of the ancient civilisation of Sumer! And his own critique of the PKK, it is fascinating. He is very open, honest, self-critical, to a degree you probably wouldn't have here. Equally stunning is how he emphasizes that women must be at the front and centre of movement.

The paradigm shift he proposes, with the Bookchin influence and democratic confederalism as a model, has helped me to re-evaluate my own position. Because, on a personal level, I felt it refreshing to break out. He is not deserting Marx and Lenin, not at all. But he is being open and critical, seeing the failures of the past for what they were, and reflecting on the significance of the collapse of the Soviet Union, the failure of state socialism. And I love his whole approach to the Nation-State, for a movement that started off as separatist movement to arrive at that conclusion is one hell of a shift!

On all of those fronts, it has been an incredible journey. I see Rojava as an inspiration. We went on a mission to Iraq last summer, just before the referendum in the KRG, which really threw up for me precisely why they are so critical of feudal nationalist Barzani politics. It is disgusting to see the KDP in bed with Erdoğan; the contrast with the YPG and YPJ could hardly be clearer, making it even more inspirational. The PYD, the YPG, the YPJ, they are doing something different on the ground, something truly admirable, something truly inspiring, and they are highly trained and battle hardened and not going to give way easily to any aggression they face or attempts to destroy what they are building.

Thomas Jeff Miley: What are the main challenges you have faced in the campaign, and what should be its priorities moving forward?

Simon Dubbins: We have good experience with Cuba, South Africa, Palestine and Colombia, all of that, the solidarity tradition of British trade union movement, of which I am proud. We are using those experiences to help us build this campaign. And that's just the UK side of the campaign.

We are also trying to internationalise the campaign, putting motions into the European and international federations. We are acutely aware how sensitive it is for Turkish unions, but we have our position. The campaign has generated lots of sympathy, sometimes from surprising quarters. The president of the American UAW has even signed a letter in support of the campaign.

I think first priority is to get people to realize, the Kurdish movement is the only real progressive force in the region, a crucial region, where the world powers all come together. Unrest there quickly spills over, as in the refugee crisis, which can affect the political situation here quite negatively, as we have seen with the surge of the far right across Europe. We have to make the case, we have to support our friends, those who support our values in the region.

The bigger question, where I think there is a lot of debate to still be had, is how some of the theory of democratic confederalism actually fits with some of the other crucial issues. For example, I am not sure how democratic confederalism exactly fits together with the struggle against global multinationals, with the fight to try to get finance capital under control. Initially Öcalan wrote positively about EU, for transcending the nation-state; but then, reflecting on the EU's complicity in his abduction, he became more disillusioned. I shared the view, to get global capital under control, we need transnational structures. I understand that how the EU has moved is highly problematic, but I am convinced nonetheless, a return to the Nation-State is not the way ahead. We need transnational structures. But I am certainly convinced that the commitment to women is very genuine, and I am extremely impressed with such a strong bottom-up, grass-roots movement. We need to rekindle that kind of energy, we haven't fully lost it.

I find it very exciting to see a left, radical, revolutionary movement, in one of the most difficult regions, scaring the vested reactionary interests and powers that be, which is why people are ganging up to stop them. But if it can help us breathe some fresh air, in terms of our own ideology, this would be a great achievement. Because frankly, since the collapse of the USSR, and the dreadful third way of Tony Blair, the left has found it very difficult to imagine an alternative to a fundamentally neoliberal market-economy oriented approach. The Kurdish movement can help us rethink things, I truly believe.

I don't know. I don't have all the answers. But for first time in a long time, I am feeling excited. This campaign has been bringing me into contact with people like Dilar Dirik and Adem Uzun, people like Estella Schmid, and many, many other inspirational people in the Kurdish movement. But it is yet to have its rightful place right at the top of international left. The women's movement is becoming more and more aware, but it is not going to be easy.

After 20 years in the apparatus, you do get conditioned and sometimes it's hard to develop new things, and we have to be aware that for many of our members their bread and butter issues about pay, jobs and conditions are quite understandably still their main focus and priority. We have a hell of an education job in front of us.

There is of course also the issue that the PKK is on the terrorist list, which makes people afraid. A lot of people are frightened. Like with the Palestine issue, where people are often intimidated by those who deliberately and misleadingly conflate any critique of Israel with anti-Semitism.

And we need the Kurdish community to get more involved with the trade union movement. In that regard, Ibrahim Dogus has been excellent. He is prepared to break boundaries, and he is well aware of the need for the Kurdish community here to get more involved in our struggles, too.

At the same time, it is essential that the Freedom for Öcalan campaign needs to have non-Kurdish faces. It needs to show that the campaign is expanding, gaining new profiles of supporters, that it is not just a front operation for another Kurdish organisation.

After all, the Kurdish movement should be an inspiration for us all. How they went in to fight ISIS. I find the hypocrisy of the UK and US, their silence and complicity in the assault on Afrin, thoroughly disgusting, especially after all of us relied on the Kurdish forces to take on and defeat those criminal thugs.

1.   Editors' Note: The 2017 TUC motion is titled "Solidarity with all progressive forces and the Kurdish population of Turkey." It reads as follows: "Conference is appalled at the continuing repression and massive human rights abuses taking place at the hands of the Turkish government. It's clear that since President Erdoğan failed to achieve an electoral majority in the June 2015 election, his government has embarked on a war against the Kurdish population, criminalisation of opposition groups, closing down the free press and intimidation and threats against anyone who challenges his rule. The failed coup attempt has been used as an excuse to radically speed up this process.

Conference is further appalled at the international actions of the Turkish government , its actions in Syria demonstrate clearly it's more intent on fighting the progressive Kurdish led administration in Rojava rather than defeating so called Islamic State.

Conference calls on the Turkish government to:

(1) Immediately end the state of emergency, restore all democratic and press freedoms and restart the peace process with the Kurdistan Workers Party (PKK);

(2) Release all political prisoners, including the imprisoned HDP leaders and members of parliament and jailed Kurdish leader Abdullah Öcalan;

(3) Withdraw its forces from Syria, and stop attacking Kurdish led forces;

(4) Immediately cease support and backing of Jihadi groups.

Conference calls on the UK government to maximise pressure on the Turkish government to comply with the actions listed above and calls on all unions to affiliate and support the work of the Peace in Kurdistan and Freedom for Öcalan campaigns. Conference calls on the TUC to organise a solidarity delegation to Turkey including a visit to the Kurdish areas.

PART THREE:
The EUTCC İmralı International Peace Delegations

The Plight of the Kurds in Turkey and the Fate of the Middle East

Thomas Jeffrey Miley

March 1, 2016

Editors' Note: This is a report on the Kurdish question in Turkey and other issues by Thomas Jeffrey Miley after his participation in the first İmralı Delegation. The report was prepared for the Iraq Institute for Strategic Studies, on whose website it was originally published (http://www.iraqstudies.com/featured13.html).

A decade and a half in, the "War on Terror" remains a disaster of increasingly colossal proportions. The Middle East is in flames. The wars of aggression against Iraq and Libya have not produced the freedoms that were promised. Thus far, they have only served to replace tyrannical states with failed states. Tyranny and chaos remain the only alternatives effectively on offer for the peoples of the region. This is the precondition or ultimate root cause of sympathy for ISIS, the objective grievance that renders the group's apocalyptic vision plausible to so many in the Sunni Arab world. The combination of lethal ineptitude and hypocrisy by Western countries certainly does not go unnoticed.

To make matters worse, the Kurdish forces in Rojava, which constitute the only group in Syria that has been an effective and reliable ally of the Western countries in the struggle against ISIS, remain subject to a cruel and debilitating embargo, having been consistently demonized as "terrorists" and threatened by NATO member Turkey, while, for the most part, the West turns a blind eye.

The Kurdish forces in Rojava possess a crucial strength: the courage of their convictions. Courage that has been on display consistently over the course of the past year, perhaps most dramatically during the heroic defence of Kobane and the liberation of the Yazidis on Sinjar mountain.

The Erdoğan government is right about one thing: the Kurdish forces in Rojava are organically linked to the PKK. Indeed, the Kurdish forces in Rojava and the Kurdish movement in Turkey share a common political program too—one called "democratic confederalism." It is a program inspired by the ideas of their undisputed leader, Abdullah Öcalan, a man whose words are treated by many Kurds as something close to sacred.

Öcalan's vision of "democratic confederalism," which he has elaborated extensively from his lonely prison cell on İmralı, amounts to a striking re-interpretation of the principle of self-determination, and provides a road map for peace in the broader Middle East. His model combines (a) an expansion of outlets in local and participatory democratic decision-making, with (b) institutional guarantees for accommodating local ethnic and religious diversities, (c) an emphasis on gender equality, and (d) respect for existing state boundaries, including an explicit and principled renunciation of the goal of a "Greater Kurdistan."

Those inspired by Öcalan in Syria are thus not only the sole effective allies in the struggle against ISIS; they are also the most significant force fighting for something other than more tyranny and/or more chaos—indeed, for something resembling democracy.

Not coincidentally, in Turkey too, the movement inspired by Öcalan has emerged as a crucial protagonist in the struggle for democracy. The impressive performance of the Peoples' Democratic Party (HDP) in the June 2015 general elections temporarily checked Erdoğan's hyper-presidentialist ambitions, a fact that does much to explain the subsequent escalation of conflict and brutal crackdown on the Kurdish movement since. The government's repression and intimidation of Turkish academics and journalists who have spoken out against its on-going atrocities in Cizre goes to show just how tight the connection is between the fate of the Kurdish question and the fate of democracy throughout Turkey.

Meanwhile, the Erdoğan government's assault on the Kurdish movement inside the country has been accompanied by an increasingly belligerent stance towards the Kurdish forces beyond the Turkish border in Syria. In recent weeks, the Turkish military has begun directly shelling the Kurdish forces advancing against ISIS, and is even threatening a ground invasion—a spectre whose realization could well trigger war with Russia, with certain dire consequences for stability in the region and the world.

It is therefore becoming increasingly clear that the domestic and international fronts of the Erdoğan government's still-escalating policy of war-mongering against the followers of Öcalan are both (a) intimately linked and (b) extremely dangerous. The war in Syria has already effectively spilled over into the Kurdish region in Turkey, and the potential for further violence and destabilization throughout the rest of the country can hardly be underestimated.

Though the Kurdish movement in both Turkey and Syria is organically linked to the PKK, it is not reducible to the PKK. Instead, the glue that holds the entire movement together is Öcalan himself. This is why the deliberate silencing of his voice—a voice that has consistently called (since at least 2005) for constraint and for commitment to a peaceful political resolution to the Kurdish question in Turkey—has been one of the most dangerous components of the criminal and polarizing policy pursued by the Turkish authorities vis-à-vis the Kurdish movement in recent months.

Thus far, the Peoples' Democratic Party (HDP) has shown great courage under fire, and its leaders remain constrained and staunchly committed to peace negotiations. For instance, at the party's congress last month in Ankara, co-chair Selahattin Demirtaş passionately implored a restive attendance:

> The correct attitude needs to be defended even in the most difficult times. We cannot subject ourselves to this time of sorrows. We cannot let our traumas undermine our principled stance for peace. We are the only party defending

the rainbow of diversity in Turkey. We aim for a new union in this country, one based not on the fascist principle of forced assimilation but on the pluralist principle of respect for diversity. Why do they claim that we aim to divide the country, when they are the ones dividing it with their monism? They call us the Kurdish party, but we are not only the party of the Kurds, but of Turks, Circassians, Armenians, and Arabs, too. We are the party of all religions, and we are the party of women. We are the party of the real Turkey, and we stand for self-governance and self-management for all the peoples of Turkey ... Turkey is our country, our motherland. What is happening to the Kurds is a disaster. The strengthening of democracy is the only way to save us from this disaster. To argue for peace in easy times is very easy. Now it is much more difficult, when the people in the palace curse peace and push for war. But you cannot be for peace according to how the wind blows. Peace is an ethical choice; we will never give up on peace.

Even so, the unravelling of the peace process, the total isolation and silencing of Öcalan, alongside the violent onslaught unleashed against the Kurds by the Erdoğan government over the past several months, is rendering Demirtaş's position increasingly difficult to maintain. The government seems bent on closing the political space opened up by the HDP in June of 2015.

Tellingly, one of the HDP's most respected elected deputies, Emine Ayna, who is currently facing charges of "making propaganda for a terrorist organization and inciting hate," resigned at the end of January from her post as parliamentarian, on the grounds that participating in the chamber gives a "veneer of democratic legitimacy" to the Turkish representative institutions, a veneer she insisted was inexcusable at a time when Kurds are being "massacred by the fascist state." In dialogue with an international peace delegation led by Nelson Mandela's former lawyer, Judge Essa Moosa, in Istanbul in mid-February, she explained with much righteous anger and indignation:

> I refuse to participate in the parliamentary pantomime. Turkey's militaristic approach leaves no room for politics. Not now, because—let me be clear— these days are most challenging for us. Things are worse now than back in the nineties. In three basements in Cizre, 173 civilians, including women and children, were massacred and burned. Sixty people in each basement, crowded in small spaces. Also in Syria, the situation is worsening. And the Turkish officials refuse all requests for talk. The time has passed for begging for peace. We can no longer afford to beg for peace. Now we must create a situation where *they* will ask for peace.

Despite such ominous words, Ms. Ayna would nevertheless still be quick to add: "We do not want to divide Turkey. That would mean only more hostility from the Turkish state. It would mean neither freedom for Kurds, nor peace for Turks."

Virtually all of the representatives of the Kurdish movement with whom Judge Moosa's international peace delegation had the chance to speak echoed Ms. Ayna's deep concerns about the polarizing consequences of the still-escalating conflict in Cizre and elsewhere in the southeast of the country. Many cautioned that the ongoing violence against the Kurdish population was on the verge of provoking a definitive rupture, a point of no return. For example, in a meeting with representatives from the Peoples' Democratic Congress (HDK), co-chair Gülistan Kiliç Koçyiğit would insist:

> An extreme war is being waged on civilians. Violence against women has risen. Despite the fact that the government doesn't define this as a war, it is a war. Literally. Crimes against humanity are being committed. Women are being killed and stripped, their bodies humiliated. These security forces have written sexist and racist things on the walls. They are traumatizing society, causing feelings of disillusionment, and cutting off the remaining links between the Kurds and the rest of society.

Likewise, co-chair Ertuğrul Kürkçü would stress:

> A new war has erupted. We are witnessing a ground-breaking episode. For the first time, urban, settled areas have become war zones. Non-partisans are also being seriously hurt ... The cities have been pounded by heavy artillery and tank fires. The gendarme special forces that have been deployed are licensed to kill. Full impunity is provided for them, and they are directly linked to the president himself ... Meanwhile, our deputies have been stripped of our parliamentary immunity. They have been denied entrance to the areas under curfew ... The state authorities have targeted certain localities, as if treating a cancer ... Among the Kurds there is a very big anger against the government. There is the widespread belief that this is being done to us because we didn't vote for Erdoğan.

The political space for a peaceful resolution to the Kurdish question in Turkey is rapidly vanishing. As HDP deputy Pervin Buldan, who had served as one of the chief negotiators on Öcalan's committee throughout the now deep-frozen peace process, warned:

> I would like to stress that a massacre is under way. The ruling AKP party and the palace, to protect their power, are attempting to get Kurds to evacuate their homes and their land. Without the end of the isolation of Öcalan, the process will not start again. In summary, I'd stress the need for peace and for a democratic solution. We are on the verge of a civil war here ... I am deeply concerned that the war will spread to the western part of Turkey. The danger is rising. The conflicts should immediately end. The only way to avoid a catastrophe is to end Öcalan's isolation and to restart negotiations with him.

The point of no return seems, indeed, to be fast-approaching. Another of the erstwhile team of peace negotiators, Hatip Dicle, would be even more explicit in this regard. According to Dicle:

> Frankly, we want peace. We prefer negotiations and peace. We want the isolation of Öcalan to be ended. But Erdoğan wants none of this now ... From the minarets, announcements are being made telling people to leave the province, or else the government will not be responsible for their safety. Cruelty reigns in Kurdistan ... The cruelty now surpasses that of the nineties. The police and the army are acting like ISIS to our people. They are beheading people, burning people alive, shooting young people in the head. It wasn't this cruel in the

nineties. Then they evacuated and burned villages. Now they want to do this to our cities. Sometimes I am ashamed of being alive… I fear what may come in the spring. If this war is not stopped in two months, there are thousands of guerrillas in the mountains, waiting for the snow to melt. The war will expand to all of Kurdistan and throughout all of Turkey. We are concerned that a great disaster will happen in Turkey.

The Erdoğan government tries to justify its actions by alleging that it is fighting against "terrorism" and the threat of Kurdish separatism; but, in fact, its belligerent course of action would seem the perfect recipe for conjuring (back) into being the very "separatist-terrorist" enemy it somehow desperately seems to need.

Joint Statement of the First International İmralı Peace Delegation

Istanbul, February 15–16, 2016

Introduction

The situation in Turkey today is critical—the recent escalation of conflict surrounding the Kurdish question seriously endangers the country and the surrounding region. The war in Syria has already created widespread hostilities and spilled out across the southeast of Turkey. President Recep Tayyip Erdoğan's AKP government is committing human rights atrocities in Cizre and other towns and cities, and there is a very real threat of a further spiralling of violence throughout the country. the State's repression and intimidation of Turkish academics and journalists who have spoken out against its war-mongering reveals the intimate connection between the struggle for a peaceful resolution to the Kurdish question and the struggle for democracy in Turkey more generally.

The Isolation of Abdullah Öcalan

The escalation of conflict has coincided with the total isolation of the leader of the Kurdish freedom movement, Abdullah Öcalan, who, from his lonely prison cell on the island of İmralı, has continued to play a crucial role as an advocate for peaceful resolutions and has been a consistent voice calling for peace.

Yet the very fact that Öcalan is in prison has been a fundamental problem for peace talks, even during the talks that occurred for two years starting in March 2013. His condition of imprisonment forces him to negotiate with his captors—an inherent disadvantage. Moreover, in prison he cannot consult with his constituency. Before substantive negotiations can commence, the State must first release him from prison just as Nelson Mandela was released before—not after or during—the South African negotiations could begin. Until Öcalan is freed, there can be no authentic negotiations, otherwise any "negotiations" are merely talk and nothing more. Just as Mandela had emphasized, a leader must be free because then they can truly negotiate on behalf of their people for a political solution.

The Ten-Member International Peace Delegation

On February 14 2016, a ten-member international delegation assembled in Istanbul to try to help restart the Kurdish-Turkish peace process, which has been suspended since the spring of 2015. The leader of the delegation, Judge Essa Moosa of the High Court of South Africa, on behalf of the delegation, wrote a letter to the Turkish Ministry of Justice on February 3 to request two meetings: one with the Ministry, to discuss ways and means to resume the peace process between the Turkish government and Öcalan, and the other discussion with Abdullah Öcalan on İmralı to discuss the same issue. We requested that the meetings take place on February 15, which coincided with the seventeenth anniversary of Öcalan's capture and detention. Judge Moosa, who had formerly acted on behalf of Nelson Mandela, while imprisoned on Robben Island and elsewhere, had also been involved in the negotiation process in South Africa.

We are convinced that neither the Kurdistan Workers' Party (PKK) nor the Turkish military can decisively prevail or avoid a war that could further exacerbate the severe humanitarian crises in the country. We believe that the peace process offers the only solution and that Öcalan, as the chief spokesperson for the Kurdish movement, is essential to this process. No progress toward a solution can be achieved, we believe, without Öcalan's participation.

Unfortunately our delegation was granted neither of the two meetings that we requested. On February 15, the Ministry acknowledged receipt of the letter but did not bother to formally accept or reject our request. Beyond that mere acknowledgment, it gave no response at all by the time we left Turkey. We are extremely disappointed that we were not afforded an opportunity to engage the minister of justice and Öcalan on the question of the resumption of the peace process.

The delegation meanwhile met with representatives from a variety of political and social organizations who briefed us on the country's disturbing situation. We also met with lawyers and lawyers' organizations who have been deeply involved in the defense of members of the Kurdish freedom movement against the many criminal charges that have been laid, and who have themselves been the subject of much intimidation and persecution by the State.

From Peace to War

All these representatives recounted to us that during the current period of Öcalan's isolation, from April 2015, the Erdoğan government has shifted from a peace footing to a war footing. The shift from peace-making to war-making has coincided with the total isolation of Öcalan. As he enters the eighteenth year of his detention, he leads a solitary life. Two other prisoners of the five who were formerly present on İmralı have now been transferred to other high-security prisons. Öcalan's only human contact is with his guards or, if so permitted, with the remaining three prisoners. Not even his family can visit him. His lawyers, who have not been able to visit him since 2011, have applied to visit Öcalan at least once a week, and this despite the fact after 600 hundred application attempts, they are repeatedly turned down, and given absurd excuses that transportation to the island is unavailable i.e. the boat to go there is broken. Since the last HDP delegates left on April 5, 2015, no one at all has been permitted to visit. No communication from Öcalan has been received since then either. Based on the fact that Öcalan's basic human rights have been denied to him regarding contact with visitors, we are also deeply concerned for his health and well-being and question whether he has proper access to medical care.

After the June 2015 elections, the peace process has decisively come to an end and the situation in Turkey has deteriorated rapidly. We are informed that cities are becoming war zones, pounded with heavy artillery and tank fire. Children are being killed. People's parents and grandparents are shot dead in the streets, but because of the curfew, their bodies cannot be retrieved for extended periods. We are told that certain police forces are licensed to shoot anyone without consequences. These Special Forces are not commanded by local governors but are directly linked to the central government.

In Cizre, people, many of them civilians who took refuge in three different basements, have been killed, even burned alive, and now the State is destroying the buildings to eliminate the evidence. Violence against women is on the rise. Women are killed, then stripped and humiliated. These constitute war crimes and crimes against humanity. They violate the Third Geneva Convention, and meet the United Nations' criteria for genocide, of which Turkey is a signatory.

On the Kurdish side, anger against the government is rising, and many are moving away from Turkish society altogether. The Kurds sense that the war on their cities is linked to the election outcome. Even as war crimes and atrocities are being committed, however, the EU and the US are averting their eyes. Internationally, the AKP controls the flow of refugees into Europe, and it uses that leverage to intimidate European powers. European governing parties fearing what increased immigration might do to their electoral prospects, stay silent as massacres are under way in Turkey. As for the United States, it repeatedly affirms its military alliance with Turkey in the war against IS, despite the fact that Turkey's prime enemies in the conflict are not IS (which it even supports) but the Kurds in Turkey, Iraq, and Syria, as well as Bashar al-Assad.

The Erdoğan government continues to bombard the Kurdish forces in Syria, the very forces which have proven to be the US-led coalition's only effective ally in the struggle against ISIS. There is even talk of a ground invasion by Turkey into the Kurdish region of Syria, which could well trigger war with Russia, with unfathomable consequences for the region and the world. The fate of the Kurds depends in large part, then, on people in the rest of the world calling on governments and international institutions to change their policies toward Turkey and stand up for the beleaguered Kurds.

Our last meeting was a round table with around fifty Kurdish and Turkish intellectuals, journalists, human rights leaders, and academics. Some emphasized the urgent necessity to resume the peace talks, while others despaired that talks are no longer relevant when people are being burned alive.

The Resolution

In light of circumstances, we, the undersigned, the members of the International Peace Delegation, unanimously resolve as follows:

• We call upon the Turkish government and Abdullah Öcalan to resume the peace process as a matter of urgency. In December 2012, the Archbishop Emeritus Desmond Tutu, as the Chair of the Elders (which was founded by Nelson Mandela), in a personal note to the then Prime Minister, Recep Tayyip Erdoğan, said that "Peace is better than war" and appealed to the Prime Minister to resume the peace process with Abdullah Öcalan.

• In order for genuine peace negotiations to take place to resolve the Kurdish issue in Turkey, Abdullah Öcalan must be released unconditionally from prison to enable him to take his rightful place at the negotiating table for the lasting resolution of the Kurdish issue in Turkey and for the democratization of Turkey.

• We call upon the Turkish government to level the playing field by, among other things, legitimizing the PKK and other banned organizations, releasing all political prisoners and permitting exiles to return to Turkey to participate in the peace process.

• We resolve to lobby our respective governments and non-governmental organizations to put pressure on the Turkish government to resume the peace process as a matter of urgency. In those countries where the PKK is listed as a terrorist organization and Abdullah Öcalan is listed as a terrorist, we resolve to pressure such governments to remove them from such lists as they are a liberation movement fighting for freedom in terms of the Core International Human Rights Instruments.

• We call upon international human rights organizations to investigate, as a matter of urgency, the human rights abuses perpetrated by the Turkish authorities against the civilian population in the areas of conflict and to assess and determine whether such abuses constitute war crimes, crimes against humanity, genocide and/or contraventions of the Geneva Convention.

• We call upon the Committee for the Protection against Torture, Inhuman or Degrading Treatment or Punishment of the Council of Europe (CPT), as a matter of extreme urgency, to visit Abdullah Öcalan on İmralı Island Prison in order to investigate the violation of his rights. In terms of the European Convention on Human Rights, as a political prisoner, (i) his right to have access to his lawyers has been violated for the last 5 years; (ii) his right to have access to members of his family has been violated for the last 14 months; (iii) his right not to be completely isolated from social contact has been violated for an unknown period; and (iv) his right to have access to medical doctors and/or treatment has been violated. The CPT is called upon to report urgently on their findings, after its visit, to the Council of Europe, to the Turkish government, and to Abdullah Öcalan and his lawyers.

• We call upon the international academic fraternity to come out in support of dissident academics in Turkey in the interest of academic freedom, and give them moral, material, physical, and academic assistance.

• We call upon members of our delegation to distribute this report as widely as possible to heads of state, foreign ministers, ambassadors, officials, the media (both electronic and print), human rights organizations and non-governmental organizations in our respective countries.

Signed:

Janet Biehl, independent author; advisory board member of the Transnational
  Institute for Social Ecology (TRISE), (US)
Dr Radha D'Souza, Reader in Law at the University of Westminster and social
  justice activist (UK)
Eirik Eiglad, writer and publisher, New Compass Press (Norway)
Andrej Hunko, MP of DIE LINKE, Aachen (Germany)
Dr. Thomas Jeffrey Miley, lecturer in sociology, Cambridge University (UK)
Judge Essa Moosa (head of delegation), International Peace and
  Reconciliation Initiative (South Africa)
Dr. Elly Van Reusel, medical doctor (Belgium)
Dimitri Roussopoulos, co-founder of TRISE and Black Rose Books (Canada)
Fr. Joe Ryan, chair of the Westminster Justice and Peace Commission (UK)
Francisco Velasco, former Minister of Culture (Ecuador)
Federico Venturini, University of Leeds, advisory board of TRISE (UK)

Addendum: Letter of Request from Judge Essa Moosa to the Minister of Justice Mr. Bekir Bozdag, Dated 3 February 2016

03 February 2016

The Honorable Minister of Justice, BEKIR BOZDAG
Ministry of Justice
KIZILAY/ANKARA
REPUBLIC OF TURKEY

Dear Honorable BEKIR BOZDAG

I write to you as a judge of the High Court of South Africa on behalf of an International Delegation consisting of well-respected members of the international community from political, cultural and public spheres of life. These influential figures with a range of expertise have been involved in peace initiatives, human rights, and human development. The names of the delegation are listed at the end of the letter. The members of the delegation are well aware that the priority of your government is the democratization of your country.

The mission of the delegation is to visit Turkey with the object of promoting the resumption of the Peace Process in Turkey between the leader of the ruling party, His Excellency President Recep Tayyip Erdoğan and the imprisoned leader of the Kurdish people, the Honorable Abdullah Öcalan. The Peace Process has unfortunately stalled due to unforeseen circumstances. The visit of the delegation to Turkey is scheduled to take place during the 14th to the 17th February 2016.

Our first step in our mission is to seek your permission for our delegation to visit the İMRALI PRISON to consult and brief Mr. Öcalan on the resumption of the Peace Process. We believe that he can play a pivotal role, like President Nelson Mandela in South Africa, in the democratization and the peaceful resolution of the Kurdish question in Turkey.

The delegation would like to have permission to visit İMRALI Prison on 16 February 2016. If it is not possible for the entire delegation to visit İMRALI then we ask for permission for a selected group from the delegation to do so.

As a prelude to the visit to İMRALI, I would request you to permit me and a selected group from the delegation to meet you and any of your colleagues to enable us to exchange views on the resumption of the Peace Process and the way forward before we meet Mr. Öcalan.

Following our visit to İMRALI, we request a consultation and briefing session with you as the Honorable Minister of Justice for the purpose of reporting to you on the deliberations and view of Mr Öcalan and to encourage both parties to resume the Peace Process.

I might mention that I was acting for Mr. Mandela and his colleagues when they were imprisoned on Robben Island and other prisons in Cape Town. As proof thereof I attach hereto a letter dated 21/08/89 addressed by Mandela to me from Victor Verster Prison before his release on 11 February 1990.

As Secretary of the ANC Constitutional Committee, I was intimately involved in the Peace Process and in the Constitutional-Making Process in South Africa. I was appointed by President Nelson Mandela in 1998 as a Judge in the High Court of South Africa.

I have been involved from 2005 to 2014 in monitoring the Peace Process in Turkey and was very optimistic that since my last visit to Turkey in July 2014, that Turkey would find a peaceful political solution to the Kurdish question and the democratization of its polity after the national elections. Unfortunately this was not to be. It behoves on us to work together to achieve a lasting peace in Turkey.

I will deem it a great honor if you will give favorable consideration to our requests contained in this letter. I await to hear from you as a matter of urgency.

I remain,
Yours sincerely

JUDGE ESSA MOOSA

LIST OF DELEGATES

Janet Biehl, independent author and advisory board member of the
    Transnational Institute for Social Ecology (TRISE) (US)
Dr Radha D'Souza, Reader in Law at the University of Westminster and social
    justice activist (UK)
Eirik Eiglad, writer and publisher, New Compass Press (Norway)
Andrej Hunko, MP of DIE LINKE, Aachen (Germany)
Edgar de Jesús Lucena González, Member of the National Assembly of
    Venezuela
Dr. Thomas Jeffrey Miley, lecturer in sociology, Cambridge University (UK)
Judge Essa Moosa (head of delegation), International Peace and
    Reconciliation Initiative (South Africa)
Dr. Elly Van Reusel, medical doctor (Belgium)
Dimitri Roussopoulos, co-founder of TRISE and Black Rose Books (Canada)
Fr. Joe Ryan, chair of the Westminster Justice and Peace Commission (UK)
Francisco Velasco, former Minister of Culture (Ecuador)
Federico Venturini, University of Leeds, advisory board of TRISE (UK)

Letter from Nelson Mandela to Essa Moosa, 1989

81/143299

1335/88: NELSON MANDELA

Victor Verster Prison,
P/B X 6005,
Paarl South. 7624.
21   8   89

Dear Essa,

Many friends have rallied around us during these
past 26 years and left us with a lot of courage and
hope. In this regard you and your firm have been
outstanding, so much so that I sometimes wonder whether
without that support we would have had the staying
power for which my fellow prisoners have become so
renowned. Many thanks for the flowers and birthday
greetings. I only hope it will be possible for me to
see you on these premises in due course. Meantime I
send you, your family and staff my very best wishes.

Sincerely,
Madiba.

RECEIVED
1989 -08- 25

Addendum 2: Number 64871687.3-10-1-2015.
Subject: About your application on getting information—Responses of the
Ministry of Justice, dated 29 February

REPUBLIC OF TURKEY
JUSTICE MINISTRY
International Law and Relations General Directorate
Human Rights Head of Department

29 February 2016

Number: 64871687.3-10-1-2015
Subject: About your application on getting information

Dear Essa MOOSA
(essa.moosa1@gmail.com)

As a summary of your petition dated 12 February 2016; you had indicated that you requested help from Ministry of Justice in order to see Abdullah Öcalan who is a convicted prisoner at İmralı Prison.

Your application has been sent to the General Directorate of Prisons and Detention Houses because of relationship of your request's content.

Respectfully submitted

Yurdagül KESKİN
Judge
Justice Ministry
Vice Head of Department

(With e-signature)

Milli Müdafaa Caddesi No:22 Bakanlıklar/ANKARA Ayrıntılı Bilgi:
U. BEKMEZ (Uzman Yrd.)
Telefon : O (312) 414 87 37
Faks: O (312) 2194528
B-posta: inhak@adalet.gov.tr
Elektronik Ağ : www.inhak.adalet.gov.tr

Turkey and the Kurds: A Chance for Peace?

Jonathan Steele, Veteran Foreign Correspondent

20 April, 2017

Editors' Note: This is a report by EUTCC İmralı delegate Jonathan Steele, a foreign correspondent with The Middle East Eye *and formerly with* The Guardian. *This was originally published as an article in the New York Review of Books.*[1]

In the months following last July's failed coup against him, Turkish President Recep Tayyip Erdoğan has mounted the biggest purge of public officials in a century. As has been widely reported, over 100,000 civil servants, teachers, prosecutors, judges, journalists, army officers, and police have been suspended or dismissed. At least 52,000 are now in prison. Most of these are accused of having links with the movement of Fethullah Gülen, the self-exiled Islamist who used to be Erdoğan's ally in curbing the political power of the military in Turkey's secular "deep state" but broke with him in 2013 and is accused of masterminding the coup.

Yet amid the crackdown, the plight of one major group has been far less in view: the country's 14 million Kurds. In Turkey's southeast, a half-million Kurds have been uprooted from their homes in Turkish military operations since July 2015. According to a report issued on March 10 by the United Nations High Commissioner on Human Rights, these actions have been brutal, leading to widespread human rights violations, destruction of property, and the killing of hundreds of Kurds. Recent actions by the government have also clamped down on every sector of the Kurdish movement, including journalists, aid groups, and politicians. A particular target has been the main Kurdish political party, the People's Democratic Party (HDP), which won 59 seats in Parliament in the November, 2015, elections and whose support comes from other minorities and left-wing Turks as well as Kurds.

There is no basis for suspecting collaboration between Gülen and the Kurds, particularly on as sensitive an issue as planning the overthrow of the leader of Turkey. In fact, the Gülen movement has long been more in favour of using military force against the Kurds than has Erdoğan. But Erdoğan is using the post-coup clampdown as a cover for undermining the HDP, claiming the party is a security threat. Twenty-nine HDP MPs have been arrested and fourteen are still in jail, along with dozens of elected local officials accused of links with the PKK, the militant Kurdish Workers' Party that has been in conflict with the government for almost 40 years.

The HDP and PKK are certainly both part of a broad-based Kurdish freedom movement, but the HDP co-chair, Selahattin Demirtaş (now also in jail awaiting trial), has denied that his party has structural connections with the PKK or is its political arm. Nor has there been any evidence that the HDP has supported violence against the government.

In Diyarbakır, the unofficial capital of Turkey's mainly Kurdish southeast, I recently witnessed a court appearance by Çağlar Demirel, one of the town's HDP MPs. Accused of insulting the president and taking actions that amount to being a member of a terrorist organization, she was forced to address a three-judge panel by video link from Kandira prison near Istanbul, almost a thousand miles away. Defiant and uncontrite, she told the judges:

> I've not been shown any evidence. I reject the accusations. There is nothing lawful about detaining MPs. We were all arrested on November 4, 2016, even though we face different charges. This shows the case is the result of political decisions.

The hearing was to decide if Demirel could be released before trial in April. The court ruled against it, the main judge declaring, bizarrely, that being in jail for two more months would not interfere with Demirel's parliamentary duties. In the public gallery Demirel's mother, in a headscarf, wept when the judgement was announced. Demirel looked unfazed. Like most female Kurdish activists she wears her hair uncovered. Gender equality is a core principle of the movement, which has introduced the concept of parity in most public positions. The HDP is led by co-chairs, a man and a woman. Kurdish towns have co-mayors.

Demirel belongs to a cohort of secular Kurdish women in their thirties and forties who have shown extraordinary toughness and determination. One of the most remarkable is Fatima Kasan, a spokesperson for the Free Women's Congress, an organization that fights for equal rights and was banned by Erdoğan last November. Kasan spent twelve years in prison from the age of 18. She told me in February, "We're trying to institutionalize gender equality. We struggle against the patriarchal system, bias against women, and the mechanisms which reproduce discrimination against women, since women were the first group to be colonized." She continued:

> Until the 1990s we were socialists. We saw the collapse of real [Soviet] socialism and decided it was because the emancipation of workers doesn't mean others were also emancipated. Freedom is not equated with seizing a state structure and having a nation-state.

Part of the problem for Turkey's Kurds is that their aspirations continue to be coloured by the long-running conflict between the PKK and the Turkish government. Thirty-three years have passed since the PKK fired its first shots against Turkish police and troops. At that time the PKK was a classic national liberation movement with a Marxist-Leninist orientation that drew comparisons with counterparts elsewhere such as the Sandinistas in Nicaragua or the New People's Army in the Philippines. The PKK's philosophy has since changed but the organization continues to engage in violent confrontations with Turkish security forces. It is exactly a year since the end of the latest clashes between Turkish security forces and Kurdish militants, which took an estimated 2,300 lives in 19 towns and districts in the southeast. Dr. Mehmet Müezzinoğlu, then Minister of

Health, said last year that some 355,000 people were displaced, though the true figure is likely higher. (In its report, the UN human rights office said that up to 500,000 people had been displaced.) Most are still unable to return to their homes because security forces are blocking access to their ruined towns. They are forced to rent apartments or live with relatives elsewhere in Turkey.

Foreign journalists rarely report on these uprooted Kurds, while Western politicians—even those who have been critical of the recent purges—say little. This has been particularly glaring since Turkey has been praised for hosting two million Syrian refugees. The hypocrisy upsets Kurdish aid organizations as they try to collect donations from private citizens in the absence of funding from Ankara.

The last 18 months have taught the Kurdish freedom movement some hard lessons. At first, activists in Turkey were inspired by what was happening next door in northern Syria. Syrian Kurds had declared autonomy and renamed their region Rojava after President Bashar al-Assad withdrew his overstretched forces to Syria's central heartland in 2012. Seeking to copy the Rojava model, Kurds in southeast Turkey started to build barricades and dig trenches in their towns after the ceasefire between the PKK and the Turkish government broke down in July 2015. The aim was to create areas that Turkish security forces could not enter. Starting with the town of Cizre, on the eastern end of Turkey's border with Syria, several places declared autonomy.

But unlike the embattled Syrian military, Turkey has a powerful army and reacted to the Kurds' challenge with enormous force. Abdullah Öcalan, the imprisoned PKK leader, called on the Cizre militants to stand down and they did, briefly. But the uprising took on a dynamic of its own and, helped by PKK commanders, the trench-digging resumed. The Turkish state imposed curfews and pounded besieged towns with artillery and tank fire. PKK fighters ambushed Turkish forces, killing almost 100 police and soldiers within three months. In some ways, this was a departure in Turkey's long conflict with the PKK. In the 1980s and the 1990s the Turkish-Kurdish conflict centred on mountain villages in the southeast. Over 36,000 people were killed, including some 6,700 civilians, according to Turkish security sources. By contrast, the new clashes amounted to urban warfare in densely populated areas. Although far fewer people were killed, the cities involved were devastated.

A year later, the damage can still be seen in Sur, the old city of Diyarbakır, which used to have some 30,000 inhabitants. In 2015, UNESCO declared the old city a world heritage site because of its four miles of eleventh-century walls, including four gates and 82 towers. Ten-foot-tall concrete walls block the alleys that lead into about a third of the city. Only the top of the pre-Ottoman, sixteenth-century square minaret, set on four basalt pillars and known as the four-legged minaret, is visible. Armed police patrol throughout Sur and none of the residents can go back into the closed area. Bulldozers are at work, removing the rubble. Large sections of other towns in the region have been similarly levelled.

Kurdish politicians accuse the Turkish government of committing atrocities, a view that is supported by the findings of the March UN report. But as Emma

Sinclair-Webb, the director of Human Rights Watch's Turkey Office, put it to me, "There is a lot of resentment among ordinary people over the trench-digging and the fact that the PKK embedded themselves in towns and brought the fight there." The government is clearing large areas of several Kurdish towns to try to prevent similar urban uprisings in the future. As Sinclair-Webb explained:

> It claims buildings are unsafe and booby-trapped but it goes far beyond that. We can speculate that they want to replace narrow alleys and small winding roads with wide streets and high-rise blocks which are much easier to cordon off and control access to. It looks like a form of social engineering.

In the actions in the southeast and the repression of Kurdish politicians, the president's short-term aim seems to be to weaken his opponents in the national referendum set for April 16 2017, in which voters are being asked to approve the establishment of what is being called a super-presidency. If the referendum is successful, the post of Prime Minister will be abolished; Erdoğan will be able to appoint ministers and dismiss Parliament at will, control the budget, and nominate senior judges; and he will be eligible to stay in power until 2029. This is the culmination of a drive toward one-man rule that Erdoğan started some five years ago.

Along with the secular Kemalists in the Republican People's Party (CHP), the HDP is firmly against these sweeping changes. In order to ensure that he wins the referendum, Erdoğan appears to be trying to silence the HDP since it represents at least 10% of the electorate. But questions remain about the president's long-term objectives. Does he need to suppress the Kurds because he wants a powerful presidency? Or does he need a powerful presidency in order to suppress the Kurds? If his campaign against the Kurds is a strategic shift rather than a mere tactical manoeuvre, then the Kurdish conflict may be one of those struggles that can never be resolved.

There are countervailing indications. The Kurdish movement's aims in Turkey are less ambitious, territorially and politically, than those of the leadership of Iraqi Kurdistan, which has, ironically, good relations with Turkey, in part because it is seen as an effective counterweight to the PKK. Turkey also enjoys economic and political leverage over Erbil since the oil pipelines from Iraqi Kurdistan go through Turkey. In Erbil, the seat of Iraq's Kurdistan Regional Government (KRG), Massoud Barzani, the president of the KRG, has—against the advice of its US government allies and to the consternation of Baghdad—called for independence and threatened to hold a referendum to break away from the larger Arab-majority areas of Iraq. The issue has been postponed by the battle to liberate Mosul from ISIS control because the Kurdish Peshmerga and the Iraqi national army need each other to defeat the jihadists. But once ISIS is driven out of Mosul a major conflict may arise between Erbil and Baghdad. Control of much of the land in Iraq's northwest has been disputed between Kurds and Arabs for decades. In the early months of resistance to ISIS the Kurds seized these lands as a useful buffer. It will not be easy for the Iraqi government to get them back.

By contrast, the Kurds of Turkey no longer talk much about secession and independence. In the years since his 1999 capture and imprisonment on İmralı island in the Sea of Marmara, the thinking of PKK leader Abdullah Öcalan has undergone a profound shift. He has long since abandoned his Marxism-Leninism as well as his aspiration for a breakaway Kurdish republic. The Kurds are now an anomaly among liberation movements. They want to be a nation without a nation-state.

In Öcalan's prison writings, published in 2013 under the title *War and Peace in Kurdistan* by a group of his sympathizers called the International Initiative,[2] the PKK leader criticized the classic nation-state as hierarchical and authoritarian. "There should be a lean state as a political institution, which only observes functions in the fields of internal and external security and in the provision of social security," he wrote. The ideal system of government, he argued, would be "democratic confederalism" or "democratic autonomy," based on collective cultural rights enshrined in the Turkish constitution, bilingual public administration with education in Kurdish, the devolution of political and administrative powers to town councils, and the sharing of sovereignty between the central government and a Kurdish regional authority. It sounds no more radical than, say, the "asymmetric federalism" that Quebec enjoys in Canada.

Thus, the PKK's initial goal of a "national democratic revolution," leading later to socialism, across all the Kurdish lands in Iran, Iraq, Syria, and Turkey, has been replaced by the aim of a "solution within Turkey" that could be a model for Kurdish areas in neighbouring countries. As Öcalan put it in *War and Peace in Kurdistan*, "It is possible to build confederate structures across all parts of Kurdistan without the need to question the existing borders."

Some may argue that Öcalan's position is a smokescreen, forced on him by his life sentence in prison and by new geopolitical realities. Against that view one has to place the fact that his opinions are echoed by his adherents across Turkey as well as in northern Syria, where the largest political grouping, the Democratic Union Party (PYD), began as an offshoot of the PKK. The display of Öcalan's picture is illegal in Turkey, but it hangs in offices across Syrian Kurdistan.

This leads to a second reason why a solution to the Kurdish conflict in Turkey may be less remote than it seems. Making the initial contact is often the hardest part in any peace process. In Northern Ireland, the British government followed years of reluctance to talk to the Irish Republican Army with years of denying that any talks had started. But the Turkish government has already broken the taboo and held peace talks with the Kurds. Turkey describes the PKK as a terrorist group and has persuaded its European neighbours, as well as the United States, to issue the same designation. But in 2013 Erdoğan authorized Turkish officials to start a dialogue with Öcalan, along with representatives of the HDP.

In Istanbul I spoke to Pervin Buldan, the HDP MP who was a member of the delegation that made the initial two-hour boat trip to İmralı island to meet government officials and Öcalan in 2013. She and other Kurdish activists like to compare Öcalan with Nelson Mandela, another leader of a major liberation movement who was detained on a prison island. There are differences of treatment. While Mandela was forced to do hard physical labour in Robben Island's quarry and was denied writing material except to send occasional letters, Öcalan was not required to work. He was allowed pen and paper and the right to transmit his manuscripts (censored, of course) to the mainland via his lawyers. But while Mandela had the companionship of fellow African political inmates, Öcalan was kept in isolation for ten years. Five other PKK prisoners with life sentences were then sent there. Three are still in the island prison but it is not clear how much contact, if any, they have had with Öcalan. He has had no visits from outsiders since his brother was allowed in briefly last September.

"I attended every one of the thirty-two sessions that the process lasted," Buldan told me. "I would also go to talk to the PKK at its headquarters in the Qandil mountains [in Iraq] and also go to Ankara. There was a ceasefire. Öcalan presented us with a perspective of a peaceful solution and democratization, not only in Turkey but throughout the Middle East. An official record was kept. It resulted in a road-map of ten points. Öcalan gave great importance to having a team of monitors to watch implementation. He said that the day the team arrived would be the day when negotiations would begin. He would call on the PKK to lay down its arms."

At the culmination of these talks, Buldan and two HDP colleagues were invited to attend a joint press conference with the Turkish deputy prime minister, Yalçın Akdoğan, and the interior minister, Muammer Dervişoğlu, in the Prime Minister's office in Istanbul's Dolmabahçe Palace on 28 February, 2015. Though the plan was to read a joint statement, the two sides each read their own statement. Only the Kurdish one mentioned Öcalan's road map as a way forward, though it did not go into detail. The government statement made no mention of a monitoring committee or the start of negotiations. Erdoğan made his own position known a few days later. He denied there was any monitoring committee or agreement on negotiations.

Why did Erdoğan turn away from the peace talks? It seems to have been largely a matter of malign opportunism. Cuma Çiçek offers a clear analysis of Erdoğan's shift in attitude towards the Kurds of Turkey. It began, he argues, with the attack by ISIS on the largely Kurdish city of Kobane on the northern Syrian border in July 2014. The battle captured world attention and drove Kurds across the region to mobilize in solidarity with the besieged city while Turkish forces watched idly by from across the border. Kurds fought desperately to defend Kobane until the US-led coalition in Iraq started bombing ISIS positions and forced the jihadists to retreat.

The victory gave a new boost to the Kurds' drive for autonomy throughout northern Syria. Erdoğan saw the contagion spreading into Turkey. He felt he could not afford to let the HDP take credit for ending the Turkish-Kurdish conflict in advance of the June 2015 parliamentary elections, especially since the HDP was vowing to thwart his ambitions to change the Constitution and establish a super-presidency. Çiçek wrote, "The open, sincere, reassuring and stable role of the HDP in the ongoing peace process increased the party's credibility throughout society." In the election, the HDP won 13 per cent of the vote, with support from many progressive non-Kurds, and took 80 of the Parliament's 550 seats even with the peace process on hold (the HDP vote fell back slightly in the next elections). A month later this détente collapsed when a clash between the PKK and Turkish security forces prompted Erdoğan to launch multiple air strikes on PKK bases in Iraq, effectively ending the ceasefire.

Could the Turkish government resume peace talks with Öcalan and the Kurds after the April referendum? The latest polls about the vote are contradictory, with several showing victory for the "No" side and others for the "Yes" side. If Erdoğan loses, his mood will not favour any kind of reconciliation with those who opposed him in the referendum. If he wins, there might be more of a chance. In an intriguing recent article in Daily Sabah, a strongly pro-government paper, Meryem İlayda Atlas, its opinion editor, described the resumption of peace talks as "inevitable." "The question now is not when, but how they restart and who will the State talk to," she wrote.

If the Turkish majority can be persuaded that Kurdish demands relate mainly to cultural rights and local power, then the basis for peace need not be hard to find. Atlas went on to say, correctly, that "a majority of Kurds now live in urban centres, enjoying a higher standard of living and traveling more than ever." In his book, Çiçek makes a similar point, arguing that in Turkey's traditional Kurdish heartland in the underdeveloped southeast the HDP and PKK rely on poor and lower-middle-class supporters, who favour cooperative arrangements for the economy. This is the antithesis of the neoliberal policies of Erdoğan's party as well as of the new Kurdish urban middle class in Istanbul and western Turkey. Yet regardless of their economic views or social status, neither Kurdish group seeks territorial sovereignty, a point that Öcalan made more than a decade ago. He needs to be freed so as to resume talks with the government on a fair basis. There is no better way to restore peace.

Notes:

1.   Jonathan Steele. "Turkey and the Kurds: A Chance for Peace?" *The New York Review of Books*. April 20, 2017. Accessed May 28, 2017. http://bit.ly/2tQSgW9.

2.   The International Initiative is not just any group of sympathizers, but includes an extremely prominent group of public figures and intellectuals from around the globe. Among its first signatories can be found three winners of the Nobel Peace Prize (Mairead Maguire, Adolfo Pérez Esquival, and José Ramos-Horta), two winners of the Nobel Prize in Literature (Dario Fo and José Saramago), and many prominent politicians and academics from Germany, Britain, and other European countries. For more information: http://bit.ly/2yQK8KM.

EU Turkey Civic Commission Cover Letter for the Report of the Third İmralı International Peace Delegation

Dear Colleagues

The Third EU Turkey Civic Commission (EUTCC) İmralı Delegation Report of March 2017 provides a first-hand account of the situation in Turkey in the early months of 2017, as the country approaches the Presidential Powers Referendum on April 16. The delegation met with a broad range of politicians, lawyers, NGOs, trade unionists, journalists and peace activists in order to assess the impact of the current deterioration of political and civil liberties in Turkey with a particular focus on the Kurdish question and the continued detention of Kurdish leader Abdullah Öcalan.

The State of Emergency imposed across the Kurdish regions of Turkey, after the ruling AKP party lost its parliamentary majority in the 2015 elections, pre-saged the wider State of Emergency, which is still in place throughout Turkey following the failed coup of July 2016.

Since November 2015, 2000 people have been killed in the renewed conflict and many more displaced. The United Nations has reported on wide scale egregious human rights violations in the region, including killings and destruction of property. As of December 2016, more than 10 Members of Parliament from the pro Kurdish HDP Party are in detention, 64 elected mayors and co-mayors have been detained in Kurdish cities, 5000 HDP members arrested over the last 18 months, of whom 2488 are still in custody.

The EUTCC has held conferences on an annual basis since the inception of the EU-Turkey Accession process in 2004, convening leading human rights institutions, political parties, academics, journalists, unionists, writers, legal experts and prominent Kurdish and Turkish intellectuals to discuss the Kurdish question in Turkey and the Middle East. The EUTCC acts as a point of contact, and a platform for different actors working on issues related to the Kurds, Turkey and the Middle East and exchanges information with the institutions of the EU as well as other governmental and non-governmental organisations. The latest report adds to a body of accurate and objective information about the political situation in Turkey.

18 March 2017

Kariane Westrheim
EUTCC chairperson
Professor at the University of Bergen, Department of Education, Norway

State Terror, Human Rights Violations, and Authoritarianism in Turkey

Report of the Third EUTCC İmralı International Peace Delegation,
Based on its Visit to Turkey, 13–19 February, 2017

Introduction

The events of the past year and a half demonstrate very clearly that there can be no democracy in Turkey without a peaceful resolution of the Kurdish question. The political situation in the country has deteriorated dramatically since the breakdown of the peace process in mid-June, 2015, and especially since the failed coup in mid-July, 2016. President Erdoğan has taken advantage of the state of emergency to repress all opposition, not just those groups allegedly implicated in the coup. Many repressive measures have violated certain European and human rights norms to which Turkey is bound. These measures not only targeted the Kurdish freedom movement with special intensity, but have also extended to dissenting voices in the media and academia, as well as trade unions, human rights organizations, and wider civil society. To make matters worse, the victims

A press conference with the Democratic Regions Party (DBP) in Diyarbakır/Amed deploring the local human rights situation in the city; February 2017. During the press conference, a large contingent of police and a water cannon truck were deployed outside the building, an example of the heavy sense of state terror throughout the city.

of these repressive measures have virtually no effective recourse to the judiciary, whose independence has been severely undermined. Indeed, the judiciary itself has experienced a massive and unlawful purge, as has the public administration and the education system.[1]

An international peace delegation was organized by the EU Turkey Civic Commission (EUTCC), consisting of ten members from Europe and North America, including members of the European Parliament and the Council of Europe, academics, and journalists. The delegation visited Turkey 13–19 February, 2017.

The delegation witnessed and noted the dire civil and human rights situation in the country. Delegates met representatives from the Kurdish freedom movement, political parties, trade unions, lawyers, academics, journalists, and representatives of other civil society organizations in both Diyarbakır and Istanbul, and attended the unlawful, politicized trial of Ms. Çağlar Demirel, an MP in the Peoples' Democratic Party (HDP) from Diyarbakır. The delegation met with many people in Diyarbakır who gave testimonies about their experiences over the past 18 months, which included military assaults, blanket curfews, various infringements of civil rights, and even human rights abuses.

Through the office of Julie Ward MEP, the delegation applied to the Turkish Minister of Justice requesting a meeting with the leader of the Kurdish freedom movement, Abdullah Öcalan, who has been imprisoned in inhumane conditions on İmralı Island since 1999 and is considered a crucial figure in the peace process. Unfortunately, the Minister of Justice did not respond to the request. The delegation noted Turkey's non-compliance with the recommendations of the Committee for the Prevention of Torture regarding the unlawful and inhumane treatment of Abdullah Öcalan.

The delegation also attempted to visit the co-chair of the HDP, Selahattin Demirtaş, currently imprisoned unconstitutionally in Edirne. The request to visit the prison was rejected. The delegation was particularly disturbed by the unconstitutional imprisonment of other elected representatives of the HDP, the country's third largest political party, as well as the unlawful persecution and detention of many of its members. These unlawful detentions escalated in a most alarming fashion during our visit, with at least 834 people detained between February 13 and 15, according to the Turkish Ministry of the Interior.[2]

The escalating persecution of the HDP is especially worrisome against the backdrop of the run-up to the referendum regarding President Erdoğan's proposed hyper-presidentialist amendments to the constitution. HDP representatives with whom we spoke consistently reiterated the very plausible claim that President Erdoğan is trying to undermine the party's capacity to operate, organize, and carry out its campaign for a "No" vote. This situation, combined with the repression of opposition media, means that the conditions for a free and fair plebiscite on the proposed constitutional changes simply do not hold, casting serious doubt on the democratic legitimacy of the outcome of the referendum. It also bodes very poorly for the peace process, not to mention the stability of the country more generally.

State Terror and Human Rights Violations

People who spoke with the delegation consistently reported state terror and human rights abuses perpetrated by the Turkish authorities since the unravelling of the peace process. On 4 September, 2015, Turkish security forces sealed off the city of Cizre and placed it under curfew. This was the first of over sixty sieges on urban neighbourhoods and cities carried out across the Kurdish region in security operations justified as attempts to "flush out" insurgents.

Numerous documented human rights atrocities have taken place during these curfews.[3] Hundreds of civilians have been killed and entire towns have been shelled to the ground during successive waves of round-the-clock blanket curfews that last from a day through several months.[4] According to a recent Human Rights Watch (HRW) report, up to 400,000 people have been displaced in the process.[5] However, Amnesty International and OHCHR (the Office of the United Nations High Commissioner for Human Rights) both estimate the number of displaced people to be closer to 500,000.[6]

The cities under curfew were pounded with heavy artillery and tank fire. Children were killed. People of all ages were shot dead in the streets but, because of the curfew, their bodies could not be retrieved for extended periods. Certain police forces were licensed to shoot anyone with full impunity. These special forces were not commanded by local governors but were directly linked to the central government. In one particularly egregious example in Cizre, civilians who had taken refuge in three separate basements were burned alive; the State then destroyed the buildings in order to eliminate the evidence.[7] In addition, in the Sur district of Diyarbakır, UNESCO world heritage sites have been badly damaged.[8] These events most certainly constitute war crimes and crimes against humanity. Mr. Ahmet Özmer, the chair of the Diyarbakır Bar Association, with whom the delegation met, explained the gravity of the situation in both human and constitutional terms:

> July 2015 was a milestone. This was when the armed conflict recommenced and the criminalization of Kurdish organizations [was implemented]. Since then, we have witnessed a step back to the old policy perspective of the deep state. We have seen urban warfare, and curfews declared, still partially continuing in the Sur district. These curfews have no bases in law. Even if Turkey were not a member of the Council of Europe nor applying to the EU, these curfews are still a violation of the Turkish Constitution, specifically Articles 13 and 15. Nor is there any basis in the Turkish legal framework. Articles 13 and 15 of the Constitution stipulate the conditions in which rights and liberties can be narrowed. There are four such conditions: (1) war; (2) war campaigns; (3) martial law approved by the assembly; (4) state of emergency. None of these were met when the curfews were declared. The Venice Commission published a report at the European Parliament, analysing the incompliance with Turkey's internal law. They came to the same conclusion.

The crimes continue. During our visit, blockades and round-the-clock curfews were implemented in several villages around Diyarbakır, as well as in the border city of Nusaybin, in the province of Mardin, with reports of serious human rights violations, including shootings, torture, and the shelling and demolishing of houses. During this period, HDP deputies and human rights activists have been barred from entering the curfew zones.[9]

Amnesty International and the Council of Europe expressed grave concerns about the situation in areas placed under curfew, condemning the use of disproportionate force and the imposition of measures that amount to collective punishment, and called on Turkey to allow independent observers. These calls went unheeded.[10] Instead, as Mr. Ahmet Özmer lamented in a meeting with our delegation, "No serious interrogation or legal actions have been pursued related to these great crimes. Impunity has been granted to state agents (to the soldiers in command), and so they don't face any consequences for committing crimes."

Worse than impunity, those who have spoken out against state terror and human rights atrocities in the Kurdish region have been persecuted and silenced. Even before the failed coup and state of emergency, academics were threatened for opposing the conduct of the war, lawyers were intimidated and subject to criminal charges for defending Kurds, journalists were prosecuted, and media outlets were closed down for questioning the descent into war. Such persecution has escalated greatly during the state of emergency.

Indeed, the HRW report includes a chilling chapter on recent events in Turkey, in which it denounces "the government's increasing authoritarianism," and emphasizes especially the "crackdown in the aftermath of the attempted coup."[11] The report documents concerted efforts by the Erdoğan government to silence dissenting voices.

The extraordinary powers granted to the president during the state of emergency have greatly facilitated his increasingly authoritarian ambitions, and enabled violations of civil and human rights in what amounts to a naked power grab. As the HRW report highlights:

> Under the state of emergency, the president presides over the cabinet, which can pass decrees without parliamentary scrutiny or possibility of appeal to the constitutional court. Many decrees passed contain measures which conflict with basic human rights safeguards and Turkey's obligations under international and domestic law.

> These include provisions allowing for dismissal without an investigation, confiscation of property without judicial review, police custody of up to 30 days, and the reintroduction of incommunicado detention in which detainees can be denied access to a lawyer in the first five days of custody, giving rise to heightened risks of ill-treatment.

Repression of Academics and Purges of the Education System

In January, 2016, in response to a petition by over 1,000 university lecturers objecting to the spiralling repression in southeast Turkey and which called for a return to the negotiating table with the PKK, the Erdoğan government embarked on an assault on academic freedom and the silencing of dissenting voices. The "Academics for Peace" signatories have been subjected to a campaign of intimidation and social and legal persecution. Signatories are facing criminal investigations for "insulting the Turkish State." Dozens were dismissed by their universities in the spring, and in the fall, thanks to the state of emergency, 68 were dismissed by executive decree, bringing the total number of dismissed "Academics for Peace" to 126.

During emergency rule, a veritable purge of the academy has taken place. More than 11,000 academics are currently under investigation. Fully 4,481 academics have been dismissed alongside another 1,102 administrative personnel.[12] Nor have university-level academics been the only educators targeted by the Erdoğan government. The assault on academic freedom at the university level has been accompanied by an even more systematic purge of faculty employed in primary and secondary schools. During our visit to Diyarbakır, trade union representatives informed us that over 10,000 members of the primary and secondary school teachers' union, Egitim-Sen, have been suspended from their posts, and that one of the main reasons for these suspensions was that they had participated in a strike at the end of 2015 calling for peace. In addition to these suspensions, to make matters worse, during emergency rule over 30,000 educators working for the Ministry of Education have been dismissed, and the contracts of another 21,000 educators in private education institutions have been cancelled. In consequence, 15 private universities and over 900 private schools were forced to shut down altogether.[13]

Attacks on NGOs, the Free Press, and Social Media

The education system has not been the sole target for government attacks. As Mr. Ahmet Özmer, put it, "the state of emergency has turned into a campaign for the elimination of all opposition in Turkey." This campaign includes the closure by decree of over 1500 non-governmental and civil society organizations, 123 foundations, and 19 unions, federations, and confederations.

The Erdoğan government has also launched a virulent attack against independent and opposition media. Indeed, even before the post-coup assault, the situation had been rapidly deteriorating. In 2016, Turkey ranked 151st out of 180 countries included in the Committee to Protect Journalists' World Press Freedom list, while Freedom House ranked Turkey 71st out of 100 countries in terms of press freedom, labelling it "unfree."[14] The Human Rights Watch (HRW) report denounced the disturbing trends in prosecution and jailing of journalists over the course of 2016. To date, 839 journalists have stood trial for articles they published, and 189 have suffered verbal and physical assaults from police and security forces. Some 151 journalists are now under arrest, "making Turkey once again a world leader in jailing journalists."[15] The Erdoğan government has arrested some journalists for alleged links to the Gülen movement, and others for alleged links to the PKK. Yet it has presented no evidence of criminal wrongdoing to substantiate the charges.

In addition, 176 media outlets have been closed down, again mostly for alleged links to the Gülen movement or, more frequently, the PKK. In the process,

Jonathan Steele with banned Turkish and Kurdish journalists; Istanbul, February 2017. Since the 2016 coup attempt, almost 200 media outlets have been shut down and around 3 000 journalists fired, blacklisted from all employment and social security benefits.

the government has seized the assets of these outlets. It has targeted outlets for ethnic and religious minorities. Indeed, "almost all of the national and local TV and radio stations broadcasting for the Kurdish and Alevi communities have been closed." As a result of these closures, 780 press cards have been cancelled and over 3000 journalists have lost their jobs.[16] Even worse, as Mr. Baris Baristiran from Özgür Gün informed the delegation, "the mainstream Turkish media will not hire journalists who used to work for media outlets that have been closed down, and the State threatens those who consider employing them." Meanwhile, the Turkish Union of Journalists has been closed down by decree.

The result is the effective silencing of critical reporting about the ongoing campaign of state terror and human rights violations in the Kurdish region. As Ms. Fatima Gul from the Democratic Regions Party explained:

> We are cut off from the Turkish regions. While the urban conflicts were going on, there was still coverage in the press, but not anymore. In the aftermath of the attempted coup, the opposition media has been decimated. And the pro-government media manipulate what is happening. Their headlines read, "Huge Operation Targeting Terror." People are even being arrested for what they post on social media.

Indeed, the crackdown on freedom of expression extends to social media as well. According to the Turkish Ministry of Interior, during the first six months of emergency rule, fully 3,170 people had been processed and 1,656 arrested, charged with "making terrorist propaganda" on social media. Some 1,203 have been released and are under judicial control. As of mid-January, 2017, some 84 people remained detained, and 767 had been released after having been detained. The Ministry of Interior added that over 10,000 cases had been filed, and that the identification details of those who had been identified as aiders-and-abettors of "terrorism" had been passed on to public prosecutors. Charges included "incitement of public hatred, praising and making propaganda for a terrorist organization, declaring links to a terrorist organization, defaming officials, attempting to damage the unity of the State, and jeopardizing the safety of the public." In addition, the Ministry of Interior has announced "higher cooperation with service providers, such as Twitter, Facebook, and YouTube." Even for simply sharing statements made by HDP co-chairs, ordinary citizens have been arrested for "supporting a terrorist organization." Such are the lengths to which the Erdoğan government is willing to go to silence dissenting Kurds.[17]

In February 2017, the Commissioner of Human Rights for the Council of Europe issued a memorandum on freedom of expression and media freedom in which it condemned the current situation in no uncertain terms. The Commissioner expressed his "utmost concern" about "the scale and speed of the deterioration of the situation regarding media freedom and freedom of expression in Turkey." He documented "numerous, blatant violations of principles enshrined in the ECHR, the case law of the European Court of Human Rights, [the] standards of the Council of Europe, as well as other relevant international standards." He also denounced that such "violations have created a distinct chilling effect manifesting itself not only in self-censorship in the remaining media which is not controlled by or sympathetic to the government and the ruling political party, but also among ordinary citizens."[18]

Purges in the Bureaucracy, the Military, and the Judiciary

"The state of emergency is a threat to all citizens and a weapon for intimidating the opposition." These words were spoken by Ms. Çağlar Demirel MP during her trial. She might have added that the state of emergency is also a means through which Erdoğan has managed to tighten his grip on power within the state apparatus, including, crucially, the education system, the military, the bureaucracy, and the judiciary. The Erdoğan government's counter-attack has extended well beyond the coup plotters. Erdoğan has used emergency rule to target and purge all checks and balances on his power, both from within the State and from without. Erdoğan himself has tended to bypass Parliament and effectively rule by decree, thereby limiting access to the judiciary. Indeed, the proposed constitutional changes aim to replace the rule of law with rule by tyrannical presidential decree. As Mr. Ahmet Özmer explained:

> Since the state of emergency was declared, there has been limited access to justice. Decrees during the state of emergency do not need the approval of the Turkish Assembly. There have been decrees made almost weekly. They are changing laws through decrees.
>
> How do these decrees work in practice? Democratically elected mayors and employees of the State have been dismissed by decree. Tens of thousands of people have been dismissed. NGOs have been closed down. Members of Parliament have been jailed. … When you look at the lists of people dismissed, some are related to the Gülen movement, but the majority are not. The main target seems to be the Kurds, but not only the Kurds. …

Even during a state of exception, there are still certain rules and regulations. It can be extended with the approval of the majority of the assembly, and lasts for a three-month period. The current state of emergency ends at the end of March. There must be a relation between the threat, which is the main cause of the state of emergency, and the actions undertaken by the State. However, this is not happening.

As lawyers, we cannot help because, especially in those cases of people dismissed by decree, there are no legal channels to help. No appeals. The right to defence is under serious threat. People are being detained for five days without being able to meet with their lawyers. People are being detained for 30 days without any charges. As lawyers, there is no space, no mechanism for us to make an impact. In hearings, we are constantly reminding the judges how the principles of democracy and the rule of law should work. But in the final verdicts, these show no impact.

More than one representative from the Kurdish freedom movement with whom we spoke during our visit aptly referred to the ongoing state of emergency as Erdoğan's "counter-coup"—a counter-coup that Erdoğan hopes to consolidate via plebiscite in the upcoming April 2017 referendum on reforms of the Turkish Constitution. During emergency rule, a major purge has been carried out in the bureaucracy and in the coercive state apparatus proper—the police and the military. According to the Ministry of Labour and Social Security, nearly 100,000 civil servants have been dismissed. A quarter of these were police officers. Even more significantly, the military has been dramatically reduced in size. Before the coup, the Turkish armed forces employed nearly 520,000 people; by December of 2016, that number had been slashed by 30%, to about 355,000.

The judge and prosecutor in Ms. Demirel's trial were both in their early thirties. This was not a coincidence. As Mr. Ahmet Özmer, who served as one of Ms. Demirel's defence lawyers in the trial, explained to us two days before:

We are experiencing the worst moment in the history of the Turkish judiciary, in terms of the lack of independence of the judiciary. Some 4,370 personnel in the judiciary have been dismissed since the coup. More than half of these have been arrested and accused of being members of a terrorist organization. Students who have recently finished law school and who have no training are being appointed as judges. To make matters worse, one of the main criteria for their appointments is political obedience to Mr. Erdoğan.

The independence, as well as expertise and competence of the judiciary has been severely undermined as a result of the massive purge. Nearly 3,700 judges and prosecutors have been dismissed, along with nearly 200 members of the military judiciary; around 250 judges, experts, and administrative personnel at the Court of Accounts and the Council of State; over 220 experts and administrative personnel at the Court of Cassation and the Constitutional Court; and another 15 administrative personnel of the High Council of Judges and Prosecutors. The compromised and politicized judiciary, combined with the extraordinary powers granted to the president during the state of emergency, has left victims of civil and human rights abuses at the hands of an increasingly authoritarian state without any effective legal protection, recourse, or redress.

To make matters even worse, Erdoğan is seeking to embed the subordination of the judiciary to the executive as part of his package of proposed constitutional amendments. Indeed, as a Turkish lawyer, Professor Bülent Çiçekli, warned in a well-argued assessment of the scope and content of the proposed reforms:

> Practically all the members of the Constitutional Court will be selected and appointed by the president, which would make it difficult for the Constitutional Court to act independently of the president. The president will also have a broad authority over the formation of the Council of Judges and Prosecutors (HSK) directly and indirectly through the parliamentary majority. The bill leaves no space for any self-representation from among the judiciary through a direct election. It would be impossible to talk about the independence and impartiality of the judiciary from the executive in the new amended constitution. (*Assessment of the Turkish Constitutional Amendment*, p. 10)

Crackdown on the HDP and the DBP

If the state of emergency has provided the means by which President Erdoğan has managed to purge the State, to undermine the independence of the judiciary, and to silence dissenting voices—in effect, to consummate a counter-coup—the "war on terror" has provided the alibi. The crackdown on the HDP, so tragic in its consequences, is most illustrative in this regard.[19]

The unprecedented success of the HDP in the June 2015 election was a reflection, a reward, and a vote of confidence for its constructive role in, and firm commitment to, the peace process. But for Erdoğan, the HDP's electoral success proved the principle parliamentary obstacle and frustration for his hyper-presidentialist ambitions. As Ms. Fatima Gul, a representative from the Democratic Regions Party (DBP), a party affiliated with the HDP, explained to our delegation:

> The general election of 2015 was revolutionary for Turkey. For the first time, all oppressed groups—Kurds, Alevis, women—could have a platform. But the government managed to turn the electoral results into a purge operation. In the aftermath of that election, the regime has targeted many groups, especially Kurds.

Indeed, in the aftermath of the election, President Erdoğan opted decisively for a strategy of war and deliberate societal polarization. He called for a new snap election and pushed aggressively for the criminalization of the HDP. He deliberately destroyed the peace process, veered to the far right, and appealed to ultra-Turkish nationalist sentiment. He chose to ignite a spiral of violence and repression by unleashing a ruthless persecution of the most persistent and courageous advocates for peace, who he rebranded as "terrorists." Or, as Mr. Ibrahim Bilmez, one of Abdullah Öcalan's lawyers, described it to us:

> To briefly summarize, in the 7 June, 2015, general elections, this overall atmosphere of hope led to a great success by the HDP—6 million votes, the third largest party, with 80 MPs. But the AKP and Erdoğan lost votes in the election. Unfortunately, Erdoğan based his calculations on votes. His conclusion was that the peace process led him to lose votes. He preferred votes to peace. Since

then, he has provoked an atmosphere of fear and terror. He calculated it would help him, and it did. On the 1 November election, the AKP got back some votes, and the HDP was less successful. But the cost is great. Today we face a gloomy landscape, and we are heading towards a referendum in which dictatorship is on the table.

Ms. Demirel expressed the gravity of the situation while defending herself at her trial. In her words:

> I am an MP elected by the people. A party with 6 million votes, the third largest party in the Assembly. We represent the will of 6 million people. This legal process is the outcome of a political decision. The will of the people is on trial. According to the Constitution, this trial means a trial of the will of the people. Isn't it strange that while they are lifting the immunity of MPs, they are granting immunity to soldiers? That is the mentality: to bring war inside of Turkey, and war outside of Turkey.

Ms. Demirel was right to mention the intimate link between the "domestic" and the "international" fronts in the drive for war. Even before the election—both chronologically and in terms of causal importance—events in Kobane had put the peace process under severe stress. The successful defence of Kobane against ISIS's genocidal siege, a heroic defence by revolutionary Kurdish forces in control in the northeast of Syria, inspired by Abdullah Öcalan and seeking to implement his project of "democratic autonomy/ democratic confederalism," had caused great concern within the coercive state apparatus.

The Turkish "national security community" not only feared contagion (i.e., a spillover of the Rojava model), but was also incensed and felt deeply threatened by the increasing collaboration between Syrian Kurdish forces and the USA in the ongoing war against ISIS. Compounding tensions further, the "national security community" was also greatly embarrassed by the exposure of its complicity with ISIS, throwing its commitment to NATO into question. Indeed, that the HDP defended those responsible for bringing such complicity between the Turkish state and ISIS to light no doubt contributed to the virulence with which Erdoğan turned on them. In fact, one of the many cases filed against HDP co-chairs Mr. Selahattin Demirtaş and Ms. Figen Yüksekdağ is related to a joint press statement that was a response to the "well-publicized prosecution of the journalists Can Dündar and Erdem Gul for [exposing] truckloads of weapons transferred by the government to jihadist groups in Syria," which resulted in their conviction for "revealing secret information belonging to the State." The co-chairs criticized the trial in their statement and recalled the president's threat that "they will pay for it," before remarking, "[t]he president exacts payment." For these comments, the co-chairs face the criminal charge of "insulting the president."[20]

This charge is but one of hundreds that have been filed against HDP members of Parliament since parliamentary immunity was lifted for 55 of the 59 in their group. The move to lift immunity gained momentum in early January, 2016, spurred on by President Erdoğan himself, who publicly "advised" the Parliament that "HDP MPs should go to prison." In the weeks and months that followed, the number of dossiers affecting immunity that were prepared against members of the HDP skyrocketed.[21] As the HDP has explained in its own thorough and incisive report on the subject:

> [t]he Turkish constitution adopted under the military junta in 1982 recognizes [only] a limited form of parliamentary immunity. … [W]hile the promise of narrowing immunities to fight political corruption has been a key agenda in many political parties' electoral platforms since [the] 1980s, parliamentary immunities were lifted only twice; both when nationalist alliances were formed to exclude Kurdish political representation in Turkey's Parliament.[22]

On both previous occasions, excluding representatives of the Kurdish freedom movement from representation in Parliament served to "aggravate the long-standing Kurdish conflict, costing tens of thousands of human lives over decades." So too with this third occasion.

Between 2013 and 2015, the Erdoğan government seemed committed to the pursuit of a "democratic resolution" to the Kurdish question. During this brief period, Erdoğan and his government proved willing to break many long-standing taboos, for starters, by even recognizing the existence of a "Kurdish question." The HDP played a crucial role throughout the so-called "resolution process." As was formally requested and sanctioned by the AKP government and state institutions, party officials agreed to serve as "mediators between the State and government bodies" on the one side, and Abdullah Öcalan and the PKK on the other. But after the breakdown of the resolution process, these same officials faced criminal charges for their role in the peace negotiations.[23]

Already in the run-up to the June election, President Erdoğan began accusing the HDP of terrorism, even when ISIS attacked and murdered its supporters. The party faced significant harassment and intimidation throughout the campaign, which escalated in the run-up to the snap election in November. Since then, the assault has been full-fledged.

Amidst a spiral of violence and repression, the HDP has suffered waves of massive state-sponsored repression. Between 22 July, 2015, and 10 January, 2017, fully 8,930 HDP members have been detained and 2,782 imprisoned. In addition, between January, 2015, and January, 2017, HDP offices were attacked on at least 494 occasions, including one attack on party headquarters, which was "set on fire by racist mobs."[24]

On 20 May, 2016, Parliament passed an Immunity Bill in which the procedures prescribed in Article 83 of the 1982 Constitution were not followed. The Parliament ignored the constitutional rules on at least three counts by: (1) allowing a blanket vote over hundreds of immunity cases at once; (2) by obstructing parliamentary review of the cases; and (3) by depriving deputies of the right to defend themselves against the accusations included in their dossiers. In addition, the constitution was violated by the fact that President Erdoğan, who is constitutionally required to remain impartial with respect to parliamentary activities, openly campaigned for the passage of the Bill, claiming, "[m]y nation wants them in prison."[25] In total, 55 HDP members of Parliament now face 654 criminal charges listed in 510 cases. The baseless and evidence-free nature of so many of the charges filed against them speaks volumes. As the HDP aptly states in its report, it is not simply the acts of individual parliamentarians that are being put on trial, but rather the very values and principles that the HDP stands for.[26] Indeed, ever since the breakdown of the peace process, many of the "key understandings, values and perspectives" defended consistently by the HDP in its party program and in its political campaigns have come to be criminalized, as constituting apologies for "terror."

For example, one of the many charges against HDP co-chair Selahattin Demirtaş is for "making propaganda for a terrorist organization." The supposed grounds for this charge were the use of the words "Kurds" and "Kurdistan" in two public speeches in 2012. It might be worth noting that President Erdoğan himself made use of those terms during the "resolution process."[27]

Perhaps even more absurdly, co-chair Demirtaş was charged again with "making propaganda for a terrorist organization" based on a photograph that was taken of him at PKK headquarters in the Kandil mountains during the "resolution process," where he had travelled many times in his role as mediator between the State, Öcalan, and the PKK, with not only the State's full knowledge, but at the State's behest.[28]

Another case against Demirtaş includes charges of "attempting to destroy the unity of the State and country," "praising a crime and a criminal," "inciting people to hatred and enmity," and "making propaganda for a terrorist organization." The grounds for these was a speech Demirtaş gave in January of 2016 at a rally in Van, in which he expressed the right to defend his ideas: "Let's get together and discuss things. We say autonomy. Why is your [defence of presidency] a right and ours is not? Let's go on live broadcast, Mr. Prime Minister. You defend presidency and I shall defend autonomy."[29]

Another example comes from Mr. Ziya Pir, an MP from Diyarbakır, who met with the delegation. Among the charges that Mr. Pir faces are those of "membership of a terrorist organization" and "inciting people to enmity and hatred" for making this remark in a speech in Diyarbakır in November 2015: "Self-governance is our right and we shall earn our right."[30] Mr. Pir faces up to 15 years in prison if convicted. These and other charges against Demirtaş and his fellow MPs reveal the extent to which the defence of the basic party program and platform of "democratic autonomy" has been criminalized by the Turkish state.

Since the unravelling of the peace process, HDP deputies have been active and outspoken in documenting and denouncing state terror and human rights violations in the zones under blanket curfew, including crimes committed against "local leaders and municipal officials who have been killed, tortured and/or threatened by the police and the military in the sieged towns."[31] This, too, has constituted grounds for criminal accusations against HDP deputies. In the words of Ms. Leyla Birlik, MP for the province of Sirnak:

A meeting with a HDP MP Pervin Buldan in Istanbul; February 2017. As a participant in the HDP/BDP delegations to İmralı during the peace talks, she has been the most frequent visitor of Öcalan since his imprisonment and was thus a central actor during the negotiations. These delegations would also meet with representatives of the Turkish military as well as PKK commanders in the Qandil Mountains.

> Turkish law has no meaning at all, not even the rules of war have been applied. People were forbidden to go to hospitals, to shops. People were shot by snipers while taking the wounded to hospitals, or while going for food. In the HDP we have reports about these incidents. This is one of the reasons they are going after the HDP. They want to leave no witness behind. They don't want us to talk about this.

Co-chair Demirtaş faces additional charges of "insulting the president" and "insulting a public officer" for a remark he made during the eight-day siege of Cizre in September of 2015: "You see children are being killed in Cizre, babies are being killed, and [families] are not allowed to bury them. I just want to remind Mr. Davutoğlu that he has made it into the historical records as the Prime Minister who did not allow children to be buried."[32]

Likewise, among the many charges against Ms. Demirel, the deputy from Diyarbakır, are those of "insulting the president" and "resisting and obstructing an officer on duty," which were filed in relation to her participation in a delegation of HDP parliamentarians to visit the town of Silvan while it was under siege for 13 days in November, 2015. All members of the delegation face the same charges, including co-chair Figen Yüksekdağ, who suffered head injuries after being shot by security forces with a gas bomb during the visit, a grievous attack on a parliamentarian and co-chair of the country's third largest party, for which no investigation has even been opened.

Among the parliamentarians in that visit to Silvan who face charges is Ms. Hüda Kaya, MP for Istanbul. The delegation met her when she accompanied us on our failed attempt to visit co-chair Demirtaş, imprisoned in Edirne. Ms. Kaya, a devout Muslim, is also co-chair of the Democratic Islam Congress, which is affiliated with the HDP, and advocates "a perspective on religion that is anti-hierarchy, anti-power, anti-sultan-style politics, and anti-patriarchal way of interpreting religion." In addition to the charges she faces for her participation in the visit to besieged Silvan, Ms. Kaya faces the charge of "making propaganda for a terrorist organization" for a public speech she gave denouncing the military siege in the Sur district of Diyarbakır. In that speech, Ms. Kaya said that she stands as "witness to the state forces' killing of civilians, abduction of corpses, bombing of holy sites, and to all massacres denied and censored by the State and the media."[33] As Ms. Kaya recounted to our delegation:

> Last year during the blockade and curfew in Sur, when the city was being destroyed and dead people were on the street, they could not be buried, we made press declaration as co-chairs. I said: "the savagery here has no place either in Islam or in the Koran." I cited evidence for this. All beliefs and faiths have their foundations in justice. We came to defend life against death. One of the accusations of the Minister of Justice, the reason why I was detained in Istanbul, was for making a call for peace there, speaking as co-chair of the Democratic Islam Congress.

The witch-hunt and cooked-up charges against the representatives of the country's third-largest political party is disturbing enough. But the extent of state violations is even greater still and includes cruel and unusual treatment towards HDP deputies while in custody. Indeed, reports of torture at the hands of Turkish security forces have surged across the country during the period of emergency rule. Tellingly, HRW also notes that in the Kurdish regions reports of torture preceded the declaration of emergency rule, coinciding with the end of the peace process and the commencement of the sieges.

HDP members of Parliament were among those tortured. Ms. Leyla Birlik, who, though still facing trial, had been released from prison not long before our visit and explained with remarkable resilience to our delegation:

> Many HDP MPs have been exposed to torture while in custody, including myself. Suicides are likely. These things should be taken into consideration by the European Parliament and the Council of Europe. I was tortured. I was taken in a Ford Ranger Special Forces SUV, they handcuffed my hands behind my back in a very stressful position for several hours, and they played racist Turkish songs at the highest volume possible. I remained handcuffed with my arms in a painful position for a three-hour helicopter ride, straight to prison, after which I was totally isolated. I was not allowed newspapers, I was not allowed to see anybody. And I am an MP! Think about how they must treat an ordinary person.

At the same meeting, Mr. Pir, a member of the Parliamentary Assembly of NATO and who lived in Germany for 35 years before returning to Diyarbakır to participate in the HDP project, stressed how painful it was to have witnessed the window of opportunity for a peaceful and democratic solution to the Kurdish question open and then be so quickly slammed shut. Mr. Pir did everything in his power to de-escalate the conflict when things were heating up. Through the German Ambassador, he even managed to set up a meeting with then-Prime Minister Davutoğlu to try to persuade him of the desirability of a peaceful alternative to blanket curfews and brutal repression. According to Mr. Pir, Mr. Davutoğlu let it be known that he himself was personally in favour of a peaceful negotiated approach, but that the order from above was for "counter-terror operations," i.e. violence and war. A few months later, Mr. Davutoğlu was replaced. Mr. Pir lamented in conclusion, "We tried to stop the tragedy. For our efforts, we are criminalized, we who fight for peace and democracy, [are] labelled terrorists."

Indeed, targeted as public enemy number one. As Mr. Pir further explained:

> By now, 17,000 HDP activists have been detained. 7,000 are in jail right now. All this since the last general election. It is impossible to operate under such conditions. Since they lifted the immunity of MPs, 29 HDP MPs have been detained, 14 are currently under arrest. Two have been very recently released, including Leyla. But we can all be detained and imprisoned at any time. I have been detained twice. I am being accused by the government of belonging to a terrorist organization. The accusation is based on speeches I have given, particularly for saying that self-government is a right of the Kurdish people. I face 15 years in prison for this claim.

The deputies have been traumatized. In addition to political persecution and even torture, they have experienced the brutal deaths of friends and family murdered by the State during the "blanket curfews" and sieges. But there is little time for mourning, as the repressive onslaught of the Turkish authorities continues unabated. Beyond the pain of the personal sacrifices, there was the palpable pain of being collectively punished and brutally victimized by the Turkish State. Ms. Birlik even used the word "genocide," and she was not the only one we met who used it. She implored us to understand:

> We can talk about the statistics. This was an attempted genocide of the Kurdish people, not an armed clash. The State didn't let people collect bodies. There were no available places in morgues, so bodies were just thrown about. Among the killed, there was a 73-year-old woman, a 3-month-old baby, pregnant women.... Funerals could not be held, so dead bodies had to be kept in refrigerators. My brother-in-law's body was tied to an armoured vehicle and dragged through the streets.

Like the other three elected HDP deputies from the province of Sirnak, which overwhelmingly supported the HDP in the last elections, Ms. Birlik faces many charges for her words and deeds during the long curfews on Cizre and Silope. Among the charges she faces is one for "making propaganda for a terrorist organization." The basis of this charge is that she attended the funeral of Aziz Yural, a registered nurse at the state hospital in Cizre who was murdered for breaking the curfew to attend to a woman who had been gunned down on the street by security forces.[34] It is perhaps mistaken to distinguish the collective pain from the personal; the two are intimately intertwined. Ms. Birlik spoke about her teenage son. He had seen his uncle brutally murdered and dragged through the streets. He was filled with rage. When speaking about this rage, Ms. Birlik shifted, for a moment, to the optic of a worried mother:

> He is not doing well. He has too much fury. He saw his uncle die up-close. He is taking the nihilist line… He is too angry; it is not good.

Ms. Sibil Yigitalp, another HDP MP from Diyarbakır, exclaimed, "The main reason we are facing this repression is because we were so close to a democratic solution. The State is asking for war. They do not want peace and democracy." The persecution of the representatives of the Kurdish freedom movement reaches beyond parliamentarians, and targets local authorities as well. As the HDP's Deputy Co-chair responsible for Foreign Affairs and a member of Parliament, Mr. Hişyar Özsoy put it, "The AKP government's crackdown on local democracy is also continuing full force."[35]

During our visit to Diyarbakır, we met with several DBP representatives operating at the local level. As Mr. Ramazan Tunç, a member of the DBP's Foreign Affairs Office, explained the morning after our arrival in Diyarbakır:

> We have had to and continue paying heavy costs for our struggle—a struggle that shapes the political ground in Turkey. What kind of costs, you may ask? We have 4,000 party members in jail right now. Eighty-five of our co-mayors are in jail. Seventy-five municipalities have been seized by the central government—actually, 76 now, since another one was seized just last night. We have 106 municipalities, which means that almost 75% of our municipalities are now under state control, with mayors dismissed and in many cases under arrest. In just the last two days, 450 HDP and DBP members have been detained.

The seized municipalities have had their democratically elected mayors removed from office and often imprisoned, on charges very similar to those filed against HDP parliamentarians. As of mid-January, 2017, 74 co-mayors, including 6 deputy co-mayors, were under arrest. Trustees, appointed by the State in Ankara and known for their loyalty to President Erdoğan's AKP, have replaced the elected mayors. Among their first actions were to close down art workshops, theatres, nurseries, and social and educational projects for women, all provided in Kurdish, and dismiss the public employees who worked on these projects. In Diyarbakır, the State-appointed trustee removed a monument dedicated to the memory of 34 civilians bombed by Turkish jets in Roboski (in the province of Sirnak). The trustee also removed a replica of the Assyrian lion statues and icons, part of the cultural heritage of the region, which were displayed in front of the municipal government building. It is perhaps worth noting, as the HDP does, that "the original forms of these statues were destroyed with bulldozers in Raqqa by ISIS."[36]

The delegation with Mehmet Emin Aktar from the Human Rights Association of Diyarbakır, and Ayşe Serra Bucak Küçük, co-deputy mayor of Diyarbakır until the municipality was seized and the mayors imprisoned. Diyarbakır/Amed, February 2017.

We also noted that the procedures used to replace the dismissed mayors did not abide with the Turkish Constitution. Article 127 stipulates that "the formation, duties, and powers of the local administrations shall be regulated in accordance with the principle of local administration" (Union of Southeastern Anatolia Region Municipalities (GABB). *Report on Local Democracy and Appointment of State Commissioners to Municipalities in Turkey*, 13 Feb., 2017, p. 10).

During our visit, the unlawful detentions of the HDP and the DBP escalated further. According to the Ministry of the Interior, 834 members were rounded up between 13 and the 15 February, 2017. On our first morning in Diyarbakır, Mr. Ramazan Tunç, from the DBP Foreign Affairs Office, offered us a plausible and disturbing interpretation of these most recent attacks while they were just getting underway:

> The April referendum is the main agenda. Erdoğan is determined to round up and arrest people working on the "No" campaign, and even people who simply attend conferences (not just speakers). Even your presence here has been received with hostility by the State authorities. The police came to notify us that we cannot have a press e outside of this building. There is martial law in Turkey, a state of emergency. These are most difficult times, and they could well get worse as the referendum approaches.

In a similar vein, Mr. Hişyar Özsoy, MP and Deputy Co-chair of the HDP responsible for foreign affairs, warned:

> The Erdoğan-AKP government will unlawfully use every means at its disposal to establish the presidential system, which means that the government's politics of terror and intimidation against each and every sector of the democratic opposition will further intensify in the coming two months. The aim is surely to prevent the opposition from carrying out an effective campaign against the presidential system.

Every passing day it becomes clearer that our co-chairs, deputies and mayors are in prison not because they had committed some crime in the past, but because the HDP [stopped] Erdoğan's ambitious presidential system in June and November elections in 2015 and can stop him again in the referendum scheduled for April 2017.[37]

The 15th of February, 2017, was a particularly tense day in Diyarbakır. In the afternoon, the delegation drove through some of the Sur district, where militarized police-presence was very heavy and check-points stopped most circulating vehicles. Our translator even tried to dissuade us from going, "especially given the date." It should be noted that our translator was not someone who seems easily nervous, nor a person unwilling to take a risk. He mentioned in passing that one of his proudest moments was when he helped some people escape from the curfew zone during the siege. When we made it through without getting stopped or interrogated, he breathed a sigh of relief, and said, "We got lucky." Nor were heightened tensions limited to Diyarbakır. The next day, journalist Günay Aksoy recounted her brush with state repression in Istanbul in the early morning hours of 15 February:

A woman friend of ours, the head of the trade union for teachers, had her home raided the other night at 2 a.m. The special forces broke down the door, searched the house, turned everything upside down, no door was left. A friend and I went to the house because we were worried. The house was surrounded by special forces vans. At first they did not let us go upstairs. But then they wanted to hand the house over to me. They called an artisan to fix the door so they could leave the house. Their behaviour was completely unlawful.

I asked, "Why are you arresting my friend?" In the order for her arrest, it says because she is a member of the PKK preparing a bomb attack or a Molotov cocktail. There are ten other people on the list, all HDP members.

There were hundreds of operations across the country the same day. One thousand people were detained in this way in the last two days. We think these operations will continue. It is possible we could be accused, even you could be accused. In such a situation, no one can say, not me.

I am quite sure this latest wave of repression is not just about February 15th, but still, you should have seen Taksim Square yesterday. Three layers of police barricades! It is horrifying what is happening.

The special significance of 15 February is that it was the 18th anniversary of Abdullah Öcalan's abduction in Kenya in 1999, an event solemnly commemorated by the Kurdish freedom movement and referred to as "the international conspiracy." Despite his life imprisonment, Öcalan is the undisputed leader of the Kurdish freedom movement and is the ideological inspiration for the project of "democratic autonomy/democratic confederalism" for which the broader movement struggles. In 2015, 10,328,623 signatures were collected expressing the wish for his freedom and that of other political prisoners in Turkey.

Öcalan's charismatic appeal is magnified by his extreme and inhumane isolation. For 18 years now, he has been, in his own words, "chained to the rock of İmralı" where he was, from 1999 to 2009, its sole prisoner. Such circumstances have led him to be compared on more than one occasion to Nelson Mandela by, among others, Mandela's lawyer, the late Judge Essa Moosa, who headed the first international İmralı peace delegation in 2016. As Ms. Fatima Gul, a representative of the DBP, told our delegation, "Freedom, stability, and peace are all associated with the fate of Öcalan." With the unravelling of the "Resolution Process," any positive mention of Öcalan's name, much less the display of his photo, have been criminalized. Among the many charges filed against co-chair Selahattin Demirtaş, there is one for "forming an illegal organization with the aim of committing crime." The basis of the charge was communicating greetings from Mr. Öcalan at the 2013 Newroz celebration in Diyarbakır, a charge all the more ironic given that the letter from Öcalan read at the celebration had declared the "resolution process" a "harbinger for 'the ending of the armed struggle and the start of a new era of democracy."[38]

Our delegation sent a letter to the Ministry of Justice requesting to visit co-chair Demirtaş and/or co-chair Figen Yüksekdağ. When the Ministry failed to reply (as it has twice with respect to our requests to visit Mr. Öcalan), we opted to go to the prison where Mr. Demirtaş is currently being held and at least force a formal decision. Accompanied by Mr. George-Henri Beauthier (a barrister from Brussels) and HDP MP Hüda Kaya, we travelled by bus to Edirne, some 240 km northwest of Istanbul, very close to the Greek border, only to have our request officially rejected, which was not a surprise. We then managed an open-air press conference in front of the prison, something technically prohibited during emergency rule but tolerated in this case. This was very much unlike our experience in Diyarbakır, where heavily armed police tanks waited outside of the building where we were scheduled to hold our first press conference. Indeed, on that occasion, security forces took extensive photos and videos of our delegation members. The building in which we held the press conference houses the Democratic Society Congress (DTK),[39] and, in fact, HDP politicians have been charged with belonging to a terrorist organization just for being photographed entering and exiting it.

But in Edirne, the atmosphere was much more relaxed, perhaps because the agents of the State felt more secure than in Kurdistan. Even a reporter for a government-sponsored news agency showed up to the press conference and managed to ask Ms. Julie Ward, Member of European Parliament from Britain, what she meant when she referred to the concept of "Kurdistan." "Where exactly is this place?" He claimed it does not exist. However comparatively relaxed the atmosphere might have seemed from the gates of Edirne prison, the fact remains that Mr. Demirtaş and other HDP MPs find themselves isolated there and in other prisons, far away from their constituencies and held in inhumane conditions not altogether dissimilar to Abdullah Öcalan on İmralı Island. In fact, they are so similar that Mr. Öcalan's lawyers registered their grave concerns about what they called "an extension of the İmralı model" to all representatives of the Kurdish freedom movement.

The night before our trip to Edirne, the delegation had a chance to meet with Mr. Ferhat Encu, an HDP MP who had been released after three months in Kandira prison just two days previously, and who would be arrested again the following day. In his brief parenthesis of freedom, Mr. Encu came to our hotel lobby near Taksim square in Istanbul and spoke softly as he described the conditions of his imprisonment. When asked by a delegation member to elaborate upon the "violations" he had experienced, he replied:

> To begin with, I was in isolation for more than 70 days. We were all alone, not able to communicate with anybody. In the prison, there are three rooms in each corridor. To isolate us, they emptied the other rooms. I couldn't hear other sounds or voices. Plus, it is an old prison, and it is very cold there. I had to wear my coat constantly. I am still cold. All I was provided with was a bed, a chair, a table. It was really hard to find other things we needed. Even the plastic spoons and forks they gave us to eat with, they were so soft and they would break and the sharp edges would cut the mouth.

> Communication with the outside world was seriously hindered. Letters were censored, their delivery delayed for a very long time. Only once a week could we buy from the canteen. The things provided did not fulfil our requirements. From the faucets the running water was so dirty, it came out yellow. I had no clean water for the first three days. When I asked for water, they said I have to wait for the canteen day.

> I had to write petitions for the smallest of things. Once every two weeks I had the right to make a phone call to my family. Under normal conditions, three people are allowed to visit. But this has been cancelled by the state of emergency. When we demanded that things be provided, the prison couldn't decide. The request had to go up to the Minister of Justice. In general, our requests were denied.

> After the isolation was ended, we were taken to cells where we were two people. But the isolation was only ended after 70 days, through the hard struggle of the co-chairs and the party. For the women, isolation only ended this week. Some of our MPs are in bad health condition, and the food is not good enough for them given their condition.

> This is how we were treated, in spite of the fact that we are MPs.

It is an extension of the "İmralı model" in multiple ways, particularly the unlawful and inhumane isolation, restrictions and bans on visits for significant periods, confiscation of lawyers' documents, audio-visual recordings of visits with lawyers, and the presence of an officer during visits. The model is an extension of İmralı in another crucial way as well, in terms of intent, which is to silence the voices of peace.

The Isolation and Silencing of Abdullah Öcalan

Which brings us again to the subject of Mr. Öcalan. One of the key components of the polarizing policy pursued by the Turkish authorities vis-à-vis the Kurdish freedom movement over the past year and a half has been the deliberate silencing of the voice of Abdullah Öcalan. Since the Turkish government's abrupt ending of peace talks in spring of 2015, Mr. Öcalan has once again been subjected to a regime of near total isolation.

As he enters the 19th year of his detention, he leads a solitary life. Two of the five other prisoners who were formerly present on İmralı have now been transferred to other high-security prisons. Öcalan's only human contact is with his guards and, intermittently, the remaining three other prisoners. The only exception was one hour granted his brother on September 11, 2016—a concession which took a hunger strike by HDP members of Parliament and his lawyers to win, and which was counterbalanced by the seizure of dozens of Kurdish-controlled municipalities on the same day. His lawyers, who have not been able to visit him since 2011, have applied to visit more than 600 times now and are repeatedly turned down, with absurd excuses such as the boat is broken. Aside from his brother and a visit from the Council of Europe's Committee for the Prevention of Torture, no one has been permitted to visit since the last HDP delegates left on 5 April, 2015. Other than a short message delivered by his brother, no communication has been received since then.

Öcalan's total isolation during the unravelling of the peace process is no coincidence. On the contrary, it is a deliberate act and constitutes one of the most dangerous components of the criminal and polarizing policy pursued by the Turkish authorities vis-à-vis the Kurdish freedom movement over the past year. Because of his charismatic appeal, his words carry a lot of weight within the Kurdish freedom movement. They exercise a powerful influence over the contours of political subjectivity amongst his many followers. And over the course of the past two decades, especially since his capture, Öcalan has been consistent, clear and unambiguous with respect to the need for a peace process that would entail sacrifice and transformation on all sides. Indeed, his has been a voice that has consistently called for constraint and for commitment to a peaceful political resolution to the Kurdish question in Turkey.

Öcalan's vision of "democratic autonomy," or "democratic confederalism," upon which he has elaborated extensively from his prison cell, amounts to a striking re-interpretation of the principle of self-determination and even provides a road map for peace for the broader Middle East. His model combines (a) an expansion of outlets for local and participatory democratic decision-making with (b) institutional guarantees for accommodating local ethnic and religious diversities, (c) an emphasis on gender equality, and (d) respect for existing state boundaries including an explicit and principled renunciation of the goal of a "Greater Kurdistan."[40] This last prong of his political model merits special attention, given the conflicts and accusations surrounding the declarations of self-rule since August of 2015 throughout the Kurdish region.

İmralı Peace Delegation meeting with HDK co-leader Güllistan Koçyiğit and MP Ertuğrul Kürkçü, honorary president of the HDP; Istanbul, February 2016. The HDK is an important umbrella civil society organization that represents a range of Turkish and Kurdish organizations involved in labour, ecological, women's, peace, and human rights movements.

The resumption of violence and the rapid descent into human rights' atrocities is all the more tragic given the fact that just two years ago a definitive peace looked so close. In Newroz celebrations in March of 2013, a message from Öcalan was read in which the Kurdish leader called for a ceasefire (the 7th time he had done so since 1993) and, for the second time, asked the PKK to withdraw from Turkish soil into the Qandil mountains. The first time he asked the PKK to do this was in August, 1999, during his trial. His request in 1999 was obeyed by the PKK, but their retreat was "met with a massive armed operation by the Turkish military and resulted in the deaths of hundreds of guerrillas."[41] Among the words of Öcalan read out at the historic Newroz celebration in Diyarbakır in 2013, the Kurdish celebration of the New Year, were these: "Let guns be silenced and politics dominate. The stage has been reached where our armed forces should withdraw beyond the borders... It's not the end, it's the start of a new era."

On 28 February, 2015, Erdoğan government officials met with HDP representatives at the Prime Minister's Office in Dolmabahçe, where the HDP representative read out a message from Öcalan sketching an outline for a definitive peace (later dubbed the Dolmabahçe Agreement). According to Öcalan:

In taking this 30-year process of clashes to permanent peace, our main target is reaching a democratic solution. On principles that form the least common denominator, I invite the PKK to summon an extraordinary congress in spring in order to make the strategic and historic decision on the basis of ending the armed struggle. This invitation is a historical declaration of intent aimed at replacing armed struggle with democratic politics.[42]

The HDP representative then went on to list the headings of ten clauses included in the framework of the Agreement: (1) democratic politics, its definition and content; (2) recognition of the national and local dimensions of the democratic solution; (3) legal and democratic reassurances for free citizenship; (4) the relationship between the State and society and democratic politics, a heading aimed towards its institutionalization; (5) socioeconomic dimensions of the solution process; (6) treatment of the democracy-security relationship in a manner that protects public order and freedoms throughout the process; (7) legal solutions and reassurances for women's, cultural, and ecological problems; (8) development of a pluralist democratic approach regarding the recognition of the concept, definition and recognition of identity; (9) definition of the democratic republic, common homeland and nation on the basis of democratic criteria, and the introduction of legal and constitutional reassurances within the pluralist democratic system; and (10) a new constitution with a vision to internalize all these democratic moves and transformations.[43]

Turkey's Deputy Prime Minister, present at the reading of the message, remarked, "We acknowledge the importance of this statement regarding the acceleration of efforts towards disarmament, the attainment of a complete state of non-aggression, and the prioritization of democratic politics as a method."[44] For his part, then Prime Minister, Ahmet Davutoğlu, referred to Öcalan's statement as marking the beginning of a new phase in the peace negotiations.[45]

But by the end of the first week of March, 2015, the government was already distancing itself from the Accord, and by 15 March, President Erdoğan was rapidly backtracking, denying altogether the existence of a Kurdish question in Turkey.[46] Shortly after, 5 April, 2015 was the last time HDP representatives were allowed to meet with Öcalan. Since then, his fate has been total isolation and, for most of the HDP representatives, persecution, imprisonment, and isolation as well. With the isolation of Öcalan and the HDP, the voices of crucial players in the difficult path towards peace have been silenced—a peace that had been so close in 2015, now seemingly so far away.

Though, perhaps not so far as it seems. In Öcalan's only message since the unravelling of the resolution process, communicated through his brother after the one-hour visit in September of 2016, he reiterated his commitment to a peaceful and democratic solution to the Kurdish question, and made an urgent call to return to peace negotiations. As the late Judge Essa Moosa once put it, "The Kurds have their Mandela, but where is the Turkish de Klerk?"

Complicity of the EU and Silence from the Council of Europe

There is of course a much longer history to the conflict between the Turkish State and the Kurdish freedom movement, a history steeped in state terror, without which this latest episode cannot be understood.[47]

During the accession process, the European Union managed to leverage significant pressure on the Turkish State, contributing to a certain liberalization, if not full convergence with European law and international human rights' norms, especially in dealing with ethnic minorities, most significantly the Kurds. But since the latest purges and abuses the carrot of accession has been taken off the table. With the rise of the xenophobic right in Europe and the associated obsession with "fortress building," the dynamics of relations between Turkey and Europe have been significantly transformed in a most problematic direction. No longer does the European Union appear capable of exercising such liberalizing leverage over the Turkish authorities. In fact, in the so-called "refugee crisis," the tables have been turned. The balance of leverage has effectively been reversed. Now the Erdoğan government gets rewarded by the European Union even as it suppresses freedom of expression and even as it pummels the Kurds.

Just two weeks before Turkey's snap election on 1 November, 2015, German Chancellor Angela Merkel, facing intense domestic pressure to stem the flow of refugees into Europe, travelled to Istanbul to meet with President Erdoğan, where she pledged to push forward Turkey's long-delayed bid to join the European Union in return for cooperation in keeping refugees out of Europe. Nor was Merkel alone in her appetite for appeasement. Indeed, as Time magazine reported, "Desperate to engage with Ankara over the migrant crisis, Brussels ... even delayed the European Commission's annual report on Turkey's EU membership application until after the November elections—a report that was expected to contain heavy criticism of Erdoğan's autocratic rule and disregard for EU principles of freedom of expression."[48] In March, 2016, Chancellor Merkel began to deliver on her promise when the EU struck a deal with Turkey at a summit, according to which all refugees and migrants arriving in Greece are to be returned, in exchange for "'reenergized' talks on [Turkey's] EU membership, and 3 billion Euros in financial support for the Erdoğan government, nominally "intended to help Syrian refugees in Turkey."[49] It should be noted that not a single euro has gone to help the Yezidi refugees coming across the land border. They are supported instead by Kurdish aid organisations and the municipalities of nearby cities such as Diyarbakır.

The deal has come under much scrutiny from human rights' advocates. Back in October, 2015, on the occasion of Merkel's visit with Erdoğan when plans were first announced, Andrew Gardner, Amnesty International's researcher on Turkey, had complained that "a deal premised on keeping refugees in Turkey fundamentally ignores both the challenges they face there and the obvious need for the E.U. to offer protection to a greater share of the world's burgeoning refugee population."[50] In April, 2016, the Council of Europe concurred with this judgment, issuing a report that amounted to a "stinging indictment" of the deal, which it warned might even "exceed the limits of what is permissible in international law." According to the report, "Even on paper, [the deal] raises many serious questions of compatibility with basic norms on refugees' and migrants' rights. It has so far given every indication of being even more problematic in practice."[51]

This represents a dark hour for the European Union, to say the least, and a veritable crisis for its self-image as a beacon of human rights and democracy. Not only does the EU look the other way while the Erdoğan government commits human rights atrocities, it even rewards it for pledging to help keep refugees at bay, safely outside the "fortress." The insidious logic of the "war on terror" thus seems to have brought the European project full circle. The chickens are coming home to roost. The brutal indifference of the European authorities to the recent resurgence of state terror and human rights' abuses in Turkey helps clarify precisely what "European values" have come—again—to mean.

Urgent Call for Action

There is still hope that European institutions, especially the European Court of Human Rights and the Committee for the Prevention of Torture, can effectively leverage pressure on President Erdoğan and the Turkish State to cease and desist from the ongoing campaign of state terror and human rights violations against the Kurds. Indeed, many of the people with whom the delegation met had important messages they wanted to deliver to the European authorities about the relevant courses of action that should be pursued to help stop the violence. For instance, in denouncing the many violations of the blanket curfews and sieges, the Chair of the Diyarbakır Bar Association, Mr. Ahmet Özmer, urged the European Court of Human Rights (ECHR) and the Council of Europe to act. According to Mr. Özmer:

> There were appeals from the people in the basement in Cizre; the war escalated afterword. Hundreds of academics who signed a peace petition have been suspended, some of these dismissed. Right now, all of these violations by the Turkish State are met with impunity. If the ECHR were to give a decision about these violations, even of a pilot case, this would have serious repercussions. It could make these violations stop. The precedent is in the 1990s, when there was the burning of some 3000 Kurdish villages. The ECHR gave a decision about just one person affected and, as a result, the Turkish State began paying compensation.

> The High Commissioner of Human Rights for the Council of Europe visited. If the Council could find a way to investigate the gross human rights violations, to form a mission—that could be useful. As for the EU, I have little faith in it right now, it appears that the reigning idea in the EU is to look the other way so as not to lose Turkey.

Mr. Abdullah Öcalan's lawyers also made specific urgent appeals addressed to the Council of Europe, its Committee of Ministers, the ECHR, and the Committee for the Prevention of Torture, with respect to the inhumane isolation of Mr. Öcalan. The appeals start from the plausible premise, summarized nicely by

Mr. Ibrahim Bildez, that "[a]ll the developments—positive or negative—related to İmralı have an impact on the country. Therefore, the situation of Mr. Öcalan is a main determining factor of what is going on in the country." To which, Mr. Bildez added, "Today Turkey claims it is a state of law, bound by European law. We are going to demand the rule of law. I say this because I attach a lot of meaning to the CPT [European Committee for the Prevention of Torture and Inhuman or Degrading Treatment or Punishment]."

On 18 March, 2014, the ECHR ruled unanimously in the case of Öcalan v. Turkey (application Nos. 24069/03, 197/04, 6201/06 and 10464/07) that there had been a violation of Article 3 of the European Convention of Human Rights (prohibition of inhumane or degrading treatment) with respect to Mr. Öcalan's sentence to life imprisonment without any possibility of conditional release. The court also ruled that during the majority of his imprisonment on the island, Mr. Öcalan had been subjected to inhumane and degrading degrees of isolation. However, in the three years since this judgment, there has been virtually no follow-up. As one of Öcalan's lawyers, Mr. Rezan Sarica, stressed, "According to Article 46 of the European Human Rights Convention, the Ministerial Committee of the Council of Europe has to monitor the implementation of ECHR decisions."

As such, Mr. Öcalan's team of lawyers implore the Council of Europe to "ask Turkey to lift all legislative restrictions on the issue." They recommend that "the Committee of Ministers of the Council of Europe should determine that the violations … raised in this case and other violations still continue." And they highlight the "need for an initiative to determine a more efficient policy of monitoring, and for making public statements on the matter." In a written statement prepared for our delegation, Mr. Öcalan's lawyers were especially emphatic in their appeals to the ECHR and the European Committee for the Prevention of Torture and Inhuman or Degrading Treatment or Punishment (CPT). In their words:

> After the exhaustion of domestic remedies in October, 2011, an application was submitted to the European Court of Human Rights (74751/11). No progress on this application has been made although the application was submitted a long time ago. The İmralı Isolation System, which has no legal ground, has been built for a long period and has spread across the country now. It might be the only prison in all over the world that no information about it is received. We have received no direct or indirect piece of information about the İmralı Prison for last 150 days. Therefore, we are seriously concerned about our client.

> After the failed coup attempt on 15 July, 2016, the 1st Office of the Judge of Execution in Bursa ruled, in summary, that "all forms of communication and visits are banned at the İmralı Prison during the state of emergency period." The appeal against this court decision (that we filed on 27.10.2016), like other thousands of applications, is still pending before the Constitutional Court of the Republic of Turkey.

> The CPT has been informed about the situation at İmralı Island Prison and Mr. Öcalan. We send our reports to the CPT on a regular basis. These reports include many recommendations and demands. However, the CPT did not take

any satisfactory steps for the İmralı Isolation during the last 6 months. Nor, did the CPT intervene in the isolation. The CPT could not make a positive impact on the İmralı case though the ban on torture is absolute. We shared all of our information and concerns in a face to face meeting.... The CPT has visited the İmralı Prison seven times since 15 February, 1999, and published all its reports after the Turkish government has requested the publication of these reports. However, the CPT has not published its report on a two-day-visit (28–29 April 2016) to the İmralı prison, though it finished the report. None of the CPT recommendations, which the Committee made in its previous reports, for family and lawyer visits as well as other aspects of the isolation at İmralı have been implemented by the Turkish government. Not taking necessary steps to implement recommendations for problems, which reports draw attention to, at İmralı indicates that Turkey acts in a contrary manner to the ban on torture and the co-operation principle of the Convention. In this regard, if the CPT authorities think that they have nothing to do (it is what we observe from the CPT authorities), it is not true. Article 10/2 of the European Convention for the Prevention of Torture and Inhuman or Degrading Treatment or Punishment, which is the basis of the CPT, refers to a procedure. The Article provides that if the situation is not improved in a certain period, the Committee—as a warning—may make a public statement on the matter. The present conditions are worse than 2007 on which the Committee made such a public statement. None of the recommendations from 2010 and 2013 CPT reports were implemented. On the contrary, conditions were worsened at the İmralı Prison.

Mr. Öcalan has been held in prison under these conditions for 18 years. The Turkish government has taken neither a legislative nor an administrative step that can be considered a process in line with this judgment. The Committee of Ministers of the Council of Europe was informed about this situation on 16 June 2016. Given that the Turkish government has taken no steps yet we believe that it will not take any steps in the future, either.

As Mr. Rezan Sarica summed up the matter in layman's terms for our delegation, "We want the CPT to do something about Öcalan's isolation at İmralı. None of the advice given by the CPT in 2010 and 2013 has been implemented. Even worse conditions have been put in place." Even more explicitly, Mr. Ibrahim Bildez concluded, "When the government keeps violating norms, the CPT can make a press statement and publicize this to the world. It can and must say: 'European law is being violated. This has to be stopped.'" Silence signifies complicity.

The Delegation

The delegation included: two current representatives from the Parliamentary Assembly of the Council of Europe, Miren Edurne Gorrotxategi (Basque Country, Spain) and Ulla Sandbæk (Denmark); a current member of the European Parliament, Julie Ward (UK); a former MEP, Francis Wurtz (France); a former Minister of Justice and trade unionist, Ögmundur Jonasson (Iceland); veteran Foreign Correspondent, Jonathan Steele (UK); the Chair of the Westminster Justice and Peace Commission, Father Joe Ryan (UK); the Chair of the Transnational Institute for Social Ecology (TRISE), Dimitri Roussopoulos (Canada); member of the TRISE advisory board and researcher at Leeds University, Federico Venturini (Italy); and a Lecturer from the University of Cambridge, Thomas Jeffrey Miley (USA).

List of Organizations and Representatives that the Delegation Met

Democratic Society Congress (DTK):
Ms. Leyla Guyen (co-chair);
Ms. Dilek Arcan (member of executive board); Mr. Moussa Fayasullani (member of executive board).

Democratic Regions' Party (DBP):
Mr. Ramazan Tunç; Ms. Fatima Gül;
Mr. Salih Yıldız; Ms. Ayse Serra Bucak.

Diyarbakır Bar Association:
Mr. Ahmet Ozmer (Chair); Ms. Nugin Uysal (General Secretary); Mr. Darket Eren (member of executive board); Mr. Mehmet Emin Aktar (Former Chair).

Free Women's Movement (TJA):
Ms. Fatma Kasan; Ms. Aysa Gokkan; Ms. Miyosa Celik; Ms. Ruker Yilmiz; Ms. Zukal Tekiner.

Peoples' Democratic Party (HDP):
Ms. Leyla Birlik (MP); Mr. Ziya Pir (MP); Ms. Sibil Yigitalp (MP); Mr. Ferhat Encü (MP); Mr. Serpil Kemalbay (Central Committee) Ms. Hüda Kaya (MP); Ms. Pervin Buldan (MP); Ms. Esengul Demir (HDP Istanbul co-chair); Ms. Ayse Erdem (MP); Ms. Gülsüm Agoaglu (Central Committee).

Confederation of Progressive Trade Unions of Turkey (DISK) and Confederation of Public Workers' Unions (KESK):
Ms. Fatma Kiliç; Mr. Üzeyir Evrenk; Mr. Hassan Eraglu.

Journalists from Banned Media Outlets in Diyarbakır:
Mr. Mehmet Ali Ertas (Dicle Haber); Mr. Baris Baristiran (Özgür Gün TV); Mr. Ibraham Aslan (Jiyantu); Mr. Gülistan Korhan (Azadi TV); Ms. Firat Yasar (Van TV).

Jarmasik Aid Organization and Rojava Aid Organization:
Mr. Serif Camci; Mr. Mustafa Ocaklik; Mr. Huseyin Durmaz; and Mr. Daynt Kesen.

Mr. Öcalan's Lawyers (Asrin Law Office):
Mr. Ibrahim Bilmez; Mr. Rezan Sarica; Mr. Serbay Köklü

Peoples' Democratic Congress (HDK):
Ms. Gülistan Kiliç Konyigit (co-chair); Ms. Çigden Kiliçgun Uçar (member of executive board); Mr. Erkan Tepeli.

Democratic Islam Congress (DIK): Ms. Hüda Kaya; Mr. Yusuf Inal; Ms. Didem Aydin; Ms. Süheyla Inal; Ms. Nurten Ertugrul; Ms. Tülay Yıldırım Ede.

Journalists from Banned Media Outlets in Istanbul:
Ms. Günay Aksoy (Özgür Gündem); Mr. Yasin Kobulan (DiHaber); Ms. Derya Okatan (Özgür Radio); Mr. Veli Büyüksahin (TV10).

Peace Bloc:
Ms. Ayse Erzan (co-chair).

Peace Academicians:
Ms. Asli Odman.

Women's Freedom Assembly:
Ms. Züleyha Gülüm.

Human Rights Association:
Ms. Gülseren Yoleri (co-chair); Mr. Oztürk Türkdogan (chair).

Notes for Online References:

1. "World Report 2017: Turkey." Human Rights Watch. Accessed April 28, 2018. http://bit.ly/2tJ70pU.

2. "Turkey: Hundreds detained over alleged links to PKK." Turkey News | Al Jazeera. February 14, 2017. Accessed February 28, 2017. http://bit.ly/2KijL5W.; "More than 830 PKK suspects detained in anti-terror operations." Daily Sabah. February 14, 2017. Accessed February 28, 2017. http://bit.ly/2N97QVW.

3. "Reports on Curfews in Turkey." Kaynak Tipleri | Hafıza Merkez. Accessed April 20, 2018. http://hakikatadalethafiza.org/en/kaynak_tipi/reports-on-curfews/.

4. "Report on the human rights situation in South-East Turkey." Office of the United Nations High Commissioner for Human Rights. March 10, 2017. Accessed April 10, 2017. http://bit.ly/2tQPtvW.

5. "World Report 2017: Turkey." op. cit.

6. "Turkey: Curfews and crackdown force hundreds of thousands of Kurds from their homes." Amnesty International. December 6, 2016. Accessed January 1, 2017. http://bit.ly/2tFcqmF.; "Damage Assessment & Forced Migration Report Aftermath the Urban Armed Conflicts in Southeast of Turkey." Hafıza Merkezi. Accessed January 1, 2017. http://bit.ly/2tP4rmi.; Jonathan Steele. "Turkey's own refugees: Now Kurds turn to Europe for help." Middle East Eye. 28 February 2017. Accessed 28 February 2017. https://bit.ly/2lVZape.

7. "79 days of Curfew: Cizre Review Report." Human Rights Association (IHD). Accessed January 1, 2017. https://bit.ly/2u3omhr.

8. "SUR (Amed) Report April 2016." Diyarbakır Metropolitan Municipality. Accessed January 1, 2017. https://bit.ly/2KAgsqY

9. "İHD: Families cannot reach their children in blockaded Koruköy." Turkey Purge. February 27, 2017. Accessed February 28, 2017. https://bit.ly/2u74Al4.

10. "Turkey: authorities must allow residents of Cizre access to basic needs during prolonged curfew," Amnesty International, 11 September 2015, Index number: EUR 44/2438/2015. https://bit.ly/1SONlcN

11. "World Report 2017: Turkey." op. cit.

12. "Turkey Freedom and Democracy Year in Review," Peoples' Democratic Party, (March 14, 2017). https://bit.ly/2IUDEdA

13. Ibid.

14. "Turkey: Freedom of the Press 2016." Freedom House. Accessed January 1, 2017. https://freedomhouse.org/report/freedom-press/2016/turkey.

15. "World Report 2017: Turkey," op. cit.

16. "Turkey Freedom and Democracy Year in Review." op. cit.

17. Ibid.

18. "Memorandum on freedom of expression and media freedom in Turkey," Commissioner for Human Rights, the Council of Europe, 15 February, 2017. https://bit.ly/2KnAwN9

19. Jonathan Steele. "Turkish opposition MPs sit in jail as president seeks more power." Middle East Eye. 22 February 2017. Accessed February 28, 2017. http://bit.ly/2tDMjMZ.

20. "The Lifting of Legislative Immunities at the Parliament of Turkey: An Assessment Report." People's Democratic Party. Accessed June 1, 2017. https://bit.ly/2tSZXvU. p. 13.

21. Ibid., p. 5.

22. Ibid., p. 3.

23. Ibid., p.4.

24. "Turkey Freedom and Democracy Year in Review." op. cit.

25. "The Lifting of Legislative Immunities at the Parliament of Turkey: An Assessment Report." op. cit., pp. 6–7.

26. Ibid., p.7.

27. Ibid., pp. 9–11

28. Ibid., p. 10.

29. Ibid., p. 11.

30. Ibid., p. 11.

31. Ibid., p. 3.

32. Ibid., p. 12.

33. Ibid., p. 12.

34. Ibid., p. 13.

35. "Increasing Pressures on the HDP in the Lead-up to the Referendum." Peoples' Democratic Party. Accessed March 12, 2017. http://bit.ly/2tPz3Ux.

36. "Turkey Freedom and Democracy Year in Review." op. cit.

37. "Increasing Pressures on the HDP in the Lead-up to the Referendum." op. cit.

38. "Towards a Resolution: An Assessment of Possibilities, Opportunities, and Problems." Turkey Peace Assembly. November 2015. Accessed January 1, 2017. http://bit.ly/2tEBoTh. p. 10.

39. "DTK." People's Democratic Party. Accessed January 2, 2017. http://en.hdpeurope.com/?page_id=912.

40. Abdullah Öcalan. "Democratic Confederalism." International Initiative. 2011. Accessed January 1, 2017. https://bit.ly/1CA8DVA.

41. "Towards a Resolution: An Assessment of Possibilities, Opportunities, and Problems." op. cit. p. 9.

42. Ibid. p.106.

43. Ibid. p.106.

44. Ibid. p. 107.

45. "Turkish government and Kurds in bid to revitalise peace talks," Financial Times, February 28, 2015. https://on.ft.com/2yINxeA

46. "Towards a Resolution: An Assessment of Possibilities, Opportunities, and Problems." op. cit. p. 109.

47. "Introducing State Crime In Turkey." International State Crime Initiative. Accessed 28, 2018. https://bit.ly/2u3pzoZ; "Building Peace in Permanent War: Terrorist Listing and Conflict Resolution." International State Crime Initiative. 2015. Accessed January 1, 2017. https://bit.ly/2h1ze6S

48. Naina Bajekal. "Why the E.U. Is Offering Turkey Billions to Deal With Refugees." Time. October 19, 2015. Accessed January 1, 2016. https://ti.me/1QSKE9x

49. Jennifer Rankin. "EU strikes deal with Turkey to send back refugees." The Guardian. March 18, 2016. Accessed March 30, 2016. http://bit.ly/2NaDxOA.

50. Naina Bajekal. Ibid.

51. Jennifer Rankin. "Council of Europe condemns EU's refugee deal with Turkey." The Guardian. April 30, 2016. Accessed April 20, 2016. http://bit.ly/2N89mHK.

The EUTCC Delegation after a live-TV interview during an advocacy trip to the Council of Europe in Strasbourg; April 2016. From left to right: Dr. Elly Van Reusel, Thomas Jeffrey Miley, Judge Essa Moosa, Kurdish intellectual Dilar Dirik, journalist Huseyin Elmali, Kariane Westrheim, unknown, Father Joe Ryan, and Federico Venturini. As follow-ups to the visits to Turkey, the EUTCC organised several delegations to the Council of Europe and the European Parliament in Brussels.

The Council of Europe and the Death of the Peace Process: Report from the İmralı Delegation to Strasbourg

(25–27 April, 2017)

Thomas Jeffrey Miley

Editors' Note: This is Thomas Jeffrey Miley's report on the Fourth EUTCC İmralı Delegation's visit to Strasbourg, originally published in The Region.[1]

Judge Essa Moosa passed away at the end of February, 2017. The timing of his death seemed symbolic. His had been a consistent voice of optimism and hope in the quest for a peaceful, political solution to the long and bloody conflict between the Turkish State and the Kurdish freedom movement.

Judge Moosa was a man with decades of experience fighting for peace and justice in the anti-apartheid struggle, a close confidante of Nelson Mandela, and served as his lawyer when the South African leader was imprisoned on Robben Island. He was fond of telling the story: "Before the ANC and its alliance partners were banned, one of the slogans often repeated at their political meetings was: 'Freedom in Our Lifetime'. As a student I thought it was a pipedream."[2] Nevertheless, he lived to see the freedom of Mandela and the end of apartheid. In the many meetings and press conferences I attended with him as a member of the İmralı delegations he spearheaded in the last years of his life, he would invariably add, "I hope that I can also see in my lifetime the freedom of Abdullah Öcalan."[3]

The İmralı delegations were the culmination of close to two decades of activism and commitment on the part of Judge Moosa to the cause of Kurdish freedom. When Abdullah Öcalan was abducted in Kenya back in 1999, he was on his way to South Africa; it was Judge Moosa who had convinced President Mandela to offer Öcalan asylum.[4] Following his abduction, Judge Moosa had been active in attempts to contest Öcalan's unlawful trial and treatment, his inhumane isolation on the island of İmralı, and in the campaigns calling for his freedom.

Not long ago, it looked like Judge Moosa might get his wish. But the window of opportunity for peace and for a political solution to the conflict between the Turkish State and the Kurdish freedom movement slammed shut in July, 2015.

The İmralı delegations were launched by the European Union Turkey Civic Commission (EUTCC), with Judge Moosa originally in the lead role, in a last-ditch effort to exert international pressure to help resuscitate a moribund peace process. To date, there have been four such delegations, though Judge Moosa's health held out only long enough for him to participate in the first two—Istanbul in February, 2016, then Strasbourg in April, 2016.

On the first delegation to Istanbul, one of the politicians with whom we met was Ertugrul Kürkçü, who has served since 2014 as the honorary president of the People's Democratic Party (HDP). The HDP is an umbrella party that seeks to re-unite the Turkish Left with the Kurdish freedom movement. Its historic success in the last cycle of general elections, in combination with the breakdown of peace negotiations, had already provoked a wave of vicious state repression by the time our delegation had arrived in Istanbul in February, 2016.

When we met Mr. Kürkçü, the military sieges of urban centres across the Kurdish region, which have displaced approximately half a million Kurds, were already well under way. Understandably, he was not in an optimistic mood. After the meeting, he approached Judge Moosa and hugged him, before addressing his comparison between the apartheid regime and the Turkish State by pointing out, "Fortunately for you, the anti-apartheid movement had the majority on your side, whereas the Kurds are a minority. Moreover, by the 1980s, it had become increasingly easy to isolate the South African government, both politically and economically. We who struggle with the Kurds unfortunately do not enjoy such crucial advantages." Points well-put; even the ever-optimistic Judge Moosa had to tacitly concede, in silence.

Mr. Kürkçü, too, is a man with decades of experience in high-stake political struggles. Born in the city of Bursa, in the northwest of Anatolia, he first came to prominence as a student activist in the 1960s, and in 1970, was elected president of the Turkish Revolutionary Youth Federation. After the "military coup by memorandum" of 1971, Mr. Kürkçü joined the armed resistance, and in March, 1972, along with ten other activists, took part in the kidnapping of three NATO technicians. In exchange for the release of hostages, the group demanded that the military junta not execute Denis Gezmis, one of the founding members of the Turkish People's Liberation Army. The Turkish Che Guevara had been condemned to death for kidnapping and holding hostage four US soldiers.[5]

Not only did the authorities not give in to the group's demand; but they bombed the house in the village where the eleven activists were hiding with their three captives. Mr. Kürkçü was the only survivor. He was tried under martial law and sentenced to death, but after a general amnesty in 1974, the sentence was commuted to 30 years, of which he served 14. Since the 1990s, Mr. Kürkçü has been active in several successive attempts to unite the Turkish and Kurdish left. He was elected to the Turkish Parliament in 2011, and in 2013–2014 served as co-chair of the HDP before becoming its honorary president. Mr. Kürkçü also represents the HDP in the Parliamentary Assembly of the Council of Europe (PACE) in Strasbourg, where we met again this past April, two months after Judge Moosa's death.

Our delegation arrived in Strasbourg on the morning of the 25 April, just in time to witness the Assembly debate and pass a resolution in favour of re-opening a human rights' monitoring procedure for Turkey. The resolution got a lot of press in the West, with The Guardian running the headline the following day: "Council of Europe Vote Puts Pressure on Turkey over Human Rights." The resolution was framed as expressing "'serious concerns' about democracy and human rights," and the vote in its favour was deemed "an unprecedented decision," meant to "put pressure on the EU to reassess relations with Ankara."[6] But on the issue of the end of the peace process and the still-escalating conflict between the Turkish State and the Kurdish freedom movement, the Council's Resolution was anything but unprecedented, perpetrating false equivalences and trapped in the limitations and contradictions of the lethally inept paradigm of the "war on terror."

Mr. Kürkçü was among the members of the group of the United European Left who proposed a formal amendment to the fifth paragraph, where the issue of "terror" was addressed. Specifically, paragraph 5 of the draft resolution read:

> Turkey has faced massive and repeated terrorist attacks perpetrated by the so-called "Islamic State of Iraq and the Levant" (ISIL/Daesh), the "Kurdistan Workers' Party" (PKK) and the PKK-affiliated "Kurdistan Freedom Hawks" (TAK). These attacks caused hundreds of casualties in Ankara, Suruç, Istanbul, Bursa, Diyarbakır, Kayseri and other cities in Turkey. In addition, the border city of Kilis was targeted by shelling from Syrian territory. The Assembly un-equivocally condemns these attacks and all terrorist action and violence per-petrated by the PKK, Daesh, or any other organization, which can by no means be tolerated.

The amendment proposed by Kürkçü and his colleagues would have stated instead:

> The Assembly clearly condemns all terrorist attacks in Turkey. Both the so-called "Islamic State of Iraq and the Levant" (ISIL/Daesh) and "Kurdistan Free-dom Hawks" (TAK) have conducted massive and repeated attacks that have caused hundreds of casualties in Ankara, Suruc, Istanbul, Bursa, Diyarbakır, Kayseri and other cities in Turkey. In addition, the border city of Kilis was tar-geted by shelling from Syrian territory. The Assembly regrets that the peace process between the Turkish government and the PKK has ended leading to a vicious circle of violence and many casualties. The Assembly urges all sides of the conflict to resume the peace process in order to reach a peaceful solution to the conflict.

But the amendment did not pass. Evidently, for the committee in charge of draft-ing the resolution, as well as for the majority in the Parliamentary Assembly, any official linking of the PKK and ISIS remains unpalatable. The situation the PKK and, by extension, the Kurdish freedom movement, finds itself in reflects the tru-ism that one person's terrorist is another person's freedom fighter. In effect, the PKK and the Kurdish freedom movement have come to be considered, in the eyes of the very same people, freedom fighters on one side of the border (in Syria), but terrorists on the other (in Turkey). Reference to the "vicious circle of violence" is explicitly rejected, even amidst a brutal wave of state terror that has led to half a million displaced Kurds and hundreds of civilians killed, including elderly women and children, with dozens burnt alive in basements. When it comes to the Turkish State's war with the PKK and on the Kurdish people, the Council of Europe still reserves its "unequivocal condemnation[s]" for non-state actors alone. And, what of the pressure to restart the "peace process" with the PKK? It remains off the agenda for now, manifestly beyond the Assembly's man-date and horizons.

The Council of Europe was nevertheless "unequivocal" in expressing clear concerns about the escalation of authoritarianism by the Erdoğan government in the aftermath of the July 2016 failed coup. It denounced the persecution of the pro-Kurdish HDP, with special focus on the lifting of parliamentary immunity and the subsequent imprisonment of many of its MPs, including co-chairs, Mr. Selahattin Demirtaş and Ms. Figen Yüksekdağ, as well as the imprisonment of pro-Kurdish mayors and the suppression of local administrations that had been governed by pro-Kurdish forces (paras. 9–11). The peace process came off the agenda, but democracy stayed on. The link between the two became somehow severed, as if the persecution of the HDP and of pro-Kurdish local administrations were unrelated to the breakdown of peace and the resurgence of war. The fate of Demirtaş and the HDP were distinguished, if not disentangled, from those of Öcalan and the PKK.

Our delegation met with the Council's Secretary General, Mr. Thorbjørn Jagland, just a few hours after the resolution was passed. Mr. Jagland's credentials are formidable. Former Prime Minister of Norway, former Chair of the Socialist International's Committee on the Middle East, member of the Mitchell Committee, former chair of the Oslo Centre for Peace and Human Rights, and member of the Norwegian Nobel Committee—an impressive institutional CV. An expert-practitioner of failed peace processes if ever there was one.

We presented Mr. Jagland with a copy of our latest report *State Terror, Human Rights Violations, and Authoritarianism in Turkey*.[7] We stressed our conviction that the isolation of Öcalan and the breakdown of the peace negotiations were central components of the Erdoğan government's authoritarian turn, and we argued that a call for all sides to return to the peace process should be a prominent item on the Council's agenda.

Mr. Jagland listened carefully to our plea, with a couple of advisors taking notes. He conceded, "I fully agree that the Kurdish issue is at the centre of the problems in Turkey. It has been the pretext. It is very important to come back to the peace process." However, he was quick to add, "The importance of Öcalan is undeniable, but the PKK's structure is a problem. Let's not be naïve about the PKK." Given his trajectory, it is perhaps not surprising that the comparison on Mr. Jagland's mind was the Israeli-Palestinian conflict. For he continued, "It reminds me of the many times I met with Arafat and had discussions with the PLO. The PLO did come to accept the existence of Israel. But on the other hand, they would go back and forth—now peace, now war; nobody trusted them when they said they were committed to peace."

Utopian tendencies; a lack of sincerity; an inconsistent commitment to peace; not to be trusted—these were the charges implicitly invoked by the Secretary General against the PKK when pressed to justify the Council's silence about the breakdown of the peace process.

According to Mr. Jagland, the Kurdish parallel to the Palestinian refusal to recognize Israel was "the idea of an independent Greater Kurdistan," an idea that he dismissed as "a fantasy, a utopia," and "unrealistic." Either he didn't know or he simply didn't believe that the Kurdish freedom movement had renounced that goal and had replaced it with the alternative model of "democratic confederal-

After a crucial meeting with the most senior representative of the Council of Europe, General Secretary Thorbjørn Jagland; Strasbourg, April 2017. Delegates present were Ulla Sandbæk, Miren Gorrotxategi, Thomas Jeffrey Miley, and Federico Venturini.

ism." Moreover, in his mind's eye, Öcalan was indelibly cast in the role of Arafat, and the PKK playing the part of the PLO—not Mandela and the ANC. As for the Kurdish freedom movement's commitment to peace, Mr. Jagland was sceptical. He criticized the PKK for what he saw as its role in reproducing a vicious cycle of violence and repression, for its recourse to "terror." In his words: "And of course, terrorism is a huge problem, in Turkey and across the globe, in terms of respect for human rights and democracy. It gives the authorities a pretext." A pretext for what? For human rights' atrocities, which he was willing to admit: "Anti-terrorist legislation leads to violations."

Indeed, Mr. Jagland was more than willing to be critical of both sides in the conflict. A plague on both their houses, he seemed to suggest. Though he made sure to clarify that he believed it wrong to pin too much blame on Erdoğan himself. He argued that "Erdoğan did a lot—remember, before him the State's official position was that the Kurds were Mountain Turks." Rather, for the Secretary General, "Turkish nationalists," not Erdoğan, were to blame—"forces who dislike talks with the PKK," some of whom, he insisted, "were behind the coup attempt." Indeed, he was even willing to add, "The same Turkish nationalist forces who leaked the secret Oslo talks, to damage the process, to reduce Erdoğan's room for manoeuvre. They succeeded." On one side was the PKK; on the other, Turkish nationalists, presumably with organic links to the so-called deep state (though Mr. Jagland was careful to avoid such a term). The two sides were locked in a vicious cycle of endemic violence and repression—the space for peace, for politics, erased.

However, in the mind and the discourse of the Secretary General, the veteran peace-negotiator, the link between justice and peace, though never denied, was clearly downplayed. Thrasymachus' conflation of might with right was simultaneously eschewed and assumed. Nor was Mr. Jagland optimistic about the ability of European institutions to exercise much leverage over the political dynamics in Turkey at this point. The resolution passed by the Parliamentary Assembly, he seemed to suggest, was a sign of weakness, not strength, and a measure that might even backfire. "You have seen the debate in the assembly," he remarked, towards the end of our meeting. "Turkey is once again under the monitoring process. But I am not sure what effect the monitoring will have on the Turkish government. Things are very unpredictable now."

The Secretary General came across as a pessimist and a sceptic, if not a cynic. He was sceptical of Öcalan and the PKK, sceptical of the Turkish nationalists, the government, and the State. Sceptical of the efficacy of the monitoring process, and even sceptical of our delegation. When our half-hour was up, on our way out the door, he obliged our request for a group photo, on one condition—that we not "put words in my mouth."

On our last day in Strasbourg, our delegation met with the Council's Commissioner for Human Rights, Dr. Nils Muižnieks. When Dr. Muižnieks speaks, he sounds like an unlikely candidate for the post. Not because of what he says, but because of his distinctively American English. He is a Latvian-American, born and raised in Los Angeles, with a Ph.D. in Political Science from U.C. Berkeley. After finishing his doctoral dissertation, on the Baltic independence movements and the dissolution of the Soviet Union, in 1993 he moved to Latvia for a post-doctoral fellowship, and never looked back. He has been a founding member of the Latvian Centre for Human Rights and Ethnic Studies, the Director of the Soros Foundation—Latvia, and has served as Latvian government Minister for Social Integration, and as a member and then as the Chair of the European Commission against Racism and Intolerance.

Dr. Muižnieks was in Turkey twice in 2016—once before the failed July coup, in April, and once just after, in August—and it is clear that he has been following events there very closely since. Indeed, two days before our meeting, on the same day that the resolution was passed, he had published his third report on the human rights situation in Turkey, two of which focus on counter-terrorism measures and the curfews in municipalities across the Kurdish region, and one on the Erdoğan government's crackdown on freedom of expression, and on the media.[8] This third report was submitted to the European Court of Human Rights as a third-party intervention, in relation to 34 cases associated with the counter-terrorism measures and curfews, and contains a clear denunciation of violations of "the protection of the right to life; the lack of effective investigations and the problem of impunity; restrictions on relatives paying their last respects to their deceased family members; and undue interference with the work of human rights' defenders."[9]

The Commissioner's report nevertheless qualifies this denunciation somewhat by also mentioning "the severe terrorist threat faced by Turkey," recognizing "the right and duty of the Turkish State to fight against terrorism in all its forms," and by referring to the "deteriorating security situation in South-Eastern Turkey, which included the building of trenches and barricades by armed terrorist groups in certain neighbourhoods" that preceded the declaration of the curfews in urban centres. Moreover, the report ends with an acknowledgement of "the predicament of the Turkish authorities and the Turkish security forces, who have the duty to fight against terrorism," before recalling "that in this fight they should show much higher regard to the human rights of populations affected by the measures they take and ensure that all allegations are promptly, adequately and effectively investigated by the judicial authorities with a view to enforcing laws and maintaining the principle of the rule of law."[10] In effect, the report thus calls for a more humane, more proportional, waging of the war on terror. But though the report refers to the "legacy of the armed confrontation between Kurdish separatists and the Turkish security forces," nowhere are the underlying issues of injustice that have motivated the Kurdish movement anywhere addressed by the Commissioner of Human Rights.

Dr. Muižnieks was affable and engaged during our meeting. He even agreed with our point about both Demirtaş and Öcalan playing key roles in the quest for peace. But like the Secretary General, he registered a certain scepticism about the prospects for peace in the near future. He originally cited the Gezi Park protests as the crucial turning point for the Erdoğan government's escalation of authoritarianism, but also agreed with our claim that Kobane was crucial as well. He admitted that the successful defence of Kobane by Kurdish forces in Rojava had "spilled over into Turkey," and were "intimately intertwined with domestic affairs," an "intertwining which leads me to be more pessimistic about Turkey."

Unlike the Secretary General, Dr. Muižnieks did not question the credibility of Öcalan's commitment to peace, but he did register scepticism nonetheless, posing the question: "Is it really true that Öcalan has the power to control the younger generation?" When we responded by suggesting that Öcalan is perhaps the only person who can control the youth, he responded, "I heard that the younger generation who dug the trenches is not interested in listening to Öcalan's calls for a peace process and for a political solution." When we pushed him on the importance of emphasizing the centrality of a peaceful, political resolution to the Kurdish question for the prospects of democracy in Turkey, he pushed back: "To what extent does it tactically make sense to stress the Kurdish question in particular instead of the human rights and freedom of expression issues more generally? I am not convinced it makes sense to stress the Kurdish question, because there are too many Turkish people who don't want to hear about it." Tactical prudence, or evasion of truth? Yet again, we seemed to witness a difficult balancing act between the logic of might and the logic of right, performed this time by none other than the Commissioner of Human Rights.

Before leaving Strasbourg, we had the chance to sit down with Mr. Kürkçü, to ask him for some reflections on the current conjuncture and to get his opinion about what the priorities for future international İmralı delegations should be.

The honorary president of the HDP was eloquent and incisive in his response. He began by alluding to the disturbing significance of the silence surrounding Öcalan's isolation, even as an issue for debate. According to Mr. Kürçü, "The Öcalan issue seems to have been pushed back to the second or third row now." The emergence of Demirtaş, especially after his imprisonment, he admitted, has something to do with the silence about Öcalan. "Demirtaş's situation has gained further priority," Mr. Kürçü argued. "He has gained a reputation of his own, especially in international circles, as also a legitimate representative of the Kurds. Around here, for example, he is praised by many as a spokesperson for the Kurds. Releasing him has become a priority."

The figure and fate of Öcalan was thus contrasted to the figure and fate of Demirtaş, before he continued, "This unfortunately also the consequence of pushing the cause of Öcalan into the shadows." He nevertheless made a point of emphasizing, "This was never Demirtaş's intention. Neither he nor anyone in the HDP would deny that Öcalan is the leader of the Kurds. It is the image, not the reality." Or perhaps more precisely, an image that has become part of the reality, since "the reality is that international circles are much more comfortable agitating in favour of Demirtaş." From this line of reasoning, Mr. Kürçü drew a first practical conclusion for our delegation: "So the challenge for your delegation is, without hurting Demirtaş's cause, to put forward Öcalan and his role." He again insisted, "Öcalan's role is not contested by the Kurds. But explaining this situation, his unique role, his uncontested leadership, this is much more difficult to explain to the international community."

It is a difficult challenge, he insisted, especially since the breakdown of peace negotiations and the resurgence of war. He contrasted the media coverage of our delegations to Turkey in February, 2016, with the one in February, 2017: "This year the İmralı delegation got no media coverage in Turkey. Last year it got some." What accounts for the contrasting receptions? "The most important factor has to do with the strict ban in the Turkish media." Even so, he continued, "But also the urgent situation has changed. When the peace process was on, this was an urgent issue. Now, relieving city sieges is what everyone is worried about most urgently. The attention of the Kurdish movement, and the broader Kurdish public, is perplexed."

Adding to and perhaps underlying such perplexion, Mr. Kürçü suggested, are differences in sensibility, associated with tactical priorities and organizational differences within the movement itself—differences between the HDP and the PKK. In Mr. Kürçü's words, "There is also another issue. On the one hand, Demirtaş has from the start insisted that the HDP campaign should be separate from the PKK campaign. He has refused to be part of the PKK campaign. He has always wanted it this way. He believes the two should not be mixed." As for the PKK? "On the other hand, the PKK is not raising Öcalan's situation as an immediate issue. Tactically, in the recent hunger strike wave, the PKK warned them [imprisoned HDP MPs] not to start the hunger strike. The PKK then issued a written statement to stop the hunger strike." Then he turned to pose the question:

"What is accepted? I do not know. What are their priorities?" He paused—a pregnant silence—before concluding instead, "But whatever these may be, there are domestic premises required to start a new campaign with a focus on the freedom of Öcalan." By way of example, Mr. Kürkçü relayed, "Today, I had a little talk with the former head of the Republican People's Party (CHP). He doesn't want to hear such issues. But he is open to talking about Kurds in general. The season is not yet suitable for a reopening, for a renewed attack on this point."

Mr. Kürkçü finished his reflections by drawing a distinction between "powerful, everlasting" issues and "urgent" ones, and by suggesting that in a climate of emergency such as the one in Turkey, the two can easily get confused. "Keep in mind," he pointed out, "there is a difference between a powerful issue and an urgent issue." He insisted that "the freedom of Öcalan is still the number one issue for the Kurdish movement. The peace process helped a lot. But when there is no peace process, Öcalan's voice is not heard as much. A new phase of the peace process would certainly help highlight the Öcalan issue." Of course, he admitted, the two issues should not be separated—Öcalan and peace. Rather, it makes more sense to frame the matter as one and the same issue: "Öcalan as a peacemaker ... Peace and Öcalan understood as one. But you witnessed the debate in the Assembly, you witnessed the rejection of our proposed amendment to paragraph five. Proposing a new peace process is understood as not right. Not now. We have to cook the idea again." There was another pregnant pause before a final conclusion—a final question: "Time is running out. He is 69 now—one year older than me. How many more years will he live?"

Notes:

1. Jeffrey Miley. "The Council of Europe and the death of the peace process in Turkey." The Region. September 8, 2017. Accessed September 30, 2017. http://bit.ly/2tQ93sn.

2. "Judge Moosa: Öcalan is the Undisputed Leader of Majority of Kurds." Kurdish Info. February, 2016. Accessed March 28, 2016. http://bit.ly/2NauPjt.

3. "Essa Moosa: We Want Turkish Government to Resume Peace Talks with Öcalan." KurdishQuestion.com. April 20, 2016. Accessed. April 28, 2016. http://kurdishquestion.com/video/9.

4. "Essa Moosa: Human rights lawyer, judge and activist—1936–2017." Sunday Times. March 5, 2017. Accessed March 28, 2017. https://bit.ly/2MMRCRq

5. "Ertuğrul Kürkçü." Wikipedia. Accessed January 1, 2018. http://bit.ly/2NauPjt.

6. Jennifer Rankin. "Council of Europe vote puts pressure on Turkey over human rights." The Guardian. April 26, 2017. Accessed April 30, 2017. http://bit.ly/2tQms3x.

7. Kariane Westrheim. "State Terror, Human Rights Violations, and Authoritarianism in Turkey: Report of the Third İmralı Peace Delegation, Based on its Visit to Turkey, Feb. 13–19, 2017." The Third EU-Turkey Civic Commission. March 18, 2017. Accessed April 30, 2017. https://www.mbl.is/media/99/10299.pdf.

8. "The Commissioner intervenes before the European Court of Human Rights in cases concerning the freedom of expression and right to liberty and security of parliamentarians in Turkey." Council of Europe Commissioner for Human Rights. October 11, 2017. Accessed January 1, 2018. https://bit.ly/2MN7OC0

9. "The Commissioner intervenes before the European Court of Human Rights in a group of cases concerning anti-terrorism operations in South-Eastern Turkey." Council of Europe Commissioner for Human Rights. May 5, 2017. Accessed May 28, 2017. http://bit.ly/2KlQHe1.

10. "Third party intervention by the Council of Europe Commissioner for Human Rights." Council of Europe Commissioner for Human Rights. 25 April 2017. Accessed May 28, 2017. https://rm.coe.int/168070cff9.

PART FOUR:
Reflections of the EUTCC
İmralı Peace Delegates

Fighting the Lion Inside the Cage

Janet Biehl

Author, Editor, and Collaborator with Theorist Murray Bookchin

On the morning of February 15, 2016, Ertuğrul Kürkçü, co-leader of the Democratic People's Congress (HDK)—a coalition of democratic left forces, from social democrats to grassroots political, ecological, and cultural movements, trade unions, and the women's movement—sat down with our delegation in Istanbul. It was here that he explained that the Kurdish movement and its allies were working to strengthen local government throughout Turkey, moving the country from an undemocratic unitary state to an inclusive democracy. To achieve this goal of "autonomy for all," the HDK works in tandem with the People's Democratic Party (HDP), which was then the third-largest political party in Turkey.

The AKP government, in response, targets the HDP and HDK for repression. The State, Kürkçü reported, identifies calls for democracy as "terrorism" and groups that advocate it as "terrorist," in order to suppress them. Kürkçü explained that the HDP deputies had already been stripped of their parliamentary immunity.

Our visit took place after the Turkish general election of November 2015 but before the coup of July 2016. The AKP government, insisting that "there's no Kurdish problem but a terror problem," had whipped up hysterical propaganda against Kurdish people and organizations and used bomb attacks on progressive gatherings to sway the outcome. After the election, it inflicted brutal military attacks on the population of cities such as Cizre and persecuted academics who merely called for peace—waging all-out war against Kurdishness. Cities had become war zones, pounded with artillery and tank fire. Police and special forces directly linked to the president were empowered to kill with impunity, persecuting academics who merely called for peace, and waging all-out war against Kurdishness. Cities had become war zones, pounded with artillery and tank fire. Police and special forces directly linked to the president were empowered to kill with impunity.

Amid these developments, Abdullah Öcalan, leader of the PKK, remained incarcerated in the island prison on İmralı that had been constructed for him ("to cut off his connection to the world," one of his lawyers explained to us). Now in his eighteenth year of detention, he suffers grievous human rights violations. He is not permitted contact with anyone apart from his guards. This degree of isolation, one of his lawyers would tell us, is "cruel torture….Conditions faced by Öcalan are severe and violent. No human could endure them."

Not even his lawyers are permitted to visit him—the last time was April 5, 2015. The human right to meet with one's lawyers is basic, and he has a large legal team in Istanbul. "We have applied to visit him every week for five years," one lawyer explained. "That's more than six hundred times." In February 2016 hundreds of them applied *en masse* to visit, but the state denied permission. "The excuses are ridiculous," the lawyers told us. "'The boat is broken.' 'The weather is bad.'" No other reasons are given. We have had five years of bad weather and the broken boat."

"Is Öcalan considered a political prisoner?" we asked. "No," one explained, "that term is not used. He was tried as a criminal." According to human rights lawyer Margaret Owen, "Turkey claims to have no political prisoners." Instead the State uses Turkey's extremely broad Anti-Terror Law "to destroy all efforts by the Kurdish people to obtain their fundamental human rights—rights to equality before the law, freedom of association, expression, rights to use their own language and to be represented in national and local government." Kurdish people see Öcalan, deprived of his legal rights, as a surrogate for themselves, deprived of their human, cultural, and political rights.

"Öcalan stands for ideological identity," one lawyer told us. "Not only is his body but the will of our people is being held hostage in İmralı."

When we met with the human rights lawyers on February 15, 2016, we wanted to be helpful and barraged them with what we hoped would be useful suggestions.

"What about making representations to the UN Human Rights Commission that genocide is taking place?"

"Yes," we were told, "applications had previously been made."

"What about the International Criminal Court in the Hague?"

"Turkey has not signed the convention," They responded, "and so is not bound by the ICC and can't be tried there."

"What about the Geneva Conventions?"

"Again, Turkey did not sign the First and Second ones and so is not bound by them. But yes, the third one—referring to crimes against humanity—applies even if it is not signed."

"What about the European Court of Human Rights (ECHR)?"

"It always decides in favor of government, never with Kurds," they said. In 2014, ECHR judges decided the restrictions on lawyers' visits and the State's eavesdropping on conversations with Öcalan were "a legitimate security measure." According to the Freedom for Öcalan Initiative, "This very unfortunate decision … justifies… the ban on visits of lawyers to the island, thereby accepting the basic logic of Turkey's anti-terror legislation."

"What about the European Committee for the Prevention of Torture (CPT)?" we asked. "We've informed them every month for the last 15 years. They're good listeners, and they say they are trying, but no outcome."

Yet the team of brilliant young lawyers standing before us were upbeat, hopeful, and resolute. They took the long view, recognizing that their struggle would be protracted. They saw their role, at a minimum, as documenting human rights violations. "Maybe Turkey will be held accountable in a court someday, we are preparing for that or for a special court. We keep records of what's happening. We may not taste the fruits of our work, but we hope it will be the future basis for convictions of crimes against humanity."

They considered themselves part of the democratic struggle in Turkey, they told us. Indeed, they were not merely documenters of abuses but agents of struggle in their own right; Öcalan's legal team has itself been prosecuted fifteen times. In 2011, Turkish police arrested several dozen Kurdish lawyers and charged them under the Anti-Terror Act of "being members of an illegal organization"— that is, by virtue of acting as Öcalan's defense lawyers, they were held to be supporters of terrorism. But it is a firm legal principle that anyone accused of a crime has an absolute right to be represented by a lawyer.

The lawyers who were met in 2011 had also been charged with "passing orders of Abdullah Öcalan," that is, conveying Öcalan's words to the PKK. No evidence whatsoever supported this charge. In fact, state officials knew it was false; the Turkish state had not only eavesdropped on all conversations between Öcalan and his lawyers but recorded them—a gross breach of client confidentiality. The prosecution authorities were trying to make it a crime to represent Öcalan.

At their trial in 2012–13, Tahir Elçi, president of the Diyarbakır Bar Association, addressed the judges on behalf of Öcalan's lawyers. They, he said, were being punished simply for practicing as lawyers. Elçi was a longtime fighter for human rights and Kurdish rights. Only three months before our delegation met with the remarkable young Kurdish lawyers in Istanbul, Elçi had been murdered, slaughtered on a street in Diyarbakır (Amed) during a press briefing. It was under the shadow of this horrific murder that the young lawyers we met were acting, knowing that the same could happen to them at any time. Yet none of them even mentioned it to us, let alone displayed fear.

These lawyers were just a few of the figures of towering courage whom our group encountered that February. As mentioned earlier, we met the HDK co-leader Ertuğrul Kürkçü a militant of the Turkish Left since the generation of '68.

Janet Biehl, author and editor, with Eirik Eiglad, publisher with New Compass Press, in a meeting with lawyers from the Istanbul Bar Association; February 2016.

As a young man, he had participated in an armed guerrilla movement (THKO), for which he was indicted and served fourteen years in a Turkish prison (1972–86). Afterward he fought indefatigably for the unification of Turkey's socialist Left, variously as an editor, a political journalist, and a parliamentarian. His present work with the pan-leftist HDP and HDK is a continuation of his extraordinary career.

We met Pervin Buldan, a HDP member whose businessman husband had been a PKK supporter. For that, in 1994, he was tortured and then murdered by the State. Buldan joined the "Saturday Mothers," a group who used civil disobedience to call attention to "disappearances in custody" cases. Every week they would hold sit-down demonstrations to demand that the State address the "reality of the disappeared." She entered politics, and in 2013, as deputy chair of the Peace and Democracy Party (BDP), she visited Öcalan on İmralı as "part of the negotiating committee [and] was the longest-standing member, attending all thirty-three meetings." In 2015, after three years, the talks suddenly ended. Thereafter, Turkey renewed its campaign of war and massacre. "The massacres taking place in Kurdish areas—it's to drive the Kurds out of their homelands," she explained. "Turkey is in huge need of peace", she said. "To that end, negotiations are essential. And before negotiations can start, Öcalan must be free."

We met many others who made me think that tenacity, high-minded commitment, and practical savvy had to be routine in the Kurdish movement. One afternoon, for example, a journalist from *Özgür Gündem* interviewed me, and I took the opportunity to ask her how she functioned under conditions where journalists can be arbitrarily jailed. "Does it make you more cautious?" I asked. "No," she told me, "it makes us bolder."

They made my own political activity in the United States seem tame by comparison. But then, I had met many courageous Kurdish militants since I first got involved with the Kurdish movement in the fall of 2011. I had visited Diyarbakır, then Rojava a couple of times; I had attended conferences in Europe. But never had I felt such a sense of high-stakes confrontation as here in Istanbul. From the comfort of my American home, I had translated books (German to English) about the Kurdish movement. But I was fighting the lion outside the cage. To use a metaphor I once learned from the Kurdish activist Nilüfer Koç, the Kurds are fighting for justice while being trapped in the cage with the lion.

In the year and a half since our delegation's February 2016 visit, Erdoğan has become ever more the lion, especially in the wake of the coup attempt and subsequent crackdown: we have seen the referendum giving Erdoğan presidential powers, the arrest and imprisonment of much of the HDP parliamentary delegation, the continuing repression of dissent, and the persecution of thousands of people. The AKP's war on the Kurds is ever more brutal. In 2016 I had asked Kürkçü whether Turkey was fascist, and he told me, "We say it is an authoritarian state heading in a fascist direction." Today it has moved much farther in that direction.

When we asked what we can do to help the Kurdish movement, a group of women told us:

> Our struggle is insufficient without support from outside… We cannot raise our own voices in Turkey because when we do, we are attacked, tortured, or killed. Raise our voices in your countries. Tell them what is being done to the Kurdish people. War crimes are being committed. Put pressure on the world to stop this violence. Forty million Kurds face genocide. Babies are being murdered in mothers' hands, grandfathers' bodies in streets, with no accountability. We ask you to urge your countries to hear our voices and find a way to stop this. Your countries that prefer to side with economic interests—get them to take human rights considerations seriously.

My Tryst with the Kurdish Freedom Struggle

Radha D'Souza, Reader of Law, University of Westminster

I stumbled upon Peace in Kurdistan (PIK) in London quite serendipitously. The huge surge in the numbers of political prisoners in India, especially after the commencement of Operation Green Hunt, the military offensive against the indigenous peoples of Central India in 2009, and the mass incarceration of Tamils in detention camps after the genocide in Sri Lanka in the same year, impelled many South Asians and Tamils like myself to seek out organisations and people in London who may be willing to help internationalise the campaign for the release of political prisoners. Political prisoners continue to fill up Indian prisons far beyond their holding capacities. I was asked to contact Peace in Kurdistan as a possible supporter. Lo and behold, my tryst with the Kurdish freedom struggle began the moment when I first met activists of Peace in Kurdistan.

When Peace in Kurdistan invited me to join the International İmralı Delegation organised by the EU Turkey Civic Commission (EUTCC), I was hesitant. What could I, a citizen of India, a country with its own problems about political prisoners, do for the release of Abdullah Öcalan and his compatriots? For a start, I did not have that magic booklet—a European or UK or Western passport—which can, like the invocation in Aladdin's story, magically swing open many immigration turnstiles at airports around the world. I did not hold positions of influence or power in British, European or Western institutions to be able to influence anything. I was not even one of the "opinion making classes"—a journalist in a prominent newspaper, a media personality, an actress, a lawyer, a judge, an influential academic or writer—or even a stand-up comedian—with capacities to do anything concrete to influence anyone in favour of the release of political prisoners in Turkey, including Öcalan, the most prominent amongst them. Moreover, going beyond these surface considerations, my hesitation had a deeper source.

As someone who has remained a participant in the democratic rights movement in India and South Asia for well over four decades, I find the problem of political prisoners to be a curious one in contemporary "democracies." The problem of political prisoners is as old as the institution of the State itself. Sultans and monarchs threw dissidents into dungeons. I know that. These rulers were considered to be endowed with "divine rights" or were viewed as "protectors of the faith," and their actions were, at least, consistent with the prevalent theories of absolutism. Then came the colonialists. When the East India Company threw Bahadur Shah Zafar, the last Mughul emperor of India, into a dungeon in Rangoon for life in 1857, it was a trading corporation that imprisoned him, not an absolute sultan or monarch. Thereafter, colonial rule established an entire legal apparatus, replete with classifications, trial procedures, prison codes, and jail manuals for political prisoners. But then, they were colonisers. Colonised subjects expect colonisers to imprison opponents of colonial rule. That is why my grandparents' generation and the generations before them joined the freedom struggle against colonialism on a continental scale.

Democracy, the ideology of modernity, befuddles the problem of political prisoners. Democracy creates an expectation of political, social, and cultural spaces for dissent even when states continue to police those spaces and imprison dissidents. The much-celebrated Indian constitution guarantees freedom of thought, expression, and beliefs, yet throughout the post-Independence era, Indian prisons have never been short of political prisoners. Strictly speaking, political prisoners in a democracy is a contradiction in terms.

So how could I refuse to join the delegation when I had also sought out support for our own cause for political prisoners in India? So join the delegation I did. In April 2016, we travelled to Strasbourg to meet with a member of the secretariat of the Council of Europe's European Committee for the Prevention of Torture and Inhuman or Degrading Treatment or Punishment (CPT). Our purpose was simple: CPT officials had visited Abdullah Öcalan in January 2013. No one had had access to Öcalan or seen him—not even his lawyers—since April 2015. The solitary confinement, prohibition of family visits, and access to lawyers breached the recommendations made by the CPT in 2013. Would the CPT undertake another visit to verify the conditions of Öcalan's detention and ascertain if the Turkish authorities had complied with the CPT's 2013 recommendations?

Sitting in the meeting room in Strasbourg, I was unable to resist juxtaposing the leaders of the two sides. The International İmralı Delegation was led by the late Judge Essa Moosa, the inspirational South African judge and former lawyer of another famous political prisoner: Nelson Mandela. On the other side, the CPT had recently elevated a Ukrainian academic as its chairperson at a time when Ukraine was under the spotlight for widespread torture and abuse of political prisoners. The Ukrainian government boasted about the appointment of its citizen on its official website, claiming, "[t]he election… is… evidence of a high level of scientific development of international law in Ukraine in general,"[1] while at the same time it denied permission to the United Nations Subcommittee on Prevention of Torture to visit and investigate allegations of torture and abuse of political prisoners in Ukraine.[2] What did the CPT's chairman do about the UN Subcommittee's visit to his own country, if he did anything at all? I wondered. But meetings of the type I was in are not moments to contemplate the truth, and most certainly not for speaking one's mind. That much I knew very well, and I was relieved that we had Judge Moosa, a soft-spoken, gentle, dignified, and principled spokesperson to speak for all of us.

Towards the tail end of the meeting, more as a concluding reflection, I said: "I teach law in a university and my students often ask me why the stated purposes of the law are frequently not achieved. I would love to be able to tell my students that the law does offer justice and hope to many." The suave and composed demeanour of the CPT official fell away instantly. "Are you challenging me?" he questioned, sounding stern. "Remember it is because of the EC, and the European Convention on Human Rights, and the prohibition on the death penalty in

Turkey as a result, that Öcalan is even alive today." I remembered something that the Commissioner of Police in Mumbai said to me when I had just joined the legal profession as a young lawyer, decades ago. "Remember, it is not enough to know your law. Your attitude must be right. Learn to speak to police officers properly with respect," he told me. Those words have stayed with me ever since and surfaced again in the Strasbourg office. Had I said anything disrespectful? Is my attitude so transparent? I continue to wonder a year and half later. Some conversations remain etched in our memories and the CPT official's response to my interjection will remain with me for a long time. In the past, there were elaborate protocols that ordinary people had to follow when seeking audience with a sultan or a monarch. They knew they had to kow-tow, swear allegiance, proclaim their loyalty, and be subservient. Modern democracies promise equality of rulers and ruled, transparency and openness, even accountability of the rulers over the ruled. And yet, in reality, those very things render opaque the existence of protocols and practices when in audience with those in power. Perhaps someone needs to write an activist handbook called "How to Conduct Yourself in the Presence of Officials When Campaigning for Your Rights!"

The fact remains that one and half years after the International İmralı Delegation met with the CPT, and four and half years after the CPT's first recommendations on Öcalan's treatment in prison, he remains in solitary confinement, without access to lawyers or family or friends. In the meantime, the situation in Turkey continues to deteriorate rapidly, and the numbers of political prisoners in Turkish prisons continue to swell—as they do around the world in India, Sri Lanka, Philippines, Rwanda, Uganda, and countries far too numerous to list here. Mumia Abu-Jamal remains in prison for his views on black nations in America since 1981, most of it spent in solitary confinement, and campaigners in the capital of the "Free World," the United States, continue to petition courts for his medical needs. We have yet to comprehend the global scope of suppression of political dissent and the sheer numbers of political prisoners around the world. If ever there was a moment in history when a sustained international campaign for the release of political prisoners was essential, that moment is now.

A tryst with the Kurdish freedom struggle is much more than a meeting with a Strasbourg official, important though such meetings are. In India, I knew of the Kurdish struggle as one of the many "nationality movements" as they are known in South Asia: Kashmir, Nagaland, Tamil Eelam, Manipur, Assam, Baluchistan, Karen, and many more. Resistance to military occupations of homelands, to the Armed Forces Special Powers Act of 1958 in India, popular aspirations for freedom, and the reasons for state repression and incarceration of leaders are familiar to many in the region. Speaking for myself, the Kurdish struggle stands out amongst the many nationality movements for one important reason: the extraordinary levels of international mobilisation by the Kurdish diaspora. Through their sustained work and inexhaustible energy, the Kurdish diaspora have brought the "Kurdish question" to the attention of officials, the general public, intellectuals, professionals, and political leaders in a way few other movements have succeeded in doing. In a globalised world of internationalised capitalism, movements and struggles that remain confined within national boundaries become invisible to the rest of the world. Their invisibility strengthens the hands of repressive states.

There is much that other diasporas around the world can learn from the Kurdish diaspora. No diaspora can organise or mobilise opinion overseas without strong movements at home that present a serious political alternative to people there. The Kurdish freedom struggle has transcended traditional nationality movements and transformed itself into a broad-based democratic movement demanding democratic change for all people in society: Kurdish and non-Kurdish, men and women, and all racial, ethnic, and religious groups. The new imperial wars in the Middle East have destroyed natural, physical, social, and cultural infrastructures needed for human life. Amidst the mayhem and destruction that we witness in the Middle East today, the very presence of the Kurdish freedom struggle offers the possibilities of hope and humane futures. In this regard too, other nationality movements elsewhere have a great deal to learn from the Kurdish freedom struggle. Slowly but surely there is growing recognition, in India at least, that the Kurdish freedom struggle is amongst the most important movements in the present time.

For me personally, the Kurdish freedom struggle has opened a whole new world of amazing, inspiring people, new friendships, and solidarities that I would never have found had I not serendipitously discovered Peace in Kurdistan UK. Beyond personal friendships and solidarities, the struggle has opened the possibilities of new internationalisms. International solidarities of oppressed peoples have disappeared from the horizons of many movements for the past seventy years. Capitalism, however, is—and has always been—international in scope with a global dynamic and outreach. Anti-colonial movements of the past were successful to the extent possible within the conditions of those times, at least partly because of their internationalist orientations. An international system such as capitalism cannot be resisted within individual nation-states alone. The Kurdish movement brings back the possibilities of reviving international solidarities once again. I sought out Peace in Kurdistan in London seeking support for movements for the release of political prisoners in India, and I have ended up asking myself how I can make movements in India more aware of the Kurdish movement. Hence, my *tryst* with the Kurdish freedom struggle.

Notes:

1. "Ukrainian lawyer Mykola Gnatowskyy elected Chairman of European Committee of Torture Prevention," Embassy of Ukraine in the Republic of Latvia, March 09, 2015. https://bit.ly/2u1hl0F

2. "UN torture prevention body suspends Ukraine visit," Human Rights House Foundation. May 31, 2016. https://bit.ly/2lP2QcD.

A Basque Politician in Kurdistan

Miren Gorrotxategi, Lawyer and Member of the Spanish Senate with *Podemos*
and Member of the Parliamentary Assembly of the Council of Europe (PACE)

Translated by Josie Hooker

I joined the third İmralı Delegation just weeks before it was due to make its one-week visit to Turkey in February 2017. Just a month before, in January 2017, I became a representative of *Podemos* in the Spanish delegation of the Parliamentary Assembly of the Council of Europe (PACE). As a professor of constitutional law at the University of the Basque Country, PACE has been an object of study for me each time that I have undertaken work in relation with human rights. It is a supranational body whose purpose is not commercial; instead, it is dedicated to the protection of democracy and human rights. It has at its disposal a tribunal whose sentences are binding and, as such, it is an institution of utmost interest for those of us who seek to widen the space for justice and equality using law as a tool.

In my recently launched new life as a politician, working directly in the Council of Europe was such a cherished opportunity for me that I was determined to take up every chance it offered me for new projects, knowledge, and action.

When I was invited to join the İmralı Delegation, my knowledge about the Kurdish people was quite poor. I had just a few vague impressions about the existence of a conflict in the Middle East that pitted a nation, the Kurdish nation, against states like Turkey and its neighbours along with the equally hazy notion that the Kurdish people were a people subjugated to the violence of war and to the humiliation of non-recognition as a political and cultural subject. The opportunity to visit a territory in these conditions as a member of a European delegation, to hear the testimonies of its people, to influence the actions (increasingly dark and undemocratic) of the Turkish government, and to transmit what we learned to the citizens of my country and the institutions of the Council of Europe seemed, to me, to be an unrivalled way of giving meaning to my political activity.

With the modesty of somebody who knew little, but the optimism of somebody who wanted to do what they could, I joined the delegation of experienced participants. I was very conscious of my personal circumstances and how they might influence my perceptions of the issues at stake. Indeed, I had a hunch that these circumstances were precisely the reason I had been invited to participate: I am a woman, Basque, a lawyer, and a parliamentarian.

My Thoughts as a Lawyer-Parliamentarian

As a parliamentarian of the Council of Europe, I was slowly learning of Turkey's capacity to influence debate in the Assembly, and not only on account of the denunciations that some Turkish parliamentarians brought to the plenary regarding their government's human rights violations, including arbitrary detentions and the withdrawal of immunity from MPs. As a privileged member of PACE (Turkey makes voluntary, additional contributions to the Council's budget), Turkey's influence in the Council was revealed to a shocked and scandalised public when, during the Assembly session of January 2017, a debate on Turkey was cancelled despite already having been included in the official proceedings. Going against significant opposition in the Assembly (94 votes in favour and 68 against, with 19 abstentions), the directive organ of the Assembly, by a majority of just one vote, decided to suspend the debate and neutralise the will of the majority.

This practice of despotism and abuse of state power by the Turkish government is something I witnessed directly from the first day of our visit to Turkey. During our first interviews with various Kurdish political parties in Diyarbakır (Amed), several armoured police vehicles "guarded" the meeting: they parked opposite the building in which we were hosted and, after we left, several of the officers, armed as if for war, photographed us a number of times in an intimidating fashion. It would not be the only encounter our delegation would have with the police, and is an example of how the Turkish state acts through its security forces.

If these actions and this threatening attitude was manifest at a private meeting of a European delegation of political representatives who would be returning to their countries of origin within the week, what on Earth could happen to the Kurdish women and men who attempt to pose political opposition on a permanent basis? Any of the people we met in Turkey could have given accounts of arbitrary detentions, rigged trials, and other human rights violations. Such accounts are only the most likely outcomes of the activity of a state that, as I myself have witnessed, is cruel with its citizens, armed in its use of force, and against pluralism. Later, we would have the opportunity to learn, via the testimony of his lawyers, of the situation of complete isolation in which the Kurdish leader Abdullah Öcalan is held in the prison of İmralı.

My Thoughts as a Basque Woman

Although I have lived my entire adult life under a political regime founded on democracy, I was born when the fascist dictator Francisco Franco was still alive. As such, the effects of dictatorship are, to me, not only recent but also directly felt in some cases.

An example would be my name. When I was born, the use of Euskera (the Basque language) was banned, as were Basque names. My parents, who had always wanted a Basque name for me, registered me legally with a Spanish name. This was the case until, after democratisation, it became possible to change the names registered in civil records, adapting them into the Basque language. I, like many other people, had two names: the real one and the official one.

The issue of my name is just one example, but it is typical of regimes that deny cultural minorities recognition of their cultural specificity, of the use and preservation of their language and of their historical references and traditions. These are regimes that are opposed to the forms of culture that distinguish these groups; they are regimes that use force against minorities' efforts to carve out their own political and institutional spaces. During Franco's dictatorship, in many schools children were beaten for speaking Euskera and made to feel even worse if they were also from rural areas. All references to difference were eliminated in school textbooks. Under Franco, the authorities could give fines for using Euskera and the right of association was denied. Simply aspiring to self-governance was a criminal offence; jails housed hundreds of prisoners of conscience.

In Diyarbakır, I met a person who shared my story about having two names, with the difference that he had still not been able register his Kurdish name officially. The same history of denial, contempt, humiliation, and repression was manifest in the testimonies we heard from civil society organisations, political parties, trade unions, and journalists about the Kurdish people's possibilities to exercise self-determination.

The drawing of borders in the Middle East in the aftermath of World War I left the Kurds spread among four nation-states: Iraq, Iran, Syria, and Turkey. Almost half—namely 25 million people—live as Turkish citizens in Turkey as a "stateless nation." They have their own language (and its dialects), traditions, and history. The Kurdish movement demands that their rights as a cultural minority are recognised: that is, the recognition of the Kurdish language as a language of schooling and communication, as well as constitutional recognition giving special legal status within the Turkish state and allowing the defence of their cultural values. However, the Turkish government conceives of social peace as the outcome of its victory against internal insurgency that, in its eyes, challenges the unity of the Turkish nation, understood in centralist, assimilationist terms.

For this reason, the current situation of Turkish Kurds is one of war, in the strict sense of the word. This is the case despite the fact that the current demands of the Kurdish movement (with the exception, of course, of the armed struggle as a method) can easily be translated into the rights of cultural minorities in the framework of a diverse democratic society; minority rights are recognised by the United Nations Declaration on the Rights of Minorities, and also by the Council of Europe's Framework Convention for the Protection of National Minorities.

All of this leads us to the conclusion that Erdoğan's government is an authoritarian one that, using terrorism and the failed coup of July 15, 2016 as pretexts, does not respect the fundamental principles of the democratic state or rule of law.

Still a Long Way to Peace:
Changing Minds about the Kurdish Issue

Andrej Hunko,
Member of the German Parliament and the Parliamentary Assembly of
the Council of Europe (PACE)

It was through my membership in the Parliamentary Assembly of the Council of Europe (PACE) in Strasbourg that I dealt more intensely with the Kurdish question and the Turkish-Kurdish conflict. Being the largest and oldest European institution regarding human rights, the Council of Europe has always drawn many people to Strasbourg who had suffered as a result of human rights violations. Representatives of the Kurdish movement, including Abdullah Öcalan's lawyers, are frequent visitors there.

Since my appointment to the Council of Europe, I have used the opportunities to inform myself about the development of the Turkish-Kurdish conflict, and on various occasions, together with other PACE members, I filed applications to the Turkish authorities for visiting Öcalan in prison. Because of this involvement, it was obvious for me to participate in the İmralı Delegation.

It is interesting to describe the debates about the Kurdish question in the Assembly. At the beginning of my activity there in the years 2010 to 2012, the Kurdish question played practically no role in this parliamentary assembly of 47 European states. I remember how a listener told me after a speech in the plenary hall in 2011 that I was the first person in years who even used the term "Kurds" in the Assembly. When I talked about the PKK and the Turkish anti-terrorism laws in a committee meeting in Paris in 2012, it was so quiet that you could have heard a pin drop. I interpreted the situation as a mix of suppression and fear that one could be associated with the topic.

An example from 2012 might illustrate this widespread fear: I had filed an application to visit the imprisoned MPs of the Peace and Democracy Party (BDP): Selma Irmak in Diyarbakır (Amed) and Faysal Sarıyıldız in Mardin (Mêrdîn). By coincidence, the proposed visit date was April 4 2012. Usually applications of that kind are used to be approved within two weeks by the Turkish authorities. In this case, I had not been granted permit after two weeks, but I had already travelled to Istanbul for political discussions. When I mentioned to a Human Rights Watch (HRW) representative that my application had still not been approved and I'd showed her my documents, she turned quite pale and told me: "you applied to visit them on Öcalan's birthday." She recommended withdrawing the application, otherwise I would be accused of sympathizing with Öcalan. Shortly after our conversation, I was nonetheless granted permission. No representative of Turkish authorities made any reference to the case. With this example, I would like to pinpoint how the term "terrorism" is used to discourage parliamentarians, journalists, and human rights organizations from this type of activity.

That prevailing mood changed slowly with the foundation of the Peoples' Democratic Party (HDP) and the Gezi protests. More and more parliamentarians from different political groups started to see the Kurdish movement not as a source of terrorist activities but as a possible force towards the democratization of Turkey. The peak of that development in the Council of Europe was in April 2013, when a huge PACE majority adopted an amendment wherein I proposed to no longer refer to PKK as a terrorist organization. Instead, focus should be limited to describing the conflict in terms of the 40,000 deaths that resulted—a more neutral expression. At that time, there were widespread hopes that the unofficial peace negotiations, between representatives of the Turkish authorities and Abdullah Öcalan, would lead to success.

The basic problem of the category of terrorism, as opposed to an armed party of a conflict, is that peace talks with a "terrorist organization" are by definition almost impossible, because contact is usually prohibited with such organizations. Additionally, there is no internationally agreed definition of terrorism, which throws the gates wide open to arbitrariness.

On my journeys to Turkey, human rights organizations like HRW have repeatedly pointed out the excessive and flexible use of the term "terrorism" in Turkey. Unfortunately, the German government in particular has adopted the official Turkish version of the conflict with the PKK: Germany was one of the first European states to classify the PKK as a terrorist organization, which it did in 1993 when Manfred Kanther (CDU) was Minister of Internal Affairs. That classification was then expanded with the inclusion of the PKK on the EU terrorist list. There is a lot of criticism towards the ways in which terrorist lists are compiled. The inclusion of organizations on the list is decided upon in non-transparent EU Council working groups, often with the participation of intelligence services. There are no rule-of-law procedures for any withdrawals from that list. PACE has already pointed out these deficits in the rule of law in 2007.

The İmralı Delegation in February 2016, led by the former lawyer of Nelson Mandela, Essa Moussa, took place at a moment when the success of a visit to Abdullah Öcalan was improbable due to internal political developments, despite the high-ranking cast of the delegation. Nonetheless, it was and is still right to make the attempt to draw public attention to the person that is viewed by large parts of the Kurdish movement as its most important leader. About half a year before the delegation's visit, after his electoral setback in July 2015, President Erdoğan had decided to reach his goal of an authoritarian presidential regime through a polarization of society. The peace talks were cancelled and the war returned to the Kurdish regions in south-east Turkey.

I was not much surprised that the competent Turkish authorities did not even respond to the delegation's request, which also sought to promote the resumption of the peace talks with an offer of dialogue. At the same time, it was important to me as a member of the German Parliament to show my support for this delegation.

For many years, Germany has played a very inglorious role in the Turkish-Kurdish conflict. The arrest of Öcalan in 1998 in Italy was based on a German arrest warrant. At the same time, the German government of Social Democrats (SPD) and Greens waived any extradition to Germany and thereby opened the possibility for an illegal abduction of Öcalan in Nairobi (Kenya) by the Turkish secret service, MİT, and his transfer to Turkey. Previously, he had applied for asylum unsuccessfully in various European countries.

Until today, Germany is one of the most important arms exporters to Turkey—arms that are also used against the Kurdish population in Turkey. In Germany, Kurdish associations are also criminalized in a close level of cooperation with Turkish authorities that continues despite the deterioration in Turkish-German relations on a diplomatic level. So far, the increasing realization in German government circles about Erdoğan's anti-democratic course has not led to a change in attitude towards the Kurdish movement, which is the most affected by that course.

The future of Öcalan and a possible peaceful solution to the Turkish-Kurdish conflict is closely connected with internal political developments in Turkey. It was only through manipulation that Erdoğan was arduously able to reach a majority in the April 2017 referendum about his authoritarian presidential regime. In all major cities, and above all in Istanbul, a majority was not gained despite the electoral manipulations. At the same time, there is a climate of fear and intimidation which is suffocating public life extensively. The necessary resumption of the peace negotiations will be accompanied by the breakup of that climate of repression. The attention of international players to this situation is of great importance. That also includes attention to the situation of Abdullah Öcalan.

An Exercise in Understanding

Ögmundur Jónasson,

Former Icelandic Minister for the Ministries of Health, Justice, and the Interior; Former Member of the Parliamentary Assembly of the Council of Europe

I come from a small country, Iceland, with 330,000 inhabitants. It was therefore an experience to attend a rally together with a million people, as I did in Diyarbakır (Amed) in Kurdistan, in March 2014. This was my first visit to these parts and I was eager to understand the politics of Kurdish-Turkish relations.

I had read about the peace talks that had been in progress for a couple of years and I was perplexed to hear the seemingly aggressive tone blasted over the loudspeakers at the rally which was held to celebrate Newroz. The political undertones were evident. There were many speeches, banners were being waved in the air, and in the crowd you could see flocks of men who—so it was explained to me—were fighters who had come over the border from Syria to celebrate Newroz with fellow Kurds and use the opportunity to express solidarity: Kurdish solidarity. The atmosphere was electric.

It was obvious to the observer that the crowds paid particular attention to the message read out from Abdullah Öcalan. All this was translated to me. Gradually it dawned upon me that the seemingly aggressive tone was all in one direction: an exhortation for peace, a negotiated peace. *"Let us be consistent in our commitment to the peace process. This requires courage, let us be courageous!"* This was the message from the podium. And not in one speech or message but in all the words spoken. The period of 2013 to 2015 had been a time of thawing relations between the central government and the Kurds. At this time, it was genuinely believed that, on the horizon, was the possibility of increased democratic rights and a recognition of cultural autonomy, including the right to not only speak the Kurdish language but to cultivate and nurture it. Everywhere I went, there was optimism in the air. That optimism had gone when I visited Diyarbakır in February 2017 as a member of the İmralı Delegation. After the elections of June 2015, with a HDP victory and Erdoğan losing his majority, developments had taken a sinister turn.

Those who had signed petitions calling for support to the peace process between Kurds and Ankara—and we met many such persons—were now branded as terrorist sympathisers. Many of them had been deprived of their jobs and would be without any means of subsistence were it not for informal community support. Many awaited trial with apprehension. They knew that their fate in the coming years would be decided in the court room. And what was decided in the court room would be dependent on political whims. Nothing of this came as a surprise to me. I had, of course, followed the deteriorating situation. It had been explained to me on numerous occasions by human rights organisations, such as Amnesty International, how the Turkish armed forces and paramilitary groups linked to the government had committed atrocities that were in serious breach of human rights. Reports to the same effect had been presented before the Parliamentary Assembly of the Council of Europe, where I was a member. These reports told of hundreds of thousands of people uprooted from their homes, deprived of electricity and water, and placed under military curfew lasting for months. Independent and unquestionably objective reports had been gathered on massive human rights violations, including murders and torture. All this I have witnessed.

Nevertheless, although one can be aware of these grave violations, it is an entirely different experience to personally meet the victims: those who had suffered persecution themselves or whose families had been harmed, or even molested or killed. This makes an altogether different impact than reading reports. Likewise, to be present at trials where democratically elected people who had been imprisoned were being tried on obviously fabricated grounds is a chilling experience.

But why the title of this chapter? An exercise in understanding what? Taking part in the İmralı Delegation helped me understand the plight of the Kurds more fully and in more depth than before. I will give three examples of where my understanding was deepened.

Firstly, I want to mention the massive in-depth information we received—information not generally portrayed in mainstream media. It was an eye opener to be systematically presented with information on the extent to which persecutions—from killings and torturing of innocent people, to depriving ordinary citizens of fundamental rights, to shutting down media and stifling free and open discussion—were taking place. Information in the international media surely told us of politicians, lawyers, and teachers being arrested, but human rights violations outside these ranks were less talked about. After our visit, we had a clearer picture of a nation being terrorised at large: democracy being stifled, society suffocated.

Secondly, I received a lesson in the way in which the outside world was playing dirty against the Kurds. We had all witnessed NATO's top-level meeting in Brussels at the end of July 2015, which turned a blind eye to rising state aggression and terrorism against the Kurds. Prior to our visit, some of us had experienced a more subtle way of siding with Turkish authorities. Some of our team members had been warned by their respective foreign services not to go to the Kurdish parts of Turkey since they would not be safe there. And insurance companies had accordingly said that they would not insure people who travelled to the Kurdish part of Turkey. Of course such statements were politically loaded since the purpose very obviously was to discourage people to take part in such missions as ours. It turned out that the only times we felt threatened were when we encountered paramilitary groups who operated as police, e.g., on our arrival to Diyarbakır, on the way into the city centre. And when we met with civil rights groups and labour union representatives, the army reminded us with its ominous presence and display of armoury that a step out of line on our part would not be tolerated. This we understood as it was meant, namely as a threat.

My third lesson from this visit was the extraordinary experience of meeting with a political prisoner by the name of Ferhat Encü and learning more about his case. Why him? The reason is the following. When I attended the conference of the EU Turkish Commission in Brussel in December 2016, we were told of the arrest of a large number of democratically elected mayors and likewise the imprisonment of members of Parliament. Inspired and urged on by friends and colleagues, I decided to select one prisoner with the idea in mind of taking him as a kind of protégé from afar, knowing full well that the only thing I could do for him was to try and understand his case and make as many people as possible aware of it. By doing that, he would serve as *pars pro toto*, an example of the fate of thousands of prisoners.

The prisoner I selected to learn all about—in particular the circumstances leading to his imprisonment and then his condition in prison—was a young Kurdish Member of Parliament, Ferhat Encü. I learned that he was just over 30 years of age, born in 1985 in Şırnak district. He had studied mining engineering and been engaged in such work until he was elected to the Turkish Parliament in June 2015 for the HDP party.

In order to understand his fate, we must go a few years back, just before the time of the thaw in relations. On December 28, 2011, the Turkish air force attacked a group of people in the mountainous border region of Turkey and Iraq. Over 30 people—34 to be exact—were killed, mainly youngsters in their teens and early twenties in what is known as the Roboski Massacre. Most of them were members of Encü's family, including his young brothers and nephews. The corpses were so badly burned after the lethal attack that they could barely be recognised. I don't want to leave these youngsters and children as mere numbers. They also had a life which was just beginning. Here are their names so that they are not forgotten and to remind us that this is more than an issue of statistics: Salih Ürek, Bedran Encü, Adem Ant, Erkan Encü, Şivan Encü, Muhammed Encü, Bilal Encü, Aslan Encü, Mehmet Ali Tosun, Savaş Encü, Orhan Encü, Nadir Alma, Celal Encü, Fadil Encü, Mahsun Encü, Şervan Encü, Yüksel Ürek, Cemal Encü, Cihan Encü, Vedat Encü, Serhat Encü, Salih Encü, Özcan Uysal, Hüseyin Encü, Nevzat Encü, Hamza Encü, Selim Encü, Zeydan Encü, Seyithan Enç, Hüsnü Encü, Selahattin Encü, Osman Kaplan, Abdulselam Encü, Şerafettin Encü.

But what reason was given for the murderous attack? It was to uproot smuggling! A group of smugglers had been detected, it was said, and hence the attack. This was the official explanation. Others understood this as an act of terror. It is widely known that traditionally there has been trade in the mountains in this region, irrespective of borders. And even if children had been transporting petrol and cigarettes on donkeys, as was alleged to have been the case, this would hardly be a justification for the execution of poor harmless children with their donkeys!

Sorrow, outrage, and an urge for justice would not let the young Ferhat alone, and he demanded that an enquiry should be carried out, but to no avail.

In a meeting with HDP MP Ferhat Encü on the evening following his release from prison. He was detained again only a few hours later; Istanbul, February 2017.

Encü's struggle for justice eventually led to his political engagement and social involvement, until he was elected to become a Member of Parliament in 2015. Just over a year later, on November 4, 2016, Encü was arrested at Istanbul Airport, while on his way to attend a meeting in Brussels. All identification documents were taken from him and subsequently he was put in prison, where he has been held ever since—with one exception, which I will discuss presently.

However, let me first tell you that 17 charges were raised against Ferhat Encü, one with a pending death penalty. This charge has to do with the visit of the governor of Uludere to the village where the victims of the massacre had lived. The governor wanted to make their families accept compensation and agree not to lodge a claim against the Turkish state. But the villagers had organised a demonstration to protest the governor's coercion and to demand a full enquiry. During this protest, government soldiers attacked the villagers who, in turn, tried to defend themselves. Amongst them was Encü. That was his "crime." This democratic action and civil defence was now termed by the Turkish prosecutor as "lynching state authorities!"

Fast forward to February 2017, when the İmralı Delegation was on its way to Istanbul; the almost unbelievable news reached us that Encü was to be released from prison almost simultaneously with our arrival. I was in contact with his lawyers and a meeting was arranged at our hotel. I had taken some newspapers from Iceland with articles I had written about Encü, hoping to have them forwarded to him. But there he now was in person, and I could show him such media coverage at our meeting, eye to eye. But this was a short-lived bliss. The following day, Encü was already back in prison. He had been arrested at the airport when he was heading home to see his family and loved ones in eastern Turkey, Kurdistan.

Of course there are many more lessons to be learned from the Kurds than those I have mentioned in this account: the importance they attach to democracy, not only in word but also in deed; likewise their emphasis on gender, again not only in word; and then, and here I refer to Abdullah Öcalan, the imprisoned leader, his willingness to re-evaluate former beliefs and methods. This is indeed a lesson to be learned by a world all too often freewheeling along old dogmatic tracks.

From prison, Encü has sent a message which was presented at the aforementioned conference in Brussels, held by the EU Civic Commission. In it, he calls for solidarity against oppression, reminding us that with solidarity we will overcome. And from Iceland I now send him back the message that neither he nor the struggling Kurds will be forgotten until justice prevails.

"Please Tell My Story"

By Fr. Joe Ryan

Catholic Priest and Chair of the Westminster Justice and Peace Commission

These four words, "please tell my story," sum up so much of why I am involved in the Kurdish/Turkish question and in the whole Justice and Peace movement. Some people have no voice of their own. They need others to relate their story.

Going back to 2003, when I arrived in West Green, in the London borough of Haringey, I very soon was aware of the Kurdish Centre in the parish to which I was assigned as a Roman Catholic priest. I was invited to visit the centre at Green Lanes. As I sat in a small cafe attached, I chatted with members who belong to the centre. They introduced themselves and very soon I had a good part of their story. Each one of those young people in their 20s had spent some time in Turkish jails for anything from three months to three years. They had been involved in student protests and demonstrations or perhaps just associated with others who were arrested. I thought to myself, "This cannot be right. It's as if the national pastime in Turkey consisted of putting people in jail. I need to find out more." And so the story continues.

Having been Chair of the Westminster Diocese Justice and Peace Commission, I was invited to be part of an international delegation attending the mass trial of 151 Kurdish politicians, lawyers, and human rights activists. Their trial began in October 2010 in Diyarbakır (Amed), Turkey. We attended in January 2011: human rights lawyers Omer Moore and Sanya Karakas, Liberal Democrat politician and human rights activist Nasser Butt, and I, as Chair of the Westminster Diocese Justice and Peace Commission, were the UK delegation as observers at the trial.

We witnessed the proceedings in the courthouse, which had been built especially for the trial of the 151 selected prisoners. They were chosen out of the hundreds who had been arrested since the March 2009 elections in which Kurdish candidates were very successful. Much of the original part of the trial was taken up with the presentation of some of the 7,500 pages of charges held against the prisoners. Things came to a halt when the court denied the prisoners the right to defend themselves in their own native Kurdish language. When the prisoners replied to their roll call in Kurdish, the judge replied, "This court does not recognise this language." Security was high to enter the court; we waited a long time for the judges to arrive. I found this time most valuable to be able to meet with the families of the prisoners. These were mothers, fathers, brothers, and sisters who explained: "We are simple folks. My sons were involved in a demonstration or just by association with others; they didn't cause trouble. What am I to do?" They thanked us profusely for being present.

Some four years later, when back in Turkey on the İmralı Delegation, I met two of the lawyers who were among the 151 tried. They made very interesting points. They said: "It wasn't so much the fact of being in prison that was difficult to handle, but the feeling of being forgotten." This is a challenging concept, and reinforces the quest of "telling our story."

A press conference took place in September 2012 in Brussels to launch the Freedom for Abdullah Öcalan campaign. Those involved were BDP deputy Ayla Akat Ata; German deputy Andrej Hunko; myself; and Reimar Heider, International Initiative representative for "Freedom for Abdullah Öcalan—Peace in Kurdistan." This effort was taken up by several movements supporting the Kurdish cause. Under two years later that same group presented 10.3 million signatures pleading for the freedom of Abdullah Öcalan to the Council of Europe in Strasbourg. Sadly he is still in prison and there is very little recognition shown by the Turkish government of his sad situation. Here lies the problem: Mr Öcalan, just like the PKK, is on the terrorist list. Despite the fact that the guns of the PKK had been silent while peace negotiations and talks were taking place, no question of his liberation has been forthcoming. The fact that Mr Öcalan is deemed as the Nelson Mandela of the Kurdish people has little credibility in Turkish eyes.

I was glad to be part of the first İmralı Delegation, led by former South African judge, Essa Moosa, in 2016. We relied very much on his wisdom and experience to guide us. He had a simple strategy to make contact with the Turkish authorities, with the direct request that some of the delegation members would be allowed to visit Abdullah Öcalan on İmralı Island. This seems to be a very simple request. To visit someone in prison is very basic. The fact that his own family are denied visits says a lot. The refusal to allow his own lawyers to see him indicates a denial of human rights. How can this be tolerated? Here we have the very heart of the denial of human rights to a person in prison; but this is but the tip of the iceberg when it comes to denial of rights to members of the wider Kurdish community.

Mr Öcalan has put forward a plan for peace and reconciliation between the Turkish authorities and the Kurdish Community. Progress has been made, but just when an agreement was imminent, the Turkish authorities backed off. Things have not been helped by the outcome of the referendum in Turkey on April 16, 2017. It is a real turning point in Turkish political history. The result of this referendum has allowed Mr Recep Tayyip Erdoğan, the current president of Turkey, the freedom to dictate all policies in Turkey and to hold the key to supreme power. The suppression, intimidation and imprisonment of minorities, especially the Kurdish people, can now continue even more. There is no accountability since he is in charge of the judicial system. Human rights are denied and democracy as we know it is obliterated. The support given by other major nations give full credibility to an unjust regime. What the future holds is unpredictable.

I have been privileged to be able to respond over the years in other ways, to show solidarity with the Kurdish struggle for peace, democracy, and recognition as a people in its own right: being part of some of the rallies and demonstrations at Trafalgar Square, London; attending rallies at the BBC headquarters seeking fair reporting in the media; reporting to meetings in the House of Commons;

and especially joining the Kurdish Newroz celebrations at Finsbury Park, North London.

In November 2017, I was glad to be present at the funeral of Mehmet Aksoy, the filmmaker and peace activist. The tributes address to Mehmet summed up how much of a role model and inspiration he was, as a young man, to the Kurdish community. His vision and inspiration must never be lost.

I wish to thank those I have met along the way. I remember with great admiration and affection, Judge Essa Moosa of South Africa who, at the time of the delegation, had recently died. As a young lawyer he was very involved in the release of Nelson Mandela and all that followed in South Africa. I have made many wonderful friends in my involvement in the struggle for human rights. We continue the struggle with the Kurdish people, in the light of the inspiration of Judge Moosa for peace and justice.

I find the words of Archbishop Oscar Romeo, a champion for the poor and oppressed in El Salvador very inspiring. He was assassinated in March 1980, but his efforts and example still live on to inspire others. He wrote:

A Step Along the Way

It helps, now and then, to step back and take a long view.
The aim is not only beyond our efforts, it is even beyond our vision.
We accomplish in our lifetime only a tiny fraction of the magnificent enterprise that is God's work. Nothing we do is complete.
No statement says all that could be said.
No set of goals and objectives includes everything.
We plant the seeds that one day will grow.
We water seeds already planted, knowing that they hold future promise.
We lay foundations that will need further development.
We provide yeast that produces far beyond our capabilities.
We cannot do everything, and there is a sense of liberation in realising that.
This enables us to do something, and to do it very well.
It may be incomplete, but it is a beginning, a step along the way.
We may never see the end results, but that is the difference between the master builder and the worker.
We are prophets of a future not our own.

This journey with the Kurdish people has allowed me to meet so many wonderful and dedicated people. As an Irishman and priest, I can identify with the struggle for justice. It is remarkable how the Kurdish people have been able to identify the struggle for Irish freedom as a parallel to their own struggle. The challenge now is for freedom of expression, being allowed your own culture and heritage, and being able to live in peace with others. These human rights are denied the Kurdish people, especially in Turkey. So the efforts must continue.

Repressing Comedians, Journalists, and Politicians

Ulla Sandbæk,

Member of the Danish Parliament and former Member of the

European Parliament (1989–2004)

In the January 2017 session of the Council of Europe's Parliamentary Assembly, of which I am a member, I was asked if I would go to Turkey as part of the third İmralı Delegation. That was prior to the referendum which was to take place in April, in which President Erdoğan planned to change the Turkish constitution in such a way as to give him absolute power. It was important that, as a member of the Parliamentary Assembly, I could see for myself and be a witness to what was happening in Turkey. So I agreed to take part in the Delegation's visit.

I first became aware of what might happen to Turkey under the rule of Recep Tayyip Erdoğan when Angela Merkel was criticised by members of her cabinet after acceding to a request from Ankara to prosecute a comedian, Jan Böhmermann, who read out an "offensive" poem about the Turkish president. The poem was read in a short clip on a late-night program screened on the German state broadcaster ZDF at the end of March 2016. Böhmermann sat in front of a Turkish flag beneath a small framed portrait of Erdoğan, reading out a poem that accused the Turkish president of, among other things, "repressing minorities, kicking Kurds, and slapping Christians."

Böhmermann's poem was deliberately framed as a test of the boundaries of satire because it was broadcast shortly after it emerged that Turkey had demanded the deletion of a satirical song from a weekly German comedy show called Extra 3. The mock music video, called "Erdowie, Erdowo, Erdoğan," shows the president playing football, falling off a horse, and wearing a huge blond wig amid clips of recent protests and unrest in Turkey. "Press freedom gives him a swollen neck, that's why he needs all those scarves," says one line, translated from German. "With tear gas and water cannons, he's riding through the night." The song takes aim at recent restrictions on press freedom in Turkey, including the recent takeover of the *Zaman* newspaper, and a crackdown on International Women's Day protests. "Equal rights for women… beaten up equally," the song continues over footage of female demonstrators being hit with batons by riot police. The video also repeats criticism over Turkey's military campaign against Kurdish groups fighting ISIS over the border in Syria, claiming Erdoğan would much rather bomb them than the so-called Islamic State. Turkish officials condemned the video and demanded that NDR stopped showing it. The broadcaster has made no move to remove the footage and was merrily tweeting out links to the song.

These two incidents alarmed me and made me concerned about the future of Turkey under President Erdoğan. My worries about the end of Turkey as a democratic state with Erdoğan as its president were so great that, contrary to everything I normally believe in, I hoped that the attempted coup would succeed; because it seemed to me that a takeover by the army might after a while preserve democracy. That is at least what I have understood to happen during previous episodes in Turkish history when the army took power.

I was shocked when every head of state without any reservation praised Erdoğan for having protected democracy. For me it was completely evident that he was now free to go down a road leading in the exact opposite direction. But nobody warned him against that.

Even so, I was unprepared to hear all the details, by people who had witnessed them in close proximity, of the atrocities carried out by the Turkish army in Cizre and Silopi in the Şırnak province and in Silvan and Sur in the Diyarbakır province. I was likewise unprepared to learn that the reason for the imprisonment of the elected HDP parliamentarians of those regions was an accusation of supporting terrorism.

One MP is Ms. Besime Konca, whose "crime" is that she attended the funeral of a militant who lost his life during a clash in Sur district of Diyarbakır province during the curfew. She stood in silent homage for him in the cemetery and made a speech there saying, "We will keep our martyr alive." "We will follow in his footsteps." Ms. Besime Konca stated in her defence:

> As a woman, I struggled for the freedom of women. I struggled for the freedom of Kurds and all the people living in Turkey. And as an Alevi, I struggled for freedom of all the beliefs in Turkey. I promised to be with my people through thick and thin. I attended that funeral to share my people's pain and I attended not only this funeral but hundreds of them because that's why they voted for us.

When I attended the hearing of MP Leyla Birlik, who was like all the MPs accused of collaborating with a terrorist organisation, I witnessed how one judge was without any doubt a very young student. Another judge was very old and slept through most of the hearing. It was a complete farce. We could not stay until the end of the hearing, but we were informed that Leyla Birlik was not released from prison to await her trial because, "she could carry out her duties as an MP from her prison cell."

Another thing which made a deep impression on me was the meeting we had with a journalist from a TV station which had been shut down. They told us that all their savings in the bank had been seized, as well as their houses and cars. This was already terrible enough, but all the possessions of their family members had also been seized. Until I heard with my own ears that this had happened I would never have believed that Erdoğan would go to such extremes to silence every thinkable opposition against him.

Equally sad was the fact that thousands of public employees were fired without any possibility at all of getting a new job and without any support whatsoever. Their passports had been confiscated so they could not even leave Turkey. How these people will survive I cannot imagine.

What is so meaningless is that, in the beginning, Erdoğan supported the İmralı peace process, but then decided that it would be more advantageous for his own lust for power to amputate it.

I only hope that what he is doing now will in the end be so unacceptable to a majority of the Turkish people that when election day arrives in 2019, and when he supposes he can harvest the fruits of the referendum which ended democracy in Turkey, he will not be elected. This is something we can all work to make happen; I for one will surely do so. I will probably not be able to make my voice heard in Turkey because the chances are high that I would be arrested on arrival. At least I might be able to reach the Turks who live in Europe and who contributed to Erdoğan's referendum win because they were led to believe that the vote was about supporting Erdoğan—not making him a dictator.

An Activist-Researcher as a Peace Delegate

Federico Venturini, Human Geographer and Social Ecologist with a PhD from the University of Leeds

This is a personal reflection on an activist-researcher's experience as a peace delegate. As with all stories, let's start from the beginning.

I believe in freedom and I work towards the elimination of all forms of domination. For this reason I am embedded in many social movements and parts of different campaigns, from social centres to environmentalism, from the student movement to union actions. As such, I believe that research can be an invaluable tool for the advancement of social and political struggles. Through research, a critical reflection is realised, endowing social movements with specific and general knowledge to understand the society in which we live and, at the same time, to develop mechanisms that help its transformation. Research is precious in order to organise and systematise this knowledge, and it allows us to develop methods and analytical tools that support and improve the performance of campaigns and movements. In a dark age of nationalism and capitalism, it seems that the Left has lost its way. The aim of research to build a culture of resistance seems crucial for analysing and re-creating practices that can enable social change. This is why I call myself an activist-researcher. I am not just a detached academic; rather, social change is at the core of my efforts.

My interest in the Kurdish question came via social ecology. Since my university years I was involved in an occupied social centre in Udine, my hometown. There I was exposed to the ideas and practices of social ecology, a philosophy founded by Murray Bookchin, based on the concepts of freedom, democracy, and self-management. In 2011 I moved to Leeds (UK) to study a doctorate on Brazilian social movements, using social ecology as a philosopical reference point. Moved by political interests, I began to develop research on Bookchin's contribution to social ecology and his influence on Abdullah Öcalan. In April 2015, I was selected to present a paper at a conference entitled "Challenging Capitalist Modernity II" in Hamburg organised by the Network for an Alternative Quest, a network of several Kurdish organisations. My contribution, entitled "Social Ecology and the Non-Western World," focused on the need for social ecology to develop by learning from outside the Western world.

In December 2015, I received an unexpected email from the EUTCC inviting me to join a peace delegation to Istanbul for the purpose of meeting with Öcalan and resuming the dialogue between Turkish officials and the Kurdish movement. This invitation was probably due to my contribution at the Hamburg conference and my academic credentials.

However, I soon had a question for myself: how could I contribute to such an endeavour as activist-researcher?

At the beginning I was sceptical, but then I realised how I could contribute. First, the academic credentials that I hold (as do others in the delegation) open doors that would otherwise remain closed. Of course, it then depends on individual skill to keep that door open and have a fruitful discussion. However, academic credentials are useful in order to initiate a debate, to be selected to give an interview, or to write an article. So, why not use them? Second, the knowledge on the subject that I developed during my studies and the mediation skills that I've developed over years of interminable activist meetings could be useful as well.

Then I had another set of questions: an activist as a peace delegate? Would it be too "institutional"? Would I dirty my hands working at an institutional level?

As an activist, I am accustomed to working with people "from below and on the Left," as the Zapatistas say, and I felt uneasy using institutional channels. However, soon I found out that no delegate from the EUTCC would take part in the trip (the chair, Kariane Westrheim, is *persona non grata* in Turkey) and that the participants were mainly, though not exclusively, academics and intellectuals. These factors reassured me as to the independence of the delegation and, after some reflection—and motivated by curiosity and trust in the organisers—I decided to take part.

Two months of preparation followed, during which time I never disclosed my participation in the trip to anyone, due to security issues. I found out that the ten-person delegation would be led by the late Essa Moosa, a retired judge of the Supreme Court of South Africa involved in the negotiation process in South Africa at the end of apartheid. Later, I would meet Moosa in person. He led the delegation with charisma and knowledge, setting the direction and giving precious advice. It was an honour to have met him.

During that first delegation I must admit I was very naïve regarding the possibility of being granted permission to visit Öcalan, imprisoned on İmralı Island since 1999. As an Italian, I felt somehow responsible for his imprisonment, given the involvement of the Italian government in his arrest and in refusing him political asylum while he was in Italy in 1999.

After the first delegation, another delegation to Turkey followed, and then another to the Council of Europe in Strasbourg. The goal of the delegation has always remained the same: pushing the Turkish government to the peace table. And in all of our delegations we met a range of politicians, lawyers, NGOs, trade unionists, journalists, and activists. However, if in the first delegation we had few politicians as members, later more were incorporated in order to increase the political pressure in the Council of Europe and in the European Parliament, institutions with a crucial role in denouncing human rights violations in Turkey.

Amongst all the information we garnered over the course of the two delegations, what do I value the most? I want to stress two key concepts that, in their simplicity, may seem almost trivial.

First, the conflict between Turks and Kurds cannot be solved militarily: there are 14 million Kurds in Turkey, representing 18% of the entire population and they cannot simply be eliminated. At the same time, Kurdish guerrillas cannot eliminate the Turkish state, a NATO force. The only solution is to sit down to negotiate. The Kurdish proposal of democratic confederalism goes in this direction: no longer do they aspire for an independent Kurdish state, but a confederalist Turkey, where all social groups can achieve autonomy and self-governed freedom. From this perspective, the Kurdish question would be better termed the Kurdish answer (Virasami 2015).

The main actor for this peace process is the leader Öcalan, who has become the unifying symbol of all Kurds in Turkey. Like many activists, I am often dubious of leaders. However, thanks to the Delegation, I came to terms with the importance of Öcalan's leadership. I am convinced that no progress towards a solution can be achieved without Öcalan, the recognised leader of the Kurdish people, who has become the symbol of the liberation movement. Since the end of preliminary peace talks in 2015, Öcalan has received very limited visits either from politicians, lawyers, or family members, increasing his isolation. It is very striking that Öcalan's lawyers have not been able to see their client since 2011. News is circulating regarding his troubling health. From this point of view, the Turkish-Kurdish situation is similar to apartheid South Africa: Nelson Mandela, leader of the Black freedom movement, was held in his cell for 27 years. Before genuine Turkish-Kurdish negotiations can begin, the Turkish state must free Öcalan, just as Nelson Mandela was released *before*—not after nor during—the South African negotiations. For as long as Öcalan remains imprisoned, there will be room only for preliminary talks, not for real negotiations. Mandela himself had pointed out that only free and non-imprisoned persons could negotiate a political solution on behalf of their people. Öcalan's freedom is therefore a fundamental prerequisite for the peace process.

Second, Turkey is on the brink of a civil war similar to Syria's. A civil war is a creeping reality in the south-eastern part of the country—in northern Kurdistan—and the chances of increasing and intensifying clashes, and of the spreading of the conflict on a national scale, are rising every day. President Erdoğan is pushing for dictatorial measures throughout society—not least tightening media control—putting in place a forced displacement, committing massive human rights violations against the Kurdish population, denying language and culture, forcing migration, and perpetuating the indiscriminate massacre of civilians. He took advantage of the state of emergency declared after the failed coup in July 2016 to intensify repression against any opposition (not just against those accused of the coup) directly influencing the constitutional referendum in 2017. Furthermore, since the summer of 2016, Turkey has occupied a portion of Syria and is a continuing threat to the Democratic Federation of Northern Syria. The latter is experiencing a new society directly influenced by the ideas of Öcalan and based on anti-authoritarian values like gender equality, ecology, nation-state refusal, confederalism, and multiculturalism. Democracy cannot exist in Turkey without a peaceful resolution of the Kurdish issue and the peace process in Turkey is interlinked with the peace process in Syria.

Let's return now to my role as an activist-researcher in a peace delegation. This kind of delegation had very clear aims, within a defined political arena, and it is just one form of supporting a freedom struggle. The Kurdish freedom movement will not achieve its goals thanks to the Council of Europe. However, the latter is an arena in which it is worth fighting for the Kurdish cause. As with many others, this struggle is composed of a myriad of different pieces of a complex puzzle. Moreover, the information gathered through the delegations has been useful to meet another goal: to acquire knowledge to be spread in Turkey and abroad in order to create a media impact in favour of the peace process. And in this case the outcome was positive; the delegation organised several press conferences and issued several press releases published in Turkey and abroad. For example, during my stay in Istanbul, I participated in a round table on social ecology promoted by the Transnational Institute of Social Ecology, with an intervention on the philosophy of social ecology and dialectical naturalism. In addition, the *Devrimci Anarşist Faaliyet*—Anarchist Revolutionary Action (DAF)—held a public meeting where I presented the theme "Social Ecology and Anarchism." In the UK, I was twice invited to public debates at the House of Commons, and, in Italy, I participated in public events organised by lawyers' organisations, the Rotary Club, and social movements, always to talk about human rights violations in Turkey.

The whole Western world is silently watching the genocide happening to the Kurds and it is crucial to raise awareness at all levels. The European Union's silence is particularly significant: beyond rhetorical and marginal mentions of human rights, the agreement with Turkey on migrants gives Erdoğan full freedom for a criminal response to the Kurdish question. All the people we met during our delegations were shocked by the silence of public opinion and the Western media around what is happening in Kurdish territory. The help that the Kurds have sought is that we not leave them isolated and without support, that we speak out loudly about what is happening there; the Delegation worked to meet this call.

As an activist I often ask the question of the necessity and consistency of participation in these initiatives. If you avoid spectacularisation, these international delegations are an effective way to gather field information, as mentioned before. Even the account we present here can be understood as the continuation of the work of the peace delegation: it is part of the effort needed to break the silence and try to build pressure from below on an international scale—and especially in Western countries—so that Turkey is convinced to sit at the negotiating table. Our task as activists from different parts of the world is to break barriers and walls of silence, building real bridges of solidarity between liberation movements around the world. Certainly a coherent and incisive revolutionary commitment cannot be confined to sporadic institutional delegations, but these are only a small part of our support for the Kurdish liberation movement.

As an internationalist, I call for unity and cooperation between all the oppressed of the world and actively help struggles for freedom all around the globe. A critical solidarity is needed between different struggles, one that should be built on respect for the historical context of each struggle and be mirrored by a theory able to accommodate the specificity and learning of different experiences. However, we should bear in mind two important aspects. First, being in solidarity does not mean uncritical acceptance:

> [S]olidarity is based on mutual respect and understanding, not agreement for agreement's sake. If real solidarity is worked at, respectful critique and disagreement are vital. (Chatterton et al. 2007: 219).

Avoiding the idealisation of any movements is necessary to maintain a critical attitude towards their theories and practices, precisely so that we may continue to move forward.

Second, being in critical solidarity is crucial because it allows us to learn from other experiences, helping us to not fossilise in our struggle and pretend that our way is the right or best way to do things. It helps us keep our minds open and receptive; it is a chance to grow. Then it is necessary to elaborate and reinvent ourselves in different contexts and times, building a culture of resistance that is able to speak to our struggles.

As Handler (2007) reminds us, activists for social change are not just "loyal" to a nation, a party, a group or collective but to the idea of social change, as against all forms of domination: in the end, our loyalty is poetically—but also truly—*to the sky*. Struggles for social change are everywhere and we should be able to move, act, and contribute wherever and whatever we can.

I believe that my contribution as an activist-researcher to the peace delegation has been fruitful, an example of what Souza (2006) called "together *with* the State, *despite* the State, *against* the State." Crucially, I contributed to the effort of the delegation. Then, I was able to reflect, comment, and analyse the events I witnessed and participated in, speaking in different events and incorporating the lessons learned in my theory and practices.

Being a peace delegate is not only limited to a few days of meeting and discussions. It also means to continue to work in solidarity with that struggle *and* continue to build our own struggles.

And from the Kurds we have much to learn.

References

Chatterton, P. et al. 2007. "Relating Action to Activism: Theoretical and Methodological Reflections." In: Kindon, S. et al. *Participatory Action Research Approaches and Methods: Connecting People, Participation and Place*, 216–222. London: Routledge.

Handler, M. 2007. *Loyal to the Sky: Notes from an Activist*. San Francisco: Berrett-Koehler Publishers.

Souza, M. L. 2006. "Together with the State, Despite the State, Against the State: Social Movements as 'Critical Urban Planning' Agents," *City*. 10(3), 327–342.

Virasami, J. 2015. "Rojava's revolution is roaring—Are we listening?" *Contributoria*. [Online]. March 2015. [Accessed 10 September 2017]. Available from: https://bit.ly/2KJkYCy.

The Experience of an Ignorant European Politician
Julie Ward, British Member of the European Parliament (Labour Party)

I first visited Turkey in 2012 as part of a pan-European cultural management project before I had entered politics. I was working as the director of a rural artists' co-operative in northern England. Collaborating with a children's arts centre in Çanakkale, I co-organised a project about recycling. Our exhibition fed into a festival in Istanbul which included audacious street theatre, provocative media art, and more. Viewed retrospectively, that world of creative freedom, urban playfulness, and critical analysis seems centuries ago.

Yet, even then, in 2012, the Turkish state was not the liberal democracy that some suggested it was. The Turkish parliament had approved education reforms strengthening Islamic elements in state schools, with Erdoğan saying he wanted to foster "a pious generation."[1] I remember a young Turkish woman who was studying international relations telling me that in her university they weren't allowed to question the status quo. Erdoğan was then Prime Minister and already thinking about his next move.

Six months later, environmental protests in Gezi Park provoked a violent state response. It was quite obvious that Erdoğan had turned a corner. According to Koray Çalışkan, a political scientist at Boğaziçi University, "Erdoğan is a very confident and a very authoritarian politician, and he doesn't listen to anyone anymore."[2]

My Turkish friends began sending messages of dismay, despair, and defiance, and some just stopped sending any messages. The shutting down of public space, both online and offline, along with an attack on independent media, has been a hallmark of Erdoğan's autocratic style.

In May 2015, two years after Gezi, I returned to Turkey, to the city of Eskişehir, as an elected politician at the invitation of a humanities professor to speak about opportunities for creative collaboration. Walking through the city we encountered an anniversary vigil for the people killed during the Gezi protest. I joined the vigil but my friend, the professor, moved away and observed from a safe distance. Later she told me that, as a government employee, her job was at risk if she participated in any kind of action criticising the authorities. It was a portent of things yet to come (for example, in the aftermath of the July 2016 coup every university dean in the country was arrested).

In April 2016, I returned to Istanbul with the European Grassroots Anti-Racist Movement (EGAM) to participate in a programme of commemorative events marking the 1915 Armenian Genocide.[3] As well as re-tracing the first leg of the journey taken by the 270 Armenian intellectuals who were rounded up and transported to almost-certain death, we attended a memorial for Sevag Balıkçı, a Turkish-Armenian soldier who was shot by a fellow conscript on the 96th anniversary of the Genocide in 2012, the killer, later being identified as an ultra-nationalist. In March 2015, fellow conscript, Kıvanç Ağaoğlu, was finally sentenced to four and a half years imprisonment after a flawed judicial process.

A few months later, a criminology report was published stating that the victim's military uniform contained 41 bullet holes, rather than the two initially reported by the military commander. I visited the boy's grave and met his grieving parents.

Over the same weekend in Istanbul, EGAM organised meetings with a wide range of NGOs, human rights activists, and a few politicians from the CHP (the Republican People's Party) to discuss the AKP's (Justice and Development Party) attack on opposition voices and the narrowing of civil society. I was deeply affected by an encounter with a young LGBT Armenian who was very frightened for himself and his peer group. It should be noted that the LGBT Pride parade has been banned for three years running in Istanbul. *Pink News* reported in September 2017, "Turkey's LGBT rallies are known to be one of the most dangerous for parade-goers. Hundreds of anti-riot police officers have been known to surround demonstrators, fire rubber bullets and use tear gas and water cannons to break up the Pride marchers."[4]

Set against this background of state repression and authoritarianism, were any of us surprised when the attempted coup happened in July 2016? Conspiracy theories abound but, whoever was behind the violence and chaos of that night, Erdoğan has subsequently used the situation to create a wall around him, whipping up nationalistic and fundamentalist feeling whilst further cracking down on critical voices, whether in politics, academia, the media, or civil society. According to a July 2016 editorial in *The New York Times*, the president "has become more vengeful and obsessed with control than ever [before], exploiting the crisis not just to punish mutinous soldiers but to further quash whatever dissent is left in Turkey."[5]

At this point, I had limited engagement with the Kurdish question specifically. Then, in September 2016, the freelance journalist, John Hunt, contacted me regarding a Kurdish student at Manchester University in my constituency. My meeting with the student, Roni Digir, was to change everything. He told me about the Turkish military dragging the corpse of 24-year-old Kurdish actor, Hacı Lokman Birlik, behind an armoured vehicle. He told me about his home village of Idil in Şırnak Province which was subject to brutal attacks by the Turkish military, leaving many dead, including youths who were Roni's close relatives. He told me that a third of the 120 bodies of so-called "terrorists" had not been returned to their families. He told me about his 15-year-old female cousin, Sevilay, who joined a youth resistance movement and was one of those killed. He told me that his family had been forcefully displaced by the Turkish authorities in 1990 and that the same thing was happening again. These stories were not circulating in the mainstream media.

Soon after meeting Roni, I was invited by EGAM to participate in a fact-finding visit to Diyarbakır (Amed) and Nusaybin. I persuaded John Hunt to join me. However, *en route* I was detained by the Turkish police at Atatürk Airport and interrogated for several hours. My phone and laptop were taken from me and my emails hacked into. I decided not to show my diplomatic passport as I feared, most of all, that any information about my mission would give my interrogators access to the EGAM organisers, some of whom were local activists. I knew that our carefully planned mission would be at risk and that what was supremely important was our observations, which would be the basis for a detailed report.[6]

I was released after several hours, possibly because the schedule I was carrying showed that we would be meeting with local representatives of the ruling AKP party. This apparent balanced diplomacy is a feature of EGAM's approach and it probably saved the mission and maybe lives too.

The four-day mission included meetings with HDP (*Halkların Demokratik Partisi*—The Peoples' Democratic Party) ministers of Parliament, co-mayors, party organisers, women's rights organisations, journalists, civil society representatives, lawyers, and more. We toured the perimeter of the bombed-out district of Sur, a historic neighbourhood on the banks of the Euphrates, where many young people had been burned alive, trapped in a basement under bombardment from government forces. We met bereaved fathers who showed us photographs of their children, alive and dead. They wanted justice and had worked with local HDP members to document the state-sponsored destruction and violence. Even as we spoke, bulldozers continued to flatten the area. The AKP representatives told us this was to ensure the safety of the inhabitants and that the young Kurdish activists were only making more trouble for their community.

We visited Nusaybin on the border with Syria, where whole neighbourhoods had been bombed by the Turkish air force, causing mass displacement. In a community centre, we met with grieving mothers who clutched photos of their missing children, presumed dead. Body parts had been found in different places strewn across the rubble, suggesting mutilation of the corpses. Dogs wandered through the ruins, picking up scraps of human flesh. As a mother, it was hard to be in the room with such intense sorrow and pain, and I was reminded of my meetings with the Mothers of Srebrenica.

We visited a Yezidi refugee camp, entirely maintained by the hard-pressed local HDP administration with no state support. There I talked to refugees of all ages who had been separated from their families, thankful for the humanitarian response but desperate to find a more permanent home, to be with their loved ones, to work, to go to school, to continue with their university education, to be self-sufficient, to contribute to society. The camp was clean and orderly, unlike any I had seen in northern France, where the British and French authorities had largely ignored the human rights of the people who had travelled thousands of miles to escape conflict, persecution, flood, famine, and other circumstances that made life unsustainable. At this refugee camp, I was struck by the humanity and inclusiveness that lies at the heart of HDP.

The most memorable encounter was a meeting with the teachers' trade union. The room was packed with people who were visibly traumatised, victims of a level of state harassment that had hitherto been reserved for politicians, academics, journalists, and more militant groups. I realised that I was in a room with nursery and primary school teachers, music, drama, and sports teachers,

MEP Julie Ward with Ayşe Berktay during the press conference outside Edirne Prison after being refused permission to visit HDP co-leader Selahattin Demirtaş; February 2017.

special needs teachers, ICT education specialists, people like my sister for whom teaching is a vocation and not simply a job. Everyone had a story to tell. We listened to testimonies from teachers, their husbands and wives, their mothers and fathers, their children and their pupils. Many had lost their jobs, removed for offenses such as running after-school clubs, teaching traditional songs, dances, and games. Some spoke for family members who were already imprisoned or too frightened to attend. They didn't know how they could make a living, their salaries were frozen, their future prospects ruined. The police were waiting outside, filming everyone as they left. I am pleased to say that teachers' trade unions in the UK and elsewhere later passed resolutions of solidarity and contributed to welfare funds for affected families. However, the situation has not improved and, as HDP co-mayors have been replaced by state-appointed "trustees", education of Kurdish children is now under the jurisdiction of distinctly hostile managers.

EGAM produced a detailed report about the study visit. We held a few press conferences in Diyarbakır, and my detention and interrogation at Ataturk Airport was reported by Middle Eastern Eye.[7] I was under pressure to complain to Turkish embassies in the UK and/or Belgium but decided, on balance, that if I wanted to continue visiting Turkey to learn first-hand about human rights abuses, especially in Kurdistan, I should maintain a low profile. This strategy paid off as three weeks later I was back in Diyarbakır with lawyer Melanie Gingell from the British organisation Peace in Kurdistan. I was shocked at how much had changed in such a short space of time. Both co-mayors were now in police detention and the municipal building was completely surrounded by barricades, armoured vehicles, and soldiers. If my town hall took on such an appearance, the population would be outraged. The business of local government cannot be best administered under such conditions.

Melanie and I gave special attention to women's issues during our short mission. JINHA, the feminist media collective I had met on my previous visit, was now proscribed and operating largely online, meeting in borrowed premises along with other women's rights organisations. I walked past the building where we had stood on the steps for a group photo with some of the bravest women I had ever met. The gates were padlocked and a large steel plate was hammered across the door. I knew that this closing down of civil society was going on across the country. This is the visible sign of a country in denial of contemporary liberal values, a government scared of debate and discussion. This is the sign of a weak leader. Melanie and I ended our mission in Diyarbakır at a Kurdish women's solidarity conference along with sisters from Ireland, Germany, Spain, and Serbia.[8] As we held hands and danced inside a city centre hotel, the Turkish military positioned themselves outside. Many of the dancers knew that it was only a matter of time before they would be arrested. Their extraordinary spirit in the face of horrendous misogyny and fascism is truly inspirational.

During this time, the Turkish government was debating a serious proposition that would effectively legalise paedophilia, through the enactment of a law to pardon and release convicted rapists provided they agree to marry their victims. It was an outrageous proposal which prompted mass protests at home and abroad so was quietly dropped—for the moment at least.[9]

As Erdoğan's post-coup purge continued, I joined a solidarity campaign to support arrested HDP politicians. I chose to reach out to Leyla Birlik, one of the imprisoned HDP politicians, and began to speak about her in the European Parliament and feature her in my blogs. After leaving Diyarbakır, I met with Leyla's parliamentary assistant, her brother, and her lawyer in Istanbul. We made a plan to visit Silivri Prison the next day in the hope of gaining access to Leyla. Our car was randomly stopped *en route* and searched and the driver reprimanded for some interior damage to the vehicle, ironically caused by police during a previous stop and search. We sat outside the prison gates drinking coffee from a mobile cafe until guards came to question us and check our passports. They ordered us to leave until we had permission from the authorities. I had been in touch with the British embassy, who were advocating on my behalf. Predictably, permission never came, and we returned to the prison with a handwritten letter from me to Leyla. We photographed me holding the letter outside the visitors' entrance. Leyla was released from Silivri Prison shortly afterwards, although she still faces charges and a possible jail sentence.

In February 2017, I was invited to join the third EUTCC İmralı Delegation. Abdullah Öcalan was almost a mythical figure to me, a friendly face on a flag I had waved at demonstrations and rallies, but I had not absorbed the story of the man and the movement he inspired. Participating in the İmralı Delegation enabled me to join up the dots at last, to understand why Öcalan's freedom was so important for the peace process: not just for the Kurds but for humanity as a whole.

References:

1. Lüküslü, D. 2016. "Creating a pious generation: youth and education policies of the AKP in Turkey." *Southeast European and Black Sea Studies* 16, no. 4 (2016): 637–649.

2. Letsch, C. 2013. "Turkey protests spread after violence in Istanbul over park demolition." *The Guardian*, June 1, 2013. https://bit.ly/2KuYAgU

3. Agos 2016. "Genocide commemorations in Istanbul: racism and war policies are not destiny." *Agos*, April 24, 2016. https://bit.ly/2tRvBcU

4. Rizvi, H. 2017. "The world's most dangerous Pride demonstrations." *Pink News*, September 1, 2017. https://bit.ly/2KHXM4H

5. The New York Times Editorial Board 2016. "The Counter-Coup in Turkey." *The New York Times*, July 16, 2016. https://nyti.ms/2u0Hdtx

6. European Grassroots Antiracist Movement (EGAM) and Elie Wiesel Network 2016. "Report on the International Fact-Finding Mission to Investigate Rights Violations of the Population in South-East Turkey Committed in and by Implementation of the Country's Security Policy." https://bit.ly/2fFREdK

7. MacDonald, A. 2016. "British MEP detained and equipment confiscated while entering Turkey." *Middle East Eye*, October 22, 2016. https://bit.ly/2lP1Vcb

8. Ward, J. and Gingell, M. 2016. "Fear of genocide in south-east Turkey." Peace in Kurdistan Campaign, December 12, 2016. https://bit.ly/2MJUE90

9. Pasha-Robinson, L. and Withnall, A. 2016. "Turkey scraps plans for law that would have pardoned rapists who marry underage victims." *The Independent*, November 22, 2016.

Ten Powerful Moments of an Outraging Experience

Francis Wurtz,

Former French Member of the European Parliament (1979-2009)

Translated by Josie Hooker

Before recounting the mission we undertook in February 2017, I would like to offer some immediate impressions, fresh from the frying pan. I write these words from Strasbourg, at the end of October 2017, at a time that extremely concerning rumours are circulating regarding the health, even the life chances, of Abdullah Öcalan. Alongside Julie Ward, European MEP, and Fayik Yaguisay, representative of the HDP in Strasbourg, I am about to leave the offices of the European Committee for the Prevention of Torture and Inhuman or Degrading Treatment or Punishment (CPT)—an important organ of the Council of Europe. There, we made an appeal—on behalf of all the members of the İmralı Delegation—that the CPT make an urgent visit to the leader of the Kurdish people, with a view to establishing the truth about his situation. During our meeting, a peaceful protest made up of Kurdish activists, visibly worried, took place outside the building.

Out of this meeting—which was cordial but cautious, on account of the confidentiality restrictions of the CPT Convention—I took two points. Firstly, the case of the İmralı prison is unique in the world: I remind the reader that, with the exception of a one hour visit by his brother in September 2016, no contact has been authorised with Abdullah Öcalan since 2015, neither from his family, nor his lawyers, nor even less from members of the HDP. The CPT is the only channel still partly-open with respect to İmralı! In response to our insistent questioning as to whether the speculations regarding Öcalan's critical health condition are true, the CPT made it known that they were monitoring the situation closely and that, in the event of serious circumstances, they would intervene immediately. We understood this diplomatic statement as confirmation that Abdullah Öcalan is alive. Upon leaving, when we recounted our meeting to the protesters, the relief was palpable; even if, of course, beyond these urgent considerations, the fundamental demand remains the liberation of the historic leader of the Kurdish people.

On a more general note, since my return last February from the mission which I was honoured to be a part of, via the 3rd İmralı Delegation, there has been a series of bad news regarding Kurdish and Turkish figures that we met during our visits to Istanbul, Ankara, and Diyarbakır. The most recent known victim is Osman Kavala—a man of culture, a renowned editor, and an internationally-regarded democrat above all suspicion—who was intercepted as he disembarked from a plane and was remanded in custody for an indefinite period. Turkey's descent into hell in terms of human rights calls upon each and every one of us to respond, inform our citizens, challenge our governments, and show that the spirit of solidarity is alive!

It is in this spirit that I want to relate what, in my eyes, were among the ten most remarkable moments during our delegation visit to Turkey.

One of the most powerful moments was indeed a meeting we held with Abdullah Öcalan's lawyers. I was shocked to learn from them that since July 2011, they themselves no longer have access to İmralı prison. Six years without contact! The small HDP delegation that was authorised to make some visits during the peace talks has suffered the same fate since 2015. As for the one-off and very brief visit by Öcalan's brother, it was only conceded by the authorities following a spectacular hunger strike undertaken by Kurdish civil society. The lawyers very strongly encouraged us to appeal to the CPT upon our return. The CPT is, in effect, the only entity that is still authorised to maintain contact with both Abdullah Öcalan and the authorities, or to secure any relaxing in the conditions of his detention. Unfortunately, as would be explained to us during our first meeting with members of this institution last February, only the Turkish government can make public a report by the CPT regarding its own country.

Another moving moment during our visit was an evening we spent with a great number of HDP parliamentarians. Not one of them appeared defeated or resigned. However, each and every one of them faced the threat of imprisonment at any moment. And the sentences! "The prosecutor has applied for 18 years of prison in my case," one told me; the next raises the bid: "It's 23 years for me!"; while a third weighs in: "For me, it's 28!" Frightening! Men and women of such incredible courage, innocent of any crime, are rare in this world!

Some days later, in Diyarbakır, we were participating in a discussion with a group of representatives from various progressive social movements on the ground floor of the headquarters of one of the participating groups. Suddenly, through the window, we became aware of the arrival of two police cars, one from the left and the other from the right. They stationed themselves in front of the building in which we were meeting. Armed men emerged. Naturally, I wondered to myself about their intentions, as I've no doubt the rest of our delegation did. However, I noted the absolute calm of our Kurdish colleagues. Not a word was said about it, nor a glance out of the window. Their contributions went on as if nothing had happened. When, eventually, we came to leave the building, the police made no move. On this particular occasion, it had been a simple act of intimidation. Our Kurdish friends knew from experience that, sooner or later, such an event could end differently. However, nothing affected their courage and dignity. It is admirable.

A further memorable episode was the evening that some friends, radiating with happiness, introduced us to another HDP MP. He had just been released from prison, and he received as little explanation regarding the reasons for his liberation as he had for his arrest. We celebrated the occasion over a drink. The following day, we learned that he had been arrested once more as he was returning to the city of his constituency. This repression is as intolerable as it is entirely arbitrary: it is an arbitrary, exceptional act of the government. As one of the prosecutors admitted when questioned by another HDP MP regarding the charges he faces: "I know nothing for the moment, it's Ankara that decides!"

Another powerful moment was our meeting with some journalists who had been brutally dismissed from their jobs. We knew already that the editor-in-chief of the republican daily, *Cumhuriyet*, a man known and respected across the world, had been arrested. Then we learned that, in addition, 1000 journalists had been made redundant, dozens of whom were also imprisoned, and that 150 press organisations had been closed. According to our hosts, this diabolic chain of events was accelerating day by day. Their testimonies made my blood freeze. Since then, every time we learn of new waves of arrests of journalists, I come back to their words; today, the figures stand at 155 journalists in prison and 600 newspapers and media outlets closed. This is the madness that is raging over Turkey.

Another shock was learning, on February 15, that, since our arrival in Diyarbakır (Amed) two days earlier, 834 arrests had been made! We were told that no sector has been spared from this "witch hunt" against so-called "terrorists," a category which has come to encompass any opponent of the regime: 10,000 teachers and 3,000 health professionals have lost their jobs! Utter lunacy! 4,000 judges have been dismissed and replaced, overnight, with jurists still in training but reputed to be close to the regime. I've never seen such a scandal!

Personally, I was particularly touched by the case of a young HDP MP named Feleknas Uca. Before 2009, she was, in effect, an MEP of German nationality and belonged to a political group over which I presided at that time within the European Parliament. Later, she decided to go and live in the country of her family and she successfully stood as MP for Diyarbakır. Abandoning voluntarily the stable and relatively comfortable conditions of her former life, she chose to offer herself to the promising democratic project of the HDP progressives. When she learned of my presence in the city, she came to meet me. We were seeing one another again for the first time. With impressive calm, she told me that the prosecutor had threatened her with 15 years in prison. Her particular case was a cruel reminder to me that, behind every abstract number that we heard about day in and day out during our time in Turkey, there is a flesh and blood person, an individual drama and a collective tragedy.

A further testimony that hit me particularly hard was that of the president of the Bar of Diyarbakır, who recounted the brutal death of his predecessor, Tahir Elçi, killed by the forces of repression in the city's historic south quarter during the murderous battles of 2016. The eminent lawyer was calmly reading in front of the mosque when he was targeted by a burst of gunfire. Now I had met this sincere man, a servant of justice and the rule of law, during a prior visit to the region as part of an İmralı Delegation. On that occasion, I was joined by the late Essa Moosa, former judge of the Supreme Court of South Africa and internationally respected humanist, who passed away last February, and by Osman Kavala, who is recognised internationally for his commitment to dialogue, his openness, and his respect for the rights of every human, and whose recent and worrying arrest I mentioned at the beginning of this text. When I learned of his death, which we can in fact consider an assassination or execution, I was reminded of the spirit of the meeting that the three of us had the pleasure to be granted with this esteemed judge.

I will not forget either the trial of Mrs. Çaglar Demirel, co-president of the HDP group (6 million votes, third political party in the country) in the Turkish Parliament. She had been arrested four months previously, in the middle of the budget vote, along with 28 other MPs from her group, including her two fellow co-presidents, Selahattin Demirtaş and Figen Yüksekdağ. Last February, she was made to appear at the Court House in Diyarbakır via video-conference from her cell, 1,000 km from her constituency. Like so many of her colleagues, she did not allow herself to be beaten and she literally put the trial that was brought against her itself on trial. "By arresting numerous MPs from my group in one go under different accusations, you confirm that this is a political decision," she accuses the Court, dismantling one by one the charges brought against her. On the attack, she goes on to list the real reasons for Erdoğan's persecution of this democratic and unifying party: "My party defends all minorities, cultural diversity, and fundamental rights," she declares. "Thanks to my party, we have so many women in parliament for the first time. We have been persecuted because we fight for equality." The judges, pathetic administrators for the regime, do not even know how to respond to this cry of truth. Impressive indeed.

I would like to recall here one final event, and one that particularly moved me, namely our presence at the doors of Edirne prison, where Erdoğan's true *bête noire* is held prisoner. This is the man who, with his capacity to unite democrats of all stripes, to embody the vision of an open and tolerant Turkey, and to reignite hope in all the oppressed, managed to prevent the president, during the last free elections in Turkey in June 2015, from legally accomplishing his megalomaniac dream of becoming the all-powerful master of "Great Turkey." His name is Selahattin Demirtaş. As we had suspected, we were not granted authorisation to enter the prison. At the very least, we had the opportunity to talk with the lawyers of the HDP leader and even the chance, which I made use of, to communicate to him a written message of solidarity. I have already had the privilege to meet him at the European Parliament, and I was impressed by his resolutely democratic and pluralist vision of a Turkey that turns its back on the archaism of Erdoğan. One of the poems he has written from his prison cell is called *"Bulaşıcı Cesaret"* (Contagious Courage). There is no better way to sum up the sentiment instilled in me by the invaluable and outraging experience that the İmralı Delegation represented for me: the terrible trials endured by the Kurdish people and, more generally, by Turks of democratic spirit, only serve to boost their impressive courage. These men and women represent the future. And they deserve more of our solidarity.

PART FIVE:
Analysing Democratic Confederalism

A Seeker of Truth
Abdullah Öcalan
2011

Editors' Note: This is a short excerpt from the legal defence that the leader of the Kurdish freedom movement, Abdullah Öcalan, prepared at the beginning of 2011. It was prepared from his maximum-security prison on İmralı Island where he has been held since 1999, mostly as the island's only prisoner, although it is guarded by hundreds of Turkish soldiers. The excerpt was included as a contribution to a conference organised by the International Initiative's Network for an Alternative Quest titled "Challenging Capitalist Modernity: Alternative Concepts and the Kurdish Quest", held in Hamburg, Germany, February 3–5, 2012. It was translated by the International Initiative "Freedom for Öcalan—Peace in Kurdistan" and edited for clarity by Nathan McDonnell.

Nothing is more valuable in one's life than the attainment of truth that one lives. This quest is the most valuable human activity because only we are capable of making the truth real.

I was completely unprepared for the adventure of my life. It was very difficult to be born and raised in a morally decomposing family that could hardly stand on its own two feet in a society breaking apart. Because of a family's deep loss of its own sense of truth and morality, there is little left to pass onto a child. The result of this is a mentality void of substance which is vulnerable to the endless deceptions of society's rulers.

It is inevitable that societies under a state of colonisation (or worse) will eventually, either through force or persuasion, accept the lies that they are given. The rulers of the world have by now developed a vast pool of experience in doing this. They know very well how to most effectively convey their lies. Only if people cross a threshold that sheds their vulnerability to such illusions can the process of revolution begin.

I am a person who knows no boundaries. The journey of my own life has inevitably led me to see beyond illusions and face the truth of society. As I was confronted by difficult circumstances during certain periods of my life, I have tried to understand the reality of social oppression both concretely and ideologically. I have continued to do so even as the powers-that-be have rejected my humanity and social identity, tried to severely punish me as if I were a fugitive, and even tried to annihilate me; those who were primarily responsible for this were the United States, the European Union, the Republic of Turkey, and their collaborators.

Though I was able to develop both in theory and action before being held captive in this open-air prison, I did not have much time to develop my perception of truth. For those who face serious challenges in their lives, the circumstances of a maximum-security prison are profoundly educational. They are not places for theoretical and practical struggle; instead, they are places where, if one's will is not crushed, one can develop a deep awareness of the truth and the means necessary to struggle for it. Imprisonment allows those who fight for exceptional causes to strive daily to attain the truth. Time that is spent doing this is, I am certain, worthwhile.

To all appearances, I arrived at my prison on İmralı Island as a result of a legal and successful operation by Turkish Security Forces; that is the story that was told to the world. But in fact my capture and imprisonment was a conspiracy that was made possible by the system of capitalist modernity led by the United States and the European Union. More specifically, the enormous operation was coordinated by NATO's unconventional and illegal force, Gladio (editors' note: "Gladio" is a term for the NATO-sponsored secret network of far-right organisations in Europe). I was brought here on February 15, 1999. Seventy-four years earlier to the day, on February 15, 1925, the Republic initiated its conspiracy against Sheikh Said. A few months after my arrest, a show trial sentenced me to death on June 25—the same date in 1925 that Sheikh Said and a few of his collaborators were hanged. Since then, for three-quarters of a century, the Turkish state has continuously carried out policies of annihilation and denial.

My trial on İmralı Island was a conspiracy that aimed to destroy our every last drop of hope. This was the reason for my death sentence and the uncertainty about my fate. The very act of delaying my execution was intentional, a means of waging psychological warfare. At first I myself was unsure as to how long I could hold out under these conditions; to survive even a year seemed unthinkable. But then I thought to myself, "How can they imprison millions of my people in such tiny spaces?" As the leader of the Kurdish people, I saw myself as the synthesis of millions. Most people can't endure being apart even from their own families—how was I supposed to endure being separated from the will of millions of my people forever? I was not even permitted to receive letters from the outside. Up to now I have been allowed to receive only a few censored letters from my fellow inmates and I have been unable to send letters. Such facts may help to convey the extent of my isolation.

In my prison on İmralı, even if the external circumstances—the State, the administration, and the prison itself—had been like a palace and I lived in optimal conditions, this alone does not explain how I have endured the isolation imposed on me. The determining factor has not been my circumstances or the State's strategy but my own ability to be clear in my mind about the conditions of my imprisonment. I needed very strong reasons to be able to endure the isolation and to prove that a great life can be lived even under these conditions. In this regard, I must share two thoughts.

The first is about the state of Kurdish society. My thinking ran like this: if I want to live a free life, the society to which I belong must be free. To be more precise, individual freedom cannot be achieved separate from society. Sociologically, the freedom of the individual is entirely dependent on the level of freedom of the society. And when we apply this hypothesis to the Kurds, with their lack of freedom, we must conclude that the life of the Kurdish people has resembled a dark prison of oppression.

The second point is the necessity to be devoted to ethical principles in order to be able to understand reality. The individual should be conscious of the absolute necessity to live as a part of their society. Modernity has successfully created the illusion that we can live untethered to society, but this is a false narrative that demonstrates the poverty of principles today. Just as truth and ethics are mutually embedded, the notion of liberal individualism is only possible through the dissolution of the moral society and the severing of its connection with the truth. The fact that liberal individualism is presented as the ultimate lifestyle of today does not mean it is right; rather, it is representative of the dominant capitalist system on which it is based. I have reached this conclusion as a result of my experience with the Kurdish phenomenon.

And here I must highlight an inner tension within myself; namely, my wish to simultaneously escape from my Kurdishness and also to embrace it. Because of the ongoing cultural genocide, there are opportunities everywhere for Kurds to flee from their cultural identity, and this can even be encouraged. But here is where ethical principles must step in. How right or good is it for one to escape from society in order to save oneself? I could have done exactly this—I almost finished my university degree, and could easily have done so, which would have practically guaranteed my career and personal survival. But it was just at that time that I tilted back toward my Kurdish identity, which signalled my return to living on the right path. The individual must become associated with a cause greater than themselves in order to live an ethical life. It was increasingly evident that I was not going to betray my people. My choice to embrace my Kurdishness, with all of its many problems, was an ethical choice made in the knowledge that the ongoing enslavement of my people rendered impossible any fulfilment of my own dream of a free life.

This world is not one in which I could live freely, even if I were living outside of this prison. Imprisonment exists outside of my prison cell as well as inside. Indeed, as I now realise, the prison out there is much more dangerous. A Kurdish person living in the outside world who believes that he or she is free is seriously delusional. A life that is lived though illusions and lies is a life betrayed and lost. In my view, life outside of prison can be lived truly only under one condition: by struggling twenty-four hours a day for the freedom of society. For a Kurdish person, an honourable and ethical life may only be had by becoming an around-the-clock freedom fighter.

In this light, when I consider my past before prison, I accept that it was an ethical life. I was responsible for many breakthroughs for my people. These advancements are only partially complete, but they are the beginnings of a free life and a free society. I had virtually dissolved all of myself into the struggle for a free society, and there was nothing of myself left behind. Just as I had overcome my ego in this way, it was at this moment in my life that I was imprisoned. Living in struggle is likely to bring consequences of death and imprisonment, but living without struggle is dishonest and dishonourable, so it would be against all my principles to find myself unable to bear my prison sentence. Sacrifice and endurance is a necessity for those who are fighting for what they believe in. For those Kurds who are imbued with socialist thought, whose minds have not been captured by liberalism or some twisted religious cult, the ethical life in such a world can only be lived through constant struggle. For such a person, there is no other way.

The second point, in connection with the first, is to develop one's appetite for the truth. This is the only way to survive in prison. Even in ordinary living, having a strong perception of truth enables one to experience the most joyful of life's moments and to grasp life's meaning. For the individual who has grasped the purpose of his or her life, its particular circumstances will no longer pose a problem. A life enmeshed in lies and error lacks all meaning—it is a degeneration and will naturally lead to discomfort, depression, violence, and degradation. But for those who have achieved an authentic perception of truth, the world appears like a miracle. Living itself is the source of excitement and pleasure. The meaning of the universe is hidden in life. As one becomes aware of this secret, albeit in prison, life is no longer merely something to be endured. Indeed if one is in prison for the cause of freedom, then one's awareness of truth can only develop further. Even the most painful emotions may be transformed into happiness if life is built upon the perception of truth.

İmralı Prison has become the arena for my quest for the truth in order to better understand the phenomenon of the Kurdish question and to find solutions. In the outside world, theory and practice were important—but here in prison, *meaning* is. The political philosophy that I have developed here through my legal defences would have been very hard to intellectually develop had I been living outside. Writing political philosophy requires robust effort and a strong perception of the truth. I was able to grasp in a profound sense that I was in fact a dogmatic positivist—I came to this understanding because of the conditions of my isolation. Here I have been able to better distinguish between different concepts of modernity—that there can be various models for the construction of nations—and it is here that I have realised that social structures are human creations and hence, by nature, are flexible.

Overcoming the ideology of the Nation-State was especially important for me. For a long time, this concept seemd to be a rigid Marxist-Leninist principle. However, my explorations of the nature of society, civilisation, and modernity have since taught me that the State has nothing to do with socialism—it is merely a residue of class-segregated society, nothing but maximal societal rule that has been legitimised by capitalism. Therefore, I didn't hesitate to reject it. If we are to ever achieve scientific socialism, then the rulers of existing socialist societies will have to fundamentally change their logic: their acceptance of the State—a capitalist concept—was a big mistake which dealt a terrible blow to the cause of socialism itself.

My realisation of the powerful ideological hegemony of capitalist liberalism helped me to better comprehend and analyse modernity. Democratic modernity, I found, is not only possible but is far more real than capitalist modernity, far more contemporary, and far more liveable. Unfortunately, socialists were not only unable to transcend the concept of the Nation-State but also considered it fundamental to modernity. This resulted in our inability to envision the possibility of a different sort of nation—a democratic nation. We thought a nation had to possess a state: if the Kurds were to be a nation, then they must have a state! But as I pondered the question, I grasped that the Nation-State is one of the most sinister realities of the last couple of centuries; it has been heavily shaped by capitalism and it is nothing more than an iron cage for societies. I then realised that concepts such as freedom and communalism are far more valuable. As I became aware that fighting for a nation-state is fighting for a capitalist political structure, there were huge transformations in my political philosophy. The narrow struggles based around nation and class would in the end result in nothing more than strengthening capitalism.

Another realisation that I came to was that the social sciences produced by modernity are nothing more than a kind of contemporary mythology—this insight deepened my historical and societal conscience and revolutionised my conceptualisation of the truth. As I tore down capitalist dogmas, I thoroughly enjoyed understanding history and society as well as the truth that they contained. At this point I began to think of myself as a "seeker of truth". When awareness of the truth develops as a holistic part of our encounter with the world, it attains a great leverage of meaning incomparable to our past experiences. Every day, under my prison conditions, I could have as many revolutionising truths as I wanted. Nothing else could have given me so much strength to resist.

The strengthening of my perception of the truth also enabled me to form better solutions to problems. Divinity and singularity have always been ascribed to the Turkish statist mentality which conceives the only possible form of administration to be the State. This mentality has Sumerian origins and continues through Arab and Iranian cultures of power. The roots of the concept of a supreme single God itself are closely tied to the origins of our societal conceptions of power. As power elites were formed, the Turkish ruling class developed its own theological justifications for political power, always shaped by their specific historical situation and by political opportunism rather than by purely theological roots. During the Seljuk and Ottoman periods, any ethical dimensions to concepts of God and power became totally meaningless, and to attain political power, brothers, sisters, and relatives were executed without a second thought. With the advent of the Turkish Republic, this took on a new guise. National sovereignty and the model of the Nation-State that were first developed in Europe were now incarnated here in a particularly intense way. Thus, the Turkish nation-state became an even more dangerous Leviathan. Anyone who dared to question it was executed. The Nation-State was to be worshipped, an imperative especially enforced on the employees in the bureaucracy. The problem of power and the State was thus to become the most complex social problem in history.

In İmralı, I applied my analysis of power and the State to the problem of Kurdish and Turkish relations. I saw what kind of role that hierarchy played and that there was a need for solutions, and so I wanted to examine the past several thousand years of historical development of power and state arrangements all the way back to the Hittites. I firmly understood the geopolitical connections between Mesopotamian and Anatolian power and state cultures. When I adapted this to the relationship of the Kurds and the Turks, I immediately understood that ignoring the question of power was a serious mistake. I saw how abandoning all governance to rulers incurred such a great loss to society and so I rejected the State as a concept that had been developed against democracy. This is when I better understood the essence of democracy and its importance.

Although I don't agree with the role of power in society, I realised, on the other hand, that the sweeping rejection of institutions of unitary power and state culture, without understanding the aspects of these institutions that can be rightfully shared for the common good, was a obstacle to finding practical solutions. I thus realised that the notion of common power was important for transforming the state.

Throughout history, hegemony and state politics have intensely manifested in Anatolia and Mesopotamia, but there have also been various attempts at shared models of governance. In Turkish-Kurdish relations, similar models have been preferred at all critical junctures, of which the War of Independence is but the most recent example. I committed to a detailed analysis of this in my last defence. Although I presented it as a theory, putting it into practice will not only solve the Turkish-Kurdish problem, but it can help solve many of the other problems in the Middle East that are currently at an impasse. Such a model is not only in harmony with historical realities, in contrast to the positivist dogmatism imposed by capitalist modernity, it also contains elements that are naturally closer to everyone's ideals in finding a practical solution. In light of historical developments, I proposed concepts such as Democratic Modernity, Democratic Nation, and Democratic Autonomy, as opposed to power and the State.

Another realisation I had was that, historically, centralised rule is but the exception and local governance is far more the norm. If we are to understand the reason why centralised nation-states are presented by capitalism to be the only and absolute model, then we should look at how these political, sociological, and economic systems of capitalism and the unitary hegemonic force of the State are interlinked as forms of social control. I thus understood the importance of democratic local solutions as an alternative to the dominance of the State.

Finally, I also drew conclusions concerning the relationship between violence and power. It was clear that gaining power and nationhood through violence cannot be our strategy. The use of arms, except in self-defence, has absolutely nothing to do with socialism—it can only be the tool of oppressors. This realisation gave me the theoretical basis to approach the question of peace in a more meaningful and ethical manner. In this way, I therefore had accumulated enough conceptual and theoretical reasons to invalidate the "separatist" or "terrorist" label that the elites of State and power used against not only Kurds but all exploited peoples.

Apart from certain health issues caused by the physical conditions of my imprisonment, I can endure life on İmralı. My morale, my conscience, and the force of my will have not retreated in the slightest; on the contrary, they have been enhanced. The more that science, philosophy, and aesthetics enlighten us with social truths, the greater our potential for a better and more beautiful life. I would much rather live alone here in my cell until I draw my last breath than live with people who have lost themselves in capitalist modernity.

I must summarise: for me, life is only possible if it is lived freely. A life that is not ethical, just, and political is not a life worth living in any social sense. In general, civilisation and modern capitalist reality use ideological pressure to cause the individual to be enslaved by lies, demagoguery, and individualism. This is how social problems form. Revolutionaries, whether they call themselves socialist, anarchist, democrat, or communist, must stand against the dominant lifestyle of a civilisation that is built on oppression and class exploitation. In no other way can a free, just, and democratic life be developed and lived. Otherwise, this is a life built on the wrong foundations where only lies and filth will thrive. All my life, I have criticised this sort of living and have fully rejected it.

Another aspect of this question, that raises significant interest, is the role of women in society. This is an issue at the heart of many social problems. In our present age, in the conditions of capitalist modernity, for men and women to live in companionship that is beautiful and liberatory requires not only serious responsibility but also a great depth of ethical understanding and creative intelligence. No matter what type of relationship is entered into, one must have a clear awareness of the status of women in the history of civilisation and in the patriarchal modern world. Without this kind of sensibility, all such relationships will lead to lives full of error, immorality, and ugliness.

Modernity's power-based civilisational morality, and the sexism it imposes upon women, has brought about a lifestyle that generates terrible ugliness and immorality. I, along with many other responsible men and women, are fighting in a great battle of liberation to overcome this and to strive for a new kind of free society. There is a need especially for women to free themselves, as well as to attain an equal level of participation in all realms of society. There is also a need to cultivate an enlightened awareness through a philosophical, ethical, aesthetic, and scientific sensibility, and to work hard to enshrine this within the mentality and institutions of a new democratic society.

Whether one is inside or outside prison, in the womb or anywhere else in the universe, a human life can only be truly lived in a society that is free, equal in diversity, and democratic in its essence. Existence outside of such conditions is perverted, and therefore can only be described as sick. We can use all forms of rhetoric, actions, and social movements to correct this—including revolution; but first we need to construct a more enlightened mindset and willpower.

In that case, from the moment that I am released from prison (*if* I am to be released), it is only natural that wherever I may live I will struggle tirelessly for the creation of a democratic nation for the Kurdish people and, then, the democratic union of nations in the Middle East. This is a true model for the peoples' emancipation. With the ethical, aesthetic, philosophical, and scientific sensibilities that guide me as a seeker of truth, I will win the struggle of my life, and I will share the victory with all!

— *İmralı Island Prison, 2011*

Capitalism and the Kurdish Freedom Movement

Reimar Heider, The International Initiative

Hamburg, February 2012

Editors' Note: This is a substantial excerpt from the intervention by Reimar Heider of the International Initiative at the 2012 Network for an Alternative Quest Conference, held at the University of Hamburg February 3–5. The conference was titled, "Challenging Capitalist Modernity: Alternative Concepts and the Kurdish Quest". Mr. Heider spoke on a panel focused on the theme of "Capitalism as the Crisis of Civilisation." Mr. Heider is one of the leading interpreters and disseminators in Europe of the political thought of Abdullah Öcalan. The paper was originally published in the conference book: Challenging Capitalist Modernity: Alternative Concepts and the Kurdish Question *(Cologne, Germany: International Initiative, 2012), pp.101–111, which is available online: https://bit.ly/2v5TVYr.*

The Kurdish freedom movement of the past 30 years is downright obsessed with history. From the first illegal speeches until today, a detailed analysis of historical processes pervades the pamphlets and other writings emanating from the movement. In the 1970s, the movement accepted the rather classic linear Marxist historical sequence of primitive communism, slave society, feudalism, and then the capitalist society that was to be replaced, eventually, by a socialist society. This understanding of history has undergone a change that I would like to illustrate here.

The point of departure for Marx was the industrial revolution and its consequences in England: high productivity and the incredible accumulation of wealth on the one hand, and the emergence of great misery on the other hand. Marx examined the mechanisms of wealth accumulation and collected his thoughts and conclusions in his most important work, *Das Kapital*.

The starting point for the Kurdish movement, however, was the colonial situation in Kurdistan. There, there had been almost no developed capitalism. Indeed, it has only been in recent years that capitalism has been enforced throughout the world. This applies not only to areas that were once dominated by socialism, but also for a relatively peripheral area such as Kurdistan that was, and continues to be, virtually non-industrialised. Of course, there is some commodity production, and Kurdistan is tied to the world market, but in the 1970s it was not permeated completely by capitalism. In this respect we can say that the starting point was a colonial situation in which the system had forced its colonial subjects to identify with the oppressor. This included the production of absurd 'truths' such as how, in the imagination of the Turkish state, Kurds are fundamentally Turkish, even if they are unassimilated and don't speak Turkish.

Thus, the starting point for many discussions centred less on the economic implications of capitalism, and rather on how the system impacts the society and transforms the people into colonial subjects. Kurdistan was initially seen as an area that needed to be developed; a region steeped in backward social structures with many pre-capitalist elements, including tribal structures and feudal ownership of land. Large landowners owned entire villages and lands as absolute rulers. From the beginning, an important impetus of the liberation movement was to challenge these pre-capitalist feudal structures. These were also the first targets in the fight, not only against state institutions and military representatives of the Turkish state, but more importantly, against feudal institutions and the despised large landowners. The underlying ideology echoed the real socialist ideology of progress. This includes the idea that development is something positive, other structures must be built, the economy needs to develop, and that the transition from feudalism to capitalism and then, possibly, to socialism demonstrates a step forward. All this influenced the movement's understanding of capitalism.

Developed out of 30 years of combat experience and from the lessons of other movements worldwide, the Kurdish movement has profoundly reconsidered this view since the early 1990s. Indeed, the movement is characterised by a lack of fidelity to dogma, documents, or beliefs, and a concomitant on-going search for new answers to historical, local, and global issues. For example, the movement's activists examined writings on state socialism, decolonisation of Asia and Africa, nationalism, and social democracy. Their questions arose from the examined historical experience of these projects. The analysis that "real" socialism did not work gave rise to the question: *what* did not work? Why did state socialism, hence the attempt to install a socialist society and a socialist economic system, not work? National liberation movements were successful in decolonising Vietnam. Why, then, is it the case that across the continent of Africa and in many other countries, national liberation movements failed to establish truly liberated societies? Why did they fail to provide alternatives that envisioned societal liberation as they built their "liberated" nation states? And why, on the other side, was social democracy, which aims for nothing more than modest reform of capitalism, unable to achieve resounding success?

The analysis of the Kurdish movement was that all these movements attempted to realise their objectives through the State. State socialism attempted to build a socialist state in order to establish socialism while, on the other hand, the social democrats have tried to gain power in the capitalist system through elections. This is a familiar story, especially in Germany. Yet liberation movements, too, have sought to achieve liberation through struggles that acquire state power. Although in all cases where state power was won, true freedom was reached only to a limited extent.

At this point the Kurdish movement reconsidered its relationship with the institution of the State. Does the goal of the establishment of a Kurdish state, even if it is only intended as a step toward a confederation of states—a confederation of the Middle East in the first place—actually represent an intermediate step? Is it possible for the State to act as a means of liberation? Today, the widest parts of Kurdish society, almost all groups in northern Kurdistan and other parts of Kurdistan, assert that the State cannot be such a vehicle of liberation. Therefore, a Kurdish state is neither a real option, nor a goal to strive for. This perspective was embraced by the advanced parts of the Kurdish liberation movement, at the forefront of which is the PKK, which revised its aim from installing its own power in a newly established Kurdish state to freeing society as a whole.

What made such a radical revision possible was the commitment to understand the deeper causes of oppression and not just to scratch the surface. The dialectical method pushed beyond the errors of the Soviet Union in the 1980s or the like, to questions regarding social conditions, power, the origins and perpetuation of hierarchy, and hegemony in human society in general. And the answer to this was found in the significant repressive mechanism that is the suppression of women by men in the patriarchal family and society—the oldest mechanism of oppression and, also, the most deeply rooted.

The movement revealed that the patriarchal system is obscured by so many layers of ideological discourses that it is hardly noticeable, allowing it to be conveniently ignored and melt into the background behind other issues. For instance, if one declares that the main social contradiction lies between capital and labour or between the bourgeoisie and the working class, then patriarchy is pushed into the background. However, the Kurdish movement defined the main contradiction of mankind differently. It has been asserting that the oldest, deepest, and most important contradiction—when it comes to free a society—is the contradiction of gender and the establishment of patriarchy.

This discourse differed radically from that of other liberation and socialist movements which generally maintained a blood-and-soil discourse. Since the mid-1990s, the Kurdish movement's answer to the question "What is a free Kurdistan?" has been centred on the freedom of women *first* in order to free wider society. They asserted that controlling a territory politically through the means of building a state does not equal a free Kurdistan. Hence, the guiding principle since the mid-1990s is that the liberation of Kurdistan can only be through the liberation of women.

From questions as to why state socialism and national liberation fail the goals of a free society, the discussion would then evolve to put society as a whole into focus. What should constitute a liberated society? How does capitalism affect our society? What is the path of resistance? What are the essential ideological ideas and what are the main subjects and groups that could lead the advance to a free society? Thus, in the last ten years of discourse, a new political reference system—as I would call it—has developed. The classical sequence of social formations from primitive communism, to a slave-owning society, to feudalism, and then capitalism has now been replaced by a consideration of the past 5000 years, as Fadile Yıldırım has also argued (2012).

State civilisation extends back 5000 years. The hierarchical division of societies started in the Neolithic period. This happened in southern Mesopotamia, in what is now considered southern Iraq, in the Sumerian city-states. These states have served as an ideological and organisational model for state civilisations which has persisted until the present. It is essentially an ideological model, and not an economic model, although the first states already had a certain degree of economic formation. This ideological model is based on legitimising the rule and domination of a certain group, class, or faith community. Consequently, the ruler's main function is to create certain mythologies, ideologies, and/or religious ideas that establish and defend their ideological hegemony.

The Kurdish movement and Öcalan would call nationalism a religion—a religion of the Nation-State and of capitalist modernity. Nationalism is an essential mechanism to whitewash contradictions, as well as to persuade people to commit incredible atrocities in its name. This leads us again to the feminist discourse: the ideological hegemony of patriarchy is so strong that it is difficult to go beyond feminist circles, and to apply the ideas to the entire society in order that all are motivated to actively organise to overcome patriarchy.

The historical reference system then encourages us to look back beyond the 5000 years of state civilisation, and ask: "What was it like before?" Has the State or patriarchy always existed? The answer is clearly "no". The next question is then, where do we find points of departure for a non-statist, non-hierarchical, non-sexist, and non-patriarchal society? Felix Padel (2012) has demonstrated a wonderful example of communities that still live in a free society. Those communities have established their own rules, which are not written laws of any code of any state, but are guided by an ethical system that serves as the basis upon which life in the community is built. For example, Padel describes communities that lack a penal system. The ethical basis of these societies is reconciliation. Hence, the community works in accordance with moral principles that are based in solidarity expressed through various forms of communal production, communal farms, communal life, and communal education. The crucial point is the essential contradiction, according to this dialectical model, that a state society has arisen as an antithesis to existing natural societies, as Öcalan calls them. Previously, these natural societies were quite universal; only two or three states existed as islands in seas of societies that were organised through communal living. State civilisation had to therefore establish itself as an antithesis to thriving and prevalent free societies.

Today we take the universal dominance of states for granted. However, today's status quo arose historically as a product of a struggle for dominance. Thus, the Kurdish movement refers to specific documents from the history and mythology of the Sumerians and other early societies to understand how so-called "civilised society" and "state society" have prevailed against the natural society. The Kurdish movement's criticism of the classic Marxist conception of the sequence of societal forms is that it ignores the solidarity basis of "natural society." Natural society, which Öcalan calls the 'stem cell' of sociality in general, has a basic understanding of solidarity: that people want to cooperate, that they do not really want to compete nor hate each other.

This mentality of solidarity did not cease to exist 5000 years ago with the rise of civilisation. On the contrary, it still exists in specific places where state civilisation has not yet taken root and destroyed these natural societies. However, it also exists in the imagination. It is an ideal of many social and religious movements seeking peace and communality, philosophical movements concerned about the nature of life, and socialist movements envisioning communist or anarchist utopias. Thus, natural society exists both in reality and in the minds of people. The principle of "competition of all against all" is not a natural state. It is rather unnatural for a human being to be seeking life in isolation from society as a completely atomised individual because the actual state of nature is rooted in cooperation. Natural society is also the enemy of capitalism. Capitalism seeks to destroy communities based in natural society wherever it finds them in order to further the goal of endless private accumulation which is obviously in conflict with the solidarity-based ethics at the root of natural societies.

Öcalan identifies three main elements of capitalist modernity, which is the current historical form of the capitalist world system. The first one is what he calls a "capitalist society." In a capitalist society the basis of capitalism is reflected in its social and legal systems. Capitalist society's legal system is based on abstract laws in contrast to what Öcalan refers to as "moral society". Each community has a moral system, an ethical foundation of human society. It would be wrong to claim that wherever no state exists, murder and manslaughter will prevail. The ethical foundation of moral society is destroyed by the capitalist state through a legal system, which is usually in the service of rulers. Another aspect of this "capitalist society" is its conflation of capitalism and economics. In a moral society, real economic livelihoods, whether defined by a subsistence economy or not, is being destroyed by capitalism and replaced by a new society that produces commodities and nothing more, leading to devastating societal and environmental consequences. Furthermore, under capitalist society, individualism is destroying "sociality", the strong sense of collectivity or togetherness of people that characterizes what are called primitive peoples or tribal societies. Kurdish society first developed this discourse by looking at the differences between the people that make up the movement from Europe, those in Turkey's major cities, and those from Kurdish villages. They each carry completely different characteristics and behave quite differently in a community. Those more enmeshed in capitalist modernity tended to have weaker commitments and affinity for "sociality."

The second pillar of "capitalist modernity" is industrialism, which destroys livelihoods, alienates people in the production process, and is responsible for much of what is inherent in the critique of capitalism.

The third pillar is the Nation State, which is the most "appropriate" form for the organisation of power in modern capitalism. The Nation State is the level at which capitalist power decides laws, conducts wars, and constructs self-supporting ideologies. All nationalisms are based on the planned construction of a nation, which necessitates the extinction of many other cultural values that are incompatible with it. In the Turkish discourse, it is always France—the *Grande nation* and the nation *par excellence*—that serves as a model for the Turkish nation state. But of course, "France" could only be established by the extinction of different languages and cultures, whether Basque, Breton, or Occitan. Vast cultural traditions were wiped out to create this nation-state. With its military and police, the Nation State serves as an instrument for all the destructive policies that have led to modern wars, colonialism, and genocide. The Nation State is the main formation that accumulates and concentrates political, military, and economic power.

In contrast to capitalist modernity, the Kurdish movement proposes the concept of "democratic modernity." Democratic modernity is drawn from the search for democratic elements of natural society, not only in 5000 years of history, but even where they have escaped capitalist modernity and continue to this day. Democratic modernity is the new expression of modern society as a society free of domination.

There are three constituent elements of democratic modernity. The first one is the "political and moral society." This means a society in which people themselves care about and collectively advance their own interests and concerns. The Kurdish freedom movement embodies this social character. I think there is hardly a comparable movement in Europe and the Middle East that is as highly organised, fights at all levels, and has such a strong political culture of discussion as that of the Kurdish people. Hopefully, this movement can transform into a society which then behaves politically, not only militarily in the context of war. The term "moral" in "political and moral society" refers to a social togetherness based on morals and ethics. Moral society is based not on laws, but on cultural norms and various forms of moral systems that have been set up by the community itself for living together.

The second point is the "ecological" or "ecological-industrial society." The aim here is to overcome destructive industrialism and replace it with a more ecological method of production. The focus on the community and the local sphere plays a very strong role in centring economic thinking on the ecological. Kurdistan was permeated by capitalism quite late in history. There was almost no industrial proletariat in the 1970s and even today there is very little of an industrial proletariat. It is a predominately agrarian society that mainly operates through livestock breeding—especially in the mountainous regions. The hope is to build new or different forms of subsistence economy in places where full industrialisation has not yet taken place. The aim is not to try to force "catch-up" development and be hell-bent on industrialisation. Instead, the goal is to leverage the "disadvantage" of under-development into an opportunity for advancing alternative ecological models of economic development.

The third component of democratic modernity is "democratic confederal society." Achun Vanaik has described this beautifully as the "deepening and widening of democracy." The "deepening of democracy" means the creation of bodies and forms that ensure direct participation in decision-making processes. Democratic confederalism is already in practice in parts of Kurdistan, for both political and economic governance of communities and cooperatives. A confederal society describes how communities within a certain area relate to each other and participate in democratic decision-making without erasing their different group affiliations. This is in contrast to the Nation State, which ultimately calls for a uniform citizen, who speaks a dominant language, follows a dominant ideology, has a certain way to do business, or—very importantly in Turkey—adopts the hegemonic set of beliefs. In a confederal society, the communities are organised according to existing diverse associations based on language, ethnic or cultural identity, religious beliefs, or professions. The confederal model is not threatened by this diversity, and diversity does not lead to conflict in a system that respects and expects differences. Ideally, such structures allow for a harmonious network that ultimately may be able to replace the State.

The point is not to just propagate the idea that "the State must go," but to build an alternative. The goals of democratic modernity is its expansion beyond borders, first within Kurdistan, then the Middle East, and then the wider world. Yet, this would be done without redefining the borders or building a Kurdish nation state. The project of democratic modernity is conceptualised as a collaboration, not only among Kurdish communities, but also with communities within the societies of the oppressor countries in order to displace the State on all levels and throughout the globe.

References

Padel, F. (2012). "Capitalism as the Arch-Enemy of Ecological Societies," in Network for an Alternative Quest, *Challenging Capitalist Modernity. Alternative Concepts and the Kurdish Question* (Cologne: International Initiative, 2012), pp.86–93.

Vanaik, A. (2012). "Capitalist Industrialization and the Nation State," in Network for an Alternative Quest, *Challenging Capitalist Modernity. Alternative Concepts and the Kurdish Question* (Cologne: International Initiative, 2012), pp.76–85.

Yıldırım, F. (2012). "The Unchanging Character of State-Based Civilisation: Sexism," in Network for an Alternative Quest, *Challenging Capitalist Modernity. Alternative Concepts and the Kurdish Question* (Cologne: International Initiative, 2012), pp.67–75.

Democratic Confederalism, Democratic Autonomy

Havin Guneser, The International Initiative

Hamburg, April 2015

Editors' Note: This is the intervention by Havin Guneser of the International Initiative "Freedom for Öcalan—Peace in Kurdistan" at the 2015 conference Challenging Capitalist Modernity, held at the University of Hamburg, April 3–5, 2015. Guneser, who is the translator and one of the leading interpreters of the political thought of Abdullah Öcalan, spoke in a session dedicated to the theme of "democratic modernity." In her paper, she sketches her understanding of Öcalan's articulation of the theory and praxis of democratic confederalism and democratic autonomy. The paper was originally published in the conference book: Challenging Capitalist Modernity II: Dissecting Capitalist Modernity—Building Democratic Confederalism *(Köln, Germany, 2015).*

Dear friends, guests, ladies, and gentlemen: welcome to our conference!

Let me start with thanking the Kurdish and German people who have opened up their homes and made it easier for this conference to take place by giving us free, warm and comfortable lodgings. There are of course a whole lot of people who have prepared all the things we are enjoying now, from coffee to our lunches, registration, the programs you are holding in your hands, headphones you need to listen to simultaneous translation and more. And yes, the whole team of translators, around 30 of them. Without them too this conference would not have been possible. This is a perfect example of the solidarity of different sections of society and communities; wherever possible this conference has been realized on a voluntary basis. And finally I thank you all for making the trip here so that we can together focus not only on the things we criticize but also discuss how we want to build things. So thank you all!

When we first had the idea for such a conference, not too many people had in fact heard about the alternative paradigm the Kurdish people were discussing and attempting to implement. But today suddenly in a town that nobody had ever heard of, Kobanê, we are witnessing something most revolutionary—just when many had been convinced that revolutions were not possible, and even if they were, not in the Middle East, not in Kurdistan!

Of course, if we do not examine the past of Kobanê, or Rojava, in general we would view it as a miracle. Today I would like to look in depth at how this "miracle" happened. Of course this is not a miracle—it is the vision of a free life that the Kurdish people, the Kurdish freedom movement, and Abdullah Öcalan have been envisaging for the past 40 years or so. But how to attain this vision of a free life has not been easy to realize. The answers to this question have transformed continuously over the years.

Abdullah Öcalan and his friends began with a Marxist-Leninist perspective back in the 1970s. In 1978 they founded the PKK as a Marxist-Leninist organization aiming to establish a united socialist Kurdistan. Although the movement's departure point was the colonial situation of Kurdistan, it did not limit itself to this—especially in terms of women's freedom and class-conflict. Let me point out several reasons why the Kurdish question had unique features:

1. Kurdistan was divided as a result of international agreements and its denial of statehood was ensured internationally.
2. Since it was divided between four separate states, two of which—Iran and Turkey—have a tradition of hegemony in the region and the greater world, it has been difficult to make headway in any single part of Kurdistan with four states uniting against it.
3. Feudal structures within Kurdish society had been largely co-opted into collaboration with the State. This served as an instrument of social control.
4. Therefore, any movement that attempted to struggle for Kurdish rights would either be demonized from the beginning or be subject to external constraints such that it would not depart from traditional roles.

Both Abdullah Öcalan, as the main strategist of the PKK, and the PKK itself went through several transformations. The reasons can be summarized briefly as follows:

1. All the points above mentioned combined to create huge difficulties for PKK to organize itself, especially because the Kurdish people had already reached a point of self-imposed assimilation. From this Öcalan reached conclusions about how the system implements its cultural hegemony.
2. Due to Kurdistan being an international colony, discussions about what independence and dependence actually mean were on the table since an early stage. Regional and world powers wanted to control various Kurdish movements and use them against one another to further their own policies. Thus, policies of the Soviet Union and other real socialist states, as well as different powers, were analysed early on.
3. During the 40 years of struggle, Öcalan and the PKK were not only able to evaluate the practices of real socialism, feminism, national liberation, and other alternative movements' practices, they also evaluated their own praxis and tried to understand what was wrong. Why was everyone repeating the same forms of oppressive political systems?
4 In the late 1990s, Öcalan attempted a set of reforms within the PKK in order to break down power-centred and centralist approaches and the increasing bureaucracy within the party. From 1993 on, he tried to find a political solution to the Kurdish question with Turkey. Europe completely ignored Öcalan's attempt to resolve the Kurdish question when he came to

Europe in 1998. This attempt ended in the tragedy of his abduction from Kenya as a result of a NATO operation.

All this signalled to Öcalan that something was profoundly wrong. He did not locate the problem in the sincerity of the revolutionaries, but rather looked for problems in their analyses, strategies, and tactics, including his own. So he came to these conclusions:

1. Öcalan realized a key methodological problem: that ideological weapons of the system play a more prohibitive role than do physical weapons. Since the present understanding of science is based on written records only, women's and people's histories are either not well documented or buried under the rubble. Thus, the system established its monopoly by controlling what and how we know as well as the fact that the contributions of peoples and women do not exist as far as historical science goes. The specific methodological problem here is mainly the empirical and quantitative method.

2. Mythology, religion, philosophy, and positivist scientific structures are tightly intertwined with the history of capital and power accumulation. Therefore ideology is closely linked to politics and power and they symbiotically protect one another's interest.

3. The positivist and functionalist theory of society, especially the linear developmental approach of society from primitivism, to slave-ownership, to feudalism, and from there to capitalism, was severely criticized. In connection with this, Öcalan broke away from equating society with a particular class and thus from equating society with that of its rulers. Both analyses are simplistic and rigidly deterministic and so too reductionist in light of the greatly diverse paths of social development.

4. Analysing the practices of alternative movements, he came to the conclusion that a free life cannot be established by using the same tools that are used to enslave society, nature, women, and everyone else. Thus, power and state structures must be totally replaced with entirely different methods, and we should not, as many revolutions have done in the past, fall into the temptation of using the very weapons of the system that would corrupt our revolutionary goals.

5. Capitalism is not unique but a continuation of the five thousand-year-old patriarchal society, which has been consistently present throughout different epochs of history. Capitalism itself has only had the opportunity to become the dominant system of our world in merely the last four hundred years.

Therefore, Abdullah Öcalan reached the conclusion that the anomaly was capitalism itself. We are made to believe that there can be no life outside of capitalism inor any other form of patriarchy. But Öcalan goes into great depth into history to uncover the truth about different historical forms of society.

Democratic Civilization

Abdullah Öcalan has also contributed to the critique of capitalist modernity. Öcalan saw that various mainstream analytical models that have been developed in relation to the social arena were far from explaining what has happened:

1. The most recognized social unit is the State and, more specifically, the Nation-State. In this model, history and society are examined as merely the processes of state's construction, destruction, and secession. The real aim of this is the ideological legitimization of the State. Instead of revealing the complex problems of history and society, it serves to only conceal.

2. On the other hand, the Marxist approach chose class and economy as its starting point of analysis, which it saw as an alternative model as opposed to the state-based approach. But this approach has also had several major flaws, especially in its definition of labor, something which feminists have subsequently criticized, as well as its failure to acknowledge different nuanced models of society and also non-class forms of oppression.

By basing his model on moral and political society, Öcalan draws a relationship between freedom, morals, and politics. In order to develop structures that expand our arena of freedom, morals are defined to be the collective conscience of society and politics defined to be its common wisdom. Moral and political society is thus the natural state of society, uncorrupted by institutionalized hierarchies and power structures as states.

While religious narratives also emphasize the importance of morals, they relegate its *political* aspect to the State and hold society to be more important than the individual. Bourgeois liberal approaches not only disguise the moral and political society whenever they get the chance—they declare war against it. Liberalism is the most anti-social ideology and practice as individualism is a state of war against society, as much as the State and power are.

Öcalan concluded that slavery was above all an ideological construction that was strengthened by the use of force and violence and the seizure of the economy. Centres of power and hierarchy have been built on top of these. He saw from his own praxis that, in the absence of developing a new approach, any efforts to change such forces are doomed to fail.

For the lives and struggle of those marginalized by the system, such as women, peoples, cultures, and craft workers, he coined the term "democratic civilization." And he has called the social sciences that will develop a libertarian perspective the "sociology of freedom." He bases the analysis of democratic civilization on what he calls the "moral and political society" or "democratic society", the modern version of this historical society. Therefore, Öcalan bases his democratic civilization on the following features:

1. On women's freedom. Democratic civilization must be feminist in character, he says. Following on from Maria Mies, he calls women the first class, nation, and colony. Socialism's major flaw is in the definition of labor, that is: how to analyse the unpaid work of women and people as well as the total exploitation of nature. This is the only way capital can be accumulated. Since no one would willingly give in to such a scheme, structural violence and even physical conflict come into play. And this characterizes all colonial relations. Thus, the relationship between woman and man, too, is essentially colonial. This fact has been disguised by declaring it to be a private sphere— an area of exploitation well protected through the use of emotions and love games. Therefore, it is of utmost importance to expose this and to re-define this relationship. No non-state and non-power solutions can be achieved while each and every individual is regenerating these power relations in their seemingly harmless ways of life.

2. Democratic civilization must be based on ecological industry. This follows from a similar logic as above and perhaps is the area most difficult to over-come due to the subject-object dichotomy and the way we live.

3. Democratic civilization must develop its own understanding of self-defense. The use of force has been monopolized by the State and power structures in order to leave the moral and political society defenceless. Any attempt of the society to defend itself faces claims of terrorism and criminalization. But, on the other hand, almost all freedom struggles have fallen into the pitfall of in-terpreting the use of force in conformity with state formations. Thus, self-defense must be tied to grass-roots structures and must not be professional-ized—it should not become a sector independent of the community.

4. Finally, the economy of a democratic civilization is a communal economy. Under captialism, the economy has been seized and all individuals have been made dependent on state structures in order to meet even the most basic needs of their lives. Housing, food, schooling, and just about anything you can think of can no longer be done without money; moreover, we have all been stripped of the necessary knowledge to fulfil these needs without money. Therefore, re-connecting and grounding every individual in satisfying their own needs in a communal manner would empower the individual and the society and prevent reproducing capitalist mechanisms.

Democratic Modernity

Thus, what is "democratic modernity"? Abdullah Öcalan says, and I am quoting: "I am neither discovering nor inventing democratic modernity. Just as modernism is uniquely named to be the hegemonic era of capitalism which is the last four hundred years of classical civilization, then democratic modernity can be thought to be the unique name for the last four hundred years of democratic civilization." The fundamental dimensions of democratic modernity are:

1. Moral and political society
2. Ecological industry
3. Democratic confederalism.

Democratic Confederalism

Democratic autonomies at local levels gather together to form democratic confederalism at a larger level. Democratic confederalism is the political alternative to the Nation-State and rests on:

1. Democratic nation
2. Democratic politics
3. Self-defence.

Democratic confederations will not be limited to organizing themselves within a single particular territory. They will become cross-border confederations when the societies concerned so desire.

Here, each and every community, ethnicity, culture, religious community, intellectual movement, and economic unit can autonomously configure itself as a political unit and thereby express itself. The most fundamental element of the political units at the local level are their ability to allow for free discussion and grassroots decision-making.

Beyond this, democratic confederalism is open to different and multi-layered political formations. Both horizontal and vertical political formations are needed due to the complex structure of present day society. Democratic confederalism balances central, local, and regional political formations in an equilibrium.

We need to return the moral and political dimensions of life back to society. Intellectualism has been restricted mostly to the universities; it needs to be returned to all of us. The subject of morals has been replaced by positive law. Politics on the other hand has been brought to an almost stand-still under the administration of the Nation-State bureaucracy disguised as parliamentarianism. Thus, in order to stop the perpetuation of capital and power accumulation, as well as the reproduction of hierarchy, there is a need to create structures of democratic confederalism—that is, a democratic, ecological and gender-liberated society. To achieve this there are many things to consider, like:

- Intellectual duties and education
- Education
- Economy, industrialism, and ecology
- Family and relationships between men and women
- Self defense
- Culture, aesthetics, and beauty
- Dismantling power and hierarchy.

As a result, we see that we, "the 99 percent," to use the phrase David Graeber is said to have coined, have always been there. But to struggle and gain a free life we first need to develop a vision of a good life that is different from that which is given to us by capitalism or patriarchy in general. That is, we should no longer foster the desire to have infinite goods and increase personal wealth or to measure everything against its financial value. Instead, we should have immediate production of a good and beautiful life at the centre of all social and economic activity, as well becoming ardent seekers of truth. And this, my friends, is an open-ended process that this conference wishes to discuss further in the coming days.

I join all the people before me who have expressed their expectation that Öcalan will join us in-person at the next conference so that we can deepen these discussions together.

Review of Abdullah Öcalan's *Manifesto for a Democratic Civilization*

Donald H. Matthews and Thomas Jeffrey Miley

September 2016

Editors' Note: This is a review essay of the first volume of Öcalan's Manifesto for a Democratic Civilization: The Age of Masked Gods and Disguised Kings, *published by New Compass Press in collaboration with the International Initiative (Porsgrunn, Norway: New Compass Press, 2015). The review by Dr. Matthews and Dr. Miley was first published on the website of Peace in Kurdistan (UK). It has subsequently been translated into both Arabic and Sorani.*

Introduction

All respect for Abdullah Öcalan, the imprisoned leader of the Kurdish freedom movement, "chained to the rock of İmralı." He is a symbol of resistance, resilience, and fortitude, a responsible leader and prophet with a powerful political vision—a vision that has inspired the revolutionaries in Rojava, in Syria, and that fuels the Kurdish resistance to Erdoğan's tyranny in the southeast of Turkey.

The heroic defense of Kobane caught the world's attention with the movement's will to struggle, its ability to mobilize the people for collective self-defense, to sacrifice, and to die for a cause. This cause is the project of "democratic confederalism," a project which represents the only alternative to the negative dialectic of tyranny and chaos currently tearing the Middle East apart and, in Öcalan's terms, the only alternative to "hierarchical and dominated civilization."

The project of "democratic confederalism" in construction in Rojava is an experiment in radical, direct democracy, based on citizens' assemblies, defended by citizens' militias. It is a radical democratic project that emphasizes gender emancipation, by implementing a model of co-presidency and a quota system that enforces gender equality in all forms of political representation, by organizing women's assemblies and women's academies, and by mobilizing women in their own militia for self-defense.

It is a radical democratic project that redefines "self-determination" as direct democracy against the State, that renounces as divisive and utopian the equation of the struggle for national freedom with the goal of an independent nation-state, and that seeks to overcome the danger of majority tyranny by institutionalizing a "revolutionary-consociational" system. The social contract of such a consociational regime guarantees multi-ethnic, multi-linguistic, and multi-religious accommodation by implementing quotas for political representation (concretely, for Arabs and for Assyrian Christians) by direct assemblies of different constituent groups, and by mobilizing these groups in their own militias of self-defense. It is a radical democratic project that stresses the importance of "social ecology" and environmental sustainability in a place where the soil bleeds oil, and imperial vultures circle in the sky. In sum, it represents an alternative to the dialectic of tyranny and chaos, an alternative to the colonial machinations of divide and conquer, a project that combines radical democracy, self-defense, gender emancipation, multi-cultural and multi-religious accommodation, as well as social ecology. This is a real road map for peace.

This road map was sketched by an imprisoned leader with a prophetic message, a man who, especially since his abduction, has, even in the harshest of conditions, been eloquent and prolific in elaborating his model of "democratic confederalism"—initially as part of his defense in his trial. Paradoxically, prison has proven a space of intellectual freedom for Mr. Öcalan, as it was for Trotsky, for Gramsci, for Malcolm X, even Mandela before him. While behind bars, he has spent much of his time reading (though with very limited access to books), writing, and reflecting upon his predicament, that of his people, and that of the modern world.

The first of his five volume *Manifesto for a Democratic Civilization* has recently been translated into English by Havin Guneser. In this volume, subtitled "The Age of Masked Gods and Disguised Kings," Öcalan sets out to uncover the deep historical roots of the tremendous problems plaguing "capitalist modernity," and to recover the even deeper historical sources of the democratic alternative he proposes. Especially considering the conditions in which the text was composed, the inhumane, indeed torturous isolation, not to mention the limited access to books, the result is an intellectual and existential accomplishment of a high order.

Against Hierarchy

In Volume One of the *Manifesto*, Öcalan mounts an assault on hierarchy in all its forms. He counters hegemonic, pseudo-scientific, social Darwinist accounts that reify competitive egoism and the penchant for hierarchy. Such accounts locate social pathologies near the very core of human nature, as the products of natural selection, as "hard-wired" in our brains and even encoded in our genes. On the other hand, Öcalan insists to the contrary, that the roots of hierarchy do not run so deep. He locates these roots not near the core of human nature, but a mere 5,000 years in the past, emerging with the "birth of civilization" in the Neolithic period. And he goes on to sketch a compelling account of a dialectic between domination and resistance, between hierarchy and freedom, that was then triggered and that continues to this day.

Like Foucault before him, whom he hails (along with Nietzsche) as a "philosopher of freedom," Öcalan stresses the "extraordinary effort" involved in the interpellation of individuals by dogmas and myths to justify quiescence and subordination to hierarchy and domination. "Socialization can only be achieved through a continuous effort," and indeed, it is impossible for any individual to "escape being constructed according to the dictates of society." Even so, Öcalan contends, such efforts can never be entirely successful. The impulse to "freedom," the urge to resist "classed and hierarchic," "oppressive and exploitative societies" can be suppressed, but never extinguished. Individuals "will not readily accept societies that construct slavery," despite the constant "endeavors not only to transform [these individuals], as they pass through oppressive educational institutions, but also to eliminate them" (p.72 in *Manifesto for a Democratic Civilization,* Volume One). The point is all the more powerful and persuasive coming from a man who has spent close to two decades in solitary confinement.

Öcalan's approach is nothing if not ambitious. It corresponds to his awareness of, and sensitivity to, the critique of the modernist faith in the trinity of science, technology, and progress; combined with his sober assessment that our imprisonment within the confines of "capitalist modernity" ultimately has less to do with the power of its "money" or its "weapons" than it does with its capacity to constrict the horizons of our consciousness. If we are to believe Öcalan, Thatcher's dictum that "there is no alternative," alongside Fukuyama's declaration that we have reached "the end of history," are best interpreted as but self-fulfilling prophecies; "the real power of capitalist modernity", allegedly, "lies in its ability to suffocate all utopias [with its liberalism], including the socialist utopia which is the last and the most powerful of all (p.28).

Moreover, the consequences of this impoverishment of our imagination are nothing short of apocalyptic. Underneath the façade of triumphalist liberal ideals, Öcalan insists, the "capitalist modern forms" have led to an increasingly pervasive culture of nihilism, rendering "the antagonistic dualism of death and life meaningless," while "detach[ing] life from all its magical and poetic aspects." The result is "an era of perpetual death, similar to judgment day" (p.37); this world is characterized by pathologies like "the proliferation of nuclear weapons, population explosion, exhaustion of resources, environmental destruction, excessive growth of social rifts, disintegration of moral bonds," not to mention "a stressful life that has lost its charm and lyricism," all of which "demonstrate that our regimes of truth have failed" (p.51).

How to escape from this dead end, from this dire fate? A revolution in consciousness is required. Such a revolution is possible, Öcalan contends, simply because "the primary characteristic of our mind is its flexible structure" (p.73). But to acquire the necessary "new mentality" requires, in turn, the elaboration of a radical critique—one that exposes the root causes and origins of the pathologies of "capitalist modernity," so as to recuperate and revive healthier, more sustainable, human potentialities that have long ago been forgotten and repressed, indeed, deliberately suppressed.

Öcalan identifies the cult of power and hierarchy and the worship of the State as deeply ingrained traditions conditioning our mentalities and constricting our ideological reflexes, even capable of co-opting movements of resistance, as exemplified perhaps most dramatically by the experience of state socialism. If the cult of power corrupts, the exercise of power corrupts even more. Indeed, Öcalan contends, "one of the most striking examples of the corruptive force of power can be found in the experience of real socialism" (p.165). Such are the difficulties faced by those who would resist the dynamics of hierarchy. They are up against "a culture of domination" that is deeply entrenched, having been prepared by "hundreds of brutal emperors and various other dominating forces." Indeed, Öcalan concludes, "therein lies the true importance of the quote attributed to Mikhail Bakunin, 'If you took the most ardent revolutionary and vested him in absolute power, within a year he would be worse than the Tsar himself'" (pp.164–165).

How can such deeply ingrained hierarchical reflexes be successfully resisted? Öcalan emphasizes, along Gramscian lines, that "activists and theorists of freedom and socialism must prepare their own fields," that they must "continuously diagnose and treat contagious diseases... generated by power relations," that they must even "keep a distance from power relations and all its institutions and characteristics." But he goes beyond Gramsci to insist as well on the construction of radical and directly democratic forms of self-rule, such as the model he has outlined in his writings on democratic confederalism. If such "rich democratic forms are not implanted and nurtured at the same time," he warns, those who engage in resistance "will not escape the power net, but just repeat the thousands of failed attempts that in the end were not at all different from the systems of power they sought to escape" (p.166).

Öcalan has abandoned the illusion of any linear notion of "progress." For him, finding the way "forward" requires a return to the deep past; only by providing "a proper historical interpretation of our problems," expansive in scope, with "reference to origin," can we hope to "illuminate our future" (pp.94, 102). Only after these origins have been revealed and comprehended will we be prepared to transcend the culture of hatred and death, "to make the transition into a life where love reigns" supreme (p.94). Yet, references to Braudel notwithstanding, Öcalan's recourse to the deep past, his provision of a "proper historical interpretation of our problems," is not undertaken with the pretense of a professional historian in pursuit of the elusive goal of "scientific objectivity." This is why his admission that his account is "amateurish and unpolished" should not be read solely as a disclaimer and gesture of humility (p.279). For Öcalan is a proponent of the "mythological method," a method he insists "should be given back" its prestige.

Öcalan's own "historical interpretation" is thus best interpreted as providing a "noble myth" of sorts, an account of humanity's fall and of its potential for redemption in this world; it is at the same time a manifesto reflexively in favor of myth and against dogma of either the religious or the secular-scientific kind. He contrasts the method of myths to those of both "monotheistic religious dogma" and "science" which succeeded it. Despite the differences amongst these successive "regimes of truth," Öcalan insists they are nevertheless similar, at least insofar as they both "alleg[e] to bow" before "absolute laws" (p.42).

Öcalan laments the conversion of science into "a new religion," one that takes "the form of positivism," with its "objective laws" representing "nothing but the modern equivalent of the 'Word of God' of antiquity" (pp.90, 53). Science, united with power and capital, comprises "the new sacred alliance of modernity" (p.91). Science has been fetishized, idolatrized, rendered a new dogma, turned into an

"-ism." Those who espouse this new dogma of "scientism" he deems guilty of hubris. In perpetuating the pretense that "science alone can render truth about the world and reality," they would belittle, dismiss, deny all that "cannot be apprehended by the scientific method" (p.79, fn.16). Öcalan emphasizes the ideological function of this all-pervasive modern "-ism." He insists that "the world of science has become the power that constructs, legitimizes, and protects the system's methods and contents" (p.48)—not only the system of "capitalist modernity," but the system of state socialism, too. Though in the end, it would sow the seeds for the demise of that false alternative.

Indeed, according to Öcalan, "the objective scientific method played a determining role in the failure of scientific socialism" (p.48). This is because faith in science is closely associated with rule by experts. "One of the biggest errors of the Marxian method" was to perpetuate such elitist convictions. In so doing, it actively inhibited "the mental revolution" required for the democratic construction of a new society, a genuine alternative of collective emancipation (p.53). Even worse, Öcalan alleges, the "rationalism" and "positivism" implicated in the new dogma of science have "paved the way for the 'fascist flock.'" They have done so by inculcating "robotic and mechanical human being[s]" as well as "simulative perceptions of life," thereby propelling us towards the destruction of "the environment and the history of society" (p.80).

Dogmatism, either religious or scientific, is an enemy of emancipation. It leads to reification, to presenting unjust, hierarchical, and oppressive social arrangements not as social constructs, but as "unchangeable," as "sacred," as "divine[ly] establish[ed]," as reflecting unchangeable laws (pp.70–71).

A Focus on Patriarchy

One of the most compelling parts of Öcalan's account is the close attention he pays to the issue of patriarchy and the links he makes between the oppression of women in particular and oppression in general. Öcalan has elsewhere equated patriarchy with "[w]oman's slavery," and diagnosed this as "the most profound and disguised social area where all types of slavery, oppression, and colonization are realized" (*Democratic Confederalism*, p.17). In Volume One of the *Manifesto*, he elaborates on this point. Ironically, he invokes Nietzsche to this end—referring to the German philosopher's talk "about how society is made to adopt wife-like features and is enslaved by modernity" (p.82). More substantially, he relies on feminist scholar Maria Mies in sketching a perceptive analysis of the links between patriarchy and hierarchy, and in tracing their mutual origins.

According to Öcalan, women systematically suffer from the oppressive status of *housewifization*—this time dubbed "the most advanced form of slavery." But to make matters worse, in capitalist modernity, such slavery of women has been compounded, perhaps even fueled, by "the housewifization of man—after his castration through citizenship" (p.91). Capitalist modernity is distinguished for its relentless pursuit of the subjection of all in the "public sphere"—a subjection of all crafted in the image and likeness of the subjection of women in the "private sphere" of the home. A democratic alternative, Öcalan insists, requires the replacement of the current family system, "based on the deep-rooted slavery of women," and the creation of an entirely "new family system, based on deep-rooted freedom and the equality of woman." Such a creation would promise in turn to "help abolish the male-based hierarchic and statist order" (p.94).

With respect to the origins of housewifization, "the most ancient form of enslavement," Öcalan contends that "it has been institutionalized as a result of woman's defeat by the strong man and his attendants," a defeat that "required a long and comprehensive war," indeed a struggle so "intense and fierce" that "it has been erased from our memories, together with the consequences thereof." The result of this, according to Öcalan, is that: "Woman cannot remember what was lost, where it was lost and how it was lost. She considers a submissive womanhood as her natural state. This is why no other enslavement has been legitimized through internalization as much as woman's enslavement" (p.163). This case of collective amnesia associated with the trauma of subjugation is compounded by the patriarchal biases built into the "his"-torical record, resulting in reification, essentialism, and naturalized quiescence by woman to the point of naturalized identification with her subordinate status in society.

This characterization is of course not uncontentious, even on feminist grounds. Something of Nietzsche's scorn—if not for women as such, at least for the feminine—can arguably be still detected in Öcalan's trans-valued employment of the category of the "house-wife." A scorn reflected in Öcalan's inclusion of "crying" among the list of symptoms of subservience and "housewifization." The ethic of care, not to mention the ethics of mourning, would seem to lie outside, or beyond, the theoretical horizons informing Öcalan's brand of feminism as militant self-defense. Even so, a brand of militant feminism it is indeed, one embodied and personified by the Kurdish freedom movement's women militias.

But let us return to the contours of Öcalan's metanarrative about the origins of hierarchy. The deep-rooted and insidious patriarchal biases plaguing the "his"-torical record help justify Öcalan's heterodox—indeed, mythical—interpretation about gender equality in the Neolithic Period—an epoch crucial to Öcalan's broader metanarrative about the emergence of hierarchy.

According to Öcalan, before humanity's "fall," that is, before its fateful descent into oppression and inequality, there had been a "moment of creation," a "quantum moment" and "chaotic interval"—its epicenter was located in the Fertile Crescent, where what Gordon Childe termed "the Neolithic Revolution" occurred. This period signaled the end of the "monotonous life of hunting, gathering and defense" of "clan communities, hundreds of thousands years old." With the transition to "settled life and farming," clan society gave way to "broader structures," including the birth of "ethnic ties." It was an era of momentous upheaval and creative fertility, in which "thousands of mental revolutions" took place. Most prominent among these, the introduction and invention of "numerous nutriments, means of transport, weaving, grinding, architecture," as well as complex symbolic forms of "religious and artistic" expression (pp.122–124).

The "symbol of the Neolithic society" was the mother-goddess, Inanna. Worship of her rose symmetrically to the decline of the *totum*, "the identity of the old clan society," which decreased in significance (p.122). The cult of Inanna in turn reflected the prominent role of women in this period. Indeed, according to Öcalan, "[d]uring the Neolithic period, the driving force had been the mother-woman" (p.139) and, thus, sacredness was attributed to her.

The residues of this "quantum moment" remain ingrained as sediments that survive in the human psyche and are capable of being revived to once again structure social relations, and not only gender relations. Indeed, a whole host of "treasured moral values... more precious" than those of capitalist modernity—values such as "respect, affection, neighborly relations and solidarity"—are products of and remnants from this period (p.123). These values thus have a deep historical basis, and they underpin the inextinguishable will to resist oppressive, hierarchical social forms. They have been congealed and transmitted in collective memories that have never been fully suppressed. As is, for example, evidenced in "the narratives of the Holy Books," where the memory of those times is sublimated "into the idea of paradise" (p.124). A paradise never fully lost; a paradise that can be recovered.

The descent into hierarchy, patriarchy, and class inequality would come, in Öcalan's account, with the rise of the Sumerians, whose main legends recount "the rivalry between the crafty male god Enki and the leading female goddess Inanna," a cosmic rivalry among the gods that Öcalan interprets as reflecting and projecting transformations in material and social relations among humans—specifically, "the transition from the Neolithic village society that had *not* allowed exploitation, to that of the urban society—newly constructed by the priests—which *was* open to exploitation" (p.139). Öcalan thus again employs a materialistic hermeneutic of religious belief. Whereas the prominence of Inanna in the religious expressions of the Fertile Crescent during the Neolithic period stands as a reflection of "the social strength of the creative and leading power of the Neolithic" woman, the rivalry with the worship for the crafty male god Enki signaled the rise in prominence of a new social class, "the priestly class," now sublimated and "exalted in the new religion" (p.140).

Religion, Monotheism, and Hierarchy

The Sumerian "priestly class" plays a particularly nefarious role in Öcalan's account. Not only does it represent and protagonize the birth of class divisions; so too is to be blamed for the subordination of women and for the transition from mythical to dogmatic belief systems. According to Öcalan, the priest's main task—a thoroughly secular one—"was to administer the requirements of the growing urban society" (p.142). But at the same time, it usurped access to the world of the gods, since "anyone wanting to hear the word of God had to listen to the high priest." The combination of these two roles rendered the priest-class "the group bearing the biggest responsibility for the formation of both the civilization of modernity and of civilization in general" (pp.140–141).

With the consolidation of priestly power, the rivalry between the crafty male god Enki and the mother-goddess Inanna was decided in favor of the former. "Over time, less and less figurines of the woman-goddess were made," and by the "onset of the Babylon period, the woman-goddess had been destroyed" alto-gether; this was another signal of the increasing oppression of woman, now sub-jugated as "an official public and private prostitute as well as a slave" (p.146).

The Sumerian priests were the first to disguise their power and legitimate their usurpations and expropriations by donning the masks of the gods whose worship they ritualized and regulated. But the kings would soon learn this most useful trick from the priests (p.149). These masked men managed to cast a spell on the exploited, on the worker who, as if hypnotized, came to increasingly ac-cept a new subservient role legitimated by the dictates of "newly manufactured gods" (p.159).

Öcalan's interest in the relatively deep past is never divorced from his con-cerns about the present. Indeed, he insists that a proper analysis and understand-ing of the process of descent into hierarchy achieved by Sumerian society promises to "enhance our understanding of our own society." This is because such analysis can help us to identify and "pull off the masks that cover," to see past dominant mystifying and legitimating tropes, to see "the true faces, the real profits and the actual status of the different role-players" in contemporary society (p.154).

Öcalan contends that the spell of submission to hierarchy first cast by the Sumerian priestly class has yet to be broken. Indeed, those who have "claimed to rebel for their tribe, nation, or religion" have in reality only usurped the "crown of power" (p.157). The class division first wrought by the Sumerian priests has remained "a fundamental characteristic of civilization" ever since. Provocatively, he insists, "in the few cases where [power systems] were overthrown *by* their subjects and proletariat, the new administration has usually been far worse than the previous oppressive and exploitative regime" (p.160). Along with the emer-gence of hierarchy, the emergence of the State was consecrated by the worship of its rulers, who don the mask of gods. Öcalan defines the State as "the unity of power relations through which the general coercion and exploitation of classed society is enabled" (p.158). The development of capitalist modernity tends to fuse the State with the Nation in "the mask-less new god—the Nation-State" (p54). The cult of hierarchy remains alive and well in the contemporary cult of the Nation-State, Öcalan concludes, as "the god that has removed its mask" and that "is being sanctified ... in all modern societies" (p.81).

To break from the spell of hierarchy thus requires a break with the State, as well as a disciplined strategy of resistance to the hypnotic powers of the modern priestly classes. A first step in this direction is to decode and understand the source of such hypnotic powers—and here is where the category of dogmatism comes into play.

The Sumerian priestly class sought to legitimate emergent inequality, the for-mation of social classes, and division of society into exploiters and exploited by overseeing and encouraging the demise of the "mythological method" and its replacement with "dogmatic religious perception." According to Öcalan, "the re-lationship between the newly formed classes of the exploited and the exploiters demanded indisputable dogmas" capable of "disguis[ing] and legitimiz[ing] the exploitation and power of hierarchical and class interests." The emergent despots, the dominators, hid behind the masks of gods, not just any gods, but ones "endowed with 'indisputable' characteristics" and revealed in sacred texts containing allegedly "infallible words" (p.43). The transition from the "mythical method" to "dogma" is thus related to the invention of the written word—and the priestly class' power was based in its role as interpreter of the indisputable, infallible words of gods contained in sacred texts. The consolidation of the priestly class' role as conduit and interpreter of the word and the will of the gods meant the cultivation of a new "slave-like submission" and a "fatalistic perception" on the part of the exploited. "A shepherd-herd dialectic was" thus "established" (p.44).

Öcalan diagnoses dogmatism as a disease first propagated by the Sumerian priestly class, and still at the core of the ideological legitimation of hierarchy. Unlike orthodox atheist critiques of religion, Öcalan's critique is not framed as an exercise of "de-mystification," but instead focuses on the usurpations of the priestly class and on their propagation of dogmas. Öcalan makes it clear that he is no enemy of the mystical, the sacred, or the divine *per se*. Indeed, among the reasons he gives for his admiration of Neolithic society in comparison with contemporary capitalist modernity, Öcalan mentions an alleged harmony between Neolithic society and nature, as reflected in their view of nature "as filled with sacredness and divinity," in their belief that nature is "as alive as they were themselves." According to Öcalan, in Neolithic society "divinity had nothing to do with coercion, exploitation and tyranny" (p.239). Instead, his problem is with those who don the mask of gods and claim to be conduits of the divine when justifying exploitation and tyranny.

It was the Sumerian priests who introduced this connection—with their penchant for dogmatism, and their novel attribution of "punishment and sin to the notion of *god*," for the purpose of developing "the sense of obedience." These innovations allowed the notion of God slowly to fuse with and mutate into the State. This is the key to the "reform brought about by the Sumerian priests" (p.167).

Punishment and sin was linked to the promise of an after-life—a connection allegedly first made in Sumer, later in Egypt, then inherited by the Abrahamic tradition. It was the "paradigm of heaven, hell and life to come." Öcalan contends that this paradigm provided a crucial and "strong legitimization device needed to convince the slaves who certainly did not have an easy life" (p.194). A "strong legitimization device" capable of conjuring submission and quiescence in this life by promising reward in the next. A utopian projection, "a promise of paradise," "talk about millennia of happiness," all of which, Öcalan adds, reminds him "of the longing for an oasis." And thus, he surmises, a reflection of "[i]ts opposite," "an infertile life." Echoes of Bob Marley's refrain—"if you knew what life was worth, you would look for yours on earth." But Öcalan goes further, concluding in a decidedly secular vein, "the quest for paradise is nothing but a promise of a future in a new world," "a harbor inevitably constructed by those who have lost hope" (p.274). A contentious point, no doubt, since belief in paradise can just as easily conjure the courage to struggle and the willingness to die for a cause than it does a quiescence and submission to the status quo.

The historical record is full of examples of the political manipulation of religion, examples of which Öcalan is well aware. Indeed, he makes explicit mention of the many "wars waged in the name of Islam, Christianity, and Judaism," though he interprets these as "in essence struggles for dominance over Middle Eastern civilization," with religion serving as but a pretext, a means of mobilizing support, "masking the real reason behind bloody wars." The instrumental efficacy of religious convictions would become all the more transparent when they were later directly appropriated by the State and "declared official state ideologies." Conversely, within and against the hegemonic religious and national projects institutionalized in given states, the mobilization of "dissident sectarian" sentiments and loyalties have reflected and channeled "class conflict" and have "signified the rebellious attitude of the marginal societies excluded from civilized societies." As with wars of religion fought between states, Öcalan insists, sectarian struggles within states are best interpreted again all too often as but "a pretext" masking "real" reasons, indeed, "a type of nationalism" (p.169).

Here Öcalan displays the profound and continuing influence of materialist thought upon his hermeneutic—even seeming to flirt with a characteristic, left-atheist, double dismissal of religious consciousness as simultaneously pacifying and dangerously divisive. This historical-materialist influence and impulse, to be precise, he marshals relatively consistently in his interpretation of Islam, both past and present. In speaking about the birth of Islam, he denies the sovereignty of the supra-natural in favor of mundane causal forces, contending that the birth "was not a 'miracle in the desert' but the product of strong material and historical circumstances" (p.269). Likewise, in speaking about the spread of "radical, or political, Islam" in the present, he emphasizes the "need to understand [the] structural aspect of it" (p.272).

Consonant with his advocacy of the mythological method, Öcalan limits his critique of religion to the critique of *religious dogmatism*. He does reject a "spirit-matter dichotomy," and even denies that the "richness of life… can be explained through the dogma of an external creator." Even so, he is openly adamant that "[i]t is meaningless to claim that there is nothing besides a physical life" (pp.62, 76–77). Perhaps most crucially, he considers the religious impulse akin to the artistic impulse, or even the impulse to cultivate knowledge—all important "metaphysical feature[s]" he alleges to be "indispensable" for "endur[ing] war, death, lust, passion, beauty, etc." (pp.76–77).

For Öcalan, religious convictions are closely connected with collective memory. This helps explain their persistence. The sacred religious books continue to be revered not due to the appeal of the dogmas and doctrines about an "abstract god" or even associated "rituals" but instead because "humans can feel the meaning and traces of their own life and story in these books." They are books which contain and congeal "the memory of living society," which humanity "will not abandon so easily" (p.117).

Öcalan's take on religion has evolved over the past decade. In *The Roots of Civilization* (the English version of which was published in 2006), Öcalan had already emphasized the link between dogmatism and official religions dedicated to the legitimation and perpetuation of hierarchy. Nevertheless, in that work, he had been relatively friendly to monotheism, contending that the monotheistic religions had "emerged at a period of profound crisis in social development, and indeed, that they triggered "a revolution in the mental and ethical character of humankind" (p.56). In comparison with the "polytheistic" and "totemic" conceptualizations that had preceded it, Öcalan then contended, monotheism had "represented a higher form of logical reasoning," potentially appealing "to the whole of humankind," relating to "a more complex stage in the history of human intellect" (p.62). Moreover, in his discussions of the history of Christianity and Islam, he explicitly distinguished between an original revolutionary and emancipatory religious impulse from below, later co-opted by rulers, and converted into an instrument of hierarchy and control.

However, in Volume One of the *Manifesto for a Democratic Civilization*, Öcalan seems to have reconsidered. He now laments the demise of the mythological method and its substitution by religious dogmatism serving to justify hierarchy, which he now associates directly with monotheism. Moreover, he now appears much more sympathetic to polytheism and to notions of immanent divinity. He even goes so far as to claim that "polytheism occurr[ed] during an era of tribal equality," and that the "decrease in number and the ranking of gods according to supremacy is closely related to the administrative protocol" (p.168). A questionable generalization, at best, given the polytheism that characterized and served to legitimate Greek patriarchal and slave-holding city-states, not to mention the Roman Empire. In fact, monotheism has been both a force for enslavement and emancipation. The same is true for polytheism, as in the cases of Greece and Rome in the moves toward democracy and domination. The grand narrative of monotheism vs. polytheism binaries fall apart under intense historical scrutiny.

In nominally monotheistic traditions, a close look at those from the oppressed classes reveals a consciousness that appreciates a polyphony of divine presences whether they be found in the Kabbalah, or the Sufi, Quaker, and other mystics of Judaism, Islam, and Christianity. The march toward a spirit-less monotheism has been led by societal elites since Akhenaton, Josiah, and Zoroaster who have made intellectual and ritual acceptance of monotheism a primary weapon against the "superstitious" peasant classes who still are in contact with the myriad expression of The One, yet without the need to curtail the expression of others. However, even in the strongest self-proclaimed monotheistic societies, the peasants and some fortunate few from other classes find themselves confronted by spirits that are beyond the doctrinal proscriptions of monotheistic religious dogma. Such freedom is free even from its monotheistic master. Nat Turner, Frederick Douglas, Harriet Tubman, MLK, Malcolm X, Sojourner Truth, John Brown, and many more experienced a spiritual presence that urged them on toward freedom.

This point against grand narratives that would pose a binary between monotheism versus polytheism is crucial, and worthy of closer attention. Indeed, one of us co-authors (Donald) spent much of last summer researching the origins of monotheism and its importance for the West. This was not intentional but, as we kept finding different views regarding its origins and place in history we had to pursue it more deeply. It is the Holy Grail of western religious ideology. Scholars expressed deep differences in opinion but carefully refrained from directing their critical comments toward any of their scholarly comrades.

Monotheism originated with the Pharaoh Akhenaton (1300s BCE) when he claimed that the other deities other than the sun (Aton) did not exist. This led him to change his name (originally "Amenhotep") and to destroy other images of other deities (Amon among them) and close down the temples of those deities that proclaimed allegiance to such other gods. However, he was more of a lover than a fighter, and his kingdom experienced military defeat—a serious mistake if you want your god to be held in high esteem. He died mysteriously and many scholars believe he was assassinated by the priests of the temples he had closed. His worship of Aton never seemed to amass popular appeal.

Other Egyptologists believe that Egyptians had shown belief in monotheism by their theological understanding that a single and mysterious high God, composed of male and female elements, began creation through a dialectical process which led to a Trinitarian or 'Triadic' structure expressed in various forms throughout Egyptian history. Others call this a henotheistic structure, with God at the apex of a creation that is immanently related to the lesser deities, as opposed to "polytheism" in which many gods operate independently.

As you can begin to see this whole business of "monotheism" is becoming increasingly complex for scholars to accurately define. Yet, the development of a "true" monotheism is seen as an important development in human consciousness. It desacralizes the world to an extent that the possibility of human invention is increased. But this has extreme political importance because it is used to distinguish "godly" societies from lesser, "pagan, ungodly" societies. The development of monotheism therefore becomes a politically charged dividing point between the wise and foolish; the good and the wicked, the civilized and the uncivilized.

Monotheism springs from the teaching of Zoroaster/Zarathustra, 600–500 BC. The Jewish exiles in Babylon recognized this and incorporated it into their post-exilic religious understanding as a form of lost knowledge that was recovered during the time of Josiah immediately before the exile of the Jewish State. In this version, Josiah discovers the Deuteronomic texts which insisted that God is one God; since the Jews had been worshipping other false gods, he preached that they were going to be punished by being taken into exile. Despite the Egyptian and Persian roots of their monotheistic beliefs, Jewish scribes never assigned credit to these cultures for their monotheistic belief.

However, there is no historical evidence that shows that the people of Israel and Judah ever really practiced a monotheistic devotion to YHWH as the only God. The historical evidence shows that the Jewish peasants practiced worship of other gods throughout the Jews' rising to power in Palestine. Even so, their belief in monotheism became a marker that distinguished the Jewish religion from that of others. This belief was passed down to Christians and Muslims who, when they gained power, made this the litmus test on steroids. Those who failed this test were persecuted. And since the three major expressions of monotheism had different understandings of what that looked like, they also persecuted each other for their "unorthodox beliefs." On a sociological and theological level this belief in monotheism holds no water since Jews, Christians, and Muslims not only differ from each other in how they conceptualize and practice "monotheism" but there have been and are competing expressions of monotheistic belief within their own traditions.

But let us return to Öcalan's account. In the *Manifesto*, Öcalan is still willing to admit some positive aspects of monotheism. For example, he contends that, with the Hebrews, their "monotheistic belief may have had much to do with [their] resistance [to] assimilation into civilization" (p.202). Nevertheless, he criticizes "the extreme formalism of Hebrew tribalism," blaming such formalism for the emergence of "the concept of the immutableness of law," and with it, the transformation of the Divine into the image of a sovereign king, a law-giver, one who has decreed "perpetual laws and orders" (p.270).

Öcalan on Islam and Christianity

With regards to Islam, Öcalan maintains that the "term 'Allah' itself is conceptually so wide that sociologically speaking it has the capacity to integrate the divine in nature with that in society," but that "the issues its followers would like to understand as 'perpetual laws and orders' are extremely unclear." He argues that such an "understanding of law as changeless might have been useful in overcoming tribal anarchy but, in later centuries, it led to great conservatism in Islamic society" (p.270).

Öcalan shows some respect for the prophet Mohammed, complimenting him for having "escaped contracting the familiar disease of being the God," though he is quick to add that "one of his failings was his inability to overcome the Judaic rigorousness" (p.270). Still, he also lauds Mohammed for his "emphasis on morals," which indicate "that he was aware of the problems inherent in civilized society." In this vein, he refers to Mohammed as "a great reformer, even a revolutionary," and remarks favorably upon "his rules about interest," his "well-known abolitionist tendencies," and his "affectionate and favorable" attitude towards "freedom," even mentioning that "[a]lthough he was by no means desirous of equality and freedom for women, he did despise the slavery of women." Finally, he notes approvingly that Mohammed "recognized the differences in class and ownership in society," though seems to chastise him for being "like a social democrat" and trying "to prevent the forming of monopolies and their social hegemony by using excessive taxation" (p.271).

According to Öcalan, "the strongest feature of Islam" is the equilibrium it has established "between the material and the ideological culture," unlike Christianity, in which "the moral aspect" allegedly prevails. To this effect, Öcalan cites approvingly one of Mohammed's *hadiths*, "work for this world as if thou will never die and work for the afterlife as if thou will die tomorrow," which he suggests captures the Islamic balance between this-worldly and other-worldly concerns (p.271).

Öcalan goes on to comment about "Saddam Hussein's relationship with the Qur'an just before his execution," calling it "quite intriguing," and concluding that the "Qur'an provides exceptional power to construct the minds of those who have no hope left." He returns to the subject of paradise, again insisting that it is a projection of hope in hopeless conditions, a coping mechanism in response to ubiquitous oppression, servitude, and slavery—"[o]ne cannot properly understand the messages brought by the Holy Books without understanding the conditions of slavery." Though he adds, *en passant*, that not only oppressive social conditions, but also the "metaphysical nature of the human," rendered the utopia of paradise (and its counterpoint, hell), as well as many other utopias, "inevitable"—since "without striving for a better future, life cannot really be lived" (p.275).

It is questionable whether the striving for paradise, for transcendence, can be captured or reduced to a "striving for a better future"—not only because, strictly speaking, according to the Abrahamic tradition, paradise is alleged to exist outside of homogenous empty time; but perhaps more importantly, because striving for paradise at least as frequently reflects deep-felt desires and longing for reunion with the past, more specifically, with loved ones who have been lost. This is not to mention a desire for immortality—for ourselves, and for those we love, a desire which Öcalan equates with the "fear of death," and contends is but a social construct, adding, in an (unwittingly) Heideggerian vein, that "the most precious part of life is becoming aware of death" (p.275).

According to Öcalan, both Islam and Christianity "held an intriguing promise for ending slavery." But the question of an alternative to servitude and oppression, he continues, "was evaded with the promise of a life that would be like living in paradise"—the retreat from the secular world into "the communities of the monasteries and madrasahs" was intended as examples of "the new society to be constructed"; later, he contends that the aim of these utopias was "not the creation of new civilizations but to salvage life and to turn it into something beautiful." However, the revolutionary potential of these religions would be subverted by their co-optation and instrumentalization in the hands of "the heads of the Christian churches as well as the conquering commanders of Islam" who "easily created a late, revised slave-owning system." Though importantly, he adds, that "although there were some revised slave-owning regimes, principalities, citystates and empires constructed in their names," to consider them "Islamic" or "Christian" represents "an ideological distortion" (p.276).

Öcalan concludes that, "despite their objectives," the utopias of Christianity and Islam ended up "serving the onset of capitalism"—even if "the conflict between those elements of Islam and Christianity that became the State itself cannot be called conflict between Islam and Christianity." Such conflicts in fact have their origin in the dynamics of hierarchy and civilization, and "religion is only used as their disguise" (p.279), their proxy. Again, the metaphor and motif of religion as a mask or disguise. Not only did these utopias serve the onset of capitalism, they "do not have the skill to [re-]enchant the world of capitalist life," something he contends "can only be procured by the power and skill of the sociology of freedom"—a new type of sociology, one we can only begin to imagine, trapped as we are in the horizons of capitalist modernity, but one that Öcalan promises to contribute to in his own forthcoming work (p.277). And so goes his performative deconstruction of the orthodox Islamic belief in Mohammad as the seal of the prophets, if ever there was one.

It is a demotion of sorts for Islam and Christianity, at least with respect to the alleged impact of these traditions upon the affairs of *this* world. But it is at the same time a partial exoneration of the worthy original core messages of Islam and Christianity, since Öcalan deftly distinguishes these from the long histories of corrupted practices, indeed, usurpations by clerics and rulers, who have sought to justify hierarchy, exploitation, and unjust advantage by distorting the meaning of Islam and Christianity.

Islam is commonly considered one of the main sources of Middle Eastern culture, just as Christianity is putatively constitutive of Western culture. However, Öcalan disputes such identification, insisting instead that "the real source of both cultures [is] the five thousand year-old hierarchic and statist structures" (p.88).

If Öcalan thus shows considerable respect for the original, putatively core, revolutionary messages of early Islam and early Christianity, he shows a good deal less for the contemporary corrupted practitioners who speak the name of their God in vain. His attitude borders on contempt when it comes to "political" or "radical" Islam. He dismisses such movements as movements of pseudo-resistance, and contends that though their organizations "criticize European modernity" and even "violently oppose it," though they may have "put on the clothes and the beard of tradition," in reality "their soul and body are loaded with the most backward remnants of modernity" (p.89). In sum, Öcalan considers so-called "radical" or "political Islam" a false resistance, a movement that perpetuates and embodies the very values it claims to resist. It is a form of nationalism, in fact (p.87).

Against Orientalism?

Which brings us to the subject of Orientalism. Öcalan is adamant that his approach is an "anti-Orientalist" one. But he would do well to study more closely the critique of Orientalism, and perhaps especially the work of Edward Said, whom he strangely criticizes as aligned with radical Islam, even claiming that, like Hezbollah, Said may "seem to be anti-Orientalist and an enemy of Western modernity" but in fact is trapped "within the boundaries of this modernity" (p.89). An ungenerous interpretation of the thrust of Said's message, to say the least.

Öcalan elaborates what could be called a "Fertile Crescent-centric" meta-narrative about the arc of human history, including a story about the rise and trajectory of "civilization." It is a metanarrative ultimately too dependent on Eurocentric historiography, one that at times even reproduces certain rather crude and dubious tropes about Aryans versus Semites. Indeed, like so much of the Eurocentric historiography on which his account relies, Öcalan's treatment of ethnicity too often displays a tendency to anachronism, essentialism, and reification, and too often ignores liminal spaces and the prevalence of hybridity.

So too does Öcalan's metanarrative reproduce certain characteristic exclusions. Most tellingly, for Öcalan, the story of human history begins with an exit from Africa. In his account, even Egypt is rendered derivative, its African-ness basically denied. This is especially problematic given Öcalan's expressed ambition to provide a metanarrative capable of underpinning and fueling resistance to capitalist modernity, in favor of an alternative "democratic modernity." For, as Cedric Robinson has rightly emphasized, "the obliteration of the African past from European consciousness was the culmination of a process a thousand years long and one at the root of European historical identity" (*Black Marxism*, p.82).

Alas, Öcalan is not infallible; but his narrative is nonetheless powerful. Quiescence and consent to the injustices of neoliberal capitalism, not to mention support for the war crimes and spiraling violence committed in the on-going Orwellian global war on "terror", are all underpinned and perpetuated by the propagation of dominant myths. Effective resistance requires that such myths need more than just deconstruction. Belief in viable and desirable alternatives to the present order need to be encouraged and elaborated as well.

In this vein, Öcalan's sweeping historical vision of the dialectical struggle between domination and resistance as the motor of history is not to be underestimated. Indeed, his "dialectical naturalist" (Bookchin) effort to denaturalize hierarchies, to identify their origins and to uncover even deeper egalitarian and libertarian alternatives is most commendable, especially given the conditions of duress in which it has been composed.

But knowledge is always social, and Öcalan's manifesto is of course not the first or the last word. He does certainly point in (at least some of) the right directions: both forward and backward (if not upward) even though the verdict is by now unanimous that Nietzsche is dead, the jury is still out on the God of Abraham.

Struggling Hand in Hand with the Kurdish Youth Movement: Dispatches from the Long March for the Freedom of Öcalan (February 2017)

Mohammed Elnaiem

Written June 2017

Editors' Note: This is an excerpt from Mohammed Elnaiem's M.A. Dissertation, which he completed in the Sociology Department at the University of Cambridge in June of 2017 under the supervision of Thomas Jeffrey Miley. The dissertation is based on rigorous, extensive, and original ethnographic fieldwork, and constitutes an exemplary contribution to the genre of "militant research," based on his discussions and experiences while embedded in the Kurdish Youth Movement in Europe over the course of the 2016–2017 academic year. The complete dissertation is titled "The Truth Will Not Run Away from Us: Militant Investigations into the Kurdish and Black Liberation Movements."

Introduction

I am a child of the emerging transnational, black, petite-bourgeoisie. My parents met in The Republicans: a religious movement that had roots in the anti-colonial resistance in Sudan. The leader of the movement was hanged on charges of apostasy for resisting the institutionalisation of Sharia Law and they were compelled to leave Africa by "the oppressive boot and the irrelevance of the foot that wears it," that is to say, by post-colonial leaders that look like us. They moved to the UK for my father to receive his training as a doctor, a job which took us all around the world.

Later, as a student in Malaysia, I was confronted by the burden of my blackness. I was only 17, but had to navigate between fascist gangs and the police to survive. African students were detested by both. After a humiliating immigration raid targeting Africans, I tried and failed to organise students against the institutional response to what the public called the "African Menace." The students were too afraid: "I'm here to study, and I don't want any trouble," they often said. By the time I left the country, I was demoralized.

When I arrived in the United States in 2013 to continue my studies, there was no relief—only more rage. Young black transgender women were being murdered and young black men were being strangled to death by police for selling illegal cigarettes. The right-wing media had no conscience, justifying the murder of 12 year-old boys. We watched in horror as the courts responded to these police killings by absolving the killers. We took to the streets and became radicalized.

This project developed out of a strategic impasse. Liberation movements across the world need to reconsider the post-colonial state, and the proposed route to self-determination that it promises. I have sought to investigate the potential connections between the Kurdish movement and the Black liberation movements in order to assess whether or not this problem can be overcome. This impasse is quite simply a result of the bleak world that confronts black radicals today. Black radicals have historically found their poetry through an idealistic gaze to other lands. This internationalist dimension of the black movement generally went beyond solidarity efforts (for example with Vietnam) and envisioned the struggle for black liberation as intertwined with movements resisting imperialism. Where can one turn to today for inspiration, in a world where, following Fukuyama, history itself has come to an end?

I ask if Kurdistan can be such a promised land. Amid the Syrian civil war, the people of Rojava (western Kurdistan) have built a contradictory revolution which, if successful, can become the largest stateless democracy in the world. The cadres responsible for instituting this project of "democratic confederalism" are committed revolutionaries who are ideologically inspired by the thought of PKK (The Kurdistan Workers' Party) leader, Abdullah Öcalan. They have constructed a bottom-up democracy, built upon neighbourhood assemblies that are federated along communal, regional and cantonal lines. They defend and expand their project while fighting the IS (Islamic State) forces. At every level of governance women share power equally with men. All religious and ethnic minorities are also entitled to autonomy, and granted an equal say in decision making. Aside from a conventional government that exists side by side with the institutions of democratic modernity (which mainly plays the role of international diplomacy), all spheres of life are being radically democratized. Expropriated factories have been converted into cooperatives. Neighbourhoods have been converted into communes with the institutionalised right to self-defence. Police have been converted into self-defence units. Communists and anarchists have flocked to Rojava in order to aid it, and the parallels with revolutionary Spain in 1936 (like the fight against proto-fascistic Islamists [ISIS], and the quasi-anarchist experimentation), have largely been the catalyst for the influx of support that they have received.

Can the Kurdish experiment be a heterotopia to the black radical tradition? The utopian gaze to another land, a "heterotopia" has animated the tradition for as long as it was conceived. Historically, Haiti, Africa, the Soviet Union, and even Maoist China have all been mythologised (usually simplistically) in order to enrich the aspirations of blacks. They have been the "heterotopias," other spaces, imagined to be lands free from slavery, lynching, segregation, and police brutality. Throughout the twentieth century in fact, one can see a clear pattern of black movements seeking to transplant these heterotopias wherever they were found. The first black woman to be elected onto a city administration, Grace P. Campbell, had successfully done so on a ticket by the Socialist Party of America in May, 1920. The Federal Bureau of Investigation (FBI) once showed anxiety towards her efforts of installing "Bolshevism in place of the present government."

But that was the era of heterotopia, where are we today? Well, first and foremost, we are privileged with historical retrospect. It was in 1955 when Khrushchev revealed that Stalin had been committing crimes of monumental proportions, right about the time in which black intellectuals were being sent to the Soviet Union on magic pilgrimages. It was in 1991 when we could clearly separate the facts from fiction (with the end of the information cold war) and definitively say that the troubled legacy of "real existing socialism" was tainted with mistakes, repression, and murder. It would be a myth to say that young black revolutionaries seek to resurrect the past.

We are at a conjecture of ambivalence: young radicals today are not as interested in seizing the machinery of the state. We are haunted by the ghosts of our antecedents, who, instead of "committing suicide as a class", became the black faces to instantiate "diverse" neoliberal domination. If there is going to be a heterotopia today, it is unlikely to be a nation-state.

It is here where the thought of Öcalan offers one route out of this impasse. Whereas he writes within the revolutionary socialist tradition, Öcalan also seeks to transcend it. Conventionally—amongst Marxist and social democratic circles and insofar as the industrial base and productive forces of capitalism emerged in Britain—it is the industrial revolution that marks the beginning of history for capitalism. It is, in other words, the event that both presupposes the misery of the world's toiling masses, and the key to their emancipation.

It wasn't, therefore, difficult for post-colonial leaders like Ghana's Nkrumah and India's Nehru to believe that the seizure of the State would lead to the very "economic independence" that was key to their self-determination. They assumed, wrongly, that if each country had their own industrial revolution, then emancipation and socialism would follow naturally. Their failure to see beyond the economic realm was their major blind-sight, and without a critique of patriarchy, traditions of religious domination, and indeed even capitalism, they opened themselves up to constructing nation-states dominated by emerging national bourgeoisies, which now facilitate the development of neoliberalism in the post-colonial world.

Öcalan demands that we consider the birth of the State, 5000 years ago, as *the event* that ought to be grappled with. To Öcalan, the birth of the State not only corresponds with the birth of patriarchy, and the subjugation of women, but also the very hierarchy and domination that would necessitate the birth of capitalism centuries later. Unearthing this key, through an exploration of history, mythology, a "sociology of freedom," and even religious traditions, is the task Öcalan believes future revolutionaries must undertake. Dialectically, there has always been a struggle between what he calls "capitalist modernity", a project that is the modern manifestation of hierarchy and domination re-entrenching its existence over society, and "democratic modernity", a bottom-up struggle resisting the domination of capitalist modernity in daily life; those democratic traditions that managed to survive between the cracks of capitalist modernity.

For Öcalan, it is the woman—the first dominated subject—who stands at the vanguard of the struggle to resolve the key contradiction of society: the domination of the nation-state. This chapter will not focus on the theoretical positions of the Kurdish movement, but rather on how they translate into the everyday work of the Kurdish Youth movement in Europe. It will be an ethnography based upon work I conducted for a year as an ambassador from the Black Struggle. It will be followed by a reflection on how the Black Liberation Movement historically dealt with the question of identity and social organization.

Identity and Social Organization

It would be an understatement to say that identity politics is one of the most controversial debates of our time. The tension between identity (a marker of difference), and emancipatory alliances (a congregation of different actors joining together for a common goal) is one that leftist movements need to reconcile if they are to build political programs that appeal to all. This vignette will be a short reflection on the relationship between identity and organization within the Kurdish Youth movement. The story begins with my introduction to the Kurdish movement at the anarchist book fair, and will end with a conference that brings together activists from seven different countries to construct a project of democratic confederalism in Europe. I will then proceed to outline a snapshot from the history of the black movement in order to assess the intricate relationship between identity, organization and building political programs.

The Encounter

I encountered the Kurdish movement on October 29, 2017. Earlier on that day, I found myself caught up in debates—the annual procession for the families of those killed under police custody was taking place, as was the yearly Anarchist book fair. I felt torn between my black aspirations and my libertarian socialist sympathies. Radicals in London had to decide which event to attend, most planned to do both. It was there where I met Josh, a co-founder of the Black Lives Matter movement in the UK. He was dressed in a yellow high-vis vest, had a trimmed beard and a shaved head. Josh is black and proud of it. I later learned that he also (I feel), sympathises with the struggle to abolish race, just as I do.

We already knew of each other through Facebook, and both of us were interested in the revolutions cascading across Kurdistan. A year prior to our meeting, I contributed to a campaign to fund his journalism trip to Bakur, Kurdistan. I found him when he was alone, sitting on the corner of the road smoking a cigarette. We were happy to see each other. He asked me what I was doing in Britain. I told him I was there to do militant research and uncover the potential relationships between the Kurdish and Black Liberation movements.

"That's amazing, and where are you going next?" he said.

"I'm going to the anarchist book fair."

"You should go," he responded, "But I'm telling you bruv, it's going to be shit."

I arrived at the anarchist book fair, located that year in a small secondary school in Tottenham, just before sunset. I decided to attend a discussion on

Rojava at the fair. It would be after that meeting where I would make my first connection with the Kurdish movement. Mehmet Aksoy was a young Kurdish journalist, with a captivating smile and awe-inspiring presence. He was wearing a black leather jacket and seemed to appreciate my contribution to the discussion on Rojava.

> **Me:** Hey there, my name is Mohammed and I would like to link up the Kurdish and Black liberation movements. I was wondering if that would be something you would help me achieve. Do you have connections with the Kurdish movement here?

> **Mehmet:** Of course man! I've been waiting for something like this. You know something, yeah? Before I even read any books by Abdullah Öcalan, I would read about the Black Panthers and George Jackson's prison writings. My radicalization happened through the black movement first, when I was in college, and then the Kurdish movement. I grew up in a Kurdish family more aligned with the Turkish left, so I wasn't even aware of my identity. The Black struggle was important in centring the idea of identity for me.

He wasn't the only one to tell me about the influence the black liberation movement had on his own political beliefs. Giran had also been forging links with the Black Lives Matter movement in the US. Elif, one of the leaders in the Kurdish Youth Assembly, and Ciwanen Azad (Kurdish Free Youth Movement) also believed that there was strong potential in the unity of both movements.

The more I started visiting the Kurdish Community Centre, the more it also became clear to me that, for years, the Kurdish and Black migrants had developed strong bonds and had even worked together on multiple projects. But I also had arrived on the organizing scene at a time that could not have been more opportune for me. Understanding its newfound solidarity, the Kurdish Youth movement was now redefining itself into a beacon for other young activists across Europe.

The Beacon

I wasn't alone in seeking out the Kurdish movement. The Rojava revolution seemed to offer a glimmer of hope to many different groups. By the time I approached the London section of Ciwanen Azad, the Kurdish Youth Movement in Europe had already extended their appendages everywhere from London to the Basque Country. It is out of this context, that I would be invited to establish a new organization. This was the first time I met Elif, one of the leaders in Ciwanen Azad—UK, and someone who would slowly become my mentor in the struggle. She told me, almost immediately about a group of internationalists who sought to converge in Switzerland to lay the blueprints for the establishment of radical democracy across Europe. She invited me to join, and, without hesitation, I did.

I first met Elif and Giran at Kings Cross Station. It was a day that would pave the way for a deep camaraderie. Like me, both had lived with the internal contradictions of diasporic identity—and both were committed to the cause of class suicide. My primary loyalty was to the black liberation movement, and they were committed to the Kurdish freedom struggle. However, all of us were committed, first and foremost, to the liberation of humankind.

A year later, I would be working with them all across Europe. Mehmed, however dedicated he was to the Kurdish revolutionary cause, decided to sojourn to Rojava in the quest to document the truth of the campaign to liberate Raqqa from the so-called Islamic State. On September 26, 2017, he was killed in an ambush by ISIS militants while working for the press office of the Peoples' Protection Units (YPG). By the time I had joined *The Region,* a successor to KOM News (a media outlet he formed), he had already left. Whenever I asked when he would come back, I was told that he might not.

"I've bought a one-way ticket to return to my homeland," he told one of our friends. None of us had expected that the man who changed our lives would die a martyr, but in a way, nothing was more fitting. Mehmet died a happy man. I credit Mehmet, along with Dilar Dirik, for introducing me to the Kurdish liberation movement.

When I met Giran and Elif, I was unaware of how life-changing that casual meeting at Kings Cross would be. I asked them what inspired the passion in their hearts for their cause. Giran, a tall man in his thirties, responded with confidence and tact, accustomed to what was obviously a common question. He spoke in a moving and compassionate way: "So for me, when I was a kid, I would ask my parents where I was from, and of course, they told me 'Kurdistan', but when I went to school and told my friends, they would tell me that it's not a place. It's so weird, growing up feeling like you're not human enough because you don't have a country. I remember wanting one, but then growing up detesting the very idea of a country."

Giran discovered Öcalan's writings in college. "I wanted to create a world without states, so that all of the democratic peoples of the world could unite." The paradigm shift initiated by Öcalan—original in its attempt to redefine self-determination as a project against, instead of for, the state—was a perfect antidote to Giran's youthful angst.

Elif was more inspired by Öcalan's dedication to the struggle of women, and what she felt was his humanistic outlook. "I was never proud to be a Kurd in a patriotic kind of way. That doesn't mean that I'm not proud now—it just means that there's no point in being a nationalist," she told me. Instead, she was attracted to the universalism she found in the ideology of the movement:

> I grew up in a society, and I won't get into the details, but here in London, many of the women I know have suffered from domestic abuse, sexual assault. I think the Kurdish freedom movement is a struggle for humanity—not just for Kurdish people. If it was just for Kurdish people, then that wouldn't be enough. In fact, with the turn to Quantum politics, the Kurdish movement is a struggle for the universe. I know that sounds weird to you, but it seriously is.

I was often awestruck by the youth I met in my journey. They spoke of a "patriotic" cause, but their ideology was diametrically opposed to nationalism, a term they often used when speaking derisively. Patriotism, at least to the ones I know, meant a commitment to liberation, not just a Kurdish people.

The Question of Revolutionary Subjectivity

The diasporic consciousness directed towards Kurdistan, inflected with the daily concerns that they face as youth in Europe, was a fascinating dimension to the Kurdish Youth movement. But even more intriguing was how Öcalan's writings offered a place for these youth to situate themselves within a broader history of struggle, how the act of telling history became a way to build a revolutionary subjectivity.

After arriving in Zurich by plane, Sara, myself, and two other students took a small train to a remote village in the German-speaking region of Switzerland. Waiting for us was a tall German man. He escorted us to a large house they had rented. "The curtains of the house are closed today, because we have Öcalan flags, and we don't want to creep out the locals," he said to me. I just laughed.

We arrived late at night at a house full of activists from many different countries. There were the Swiss (who had come from Geneva), the Italians, the Germans and ourselves. We were sent up to sleep on bunk-beds, which were segregated: the men in one room and the women in the other. Over the course of the next few days, we discussed the nature of our project, the flag we wanted to use, its name. Every day, women held autonomous meetings and had the veto power to alter all decisions made. Men were assigned kitchen duty for breakfast and dinner and two individuals would be woken up for night guard every hour.

Never before in the course of my activism, in any meeting, had I seen young people deliberate and debate the revolutionary subjectivity of the "Youth" through the act of historical construction. Youth, whenever I had come across the term in activist circles, was an adjective, not a subjective position. But here, in this abandoned house in the middle-of-nowhere Switzerland, young men and women would spend hours developing the story of youth struggles against capitalism and statism over the *longue durée,* and they did so through Öcalan's analysis. Much like how the woman in Mesopotamia was dethroned with the birth of the Ziggurat temple, they argued that the birth of patriarchy was also the moment when the youth had been side-lined in favour of a gerontocracy (the rule of old men) of Shamans, and ruling elites. The two men who sat at the corner of the long table, continued their narration: "youth initiated the most heroic struggles of the 20th century, but they were side-lined and condemned by the older 'revolutionary leaders.'"

The lecture they gave to the broader group covered everything from ancient struggles against theocratic empires, to the uprisings of 1968—but some complained that the struggles of young women were overlooked.

After the lecture a young German woman offered her criticisms of the analysis prepared by the young men. "You spoke about Lenin, Kropotkin, but I heard nothing about Rosa Luxemburg, Clara Zetkin. How can you claim to be against gerontocracy, if your analysis itself is patriarchal?"

The men agreed, and opened up the space for further discussion. I proposed a motion to further complicate the analysis: "Many here believe that to be fully human means to know who we are, because a people without a history cannot have a future. But we've made a mistake, we've tried to explain the situation of youth, but have assumed all youth are the same. What of black youth, of black women youth, etc. Are all youth the same?"

In other words, if Fanon recognized that "a Marxist analysis should always be slightly stretched every time we have to deal with the colonial problem," then many of the internationalist Youth challenged their Kurdish counterparts to do the same. They believed, we believed, that Öcalan's thought provided a broad framework to both interpret struggles and intervene in history. But they also thought that this potential wasn't fully realised yet.

It was a contention that Josh brought up at the third Challenging Capitalist Modernity conference on April 14–16 in Hamburg Germany. Academics from Bakur, Europe, North America and Latin America shared the stage with young activists working in different movements. Archaeologists presented their findings on ancient architecture that seemed to substantiate Öcalan's thesis on direct democracy in early Mesopotamia. Activists from Rojava, the MST in Brazil, and the People's Congress in Colombia entered into strategic conversations on the path to global grassroots democracy. Even Salih Muslim, a former co-chair of the Rojava administration was present to give a talk on the dangers of militarism.

But Josh, a fellow activist in the black liberation movement, wondered why blacks—particularly black women—were excluded in the broader project to construct the human story of resistance.

"If some of my sisters were here, they wouldn't be happy with the silences in that history," he said. "It's not like we don't already have the work of black women to draw from. It's not like we don't have our own tradition to work with. It'd be interesting to see more of a conversation." And interesting it would be. Although I remember thinking that it was also on us, activists in the black liberation struggle to reach out and begin such a project, I felt his criticism was valid. Yet the very act of situating yourself within the thought of Öcalan was something many did, particularly Kurds.

I remember when, on a long march for the freedom of Öcalan in Europe, I met Agit. Agit, a young married man, was dressed in the outfit of the guerrilla units in the mountains. He was on the security team and brandished a stick to warn any potential Grey Wolves (Turkish neo-fascists who often attacked us as we marched) that we were serious about defending ourselves should they decide to attack. I woke up early one morning and saw him doing his morning Muslim prayers (*Subh*). It was a pleasant surprise; I had assumed, quite naively, that the backbone of this movement was secular (after all, most of the leadership were socialist and atheist). The next day, Agit and I discussed his devoutness:

Me: I noticed that you pray. If you don't mind me asking, I've always assumed that Öcalan held religion in disregard. I'm aware that in his books, he attaches a democratic spirit to Islam, and calls it an early liberation movement, but then he proceeds to declare that Islam was transformed into a project of Empire. Do you feel that the PKK embodies Islam?

Agit: You know what Serok Apo (Öcalan) said? He said, "People think that I hate Islam, but I don't. Sheikh Saïd (who led the first Kurdish uprising against the Turkish State in 1925) came and he showed us the true Islam." I hope that Muslims will remember the legacy of Saïd.

Me: ISIS today claims that they are fighting for Islam, and the SDF (Syrian Democratic Forces—armed wing of the Rojava administration (The Democratic Federation of Northern Syria—DFNS) claims that they are fighting Islamism for the sake of humanity. As a Muslim, what do you think about this situation?

Agit: To me, the SDF is fighting for the ideals of a true Islam; for the freedom of women and everybody in humanity. Even me, I'm just in this movement, and I'm here to protect you all. This is my Islam.

The Alevi disagreed with me. One of the organizers of the march, and the man with whom I corresponded with before I took off to Luxembourg, believed his cause was secular, and a fight against oppression, be it theocratic or not. They courteously debated for a little bit, and then we marched together. This is when I realized that "the ideology of Öcalan" means many different things to many different people. Insofar as the proponent of it can see themselves in the liberationist trends of democratic modernity, the devout Muslim can find themselves within it, the secular (and religious) Yezidi can find an escape from theocracy, the disillusioned student can find a liberation organization, and the expansive reach of Öcalan's thought can provide answers to all of his adherents. "What the Kurdish movement has managed to do," said Elif, when I reported back in London, "is to unite Kurds of all backgrounds. If you look at history, you'll realize that many Kurdish rebellions were divided on sub-ethnic or religious lines—this isn't happening here."

So, too, had Öcalan's writing given subjectivity to struggling women everywhere, particularly in Rojava. I recall that, as we were concluding the congress in Switzerland, activists gathered around a fire to commemorate the fallen martyrs of the Rojava revolution and sing old anti-fascist songs. I struck up a conversation with a German feminist activist who had been to Rojava, and asked her what it was like to see politicized women in Kurdistan challenging a legacy of patriarchy that extends back for millennia. She paused, stopped to warm her hands, and simply responded that it was "surreal."

She told me about her work with the *Jineoloji* (women's science) committees, the difficulties of getting reluctant women to join, and the challenges of bringing women to the newly formed communes.

"I would follow the cadres in the movement, and you know what the secret to get really old women who were so tied to old conceptions of patriarchy was?

You just have to argue that this is what Öcalan believes, and this is what the PKK argues." She told me about a day where she got to sit in with the women's *Asayish*, an all-female security force: "They brainstormed on how to develop a concept of self-defence that completely rids itself of masculine thinking. This wasn't some Western abstract argument by some academic. This was a debate that included 50-year-old women and 21-year-old women who put their lives on the line every day. I felt like crying."

This is all to say that though the Kurdish movement—like all of its contemporaries—did have its silences, it also had the vision to expand its historical scope. It redefined subjectivity in a way that empowered many, and it did so without resulting in fragmentation. Whether you were a Muslim Kurd, an Alevi, a woman, or anyone else—your identity wasn't a "facet" of your personhood. It is part of the human story in which you situate yourself.

Theoretical Reflections

In Europe, Kurdish activists distinguish themselves from other Western leftists with the sophistication of how they weave identity into social movement organization. Unlike, for instance, Cell 16, which in 1968 called for celibacy within its ranks and sought to operate autonomously, or unlike the Furies commune that only allowed lesbian feminists into its organization, the Kurdish women's movement works and struggles from within the broader Kurdish freedom movement, both at home and in the diaspora (Crow, 2000). In a word, they are not separatists.

In 1969, the Black Panther Party, after years of building a popular front which included the Puerto Rican Young Lords, Chinese-American Red Guard, Chicano-oriented *Los Siete de la Raza*, the white working class "Young Patriots"; the student led Syrian Democratic Forces (SDS); and even the Gay Liberation Front (it was the first black organization to support gay liberation), attempted to construct (however briefly) what Öcalan has called a "democratic nation". This coalition against fascism was a concept predicated on an idea that challenged black separatism. As Bobby Seale put it, "black racism is just as bad and dangerous as white racism." (Bloom; Martin, 2013, p.300). To differentiate themselves from black nationalists, they sought to form a rainbow coalition against fascism, and they argued that this epitomized class struggle. The Black Panther Party had a peculiar conception of class struggle with no precedent in the United States. In their hands, it was a reconciliation of the particular (black, gay, etc.) with the universal. It had a paradoxical character: while conceived as a class struggle, it was simultaneously a repudiation of class reductionism. In his speech, "it's a class struggle goddammit!" Fred Hampton complained about the people who have "hang-ups with the Party because the Party talks about a class struggle. [They say,] 'well I can't dig the Panther Party because the Panthers [are] dealing with oppressor-country radicals, or white people, or honkies, or what have you," (Hampton, 1969). Hampton insisted that the party knew that "black people are most oppressed," for why else would they "be running around talking about the black liberation struggle has to be the vanguard for all liberation struggles," but neither was fetishizing the black identity liberationist, nor pretending that differences don't exist.

While they succeeded in constructing a universal polity, they failed tremendously when it came to questions concerning gender. In 1969, in the United Front Against Fascism conference, the Black Panther Roberta Alexander argued that women in the Black Panther Party, while carrying most of the burden of the work (they were ⅔ of the membership), were unrecognized and denied access to power. She argued that, "black women are oppressed as a class, part of the super-oppressed class of workers and unemployed in this country. Black women are oppressed because they are black, and then on top of that, black women are oppressed by black men. And that's got to go. Not only had it got to go, but it is going." (Bloom, Martin, 2013, p.30). She was, in many ways, drawing upon her predecessors like Claudia Jones, who sought to push the same position from within the Communist Party of the United States.

The problem, however, is that gender oppression didn't go away and instead further entrenched itself. When Huey Newton failed to confront sexual assault in the party and his role in the epidemic, Elaine Brown finally had to resign from her position of leadership. The Black Panther Party (BPP) refused not only to expel patriarchy and male-chauvinism from within its ranks, but indeed, it imploded because of this fact. By the time the BPP had been effectively neutralized by the United States government, the question of gender was more pertinent than ever.

In 1974, the Combahee River Collective, a group of black feminists and lesbians, became the first organization to coin the term identity politics. They represented an assembly of the disillusioned. They decried the racism of the white feminists, and the sexism of the black liberation movement, and bade their farewell to the homophobic quarters of the broader New Left. They felt that a "class struggle" that refused to programmatically incorporate the needs of the most oppressed was a project that was bound to fail. They called, instead, for a conception of struggle that accounted for "the major systems of oppression [which] are interlocking":

This focusing upon our own oppression is embodied in the concept of identity politics. We believe that the most profound and potentially most radical politics come directly out of our own identity, as opposed to working to end somebody else's oppression (Combahee River Collective Statement, 1974).

They were "in essential agreement with Marx's theory as it applied to the very specific economic relationships he analyses," but believed "his analysis must be extended further to understand our specific economic situation as black women" (ibid.). They believed that, if social movement organizations were not going to change, then they would have to declare their own autonomy.

It was a programmatic (and not moralistic) statement, similar to that of Noel Ignatiev and Theodore Allen. Within the Students for a Democratic Society, they argued that if the white working class refused to repudiate their "white skin-privileges", i.e. their "gentleman's agreement" with the white bourgeoisie instead of the black working class, then their revolutionary program was bound to fail. Both white privilege and identity politics can be traced back to these revolutionary movements.

In many ways, the failure of the left to confront the complexity of race and gender led to the emergence of identity politics and the focus on white skin privilege. But neither of these terms carry the same connotations today. Neoliberal capitalism has captured the political imagination of even the most radical. Thatcher's dictum states that "there is no such thing as society. There are individual women and men, and there are families." It is this the case then newer generations of radicals believe that the role of politics is to change the ideas and beliefs of individual women and men. The disintegration of the New Left organizations in the 1970s took identity politics outside of social movement organizations and into the neoliberal sphere.

This explains the qualitative transformation from Ignatiev and Allen's concept of "white skin privilege" to Peggy Mcintosh's "white privilege" knapsack. As opposed to the programmatic imperative of constructing a politics based both on uprooting white supremacy *and* capitalism, McIntosh's concept of white privilege denoted a list of 26 "I" statements; "I can be pretty sure that if I get into an argument with a colleague of another race, it is more likely to jeopardise her/his chances for advancement rather than mine." (McIntosh, 1988, 30)

There was a historic shift, which took anti-racism and feminism outside of social movement organisations, and into the domain of ethics and white guilt. Revolutionary organizations were supplanted by "diversity workshops" in universities and corporations. I believe that our generation of radicals have yet to recover from this problem.

What can the paradigm shift in the thought of Abdullah Öcalan offer in breaking through this impasse? I think that the answer lies, first, in the construction of popular power through radical democratic assemblies. This removes the ability of "leaders" to ignore and block the complaints from the most oppressed groups operating within social movement organizations. Secondly, the cardinal principle of autonomy provides not only the institutional mechanisms for addressing domination from within organizations, but also the power for the most marginalized to enact change. This is still an imperfect process, even in the Kurdish movement. LGBTs, for example, have not yet been granted the same power that women have. This too is an oppression that needs to be fought, but it cannot be accomplished through moralistic denunciation from the outside; it has to be done from within.

If there is one important lesson to be learned here, it is the question of how we can return identity politics to its rightful place within social movement organizations. Of course, there are many existing social movements—some that are revolutionary, and others that are trapped within a non-profit industrial complex—but there is yet to be anything similar to the Kurdish freedom movement in Europe. The solution to this specific problem lies therein.

Bibliography:

Bloom, J. and Martin, W.E., 2013. *Black Against Empire: The History and Politics of the Black Panther Party.* University of California Press.

Crow, B. A. (Ed.). (2000). *Radical Feminism: A Documentary Reader.* NYU Press.

Kelley, R.D., 2002. *Freedom Dreams: The Black Radical Imagination.* Beacon Press.

Küçük, B. and Özselçuk, C., 2016. *The Rojava Experience: Possibilities and Challenges of Building a Democratic Life.* South Atlantic Quarterly, 115(1), pp.184–196.

McDuffie, E.S., 2011. *Sojourning for Freedom: Black Women, American Communism, and the Making of Black Left Feminism.* Duke University Press.

McIntosh, P. (1988). *White Privilege: Unpacking the Invisible Knapsack.*

Combahee River Collective. "The Combahee River Collective Statement," in *Home Girls: A Black Feminist Anthology* (1983).

Öcalan, 2011. *Prison Writings: The PKK and the Kurdish Question in the 21st Century.* Transmedia Publishing.

Öcalan, A., 2011. *Democratic Confederalism.* London: International Initiative Edition.

Öcalan, A., 2013. *Liberating Life: Woman's Revolution.* International Initiative Ed.

Öcalan, A. and Happel, K., 2007. *Prison Writings: The Roots of Civilization.* Pluto Press.

Özcan, A.K., 2012. *Turkey's Kurds: A Theoretical Analysis of the PKK and Abdullah Öcalan.* Routledge

Von Eschen, P.M., 1997. *Race against Empire: Black Americans and Anti-Colonialism, 1937–1957.* Cornell University Press.

The Perils and Promises of Self-Determination:
From Kurdistan to Catalonia

Thomas Jeffrey Miley, Lecturer of Political Sociology at Cambridge University

October 2017

Editors' Note: *This is an attempt by Thomas Jeffrey Miley to interpret and criticise, through the paradigm of "democratic confederalism", the political dynamics surrounding the 2017 referenda for self-determination in Catalonia and in Iraqi Kurdistan. The article was originally published in ROAR magazine[1] and has subsequently been published in Arabic, Spanish, and Turkish.*

The images are shocking—from police violence against peaceful demonstrators in Barcelona to military occupation by the Iraqi army in Kirkuk. The State's coercive forces brutally intervening into institutions of autonomy while self-rule is severely undermined: the repression is certainly repulsive. How did such nationalist conflicts become so polarized? What triggered such aggressive state responses? How are these ongoing conflicts likely to develop? And what are the prospects for rights-expanding, emancipatory denouements in each case?

It's been over a century since Rosa Luxemburg rightly insisted upon the need to critically evaluate all claims about abstract utopian principles, such as the principle of self-determination, in terms of their concrete impact on both local and global constellations of power relations. However, Luxemburg's prescient warnings were long drowned out by the triumph of Marxism-Leninism and its influence upon the terms and horizons of so many anti-colonial struggles. Nearly a generation after the demise of state communism, and nearly sixty years since the transition from colonialism to neo-colonialism, it is high time for us to heed Red Rosa's sage advice and strike a consistent chord in favour of internationalist revolutionary ideals. The global scope of the urgent problems that beset humanity, and threaten its very future, require globally coordinated forms of resistance. The global scope of "intersecting" and unjust hierarchies—of deeply-entrenched systems of domination of class, race, and gender—means that now, less than ever, the fatal formula of socialism in one sole country will simply not suffice. Even so, the "internationalist Left" remains confused, still clinging to hollow dogmas about the principle of self-determination, all-too-often mystified by reified, essentialist, and nationalist visions and divisions of the social world. It is all-too-rarely capable of providing sober and "ruthlessly critical" analyses of the dynamics of mobilization and counter-mobilization at work in particular power struggles and "peoplehood projects," much less how such particular projects and struggles relate to broader global trends.

We need look no further than the cases of Catalonia and Kurdistan, both dominating the headlines in recent times, where two highly contested, unilateral referenda on "self-determination" have taken place, in both instances reflecting, as well as exacerbating, already-spiralling dynamics of polarization and repression. The discussion of these conflicts in left-wing circles, perhaps especially in the English language, leaves much to be desired. In both cases, even the most critical of analysts tend to bow before the sacred principle of self-determination, and thus tend to avoid interpreting and evaluating secessionist tactics in "ruthlessly critical" terms of their impact on local and global constellations of power relations. In both cases, "the Catalans" and "the Kurds" tend to be referred to as though they were unitary actors. In both cases the serious differences and divisions within these reified "national communities," especially at their margins, have been either systematically ignored or conflated. That there are competing projects of "self-determination" is forgotten. The same can be said for the serious differences and divisions within their reified "national" opponents. Such are the insidious effects of nationalist reification.

In the case of Catalonia, there has been much enthusiasm expressed in favour of the tactics and strategy of the expressly anti-capitalist Candidatura d'Unitat Popular (CUP). And indeed, the CUP's programmatic emphasis on feminism, social ecology, and direct democracy is certainly to be lauded. Even so, its relative strength within secessionist ranks has tended to be overestimated; its exclusive commitment to tactics of unilateral rupture, and its dogmatic faith in the formula of "national independence" as the route to rupture with capitalism, must be critically interrogated. This dogmatic formula has predictably led the CUP into coalition with kleptocratic, bourgeois, secessionist forces, legitimated via a miraculous 1,515 to 1,515 assembly vote. In this capacity, in 2015, the CUP even voted in favour of the regional austerity budget. The CUP's insistence upon the urgency of unilateral secession has also, predictably, had little success in attracting much support in the old industrial belt. Indeed, all too little has been said about the limits to the appeal of the secessionist project in Catalonia, or its impact upon the broader terms of political contestation throughout all of Spain. For starters, as Antonio Santamaria has rightly emphasized, a look at participation rates in different municipalities proves most illustrative of the definite limits to secessionist appeal among the working class in Catalonia. For example, in the emblematic industrial belt town of Santa Coloma de Gramenet, participation in the referendum was less than 18% of the electoral census; whereas in the emblematically wealthy town of Sant Cugat del Vallès, the rate of participation was over 54%.

To make matters worse, polarization around the "national question" has served to legitimate austerity politics and to keep corrupt, demagogic politicians unaccountable on both sides of the Ebro River. At the same time, it has served to shift the terms of debate forced onto the agenda by the *indignados*, who framed the basic antagonism in fundamentally class terms, as a struggle between the haves and have-nots, rather than as a conflict between territories, or a struggle between "nations". Given the concrete constellation of social relations in the Iberian Peninsula, it is very difficult for a struggle framed primarily in "national" terms to avoid the *fait accompli* of dividing and conquering the working class, not only in Catalonia but, perhaps especially, in the rest of Spain too. Given the balance of both legal and brute force, unilateral independence for Catalonia is nothing short of a pipe dream; negotiations with the political forces in Madrid would be required to achieve a successful secessionist outcome. And, of course, the ideological orientation of the Spain-wide hegemonic bloc, with whom would-be secessionists would have to negotiate, matters quite a bit. So, even out of self-interest, one might have expected the secessionist bloc to work on strengthening the prospects and voice of the broader Spanish Left. But, instead, their unilateral secessionist tactics have played right into the hands of the Spanish Right.

Not that the broader Spanish Left is blameless. The "parliamentary cretinism" and opportunism of Podemos and, to a lesser extent, the *Comunes* (a coalition of the Initiative for Catalonia Greens (ICV), United and Alternative Left (EUiA), and Barcelona en Comú), with their co-optation, usurpation, and at least partial undermining of the grassroots' demands and direct-democratic logic of the *indignados* movement, has undoubtedly limited the appeal and potential of their counterhegemonic "new-New Left" project. Thus, by extension, they helped pave the way for substituting class conflict with national conflict, with horizons of contestation polarized not for and against the painful policies of austerity, but, instead, around the so-called *procés*, the process of Catalan independence. Pablo Iglesias and, especially, Ada Colau, the mayor of Barcelona and leader of the *Comunes*, have done their best to maintain a posture of calculated ambiguity, to keep the prospects for a "third way" between unilateral secession and state repression alive, but such efforts often get drowned out in the successive waves of polarizing confrontations between Spanish and Catalan nationalisms. Meanwhile, the politically bankrupt neoliberal "social democrats" of the Partido Socialista Obrero Español (PSOE) have fallen into line with the authoritarian tactics of repression pursued by the Spanish authorities. The party itself has been riven with conflict over the past year, with current leader Pedro Sánchez already deposed once, but now back again, marginally more prone to accommodation and democratic compromise on the national question than his intra-party foes, who prefer to mimic the Spanish Right's belligerent language about an alleged Catalan "coup" from the pages of *El País*, and who do their best to legitimate and applaud (when not denying) state repression and police violence.

The Balance of Forces in Struggle

If Luxemburg was right to stress the importance of critically evaluating abstract claims for "self-determination" in terms of their impact on concrete constellations of power relations, Lenin was nevertheless also right to retort that the dangers of "big-nation" chauvinism should never be underestimated when making such evaluations. Indeed, big-nation Spanish chauvinism has certainly been on abundant display in recent months and weeks. In the social media and mainstream Spanish press, every aggression by the Spanish authorities has been celebrated— the more repressive and violent, the better. The patriarchal core of Spanish nationalism has thus re-emerged with a vengeance. Like an abusive husband, the very same excuses used to justify violence against a wife who wants to leave. Union by force, because—you know—we love her so much.

The Spanish Right has even proven a disturbing capacity for popular counter-mobilization, with close to a million patriots filling the streets of Barcelona the weekend after the contested referendum, rallying around a Spanish flag already soaked in so much blood, cynically justifying the coercive defence of the Constitution as the "rule of law," or even "civil rights". Meanwhile, far-right elements blended easily into the crowd as if imperceptible, swimming freely in their natural habitat, like fish in water. Such popular counter-mobilization is officially led by "civil society," though of course it is organically linked to the right-wing Spanish political forces who control the Spanish State. The ability to mobilize supporters onto the streets is a relatively novel element in the Spanish nationalist repertoire, at least in Catalonia. At the same time it is a reflection of the polarizing spiral in which the polity seems trapped. A relative novelty, but it is one that both mimics and reflects tactics long practiced by their erstwhile opponents, the Catalan authorities.

Make no mistake—the image of the conflict under way as one pitting the Spanish "State" against the Catalan "people" is an oversimplification at best. All too often ignored is the crucial role played by the Catalan regional authorities and the regional mass media in pushing forward the procés, as well as the organic links between the Catalan government and its regional administrative apparatus with such "civil society" organizations as the Assemblea Nacional de Catalunya and Òmnium Cultural, whose leaders were unjustly imprisoned without bail. Nor can be forgotten the fawning over the Catalan regional police for its "professional" and "impressive" hunting down of Moroccan-Catalan teenage terror suspects, their extra-judicial extermination, with extreme prejudice, applauded in so many secessionist circles. It just goes to show how close the Catalans already are to having a state of their own. Nevertheless, we must insist, multiplying "independent" state apparatuses is not the same thing as smashing the State.

The ongoing conflict between central and regional state apparatuses is one in which both sides have benefitted from polarizing and utopian demagoguery. This is not to deny that either side enjoys a niche of genuine popular appeal, especially in the ranks of the secessionist popular forces, whose core constituency can be found among austerity-era squeezed and threatened, Catalan-speaking, middle classes. Even so, a realistic assessment of the balance of forces within the present struggle requires a sober recognition of the role of political elites in control of those state apparatuses on both sides of the conflict. But let there be no confusion. If the still-spiralling conflict is understood as fundamentally a stand-off between central and regional political elites and state apparatuses, both willing and increasingly able to mobilize a considerable degree of "popular" support, the balance of legal and coercive power nevertheless remains squarely with the Spanish State, as does the balance of economic force. The commanding heights of the Catalan economy have consistently voiced a preference for a negotiated solution to the current impasse, emphasizing, of course, the need for concessions of greater fiscal autonomy. Even so, the clear opposition to a unilateral declaration of independence on the part of the Catalan authorities may end up being the decisive factor in determining the conflict's denouement. Crucially, the Catalan authorities had sold their utopian project of secession as low-cost, and had repeatedly promised that secession would mean more prosperity for all Catalans, once the yoke of Madrid had been shaken off. Many Catalans were likely disabused of such illusions in the weeks following the contested referendum.

The business community in Catalonia reacted swiftly; big businesses have simply too much to lose, particularly given the very real possibility of forced exclusion from the EU in the case of a successful unilateral declaration of independence, as European authorities have repeatedly insisted. And so, the Catalan business community acted with a wave of corporate flight, thereby delivering a devastating, perhaps decisive, blow to the secessionist roadmap after at least 45 large and medium-sized firms transferred their corporate headquarters to other regions of Spain, including six of the seven largest corporations that are listed in the Spanish Ibex, the index comprised of the 35 Spanish companies with the most liquidity.[1] This swift blow from the corporate sector of the Catalan economy may or may not yet prove decisive. Certainly, though, it has been far more effective in bringing the separatists to heel than beating up grandmothers trying to vote, taking political prisoners, or suspending Catalan autonomy, although an economic jolt is perhaps not so satisfying for those whose Spanish-nationalist appetites seem to demand more heavy-handed forms of state repression. Such a penchant for heavy-handedness might just backfire in the short run, and certainly won't be forgotten anytime soon; indeed, it will only reinforce the sense of grievance that permeates and motivates secessionist imaginaries and convictions.

Meanwhile, many on the Eurosceptic Left, certainly in Britain, appear willing to cheer the secessionist movement on in its forward flight, urging it to jump off any cliff, and applauding anything that exacerbates the contradictions in the political system. That is, anything that promises to pile more instability upon the EU project, without so much as a realistic assessment of which concrete social forces will benefit from the climate of increased turbulence and nationalist discord. This is pyromania disguised as revolutionary courage. Never mind the fact that the vast majority of secessionists have consistently insisted upon their deeply-felt European convictions—even their commitment to austerity, despite the official position of the minority CUP. Even more crucially, the Eurosceptic Left seems to ignore the danger that, in the case of Spain, the potential for the victory of a right-wing, authoritarian backlash is indeed very real. The secessionist dream of establishing a left-wing independent Catalan republic is bound to remain a utopian fantasy, certainly so long as it fails to generate support among the working class of Barcelona's metropolitan area, who, given the deep history and legacy of internal migration from the South of Spain, find themselves all too frequently torn, caught in the crossfire, and alienated from both sides—each of which increasingly demands exclusive allegiance and loyalty.

Conflict in Iraqi Kurdistan

Speaking of pyromania, let us now briefly turn our attention to a region of the world that two war-criminal pyromaniacs, Bush and Blair, set on fire close to a decade and a half ago now, with the help of their good buddy José María Aznar, it should not be forgotten, their loyal lap-dog and junior-partner in the catastrophically destabilizing "Coalition of the Willing". In Iraqi Kurdistan, a contested referendum stands as another exemplar of an exacerbated conflict and stand-off between central and regional authorities. Another case, too, with a beleaguered regional president, Masoud Barzani, as protagonist—here, even more beleaguered than the corruption-plagued Catalan ruling elite. Indeed, Barzani finds himself unconstitutionally clinging to power, having served as regional president for close to two-and-a-half years longer than the constitutional limit. The regional administrative and coercive apparatuses remain divided between those loyal to his KDP and those loyal to Jalal Talabani, the recently deceased former Iraqi president, and his rival PUK. Meanwhile, payments from the central authorities have been frozen since January, 2014, over ongoing disputes about the distribution of oil resources. This, combined with falling oil prices, has meant a climate of serious economic difficulties for the regional authorities. To offset the predictable rise in discontent, Barzani responded with a ratcheting-up of political repression, including repression of opposition forces in the regional parliament. But since consent cannot be manufactured through coercion alone, he decided to combine this with a populist power-move via recourse to a plebiscite. The unilateral referendum on "self-determination"—a demagogic and utopian ploy—was meant to legitimate, secure, and tighten his grip on power. Even if, like his counterparts in Catalonia, he over-played his cards, he probably also underestimated the counter-currents that his attempt at unilateral rupture would unleash.

The referendum, held on 25 September, 2017, brought out a fairly impressive 73% of voters, close to 93% of whom voted yes. Such clear evidence of a super-majority in favour of Kurdish independence was, perhaps, not surprising given the genocidal violence they have suffered. Even so, Talabani's PUK had nevertheless warned against the referendum. As, of course, had Barzani's American backers, who, after failing to persuade him to desist, were little-inclined to defend their "self-determining" oil revenue-based, kleptocratic client. Not surprisingly, even more angry were Barzani's other erstwhile backers, the Turkish authorities. Barzani's referendum predictably stoked paranoia among the far-right upon whom Turkish President Erdoğan currently depends. It cannot be forgotten that Barzani's complicity with the Turkish authorities, including collaboration and coordination in their ongoing war against the PKK, was essential to Barzani's project from the start. In the wake of the referendum, the Turkish authorities threatened to block oil exports and close the borders—threats that, if fulfilled, would have certainly brought the Barzani regime to its knees.

As for Barzani's opponents in Baghdad, they responded almost immediately by stopping international flights into and out of Erbil and Sulaymaniyah, along with demands for KRG authorities to hand over control of airports. Before the week was out, the Iraqi and Iranian armed forces were holding joint border drills on Iran's border with the KRG. On 15 October, 2017, the Iraqi army took Kirkuk without a fight, after having presumably cut a deal with the PUK forces who had controlled the contested oil fields ever since the surge of ISIS in the summer of 2014. In turn, the PUK's retreat from Kirkuk triggered retreats from over 40% of disputed territory previously gained, and which had showcased Barzani as a constituent part of the KRG during the referendum. This represented a stunning reversal—the result of an overplayed hand—and a human rights' catastrophe in its own right, despite the avoidance of war, with reports of over a hundred thousand people fleeing from their homes in Kirkuk.

The Democratic Confederal Alternative

Discussions in Western leftist circles of events in Iraqi Kurdistan have been divided, due to the prevalence of suspicions about the geopolitical alliances binding "the Kurds" to the Americans, and even, on some accounts, to the Israelis. And yet, such discussions have been even more greatly oversimplified and misleading than discussions regarding Catalonia. Principally, references to the forces behind the referendum are often reduced, ignorantly, to "the Kurds," thereby overlooking the deep divisions within the KRG, much less between the KRG and other parts of Kurdistan. Perhaps the ignorance most problematic of all is the radical difference between Barzani's nationalist project of "self-determination" and the tactics and strategy of the Kurdish freedom movement, including the PKK and the revolutionary forces in control in Rojava, which takes its inspiration from the imprisoned leader Abdullah Öcalan and his program and model of "democratic confederalism".

Democratic confederalism is a radical democratic project based on citizens' assemblies, defended by citizens' militias. It is a program which constitutes a radical reconceptualization of self-determination, one defined in terms of direct democracy against the State. It reconceptualises "self-determination" in a way that renounces as divisive and utopian the equation of the struggle for national freedom with the goal of an independent nation-state, and seeks to overcome the danger of majority tyranny by institutionalizing a "revolutionary-consociational" regime. Its "social contract" guarantees multi-ethnic, multi-linguistic, and multi-religious accommodation by implementing quotas for political representation (concretely, in Rojava, for Arabs and Assyrian Christians), by direct assemblies of different constituent groups, and by mobilizing these groups into their own militias of self-defence. At the same time, democratic confederalism is a radical democratic project which also emphasises gender emancipation, and implements a model of co-presidency and a quota system that enforces gender equality in all forms of political representation, by organizing women's assemblies and women's academies, and by mobilizing women into their own militia for self-defence. Finally, democratic confederalism is a radical democratic project which stresses the importance of "social ecology" and environmental sustainability—in a place, note, where the soil bleeds oil. Indeed, in striking contrast to Barzani's project of "self-determination," Öcalan and the Kurdish freedom movement's democratic confederal project constitutes the only feasible alternative to the negative dialectic of tyranny and chaos currently engulfing the region. Theirs is a project that combines radical democracy, self-defence, multi-cultural and multi-religious accommodation, gender emancipation, and social ecology. Theirs is a real road map for peace in the Middle East, and beyond—perhaps even for Catalonia and Spain, where the CUP and the *Comunes*, as well as the broader Spanish Left, could all certainly learn a thing or two from the valiant example of the revolutionary sisters and brothers in the Kurdish freedom movement. As Abdullah Öcalan powerfully put the point, in a moment of critical self-reflection while trying to explain the motivations behind his principled renunciation of the goal of an independent nation-state:

> If I am guilty of anything, then it is the fact that I accepted the culture of power and war. I became part of it since I was almost religiously convinced that we needed a State to become free, and that, therefore, we had to fight a war. Only few of those who fight for freedom and for the oppressed can save themselves from this disease. Thus, I have not only become guilty in the eyes of the ruling system but also with respect to the struggle for freedom for which I have given all I had.[3]

References:

1. Thomas Jeffrey Miley, "The perils and promise of self-determination," *ROAR Magazine*, October 21, 2017. https://bit.ly/2to2zl9

2. Más de 3.000 empresas han llevado su sede fuera de Cataluña desde el referéndum [More than 3,000 companies have moved their headquarters out of Catalonia since the referendum], *El País*, December 31, 2017. https://bit.ly/2IkwXkI

3. Abdullah Öcalan, *In Defence of the People*, 2004.

PART SIX:

Geopolitics, Dilemmas, and the Scramble for the Middle East

Selected Interventions Mostly from the Panel "Consolidating Peace, Democracy, and Human Rights after Raqqa: Prospects for the Region and the Kurds"
14th Annual EUTCC Conference, European Parliament, Strasbourg, December 7, 2017

(Video recording of the full conference
is available at: https://bit.ly/2h5Rz6Q)

Regional and Global Power Politics in the Syrian Conflict

Jonathan Steele, Foreign Correspondent

Speech Delivered at the 14th Annual EUTCC Conference

Brussels, Dec. 7, 2016

If you forget the Arab-Israeli conflict for a moment, the recent history of the Middle East has been remarkably free of war. Tension between regional countries has frequently been bitter, but the various powers' rivalries and suspicions have stopped short of unleashing outright war. The two exceptions, both caused by the Iraqi dictator Saddam Hussein, are Saddam's invasions of Iran in 1980 and Kuwait in 1990, and his attacks on the Kurds of Iraq. So too was the US-led invasion of Iraq in 2003, a war which was entirely instigated and managed against a sovereign Arab country by an outside power. There was no direct involvement by Arab armies themselves.

In 2011 things changed. The Syrian conflict turned a new page in the history of the modern Middle East. What began as an internal uprising became, for the first time, a war with massive external interference—giving rise to a new piece of terminology, the phrase "proxy war". No foreign armies were openly engaged in Syria but several foreign governments saw fit to militarize and expand the conflict by supporting and arming mercenaries and other non-state actors.

It is an alarming precedent which threatens the peace of the entire region and creates massive difficulties and complications for those who would like to find diplomatic solutions.

There have been five stages in the disastrous growth of outside intervention in Syria.

Stage one involved Saudi Arabia, Qatar, and the United Arab Emirates in funding and encouraging foreign fighters to move into Syria from 2012 onwards to confront the Syrian government's army. They were supported by Turkey, which allowed fighters to move freely across its long border into Syria.

As US Vice-President Joe Biden put it in October 2014, "The Turks … the Saudis, the Emirates, etc., what were they doing? They were so determined to take down (Syrian President Bashar al) Assad and essentially have a proxy Sunni-Shia war—what did they do? They poured hundreds of millions of dollars and tens of thousands of tons of weapons into anyone who would fight against Assad."

Biden's comments were an important confirmation of what had long been reported by journalists, but they were also disingenuous. He spoke as though the United States was an innocent bystander in the Syrian conflict. In fact, the United States was as much involved in the war as Turkey and the Gulf Arabs were. Along with Britain and France the Americans had supported the armed insurgency from its outset. They tried to select groups of Syrian fighters who could be described as secular and non-sectarian rather than jihadists. These included the so-called Free Syrian Army, even though it contained supporters of the Muslim Brotherhood and other Sunni groups which had long opposed Assad's Alawite regime. In addition to their military aid, the United States and its allies formed the Friends of Syria international support group, which cut diplomatic links with Damascus and called on Assad to resign. This created another significant precedent. Not since the Second World War had there been anything comparable in the Middle East—a group of Western countries unashamedly backing the rebel side in a civil war in an Arab country.

It was not surprising that in order to counter this external interference, Syria's main supplier of tanks, war-planes and other military equipment, Russia stepped up its arms deliveries to Assad. Iran also sent weaponry. From 2012 onwards Iran and the Lebanese militia, Hezbollah, also sent fighters to help the Syrian army, initially as trainers but increasingly in a combat role as well.

The second stage of the foreign intervention in Syria began in the summer of 2014 when Barack Obama ordered the United States Air Force to begin bombing in Syria and put together a coalition of European and Arab states to take part in the air campaign alongside the Americans. The target was Islamic State fighters, and not the Syrian government's forces or assets, but the insertion of US air power marked another dramatic escalation of the war. The Syrian conflict was no longer just a proxy conflict. It now involved the direct and illegal violation of a foreign country's sovereignty, since the US-led coalition had not been invited by the Syrian government nor did it have UN Security Council backing.

The US also took an interest in the Kurdish militias in Rojava in northern Syria, seeing them as the best "boots on the ground" to counter IS militants in Raqqa and other areas along the Euphrates valley. IS had begun as an anti-US movement during the US occupation on Iraq but with the departure of US troops at the end of 2011 IS developed ambitions to become the principal defender of Sunni interests against the Shia-led government in Baghdad. After 2012 it also set itself the aim of seizing power in Syria too.

The United States was caught in a dilemma of its own making. Should it prioritise the fight against IS or the removal of Assad? Throughout 2013 and 2014 it followed both goals. The Kurds of northern Syria, the YPG militias, were supported as useful allies for both purposes. From the summer of 2015 and onwards, the US began to deploy special forces on the ground in Syria to arm and train the YPG.

Stage three of the Syrian conflict began at the end of September, 2015, when Russia's president Vladimir Putin sent his own air force into action in a bid to help the Syrian army resist the advance of rebel forces in Syria's heartland, the north–south line of cities which runs from Aleppo, via Hama and Homs, to Damascus.

The Russian intervention made a crucial contribution to Assad's fortunes and, by the end of 2016, the Syrian government's army, aided by Hezbollah and Iranian militias, had recaptured the rebel-held areas of Aleppo and Homs. Most of the Damascus suburbs were also brought back under government control.

What began as a conflict fought largely, at least on the rebel side, by non-state actors had become a hybrid conflict. On the ground foreign governments' special forces were in action alongside non-state actors on the rebel side while Russian and Iranian special forces and Hezbollah were helping the Syrian army. In the air, foreign air forces were also in action. What made the conflict even more complex and dangerous was that while the US and Russian air forces ostensibly had the same goal, namely the destruction of IS, the US had a second goal. It also hoped to see the removal of Assad. The risk of clashes between the two air forces remains ever-present.

Now let me come to stage four of the Syrian conflict—the insertion of Turkish forces. In August 2016 they entered northern Syria and captured the city of Jarabulus. In November, there were further Turkish moves when their planes and artillery helped rebel forces seize the town of al-Bab. Turkey's invasion was not aimed primarily at supporting the rebels in their struggle against the Assad regime. The purpose was to prevent the Kurdish YPG from linking Rojava to the largely Kurdish area of Afrin in north-western Syria. If they succeeded the Kurds would have forces along Turkey's entire southern border with Syria.

Thanks to the Astana negotiating process, which brings Russia, Iran and Turkey together in an effort to work out local ceasefires, the Turks have now gained a third foothold. They have been authorised to set up a so-called de-escalation zone in the north-western province of Idlib. This gives them authority to deploy military police there.

Finally, as if the role of foreign governments in the Syrian conflict was not big enough already, a new menace emerged in 2017. Long-simmering tensions between Saudi Arabia and Iran over several regional issues reached fever pitch. Saudi military had intervened in Yemen in 2015 using the claim that it was necessary to forestall Iran's growing influence there. In November 2017, this was followed by direct Saudi interference in Lebanese politics. Under Saudi pressure Saad Hariri resigned as Lebanese prime minister, plunging the country's politics into turmoil. The Saudi argument was that Iran's ally, Hezbollah, was dominating Lebanon and that this should no longer be tolerated. Hariri later defied the Saudis by suspending his resignation.

In conclusion, let me say that the paradox of the Syrian conflict is that even as the intervention by outside powers has grown more intense the actual course of the fighting on the ground has become somewhat simpler. The power of Daesh, the so-called Islamic State group, has been dramatically reduced. They have lost almost all the territory they had won since 2014. The main beneficiaries have been the YPG and the Kurds of Rojava, who have borne the brunt of the struggle against Da'esh. Meanwhile, in the rest of Syria major advances have been made against the non-Da'esh opposition forces by the Syrian government's army and its allies.

This potentially opens the way for a peace deal between the Syrian opposition and the government, provided both sides are willing to make compromises. The opposition is in the weaker position on the battlefield and in terms of diplomacy.

It will have to accept that Assad is going to stay in power at least until the next elections, due in 2021. For his part, Assad should offer some members of the opposition a share in power in some sort of government of national unity.

Russia supports a compromise on these lines. Whether the opposition is willing to support one depends on the United States and its Gulf allies. They may prefer to continue a war of attrition against Assad rather than admit publicly that they have failed in their main aim of toppling him. Accepting defeat is always hard.

The Kurds face a separate dynamic. Their primary concern is not who governs in Damascus, but what sort of policy is pursued by the Syrian government, whoever the government consists of. Will Damascus accept that Syria's Constitution needs to be reformed so as to permit a substantial degree of decentralisation which allows for autonomy for different regions of the country on a federal basis? Assad has made it clear that he wants to restore his sovereignty throughout the country, but his foreign minister, Walid Moallem, has also talked about the option of local autonomy. This upsets Turkey and is probably not welcome in Iran either. Is it a bargaining chip to get the Kurds to withdraw from Raqqa? How will the Trump administration react? There have already been reports that the US is cutting its aid to the YPG. Will Washington press the YPG to give Raqqa back to the Assad regime or will they insist on actual concessions from Damascus before they do so?

I'm sorry to raise so many questions and leave them unanswered. But we have to be realistic. The complexity of the Syrian conflict makes it hard to predict anything. There are only three certainties. ISIS has been defeated. The Assad regime is winning the war in Syria's urban heartland. The third certainty is that, however much the international context has changed in the last twelve month, the human tragedy facing Syrians remains acute. Millions are still displaced from their homes. The material destruction of towns and cities is huge.

The War on Terror and Europe's Refugee Crisis

Thomas Jeffrey Miley, Lecturer of Political Sociology at Cambridge University
Speech Delivered at the 14th Annual EUTCC Conference
Brussels, 7 December, 2017

Thank you very much for giving me the opportunity to speak in this forum about such an important issue: the question of the war on terror and its relationship to the refugee crisis and, what I would say, a crisis of European values. People talked yesterday about NATO as a community of values. The European Union likes to think of itself as a community of values standing up for human rights and democracy. But I think that recent events show a much uglier side of what the European project has become, what the NATO project certainly is about, and what it means for people struggling for self-determination. Self-determination, in the way that the Kurdish movement is valiantly struggling for—an alternative to the tyranny and chaos in the Middle East, but also around the globe. The tyranny unleashed by the contradictions of capitalist modernity, as Abdullah Öcalan would put it.

But I want to focus on what is happening in Europe, because what is happening in Europe is ultimately also very crucial for the plight of the Kurds in Turkey, and the plight of the Kurds in Europe.

A first piece of news which I think is very indicative of what's happening is the stabbing of a mayor in a small town in Germany less than a month ago. It was a politically-motivated stabbing of the mayor, and it was motivated by the fact that this mayor had stood up, had taken a stance in favour of refugees. And this comes on the heels of the unprecedented success in the elections of the neo-fascist right in Germany, which is not an isolated incident in the European context. We have a resurgent, xenophobic, racist nationalist right. It is resurgent in Denmark, in France, in Hungary, in Poland, in Finland, in Austria, in Sweden, in Greece, not to mention Brexit, where I am living, in the United Kingdom, and the United States with Donald Trump, where I am a citizen.

So this is a global trend, the resurgent neo-fascist right in the heart of these communities that present themselves as the standard-bearers of human rights and democracy. And this is a systemic problem. It's not isolated. It's happening across Europe and beyond, and it's linked to two issues—two policies which are firmly entrenched—the first being policies, let's say, of plutocratic plunder. So the plutocrats are colluding to undermine the historic class compromise that marked the era of the post-war period in Europe, during the more benevolent side and story of the European project, of expanding social rights, expanding the welfare state, etc., etc. So this more benevolent image of the European State and what Europe stands for is being undermined by a politics of neoliberal austerity—indeed, of plutocratic plunder.

This on the one hand. And then also, crucially, the warmongering that has been going on for the last two decades now, at least. The war on terror. It is an

Orwellian war on terror, and I want to hone in and talk about the ramifications of the insidious logic of the war on terror, and how it affects the Kurdish freedom movement in particular.

So, with respect to the refugee crisis, what we see that is particularly indicative is the dirty deal between the European Union and president Erdoğan, which is now a year-and-a-half into existence, and it's a dirty deal which, in many respects, undermines the narrative of the European Union holding a carrot of accession in front of the Turkish State, urging it to converge with democratic norms, human rights' norms, etc. This is, I think, an oversimplification, and I'll have more things to say about what the real record of the European Union is in the dynamics in Turkey.

But nevertheless, there was some element of truth in this, and now this has been reversed very much, and we see a state of affairs where there is much conflict between the European Union and Turkey, but also a situation in which President Erdoğan has an ability to blackmail the European Union with respect to this question. Given the toxic ideological climate in Europe, and this idea that there can be no more refugees in Europe, even though in reality a very small number of refugees around the globe are in the rich countries in general, but in the European Union in particular. I think that the figures are 85% of global refugees are in so-called "developing" countries. So what that means is that in the countries that did a lot to cause the problems in places where people are fleeing from, and that in these countries, as well, that have the most resources, there is the least amount of political will to deal with this refugee question.

And in fact, at a moment where you have a severe authoritarian turn in Turkish politics, President Erdoğan has a kind of stick that he can leverage against the European Union.

So what is this dirty deal between the European Union and Turkey mean in practice? A third piece of news from the last couple of weeks. There is a human rights catastrophe going on in the islands of Greece, in which just two weeks ago, last week in fact, Human Rights Watch, among twenty human rights organizations, decried the human rights' situation of these overburdened camps. These refugee camps in the heart of Europe, where Human Rights Watch coordinator, quoted in the Guardian last week says, "This remains a matter of life and death. There is absolutely no excuse for the conditions on the islands right now. Thousands of people crammed into overcrowded and desperately under-resourced facilities. We are in a race against time. Lives will be lost again this winter, unless people are allowed to move in an organized and voluntary fashion to the mainland."

And this situation of these human rights atrocities happening inside of Europe with respect to the treatment of refugees is part and parcel of this deal with Turkey, which is linked to an attempt ultimately to keep refugees out of Europe at all costs. So what does it mean to keep refugees out of Europe? It means that refugees will be elsewhere, obviously also in Turkey—close to 3 million refugees in Turkey.

And what is the plight of the refugees in Turkey? The European Commission has a report on this. It is concerned—some sort of lip service—at least for the human rights situation of these refugees. Estimates from the World Food Program suggest that as many as one in three refugees in Turkey are living below the survival threshold. This means that refugees are not able to cover their most basic needs. And meanwhile, in Turkey, for the last two years there have been tight controls put on the border to stem the flow of refugees into Turkey. And what this has done is to expose civilians fleeing from human rights atrocities to more human rights atrocities, to the dangers of irregular crossings and smuggling networks.

Now, another interesting thing that the European Commission notes is that when we talk about refugees in Turkey, it's not only Syrian refugees in Turkey, but there has also, in the last two years, been a massive wave of Kurdish refugees in Turkey—refugees who are fleeing their homes in the southeast of Turkey, from the Kurdish region in Turkey, because of the war that has been unleashed on the Kurdish population in Turkey. Estimates say around 500,000 people have fled. And this, of course, also affects the Syrian refugees, who are displaced once, and then find themselves in the midst of another war.

And so what we see is that the war on terror, this catastrophic war on terror, which has brought so much chaos to the Middle East, spilling over into Turkey, and also undermining the peace process in Turkey, with grave human rights' consequences. Not only for Syrian refugees, but also for the victims fleeing from state terror—state terror by the Turkish State against its own citizens.

We've already heard the salutations going out to co-chair Demirtaş. Let me just say something, a little bit more about the persecution and plight of the Kurdish freedom movement, not only in Turkey but also in Europe. Because when we talk about the European Union as a community of values, let us not forget that for decades now the Kurdish freedom movement has been persecuted in Europe as well. And this is linked to the insidious logic of the war on terror. And the Kurdish movement finds itself at the core of this war on terror logic, and victims of this war on terror logic in Europe.

Last year as a member of the İmralı delegations, I was in Strasbourg with other delegates trying to intervene, to witness and also to talk to the people in the Council of Europe about the situation. And I just want to end by getting us to think a little about the deeper issues, because when we think about this story, there is a longer history—and then there is what's happening now. I'll just make these two points.

The longer history: in that benevolent story of the European Union giving the carrot of accession in order to achieve compliance with human rights norms, it's often forgotten that at the same time that this stuff is happening over the course of the nineties—into the 2000s, but particularly in the 1990s—it was German arms, German tanks that were crushing Kurdish villages. So at the same time that they are telling this story about human rights and demanding human rights compliance, there is a longer history of complicity with state terror exercised against the Kurdish freedom movement.

And I just want to end with a point about limits, linked to this insidious logic of the war on terror, that trap the European Union, and make it impossible for the European Union to speak with anything close to moral clarity about what's going on in Kurdistan. Instead, what we see is a conflation of the logic of might and the logic of right, and false equivalences between different kinds of groups, as well as a concealment of the reality of state terror. And so this is, I think, part and parcel of a European Union, a Council of Europe, and the "Western" countries, all caught in this paradigm of the war on terror, which is bringing the chickens home to roost, in Europe, and also contributing to the ongoing war on the Kurdish freedom movement.

Dancing with the Devil

Darnell Stephen Summers, US War Veteran and Anti-War Activist
Speech Delivered at the 14th Annual EUTCC Conference
Brussels, December, 2017

Hello, my name is Darnell Stephen Summers. I'm a member of the "Stop The WAR Brigade" and the "Viet Nam Veterans Against the War/OSS". We organize active duty soldiers and veterans from all armies who are opposed to all wars of aggression, plunder and domination.

It's an honor to be here at this event organized by forces in the Kurdish freedom movement. As a black man from the belly of beast, I have a special affinity for the oppressed of other nations—in particular with the Kurds, who have been brutally subjugated by NATO's Gladio. I too have had my run-ins with NATO's Gladio, the secret enforcers of NATO!

I will never forget the hospitality and warm greeting that the Turkish and Kurdish activists gave me in 1982 upon my return to Germany to visit my family while still falsely charged with the murder of a police agent.

From some things that people have said here, it sounds as if the Kurdish movement and the United States are friends. Let us not forget NATO's Gladio and the role of NATO's Gladio in the oppression and the human rights atrocities over decades.

As Abdullah Öcalan emphasized: "NATO's Gladio is the real ruler." Not only that. We must not forget that NATO's Gladio was behind the abduction of Abdullah Öcalan in Kenya. In 1999, after being rejected asylum by many countries and then kidnapped by NATO, Öcalan came truly to see and understand that the enemy was not only Turkey, but also the capitalist world system. His capture, he realized, had been arranged by Israel, the USA, Russia and the EU. Meanwhile the role of the Turkish State was only secondary. As Öcalan explains in the first volume of his book, *Civilization*, "The role that has been assigned to Turkey is to be the vulgar Gendarme, the watch dog and the prison guard of all Middle Eastern peoples in order to make them more susceptible to the oppression and exploitation of the Capitalist System."

My duty and task as a Viet Nam War veteran is to convey to all, in no uncertain terms, the true nature and horror of US/NATO-instigated conflicts and the unbearable suffering that they and their allies have brutally imposed upon humanity. This is a fight for our very survival on this planet, our only home.

There's a quote I would like to share with you. This quote is from US Marine General MG Smedley Butler. He is a two-time recipient of the coveted "Medal of Honor," which is bestowed upon the bravest of the brave:

> I spent 33 years and four months in active military service and during that period I spent most of my time as a high class muscle man for Big Business, for Wall Street and the bankers. In short, I was a racketeer, a gangster for cap-

italism. I helped make Mexico and especially Tampico safe for American oil interests in 1914. I helped make Haiti and Cuba a decent place for the National City Bank boys to collect revenues in. I helped in the raping of half a dozen Central American republics for the benefit of Wall Street. I helped purify Nicaragua for the International Banking House of Brown Brothers in 1902–1912. I brought light to the Dominican Republic for the American sugar interests in 1916. I helped make Honduras right for the American fruit companies in 1903. In China in 1927 I helped see to it that Standard Oil went on its way unmolested. Looking back on it, I might have given Al Capone a few hints. The best he could do was to operate his racket in three districts. I operated on three continents.

US Marines General Smedley's words are powerful and dangerous. They speak a truth that some do not want to hear. That leaves you two choices, either act accordingly or you ignore the cold hard truth. General Smedley's message is clear to me. No one should cooperate with such a government. You put your cause at great risk when you consort with them. They cannot be trusted and they have demonstrated it time and time again throughout history.

General Smedley was talking about events, some of which transpired more than 100 years ago. Fast forward to today and what we are witnessing is the strategic importance of the oil-rich Kirkuk area and the potential for exploiting the other vast mineral deposits of the region and beyond. The imperialists need raw materials for their machine to maintain their way of life. Winner takes all. Keep that in mind as we continue.

The US Military has a long history of soldiers in its own ranks criticizing and fighting actively against US national and foreign policy. It's happening right now. I'm proud to say that I belong to that group of soldiers and veterans. I can say without reservation that I represent the sentiments and interests of many who are actively serving in the military, and the veterans of course. From My Lai to Abu Ghraib, soldiers were the first to expose the crimes of the US War Machine. The murder, the merciless torture, the rape of its prisoners and also of its fellow soldiers.

Desertions in the military number in the tens of thousands and counting. Who wants to die for a criminal and unjust cause? The "War On Terror" is a farce. The coalition has members that terrorize their own citizens on a daily basis. They deny them fundamental human rights. The historical narrative has been doctored from the very beginning to justify mass murder, rape, pillage and plunder, and as we can witness today, most people in America and throughout most of the western world, for that matter, have a distorted and, quite frankly, a childish, flawed and incorrect view of world history.

That condition will put you at a distinct disadvantage when trying to understand today's world and its problems. Add to that the spectre of the corporate media monopoly and you have a recipe for manipulation and deception on a grand scale.

The Viet Nam War was set in a time of great social and political upheaval in the US and abroad. American cities were burning in the fire of rebellion and despair and those conditions still exists today. The Anti-War Movement, the Black Panther Party, the SDS, the Women's Movement were all in full swing—too many to mention them all now. National liberation movements spanned the globe and the European colonial masters were being challenged in a manner that spoke to fundamental change. It was an exciting period and I was there experiencing it in real time. The whole world was in an uproar condemning the Genocide of the Vietnamese People.

Standing together against US imperialism internationally was the rallying point. But as the war dragged on, many US soldiers began to see the lies for what they were and started to rebel. Over 1,000 officers and NCOs were killed by their soldiers during the Viet Nam War—a fact that is not widely known or talked about, and for good reason. They never want the new recruits to know about their treachery and their utter disregard for human life and their lives in particular. They want to write us out of history, but they can't. They want to silence us, but we are too many, too strong. We are here to share our views and give testimony.

The question to be asked is: where are we today in our fight against US imperialism, perpetual war and the constant threat of disaster in all of its forms. Betrayal is an integral part of US foreign policy. Everyone who has eyes and the interest to see should realize that. If you don't realize that, then you're in trouble.

A friend asked me a few weeks ago a difficult question: "What other alternative was there to cooperating with the US coalition in the battle for Kobanê?" For me, any cooperation with thieves and murderers is not an option. It is out of the question. But it seems that a few may find a rationalization to justify coalescing with the US band of criminals. What could be worse than knowing you're going to be betrayed and realizing that there's nothing you can do about it, but yet you acquiesce in the fraud? Even worse is not knowing that your betrayal was inevitable, that it's going to happen and you have no idea about the impending crisis, and you don't have a clue as to what to do. You're just ignoring history. In the end you're just looking at the problem through the bottom of a coke bottle. Everything is distorted, out of focus.

I was born in Detroit Michigan in 1947. A black baby born into a racist society with all that that implies. Relatively speaking that's a long time ago, but for me it feels like yesterday. I grew up in a society that I would grow to despise. I grew up in a society full of hate and hypocrisy, that didn't appreciate or accept my worth as a human being just because of the color of my skin. Not everyone felt that way, but it was the System that gave life to this horrible ordeal. Those conditions can either literally destroy you—and yes, many were destroyed—or inspire you to fight back and end the misery and that system of oppression.

We have a term in America: "Indian giver." It literally means that you give with one hand and you take it back with the other. I first heard that term as a child, and it was a part of my vocabulary. I, and my little playmates, used that despicable term. It was part of the culture. We heard it in the cowboy movies and on television watching as white men depicted themselves as righteous saviours while slaughtering the Indigenous Peoples for the good of humanity. That's the way it was presented. Take a look. If someone didn't keep his word and stole from his friends he was an "Indian giver." We didn't know it then but it wasn't long before we learned that, through our own experience, the "Indian giver" was the US government.

The US presently houses 25% of the world's prison population with the vast majority being People of Color. Some 1.5 million blacks, 600,000 Latinos & 200,000 Whites at last count. That represents at least 25% of the world's prison population, while the US accounts for only 5% of the world population. How can this be? America consistently leads the world in death by gun violence every year. Around 100,000 persons either shot dead or seriously wounded as a result of that situation. America is a society constantly at war with itself. So it is no small wonder that that situation would bleed over to the rest of the world, leaving death and destruction in its wake. Conservatively speaking, the US consumes half of the world's resources just to keep the wasteful juggernaut rolling. I mention these facts to set the stage for understanding the nature of the entity that poses and self-proclaims itself as the protector and leader of the "Free World." Nothing could be further from the truth.

So, what role do they play? It is interesting to note the analysis being disseminated by some in the western media. For instance, Trudy Rubin, syndicated columnist, writes: "A record of abandoning one's allies can come to haunt the betrayer, the US. So the time for Washington to act on the Kurdish question is now. The Iraqi Kurds' dreams of independence, endorsed by a Kurdish referendum last month, have come to a crushing halt. This week the hostile Baghdad government clawed back the key oil town of Kirkuk from Kurdish forces, along with other territory that both sides claim. More important is how Washington deals with the Kurdish issue in the future—in both Iraq and Syria, Kurdish fighters have been crucial US allies against the Islamic State group. … Yet signals from Washington indicate small interest in the Kurds' fate once their fighters are no longer needed."

Ms. Rubin's world-outlook governs the way she formulates her viewpoint. She clearly suggests that the US would be an honest broker in any dialogue between "the Kurds" and the Iraqi government. That's outrageous. Malcolm X once remarked, "You don't take your case to the criminal. No, you take the criminal to court."

But one fact is irrefutable. The Kurdish people have been betrayed on all sides. Intentionally or unintentionally? That is irrelevant. The damage has been done. This, my friends, is a defining moment in more ways than one, considering the fact that some forces want to align themselves with a lunatic regime in the White House. The leadership in the White House is unpredictable with a racist, fascist, sexist, maniacal, warmongering idiot at the titular head of it all. Trump just recently retweeted a post from "Britain First," a right-wing, fascist cesspool. Tell me. "What's on Trump's mind? What's his message?" It's disgusting. Beware. Every day they're rattling their sabre.

"The enemy of my enemy is my friend" is a convoluted argument. At the outset of the Gulf War the US stated in clear terms that the cost of the conflict would be paid for from the expropriated oil plunder of the region: "We will attack you and the victims will pay for it."

Who can doubt the suffering of all the people of Iraq and Afghanistan? The death and destruction. The "collateral damage," as they cynically called it. I haven't forgotten, and you shouldn't either. The US—always deciding who lives and who dies, on a global basis. They brag and boast about their world-wide network of military installations, which allows them to strike at the heart of any nation on the planet with relative ease. Yes, there are limitations to their power, but what power they do possess is a constant threat to any potential for world peace and the ultimate threat to the continued survival of humanity on this planet. Yes, they have allies who aid and abet them, but the US leads the whole pack.

There is very little discussion going on between the anti-war/peace movement and the political organizations fighting for their right to be recognized as a people with a homeland. How will all of these struggles coincide with the spirit of the anti-war/peace movement? We are being pitted against each other. We are sounding the alarm. "The Stop The WAR Brigade" is calling on soldiers to "REFUSE, RESIST & REBEL." The anti-war/peace movement is actively opposing the war plans of the US/NATO alliance, who cynically proclaim to the world that they are trustworthy and responsible allies of certain liberation struggles. Those forces are fighting for self-determination, a noble cause, but not in their allies plans.

Who would deny them the right to live in peace without fear of war, persecution and exploitation and having the right to decide their just future? However, their US/NATO allies are the very people who put them in that situation in the first place. Now that's a paradox.

People can come up with rationalizations to support dancing with the Devil, but those arguments are just not convincing. You pay the Devil now or you pay him later. That's your only option when you deal with them. The bill is invariably paid with someone's blood. Those are the dangers and pitfalls in such an arrangement. You're locked in a death dance with no sense of what the future holds.

Hip Hop has played a major role in culture, worldwide. For many artists it is a platform to expose the ills of society, to offer solutions, to inspire, to enlighten, to criticize, to reflect, and a call to action. I'll leave you with this excerpt from a rap song, from Immortal Technique: "So when the Devil wants to dance with you, you'd better say never. Because a dance with the Devil might last forever."

Delisting the PKK and the Resulting Benefits

Remarks prepared for the 14th annual EUTCC conference.
Michael M. Gunter, Scholar and Secretary General of the EUTCC
Tennessee Technological University
Brussels, 7 December, 2017

US President Donald J. Trump declared during his presidential campaign in 2016: "I'm a big fan of the Kurdish forces. At the same time, I think we have a potentially... very successful relations with Turkey. And it would be really wonderful if we could put them somehow both together." The US working with the Kurds in Syria was very smart, but only tactically in the short run. Strategically, in the long run, it alienated Turkey, the much more important US NATO ally. Thus, as Trump observed, the US needed a new strategy to bring Turkey and the Kurds together. But this was like squaring the circle as the PYD/YPG in Syria was a PKK friend. The US looked hypocritical, claiming the SDF was not the YPG since the SDF largely was. Of course, Turkey too looked hypocritical given its earlier support for ISIS.

So what can the US, the EU, Turkey, and the Kurds do to try to square the circle and bring Turkey and the PKK/PYD Kurds together? The Oslo Talks between Turkey and the PKK from 2008 until May 2011, along with the on-again, off-again Kurdish Opening between 2009 and 2013, and the cease-fire from 2013 until July 2015—although ultimately unsuccessful—demonstrate that it is not impossible to bring the two sides together. Indeed, during the Turkish-PKK ceasefire, the mainline US weekly magazine Time, in its issue of 29 April/6 May, 2013, named the previously obscure Öcalan as one of "the 100 most influential people in the world" and called him a "voice for peace." Previously, such praise would have been inconceivable.

To further this peace project, the EU and US should delist the PKK as a terrorist group and encourage Turkey to do so too. After all, the EU and US largely list the PKK as a terrorist organization to please Turkey. Once the EU and US realize how this prevents peace, they will have an incentive to delist the PKK and encourage Turkey to do so, too, for its own good and to renew the peace process. After all, one does not normally negotiate with terrorists or expect to do so seriously by calling the other side such names. Too often the term "terrorist" is used mainly for political reasons to brand one's opponent as illegitimate, and largely that is so in this case. For example, for more than a quarter of a century, the United States so branded Nelson Mandela and his African National Congress. Indeed, although the US lists the PKK as a terrorist organization, the US still supported the PKK affiliate PYD/YPG against ISIS in Syria and even worked directly with the PKK in the Sinjar region in Iraq against ISIS to save the Yezidis in the summer of 2014. In the past the US has also listed Fidel Castro's Cuba, the Mujahedin-E Khalq, and even the KRG's [Kurdistan Regional Government's]

Barzani and Talabani as terrorists for narrow political reasons. Again the political nature of the usage of the term terrorist is obvious.

Delisting the PKK will encourage both Turkey and the PKK to renew peace negotiations, which if successful would alleviate one of Turkey's long-standing security/political/economic/social problems. Once the PKK is delisted, both Turkey and the PKK will be challenged this time to take up the mantle of negotiations more seriously and responsibly. However, if it does not work, the PKK can always be relisted.

What went wrong with the earlier ceasefire? When the HDP won 13% of the vote for the Turkish parliament in the elections of 7 June, 2015, it helped deny Erdoğan's AKP a new ruling majority. Erdoğan successfully calculated, in the short run at least, that he could regain his majority by turning on the Kurds and appealing to the Turkish ultra-nationalists. The HDP leader Demirtaş is also partially to blame for what happened because he needlessly provoked Erdoğan by declaring that the HDP would not allow Erdoğan to become as constitutionally strong a president as he wanted. In retrospect, it might have been better for the HDP leader not to have said this, but instead try to work with Erdoğan as he consolidated his power. Instead, Erdoğan perceived Demirtaş' declaration as a threat and contributed to this turning on the HDP and eventually imprisoning Demirtaş and other HDP leaders, as well as renewing the war against the PKK.

Delisting the PKK might also encourage Turkey not to view Rojava and the PYD/YPG with such hostility because, once Turkish-PKK peace negotiations begin again, Turkey would also be prone to deal more peacefully with the PKK friend PYD/YPG. This would also help lessen the US-Turkish quarrel over US support for the PYD/YPG. Even more, for the Kurds, this would pay dividends because once ISIS is defeated—an event about to happen in Syria—the US is likely to drop its support for Rojava and the PYD. In the long run Rojava and the PYD need an understanding with Turkey because the US is not always going to be there to help. The analogy with what just happened to the KRG should be obvious!

As already mentioned, the US has worked with the PKK friend PYD/YPG very successfully in Syria and even the PKK itself to help save the Yezidis in Iraq's Sinjar region despite the US officially branding the PKK as terrorist. Therefore, delisting the PKK would help renew the peace negotiations between Turkey and the PKK, brighten Rojava's long-term prospects, and help end the NATO crisis between the US and Turkey. Delisting the PKK would be a bold, imaginative move by the EU and US that would contribute to the Turkish-Kurdish peace process.

How might these new Turkish-PKK negotiations proceed? While Turkish territorial integrity must be maintained, some Turkish state decentralization is in order to satisfy the Kurds' legitimate right to local self-government or what the PKK terms "democratic autonomy." The Kurds should be recognized as a people, with all legitimate rights. This should be written in the Turkish

Constitution. Indeed, over-centralization of the State is a bane that many other modern states have sought to adjust. Most large states have decentralized today to achieve greater efficiency. The US, UK, Germany, even France and Spain (despite the current crisis involving Catalonia) have effectively done so.

Such provisions for the Kurds will not destroy Turkey, but actually make it stronger by strengthening the loyalty of its ethnic Kurdish population, the majority of which already lives west of Ankara, Istanbul being the largest Kurdish city in the world. Most ethnic Kurds in Turkey do not desire to secede from Turkey. The United States, European Union, United Nations, NATO, and the KRG should eventually be brought in as witnesses and guarantors of these new Turkish constitutional principles. However, Turkey presently does not want to acknowledge collective rights for its ethnic Kurds, and is willing to grant merely limited individual rights such as mother-tongue language in the schools and a Kurdish TV channel.

In addition, a Truth and Reconciliation Commission should be established as was done in South Africa. The permanent cessation of hostilities, the fate of PKK fighters, and provisions for post-conflict security, among others, should also be considered. On the other hand, US support to Turkey in an attempt to assassinate PKK leader Cemil Bayık, an idea floated in the summer of 2017, is not a good idea. Historically, the PKK has used little violence against third parties. This would surely end if the US helped kill Bayık.

Currently, the US State Department mainly supports Turkey to keep its NATO ally in the alliance, while the US Defense Department largely supports the PYD/YPG to fight ISIS in Syria. I am recognized as a supporter of the Kurds for all the well-known reasons of democracy, justice, self-determination, etc. However, my writings also testify to my defense of Turkey. As James F. Jeffrey, the former US ambassador to Turkey and Iraq, has said, "We are just bred on the importance of Turkey." However, as President Trump has also said: "We should bring Turkey and the Kurds together." As difficult as this will be, I have suggested some ways to get started by delisting the PKK.

Consolidating Peace, Democracy and Human Rights after Raqqa: Prospects for the Region and the Kurds

Panel Discussion at the 14th Annual EUTCC Conference
European Parliament, Brussels, 7 December, 2017

MEP Takis Hadjigeorgiou, Confederal Group of the European United Left, Nordic Green Left (moderator): People who are not very familiar with the problems of the issue, they think—and maybe they are a bit naïve—that the Kurds have to initiate a new movement as Kurds from Turkey, from Iran, from Iraq, from Syria, a new movement towards one State. Because now, we all of us know that the Kurds are a very, very divided people. The Kurds from Iraq have different views on their own future than the Kurds in Turkey, and the Kurds in Iran have different views for their future than the Kurds in Syria. Is there any possibility for this new movement which will, in my view, create the atmosphere and the spirit needed to combine forces in order to see a better future for all of them?

That's the first question, and the second one is, do you think that in the United States there are think tanks who believe in the division of Turkey, towards the idea of creating a new state for Kurds within Turkey, or without Turkey, or outside of Turkey, to put it in a better way? And I think sometimes that the Americans—and I mean here the American government, and not only the one that is now in power but also the previous one—I think that they don't work on the idea of dividing Turkey, but I believe, though, that they will welcome such a development. So please, if someone can deliver on these very extreme ideas, maybe, to give us a new element to the discussion. Thank you.

Michael Gunter: Well, I don't know if I fully, completely understood that question, but the idea of think tanks in the US—the US is a huge country, and we have, as you just heard in this panel, a variety of different opinions from Americans, so maybe there are think tanks that want to divide Turkey. But of the mainline think tanks that I have recently dealt with in Washington, and there are many of them, I would say two things: (1) I've seen nothing about dividing Turkey. The problem the think tanks have in Washington would be that, as we heard from David Phillips yesterday, there is a deep feeling of betrayal in the United States, on the part of Turkey's support for ISIS in earlier years.

And one thing that Mr. Phillips did not mention that has deeply disturbed American military and political authorities is that the Turks have recently revealed, printed in Sabah, one of the few remaining newspapers in Turkey, locations of American, supposedly secret, military installations in Northern Syria—opening these installations up to being attacked by enemies, and even getting Americans killed. And US people say, what kind of ally is that?

And of course, Turkey is also a member of NATO. What kind of ally in NATO is buying its military equipment from Russia, when all the NATO equipment is supposed to be integrated among the NATO allies? So, what I have seen among think tanks in the United States is a deep disappointment at the best, and even a hatred of what Turkey has done. And there is even some talk of kicking Turkey out of NATO. I am not quite sure how that would be done. I don't think NATO actually has a procedure for delisting a member of NATO. But anyway, those are my impressions. Thank you.

Thomas Jeffrey Miley: So, I am not an expert on the state of opinion inside of US think tanks. But I do think that there is concern about the future of Turkey that you've heard expressed yesterday by people closer to the foreign policy establishment than myself. And I think this goes back ultimately to the decision, what was it, in 2002, by Erdoğan that the United States could not use Turkish bases for the illegal, criminal invasion of Iraq. So I do think that some of the concerns about Turkey are linked to those sorts of questions, which I think are important to not overlook. Just because of the fact that the Kurdish freedom movement is so brutally pummelled by Turkey, not all of the reasons why the United States is opposed to Turkey are legitimate or just ones.

But with respect to the question of a united Kurdistan, I think we are here talking about the alternative to tyranny and chaos in the Middle East. And I think it is really important to stress a few things about Abdullah Öcalan's vision of what Kurdish self-determination can mean in the twenty-first century, along the lines of a democratic confederal model. I think Öcalan will go down in history as making a very important contribution to rethinking and reformulating what self-determination can mean in the twenty-first century.

So why the Kurds? Why are the Kurds at the centre of so much of this discussion? Why are they on the receiving end of so much state violence? This has to do with them being situated across these, in many ways, historically illegitimate borders that were drawn by the Imperialist powers at the end of the First World War. And Öcalan came to the conclusion that the dream of a Greater Kurdistan, and the dream of a Greater Kurdish nation-state, was in fact just an inflection, so to speak, of the same kind of nation-state mentality that had inflicted so much suffering on the Kurds.

So he has re-articulated what self-determination means, so that it is not about changing borders, and it's not about trying to get a nation-state for the Kurds; but it's about radical democracy against the State, radically democratizing the State, and we move towards something like a confederation of peoples in the Middle East governing themselves democratically, rather than thinking of it as all of the different ethnic peoples need to create a state of their own, and then repeat on a smaller level the same kinds of atrocities against the different minorities amongst them. So I think that re-articulation of self-determination in a way that moves it away from the goal of a Greater Kurdistan, I think is a very important contribution that other people have mentioned.

And I think it's an important issue, that a lot of people don't understand this, as you see, the Human Rights' Commissioner talking about the "separatist" forces in Turkey. It's very important to understand that the Kurdish freedom movement, for over a decade now, has—not just for tactical reasons, but for reasons that have been very well articulated, and explained as a matter of principle—rescinded this idea of a Greater Kurdish nation-state as the goal, or what it means to achieve self-determination.

Question from Federike Geerdink (journalist, the Netherlands): My question is about the referendum outcome in South Kurdistan. There were some significant differences between different parts—some with over 90% yes, others around 80%. I wonder if many people voted not "yes" because of a protest against the whole procedure of the KDP [Kurdistan Democratic Party]. I also wonder how many did not vote or voted "no" because they are against the nation-state as such and they don't want that for Bashur.

Michael Gunter: The referendum, to me, is somewhat troubling. I think there is a misunderstanding here. This was not a referendum on declaring independence. It was sort of the voice of the people recommending that the KRG pursue negotiations with Baghdad. It was not an out-and-out declaration of independence. Now the KRG, the Kurds, have been without a state for over a hundred years, after the modern creation of the state system after World War I in the Middle East. Barzani has specifically said for the last four years that he is thinking about calling a referendum.

Frankly I think that if Baghdad had not had the excuse of the referendum, Baghdad would have found another reason to intervene. Now, it is true that the referendum turned out to be a disaster; but how are the Kurds ever going to become independent? So many people say, when will you give us our independence? Well I'll tell you, nobody's going to give you your independence. You're going to take your independence. And to some extent, you know, I made a mistake here too, I admit it. But I thought maybe the time was ripe to move toward independence.

Now, it turned out the time was not right, and Barzani made some crucial mistakes. But these were mistakes of the heart, and these were mistakes of omission. This was not the kind of a mistake that was an error of commission, where he should not have thought of the dirty idea of independence. Independence is for the Kurds, they deserve it, and they are going to get it. It is a temporary setback. But Kurds always climb out of the hole and come back again to please us.

Question from audience: My question to you, Michael Gunter, is: so you want the PKK to be delisted. So I give a comparison with an organisation that was on the terror list in America but was delisted, the Mujahedin-e Khalq, which had done things directly against the interests of Americans. Whereas the PKK has never, for instance, been involved in assassinations or anything against the American personnel, nowhere. On the other hand, we have also this problem of duplicity on the other side of the border—they are supporting the friends of PKK, according to your own description. So how can it be processed? How can you work in the United States to get the United States to delist the PKK? Because if the United States does that, the European Union does it the day after. Thank you.

Michael Gunter: Thank you for your question. I think on this issue of delisting terrorist organisations, it should be a one-by-one process. I am not qualified really to talk about the Mujahedin-e's terrorism, but I do think my point was valid—the United States has used this terrorism list again and again for narrow political reasons rather than legitimate reasons. And we heard it today, one person's terrorist is another person's freedom fighter. There is no definition of terrorism. It is simply a political propaganda term many times, not always, I think ISIS, we can agree, was legitimately considered a terrorist movement. But many times this word terrorism is a narrow political term used for political propagandistic reasons. And largely I think that is so for the PKK. I simply suggested that if we want to seriously start up peace negotiations again, one step would be to take the PKK off the terrorism list. I think the United States should take the lead, because if the US takes PKK off the terrorist list, then Turkey will be encouraged to do so too. If we wait for Turkey to do it first, we'll wait forever.

Darnell Stephen Summers: I would like to comment on the statement that Professor Gunter made. There certainly is a definition for terrorism. And the way I interpreted your statement, it was like a back-door out for the United States. Because I am assuming that you would not designate the United States a terrorist organisation. As I said, I am a Viet Nam veteran; and certainly what went on in Viet Nam, and I talked specifically about that, was a state of terrorism, in every regard. I, along with many other Viet Nam veterans are applying for compensation for being contaminated with Agent Orange. Not only did they spray it as a defoliant, to ostensibly reveal the supply routes of the so-called enemy; they also sprayed it on us, without our knowledge. And I'll just read the definition: "The use of violence and threats to intimidate or coerce, especially for political purposes." There is a working definition of terrorism. No-one can say we don't have a definition for terrorism, or we cannot define it. I mean, it's in our colloquial speech, it's in the dictionary, it's in articles, it's everywhere. And the war on terror, what are we talking about? You know, so, the United States, and we say it—you may disagree or agree—it is the biggest terrorist organisation on this planet, in the history of this planet. With all of its crimes, you know, since its inception. You know, slavery is terrorism! Genocide is terrorism! War is terrorism! Exploitation, you know, I mean, I could go on and on and on. We are not going to let them go out the back door, you know, because that seems to be the underlying concept of your statement, all right. And I wish you would clarify that please.

Michael Gunter: Very briefly, this is a conference on the Kurds, not the United States, and certainly not the Viet Nam War. So I will have to not go into that. I think, recently, the Ken Burns documentary on the Viet Nam War, which—I don't know how much you've seen that in Europe—but, it's excellent. It shows both sides to the issue. And there is no doubt that my country has committed many sins in the past. But when you look at the overall history of the United States, over the two hundred years of its existence, I don't think there is any better force for humanity, human rights and decency in this world than the United States, and I'm not going to back off of that statement.

Question from audience: Talking about getting united among the Kurds, we have to improve and bring all the Kurds together. But we mentioned, fighting the terrorists we get together and then we are all equal, and we know, we haven't seen any terrorist attempts in the Kurdish region. But my question is, I agree with the speaker who mentioned that we are dancing with the Devil. The United States is supporting Syrian Kurds, maybe showing sympathy for Selahattin Demirtaş in Turkey; but on the other hand, they are targeting the PKK. We shouldn't dance with the Devil, that's what I think.

Thomas Jeffrey Miley: Can I just say one thing with respect to people talking along the lines of unity among Kurds? One concrete step towards that would be to end the brutal embargo on Rojava, which, as far as I know, the KRG continues. So, to appeal abstractly to the unity of the Kurdish nation is one thing, but on the ground, since we are here talking about democratic alternatives, we have to ask the question, why has not the KRG been able to behave in a democratic fashion? And it's linked to the way in which they are inserted into capitalist modernity. So I think it is very important to keep Öcalan's vision of what this democratic alternative is, and when the conversation becomes a conversation about how we can organize to achieve a Kurdish State, I think we are going very much against the spirit of Öcalan's idea—that we want a democratic alternative which moves beyond what he would term "feudal nationalism"—to think about democracy—democracy as an alternative to capitalist modernity.

Question from the audience: Thanks for allocating time for me, addressing a question to the broad panel. In fact, I was motivated by a comment by Mr. Gunter, about what would have happened if Mr. Demirtaş had chosen to collaborate or work with Erdoğan. It was a question which was left open, but made me wonder if there is any possibility for Kurds to imagine a future in the four parts of Kurdistan, even in Turkey, across the Middle East—a counterpart to work with. It is a two-fold question: first, can we imagine a situation in which Erdoğan is pushed towards the lanes of democracy again, and turn into a legal counterpart, together with the Kurds, considering the prospects for the region? If not, to what faces should Kurds turn themselves? In other words, whom can we expect Kurds to work with in Middle East, in order to constitute peace and democracy in Middle East?

Jonathan Steele: On the question of whether Demirtaş should have worked with Erdoğan, I think I have a slight disagreement with Professor Gunter about the timing of this, because the Dolmabahçe Accords, as I understood, broke down in February, 2015, four months before the election of June, 2015, which you had said was the reason why Erdoğan had turned against the HDP. I think that Erdoğan had turned against the peace process long before the elections, four months before. He may have been worried that the HDP was growing in strength and might do well in the elections—that's possible. So there is a potential connection with the elections, but the sequence of events was a bit different from the way it was described. But how can that be reversed? I don't know.

Sorry, I also think it is true that Demirtaş did make some rather provocative statements after winning 13% of the vote in the June, 2015, elections, so perhaps that is correct that he should have been a bit more diplomatic and said he would work with Erdoğan in some way, but he didn't agree with the authoritarian presidency and was against the idea of a referendum. So there are nuances there of diplomacy and tact which could have been followed better. But the basic understanding is, I think, that Erdoğan had decided for other reasons to stop the peace process. He just didn't think it was productive from his point of view.

Who can the Kurds work with? It is very difficult. They have to work on their own, I think, and they've shown fantastic initiative, and example, and energy, in creating this democratic confederalism system in Rojava, which they are also trying to do in the southeast of Turkey—when they were able to do it before the repression became so massive. I think the Kurds have to rely largely on themselves, and they have done a much better job in doing that than most other small minorities in the world.

Thomas Jeffrey Miley: Can I just say one thing with respect to this question of the relation between the HDP and the authoritarian turn in Turkey? I think it would be a terrible thing for the HDP to be complicit with this authoritarian turn in Turkey, because it's not just a question of Kurds for themselves. It's also a question about politics—politics of left versus right. And the future of the Kurdish project, the Kurdish freedom movement's project, is inextricably intertwined with the future of freedom in Turkey, freedom in the Middle East more generally, and so it has to be in coalition—as the HDP has very valiantly done—trying to make coalitions with, and reinvigorate, the broader Turkish and Arab lefts.

Last question, from Rahila Gupta: This is a question for the whole panel. It's a somewhat speculative question about the future of Syria. Assad wants to assert his sovereignty over the whole country, it is quite likely that he might attack the DFNS [Democratic Federation of Northern Syria] or Rojava, and I understand from informal conversations with PYD members that they would be prepared to take on the challenge to fight back, to fight Assad. And if that was the case, is it likely that the US might re-engage? Because it was always their aspiration to get rid of Assad, but they had such unreliable allies on the ground that they've given up on that and Russia has taken the upper hand. But is it likely that we might be entering another, very dangerous stage in the war in Syria?

Michael Gunter: Okay, very briefly, Syria has been a Hobbesian war of all against all, so anything is possible. What you said is true: the United States would like to get rid of Assad, but I don't think this is Trump's top aim. I think an even more likely situation that could get the United States more involved in Syria is Iranian influence. The Iranians are very influential in Syria right now, and the United States—and Trump has said so repeatedly—the United States is going to oppose Iran. Trump's not talking about doing that against Assad. And also Israel is not going to tolerate an Iranian force on the Israeli border. So anything's possible in Syria, but I think the Iranian situation is maybe the most immediate thing that might call forth US and Russian and Turkish—Turkey is very opposed to Iran, too. So all these things are possible, yes.

Jonathan Steele: I'll just say a few words in answer to your question. I was in Damascus in September, three months ago. And I was told by Samir Suleiman, who is the Deputy Head of the Syrian Army's political administration. He said, "We don't recognise the Kurdish forces"—so he was very dismissive—"and we have no coordination with them. But they are there and the US supports them." So the implication of what he was saying is that we will not challenge them because the US is behind them. And also Bouthaina Shaaban, another person I managed to interview in Damascus in September, said, "This small force"—very demeaning about the YPG and YPJ—"this small force does not express the opinion of all the Kurds in Syria. Millions of Kurds in Syria are very good citizens, who want the unity of Syria, and the sovereignty and territorial integrity of Syria. So—very patronising comments. So it shows that the rhetoric is very anti-YPG, but the reality of the Syrian government at the moment is that they are not going to confront the YPG, I think. And I don't think Russia would allow them to do it. Russia doesn't call all the shots. There are many instances where Assad has not done what Russia wants him to do, and we still don't know whether he will accept the kind of political solution that the Russians are advocating. But I think, on such big military issues, to turn their forces against the YPG on the battlefield, I think, Russia would be able to exert a powerful veto.

Jonathan Spyer (Director of the Rubin Centre for Research in International Affairs, second panel moderator): I do think it is certainly the key issue that Rahila brings up, in my opinion at least, and she has spent a lot of time in Rojava. The issue is, what will happen now, at these crossroads in time, when the war against ISIS is winding down, when the US is either going to go home or not go home. Then the issue, if the US leaves, will certainly be: is Assad then going to move against a depleted Kurdish force without air power? Without air power it is very hard for even a very hardened and brave force to fight against an oncoming attacker with air power. It's a crucial point. On this note we are going to close. It has been a fascinating discussion.

Afterword
Cihad Hammy

This book, as the title suggests, deals primarily with the Kurdish question in Turkey. It provides a profound reflection on the social-historical, economic and the world-systemic dimensions through which the Kurdish question first emerged and has subsequently developed. Any approach that overlooks these dimensions in seeking a solution to the Kurdish question will instead further aggravate it and bring it to an impasse.

This book was born out of an international peace delegation organized by the EU Turkey Civic Commission (EUTCC). The international peace delegation consisted of 10 members from Europe and North America, including Members of the European Parliament and of the Council of Europe, academics, and journalists, who visited Turkey twice and Strasbourg twice, between 2016 and 2017. The delegation aspired to help revive the peace process by searching for ways to restart it and by ending the isolation of the Kurdish freedom movement's leader, Abdullah Öcalan. In this vein, in 2016, the delegation applied to the Turkish Minister of Justice, requesting a meeting with Öcalan, who has been imprisoned and isolated in inhumane conditions on İmralı Island for nineteen years now, who plays a crucial role in the peace process. Unfortunately, there was no response to their request. In their trips to Turkey, the delegation met with representatives from the Kurdish freedom movement, political parties, trade unions, lawyers, academics, journalists, and representatives of other civil society organizations in both Diyarbakır and Istanbul. By doing so, the delegation collected valuable information about the peace process that lasted from 2013 to 2015. By meeting with many people in Diyarbakır, the delegation witnessed and gathered testimonies concerning the year and a half—after the ending of the peace process—of their experiences with military assaults, curfews, countless violation of civil rights, and human rights atrocities. Insistent upon creating a window of opportunity for peace, the delegation also attempted to visit the co-chair of the Peoples' Democratic Party (HDP), Selahattin Demirtaş, currently imprisoned unlawfully in Edirne. That request was also rejected.

Written by internationalist academics, politicians, lawyers, students, and activists who were part of the delegations seeking to restart the peace process between the Kurdish freedom movement and the Turkish state, this book offers rich, diverse, compelling, impressive, and exhaustive perspectives, illuminating the Kurdish question and the ongoing conflict in Turkey.

Structural Problems Impeding Democracy and Peace in Turkey

The existence of the Kurdish question is closely intertwined with the historically deep-seated structural basis of the Turkish state, which suffocates any attempt at democratization and peace in Turkey. These historical structures that cemented modern Turkey, namely the centralized Nation-State and Turkish nationalism, still brutally haunt us today. The massacres and genocides—the Armenian genocide among many other atrocities—that plague the history of modern Turkey are directly caused by these underlying structures. In addition, the role of major powers, namely that of Great Britain and the US, has been divisive, further preventing any move towards democratization and stability in Turkey, as they preserve their interests through the old colonialist tactic of "divide and rule."

The ideology of Turkish nationalism and the emergence of the Nation-State in Turkey during the breakdown of the Ottoman Empire in the late 19th and early 20th centuries was pioneered by the Young Turk movement and their Committee of Union and Progress. The leading figures of the Young Turks and founders of the Republic were a group of intellectuals and military officers educated in European universities, especially in France. These figures could impose the centralized model of the French nation-state, underpinned by secularism and positivism, on Turkey. It is worth noting that this model was created from above, by the elites in control of the State and was implemented through either violence or a controlled educational system. It is therefore an artificial model of a state that is alien to the rich and diverse fabric and traditional forms of society in Turkey. Moreover, the State forged the transition to capitalism and created a dependent bourgeois class. Turkish nationalism, xenophobic, exclusionary, and capitalist in its thinking, would be entrenched and institutionalized in the First Republic, led by Mustafa Kemal Ataturk.

Since its inception, the centralized Turkish nation targeted Islam, which it saw as backward, reactionary, and a threat to secularism. It also went after leftists and communists, called "saboteurs," and then specifically targeted the Kurds, called "separatists." The aim behind this was to have an extreme monopolization of social life under a highly centralized, bureaucratic and monolithic Turkish state. Thus, the Kemalist State banned the Communist Party and murdered its leaders during the War for Independence in 1921, crushed the revolt of Shaykh Said in 1925, and committed the massacre in Dersim in 1938. The introduction of multi-party elections in 1946 could not lead modern Turkey towards genuine democratization, as this transition did not alter the State's basic structures: centralized nation-statism and Turkish nationalism. Beginning in the sixties, a sequence of coups strengthened and protected the Kemalist legacy against the threat of reformist democratic moves. In the wake of the first coup in 1960, a new constitution birthed the Second Republic. As in the First Republic, however, the denial of Kurdish rights continued.

The Turkish Republic came to be incorporated into the global capitalist system under the hegemony of the US at the end of World War II. As a NATO member and as an ally of the US, the Turkish state intensified its extreme oppression with mass arrests against leftist groups. The effects of capitalism, industrialization, and a political economy produced economic crises for the Turkish and Kurdish people on the one hand, and brutal repression and socio-political threats posed the threat of annihilation on the other, sparking significant uprisings of the Left and of the Kurdish people. The wave of national liberation movements and class struggles occurring during these same years around the globe further fuelled such uprisings.

Within this conjuncture, the insurgency of the PKK against Turkish oppression emerged. Since 1984, the PKK has been involved in an armed conflict with the Turkish state, resulting in more than 40,000 deaths. Most of these deaths were the product of collective punishments and Turkish state terror against the Kurdish people. Since then, Turkey has been immersed in a spiral of violence that continues to this day.

Same Structures, Different Clothes

After the third coup, the constitution of 1982 opened the way for a neoliberal class of entrepreneurs who did not share the westernized style and militant secularism of their Kemalist forerunners. As Miley puts it, "the seeds for a future Islamist rival to Kemalist hegemony were certainly being sown."[1] Indeed, the era of "Green Turkishness" to use Öcalan's phrase emerged. Green Turkishness is a mixture of Turkish nationalism and authoritarian Islam which seeks to preserve the centralized Nation-State, dressed in religious clothes. This model was backed by the USA and NATO in the 1980s to achieve certain aims at that time. The first aim was to block Russian expansion, and the second was to destroy the Left, thereby preventing communities in the Middle East from achieving socialism. The AKP is the offspring and outgrowth of this Green Turkishness.

Despite the diversity of parties within parliament and government, be it the CHP, the MHP, or now the AKP, in the modern history of Turkey, Turkish nationalism is still powerfully preserved in the State's politics. A serious attempt at peace between the PKK and the Turkish state, through a democratization process during the era of Turgut Özal, was blocked by undemocratic and nationalist elements backed by NATO or "Gladio"—as Öcalan calls it—within the Turkish state. By assassinating Turgut Özal, they effectively eliminated the peace process. Efforts towards a genuine peace process, and the democratization this requires, continue to be suffocated by the undemocratic structures of the Turkish state and by its unwillingness to recognize the collective rights of the Kurdish people. This includes the peace process of 2003, the Oslo peace process of 2008–2011, and the most recent peace process of 2013–2015. As long as the Turkish state continues with its genocidal mentality towards the Kurds, resistance, escalation of violence, and bloodbaths will also continue.

A just peace will require transcending the undemocratic structures of the Turkish nation-state based on one flag, one nation, one language. In contrast to this centralist nation-state mentality, Öcalan has proposed the concept of a "Democratic Nation" as a model and solution that seeks democratically to grant individual and collective rights to all ethnicities and religious groups, and to guarantee gender equality in Turkey. This model will function within a Democratic Republic of Turkey, or the "Third Republic," to use Öcalan's terms. Öcalan has sketched a path that could lead in such a direction in one of his many books, *The Road Map to Negotiations*.

A Note on Violence

The Turkish nation-state, in its centralized, monopolized, militarized, and bureaucratized institutions, legalizes violence under the name of protecting "national security." By doing so, it permits itself to violently crush any movement that threatens the basic structures of the Turkish nation-state.

In the face of extreme repression, the genocidal, annihilation mentality that is structurally entrenched in the heart of the Turkish state, resistance and self-defense not only become an inevitable and imperative choice, but, in fact, a duty. People must seek all available means to defend their existence, socially, culturally, and politically. As Öcalan has put it, "societies without any mechanism of self-defense lose their identities, their capability of democratic decision-making, and their political nature."[2]

Herbert Marcuse, the German philosopher and Frankfurt School theorist, distinguished two forms of violence: the institutionalized violence of the established system and the violence of resistance. In his words: "Each of these forms has functions that conflict with those of the other. There is violence of suppression and violence of liberation; there is violence for the defense of life and violence of aggression." Moreover, for Marcuse, the duty of resistance is "a motive force in the historical development of freedom, a potentially liberating violence."[3]

Not far from Marcuse, Angela Davis, the philosopher-activist and professor, gave an insightful interview while serving a sentence in a Californian jail for a crime she did not commit. Discussing the Black Panthers and their conflict with the government and white supremacy in the USA, Davis argued that, since violence is exercised and permeated in every cell in society by the State's forces, violence, in turn, becomes an inevitable reaction. As she put it,

> Because of the way this society is organized, because of the violence that exists on the surface everywhere, you have to expect that there are going to be such explosions. You have to expect things like that as reactions.[4]

Likewise, in his recent manuscript *A Black Theology of Divine Violence*, Donald H. Matthews, an African-American liberation theologian trained at the University of Chicago's Seminary School, affirms three principles of Black self-defense as both a duty to protect oneself and also a divine response to injustice. As he puts it:

> 1. Self defense: Blacks have a God-given right to self-defence.
> 2. Violence is a divine response to oppression.
> 3. When non-violence is not effective in gaining freedom from oppression, the use of violence is justified.[5]

Even Theodor Adorno, who was a deep adherent of non-violent resistance, when asked what one should do under a fascist dictatorship, responded: "To a real Fascism, one can only react with violence."[6] In the same vein, Miley has quoted Buenaventura Durruti, an anarchist revolutionary in the Spanish Revolution, in a detailed manuscript on the question of violence:

Buenaventura Durruti was interviewed just a few months before he fell in battle while defending Madrid. He was put a tough question, one most likely motivated by a well-intentioned pessimism-of-the-intellect on the part of the journalist who posed it, Pierre Van Passen. A question reminiscent of Benjamin's reference to the "catastrophe, which keeps piling wreckage upon wreckage." For Van Passen would remark in passing: "You will be sitting upon a pile of ruins if you are victorious." To which, the soon-to-be revolutionary martyr Durruti would reply: "We are not in the least afraid of ruins. We are going to inherit the earth. There is not the slightest doubt about that. The bourgeoisie might blast and ruin its own world before it leaves the stage of history. We carry a new world, here in our hearts. That world is growing this minute."[7]

Miley continues: "His state of consciousness, in the pitch of the battle, near the eve of his martyrdom, showed signs of transcendence into the realm of the eternal 'now'."[8]

Let us not blame the revolutionary violence exercised by many leftist groups in the 1960s and 70s and the PKK since the 80s on these groups themselves, based as they are on the duty of self-defense. Instead, it is necessary to grasp the structural causes that have led to violence, and it is a political and moral imperative to work to eliminate these causes in a free and rational way in order to move towards a democratic Turkey.

Why is Öcalan Significant?

To understand the significance of Öcalan, one must surpass individualism and orientalism. Individualism is based on the crude divorce of the individual from society, thereby glorifying the individual at the expense of society, and at the same time diminishing the historical and societal context in which a given individual comes into being. Furthermore, the advocates of this ideology tend to degrade the importance of the charismatic personality without trying to grasp why and how this personality is essential to the people's political and social reality.

Many western leftists who consciously and subconsciously are plagued with orientalism tend to undervalue or dismiss Öcalan's writings. Let us not forget, however, that Öcalan's writings inspired the most democratic and radical revolution in the 21st century, the Rojava Revolution.

Dominated by a positivism which confines analysis within shallow appearance, liberals and some leftists in the West criticize the Kurdish freedom movement because of the ubiquity of Öcalan's images without deeply analysing what these images represent to the social and political memory of the Kurdish people. At the same time, confining Öcalan's philosophy to images is another form of injustice to him.

By overcoming the ideologies which underpin capitalism and colonialism, one can come to understand that Öcalan, as a political philosopher and Kurdish leader, is indispensable in solving the Kurdish question, or for any attempt towards a political peace process. Knowing this reality, the Turkish state tries to exclude Öcalan from any just Kurdish solution in order to hollow out and dilute the political and cultural rights and demands of the Kurdish people. In this context, Öcalan once said about his arrest in 1999: "They are targeting the Kurdish social reality through my personality." Back in the seventies and eighties, in a time when the Kurdish people experienced all the forms of exclusion and denial by systemic policies of the Turkish state, the Kurdish freedom movement led by Öcalan was an answer to save the Kurdish identity from annihilation.

What the Kurdish freedom movement, with the leadership of Öcalan, has done through their action and revolutionary struggle is to assert and preserve the existence of the Kurds culturally, socially, and politically. As Hannah Arendt put it, "Action, in so far as it engages in founding and preserving political bodies, creates the condition for remembrance, that is, for history."[9]

In other words, both Öcalan with the Kurdish freedom movement become the political and social memory of the oppressed Kurdish people. Therefore, it can be understood that the Kurdish existence at least in Bakur is closely tied to the Kurdish freedom movement and its widely revered leader, Öcalan. This can be easily noticed through Kurdish literature, art, and music. Thus, any solution that excludes Öcalan from solving the Kurdish question in Bakur signifies the exclusion of the political and social memory of the Kurds. In this case, resistance emerges, and war begins.

Since any revolutionary project is an educational project, Öcalan spent most of his time in Bakur and Rojava educating and building Kurdish identity and personality. His education focused on creating a free and strong Kurdish personality empowered by free will and a readiness to engage in political and social life. In other words, he created an active and highly politicized Kurdish personality that struggles to obtain his or her social, cultural, and political rights in a free and just way. On a daily basis, Öcalan taught face to face thousands of people in Bakur and Rojava for decades. He taught them radical history, philosophy, sociology, and revolutionary traditions, as well as the hidden history of women. He taught them how to be revolutionaries. Öcalan is therefore not only a Kurdish leader but also a revolutionary thinker, instructor, and teacher. In parallel with his commitment to education, he is a prolific writer, with more than 40 books. For him, theory and practice cannot be divided. He would envision ideas and put them into practice while the ink was still fresh. Öcalan is strongly tied to the Kurdish people at a very rooted level.

One of the most important things that Öcalan achieved is to have provided women with the political and philosophical tools to transform themselves from passive and powerless citizens to active, powerful, and highly intellectual revolutionaries. He was able to do this in a region where patriarchy is deeply ingrained in every cell of society. After a long process of educating the Kurdish people and by declaring the need to "kill the dominant male" representing the patriarchy inside each and every member of society, women left their domestic life and engaged in public and political life. Interestingly, before the rise of the Kurdish freedom movement led by Öcalan, women could not leave their homes without the permission of the dominant men. In the very same society, thanks to the Kurdish freedom movement and its leadership, women became revolutionaries and fighters against the fascism of the State. Though Öcalan provided the philosophical tools to empower women, he also protected their autonomous agency leading up to the revolution. The very same women who are leading the Rojava Revolution, and who have liberated Raqqa, which was the so-called capital of the Islamic State, are applying and implementing his ideology in order to protect and advance the freedom of women in all parts of society. This shows that the Kurdish revolutionary women are not reducible to Öcalan or any other outside figure—rather, they are self-empowered. Öcalan's path to socialism is through killing the dominant male. As he put it, "to kill the dominant man is the fundamental principle of socialism." For him, killing the dominant male "is to kill fascism, dictatorship, and despotism."[10] If this means one thing, it is the transformation and development of Kurdish society towards freedom, through the advancement of women's freedom and destruction of patriarchy. That is why revolutionary Kurdish women always linked their own freedom with Öcalan's.

When I was writing this afterword, I reached a point where I wanted to write about Öcalan's role in liberating women. My mother, aged 50, came to my room and was busy searching her bag. Accidentally she pulled a yellow photo of Öcalan with the emblem on it: "Free Öcalan!" She always keeps that photo in her bag. My mother is illiterate because, according to her, her father did not let her attend school because it was shameful at the time. She had loved going to school and spent days crying after she was prohibited from going.

"Why do you keep Öcalan's photo in your bag, Mom?" I asked her.

"Because I love him," she answered, smiling.

"Why?" I asked.

She explained: "Women were afraid of talking in front of men. But after the intense educational process by the Kurdish movement, women could face men and bravely talk, and even challenge them. Öcalan killed the fear inside women. He killed the weakness and powerlessness in us." In other words, Öcalan was instrumental in transforming women from objects into subjects.

After Öcalan was abducted and held in solitary confinement on İmralı Island, he started spending much of his time reading political and philosophical books reading more than 3000 books of social and natural sciences—to remain sane, and to try to find a peaceful solution to the Kurdish question, and for the democratization of Turkey as well. In İmralı, despite inhumane and harsh treatment in prison, he has developed his ideas about the path towards freedom and democracy. In prison, he undertook a deep self-criticism, rejecting some dogmatic and fundamental notions, such as the Nation-State and statism. As he put it in his book *In Defense of the People*:

> If I am guilty of anything, then it is the fact that I accepted the culture of power and war. I became part of it since I was almost religiously convinced that we needed a state to become free, and that therefore we had to fight a war. Only few of those who fight for freedom and for the oppressed can save themselves from this disease. Thus, I have not only become guilty in the eyes of the ruling system but also with respect to the struggle for freedom for which I have given all I had.[11]

There he came to the conclusion that the centralized nation-state is not an answer for the Kurdish question, and instead he proposed the "Democratic Nation", a project that he developed under the influence of Murray Bookchin's libertarian municipalism. As a political vision, the Democratic Nation stands at odds with the Nation-State. Whereas the centralized Nation-State seeks to create a hegemonic nation, assimilating all cultures and languages through social engineering and, when necessary, pure violence, the Democratic Nation aims to engender fraternity, democracy, peace, and freedom, not just within the political governance of Kurdistan, but also across the rest of the Middle East. Furthermore, political subjects under the Democratic Nation reclaim revolutionary politics and the power to run their lives by engaging in local-level institutions and assemblies created by all people. These assemblies confederate with each other on the local, regional, national, and international levels.

Because of the indispensable role of Öcalan in the peace process, the ultimate goals of the delegations were "to monitor the political and human rights situation in Turkey and to place high-level attention on Mr. Abdullah Öcalan's situation in İmralı prison by asking permission to visit him," with the aim of contributing "to the resumption of the peace talks".[12]

On the total isolation of Öcalan during the unravelling of the peace process, the EUTCC delegations, in this book, saw it as, "a deliberate act" that "constitutes one of the most dangerous components of the criminal and polarizing policy pursued by the Turkish authorities vis-à-vis the Kurdish freedom movement over the past year." The delegation went on to explain the reason behind such an act: "This is because Öcalan remains a symbol of the Kurdish nation for many Kurds. Because of his charismatic appeal, his words carry a lot of weight within the Kurdish freedom movement. They exercise a powerful influence over the contours of political subjectivity amongst his many followers".[13]

In a letter sent from Judge Moosa's Office to the Members of the European Committee for the Prevention of Torture and Inhuman or Degrading Treatment or Punishment, Judge Moosa stressed the crucial role of Öcalan:

> The International Peace Delegation sponsored by the EU Turkey Civic Commission has concluded that, in order for genuine peace negotiations to take place to resolve the Kurdish issue in Turkey, Abdullah Öcalan, who is a crucial actor, should be released unconditionally from prison. This would enable him to take his rightful place at the negotiating table for the lasting resolution of the Kurdish issue in Turkey and for the democratization of Turkey.[14]

In short, Öcalan must be the main and active player in any peaceful solution. Without him, there will be no solution because of his organic connection with the Kurdish people and the Kurdish freedom movement. Also, he is the initiator of an emancipatory project that aims at the democratization of Turkey and a solution to the Kurdish question in a free and rational way. Furthermore, Öcalan and his ideas have great power and meaning for the Kurdish freedom movement. In this sense, his role is crucial and decisive in pushing the Kurdish freedom movement towards freedom and democracy, and in empowering people in grass-roots political self-determination.

References:

1. Thomas Jeffrey Miley, "A History of the Conflict between the Turkish State and the Kurdish Freedom Movement," in Part One of this volume.

2. Abdullah Öcalan, *Democratic Confederalism* (International Initiative and Mesopotamian Publishers: Cologne, Neuss, 2017) p.26.

3. Herbert Marcuse, "The Problem of Violence and the Radical Opposition," 1967. (http://bit.ly/2KuEUpB).

4. Angela Davis, "Talking about Revolution," (Video: 4:17 min), April 10, 2018, (http://bit.ly/2KrBF1Y).

5. Donald H. Matthews, *A Black Theology of Divine Violence*, (PARE: Program Against Racist Education, Kindle Edition, 2017) p.55.

6. Theodor Adorno, "A Conversation with Theodor W. Adorno" *Der Spiegel*, 1969, (https://bit.ly/2GX2Yj7).

7. Thomas Jeffrey Miley, *Reflections on Revolution and the Spiral of Violence*, (unpublished).

8. Ibid.

9. Hannah Arendt, *The Human Condition*, (University of Chicago Press: 1998) pp.8–9.

10. PKKOnline.net. (Broken link.) https://bit.ly/2yQCAYt.

11. Öcalan, *In Defense of the People*, (2004) p.2.

12. Kariane Westrheim, "My Encounter with the Kurdish Movement." In Part Two of this book.

13. "State Terror, Human Rights Violations, and Authoritarianism in Turkey." In Part Three of this volume.

14. Essa Moosa, "Addendum: Letter of request of Judge Moosa to the Minister of Justice Mr. Bekir Bozdag dated 3 February 2016," in "Joint Statement of the First International İmralı Peace Delegation," in Part Three of this volume.

Notes on the Contributors

Janet Biehl is the author of numerous works on social ecology and the renowned social theorist, Murray Bookchin. After meeting at the Institute for Social Ecology in Vermont, they would collaborate for two decades to advance and explain social ecology. During this time, Biehl authored several books both alone and in collaboration with Bookchin. Since 2011, she has written frequently about Rojava and the Kurdish movement in Turkey.

Dilar Dirik is a PhD student at the Department of Sociology, University of Cambridge. Her research in Kurdistan is based on different concepts of freedom in modern Kurdish politics, with particular focus on the women's struggle against patriarchy. She writes for an international audience on the Kurdish freedom movement in a variety of media outlets.

Radha D'Souza practiced as a barrister in the High Court of Bombay and taught at the Universities of Auckland and Waikato in New Zealand before coming to University of Westminster. She is a writer, critic, and commentator on Third World issues and a social justice activist. She has a L.L.B. from the University of Mumbai and a Ph.D. in Geography and Law from the University of Auckland.

Simon Dubbins is the International Director at UNITE the Union in the UK. He has worked for the Graphical, Paper and Media Union, and served as the International Head of AMICUS. He now co-ordinates the European and International work of UNITE across all its sectors.

Mohammed Elnaiem is an editor at *The Region* and an activist in the Black Liberation Movement and writes on the Black radical tradition, with particular focus on internationalism and the history of Black socialist thought. In 2017, he earned his M.Phil. in Political and Economic Sociology from the University of Cambridge

Miren Gorrotxategi is a Basque politician and member of Podemos. She has been a member of the Spanish Senate from the province of Biscay since December 20, 2015, for the eleventh and and twelfth parliaments. Since April 2016, she has served on the Parliamentary Assembly of the Council of Europe, and is also a member of the Group of the Unified European Left, as well as a full member of the Committee on Equality and Non-Discrimination.

Havin Guneser is a Kurdish writer, journalist, women's rights activist, and a spokesperson for the International Initiative "Freedom for Abdullah Öcalan— Peace in Kurdistan." She is a translator and publisher of the works of Öcalan. Among other initiatives, she launched and coordinated a petition campaign that would collect 10.3 million signatures calling for Öcalan's freedom.

Michael M. Gunter is a scholarly authority on the Kurds in Turkey and Iraq. He is a board member of the Centre for Eurasian Studies (AVIM), the secretary general of the EU Turkey Civic Commission (EUTCC), and an important analyst of breaking news in the Middle East. Gunter has written more than 75 articles in scholarly journals and has authored nine books about the Kurds—two of which were among the first analyses in English of Kurdish unrest in the Middle East. He received the Kurdish Human Rights Watch's Service Award in 1998.

Cihad Hammy was born in Kobane in 1991. He studied English literature at Damascus University but left his studies because of the war in Syria. From 2012–2014, he worked as a translator for the Democratic Self-Administration in Kobane. He currently resides in Germany.

Andrej Hunko is a Member of Parliament in Germany (*Bundestag*) and spokesperson on European affairs for the Left Party (DIE LINKE). He is also a member of the Parliamentary Assembly of the Council of Europe (PACE), serving as first Vice-Chair on the Committee on Social Affairs, Health, and Sustainable Development and as a member of the Monitoring Committee. In April 2017, Hunko was part of the official PACE mission to observe the controversial Turkish constitutional referendum.

Reimar Heider is a physician by training and a human rights activist based in Cologne, Germany. He is a spokesperson of the International Initiative "Freedom for Abdullah Öcalan—Peace in Kurdistan," which has led him to translate several books by Öcalan and to organise their biennial conference in Hamburg.

Ögmundur Jónasson was a part-time lecturer at the University of Iceland from 1979 to 2009. From 1995 to 2016, he served as a Member of the Icelandic Parliament and was the Chair of the Parliamentary Group of the Left Green Movement for ten years. Jónasson has served as Iceland's Minister of Health, Minister of Justice, and Minister of the Interior. He was a member of the Constitutional and Supervisory Committee of the Icelandic Parliament and was a Member of the Parliamentary Assembly of the Council of Europe (PACE). Jónasson was made an Honorary Associate of PACE in 2017.

Rev. Donald H. Matthews is an ordained Methodist minister who received his Ph.D. from the Divinity School at the University of Chicago. He has written numerous books, articles, and papers, and has taught at several universities and seminaries, including the University of California at Santa Cruz, St. Louis University, Colgate-Rochester-Crozier Divinity School, and the University of Puget Sound. He directed the Black Studies Program at the University of Missouri, Kansas City, and the Master of Divinity Program at Naropa University.

Thomas Jeffrey Miley is a lecturer of political sociology at the University of Cambridge. His research interests include nationalism, religion and politics, and empirical democratic theory. He has published widely on the dynamics of nationalist conflict and accommodation in Spain and, increasingly, in Turkey. His current research project is on comparative struggles for self-determination in the twenty-first century. He has participated in several delegations to Turkey and different parts of Kurdistan, including to Rojava, and is a member of the executive board of the EU Turkey Civic Commission (EUTCC).

Abdullah Öcalan is the founder of the Kurdistan Workers Party (PKK) and leader of the Kurdish freedom movement. Since his kidnapping and arrest in 1999, he has been held in isolation at the İmralı Island Prison, where he has been largely the sole prisoner, although it is guarded by hundreds of soldiers. Öcalan has written extensively on Middle Eastern and Kurdish history and politics and, often known as the "Kurdish Mandela", he is widely regarded as a key figure for a political solution to the Kurdish issue.

Dimitrios Roussopoulos has been a lifelong political activist, writer, publisher, and public speaker. Since the late 1950s, he has spearheaded campaigns for peace, community control, housing justice, ecological movements, municipal movements, and participatory democracy. He is a cofounder of the publisher Black Rose Books and the European-based Transnational Institute of Social Ecology as well as many other grassroots political and intellectual organisations. He is based in the Milton Parc neighbourhood in Montreal, Quebec, Canada.

Father Joe Ryan is a Catholic priest from the Diocese of Westminster, UK and over the past ten years, he has served as Chair of the Westminster Justice and Peace Commission. He has joined fact-finding teams on visits to various countries such as the Philippines, El Salvador, Pakistan, Ghana, and Nigeria and has also organized study days on migrants, asylum seekers, homelessness, ecology, and climate change.

Ulla Sandbæk is a former Member of the European Parliament (1989–2004), focusing mainly on women's reproductive rights, and is currently a Member of the Danish Parliament for Greater Copenhagen. She is active with the green political party *Alternativet* (The Alternative) for which she is a spokesperson on development co-operation and ecclesiastical affairs. She is also involved in the Palestinian territories, where she has held courses in breathing practices, yoga, and meditation for former female political prisoners. She holds an M.A. in Theology and practiced as a vicar for 30 years.

Jonathan Steele is a veteran foreign correspondent who has spent most of his journalistic career with *The Guardian*. Educated at Cambridge and Yale, he has been the paper's Bureau Chief in Moscow and in Washington. Steele has covered wars in Afghanistan, Iraq, Syria, the Balkans, Central America, as well as east and southern Africa. Twice named International Reporter of the Year by the British press, he has won many prestigious journalism prizes including the James Cameron award, the Martha Gellhorn Special award, the Amnesty International Human Rights award, and the London Press Club's Scoop of the Year award. Since 2002, he has concentrated on Middle Eastern politics.

Darnell Stephen Summers enlisted in the U.S. Army in 1966 and, after serving stateside, as well as in Germany and Vietnam, he soon became an ardent anti-war spokesperson and political activist. He was a founding member of the Malcolm X Cultural Center, a member of the Black Workers' Congress, and was also associated with the Black Panther Party. In 1968, Darnell was targeted by the infamous COINTELPRO, accused of killing a Michigan State Red Squad Police Detective.

Adem Uzun was an engineering student in Germany when he first chaired the Turkish (TÖD) and then the Kurdish (YXK) student associations. Since the early 1990s, he has been involved in Kurdish politics and has belonged to many Kurdish organisations and associations, and also worked in the diplomatic sphere—mainly among Kurds in Syria and Iraq. He is currently a member of the Administrative Council of the Kurdistan National Congress (KNK).

Federico Venturini is an independent activist-researcher. In 2016, he earned his Ph.D. at the University of Leeds on the relations between contemporary cities and urban social movements. He holds an M.Phil. from the University of Trieste as well as a Master's in History and European Culture from the University of Udine (Italy). He has been a member of the Advisory Board of the Transnational Institute of Social Ecology since 2013.

Julie Ward is a Labour MEP for the North West of England. She is also a writer, poet, and cultural activist who was a factory worker before becoming a community arts worker. Ward is a member of the European Parliament's committees on Culture and Education, Women's Rights and Gender Equality, and Regional Development. A champion of children's rights, she co-founded the cross-party Intergroup on Children's Rights and sat on the Labour Party's Children and Education Policy Commission. Moreover, Ward is a board member on the European Internet Forum, and a founding member of the European Caucus of Women in Parliament.

Kariane Westrheim is a professor of Educational Science at the University of Bergen, Norway. She has been involved in the Kurdish movement since 2002, both professionally and as a supporter. Her doctoral thesis deals with educational perspectives and practices in the Kurdistan Workers' Party (PKK) and she has conducted fieldwork in Bakur, Bashur, and Rojava. Since 2004, Westrheim has been the chairperson the EU Turkey Civic Commission (EUTCC).

Francis Wurtz was a Member of the European Parliament (MEP) from 1979 until 2009, in addition to serving as Chair of the European United Left–Nordic Green Left group of the European Parliament and Vice President of the Africa-Caribbean-Pacific-European Union Joint Assembly. He has been the Deputy Chair of the Development Committee, and a member of the EU–Mediterranean Parliamentary Assembly, the EU–Latin America Parliamentary Assembly, and the European Parliament Committee on Foreign Affairs. He has taught at the Institute of International and Strategic Relations in Paris, and served as Vice-President of the Gabriel Peri Foundation, as well as President of the Institute of European Studies at the University of Paris.

Glossary of Acronyms

Courtesy of Michael M. Gunter, author of *Historical Dictionary of the Kurds*,
3rd. ed. (Lanham, MD: Rowland & Littlefield, 2018).

AKP: *Adalet ve Kalkınma Partisi* (Justice and Development Party) [Turkey]

ARGK: *Artêşa Rizgariya Gelê Kurdistan* (Kurdistan Peoples Liberation Army)

BDP: *Barış ve Demokrasi Partisi* (Peace and Democracy Party) [Turkey]

CHP: *Cumhuriyet Halk Partisi* (Republican People's Party) [Turkey]

DBP: *Demokratik Bölgeler Partisi* (Democratic Regions Party) [Turkey]

DEHAP: *Demokratik Halk Partisi* (Democratic People's Party) [Turkey]

DEP: *Demokrasi Partisi* (Democracy Party) [Turkey]

DİSK: *Devrimci İşçi Sendikaları Konfederasyonu* (Confederation of Revolutionary Worker Unions of Turkey)

DTK: *Demokratik Toplum Kongresi* (Democratic Society Congress) [Turkey]

DTP: *Demokratik Toplum Partisi* (Democratic Society Party) [Turkey]

ECHR: European Court of Human Rights

ERNK: *Eniye Rizgariya Netewa Kurdistan* (National Liberation Front of Kurdistan) [Turkey]

EUTCC: EU Turkey Civic Commission [Europe]

FSA: Free Syrian Army

HADEP: *Halkın Demokrasi Partisi* (People's Democracy Party) [Turkey]

HDK: Halkların Demokratik Kongresi (Peoples' Democratic Congress) [Turkey]

HDP: *Halkların Demokratik Partisi* (Peoples' Democratic Party) [Turkey]

HEP: *Halkın Emek Partisi* (People's Labor Party) [Turkey]

HPG: *Hêzên Parastina Gel* (People's Defense Force) [Turkey]

HRK: *Hêzên Rizgarîya Kurdistanê* (Kurdistan Freedom Brigades) [Turkey]

ISIS: Islamic State of Iraq and Syria [al-Sham/Levant]

KJK: *Komalên Jinên Kurdistan* (Kurdistan Women's Committees) [Turkey]

KADEK: *Kongreya Azadî û Demokrasiya Kurdistanê* (Kurdistan Freedom and Democracy Congress) [Turkey], replaced by the Kongra-Gel

KCK: *Koma Civakên Kurdistan* (Kurdistan Communities Union) [Iran, Iraq, Syria, and Turkey]

KDP: *Partiya Demokrat a Kurdistanê* (Kurdistan Democratic Party) [Iraq]

KGK: *Kongra-Gel* (Kurdistan People's Congress) [Iran, Iraq, Syria, and Turkey], aka KNC/KNK

KKK: *Koma Komalên Kurdistan* [Turkey], replaced by the KCK

KNK: *Kongreya Neteweyî ya Kurdistan* (Kurdistan National Congress) [Europe]

KRG: Kurdistan Regional Government [Iraq]

MEP: Member of the European Parliament

MHP: *Milliyetçi Hareket Partisi* (Nationalist Action Party) [Turkey]

MİT: *Milli İstihbarat Teşkilatı* (National Intelligence Organization) [Turkey]

NATO: North Atlantic Treaty Organization

OSCE: Organization for Security and Cooperation in Europe

PACE: Parliamentary Assembly of the Council of Europe

PJAK: *Partiya Jiyana Azad a Kurdistanê* (Kurdistan Free Life Party) [Iran]

PKK: *Partiya Karkerên Kurdistanê* (Kurdistan Workers Party) [Turkey]

PUK: Patriotic Union of Kurdistan [Iraq]

PYD: *Partiya Yekîtiya Demokrat* (Democratic Union Party) [Syria]

SDF: Syrian Democratic Forces

SNC: Syrian National Council/Coalition

TAK: *Teyrêbazên Azadiya Kurdistan* (Kurdistan Freedom Falcons/Hawks) [Turkey]

TEV-DEM: *Tevgera Civaka Demokratîk* (Movement for a Democratic Society—Democratic Popular Movement) [Syria]

TSK: *Türk Silahlı Kuvvetleri* (Turkish Armed Forces)

YDG-H: *Yurtsever Devrimci Gençlik Hareketi* (Patriotic Revolutionary Youth Movement [Turkey]

YPG: *Yekîneyên Parastina Gel* (People's Defense Units) [Syria]

YPJ: *Yekîneyên Parastina Jin* (Women's Defense Units) [Syria]

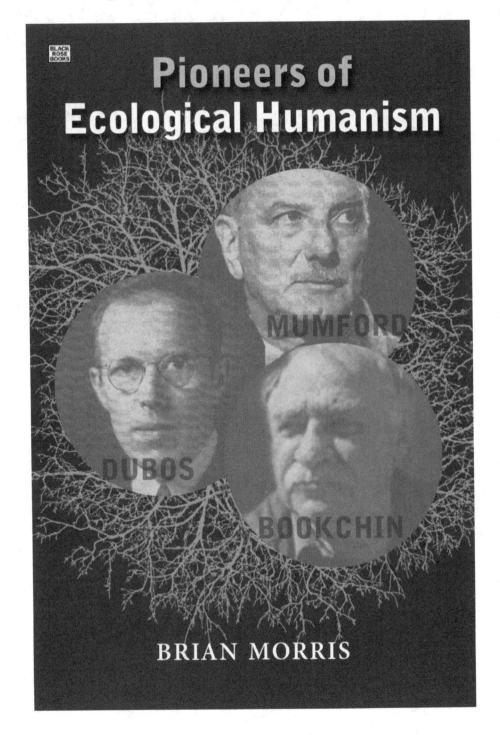

BLACK
ROSE
BOOKS

Pioneers of
Ecological Humanism

MUMFORD

DUBOS

BOOKCHIN

BRIAN MORRIS